SANJANA

Feasts

SANJANA

Feasts

Modern vegetarian and vegan Indian
recipes to feed your soul

Sanjana Modha

unbound

For Bodhi

With thanks to
the Natalyas

Contents

Introduction	7
But First, Chai	19
With Chai	31
Not Curry	59
Curry	105
Daal	131
Roti and Rice	147
Sides	179
Sweets	201
Fridge Stash	229
Magic Masalas	253
My Indian-ish Pantry	275
Oven Temperature Guide	306
Build-a-thali Menu Guide	307
Glossary	308
Tips and Tricks	310
Index	314
Supporters	318

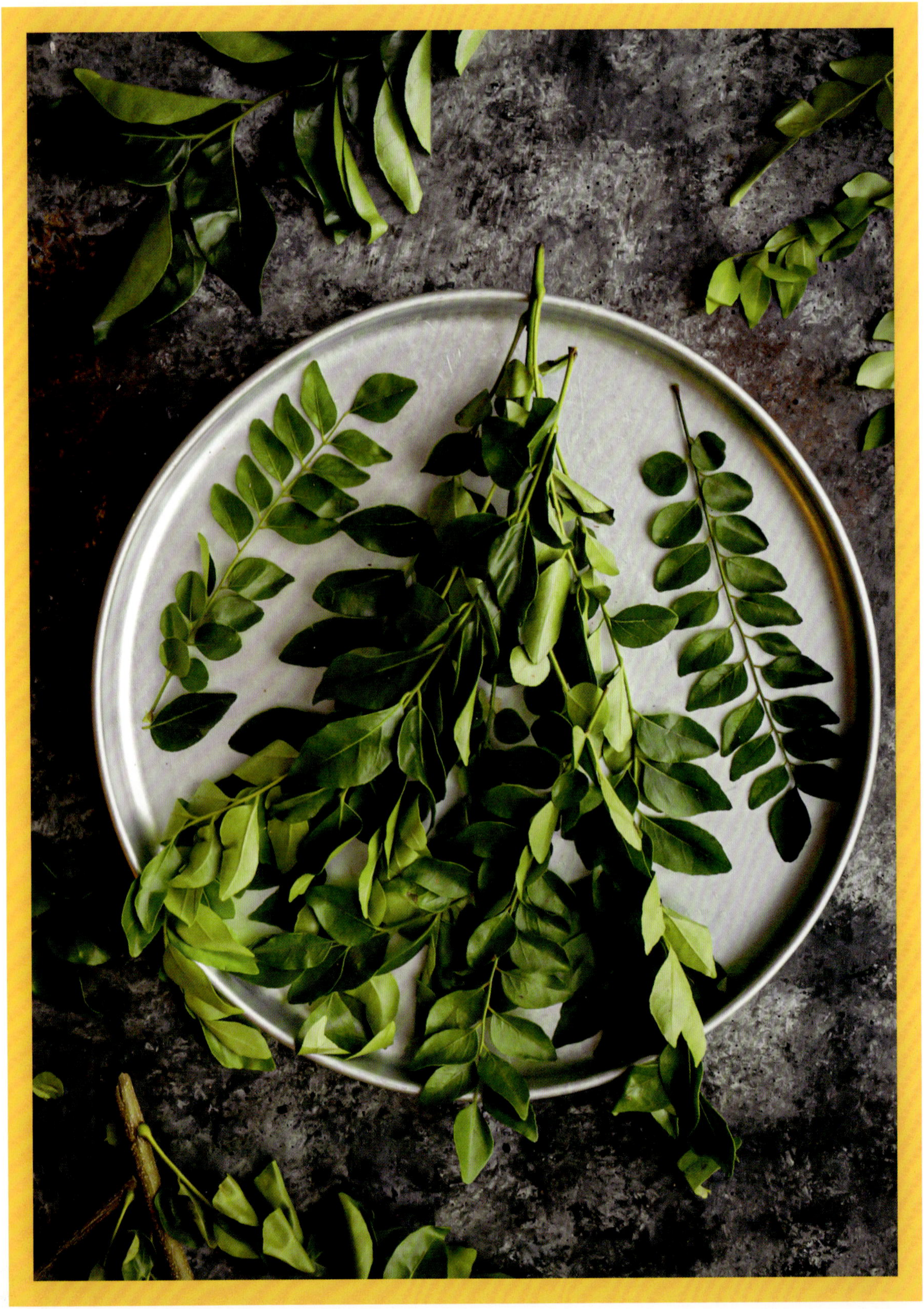

Introduction

I grew up eating the typical Gujarati meal of daal, bhaat, shaak and rotli - our practically sacred plate of lentils, rice, curry and chapati. It's so significant to our food culture that the global Gujarati community refer to it by an abbreviated term of endearment: DBSR. Sunday lunch was always the most wholesome meal of the week. My mum would often prepare a roasting pan full of akhu shaak, a dish of whole vegetables stuffed with peanut masala. Anise and cinnamon-laced Gujarati daal was ladled over boiled white rice; the steam that lapped the surface of the daal never failed to transport me back to the very first meals that soothed me as a child. Since it is usually of a flowing consistency, Gujarati daal tends to separate from the water if left undisturbed too long. After a gentle stir, the shade of warm sienna rippled with the opaqueness of pulverised pigeon peas and nuts boiled so long they turned creamy. A butter-slicked stack of our daily bread, rotli, was kept suitably warm in a trusty 30-year-old insulated container etched with the family name. Salads, raw chillies, various achaars and a buttermilk drink called chaas brought freshness, heat and a cooling element to this consistently comforting meal. A sweet would follow, usually in the form of canned mango pulp thinned with evaporated milk. This milk was instinctively referred to by its brand name, Carnation.

The way I cook DBSR - and Indian food in general - is not the way my ancestors cooked it. It's not entirely the way my mother cooked it either. As a UK-born child of Kenyan and Tanzanian immigrants, both with Indian Gujarati ancestry, the concept of cultural fluidity or 'fusion food' was deep-rooted in the meals I grew up eating. Regardless of what was on our table, or whose table we were sat around, eating together was a moment in the day to love, to laugh, and to just be. In Gujarati we call this jamvanu, which simply refers to the act of eating together. I'd like to invite you to sit at my table to experience the same feelings of joy I experience when I sit down to eat with the people I love. What's on my table may not always be in the DBSR league of traditional, but I won't apologise for that. Today, I adopt flavour combinations that raise eyebrows, even through the lens of today's modern society. A curiosity for the ingredients now at my fingertips have influenced the meals that bring warmth, comfort and life to my home. The khichdi I fed my son for his first solid meal was pressure-cooked with the unconventional addition of Scotch broth mix (a combination of pearl barley, lentils and split peas). I spread Marmite on my naan, temper my baked beans with spices and make cheese toasties with leftover samosa filling. The fact of the matter is that many other Brits with roots in the Indian subcontinent do the same.

The way the diaspora cook is antithetical to the perception of inflexibility many might assume is cultivated within the 'traditional' Indian family kitchen. We embrace our beautifully muddled experiences, despite the rocky roads that may have led us to them. We're proud of how generations of adaptation have shaped the food we cook. To the diaspora, the way we create our meals is not a mindless fudging up of ingredients, nor is it an intentional stray from 'the old ways'. It's food shaped by our experiences. Over time, a mishmash of culinary principles became a cherished by-product of the complex history of South Asian settlers across the globe. After the abolition of the African slave trade in the 1800s, Britain's Indian indenture system was created as a classification of servitude. It contributed to the creation of the world's largest diaspora of around 32 million people of Indian origin. Indian people were displaced to many parts of the globe; they worked on plantations and built infrastructure in Britain's other colonies, such as in South and East Africa, the Indian Ocean, the Caribbean, Fiji, British Guyana, Malaysia and Singapore. Entwined with the problematic history our ancestors encountered comes the fact that, today, much of the food culture of the Indian diaspora dovetails with lessons learned hundreds of years ago. Indian diasporic cuisines, and diasporic cuisines in general, are forces in their own right. Like many, I'm neither fully Indian, nor British, nor Kenyan, nor Tanzanian, but I'm a child of mixed cultures. Like the mythological ghost, Betaal, who piggybacked on King Vikramāditya's shoulders in Mahakavi Somdev Bhatt's saga *Baital Pachisi*, an awareness of this mixed identity has clung to me for as long as I remember.

My ancestors were farmers, traders and chefs from the state of Gujarat in western India. Aboard boats in the 1930s and 1940s, my grandfathers sailed across the Indian ocean, directly to the ports of East Africa. This was long before the political upheaval and expulsion of Asians in 1970s Uganda. It was in Tanzania, Kenya, Mozambique and South Africa that they laboured and lived for decades. Equipped with farming experience, both worked on plantations, chopping sugarcane, pulverising and boiling it down into bubbling syrups to produce cane sugar. My Bapuji (paternal grandfather) had shoulders like boulders and hands of steel, able to test the multiple stages of candying using his bare fingers. One string, two strings, three strings, four... He went on to become a wonderful chef.

A glut of multicultural influences has whacked my taste buds from every angle as a ripple effect of migration. The millet bread and green garlic curries of my Indian ancestors, as well as the coconut cassava and roasted chilli maize of my East Africa-born parents. And as the only vegetarian at my school, pasta bakes, potato smiles and jam sponges were firm favourites when it came to school dinners. Sherbet Lemons and Yorkshire Mixtures boiled sweets (candies) for breaktime, of course. I have a great respect for what are deemed to be 'traditionally Indian' methods of cooking, but I have never felt bound by them. Born and raised as a first-generation Brit, I was a stereotypical Asian corner-shop kid in the middle of a sleepy West Yorkshire village. We lived in the flat above the shop. Every day I'd come home from school eager to see my dad's pasta daal on the table, simultaneously worrying if the smell of perfectly caramelised onions had permeated down the stairs and into the shop, ready to make all my friends wince. For my brother, Ravi, and I, pasta daal was a compromise dish created to satisfy our urge to eat Western food like our friends, but at the same time give our parents peace of mind in knowing we hadn't offended the ancestors by cutting loose our Indian-ness.

Riley's

BEN SHAWS
Yellow Lemonade
Cola
Lemonade
Fanta
Schweppes
Soda Water

BEN SHAWS
CONNALLY
NEWSAGENTS

OUR
3 FOR £1
Thomas

The recipes you'll find in this book are an ode to the British Indian diaspora take on Indian cuisine. Many dishes are the bountiful products of an assimilation of cultures, just like the people of modern society so brilliantly are. I hope the dishes that await are respectfully curious and interesting; they lie in a spot somewhere between soulfully old and delightfully new. You might see a generous blob of mango chutney meander through a twisted Cheddar loaf, baked potatoes topped with rich keema and that blistered naan slathered in Marmite. Hell, you may even bear witness to a slow pour of sticky toffee sauce as it engulfs a bowl of bouncy gulab jamuns. This is the food I cook from my experiences, not to be rebellious, but because it feels right and tastes sublime. In any case, a flavour-forward approach with spectacularly delicious results is the goal with every recipe I'm sharing here. My instincts tell me to balance dishes with savoury, sour, sweet and bitter flavours, for these elements are ingrained within the Gujarati cuisine my palate is accustomed to. Most recipes you'll find in this book embrace this ancient philosophy – adding fats and flavours as though they're old friends.

I hope this collection of soulful meals may empower you to see Indian vegetarian cuisine with a fresh perspective; a window into what is beyond a bowl of aloo gobi. The tips peppered throughout these pages are there to provide context and background, just like an Indian grandma would most certainly do during the daily dinner prep. I won't be there to look over your shoulder and tell you that you're doing it wrong, don't worry. I come from a place where you can't really get anything wrong, anyway. Every meal I've ever cooked has been an experiment, with both rights and wrongs. Some of the wrongs have been the most delicious and exciting of all. Like my mother, I'm incapable of following recipes exactly, so I share these with you as guidelines. Rely on them for a great meal, or adapt and flex, following your intuition to create your own personal magic. For example, the bread chapter contains six mighty flavours of naan, but the base dough can easily be customised with your favourite ingredients. From everyday heroes to fabulous sharing feasts for special occasions, these recipes will allow you to explore a vibrant wave of Indian cuisine from angles that are mindful of heritage and roots but are unbound in how they manifest onto your plate. I hope the accompanying stories are a stirring read, even when you aren't planning to bake your own tiger bread for tiger pav bhaji anytime soon. Together, let's be bold enough to break a few rules and take a deep dive into Indian vegetarian cuisine, reimagined.

Why 'making do' is not a burden

They say that the regional cuisines of India change every two miles, influenced by local culture, trade, migration and not forgetting the imperial rulers of the past. The Mughal Empire, from 1526-1857, followed by The British Raj from 1858-1947, when Hindustan became what we know today as the independent nations of India, Pakistan (and in 1971, Bangladesh, which was formerly known as East Pakistan). Local cuisine was also heavily influenced by trade, which began around 500 bc, maritime trade, and The Silk Route (around the fourteenth and eighteenth centuries). Today we live in a connected world, a melting pot more diverse than ever before. For generations, migration has meant that people have adapted and assimilated when it comes to unknown ingredients, using local produce to cook the foods they know and love in their adopted foreign lands. For British Indians, spicy, oniony masala baked beans on

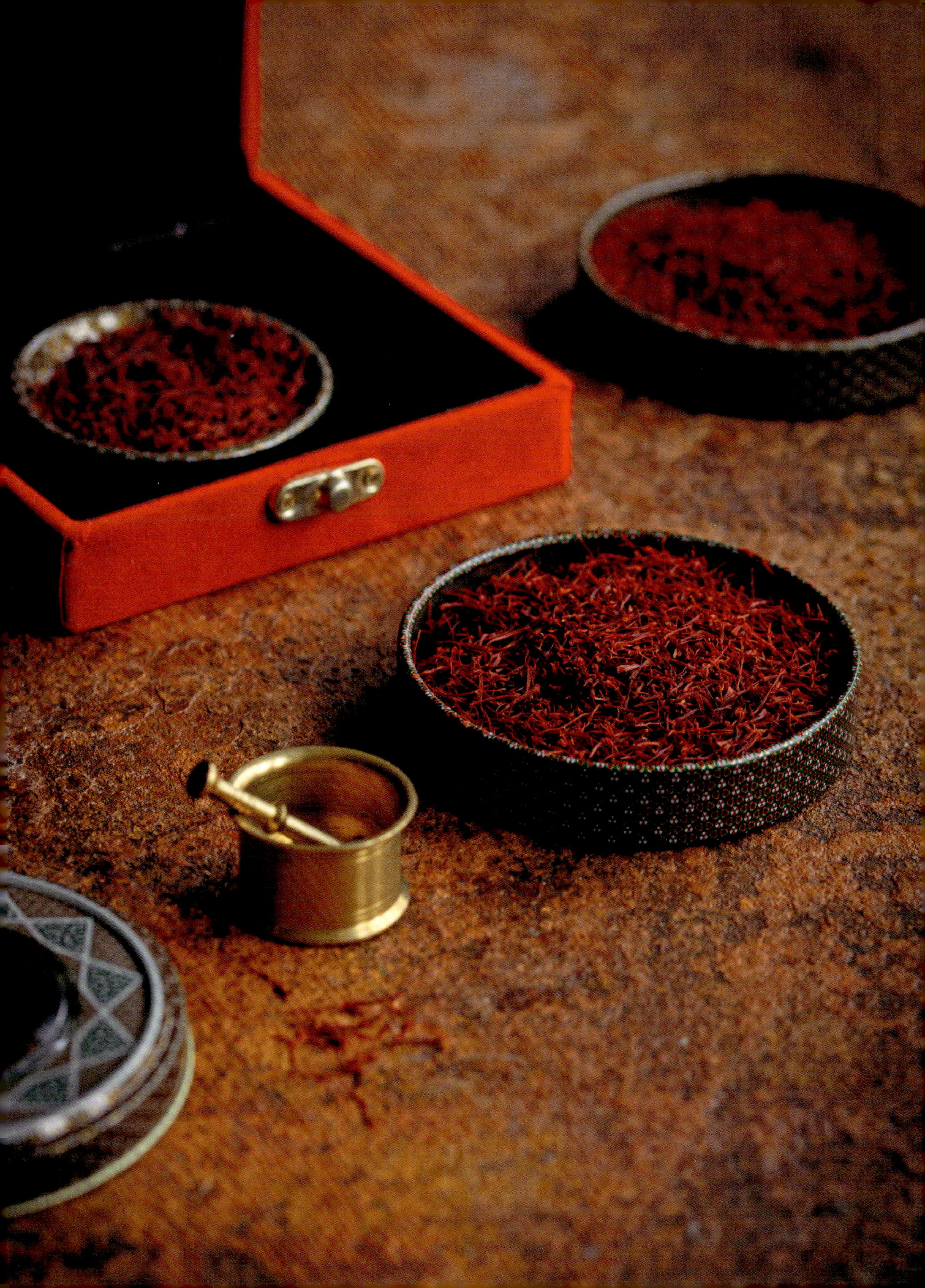

toast, or canned tomato soup with a ghee and curry leaf tempering are two prime examples. My Tanzania-born father is a fan of 'fruit jelly salad' made with Princes canned fruit, strawberry jelly (jello) and evaporated milk. His mother baked Bird's custard powder cakes inside a sand oven in Mombasa, Kenya. For years in our home, we used mushy peas in place of yellow peas when making my mother's recipe for raghda pattice (Gujarati potato cakes). This is something she picked up in the 1970s when the customary ingredients were not as readily available as they are today. Why am I telling you this? Well, when in conversation, much of this is perceived as diasporic communities 'making do'. Whilst this may have been true for some, especially those earlier generations who had to replace India's hero herb coriander (cilantro) with parsley, jaggery with brown sugar, and nuts with Weetabix (for multiple reasons from financial to seasonal), I believe it was much less of a compromise for generations like mine who were born into this fluid style of eating. We flit between food cultures because it's what we know. In fact, assimilation food is more than simply 'making do'. It is an opportunity to delve face-first into exciting foods that have a sense of the new whilst still feeling the comforting connection of familial roots. Assimilation food is as uniquely interesting as those who cook it. It also tells a story of heritage interlaced with movement and cultural change. With claims of authenticity comes bags of subjectivity. Does authenticity mean I only cook millet in the winter and sorghum in the summer, according to a centuries-old custom in India? Does cooking authentically mean we should always add asafoetida when cooking lentils and pulses like Ayurveda tells us? Should tadka or spice tempering happen at the beginning of the recipe, at the end, or both? Ask ten different people and you'll probably get ten different answers because the nuances of Indian food are both hyper-regional and personal. If you think about it, what is now deemed to be authentic, wasn't always. Historically, through trade routes came potatoes, tomatoes and chillies; all used abundantly in Indian cuisine today, and introduced by Europeans (the Portuguese, Dutch, British, and others), and with origins in the Americas and Caribbean. By no stretch does this render India's modern favourite – the tomato-laden curry, butter chicken – inauthentic because innovation doesn't cancel tradition, or vice versa. Today, tradition and innovation coexist quite happily, creating some of the most remarkable tasting dishes, many inspired by global cuisines.

The 'f' word

I'm thankful for the lessons I've had in Indian cookery from my mother, but even she hasn't always stuck to 'the rules'. Cheesy naan dough balls were her nineties dinner-party showstopper. Fluffy balls of nigella seed-infused, yeasted dough, stuffed with melting mozzarella and brushed with garlic and coriander (cilantro) butter. I still make them today. Her father was a chef and confectioner of Indian sweets (candies), trained in hotels across Mumbai. Upon migrating to East Africa in the 1930s, he had his first taste of vanilla. Since then, he added it to his signature jalebi recipe (a syrupy, spiral-shaped sweet). They were famous across Nairobi. Even after moving to the UK, the orders for his delicious vanilla jalebi came in from the local Gurdwara in Southampton. Food is an ever-evolving landscape and history has proven time and time again that change can be fruitful. So many dishes, as we know them today are products of 'fusion', whether it's an ingredient, style or technique. 'Fusion' is a term often used to connote a lack of thoughtfulness, a half-baked idea, when in fact, almost everything we eat is a form of fusion food. As human beings, we're all a little bit of fusion, aren't we? I believe that we are products of our environment. We use the ingredients we can access to create the meals that enable ourselves and our loved ones to live well. The familiar sizzle of bhajiya (pakora) on rainy days bring comfort to me and my family – and we somehow always seem to have gram flour in the cupboard. It is through embracing our cultural diversity that we have the tools to create incredible new meals that continue to enrich our lives.

This is a cookbook for everyone

It really is. The recipes you'll find in this book are vegetarian and they have been created with a flavour first approach. A quick rummage in your cupboards or at the back of the fridge will hopefully inspire you to cook one of the dishes you find here or adapt the recipe using what you have. I'm not going to say you won't miss the meat, if you are indeed a meat eater, because that is not my intention. What I will say is the recipes in this book will offer some new and interesting Indian-inspired options to add to your meal rotation. They just happen to be vegetarian.

Vegetarianism in India goes back centuries and whilst around 30 per cent of the population follow a vegetarian diet, you will find many adopt a more flexible approach. There are many ways to define 'vegetarian' in India; ovo-vegetarian (rather amusingly referred to in the Desi community as 'eggetarian'), pescatarian, lacto-vegetarian, Sattvic, vegetarian on certain religious days, vegetarian but eats chicken, vegetarian but sometimes eats the non-veg curry sauce (and not the meat), eats eggs and gelatine only in desserts but vegetarian the rest of the time and of course, non-vegetarian and vegan. It's the subject of many debates.

I have been brought up in a family of lacto-vegetarians (dairy-eating vegetarians, but no eggs) and lucky enough to have ingredients and options at my fingertips. Pushing the boundaries of plant-based cuisine has been a passion since I was very young. With Indian cuisine being so rich in vegetarian options, I've never felt like I'm missing out.

Where I've taken inspiration from India's regional non-vegetarian dishes, I've made a meatless version that tastes great and offers an interesting texture. For example, the Artichoke Pakora (see page 55) is a dish inspired by Punjab's famous Amritasri fish tikki sold on almost every street. I have found that artichokes (and I use canned for maximum convenience) lend themselves to the dish due to their naturally delicate flavour and succulent texture. A melange of carom seeds, citrusy coriander seeds, mustard oil and ginger paste imparts all the flavours of northern India in this plant-based ode to the traditional river fish version. I don't see these ingredients as meat replacements, rather as delicious elements cooked in a way that keeps things fresh and exciting.

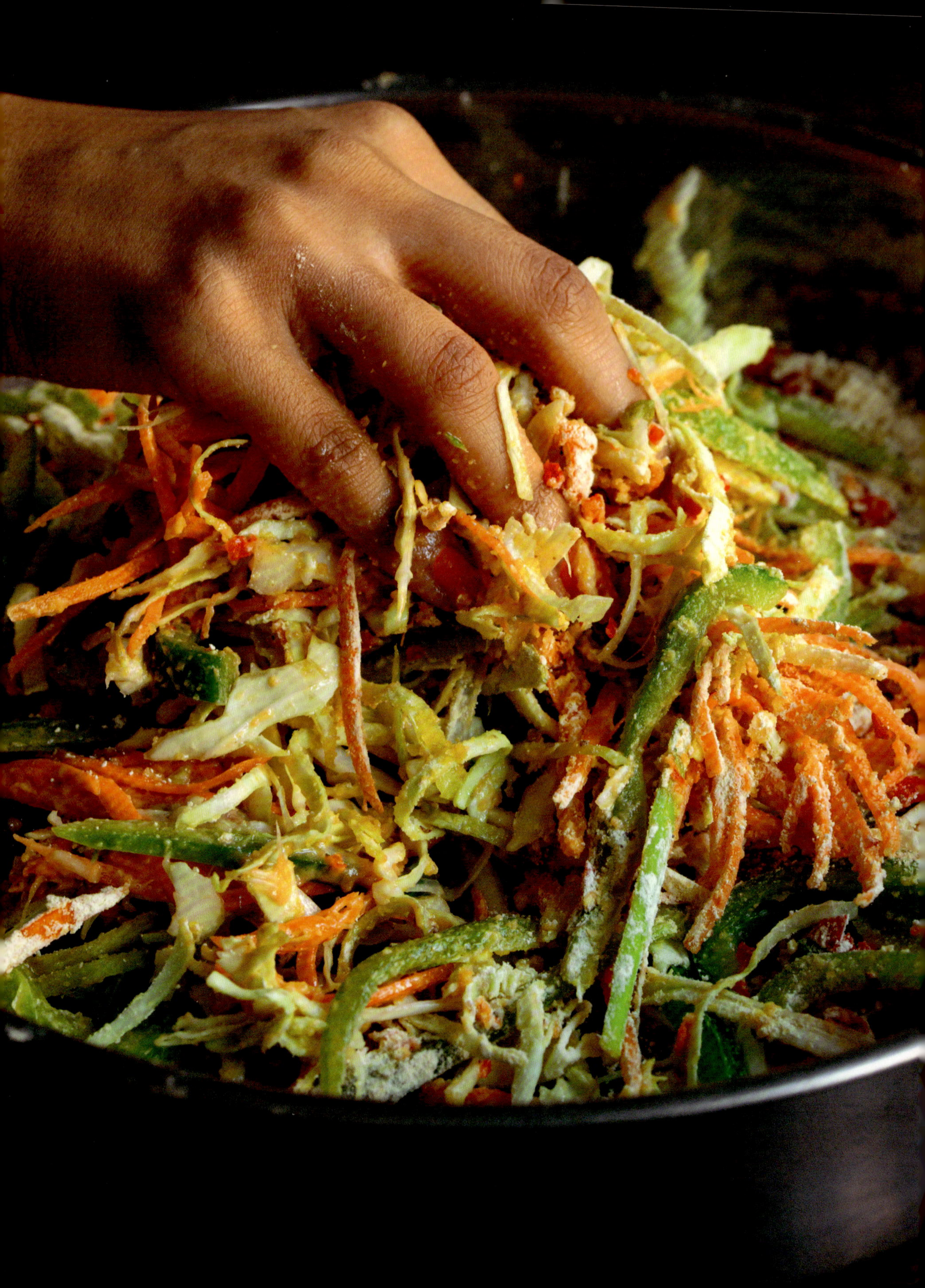

Vegan

Whilst India is known for having a big dairy culture, many recipes in this book can be adapted to suit a vegan diet. Where possible, I've included notes for how to veganise recipes. With the abundance of dairy-free milk, cream, butter, cheese and meat substitutes available in supermarkets, you'll find that a lot of recipes require just a few straightforward swaps. I use the Indian cheese, paneer, in abundance, and for this you can simply replace it with my Fauxneer (see page 251) – a vegan substitute with a richer flavour and bouncier mouthfeel to firm tofu, although tofu is also a good alternative.

Gluten free

Many of the recipes in this book are suitable or can be adapted to suit a gluten-free diet. In many cases, making a simple switch to a gluten-free plain (all-purpose) flour alternative will suffice. If you have a severe allergy or coeliac's disease, be mindful of flour blends that are processed in the same factory as wheat flours. Store-bought ground asafoetida, a spice I use widely throughout my recipes, is often combined with anti-caking agents (usually in the form of wheat flour). If you are unsure, always check the label, or use pure, compound asafoetida (you will need to pound this yourself at home).

I understand that coming up with menus can be quite a chore. If you're looking for menu options, flick to the back of this book where you'll find my suggestions for creating vegan and gluten-free meals.

A pinch of this and a fistful of that

Cooking by eye is an age-old tradition in many cultures across the globe. In Indian cuisine, a fistful or ek mutthi (one fistful) is a common phrase in Gujarati when describing how to cook a recipe. It usually refers to dry but not floury ingredients like rice, lentils, nuts and beans. A pinch or ek chutki (one pinch) is used for ingredients you use less zealously, like strong spices or salt. I have aunties who share recipes measured in 'cornflakes bowls', 'steel glasses', 'mugs' and 'eating spoons', too, although none ever specify the proper size. Whose thumb do they mean when they say, 'a thumb-sized piece of root ginger'? Exactly how big is a 'lemon-sized ball'? Their recipes will state to add 'enough water to make a dough' or to cook 'until done'. My Kishor kaka, a well-seasoned cook, is known for passing recipes on with the instruction, to add 'all the usual masalas'. As much as I am in awe of their skills to adapt and flex based on years of cooking experience, I understand that for some this might be problematic, and in particular, for those who are less familiar with Indian cuisine. I believe that anyone can cook Indian food and I'm here to show you the way I do it.

In this book, you will find metric weights and measures, as well as imperial weights and volumetric cups for most ingredients. Garlic cloves are large and peeled. All ginger should be peeled before being further prepared, and onions are peeled. Lemons refer to the large, European variety rather than the small Indian type. Ghee and oil can be used interchangeably, unless noted otherwise in the recipe. Unless specified, 'oil' refers to any flavourless cooking oil like vegetable, sunflower or rapeseed. Ghee can also be replaced with Homemade Vegan Ghee (see page 244), if required. I always recommend cooking lentils and beans in ghee because the flavours are next-level tasty when you do. The longer you boil daal with whole spices, the better it will taste, and any Indian daal or curry often tastes better the next day. Recipes for commonly used spice blends (mixed masalas) are included towards the back of this book. Whilst some store-bought varieties can be of good quality, a freshly ground homemade masala is even better. For the softest breads, I like to work with high moisture doughs; for this reason, you may find some bread doughs in this book are on the stickier side, but after the specified resting periods, they will become easier to work with. All the desserts in this book are free from eggs. Where possible, I have included notes on how to veganise the recipes in this book. Some recipes may need several substitutions, whilst others can be made vegan friendly or, indeed, free from gluten by switching out one or two ingredients.

Serving sizes

After years of writing recipes, the one thing that still makes me uncomfortable is stating serving sizes. The serving sizes in this book are a rough approximation. The real measure will be determined by your appetite on any given day. In other words, please don't listen to me and eat as much daal, roti and rice as you like.

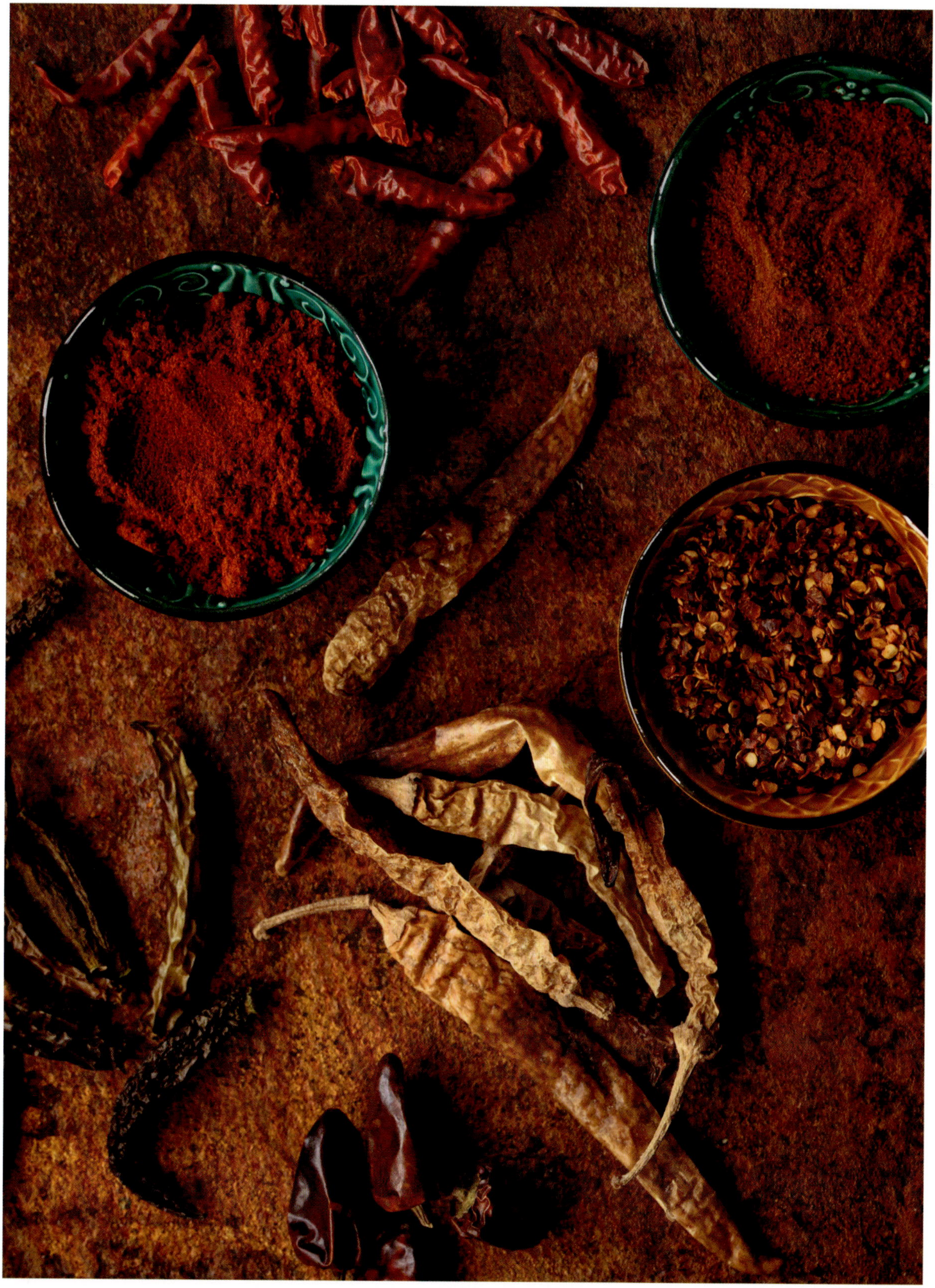

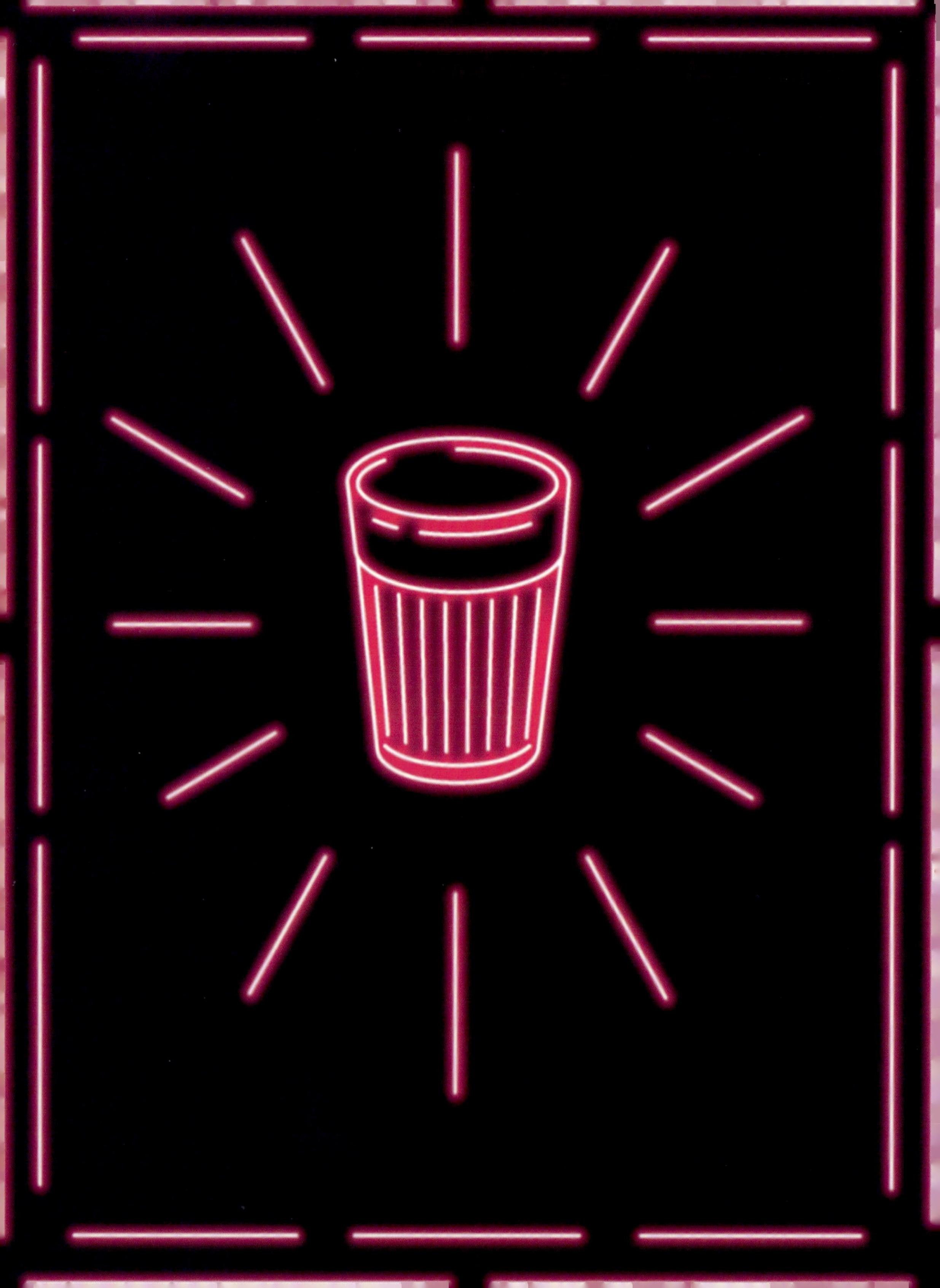

BUT FIRST, *Chai*

Pull on your stretchy pants...

'Atithi Devo Bhava' is the foundational mantra of our hospitality. This Sanskrit phrase carries the meaning 'Guest is God' and it's taken very seriously. Just as offerings of food and drink are brought to temples as a means of worship, it is customary to treat those who visit our homes with the same generosity and warmth. From the host's perspective, this is simply a way of appreciating the presence of their guest. To acknowledge the journey another soul has taken to be with you at that very moment is regarded as an act of true compassion. So, we will begin at the beginning.

'Chai?' I asked my mother as she looked up from the cash register in our shop. The first time I ever switched on a stove was to make chai. It was for my mother – an avid tea drinker and somewhat of a chai masala connoisseur. I was eight years old and had taken it upon myself to impress her with my tremendously grown-up skills. How hard could it be? I'd seen the classic pan-on-a-stovetop method a hundred times before. I knew it had to be boiled for a while after adding the milk to cook off the flavour of raw milk. I knew this lengthy boil would also give the spices time to infuse. My mother tentatively wrote out the instructions on the back of an empty paper bag, the kind we used for weighing out sweets (candies) in the shop. Grabbing the paper bag emblazoned with the nineties Trebor Bassett logo, she shot me a bemused look. Did she think I couldn't do it?

After a mad dash up two flights of stairs, I pulled out the ingredients from the cupboard, my heart walloping as I thought about how freaking perfect this chai was going to be. Tea leaves, mum's homemade chai masala, sugar and milk from the fridge all lined up like a battalion of toy soldiers ready to go into combat. This was it, my moment to prove I could make chai like all the aunties do. I filled our fatigued stainless-steel chai pan with a non-specific amount of water and lit the stove. The crackle of the ignition reminded me of my morning Rice Krispies popping as soon as milk was poured on. Next, I added two teaspoons of black tea leaves and one teaspoon of chai masala. The steam began to waft, level with my nose and not under it, for I was a solid 4 feet 5 inches. Once it boiled, I added half a cup of milk and probably too much sugar. The water ceased to boil as the heavy cloud of milk rippled through it like a tornado. It looked right to me. As the tan-coloured liquid began to bubble at the edges, I knew it was showtime. This was the moment it could all go wrong. You see, chai takes no prisoners when it comes to the boiling stage. If you take your eye off it for a moment, it can overflow and turn mum's shiny cooker into a basin of brown sludge. I moved the dial on the old stove back and forth, causing the tea to rise and fall in sync with the intensity of the flame. It climbed higher towards

and leave your shoes at the door.

the top of the pan as the flame roared louder, and then retreated into position when lowered. The tension mounted as I repeated the rise and fall action, suspicious it was controlling my breath. Inhale, exhale. In retrospect, making chai is a great prompt for practicing mindfulness. The chicken-shaped egg timer clucked to say my ten minutes were up and judging by the colour of the tea, it was ready. Gas off. The Forever Friends mug I picked out for Mother's Day was, of course, my drinking vessel of choice. A tea strainer was balanced on top of the mug, then I grabbed the pan with a sansi (pot holder). It took all my focus to pour the chai without spilling a drop. I could smell sweet cardamom, followed by the spicy ginger and black pepper that always ambushed the back of my throat. It was perfect.

As I meandered down the corridor, taking care to tread carefully down the stairs, I thought about how proud my mother was going to be. I got halfway down the stairs before a tiny wave of tea shimmied up the side of the mug and splashed onto my thumb. The burn was well and truly felt. Not one to be put off my mission, I continued down the remaining steps and appeared in the shop. I presented the mug like it was a very hot trophy. It was still too warm to drink so I sat on the step and told her all about my epic tea-making saga, being sure to leave out the details of my battle wounds so she wouldn't say no to me making it again next time. After what felt like hours, she finally took a sip. I held my breath and looked on with eager eyes. 'That'll do, Poppet,' she said.

Chai making is more of a ritual than it is a recipe; a process steeped in a 170-year history. Tea was introduced to India by the British in the nineteenth century. It was planted across Darjeeling and Assam, for these regions had the ideal climate for growing tea leaves. For Indians, it is not only the quality of the tea that matters, but also the masala blend and cooking process that determines the deliciousness of the cup. How one likes their tea is deeply personal and unique to them. In the West, we may ask a guest if milk and sugar are required. With regular masala chai, both are a given, unless a sugar-free cup is requested. These days it's common to use plant-based milks as a vegan alternative to dairy milk. I find oat milk, almond milk and rice milk are all good options. Condensed milk is a delightfully decadent addition to masala chai. The practice of swirling a typhoon of sticky condensed milk into strong-brewed chai is a longstanding tradition across the Subcontinent, as well as in the Middle East, in parts of eastern Asia and Africa. This shelf-stable alternative to milk was a European import, invented in the mid-1800s. My father's dear friend, Bryon Rollinson, would visit our newspaper shop often, perching on the steps beside the royal blue counter, sharing stories of his days serving in the British navy. While stationed in India, he recalled drinking karak chai (a type of strong masala tea), which he requested the Indian chefs prepare using the condensed milk supplied in his rations. My mother would jokingly offer him a cup of the same whenever he visited. He politely declined, since he much preferred coffee, sipped leisurely enough to share a few stories over. Mr Rollinson would always vanish before the noisy school kids arrived in from the double-decker bus that pulled into Town Road at 15.32 every weekday afternoon.

When making chai masala at home, there is no need to pre-toast the spices in a dry pan. Since this encourages the spices to release their natural oils, the aromas will simply dissipate as they sit in the jar. The heat from the spice grinder will also encourage the spices to develop, so it's best to make chai masala in small batches and to use it within three months. Store it in an airtight container, preferably somewhere cool and dark.

I'd like to welcome you by offering up a trio of my favourite hot drinks, including Masala Chai (see page 24) and a few other tealess, hot-drink options, like Maple-cardamom Masala Coffee (see page 28) and Narangi Hot Chocolate (see page 27), which is infused with orange zest and aniseed-like fennel seeds. Make these drinks for guests and, of course, for yourself.

Mind your thumbs!

Six tips for the perfect cup of chai

1. Balance your spices

My homemade chai masala recipe delivers aromatic flavours as well as a warming whack of dried ginger and peppercorns. When cooler aromatic spices and warm spices work in tandem, beautiful things happen. For me, it's the spiciness of the ginger and peppercorns offset by cooling cardamom that takes a standard cuppa chai to the next level.

2. Choose your favourite tea

Use good-quality black tea. It doesn't have to be premium, just strong and with great flavour – or a flavour you like! Assam and Darjeeling are both suitably strong. My family use Kenyan black tea. Loose leaf tea is popular, but tea bags make for an easier clean up. Choose whatever works for you.

3. Boil it in a pan, on the stove

Never use a teapot or cup for brewing. To make proper Masala Chai, you need a saucepan and a good 15 minutes or so. It's a no-shortcut zone. Before adding the milk, brew the tea for 2 or 3 minutes. I like to give it a hard boil to extract as much tea flavour as possible. Once you've added milk, it needs a further 10 minutes to simmer. The spices and tea require time to mingle, and the milk must lose that raw milk flavour. This is crucial.

4. Stir often

To stop anything burning on the base of the pan.

5. Skim and strain

Skim off any malai (skin) that forms on the surface of the chai. It's totally fine to consume but it does make pouring rather difficult. It's a bit like when skin forms on the top of hot custard – some people love it! Malai is less likely to form with plant-based milks. Pour the chai through a tea strainer into a mug.

6. Don't forget the snacks

Biscuits (cookies), buns, bhajiya (pakora), samosas, cake and beyond. It's basically the law to serve chai with various sweet and savoury snacks. This is customary during monsoon season in India, and all year round when it comes to entertaining visitors. You can explore my favourite chai-time snack options in the next chapter, With Chai.

Masala Chai

SERVES 2 • PREP: 20 MINS • COOK: 15 MINS

2 tsp strong black tea leaves (or 2 tea bags)

2 tsp Chai Masala (see page 267)

400 ml (13½ fl oz/1⅔ cups) whole (full-fat) milk or your favourite plant-based milk

Sugar, sweetener or sweetened condensed milk, to taste

Vegan?

Use any plant-based milk to make this chai. Oat milk and almond milk are both excellent options.

This is my take on the classic chai, with a heavy Gujarati influence. This Masala Chai has a generous kick of black peppercorns and dried ginger, balanced with aromatic spices like green cardamom, cinnamon and vanilla. The flavours of the chai masala are a nod to the warmly spiced bakes that couple so well with tea, too. Goes with: everything.

1. Over a medium-high heat, bring 400 ml (13½ fl oz/1⅔ cups) water to a boil in a saucepan, milk pan or chai pan. Add the tea leaves or tea bags along with the chai masala. Continue to boil for about 2 minutes.

2. Add the milk of your choice and stir well. Bring to a rolling boil, stirring often. Once the chai begins to foam up, you can turn the heat down a little but continue to boil it quite vigorously for about 10 minutes. Do not leave the chai unattended as it boils. It tends to froth up and overflow, meaning the clean-up isn't so much fun.

3. Once the chai has boiled for 10 minutes, remove the pan from the heat and strain the chai into cups. Sweeten to taste. Serve hot with your favourite biscuit (cookie), bun or savoury snack.

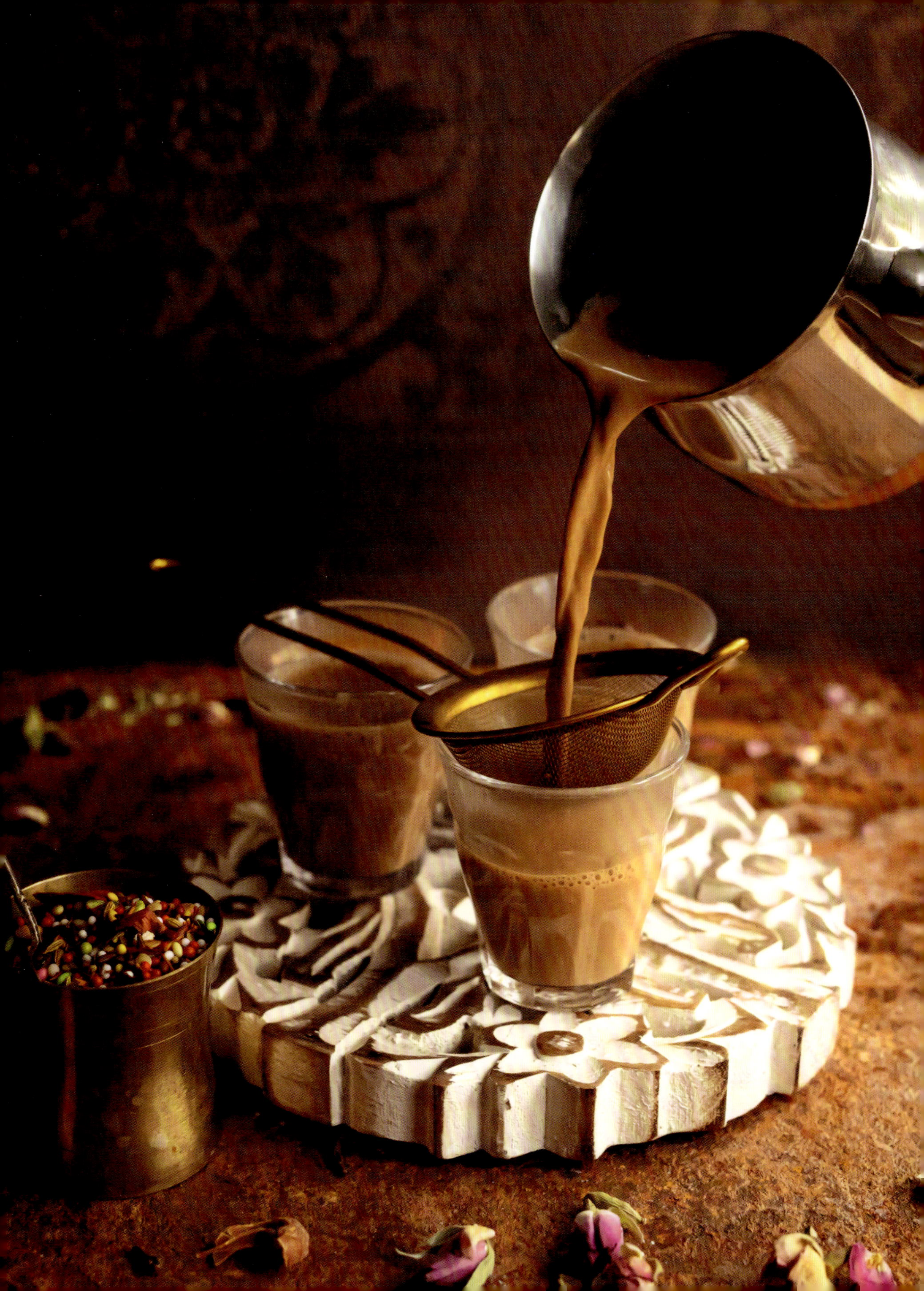

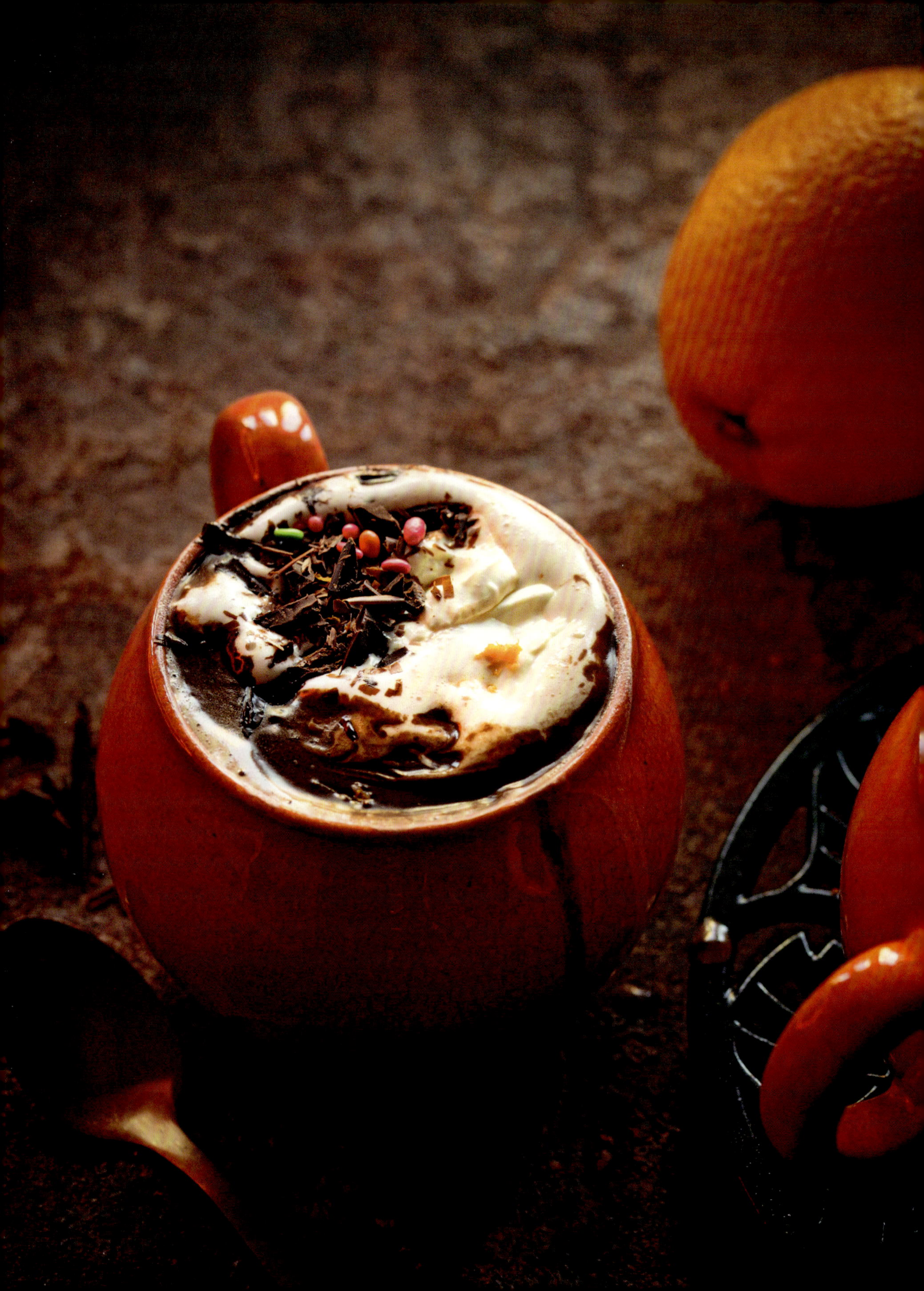

Narangi Hot Chocolate

SERVES 2 · PREP: 15 MINS · COOK: 5 MINS

100 g (3½ oz) dark (bittersweet) chocolate (70% cocoa solids), finely chopped, plus a few extra shavings to serve

50 g (1¾ oz) milk chocolate, finely chopped

1 tbsp unsweetened cocoa powder

1 tbsp cornflour (cornstarch)

475 ml (16 fl oz/scant 2 cups) whole (full-fat) milk

1 tsp ground fennel seeds

Grated (shredded) zest of ½ large orange, plus a little extra to serve

A small pinch of flaky sea salt

Whipped double (heavy) cream, to serve

Candied fennel seeds, to serve (optional)

A thick and creamy hot chocolate with sweet orange and fennel seeds. Serve as it is, with spicy Indian snacks, or alongside churros for a decadent pudding. Colourful candied fennel seeds are usually served after meals as a mouth freshener, but I love using them as sprinkles to decorate drinks, cakes and cookies. Use a combination of milk and dark (bittersweet) chocolate for the perfect balance of bittersweet flavours.

1. In a bowl, combine the chopped dark (bittersweet) and milk chocolate, cocoa powder and cornflour (cornstarch). Stir well to ensure the powdered ingredients evenly coat the chocolate.

2. Over a medium-high heat, add the milk to a saucepan along with the ground fennel seeds, orange zest and sea salt. Bring to a boil then lower the heat and simmer gently for 3–4 minutes. Switch off the heat and whisk in the chocolate mixture. Continue to whisk until the chopped chocolate has completely melted and the mixture has thickened.

3. Pour into mugs and top with the whipped cream, some extra chocolate shavings, a little grated (shredded) orange zest and optional candied fennel seeds.

Notes

For an extra-dark hot chocolate, use all 70% dark (bittersweet) chocolate in place of the milk chocolate.

This thick and creamy hot chocolate is truly decadent, so you can serve it as an afternoon treat or as a beautiful end to an Indian meal. If you reduce the quantity of milk to 350 ml (11¾ fl oz/scant 1½ cups), you can even pour it over cake as a hot chocolate sauce.

If you prefer a thinner hot chocolate, reduce the amount of cornflour (cornstarch) to ½ tablespoon and add an additional 50 ml (1¾ fl oz/scant ¼ cup) milk.

Search for candied fennel seeds in your local Indian supermarket or online. They're sometimes mixed with different seeds like roasted sesame or edible dried rose petals.

Maple-cardamom Masala Coffee

MAKES 1 LARGE OR 2 SMALL CUPS • PREP: 15 MINS • COOK: 10 MINS

275 ml (9¼ fl oz/generous 1 cup) whole (full-fat) milk or your favourite plant-based milk

6 green cardamom pods, lightly bashed

2.5-cm (1-inch) cinnamon stick

6–8 gratings nutmeg

4 tsp instant coffee powder

1 tbsp maple syrup, or to your taste

Vegan?

Use any plant-based milk to make this coffee. Oat milk and almond milk are both excellent options.

A latte-style masala coffee with warming cinnamon and aromatic cardamom. The creamy coffee pairs particularly well with maple syrup for an autumnal feel. Feel free to replace the maple syrup with hazelnut or coconut syrup if you prefer.

1. Pour the milk into a saucepan set over a medium heat. Once it comes to a boil, add the cardamom, cinnamon and nutmeg. Allow to simmer over a low heat for 5–10 minutes.

2. Add the coffee and maple syrup, whisking to incorporate. Continue to whisk vigorously or use a milk frother to achieve a creamy consistency.

3. Strain the hot coffee through a fine-mesh sieve or tea strainer into one large or two small cups.

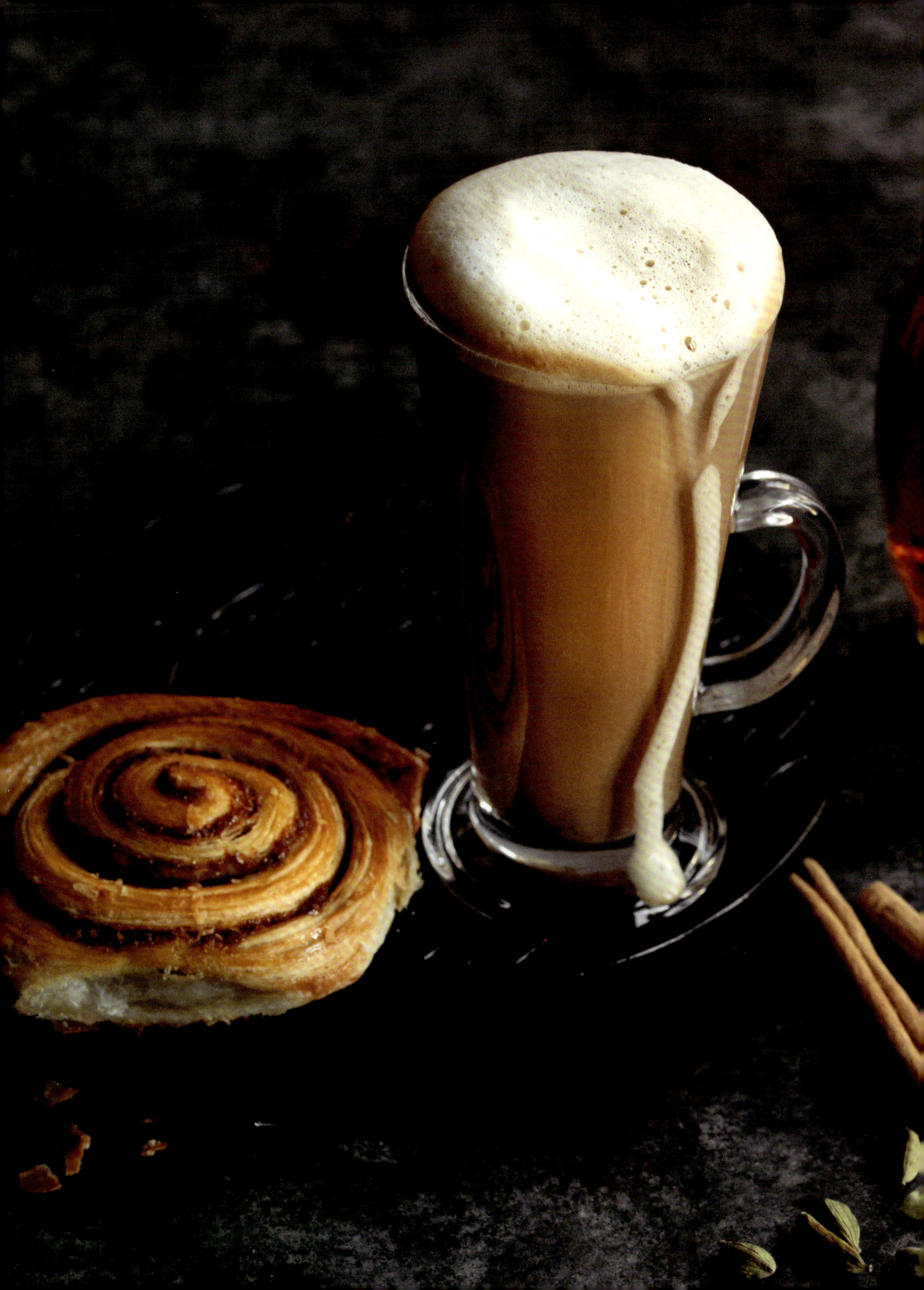

WITH
Chai

Make extra for when...

One bite of a spicy snack, one sip of chai. Repeat as necessary. Tea-time snacks are a must in most South Asian homes. Indians held on to the practice of afternoon tea long after gaining independence. It has developed into a ceremonial act of love, shared between friends and families. Samosas, pakoras, kachori, biscuits (cookies), buns, rusks and cakes are all welcome at chai time. Entire books could be written on Indian afternoon-tea favourites and, still, there wouldn't be enough pages to include them all.

The snack options are infinite and vary from region to region and home to home. Lentils, vegetables, grains, pastries and bread-based dishes feature heavily. Almost every snack has a perfect chutney partner for dipping, too. There's never been one I haven't liked. I think it's because many of them are deep-fried and laden with interesting textures and flavours. The craggy, crispy bits around the edges of Maharashtrian kanda bhajji (onion bhaji), the pillowy interior of Mysore bonda made with rice flour, ginger and finely snipped curry leaves and, of course, the melting crunch of Gujarati lamba gathiya alongside sweet jalebi and fried chillies. It's warming food for the soul that invites loved ones and perfect strangers to gather around a table and share a few moments of downtime during a busy day. One whiff of fried gram flour and suddenly a kitchen is buzzing. I'm not sure if it counts, but the ritual of enjoying sweet and savoury tea-time snacks with chai is my most favourite type of meal. There's variety and texture on the table that surpasses any other meal. Hot and spicy aloo tikkis, daal bhajiya, Parsi buttered buns called bun maska, pakoras of every kind, nankhatai (semolina biscuits) and Indian-style tea sandwiches are always welcome at chai nashta (teatime).

Not all the options are fried, but a great many are and this is what makes them feel like a treat. For lighter options, there are dhokla (steamed cakes of soaked and ground lentils or flours), poha (spicy flattened rice), khakhra (a type of roasted multigrain cracker), handvo (fermented lentil cake) and Bhojpuri bafauri (made from steamed channa daal). I've taken inspiration from dishes such as these (and others) to create snacks that'll go down a treat with a cuppa chai. Whether you choose to dunk or not is your call. A mug of sweet chai and the fried bread, masala poori, is my go-to sweet and savoury combo for dunking.

the guests are gone.

In this chapter, you'll find recipes for Indian-inspired savouries and sweets, plus some, like the Cheddar and Mango Chutney Loaf (see page 38), that blur the boundaries between east and west. In addition to the recipes here, I'd like to add that it's a perfectly common (and thrifty) snack-time practice to prepare toasted sandwiches from leftover curry – any curry will do, as long as it's a little dry. You'll get bonus points for slathering the outside of the bread with salted butter and the inside with Green Coriander and Mint Chutney (see page 197). A slice of cheese never goes amiss either (Cheddar, mozzarella and Gouda are all excellent choices), but I'll leave that up to you. My recipe for Aloo Croissants (see page 41) was inspired by a container of leftover samosa filling and an open packet of croissants that were becoming staler by the minute. Stuffed and toasted, this combination makes a dreamy carb-on-carb arrangement of flavours and textures. In fact, there's a world of snacks that require little to no preparation, which is great for when unexpected guests turn up. An electric toaster or Indian-style sandwich toaster are both handy to have, but a frying pan (skillet) will do if neither are available. Place a weight the size of the sandwich on top to create close contact between the sandwich and pan for the crispiest finish. Serve with any chutney you have, either homemade or store-bought. There are three homemade chutney options in the Sides chapter of this book.

I like to batch blend fresh chutneys and then freeze them in portions for speedy samosa dips or topping chaat. Speaking of chaat, a plethora of storecupboard snacks can save time when it comes to throwing together afternoon tea or sharing dishes on the fly. Frozen stuffed parathas, samosas and spring rolls are always great to keep on standby. Jackson Pollock a samosa chaat with splashes of homemade or store-bought chutneys, and then sprinkle with sev, chevdo or even crushed crisps; a fast and fabulous snack that's ready in under 20 minutes.

In true Gujarati fashion, I've included a few sweet options to balance the spicy recipes. An Indian-inspired Rocky Road (see page 45), as well as some very pink Raspberry and Rosewater Iced Buns (see page 52). Both are nods to my favourite childhood sweet treats. I hope they delight you too.

1

2

3

Nine Indian snacks to look out for next time you're shopping

Chevdo (1)

What is it?
A mix of puffed rice, fried gram flour noodles, nuts, fried daal, spices and more.

How do you eat it?
As it is, with a spoon. Or with a dollop of plain yogurt. Sprinkled on chaat. In cheese sandwiches, à la crisps sandwiches.

Sev

What is it?
Thin fried gram flour noodles.

How do you eat it?
Sprinkled on chaat. Or as a topping for daal, mixed with onions, tomatoes, chillies and coriander (cilantro).

Gathiya (2)

What is it?
Thick or thin fried gram flour noodles. Often flavoured with chilli powder, carom seeds and/or black pepper.

How do you eat it?
As they are, by the fistful. My dad tells stories of drowning his gathiya in a bowl of chai as a young lad, like a savoury Indian cereal. I can't say I've tried that, but he insists it's delicious – I say it's a crime against cornflakes.

Pani Puri

What is it?
Thin and crispy discs of wheat flour. Deep-fry or air-fry to make them pop up into perfectly spherical bubbles.

How do you eat it?
A popular street food snack across India. You may also know them as puchka or gol gappe. Each one has a mouth-puckering mint and coriander (cilantro) flavoured water poured inside. Simply press the tops to create a crispy cup and fill with mashed potato, black chickpeas, sev, onions, tomatoes and a pani flavour of your choice.

Chakri (3)

What is it?
A craggy spiral of rice flour, cumin seeds and chillies. Chakri is the diminutive term for Sudarshana Chakra, the auspicious disc carried by Lord Vishnu according to Hindu belief. Dangerously moreish.

How do you eat it?
As it is. I'm an advocate of going in cinnamon-roll style, breaking off the spirals and eating from the outside in.

Rusk (1)

What is it?
Double-baked sweet biscuit (cookie). Not unlike biscotti, but with a caramelised sugar or condensed milk quality. Flavours often include a plain type, cardamom and tutti frutti. Thick and crunchy, you'll find an Indian rusk can withstand double the immersion time of a Hobnob – it has the dunking longevity of a US Navy SEAL!

How do you eat it?
Dunk it in chai. Or don't.

Far far (2)

What is it?
Colourful crackers of tapioca, rice or potato starch. They're typically unflavoured with a texture that is similar to prawn crackers. They're the reason I agreed to go to Indian weddings as a kid because the buffet table was never in short supply of them. Food that speaks to your inner 5-year-old is the best. Buy dried far far by the packet. They come in a wealth of different colours and shapes, from tubes and waffles to stars and twists.

How do you eat it?
Far far are ready to deep-fry straight from the packet (the oil needs to be very hot). Fry just a few at a time since they puff to an absurdly large size in seconds. You won't believe your eyes.

Makhana (3)

What is it?
Makhana or lotus seed puffs are made from roasted lotus seeds, bashed while hot to create popcorn-like clouds that are ideal for snacking. Buy makhana ready puffed in a multitude of flavours.

How do you eat it?
Choose plain makhana and customise with your favourite seasonings. They're also delicious folded into creamy curries. Try a handful in my Brown Butter Cauliflower and Pea Makhani (see page 113) for a makhana-makhani of sorts.

Khichiya (4)

What is it?
Rice flour-based crackers made from dehydrated dough. The Gujarati grandmother's favourite. Rice khichiya and papad (lentil-based poppadoms) are somewhat of a community project that would be made in their hundreds at first sight of the summer sun. Rows and rows of people, rolling the dough and drying it under the sun to be fried or roasted into crackers later. The green chilli and cumin variety are especially moreish.

How do you eat it?
Deep-fry in very hot oil until the small disc grows to the size of what could be a bedsheet for a guinea pig. Serve them with tea or alongside meals. They're particularly delicious with khichdi. If you fry them in a high-sided pan that's around twice the width of the cracker, you can create a fabulous bowl shape to fill with chaat ingredients like boiled potatoes, black chickpeas, onions, tomatoes, masala yogurt and chutneys.

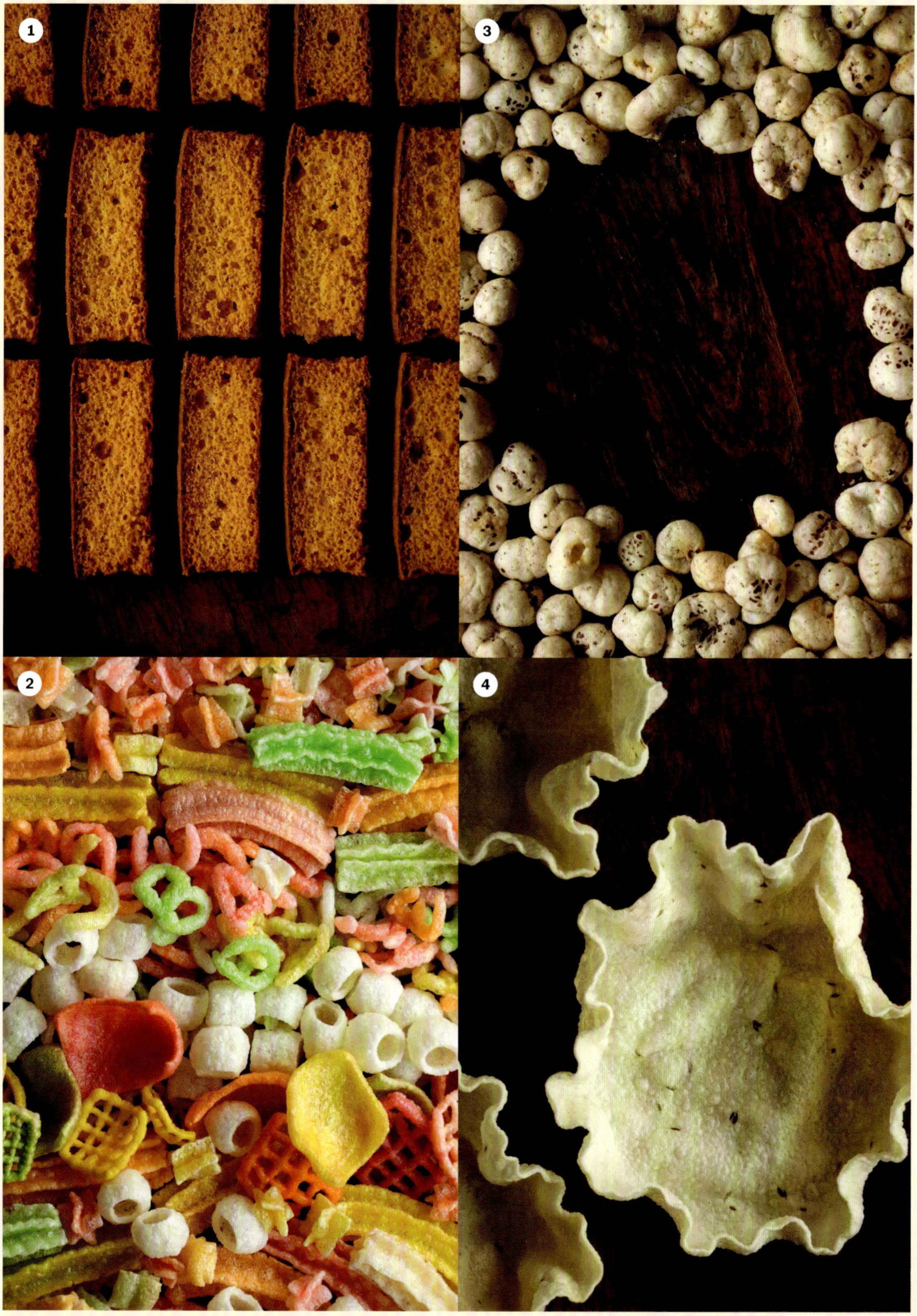
1
3
2
4

Cheddar and Mango Chutney Loaf

SERVES 4-6 • PREP: 40 MINS, PLUS 1½ HOURS RESTING • COOK: 30 MINS

225 g (8 oz/1¾ cups) strong white bread flour

7 g (2¼ tsp) fast-action dried yeast

2 tbsp full-fat milk powder

1 tbsp sugar

½ tsp salt

150 ml (5 fl oz/scant ⅔ cup) whole (full-fat) milk, slightly warm (around 26°C/78°F)

2 tbsp unsalted butter, very soft

1 tbsp milk, for brushing the loaf before it goes in the oven

2 tsp mango chutney, for brushing the loaf after it comes out of the oven

For the filling

1 spring onion (scallion), finely chopped

75 g (2⅔ oz) full-fat cream cheese

50 g (1¾ oz) mango chutney

50 g (1¾ oz/½ cup) grated (shredded) mature (sharp) Cheddar

Whilst my school friends munched on jam (jelly) sandwiches at lunchtime, I would tuck into cheese and mango chutney sandwiches. This pillowy loaf is a grown-up version of those sandwiches I'd find lovingly wrapped in my WWE branded lunchbox. If, by some miracle, you have any leftovers, toast and spread generously with butter for a carb-induced high.

1. In the bowl of a stand mixer fitted with a dough hook, combine the flour, yeast, milk powder, sugar and salt.

2. Add the milk and switch the mixer on, slow to begin with. Turn the mixer speed up and knead at medium for around 5 minutes.

3. With the mixer still running, add the butter a little at a time until it's all incorporated. Continue to knead for a further 10 minutes until the dough is soft, smooth and elastic. The mixer should run for a total of around 15 minutes.

4. Lightly grease the bowl and wrap with cling film (plastic wrap). Allow to rise in a warm place for 1 hour, or until doubled in size.

5. Meanwhile, make the filling. Set aside a teaspoon or so of the spring onion (scallion) greens to sprinkle on top of the finished loaf. Place all the remaining ingredients for the filling in a small bowl and stir well to make a thick paste.

6. Grease and line a 25 x 16-cm (10 x 6¼-inch/4 lb) loaf tin with parchment paper.

7. Knock back the risen dough and bring it together to form a ball. On a lightly floured surface, roll out the dough into a 40 x 30-cm (16 x 12-inch) rectangle. Spread the cheese filling mixture evenly over the dough. Starting from the longest side, roll the dough to form a log. Leaving about 2 cm (¾ inch) at the top intact, using a large, sharp knife, cut the dough in half lengthways to expose the layers. Carefully twist the two strands together to create a loaf, tucking the ends under to neaten. Place into the prepared loaf tin. Loosely cover the loaf with cling film and leave in a warm place for 30 minutes, or until slightly risen.

8. Preheat the oven to 190°C/170°C fan/375°F/Gas mark 5.

9. Remove the cling film and brush the top of the loaf with milk and bake in the preheated oven for 30 minutes.

10. Remove the loaf from the oven. While still warm, brush the loaf with more mango chutney and sprinkle over the reserved spring onion greens.

Notes

Swap the mango chutney for Green Coriander and Mint Chutney (see page 197) and use low-moisture mozzarella in place of Cheddar for Desi garlic bread vibes.

Vegan?

Replace the butter, cream cheese and Cheddar with your favourite dairy-free alternatives. A good vegan mozzarella or smoked vegan Cheddar will work perfectly.

Make it a feast!

Whilst this warm, sticky loaf is perfect alongside masala chai, it's also delicious for tearing and dunking into Curry Leaf Cream of Tomato Soup (see page 81).

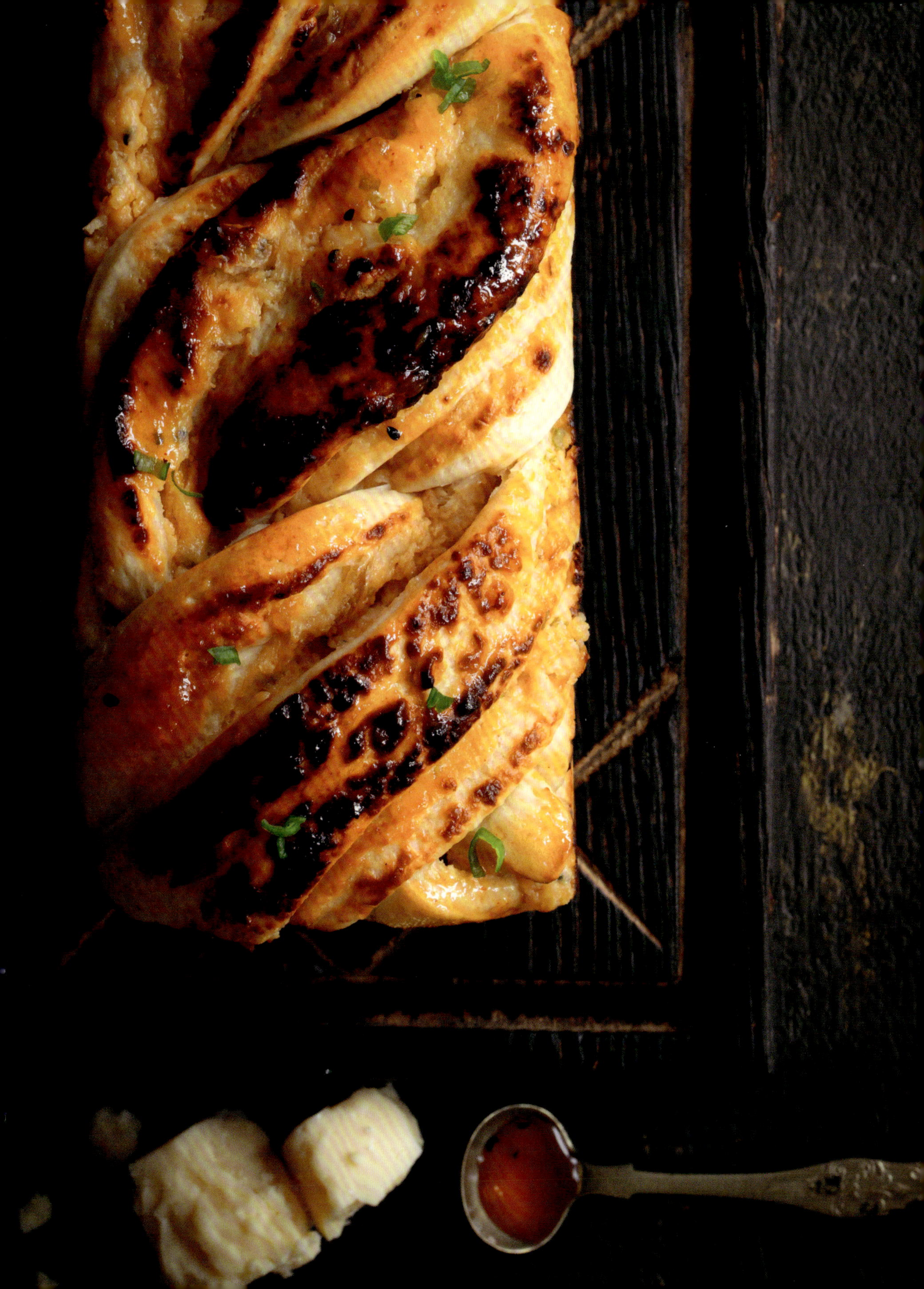

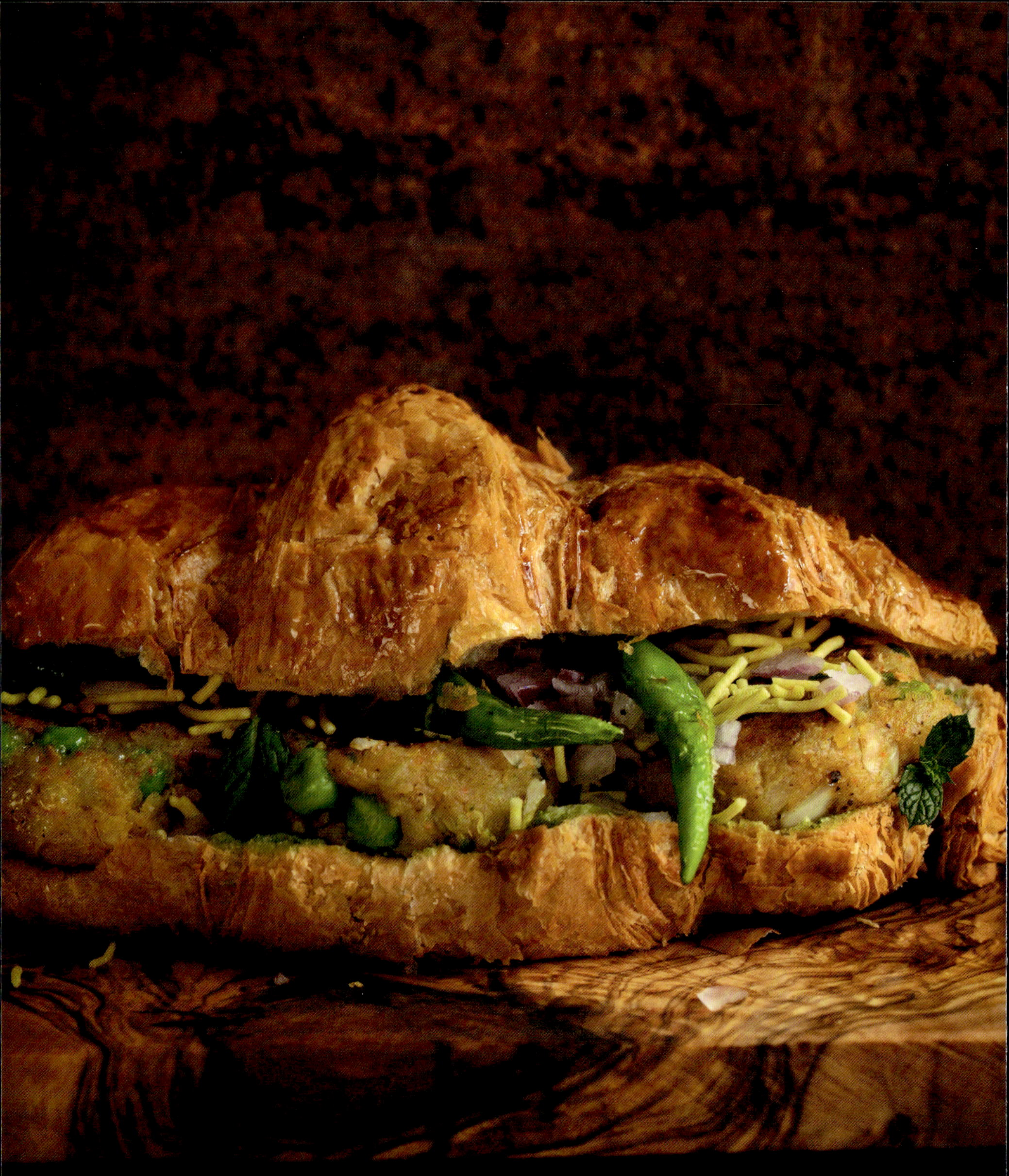

Aloo Croissants

SERVES 2 • PREP: 20 MINS, PLUS 15 MINS COOLING • COOK: 20 MINS

4 all-butter croissants
½ red onion, finely diced
1 tomato, diced
4 tbsp Green Coriander and Mint Chutney (see page 197)
100 g (3½ oz) thin sev
A few fresh mint leaves, to garnish
Deep-fried whole green chillies (optional) (see note below)

For the filling
3 large potatoes (about 500 g/1 lb 2 oz)
2 tsp oil
1 tsp cumin seeds
½ tsp ground coriander seeds
½ tsp chilli powder
1 tsp dried mango powder
¼ tsp ground turmeric
1 tsp dried fenugreek leaves, rubbed between your palms
1 tbsp chopped fresh mint leaves
¼ tsp salt

Stuff flaky croissants with a spicy potato filling for a snack that hits all the spots when you need a dose of comfort. This idea came about because I had a batch of leftover samosa filling stashed in the fridge and a packet of croissants ominously going stale on my kitchen counter. It's fast, easy and a go-to brunch in my home.

1. First, make the filling. Wash the potatoes and use a fork to prick holes all over the skins. Microwave on high power for 10 minutes, or until cooked through. Alternatively, boil the potatoes in their skins until tender. Allow to cool for 15 minutes and then peel the skins off. Roughly mash the potatoes with the back of a fork.

2. Heat the oil in a large, non-stick frying pan (skillet). Add the cumin seeds and allow to sizzle for a few seconds. Add the mashed potatoes, ground coriander seeds, chilli powder, dried mango powder, ground turmeric, dried fenugreek leaves, chopped mint and salt. Stir well and cook for 4–5 minutes, stirring continuously. Remove the pan from the heat.

3. Warm the croissants in a low oven. Split them across the middle lengthways, but do not slice all the way through. Stuff the potato filling inside the croissants, then top with diced red onion and tomato, some chutney, the sev and a few extra mint leaves before serving.

Vegan?

Vegan-friendly croissants are available in most large supermarkets. If you can't find them, try sandwiching the filling between slices of toasted sourdough.

Make it a feast!

I love a deep-fried green chilli and I think you will too! To make them, pierce several holes in as many long, thin green chillies as you like and deep-fry until the outside turns an ash grey and crinkled. Toss in a pinch of Chaat Masala (see page 263) and serve inside or alongside the potato-filled croissants. Alternatively, you can coat 4 pierced chillies in a teaspoon or so of oil, place into a microwave-safe bowl, cover and cook for around 2 minutes. Sprinkle with Chaat Masala (see page 263) and serve. These are also great with samosas and pakoras. Strictly for spice lovers.

Hara Bhara Rolls

SERVES 6-8 • PREP: 20 MINS, PLUS 20 MINS RESTING • COOK: 20 MINS

For the filling
- 2 tbsp oil
- 1 leek, finely sliced
- 3-4 hot green chillies, minced
- 150 g (5¼ oz) spinach leaves, blanched and squeezed dry
- 100 g (3½ oz/½ cup) frozen peas, defrosted
- 225 g (8 oz) paneer, grated (shredded)
- ½ tsp ground ginger
- 1 tbsp chopped fresh mint leaves
- ½ tsp Garam Masala (see page 259)
- ½ tsp Chaat Masala (see page 263)
- ½ tsp coarsely ground black pepper
- ½ tsp salt
- 1 tbsp instant mashed potato powder (potato flakes)
- 1 tbsp rice flour

For the pastry and topping
- 2 tbsp honey
- 1 tbsp English mustard
- 320 g (11¼ oz) ready-rolled puff pastry, fridge cold
- 1-2 tsp fennel seeds, to sprinkle on top
- 1 red chilli, sliced, to sprinkle on top (optional)

Hot, crispy rolls with a super-green, Indian kebab-style filling. Hara bhara kebabs are one of India's many vegetable-based kebabs, made from a medley of greens. My version calls for spinach, peas and leeks, but you can use any leafy greens, alliums or beans. Broad beans, spring onions (scallions) and finely minced French beans work particularly well. Paneer works as the ideal binder, however, if you're vegan, a mashed potato will also bring it all together. These rolls will transport you to a summer picnic at any time of year. The honey-mustard glaze gives the pastry a peppery hint, as well as a gorgeous golden colour. Since they're also delicious at room temperature, hara bhara rolls are an elite-level addition to lunchboxes. Feel free to skip the chillies for kids.

1. To make the filling, heat the oil in a large frying pan (skillet). Add the leek and chillies, then sauté for a few minutes until softened.

2. Tip the cooked leek mixture into the bowl of a food processor. Add the rest of the ingredients for the filling and pulse the mixture 6-8 times to create a thick, coarse paste. It should come together as a soft ball. If it doesn't, there may be some excess liquid in the mixture and so stir in a little more instant mashed potato powder (potato flakes), 1 teaspoon at a time, until it comes together.

3. To make the glaze, mix the honey and mustard together in a small bowl.

4. Unroll the pastry sheet and cut it in half lengthways. Place the filling mixture along the centre of each pastry strip and brush the edges of the pastry with some of the honey-mustard glaze. Fold the pastry over lengthways to cover the filling and make a log. Press the pastry edges together to seal.

5. Cut each pastry log into 4 equal pieces. Score the tops with a sharp knife. Arrange the individual rolls on a large baking sheet lined with parchment paper, leaving a 2-cm (¾-inch) gap between each roll. Brush the rolls with the remaining glaze and sprinkle with the fennel seeds and red chilli. Refrigerate for 20 minutes while the oven is preheating.

6. Preheat the oven to 200°C/180°C fan/390°F/Gas mark 6.

7. Bake the rolls for 18-20 minutes, or until the pastry is puffy and golden on the outside.

Notes
This is a wonderful make-ahead recipe to freeze for baking later. Freeze unbaked and unglazed rolls on a baking sheet for 6-8 hours, or until frozen solid. Pack into freezer-safe bags or arrange in an airtight container and store for up to 3 months. When ready to serve, glaze and bake the rolls following the directions given above, although they may take an extra 5-8 minutes to brown.

Vegan?
Replace the paneer for cooked mashed potato, chickpeas (garbanzo beans) or any other white beans of your choice. The honey can be swapped for agave syrup or maple syrup.

Gluten free?
Swap the pastry for a shop-bought gluten-free option.

Make it a feast!
Serve these little rolls with your favourite chutney. They're particularly good with tamarind chutney, mango chutney, or even with ketchup. Make bigger rolls for lunch or dinner to serve alongside baked beans and salad.

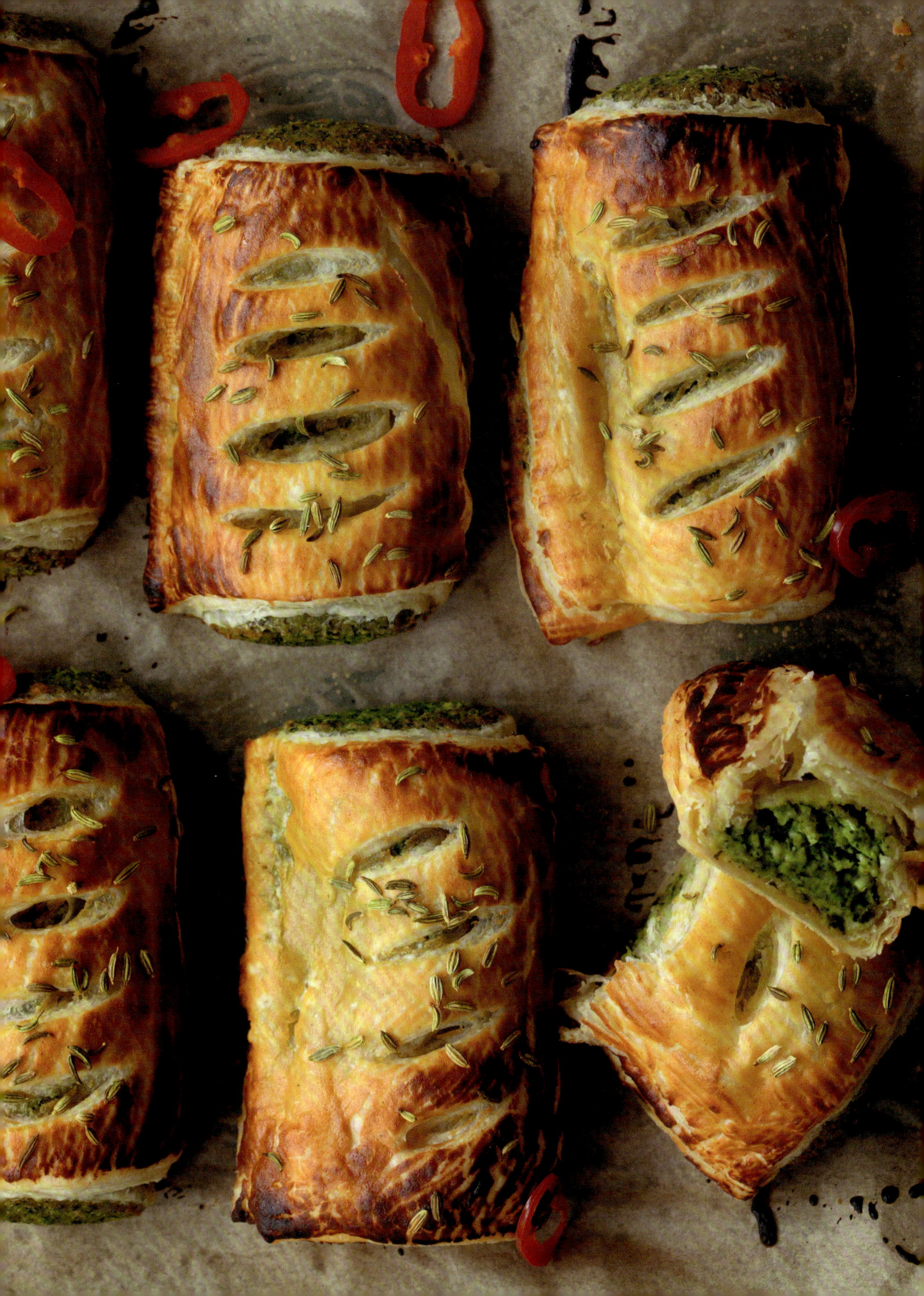

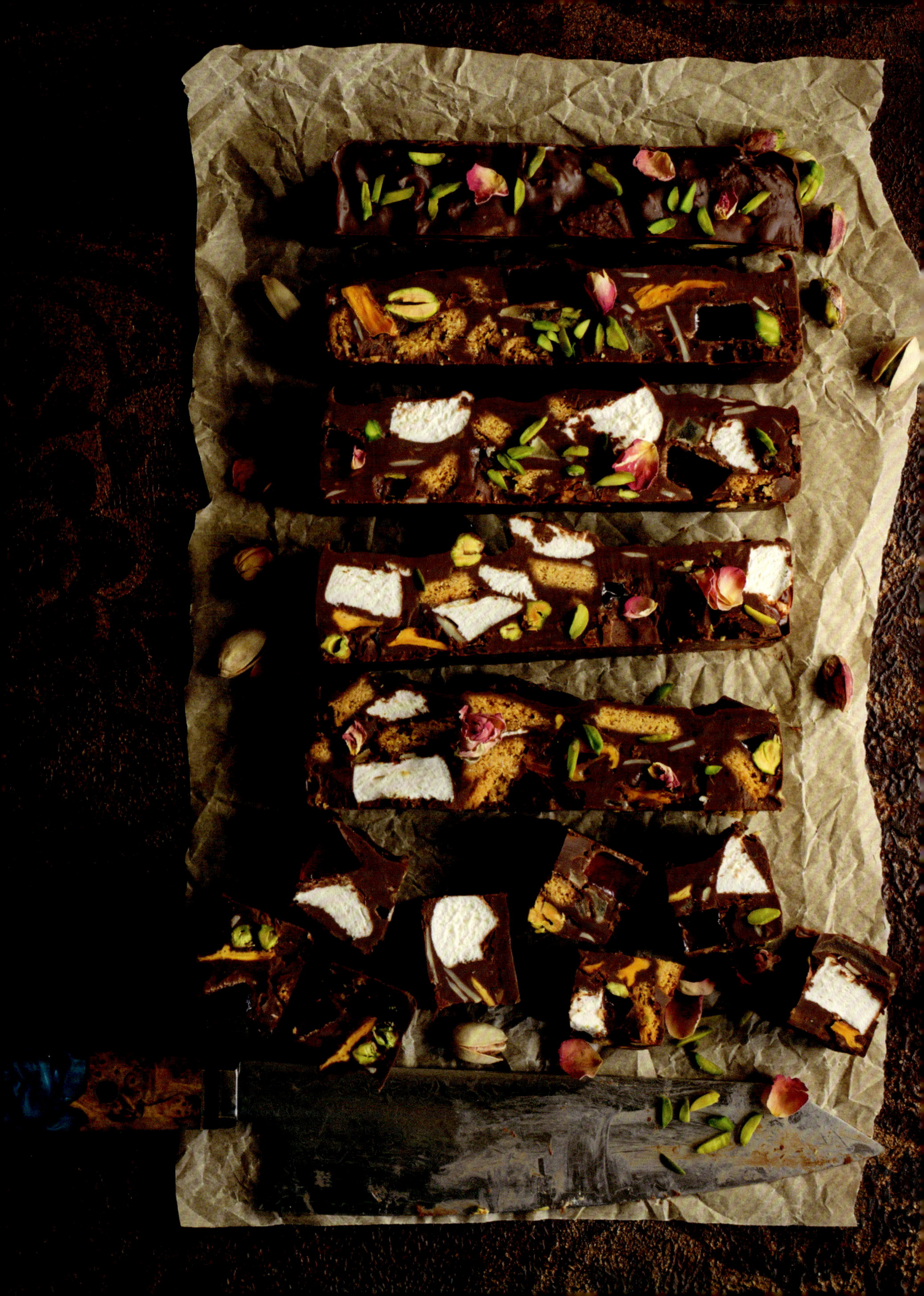

Indian-inspired Rocky Road

MAKES 24 PIECES • PREP: 20 MINS, PLUS 20 MINS FREEZING • COOK: 10 MINS

100 g (3½ oz) gelatine-free Turkish delight, cubed
60 g (2 oz) gelatine-free marshmallows, cut into pieces if they're large
300 g (10½ oz) milk chocolate
300 g (10½ oz) dark (bittersweet) chocolate
140 g (5 oz /⅝ cup) unsalted butter
3 tbsp golden syrup
¼ tsp salt
100 g (3½ oz) ginger biscuits (gingersnap cookies), broken
40 g (1½ oz) toasted pistachios
20 g (¾ oz) flaked (slivered) almonds
20 g (¾ oz) dried mango, cut into 2-cm (¾-inch) pieces
20 g (¾ oz) crystallised ginger, cut into 2-cm (¾-inch) pieces
2 tsp edible dried rose petals

An easy, no-bake slice that looks like you spent ages making it. It's crammed with biscuits (cookies), nuts, crystallised ginger, dried mango, Turkish delight, marshmallows and edible dried rose petals. I'm yet to meet a person who hasn't gone back for a second piece.

1. Pop the Turkish delight and marshmallow pieces into a freezer bag and freeze for 20 minutes. This helps them keep their shape.

2. Place the chocolate, butter, golden syrup and salt in a heatproof glass bowl over a pan of simmering water. Give it a gentle stir every few minutes until fully melted and well combined. Alternatively, melt everything together in a microwave-safe bowl. Stir until smooth and set aside to cool slightly.

3. Add the broken ginger biscuits (gingersnap cookies), frozen Turkish delight and marshmallow pieces, pistachios, almonds, dried mango and crystallised ginger. Stir to combine and coat all the add-ins.

4. Spread the mixture into a 23 x 15-cm (9 x 6-inch) cake pan lined with parchment paper. Leave a little of the parchment overhanging at the sides of the pan so that you can use that to lift out the rocky road later. Flatten the top and scatter over the edible dried rose petals. Wrap the cake pan with cling film (plastic wrap) and allow the rocky road to set in the fridge for 6–8 hours, until solid. Slice into squares and serve.

Vegan?

This recipe is so easy to adapt. Vegan alternatives for the ingredients used are available in most major supermarkets. Dairy-free butter, vegan chocolate, biscuits (cookies) and marshmallows, to name a few substitutions.

Gluten free?

Swap the ginger biscuits with any gluten-free biscuits.

Chole Samosa

SERVES 6 • PREP: 1½ HOURS, PLUS 30 MINS RESTING • COOK: 55 MINS

For the chole
3 tbsp oil
½ tsp carom seeds
3 green cardamom pods, cracked
1 large onion, finely chopped
1 tbsp gram flour
1 x 400-g (14-oz) can chopped tomatoes
2 tsp Kashmiri chilli powder
½ tsp ground turmeric
1½ tsp salt
1 tsp sugar
2 x 400-g (14-oz) cans chickpeas (garbanzo beans)
1½ tsp Garam Masala (see page 259)
1 tsp dried fenugreek leaves

For the samosa filling
375 g (13¼ oz) potatoes
75 g (2⅔ oz/scant ½ cup) frozen peas, defrosted
1 onion, finely diced
2 thin green chillies, finely chopped
2 tsp minced root ginger
1 tbsp oil
1 tsp coriander seeds
1 tsp cumin seeds
½ tsp fennel seeds
1 tsp dried mango powder
½ tsp ground turmeric
1 tbsp chopped fresh coriander (cilantro)
1 tsp salt

For the samosa pastry
250 g (9 oz/2 cups) plain (all-purpose) flour
1 tsp carom seeds
¾ tsp salt
50 ml (1¾ fl oz/scant ¼ cup) oil
100 ml (3½ fl oz/scant ½ cup) warm water
1.5 litres (50 fl oz/6⅓ cups) oil, for deep-frying

Palm-sized potato and pea samosas propped up on a pile of rugged, masala-bathed chickpeas (garbanzo beans). The pastry is short, crisp and forgiving to work with. If that Punjabi samosa can't be used as cannon fodder, it's not worth having, so be sure to fill each one generously.

1. First, make the chole. Heat the oil in a saucepan. Add the carom seeds, cardamom pods and onion. Cook over a medium-low heat, stirring continuously, until the onion has caramelised to a golden colour, about 8 minutes. Sprinkle in the gram flour and stir to coat the onion. Cook, stirring continuously, until the gram flour has toasted up, releasing a nutty aroma.

2. Add the chopped tomatoes, chilli powder, ground turmeric, salt and sugar. Pour in 200 ml (7 fl oz/generous ¾ cup) water and the liquid from one of the cans of chickpeas (garbanzo beans). This, along with the gram flour, will help the sauce thicken to a chickpea-slicking consistency. Stir well and cover the pan with a tight-fitting lid. Simmer over a low heat for 8–10 minutes.

3. Drain the remaining can of chickpeas and add them to the sauce, along with the ones you drained earlier. Cover again and simmer for a further 10 minutes.

4. Remove the lid, add the garam masala and rub the dried fenugreek leaves between your palms into the pan, adding it to the chole. Stir well and remove the pan from the heat.

5. Next, make the filling. Boil the potatoes in plenty of water until tender. Drain and allow to cool completely. Once cool, peel the potatoes and roughly mash using a potato masher or the back of a fork. Add the defrosted peas, onion, chillies, ginger and oil.

6. Toast the coriander seeds, cumin seeds and fennel seeds in a small, dry pan. Once you can smell the aromas of the spices and they look lightly golden, transfer to a pestle and mortar and coarsely grind them. You can also use a rolling pin to crush them. Add this to the potato mixture, along with the dried mango powder, ground turmeric, fresh coriander (cilantro) and salt. Mix well, until all the spices are well distributed.

7. To make the pastry, sift the flour into a large bowl and mix in the carom seeds and salt. Make a well in the centre of the flour. Add the oil. Using your fingertips, begin to rub the flour and oil together to create a fine, breadcrumb-like texture, as if you were making shortcrust pastry. Add the water and combine using your hands to create a rough, shaggy-looking dough.

8. Knead for 10 minutes, until smooth. Cover with a damp dish towel and allow to rest for 30 minutes.

9. Once rested, divide the dough into 3 equal pieces. Smooth into rounds between your palms and cover again with the damp dish towel to stop the dough from drying out. Each round will make 2 large samosas, for a total of 6 samosas. You can choose to make them larger or smaller by making fewer or more dough balls.

continued overleaf

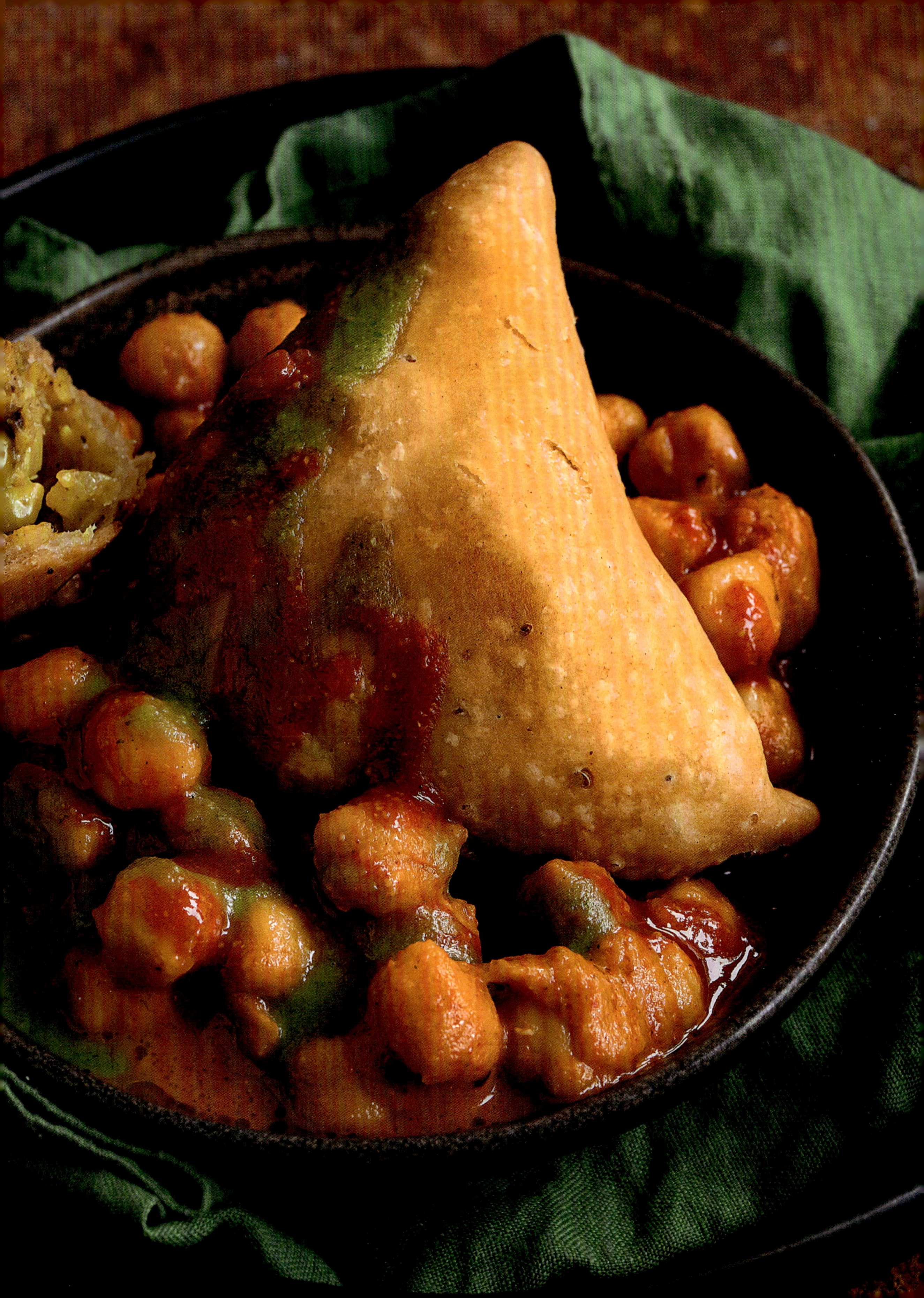

Notes

This recipe can just as easily be made with store-bought samosas but once you try homemade, your samosa standards will never be the same again.

Make it a feast!

Since chutney is the glue that holds everything together in life, serve this with your favourites. I choose the red and green chutneys from the Traffic Light Chutneys on page 196.

Whilst this is undoubtedly satisfying as it is, you can easily turn it into Chole Samosa Chaat by adding a swirl of sweetened yogurt (see page 90 Halloumi Fries Chaat), chopped onions, tomatoes, chutneys, sev and a sprinkling of Chaat Masala (see page 263).

10. Take one dough ball and dip each side in a small amount of flour (1). On a clean surface, roll it into a 22-cm (9-inch) long ellipse. It doesn't have to be perfect.

11. Cut the ellipse in half, widthways. You should be left with two tall semicircles (2). Take one of the semicircles and place it flat on the surface in front of you, straight side facing north. Roll it with your rolling pin a few times to make it a little thinner and taller. Take the upper right corner and bring it to the centre of the semicircle (3). Place some cool water down the middle and bring the upper left-hand corner of the semicircle to the centre to meet the waterline. Press both sides together very gently (4).

12. Lift the samosa pastry up and open the pocket you just created. At the same time, press the seam together a little more to ensure it is well sealed. You should have a little pouch ready for filling (5). Stuff the samosa with the cooled potato and pea filling. I use around 3 tablespoons of filling per samosa (6).

13. Create the little crease in the back of the samosa so it can stand up by itself. Along the open seam of the filled samosa, place your finger in the centre of the round edge of the pastry, create a tiny fold, about 1 cm (½ inch) wide and pinch to seal (this will create a small dimple for the back base of the samosa (7). Now dab some cold water on the inner seams of the open edge of the pastry and press together and seal to close, pushing out any air as you go (8).

14. Repeat these steps for the remaining samosas. Ensure the dough portions are always covered to prevent them from drying out.

15. Once all the samosas have been folded, allow them to air-dry for 45 minutes, until the surface of the pastry feels rough and sandy to the touch (9). This is an important step to eliminate air bubbles in the pastry and to stop your samosas from getting what we in my family call a 'gremlin' skin.

16. Heat the oil in a large, heavy-based pan with deep sides or a wok until warm, not hot, about 40°C (105°F). To test, drop a small piece of dough into the oil and look for very small, slow-moving bubbles around it. Be careful not to overheat the oil as this will result in uneven cooking. For the crispiest pastry, always start frying samosas with this style of pastry in warm oil.

17. Cook the samosas in batches. I managed to get all 6 in my large wok without it feeling overcrowded. Fry over a low heat for 20 minutes before increasing the heat to 160°C (320°F). The samosas can remain in the oil until they reach the correct temperature. Continue to fry for a further 15 minutes until golden and crispy. It sounds like a long time for the samosas to be sitting in oil, but I promise they won't be as greasy as you think – quite the opposite in fact. If you feel the samosas are browning too quickly, turn the heat down. Allow the oil to cool down in between frying the samosas in batches.

18. Drain the samosas on a plate lined with absorbent kitchen paper.

19. Spoon the chole into bowls and top with a samosa (or two – I won't tell!). Drizzle with your favourite chutneys. Devour immediately.

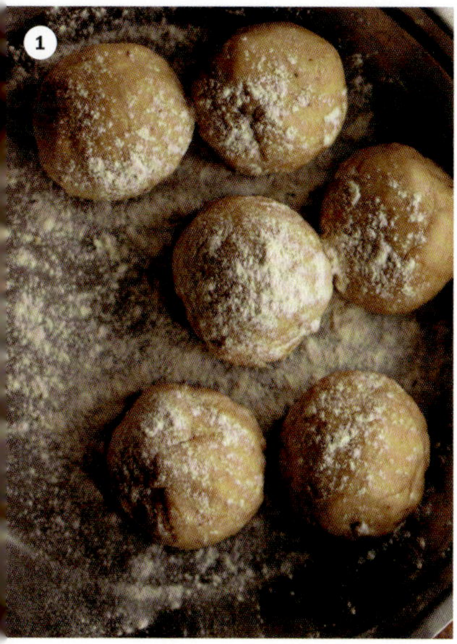
1
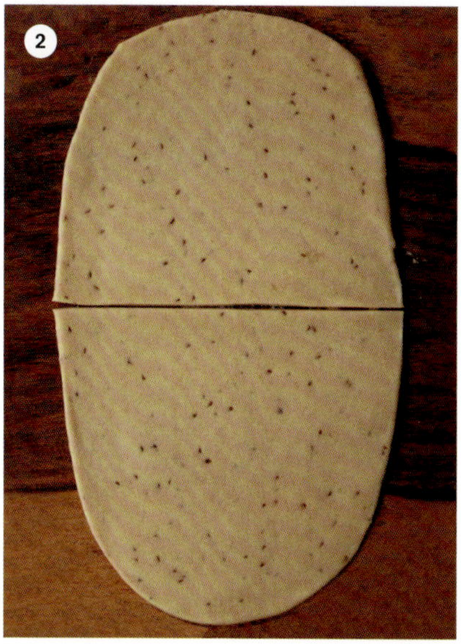
2
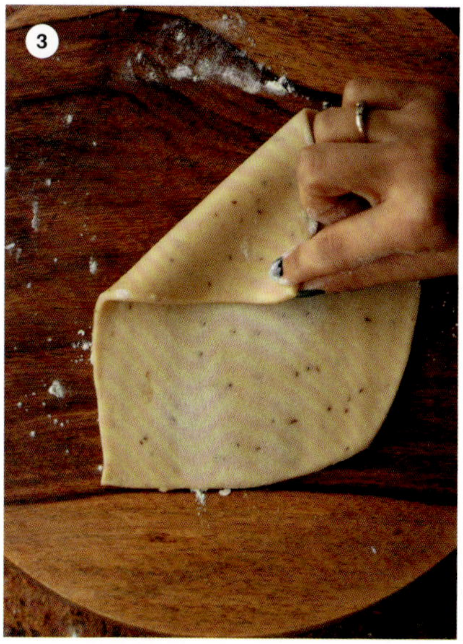
3
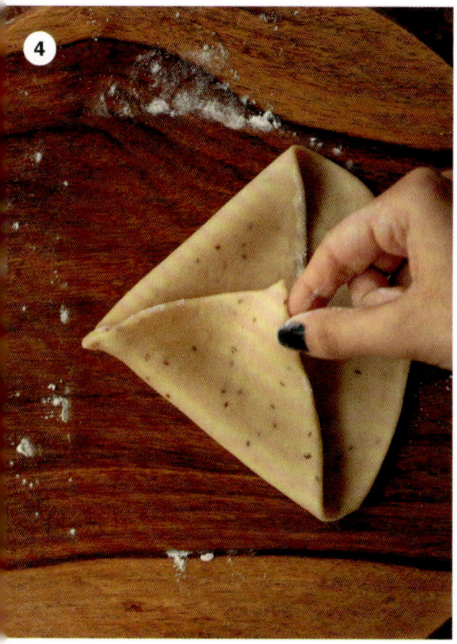
4
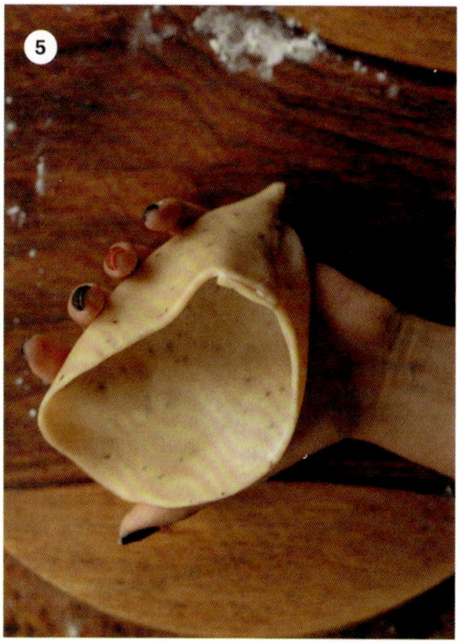
5
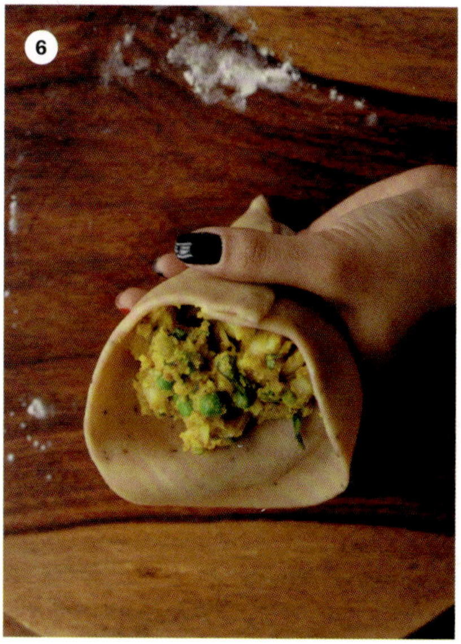
6
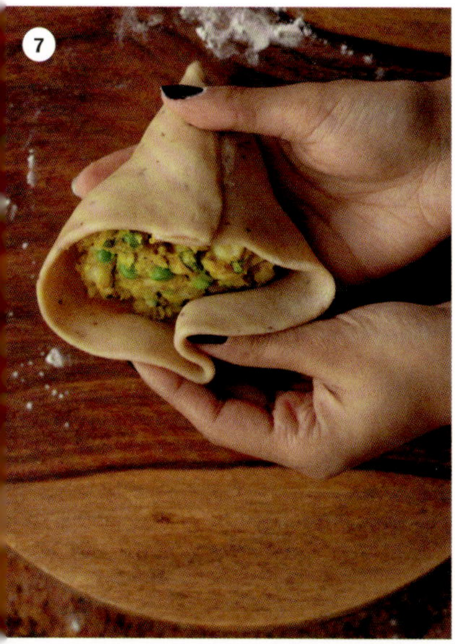
7
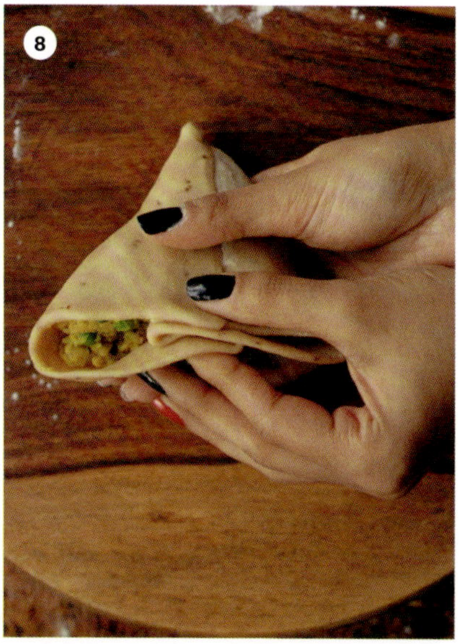
8
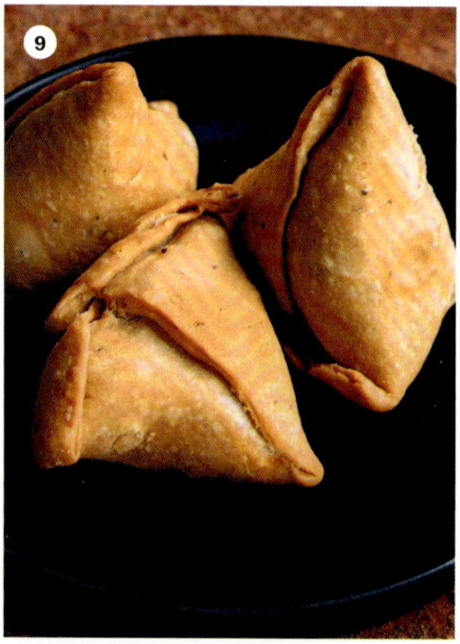
9

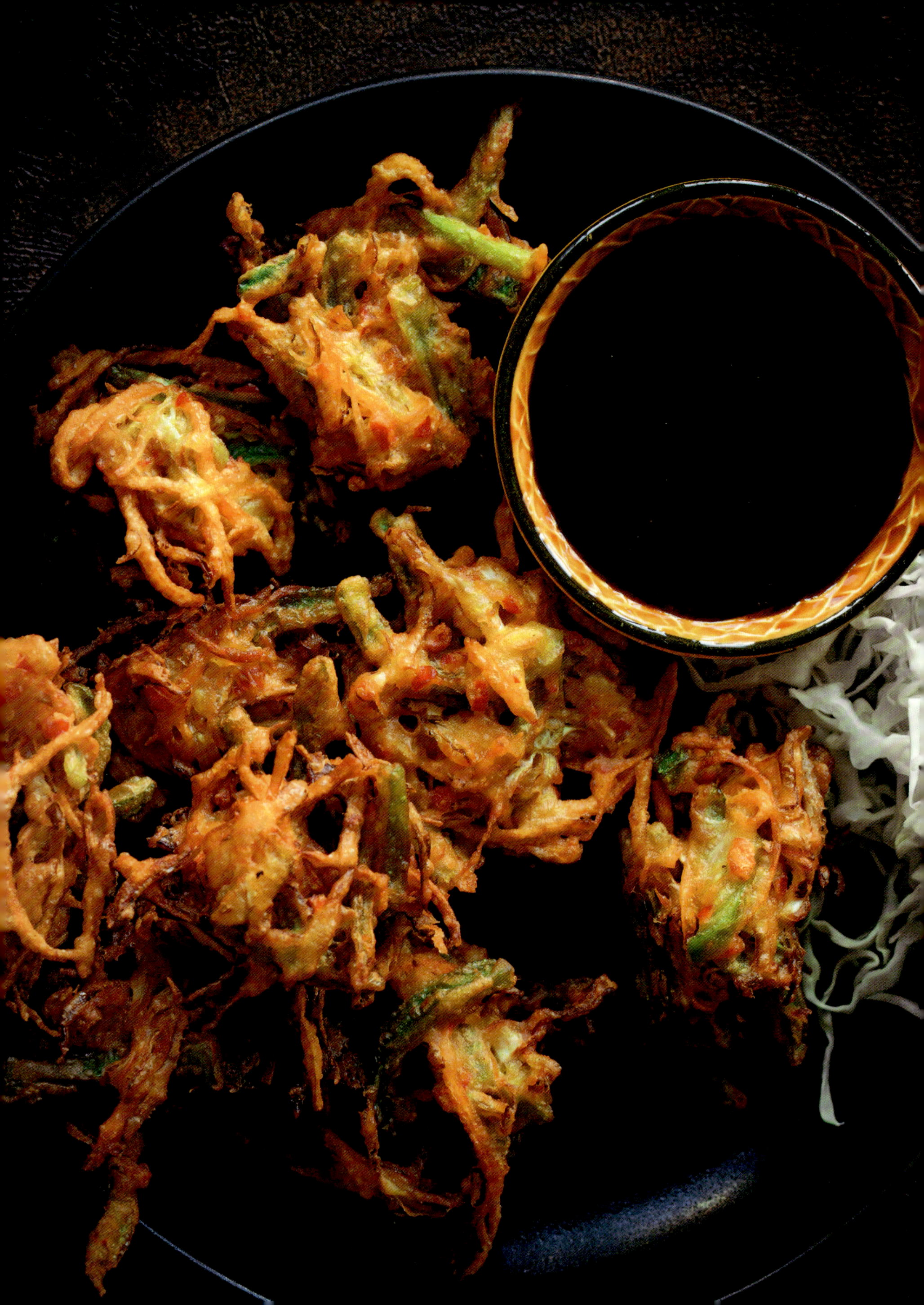

Indo-Chinese Bhajiya

SERVES 4 • PREP: 30 MINS • COOK: 10 MINS

V VG GF

100 g (3½ oz/¾ cup) gram flour
1 tbsp cornflour (cornstarch)
75 g (2⅔ oz) white cabbage (such as Chinese leaf), shredded
1 green bell pepper, cut into thin matchsticks
1 large carrot, cut into thin matchsticks
2 spring onions (scallions), cut into thin matchsticks
1–2 hot red chillies, finely chopped
1 tbsp oil
1 tsp grated (shredded) root ginger
1 tsp Sichuan peppercorns, coarsely ground
½ tsp sugar
¼ tsp salt
¼ tsp MSG
Oil, for deep-frying

An Indo-Chinese spin on bhajiya (pakora), the monsoon-season staple made with gram flour and basically any ingredient(s) you can fry. Here, shredded veggies, ginger and Sichuan peppercorns are bound into a fritter-like mixture before they hit the oil. Their moreish wisps, craters and craggy edges are reminiscent of their better-known onion counterpart.

1. In a large bowl, combine all the ingredients for the bhajiya (pakora). Use your hands to squeeze the mixture together. As you squeeze, the vegetables will release moisture that mixes with the gram flour and creates a thick, droppable, fritter-like mixture. The batter should be light and just coat the veggies.

2. Heat the oil in a large, heavy-based pan to 170°C (340°F). Immediately before frying, give the bhajiya mixture a minute-long beat with your hands. This will trap in air for a lighter, crispier finish.

3. Working in batches, deep-fry tablespoon-sized balls of the mixture for 3–4 minutes per batch until crispy and golden. It's okay if the bhajiya are misshapen; that's what gives them their unique, crunchy texture. Do not overcrowd the pan. Use a slotted spoon to lift the bhajiya from the oil and drain in a colander or on a plate lined with absorbent kitchen paper.

Notes

If the batter is too thin and the bhajiya (pakora) begin to fall apart in the oil due to the high water content of the veggies, add another tablespoon of cornflour (cornstarch).

If you happen to own a waffle iron, grease the plates well and dollop spoonfuls of the batter in. Close and cook until crusty and perfectly waffled. This is the best alternative to deep-frying I've found for this style of bhajiya.

These bhajiya are perfect with bottled tamarind chutney or Green Coriander and Mint Chutney (see page 197).

Make it a feast!

Transform these into an epic Manchurian-style dish by using them in place of the battered chestnuts in my Chestnut Manchurian (page 98).

Raspberry and Rosewater Iced Buns

SERVES 6 • PREP: 20 MINS, PLUS 1½ HOURS RESTING • COOK: 15 MINS

260 g (9¼ oz/2 cups) strong white bread flour
35 g (1¼ oz/2½ tbsp) caster (superfine) sugar
7 g (2¼ tsp) fast-action dried yeast
½ tsp ground green cardamom (about 4 pods)
¼ tsp fine salt
165 ml (5¾ fl oz/⅔ cup) warm whole (full-fat) milk
2 tbsp vegetable oil

For the icing (frosting)
50 g (1¾ oz) raspberries
½ tsp good-quality rosewater
175 g (6¼ oz/scant 1½ cups) icing (confectioners') sugar
Freeze-dried raspberries, to decorate
Edible dried rose petals, to decorate (optional)

Notes
If you don't like the taste of rosewater, you can leave the icing (frosting) plain or flavour it with coconut or vanilla extract.

Vegan?
Use any plant-based milk in place of dairy milk.

Make it a feast!
For afternoon tea vibes, split the buns in half lengthways and fill with whipped cream and fresh raspberries.

Pillowy, sweet bread fingers with sugary, set icing (frosting) are a quintessential British bakery treat. These rosy, raspberry-glazed buns sing just as they are, but they're even better filled with fresh cream and berries. Six-year-old us would totally approve.

1. In the bowl of a stand mixer fitted with a dough hook, combine the flour, sugar, yeast, cardamom and salt.

2. Add the milk and switch the mixer on, slow to begin with. Turn the mixer speed up and knead at medium for around 5 minutes.

3. With the mixer still running, add the oil a little at a time until it's all incorporated. Continue to knead for a further 5 minutes until the dough is soft, smooth and elastic. The mixer should run for a total of around 10 minutes.

4. Lightly grease the bowl and wrap with cling film (plastic wrap). Allow to rise in a warm place for 1 hour, or until doubled in size.

5. Knock back the risen dough and divide it into 6 equal portions. Shape each piece into a ball and then form into a finger shape, around 7 cm (2¾ inches) long.

6. Arrange the dough fingers in a greased 20-cm (8-inch) square cake pan. Leave some space around each one since they will rise again. Loosely cover the pan with cling film and once again leave in a warm place for 30 minutes, or until they double in size. After rising, it's okay if they are touching a little.

7. Preheat the oven to 210°C/190°C fan/410°F/Gas mark 6½.

8. Bake the buns in the preheated oven for 12–15 minutes, or until lightly golden on top. They should sound hollow when the tops are gently tapped. Remove the buns from the oven and leave to cool in the pan.

9. In a bowl, mash the raspberries with the back of a spoon. Pass the mixture through a fine-mesh sieve (strainer) and into another bowl to remove the seeds. Add the rosewater and icing (confectioners') sugar to the raspberry juice and stir to form a smooth and pourable icing (frosting).

10. Once completely cool, carefully remove the buns from the pan. Dip the tops of each bun in the icing, allowing any excess to drip away. For an extra neat finish, use your finger to smooth the top of the icing. Sprinkle the freeze-dried raspberries over the icing and allow to set at room temperature before serving.

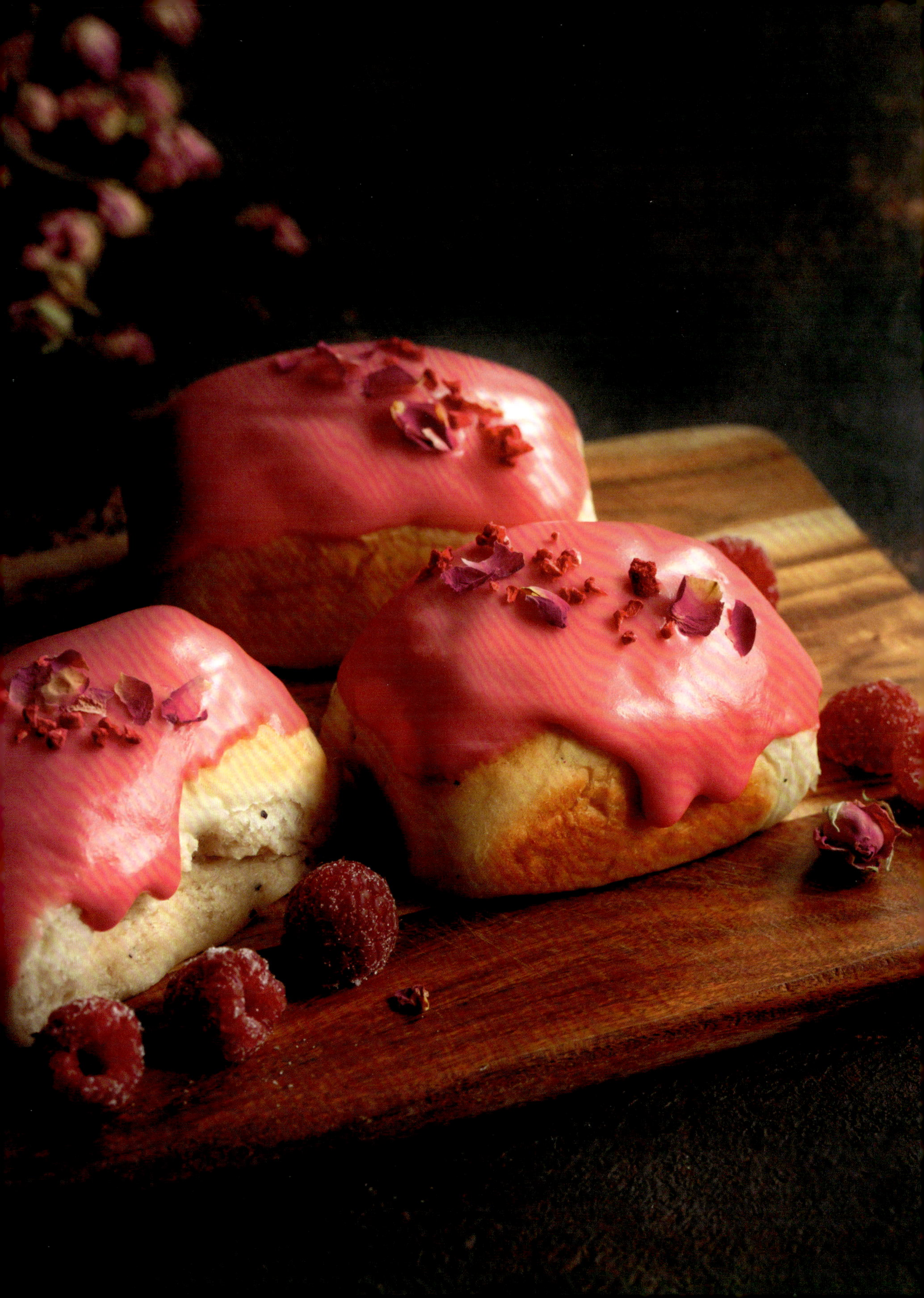

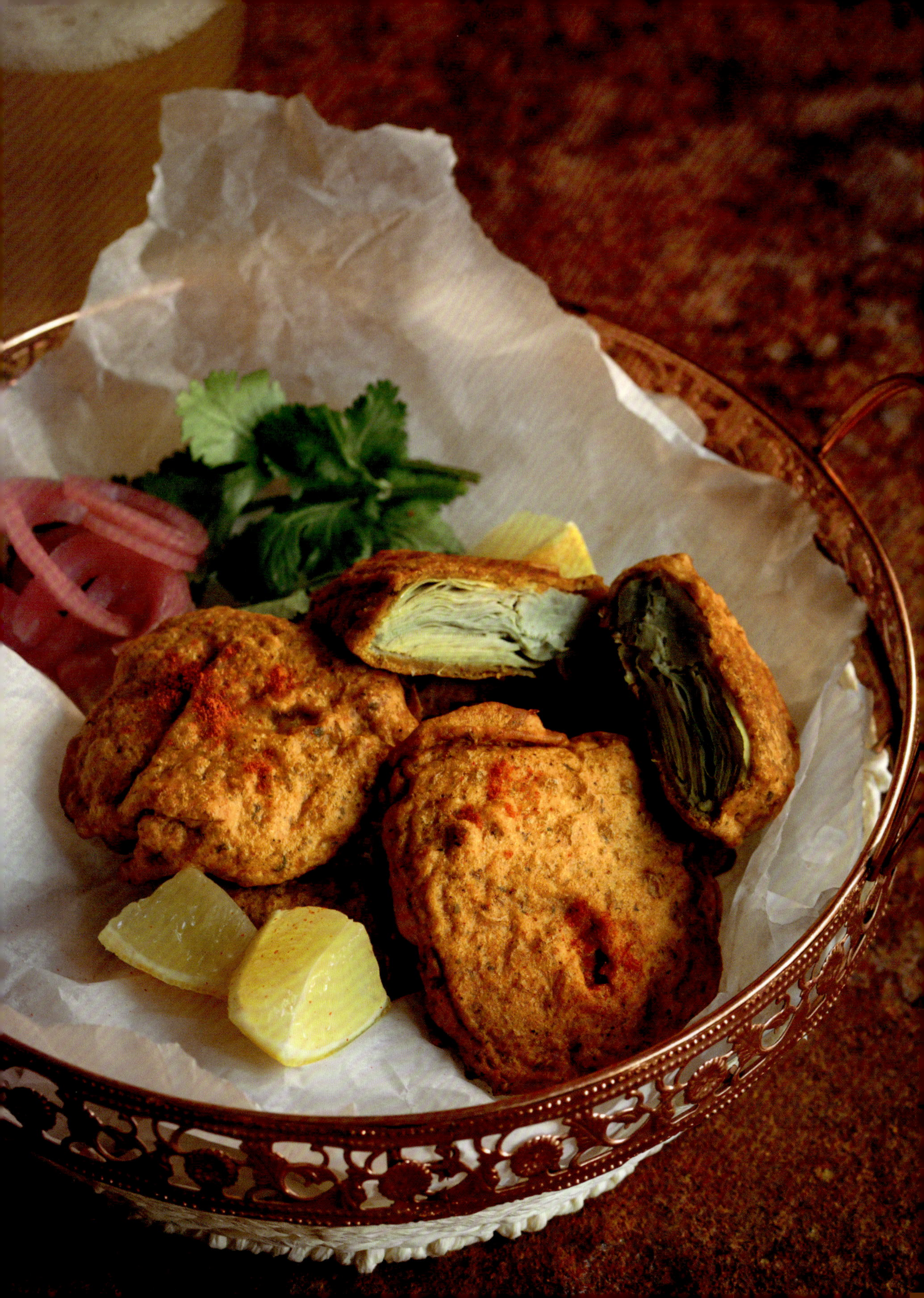

Artichoke Pakora

SERVES 4 • PREP: 20 MINS • COOK: 10 MINS

1 x 400g (14-oz) can artichoke hearts in water
2 tbsp rice flour
Oil, for deep-frying

For the batter
65 g (2⅓ oz/⅔ cup) gram flour
60 g (2 oz/½ cup) rice flour
1 tbsp cornflour (cornstarch)
2 garlic cloves, minced
1½ tsp minced root ginger
2 tsp carom seeds
1 tsp dried mango powder
2 tsp Kashmiri chilli powder
1 tsp dried fenugreek leaves, rubbed between your palms
¼ tsp ground turmeric
¼ tsp asafoetida
½ tsp salt
1 tbsp edible mustard oil

Gluten free?
Use a gluten-free asafoetida or omit this ingredient.

Make it a feast!
Serve with Pink Peppercorn Pickled Onions (see page 240) and lemon wedges.

Taking inspiration from the Punjabi delicacy, Amritsari Fish, these golden artichoke pakoras are soft and flaky on the inside. Use canned artichokes in water for the quickest version but be sure to give the hearts a gentle squeeze between kitchen paper to remove any excess moisture. Jarred artichokes in oil will need to be drained, rinsed well and patted dry prior to using.

1. In a bowl, beat together all the ingredients for the batter, gradually adding 180 ml (6 fl oz/¾ cup) cold water, so there aren't too many big clumps of flour. A few small lumps are fine. Set the batter aside for 10 minutes while you prepare the artichokes.

2. Drain the artichokes and gently squeeze them, one at a time, to remove any excess water. Lay out kitchen paper, a few sheets thick, and arrange the artichokes on top. Use another few sheets of paper, gently pressing the artichokes to flatten and compress the layers so they resemble flakes.

3. Heat the oil in a deep, heavy-based pan. Once the oil reaches 180°C (355°F), or a small piece of bread sizzles and browns in 50–60 seconds, it is ready. Working in batches, dip each artichoke first in the rice flour and then into the batter. Next, carefully lower the pakora directly into the oil. Do not overcrowd the pan as this may cause the temperature of the oil to drop. Deep-fry the pakoras, turning often, for 2–3 minutes, or until golden brown and crispy. Remove the pakoras from the oil and place into a colander, or a plate lined with kitchen paper while you fry the rest of the pakoras.

Carrot Cake Scones with Cardamom Cream and Marmalade

SERVES 6 • PREP: 30 MINS • COOK: 20 MINS, PLUS 15 MINS COOLING

250 g (9 oz/2 cups) self-raising flour
75 g (2⅔ oz/⅜ cup) light brown sugar
1½ tsp baking powder
1 tsp ground ginger
1 tsp ground cinnamon
¼ tsp grated (shredded) nutmeg
¼ tsp ground cloves
⅛ tsp salt
100 g (3½ oz/scant ½ cup) unsalted butter, cold and cubed
1 large carrot (150 g/5¼ oz), grated (shredded), squeezed and juice reserved
25 g (¾ oz/¼ cup) raisins
40 ml (1⅓ fl oz/3 tbsp) cold whole (full-fat) milk, plus an additional
4 tsp milk, for brushing on top

To serve
300 ml (10 fl oz/1¼ cups) double (heavy) cream, cold
2 green cardamom pods, seeds finely ground
3 tbsp your favourite orange marmalade

Lightly spiced with ginger, cinnamon, nutmeg and cloves, these scones are best served with a dollop of thick cardamom cream and orange marmalade. Paddington Bear would be doing cartwheels for these. They taste far more luxurious than the effort they take to prepare.

1. In a large bowl, combine the flour, sugar, baking powder, ground ginger, ground cinnamon, grated (shredded) nutmeg, ground cloves and salt.

2. Add the butter and rub it into the flour to achieve a coarse, breadcrumb-like texture. Use a light touch and try to work as quickly as you can. Some larger lumps of butter are okay.

3. Pile the grated and squeezed carrots into the flour mixture along with the raisins, then stir with a fork to coat all the carrots. Gradually add the reserved carrot juice (mine was a total of 4 tsp) and 40 ml (1⅓ fl oz/3 tbsp) ice-cold water or milk. You may not need all the liquid, so add it bit by bit. Mix with a fork until the scone dough just comes together. Do not overwork the dough and do not knead it. The scones will be lighter in texture the less you handle the dough.

4. Flour a clean work surface and pat or roll out the dough to a thickness of about 1½–2 cm (⅔–¾ inch). Stamp out 6 rounds using a round or fluted scone or cookie cutter. Re-form any scraps of dough to cut out more rounds. Handle the dough quickly and with a light touch. Cracks on the surface are fine.

5. Arrange the scones on a large baking sheet lined with parchment paper, leaving a small gap around each one. Refrigerate for 5 minutes.

6. Preheat the oven to 220°C/200°C fan /425°F/Gas mark 7.

7. Brush the scones with milk and bake in the preheated oven for 16–18 minutes, until risen and slightly golden on top. Allow to cool on the sheet for 15 minutes before eating.

8. Whip the cream and cardamom together until you have soft peaks. Refrigerate until required.

9. When ready to serve, split the scones horizontally and pile with the cardamom whipped cream and marmalade. Serve immediately.

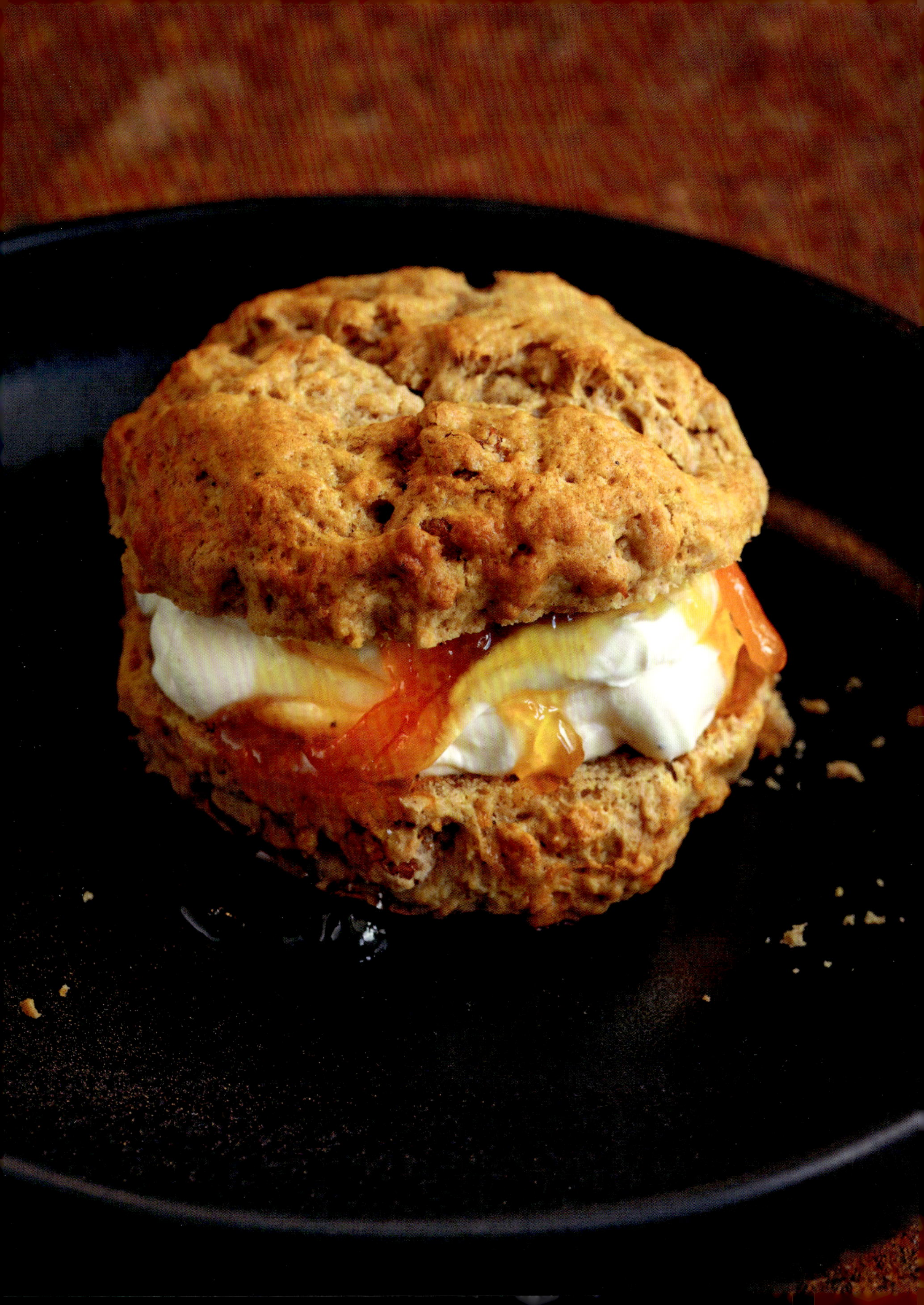

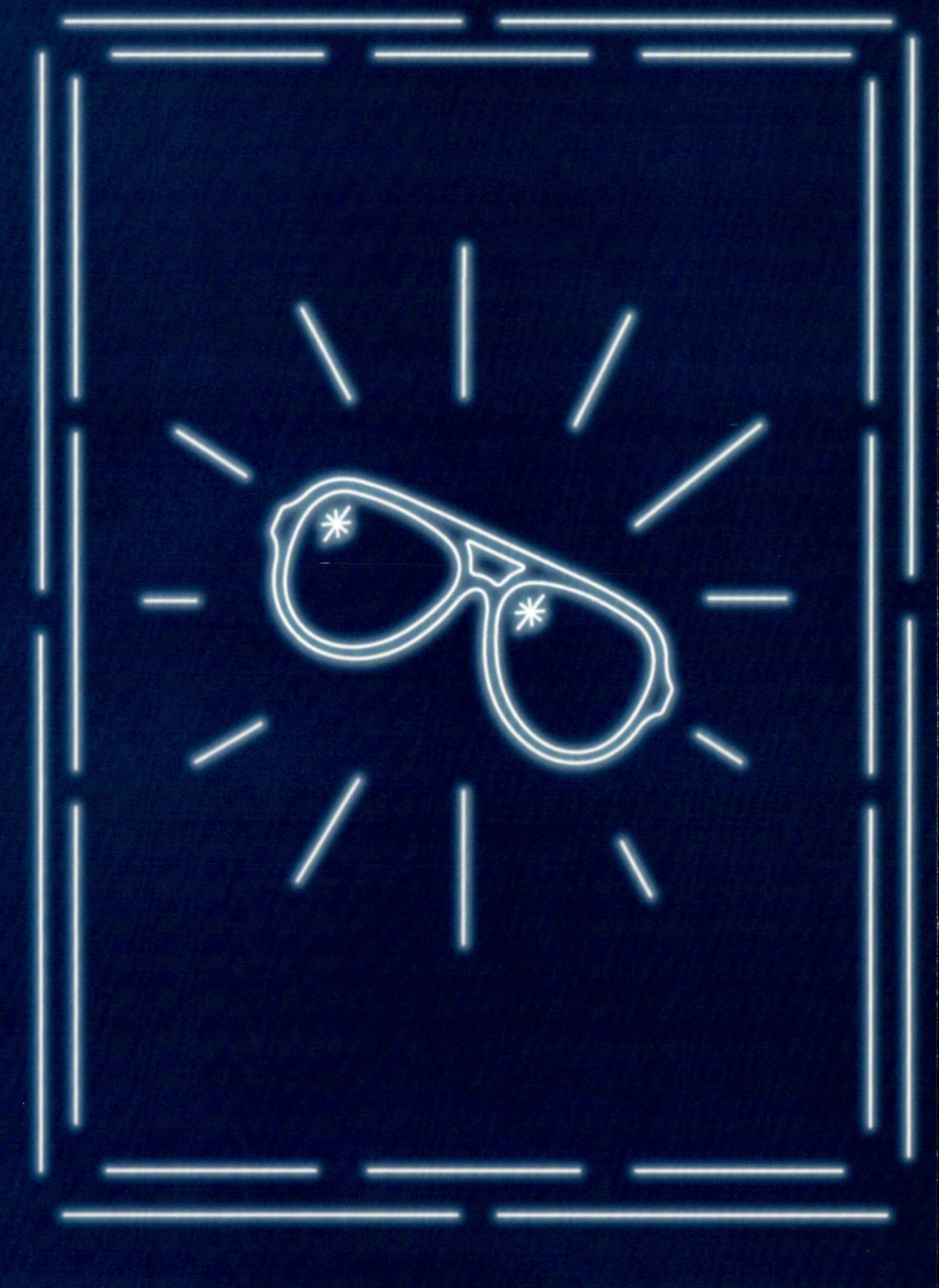

NOT
Curry

Everyday comfort food, with an Indian spin.

'Indian soup again?! Urgh!' I said, as my mum prepared a weeknight meal of Indian-style tomato soup after a long day at work. I grabbed a scrunchie and bolted through the door in fear that my freshly washed hair would smell like curry at school the next day. I wondered why we couldn't just be like everyone else and eat plain Heinz cream of tomato soup, with not a speck of masala in sight. No curry leaves or cumin, no ginger or asafoetida – just plain. What I was really asking for was the soup my English friends had for their supper. I wanted so badly to assimilate.

What I didn't appreciate at the time was that the meals on our table were a product of my ancestral roots, socio-economic struggle, hardships, and the will of my family to strive for better opportunities. Many things have changed since my teenage years. The spicy, masala-laden meals that put meat on my vegetarian bones were like boot camp for the taste buds. They trained me to understand aromas and textures, and how to make spices work in harmony.

With a library of culinary blueprints to ground my understanding of flavours, I've delved into making the meals I longed to master as a teen. Of course, it wasn't long before I found myself wielding mum's double-decker masala tin during marathon pasta-making afternoons (insert raised eyebrow emoji here). It wasn't intentional, it was instinctive and innate. I started off very innocently; a dried Indian bay leaf and a dash of tamarind paste in bolognese, or a quick French bread pizza with a schmear of tandoori butter under the sauce for lunch. I graduated to making bolder moves like whizzing up a crispy garlic naan breadcrumb topping for pasta bakes or scattering freshly ground masalas into my Sunday evening bubble and squeak. Before I knew it, I was making giant trays of spicy cauliflower only later to bathe the charred, spice-crusted florets in mature (sharp) Cheddar sauce for the most Desi cauliflower cheese ever. Putting a South Asian spin on meals has become second nature.

So, here is the product of my endless experiments, led almost entirely by tasting as I go, but also by what's available in the fridge, freezer or store cupboard. To me, this collection of comfort food recipes represents more than just dinner, but a celebration of identity. As someone raised in a realm of hybridity, it has been, and continues to be, a journey of personal growth and self-acceptance. Not only do I hope this collection of meals inspires you to be bold and follow flavour in your everyday cooking, but I'd also like for it to champion the culinary ingenuity of Indian diasporic communities in the UK and beyond. Every dish here is a satisfying comfort meal, made a little bit Indian. Desi-inspired French Bread Pizza (see page 65), Halloumi Fries Chaat (see page 90), Upma 'Summer Rolls' (see page 66) and that Curry Leaf Tomato Soup (see page 81), to name but a handful of recipes.

Weeknight meals that use up fridge scraps often require some level of creativity. We are creatures of comfort and I often find myself springing back to the flavours I know and love, even if that means throwing in some left field ideas and that forgotten head of yellowing broccoli. I would encourage you to look at what you have in the fridge, cupboard and freezer, and adapt the following recipes to suit if all the ingredients aren't available to you. For example, a few cans of chickpeas (garbanzo beans) work well in the Spicy Bean Tawa Burgers (see page 77) if the specified pinto and black beans aren't to hand. A handful of frozen mixed vegetables will give Singapore Poha (see page 93) its rainbow vibrancy if an assortment of fresh mixed vegetables isn't something you have in. Kolkata Chow Mein (see page 78) can very easily be made with rice noodles or even spaghetti in the absence of dried wheat flour noodles. These recipes are forgiving by their very nature, so if you don't have a particular spice to hand, leave it out or replace it with something else. Led by intuition, this is the kind of adaptability my mother modelled for me, and I hope to encourage my son Bodhi to develop. It's a flexible, and therefore a liberating, approach to cooking. Playing with flavours is how tremendous combinations are discovered, after all. No mention of the laced-in-subjectivity 'A' word in sight (authentic)!

Madras Mac and Cheese with Naan Crumbs

SERVES 6 • PREP: 15 MINS • COOK: 40 MINS

60 g (2 oz/¼ cup) butter

50 g (1¾ oz/scant ½ cup) plain (all-purpose) flour

700 ml (23½ fl oz/scant 3 cups) whole (full-fat) milk

200 g (7 oz/scant 2 cups) grated (shredded) extra-mature (sharp) Cheddar (or Monterey Jack)

165 g (5¾ oz/¾ cup) full-fat cream cheese

100 g (3½ oz/scant 1 cup) grated (shredded) low-moisture mozzarella

2½ tsp Madras Curry Powder (see page 273)

2 spring onions (scallions), finely sliced, plus extra greens to garnish (optional)

2 green chillies, minced (optional)

1 tsp salt

300 g (10½ oz/2 cups) elbow macaroni, or your favourite pasta shape

For the crispy crumb topping

50 g (1¾ oz/scant ¼ cup) butter

2 large garlic and coriander (cilantro) naans, blitzed to coarse crumbs (150 g/5¼ oz)

50 g (1¾ oz/scant ½ cup) grated (shredded) low-moisture mozzarella

For those who like their mac obscenely cheesy, this bubbling dish of pasta and three-cheese Madras sauce is topped with a crunchy, garlic and coriander (cilantro) naan crumb. A supreme way to use up leftover naan. If you don't want to make this mac right away, blitz any naan scraps you have, allow them to air dry on a baking sheet (or do it in a very low oven for an hour) and bag them up. Stash them in the freezer until you're ready to turbo charge any gratin-style dish.

1. For the crispy crumb topping, melt the butter in a frying pan (skillet). Add the naan crumbs and sauté over a medium-low heat for 4–5 minutes, or until lightly golden brown. Do not brown them too much as they'll finish browning in the oven. Remove the pan from the heat and set aside to cool.

2. Preheat the oven to 200°C/180°C fan/390°F/Gas mark 6.

3. To make the sauce, heat the butter in a saucepan and add the flour. Sauté the butter and flour, stirring continuously for 30 seconds and then switch the heat off. Gradually whisk in the milk. Once all the milk has been incorporated, switch the heat back on and continue to whisk until it thickens slightly. Switch the heat off again and whisk in the three cheeses, as well as the Madras curry powder, spring onions (scallions), chillies and salt.

4. Bring a pan of water to a boil and cook the macaroni for 3–4 minutes less than the cooking time stated in the package instructions. It should be very al dente. Drain.

5. Fold the partially cooked macaroni into the sauce. Spoon into a gratin dish and top with the additional mozzarella. Sprinkle generously with the naan crumbs. Bake in the preheated oven for 20–25 minutes, or until golden, gooey and bubbling. If the breadcrumbs are browning too much, cover with a piece of kitchen foil. Remove from the oven and garnish with some extra spring onion greens, if desired.

Vegan?
Use any plant-based milk in place of dairy milk. Swap the cheeses for your favourite vegan cheese alternatives. A nut-based cream cheese will help create a smooth and velvety sauce.

Gluten free?
Use both gluten-free plain (all-purpose) flour and pasta in this recipe. The naan flavour can be recreated by adding a generous pinch each of dried garlic, dried coriander and nigella seeds to gluten-free breadcrumbs.

Make it a feast!
Serve with Pink Peppercorn Pickled Onions (see page 240) and a leafy salad.

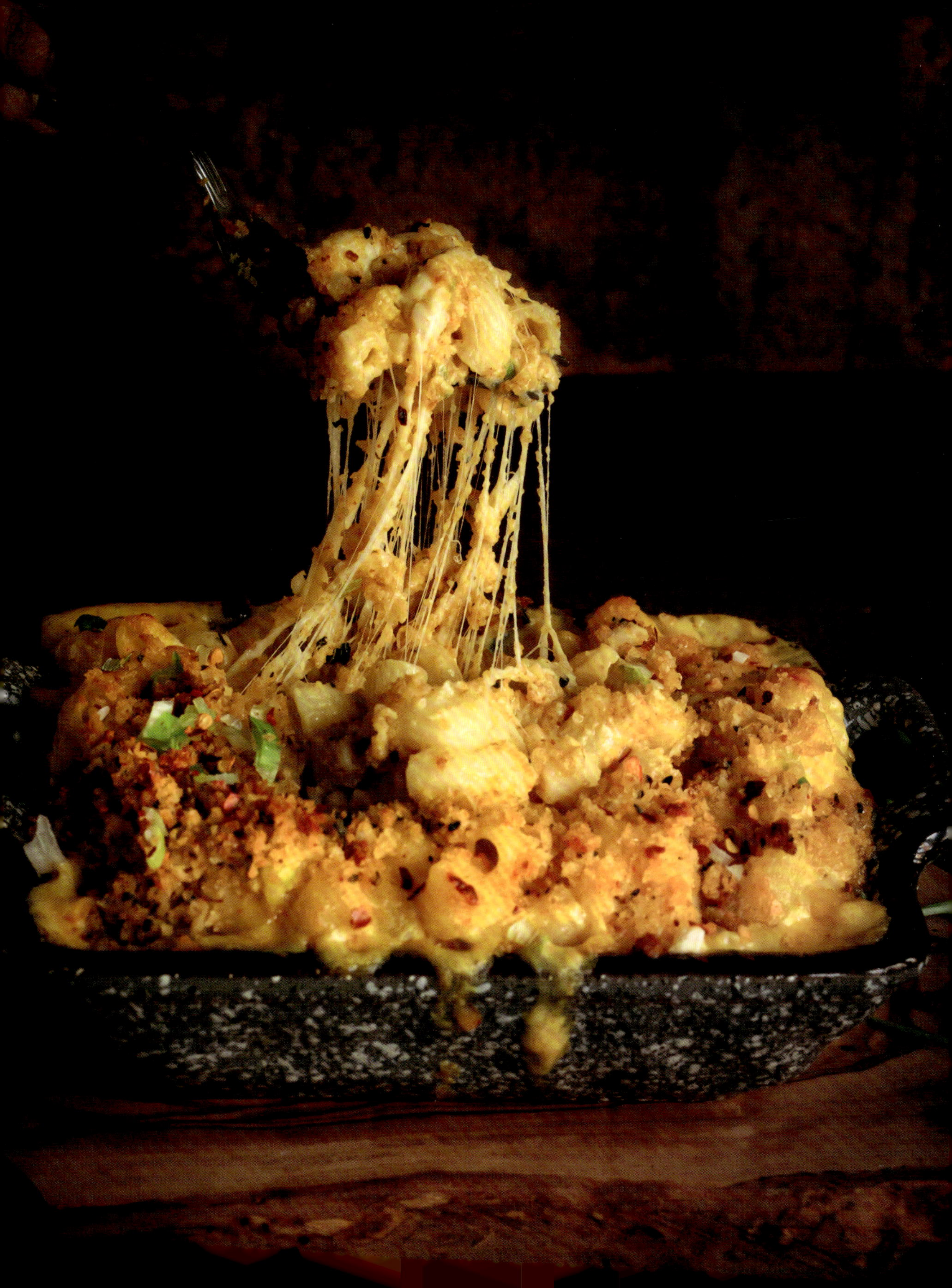

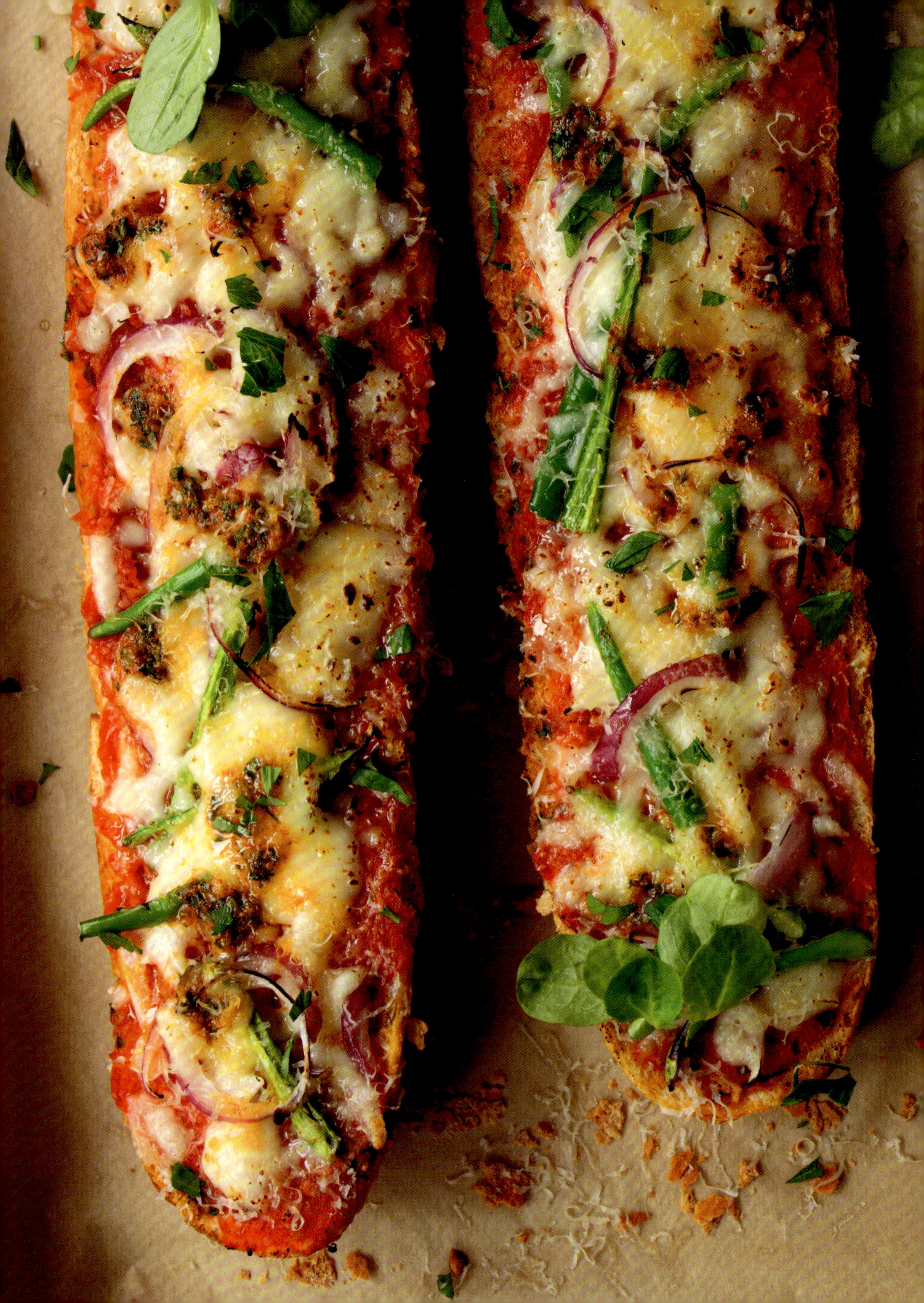

Desi-inspired French Bread Pizza

SERVES 4 • PREP: 15 MINS • COOK: 25 MINS

Hello, 1999 calling. Crusty baguette pizza slicked with tandoori butter, onions, chillies and cheese was the revision-break snack of choice throughout my teens and is still a favourite today. There was a summer when only Gregg's French bread pizzas would power me through GCSE French and Latin revision. You can indeed make this using store-bought naan too, but crusty French bread is both robust and satisfying. Be sure to flatten the baguettes with as much force as you can without tearing them. This creates a greater surface area, as well as a dense, sturdy foundation for toppings galore.

2 medium-sized French baguettes or batons (around 35 cm/14 inches)
175 g (6¼ oz/1½ cups) grated (shredded) low-moisture mozzarella
1 red onion, finely sliced
2-4 green chillies, sliced into thin strips
A handful of grated (shredded) Pecorino Romano, or any vegetarian hard cheese
1 tbsp chopped fresh parsley

For the tandoori butter
100 g (3½ oz/scant ½ cup) salted butter, softened
1 tbsp Tandoori Masala (see page 269)
2 large garlic cloves, minced
1 tbsp chopped fresh parsley

For the pizza sauce
1 x 300-g (10½-oz) can crushed tomatoes
1 tsp sugar
½ tsp salt

1. Preheat the oven to 200°C/180°C fan/390°F/Gas mark 6.

2. Place the ingredients for the pizza sauce into a small saucepan and simmer for 10 minutes, or until reduced by half. Set aside to cool slightly.

3. Next, make the tandoori butter. In a bowl, mix the softened butter, tandoori masala, garlic, and chopped parsley until smooth.

4. Split the baguettes lengthways. If you're using one very large French stick, you will need to cut it into lengths to shorten. Place the bread on a large, flat oven tray and use the back of a spoon to firmly press down the soft middles, compacting the fluffiness to form a firm base that won't turn soggy. Keep pressing until the bread feels solid at the base. You can weigh them down with something flat and heavy if they're springing back too much.

5. Spread the insides of each baguette with a generous amount of the tandoori butter and top with a light sprinkling of mozzarella. Bake in the preheated oven for 3-4 minutes until the cheese has melted and the bread is lightly toasted. Remove from the oven.

6. Spread the baguettes with the thick pizza sauce, then top with the sliced red onion, chillies, more mozzarella and, if you have any left, extra dabs of tandoori butter.

7. Bake for a further 8-10 minutes, or until the tops of the pizzas are golden and bubbling and the bread is a deep golden colour.

8. Finish with a fine grating of hard cheese and the remaining chopped parsley.

Notes

Fully build a few of these pizzas as per the recipe up to step 6. Do not bake a second time. Freeze for baking later. They're so convenient for busy weeknights.

Pause after the first bake for a glorious Tandoori Garlic Bread. You can cheese or don't cheese – simply omit the mozzarella. This is particularly good with my Curry Leaf Cream of Tomato Soup (see page 81).

Gluten free?

Replace the bread with a gluten-free baguette.

Make it a feast!

These pizzas are great alongside a fresh green salad for lunch, or my Mogo Dirty Fries (see page 186) for a more filling dinner.

Not Curry

Upma 'Summer Rolls'

SERVES 4-6 • PREP: 40 MINS • COOK: 10 MINS

Fresh, crunchy veggies and lightly spiced noodles are packed snugly inside rice paper rolls. Seviyan upma is a casual preparation of tempered spices tossed with vermicelli, typically eaten for breakfast, or stowed away inside a lunch box. It's popular throughout the southern states of India and lends itself beautifully to these vibrant, Vietnamese-inspired summer rolls. They're perfectly portable for breakfast or lunch on the go. Serve with a quick peanut-tamarind dip.

1. First, make the upma. Cook the rice vermicelli according to the packet instructions and rinse under cold water.

2. Heat the oil in a wok. Add the mustard seeds and allow them to pop. Once the popping subsides, add the asafoetida, sesame seeds, garlic, chillies and ground turmeric. Sauté for a minute, then add the drained noodles and salt. Stir-fry for 2 minutes and then set aside to cool.

3. Make the dipping sauce. In a small saucepan, combine all the ingredients for the sauce. Whisk well and cook until the sauce comes to a boil. Switch the heat off and allow to cool completely at room temperature. Refrigerate for 30 minutes, if you have the time (and patience).

4. Fill a large, shallow dish with room-temperature water. Immerse the first rice paper wrapper in the water until you feel it just begin to soften, about 10-12 seconds. It will continue to soften out of the water so do not soak it for too long as it could become sticky. Carefully lift the wrapper out of the water and lay it flat on a clean work surface, making sure it doesn't fold in on itself.

5. Place a lettuce leaf across the wrapper, about 2 cm (¾ inch) in from the edge. Top with about a tablespoon of the upma. Continue to add the fillings, with a few strips each of carrot, cucumber, cabbage and beansprouts. Take care not to overfill.

6. Roll the rice paper wrapper over once to form a log and enclose the veggies. Add a few mint leaves, coriander (cilantro) sprigs and roasted cashews. Roll again and tuck the sides in to close the two open ends. Roll the summer roll tightly to seal the remaining open edge. Repeat for the remaining rolls, one at a time.

For the upma
- 100 g (3½ oz) rice vermicelli
- 2 tsp oil
- 1 tsp mustard seeds
- ½ tsp asafoetida
- 2 tsp white sesame seeds
- 1 garlic clove, minced
- 2 red chillies, finely chopped
- ¼ tsp ground turmeric
- Salt, to taste

For the quick peanut-tamarind dip
- 75 g (2⅔ oz) smooth peanut butter
- 100 ml (3½ fl oz/scant ½ cup) full-fat coconut milk
- ½-1 tbsp tamarind paste
- 1 tbsp jaggery or brown sugar
- 1 tsp toasted sesame oil
- ⅛ tsp salt
- 4 curry leaves, cut into thin ribbons

For the wrapping and extra fillings
- 10-12 large rice paper wrappers
- 12-15 gem or romaine lettuce leaves, 2-3 shredded, the rest set aside
- 50 g (1¾ oz) carrots, cut into fine matchsticks
- 50 g (1¾ oz) cucumber, cut into fine matchsticks
- 25 g (¾ oz) red cabbage, shredded
- 25 g (¾ oz) beansprouts, washed and dried
- 15 g (½ oz) fresh mint leaves
- 15 g (½ oz) fresh coriander (cilantro) sprigs, leaves and stalks intact
- 10-12 roasted salted cashews, whole

Note
These summer rolls are best eaten fresh. If you need to store the rolls, keep them refrigerated in an airtight container for up to 24 hours.

Gluten free?
Use a gluten-free asafoetida or omit this ingredient.

66 Sanjana Feasts

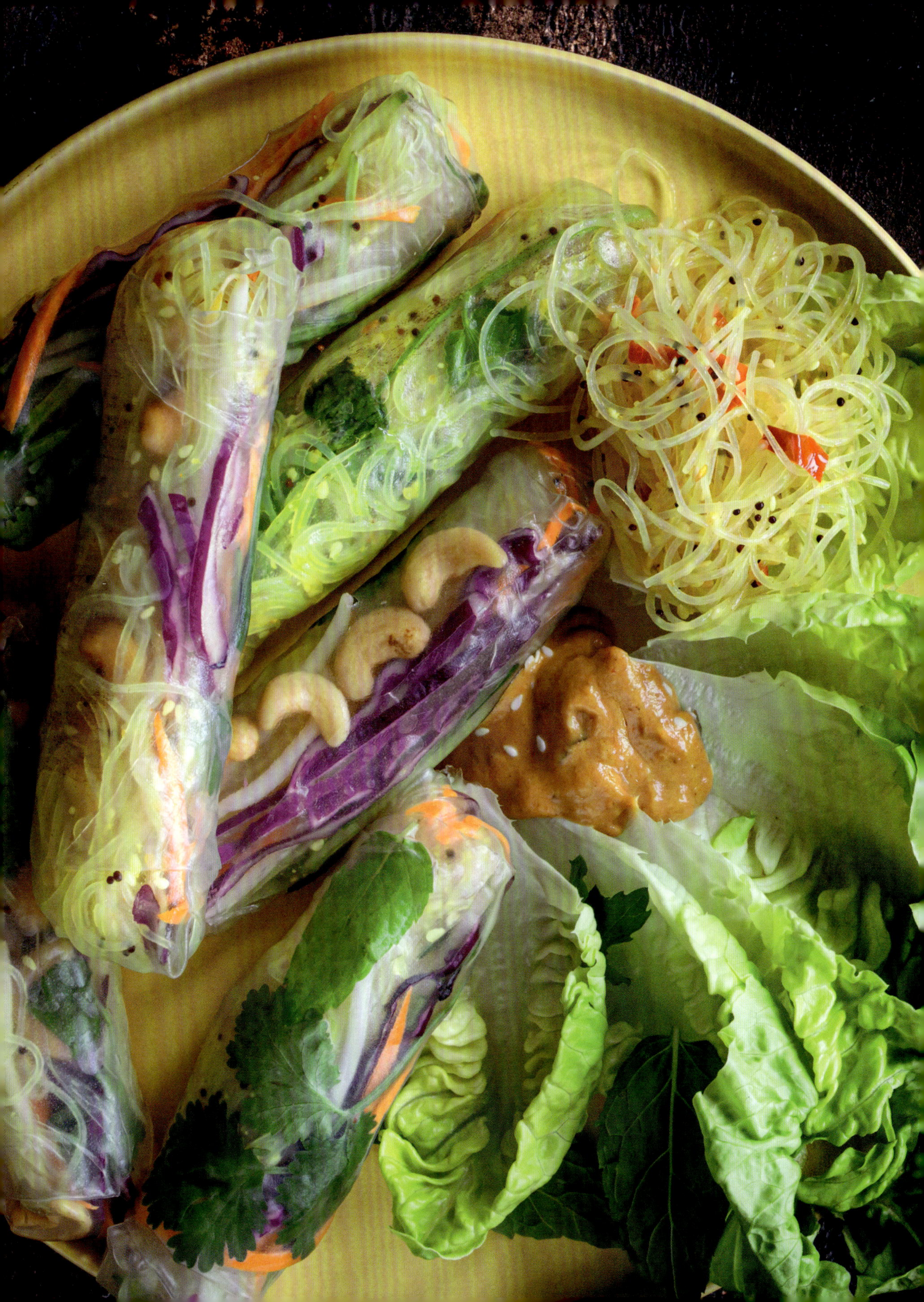

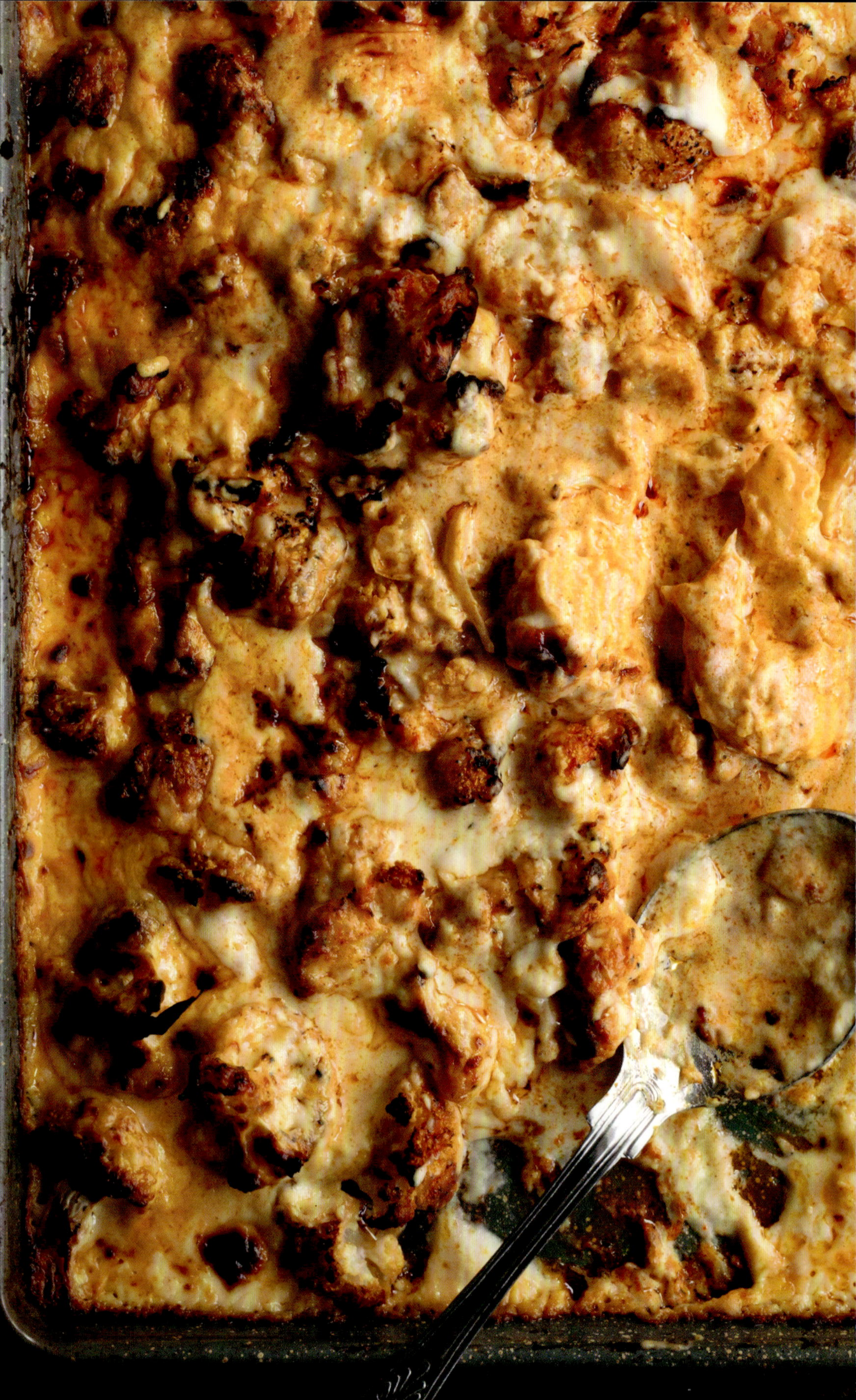

Tandoori Cauliflower Cheese

SERVES 6 • PREP: 10 MINS • COOK: 45 MINS

(V)

1 large cauliflower (about 1.5 kg/3 lb 5 oz), broken into bite-sized florets

For the tandoori marinade
150 g (5¼ oz/⅔ cup) plain yogurt
2½ tbsp Tandoori Masala (see page 269)
2 tbsp gram flour
2 large garlic cloves, minced
1 tsp grated (shredded) root ginger
¾ tsp salt
1 tbsp vegetable oil or edible mustard oil

For the cheese sauce
75 g (2⅔ oz/⅓ cup) butter
40 g (1½ oz/⅓ cup) plain (all-purpose) flour
800 ml (1½ pints/3¼ cups) whole (full-fat) milk
250 g (8¾ oz/1 cup) mascarpone
200 g (7 oz/scant 2 cups) grated (shredded) extra-mature (sharp) Cheddar (or Monterey Jack)
1 tsp salt

For the topping
100 g (3½ oz/scant 1 cup) grated (shredded) extra-mature (sharp) Cheddar (or Monterey Jack)
½ tsp sweet smoked paprika

A spicy, smoky tandoori rub is one of the fastest ways to supercharge cauliflower. This recipe calls for the florets to receive the tandoori treatment ahead of being drenched in a cheese sauce made with extra-mature (sharp) Cheddar and creamy mascarpone. From one turophile to another, baking the cauliflower cheese (or any gratin-style dish, for that matter) in a wide tray or roasting dish allows for a greater surface area of golden, crusty, bubbling cheese. We all know that's the best bit. Make it now, thank me later.

1. Preheat the oven to 240°C/220°C fan/465°F/Gas mark 9.

2. In a large bowl, whisk together all the ingredients for the tandoori marinade except the oil.

3. Heat the oil in a small saucepan until smoking hot. Carefully add it directly to the marinade and allow it to sizzle. Whisk again to combine.

4. Add the cauliflower florets to the bowl and coat each piece in the marinade.

5. Arrange the coated florets over a large roasting pan or baking dish with sides at least 2 cm (¾ inch) high and roast for 10 minutes, or until slightly softened and charred in some spots. Set aside.

6. To make the cheese sauce, heat the butter in a saucepan. Add the flour and stir well to form a roux. Cook for a minute or two until the roux is a medium blonde colour. Gradually whisk in the milk while you bring it to a boil. Once it begins to bubble a little, add the mascarpone, Cheddar and salt. Whisk until the sauce is smooth and has thickened slightly.

7. Pour the cheese sauce over the roasted cauliflower florets. Top with more Cheddar and return to the oven for 35 minutes, or until golden and bubbling. Sprinkle over the smoked paprika before serving.

Notes

If gram flour is unavailable, replace it with an equal quantity of plain (all-purpose) flour.

Edible or food-grade mustard oil is usually made with a blend of mustard and vegetable oils. It's available in most South Asian stores but if you can't get it or don't fancy buying a bottle, add 1 teaspoon of English mustard powder to the marinade and use your usual vegetable oil as directed in the recipe.

Make it a feast!

Partner the cauliflower cheese with a salad, serve it as the centrepiece of a roast dinner or eat it just as it is, with a spoon. Leftovers are particularly welcome in granary toasties (add a slick of mango chutney, too).

Gunpowder Tofu

SERVES 2 • PREP: 30 MINS • COOK: 20 MINS

400 g (14 oz) firm tofu
4 tbsp cornflour (cornstarch)
2 tbsp oil
2 tbsp ghee
6 garlic cloves, minced
1 tsp minced root ginger
8–10 curry leaves (optional)
1 red onion, cut into wedges and separated into petals
1 green bell pepper, cut into 2-cm (¾-inch) pieces
120 g (4¼ oz/½ cup) plain yogurt
3 tbsp Gunpowder (see page 268)

Vegan?
Swap ghee for oil or Vegan Ghee (see page 244), and use any plain, unsweetened vegan yogurt instead of the dairy yogurt.

Gluten free?
When preparing the Gunpowder, use a gluten-free asafoetida or omit this ingredient.

Make it a feast!
Chips (potato fries), some crisp lettuce and a bowl of mayo or aioli is all that's required alongside this tofu dish. Cooling flavours are essential when tofu has this firecracker level of heat.

A banger of a way to spice up a humble block of tofu. Roasting whole spices and daal for the gunpowder takes around 20 minutes, but it makes enough for more than a couple of batches of gunpowder tofu. You can also stir a small mound of gunpowder into hot ghee to form a spicy paste for spreading or scooping up with dosa and idli. I may be excommunicated for this, but I can't help but enjoy gunpowder on buttered crumpets, tossed with chips (potato fries) and even sprinkled into a speedy batch of instant ramen. The world is your cannon.

1. Rinse and drain the tofu. Press the block of tofu between a few layers of kitchen paper using your hands. Try to get as much liquid out as possible. You can also place a chopping board on top of the wrapped block of tofu and rest some heavy cans on top to press the water out while you prepare the rest of the ingredients.

2. Cut the tofu into 2-cm (¾-inch) cubes and dust in cornflour (cornstarch). Heat the oil in a large, wide frying pan (skillet) or wok and shallow-fry the tofu, turning every 3–4 minutes, until crispy and golden brown on all sides. Remove from the pan and set aside.

3. Give the pan a quick wipe with dry kitchen paper and heat the ghee in the same pan until smoking hot. Add the garlic, ginger and optional curry leaves. Sauté for 10–15 seconds and then add the onions and bell peppers. Stir-fry for a minute.

4. Beat together the yogurt and gunpowder and pour it into the pan. Cook for a further minute or two, until the onions and peppers soften a little. Some charring is good, so try not to add any water if you can help it.

5. Finally, toss in the fried tofu and stir until the masalas coat the cubes.

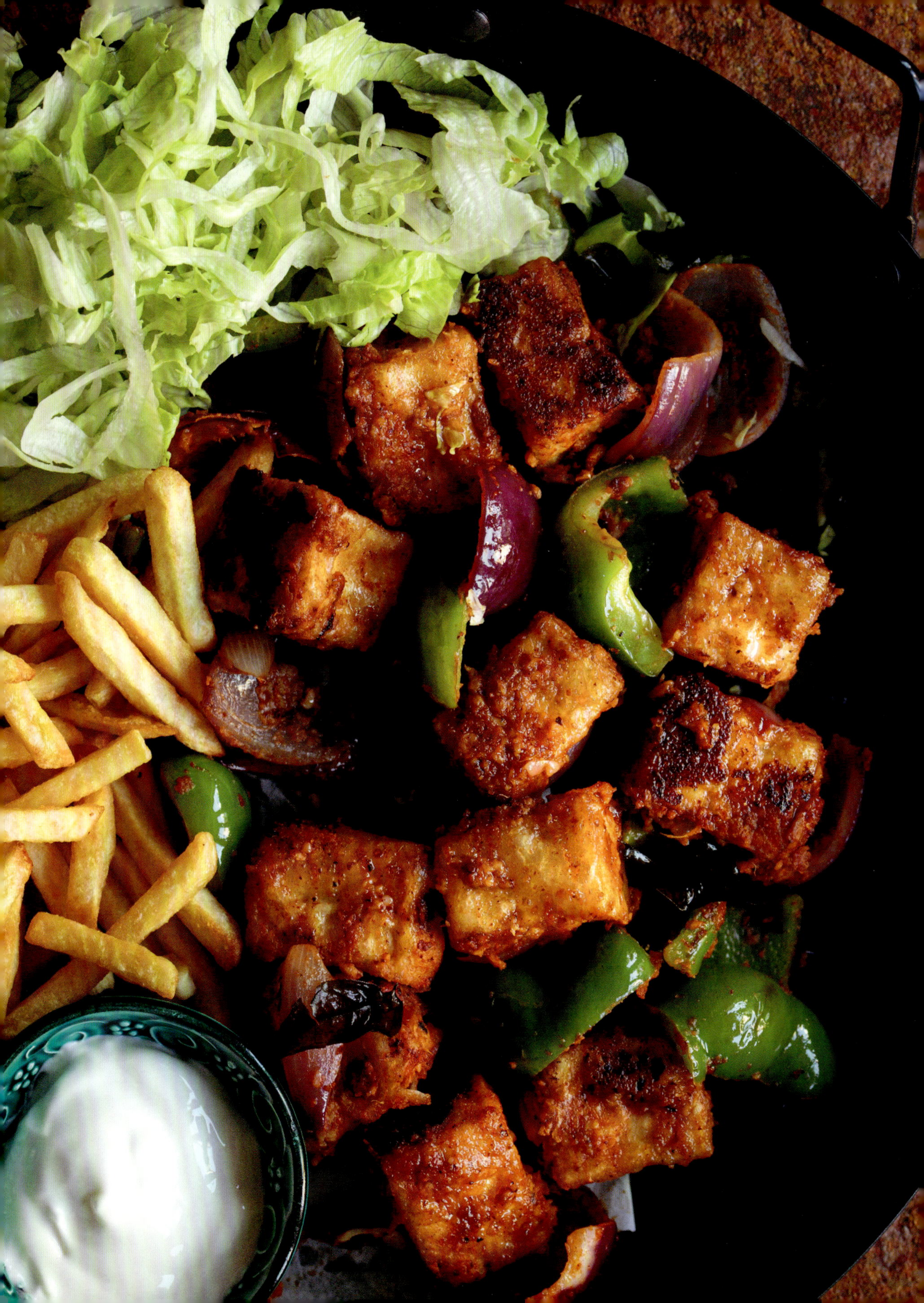

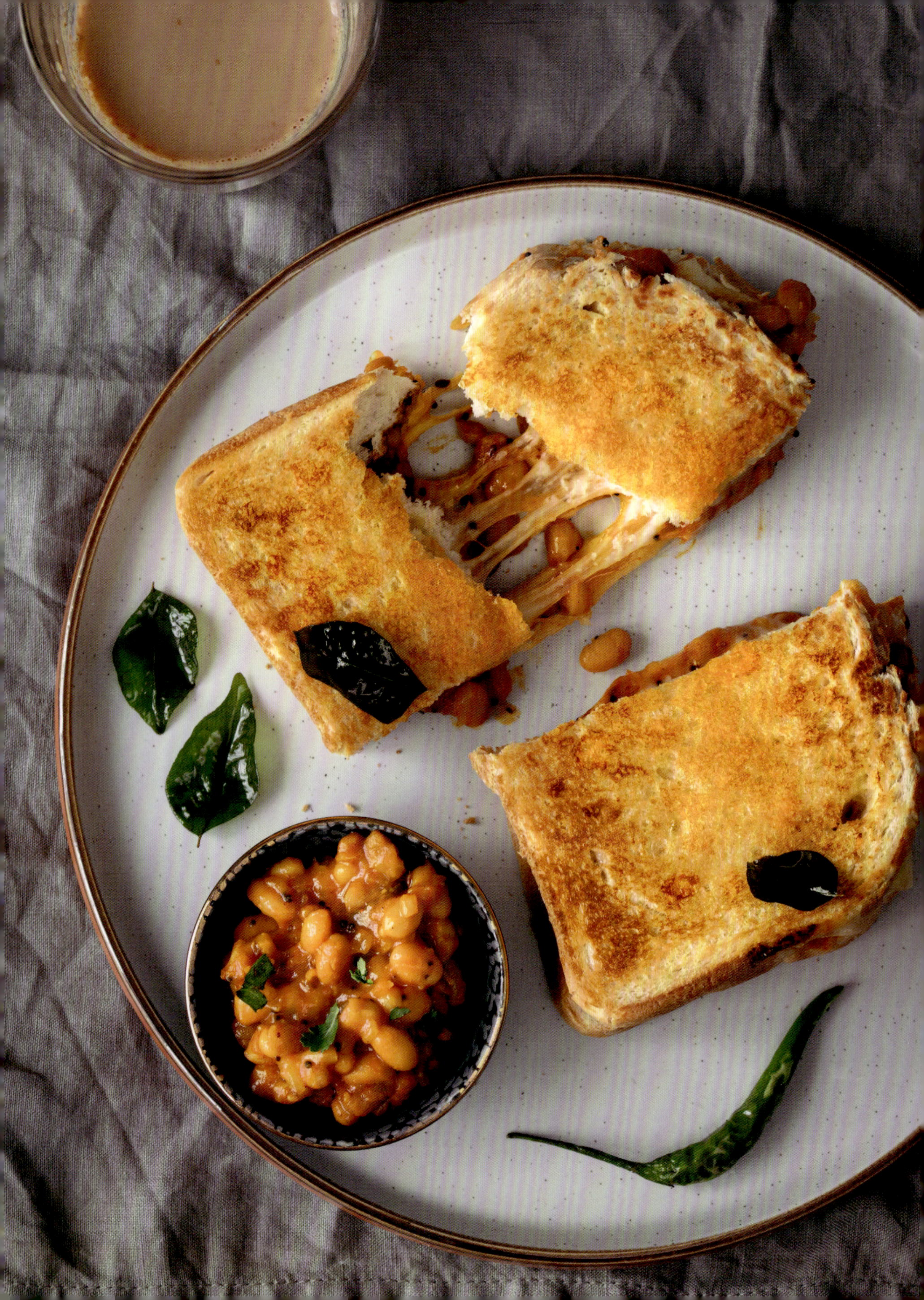

Indian Hangover Cure: Masala Baked Bean Toasties

SERVES 2-4 • PREP: 10 MINS • COOK: 15 MINS

1 tbsp ghee or oil
½ tsp mustard seeds
½ tsp cumin seeds
5-6 curry leaves
1 onion, finely chopped
1 x 410-g (14½-oz) can baked beans
¼ tsp ground turmeric
½ tsp chilli powder
½ tsp Garam Masala (see page 259)
8 slices bread of your choice
2 tbsp butter
75 g (2⅔ oz/scant ¾ cup) grated (shredded) Cheddar or Monterey Jack
Fried curry leaves and green chillies, to serve

Vegan?
Replace both the butter and cheese with your favourite vegan alternatives.

Gluten-free?
Use any gluten-free sliced bread.

Make it a feast!
Serve the masala baked beans with Everyday Roti (see page 157) for a comforting main meal. They're also delicious in a baked potato, on toast or with potato waffles. When I worked as an editor at Food Network, my fellow digital team comrades and I would partake in Waffle Wednesdays, which we always cooked together. It was a masala baked beans, potato waffles and cheese affair, and the type of office lunch that powered you through an afternoon of meetings.

Hangover optional. Stuff two slices of bread with cheese and spice-tempered baked beans and then toast for a delightfully British Indian sandwich. I'm yet to meet a South Asian family from Britain to South Africa who doesn't give their baked beans the spice treatment. It's our #1 avatar of the storecupboard staple. In South Asian homes, it's an unwritten law that masala-fying your baked beans takes them from blah to bourgeois. They're especially effortless when you make the beans the night before, then stow them away in the fridge for breakfast the next morning.

1. Heat the ghee or oil in a saucepan. Add the mustard seeds and wait for them to finish crackling. Next, add the cumin seeds, curry leaves (stand back, they will splutter) and onion. Cook for 3-4 minutes, or until the onion has softened and started browning.

2. Add the baked beans, along with the ground turmeric, chilli powder and garam masala. Stir well and simmer for a further 2-3 minutes. The beans should be a little thicker than they are when they come out of the can. Do not add any extra water.

3. Take a slice of bread and butter one side. Flip so that the buttered side is on the outside and place 2-3 tablespoons of masala beans on top and sprinkle with cheese. Place another slice of bread on top and butter the outside.

4. Press the sandwich in a sandwich toaster or cook in a frying pan (skillet) until the cheese has melted and the outside is golden brown. Slice in half and serve immediately with fried curry leaves, fried green chillies and a strong cup of Masala Chai (see page 24).

Beetroot Paneer Tikka

SERVES 4 • PREP: 25 MINS, PLUS 1 HOUR SOAKING AND 30 MINS MARINATING • COOK: 15 MINS

My favourite part of this recipe is whisking the blitzed beetroot (beets) in with the yogurt and watching it turn dusky pink. To partially temper the spices, pour smoking hot oil onto the marinade and mix to see the colour change yet again. It's like a mood ring, except there's only ever one mood and that's 'hungry'.

1. Soak 6 large wooden kebab skewers in cold water for 1 hour, or alternatively use metal skewers.

2. Roast the gram flour in a dry pan until lightly toasted. It will turn a few shades darker and smell nutty. Set aside.

3. In a large bowl, whisk together all the ingredients for the marinade, including the roasted gram flour but do not add the oil yet. Heat the oil in a small saucepan until it's smoking hot. Carefully pour the hot oil onto the marinade so it sizzles and tempers the spices. Whisk to form a smooth paste.

4. Toss the paneer, peppers and onions into the marinade and stir to coat every piece. Cover the bowl and allow to marinate at room temperature for 30 minutes.

5. Preheat the oven to 230°C/210°C fan/445°F/Gas mark 8.

6. Thread the paneer, peppers, and onions onto the skewers, alternating each ingredient so they're evenly composed.

7. Set a wire rack on top of a baking tray and arrange the skewers on top. Brush over any of the leftover marinade. Bake for 10 minutes if proceeding to the next step, or 15 minutes if skipping the next step.

8. For a restaurant-style finish, follow this optional step: once the paneer tikka is out of the oven, hold each skewer directly over an open flame on your hob (stovetop) burner and roll to char the outsides. Open a window before you start and be very careful not to burn yourself. Brush the paneer tikka pieces with melted ghee and serve immediately with a mixed salad and naan or flatbreads, or any other accompaniments of your choice.

Ingredients

- 400 g (14 oz) paneer, cut into large chunks
- 2 green bell peppers, cut into large squares
- 2 red onions, cut into wedges and separated into petals

For the marinade
- 3 tbsp gram flour
- 100 g (3½ oz/scant ½ cup) plain yogurt
- 2 large or 4 small cooked beetroots (beets), blended
- 2 thin red chillies, minced
- ½ tsp freshly ground black pepper
- 1 tbsp lemon juice
- 1 tsp ground cumin seeds
- 1 tsp ground coriander seeds
- 2 green cardamom pods, seeds ground
- ¼ tsp black salt
- ½ tsp Garam Masala (see page 259)
- 1 tsp dried fenugreek leaves, rubbed between your palms
- 3 garlic cloves, crushed
- 1½ tsp minced root ginger
- ½ tsp salt
- 2 tbsp edible mustard oil, or any cooking oil of your choice

To serve
- 1 tbsp melted ghee, for brushing the cooked tikka
- Mixed salad leaves
- Grilled naan or flatbread of your choice

Note

The paneer tikka can also be cooked on a preheated griddle pan or on the barbecue. Turn and cook on all sides until grill marks appear, around 8–10 minutes.

Vegan?

Swap paneer for pressed, firm tofu, cooked new potatoes, button mushrooms, large florets of cauliflower, or a mixture of all of these. Use any plain, unsweetened vegan yogurt.

Make it a feast!

Slip these rosy beetroot paneer tikkas into wraps or pitta bread, along with fresh salad and Fried Caper Raita (see page 194). They make for a super-fresh and filling meal.

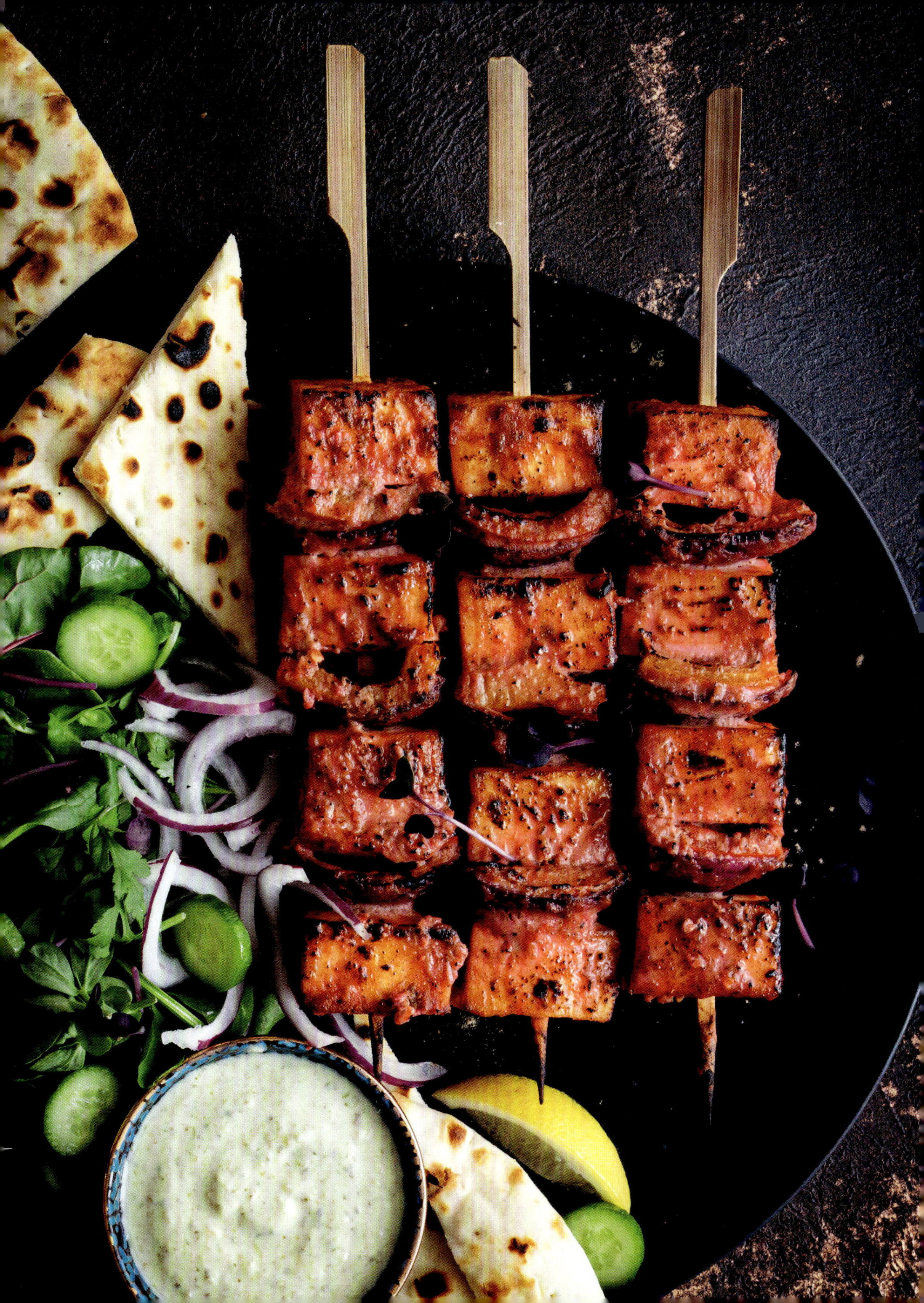

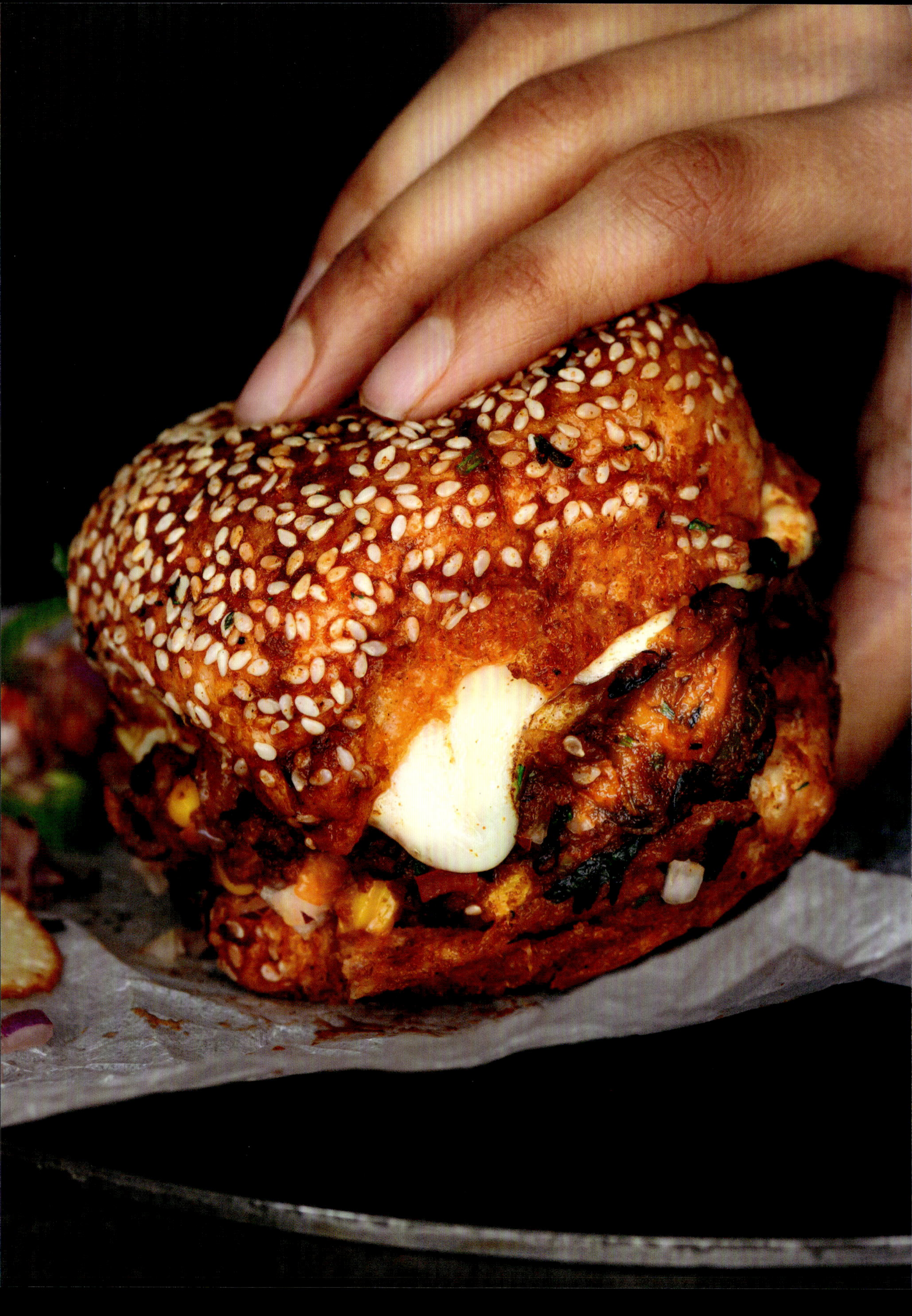

Spicy Bean Tawa Burgers

SERVES 6 • PREP: 20 MINS • COOK: 35 MINS

For the bean burgers
- 1 tbsp oil or butter
- 1 small onion, finely diced
- ½ green bell pepper, finely diced
- 1 carrot, grated (shredded)
- 1 tbsp chopped pickled jalapeños
- 2 tbsp tomato purée (paste)
- 1 tsp garlic powder
- 1 tsp ground cumin seeds
- 1 tsp ground coriander seeds
- ¼ tsp ground turmeric
- ½ tsp sweet smoked paprika
- ½ tsp chilli flakes
- 2 tsp dried oregano
- 150 g (5¼ oz/1 cup) cooked sweetcorn kernels
- 200 g (7 oz/1 cup) cooked pinto beans
- 200 g (7 oz/1 cup) cooked black beans
- ½ tsp salt
- 2 tbsp instant mashed potato powder (potato flakes), or 1 small potato, boiled and mashed

To cook the burgers
- 6 burger buns with sesame seeds
- 6 slices mozzarella or Cheddar
- 2 tbsp butter
- 1 tsp oil
- 1 tsp paprika or chilli powder
- 1 tbsp chopped fresh coriander (cilantro) leaves
- ¼ tsp Chaat Masala (see page 263) per burger

With soy, wheat gluten and pea protein meat substitutes increasingly taking centre stage in restaurants, I still crave great veggie burgers made with unprocessed natural legumes, pulses and vegetables. Here's the recipe for one I make often at home. Beany veg masala and cheese inside a squishy sesame seed bun. Toast these achingly good burgers in melted butter and smoked paprika atop an iron tawa (or in a frying pan/skillet) for the searing warmth of flat iron-cooked Indian street buns.

1. First, make the burgers. Heat the oil or butter in a large, non-stick saucepan. Add the onion and bell pepper. Sauté for a minute and then add the carrot. Sauté for a further minute before adding the chopped jalapeños and tomato purée (paste). Mix well and cook out the tomato purée for 90 seconds to remove any bitterness.

2. Next, add the following dry ingredients in quick succession: dried garlic powder, ground cumin and coriander seeds, ground turmeric, smoked paprika, chilli flakes and dried oregano. Add a splash of water, but no more than 75 ml (2½ fl oz/generous ⅓ cup), to ensure the spices can cook out without burning. Stir and cook for a further 90 seconds.

3. Add the sweetcorn, beans and salt. Stir well and cook for 2 minutes. Remove from the heat and mash the mixture with a potato masher – the beans should be a mixture of fully mashed, partially mashed, and whole for fabulous texture and a mixture that binds well. Finally, sprinkle over the instant mashed potato powder (potato flakes) or add your mashed potato, and stir well. Set aside.

4. Split the burger buns in half and fill with a generous amount of the bean mixture. I find an ice-cream scoop makes light work of this. Place a slice of cheese on top of the bean mixture and pop the burger bun top on. Press lightly.

5. To cook the burgers, add the butter and oil to a preheated tawa or frying pan (skillet). Sprinkle in the paprika or chilli powder if you like things spicier, and the chopped fresh coriander (cilantro) leaves. Mix well. Take one of the burgers and dip all sides in the butter masala in the tawa, and then the top and bottom. Lightly press the burger with a turner or spatula. Cook the burger in the hot tawa until it is perfectly toasted all over. Finally, sprinkle with a small pinch of chaat masala and serve immediately.

Note
Historically, India's native version of bread referred to unleavened flatbreads such as roti, paratha and rotla. Some were fermented with alcoholic toddy or left to ferment naturally. With the arrival of the Portuguese in Goa came the wonders of using yeast in everyday cooking. Soft Portuguese bread rolls, called pão, were thus introduced to the Indian subcontinent. Locals embraced the delicious fluffiness of pão and embraced the art of cooking with yeast. New dishes developed from this and over time, they became known locally as pav, laadi pav or pau.

Vegan?
Slide a slice of your favourite vegan cheese inside the burger, then toast in dairy-free butter or my Vegan Ghee (see page 244) for a delicious plant-based burger.

Gluten free?
Swap the buns for gluten-free burger buns.

Kolkata Chow Mein

SERVES 4 • PREP: 20 MINS • COOK: 15 MINS

A vegan take on Kolkata's treasured street-style noodles, complete with the customary scrambled 'egg', which I make with silken tofu. My recipe for Desi-style noodles has remained the same for years and puts any leftover veg to good use. It's a dish you can count on when the contents of your fridge look sparse and you're short of time.

For the noodles
325 g (11½ oz) egg-free chow mein noodles
½ tsp ground turmeric
2 tsp oil
1 tbsp light soy sauce
3 spring onions (scallions), sliced diagonally

For the scrambled 'egg'
1 tbsp oil
300 g (10½ oz) silken tofu
½ tsp ground turmeric
⅓ tsp black salt
2 tbsp gram flour

For stir-frying
2 tbsp oil
2 large garlic cloves, minced
2 green chillies, sliced
1 carrot, cut into matchsticks
80 g (2¾ oz) Chinese cabbage or white cabbage, finely shredded
60 g (2 oz/⅓ cup) beansprouts
60 ml (2 fl oz/4 tbsp) vegetarian oyster sauce
½ tsp Garam Masala (see page 259)
¼ tsp ground white pepper
¼ tsp salt
¼ tsp MSG
1 tbsp distilled white vinegar

1. Parboil the noodles in plenty of water with the ground turmeric, until 80 per cent cooked. They should be quite al dente. Drain the noodles in a colander, refresh under cold, running water, drain again and then transfer to a bowl. Add the oil, soy sauce and half of the spring onions (scallions). Toss well.

2. To make the scrambled 'egg', heat the oil in a wok. Add the tofu and use a spatula to break it into large chunks (not too small as the tofu will continue to break up as it cooks). Cook over a high heat for 2 minutes, mixing often. Sprinkle the ground turmeric, black salt and gram flour over the tofu and continue to mix and cook for a further 2–3 minutes, until it begins to look scrambled. Remove to a plate or bowl.

3. Wipe the wok with kitchen paper and heat until smoking hot. Heat 2 teaspoons of the oil in the very hot wok. Add the garlic, chillies and remaining spring onions. Stir-fry for a few seconds, then add the carrot, cabbage, beansprouts, vegetarian oyster sauce, garam masala, white pepper, salt, MSG and vinegar. Stir-fry for 90 seconds before adding the partially cooked noodles and scrambled 'egg'. Cook for a minute or two longer until some of the veggies and noodles are scorched on the base of the wok. Toss well and serve immediately.

Note
Vegetarian oyster sauce is available in most East Asian supermarkets. It's sometimes labelled 'mushroom sauce' and can be found in the stir-fry sauces and seasonings aisle.

Gluten free?
Make this with rice noodles (instead of chow mein noodles) and tamari (instead of soy sauce) for a gluten-free version. Also, check the ingredients on the vegetarian oyster sauce before using.

Make it a feast!
Indo-Chinese night wouldn't be complete without a selection of snacks to enjoy alongside, buffet-style. A side of Indo-Chinese Bhajiya (see page 51) and Chestnut Manchurian (see page 98) is ideal.

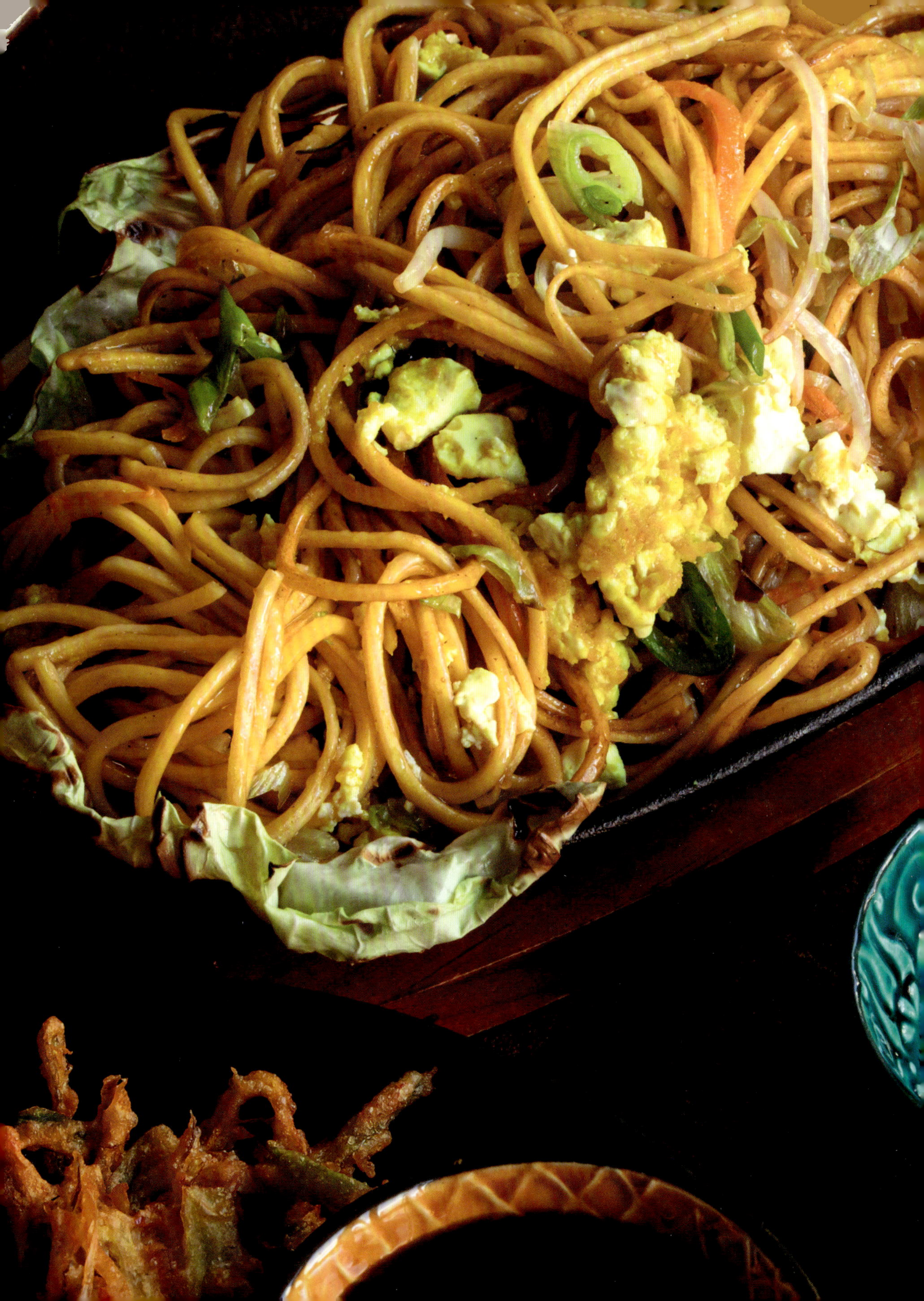

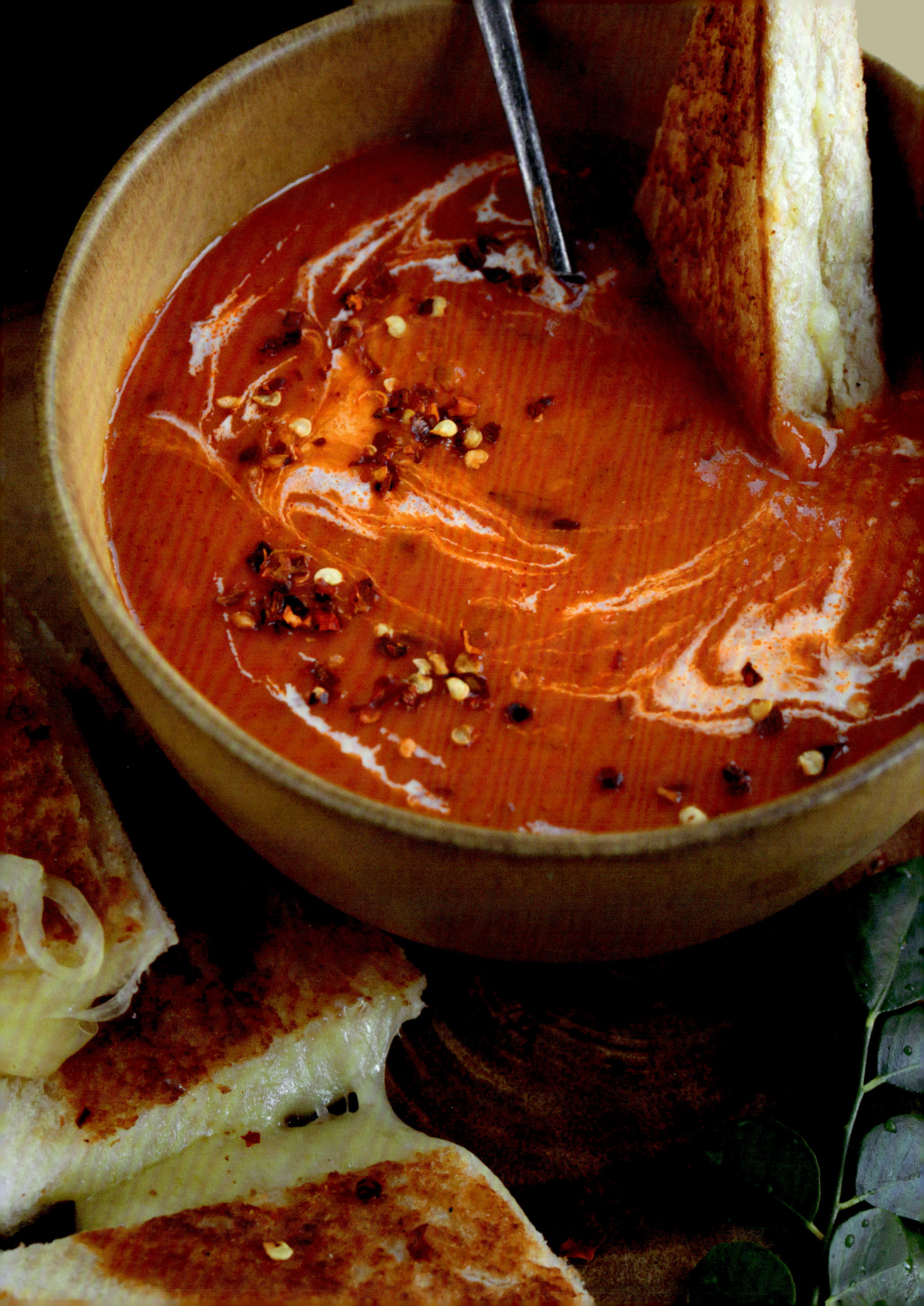

Curry Leaf Cream of Tomato Soup

SERVES 2–4 • PREP: 20 MINS • COOK: 20 MINS

2 tbsp ghee
2-cm (¾-inch) cinnamon stick
2 tsp cumin seeds
10–12 curry leaves
½ tsp asafoetida
2 tsp minced root ginger
1 large onion, finely diced
½ tsp chilli flakes (reserving some to sprinkle on top)
2 x 400-g (14-oz) cans cream of tomato soup
250 ml (8½ fl oz/1 cup) hot water
Double cream (heavy cream), to drizzle on top

Meet the soup I never wanted to eat when I was growing up. It starts with tadka, the flavour foundation to most of the dishes cooked in my childhood home. Curry leaves and whole spices are sizzled in ghee until the aromas waft under your nostrils and right through to your P.E. kitbag hanging up in the corner. Then come the big guns: cans of cream of tomato soup, directly from the back of the cupboard. I used to question why we would masala-fy everything at that age. Now the masalafication of every meal is instinctive.

1. Heat the ghee in a saucepan. In quick succession, add the following ingredients to the hot ghee: cinnamon stick, cumin seeds, curry leaves (stand back, they will crackle), asafoetida, ginger, onion and chilli flakes. Sauté for 4–5 minutes until the onion has turned a light golden brown.

2. Add the cans of tomato soup and hot water to the pan. Bring the soup to a boil. Simmer gently with a lid on for 10 minutes.

3. Ladle the soup into bowls, drizzle in a swirl of cream and top with a few extra chilli flakes.

Vegan?

Use Vegan Ghee (page 244) in place of ghee and try oat cream or coconut milk in place of dairy cream.

Gluten free?

Use gluten-free asafoetida or omit this ingredient.

Make it a feast!

Serve this comforting soup with cheese toasties (grilled cheese sandwiches).

Sambharo Spiral

SERVES 2-4 • PREP: 15 MINS • COOK: 35 MINS

For the filling
2 tbsp oil
1 tsp mustard seeds
¼ tsp asafoetida
500 g (1 lb 2 oz) white cabbage, finely shredded
400 g (14 oz) carrots, grated (shredded)
4-6 green chillies, sliced diagonally
½ tsp ground turmeric
1¼ tsp salt
1 tbsp cornflour (cornstarch)

For the spiral
12 ready-rolled filo (phyllo) pastry sheets
2 tbsp olive oil
2 tsp sesame seeds

Make it a feast!

A light salad and a pot of sweet chilli sauce is ideal alongside this spring roll-like Sambharo Spiral. Serve one spiral per person as a main or cut them in half for a starter-size portion to serve four.

Here's a new way of serving a simple Gujarati side dish. Between the layers of crispy filo (phyllo) pastry is a mixture of cabbage and carrots stir-fried with mustard seeds. Sambharo is typically eaten as an accompaniment with roti, or for breakfast alongside gathia (long gram flour snacks) and jalebi (sweet and swirly sweets (candies)). I make this when all I want for dinner is a plate of spring rolls but feel like doing none of the fiddly folding and frying.

1. Preheat the oven to 200°C/180°C fan/390°F/Gas mark 6.

2. Heat 2 tablespoons of oil in a large frying pan (skillet) or wok. Add the mustard seeds and allow them to finish crackling. Sprinkle in the asafoetida and then quickly add the cabbage, carrots, green chillies, ground turmeric and salt. Stir-fry for 4-5 minutes until everything has softened but the cabbage and carrots still have some crunch.

3. Remove the pan from the heat, sprinkle over the cornflour (cornstarch) and stir well. Set aside to allow the mixture to cool.

4. Place a sheet of filo (phyllo) pastry on a large, clean work surface. Brush with olive oil and place another sheet directly beside it, overlapping slightly so you have a longer sheet. Brush the second sheet and add a third sheet next to this one, so you have a long sheet, about a metre (3 feet) wide. Place three more sheets directly on top of these so the long sheet is double thickness.

5. Place half of the cooled Sambharo filling along one long edge of the filo pastry, leaving a 2-cm (¾-inch) gap around the borders. Roll the filo around the filling into a very loose, long rope. It's important not to roll it too tightly or the pastry will rip as you try to build the coil.

6. Starting at one end, begin to coil the rope of pastry around itself in a spiral. Carefully lift the coil and place it onto a large oven tray lined with parchment paper. Repeat with the remaining filo pastry sheets and filling so you have two spirals.

7. Brush the top of each spiral liberally with olive oil and scatter over the sesame seeds.

8. Bake in the preheated oven for 25-30 minutes until the spirals are golden brown.

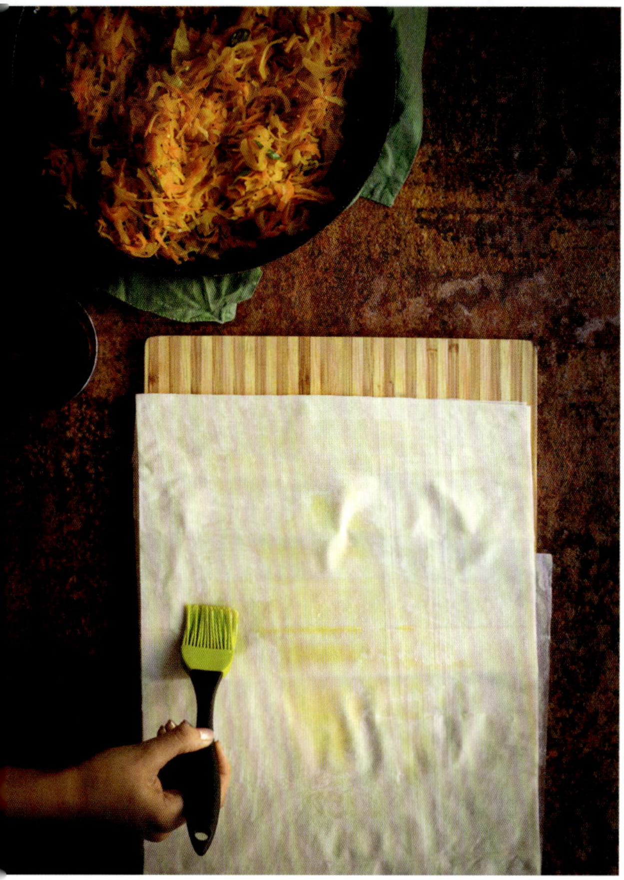
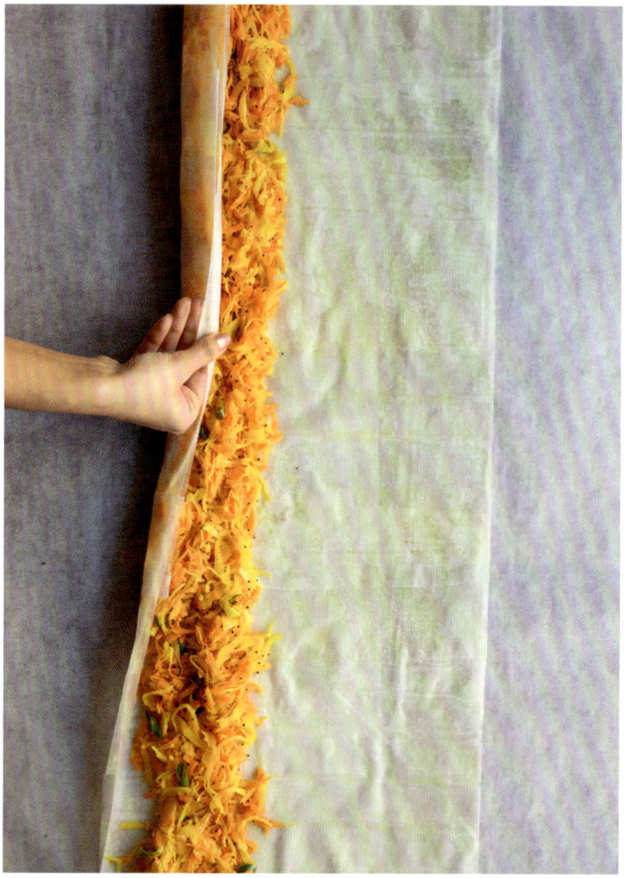
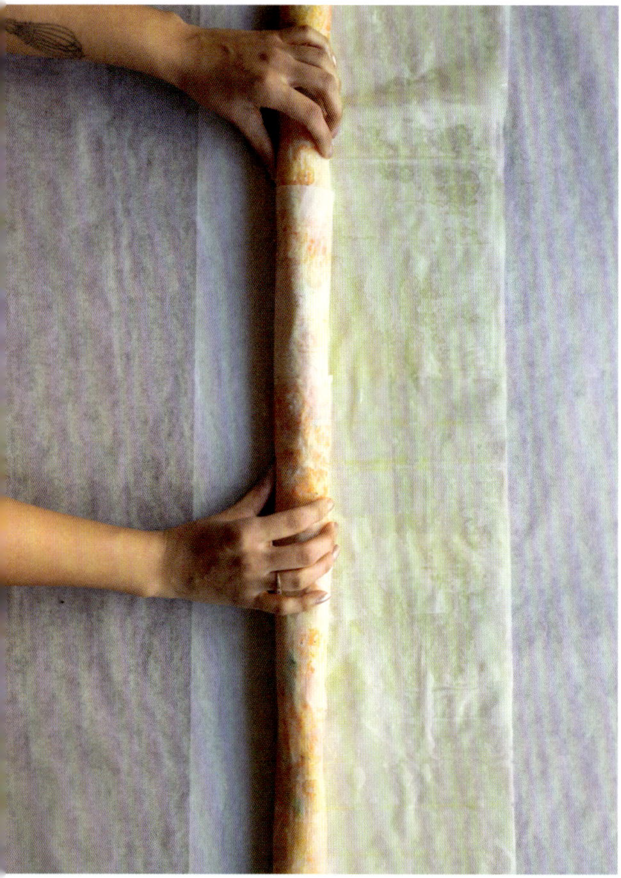
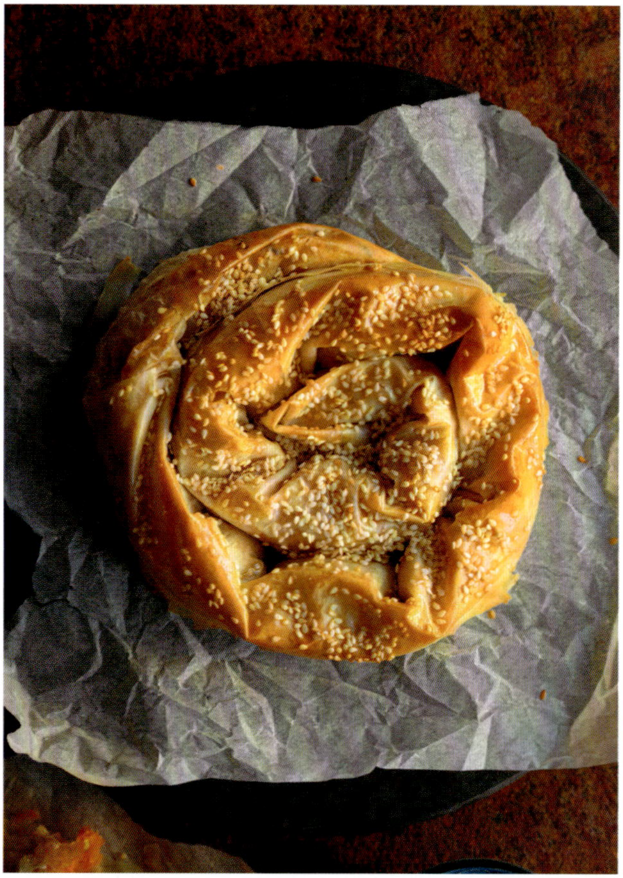

Paneer Katsu Curry

SERVES 4-6 • PREP: 30 MINS • COOK: 80 MINS

500 g (1 lb 2 oz) store-bought paneer
40 g (1½ oz/⅓ cup) cornflour (cornstarch), plus 40 g (1½ oz/⅓ cup) for the coating
40 g (1½ oz/⅓ cup) plain (all-purpose) flour
125 ml (4¼ fl oz/½ cup) ice-cold water
⅛ tsp salt
150 g (5¼ oz/3 cups) panko breadcrumbs
1 l oil, for deep-frying

For the curry sauce
3 tbsp oil
1 large onion, sliced
250 g (8¾ oz) sweet potato, peeled and diced into 2-cm (¾-inch) pieces
1 carrot, peeled and diced into 2-cm (¾-inch) pieces
1 apple, finely chopped (no need to peel)
1 ripe banana, peeled and cut into chunks
3 garlic cloves, finely chopped
2 red chillies, finely chopped
2 tbsp plain (all-purpose) flour
400 ml (13½ fl oz/1⅔ cups) full-fat coconut milk
2½ tbsp light soy sauce
1 tbsp mango chutney
2 tsp mild curry powder
2½ tsp Chinese 5-spice
½ tsp Garam Masala (see page 259)
½ tsp ground white pepper
2 dried Indian bay leaves
2.5-cm (1-inch) cinnamon stick
1 star anise
1 tsp salt, or to taste

The concept of 'curry' comes full circle with this Japanese-style Paneer Katsu Curry, so to speak. It's made with crunchy, panko-coated paneer and the sauce is crammed with sweet and gentle flavours. After colonising vast parts of the world, including the Indian subcontinent, the British invented curry powder to make cooking with spices accessible. Whipping up a 'taste of the East' had never been easier. This simplified method of cooking curry was introduced to Japan by British military personnel during the Meji period (1868-1912). Remember to caramelise the aromatics well to develop the deeply rich aromas that Japanese karē is so well known for.

1. To make the pickles, finely slice the radishes and baby cucumbers. Place them in a sterilised jar. Bring the water, vinegar, sugar and salt to a boil in a saucepan and simmer for 5 minutes. Pour this hot pickling liquid over the radishes and cucumbers. Screw the lid onto the jar and allow to cool.

2. To make the curry sauce, heat the oil in a large pan. Add the onion and cook for 10 minutes or until golden brown. Next, add the sweet potato, carrot, apple and banana. Cook for a further 15 minutes, until everything has turned a deep brown colour. The potatoes should be mushy and the mixture very well caramelised. This is the flavour foundation.

3. Add the garlic and chillies. Sauté for 2 minutes before adding the flour. Stir very well and continue to cook for a further 5 minutes. Everything should be looking soft and mushy.

4. Pour in 550 ml (18½ fl oz/2¼ cups) water and the coconut milk, then stir in the soy sauce, mango chutney, curry powder, Chinese 5-spice, garam masala and white pepper. Mix well. Switch the heat off and allow to cool for 10 minutes before blending to a very smooth sauce.

5. Return the blended sauce to the pan and add the bay leaves, cinnamon, star anise and salt. Stir well and cover with a lid. Allow the sauce to simmer for 20 minutes, stirring at regular intervals.

6. To prepare the paneer, cut the paneer into slabs about 3 cm (1 inch) wide and ½ cm (¼ inch) thick. In a bowl, mix 40 g (1½ oz/⅓ cup) of the cornflour (cornstarch), the plain (all-purpose) flour, water and salt. Whisk until the batter is smooth. Place the remaining 40 g (1½ oz/⅓ cup) of cornflour on a separate plate. Spread the panko breadcrumbs over a large plate. Your breadcrumbing station awaits. Try to keep one hand for dry dunking in the panko breadcrumbs and the other for the wet batter to avoid a big, sticky mess.

7. First, dust the paneer in the dry cornflour until coated. Next, dip each cutlet in the batter and then immediately in the panko breadcrumbs, making sure they're well stuck all over the paneer. Place the breaded paneer cutlets onto a separate plate. Repeat for the remaining pieces.

For the quick pickles

300 g (10½ oz) mixed radishes and baby cucumbers

300 ml (10 fl oz/1¼ cups) cold water

300 ml (10 fl oz/1¼ cups) distilled white vinegar

4 tbsp sugar

3 tsp salt

To serve

Steamed white rice

Salad leaves or steamed greens

Notes

If you don't fancy the deep-frying, make a curry! Simply add a handful each of chickpeas (garbanzo beans), roughly chopped potatoes, carrots and onions to the curry sauce. Simmer with a lid on until the potatoes are tender.

The paneer can also be spritzed with cooking oil and baked or air-fried. Saying this, the crunch factor will be slightly compromised.

Vegan?

Swap paneer for tofu, seitan or your favourite veg. Slices of aubergine (eggplant), squash and cauliflower all work a treat.

8. Heat enough oil for deep-frying in a pan. Once the oil reaches a temperature of 180°C (355°F), or a piece of bread sizzles and browns in 50-60 seconds, carefully place the breaded paneer cutlets into the oil. Do not overcrowd the pan and allow them to sizzle in the oil for at least a minute before moving them around to avoid all the breadcrumbs falling off.

9. Once the panko breadcrumbs are golden brown all over, lift the paneer cutlets out of the oil and place them on a plate lined with absorbent kitchen paper. Each batch should take around 3 minutes.

10. Serve the paneer cutlets and curry sauce alongside the pickled radishes and cucumbers with some steamed rice and any salad or steamed greens of your choice.

Pudla Traybake

SERVES 4 • PREP: 25 MINS • COOK: 22 MINS

V VG GF

- 2 tbsp oil, for greasing the tray (pan), plus an extra 1 tbsp, for the batter
- 300 g (10 oz/scant 2½ cups) gram flour
- 3 tbsp rice flour
- 2 tbsp plain yogurt
- ¾ tsp ground turmeric
- 2 green chillies, minced
- 1 tbsp minced root ginger
- 1 tsp citric acid
- 1 tsp salt
- 1 tbsp sugar
- ¼ tsp bicarbonate of soda (baking soda)
- ¼ tsp asafoetida
- ½ tsp carom seeds
- 420 ml (14¼ oz/1¾ cups) room-temperature water
- 3 tbsp chopped fresh coriander (cilantro), leaves and stalks
- 200 g (7 oz) mixed vegetables of your choice (for example, cabbage, onions, bell peppers, peas, French beans, carrots and corn), finely chopped
- 1 green chilli, sliced, to garnish (optional)

A 30-minute, frittata-style affair. This oven-baked gram flour slice is a speedier version of Gujarati pudla, known in other regions of India as cheela. It's naturally a fast recipe, but this traybake version cuts out the manual labour of cooking each pancake individually in a frying pan (skillet). Breakfast, lunch and dinner goals.

1. Preheat the oven to 200°C/180°C fan/390°F/Gas mark 6.

2. Grease a 42 x 28-cm (16½ x 11-inch) roasting tray (sheet pan) with oil, making sure to coat the base and sides.

3. To make the batter, whisk together all the ingredients for the pudla, except the mixed vegetables, in a large mixing bowl. Beat well making sure there are no lumps. Fold the vegetables into the batter until they are all coated. Cover the bowl and allow the batter to rest at room temperature for 15 minutes.

4. Pour the batter into the greased roasting tray. Gently wiggle the pan to evenly disperse the vegetables. Bake in the preheated oven for 20–22 minutes or until the top is golden brown. Allow to cool for a few minutes before sprinkling over the sliced green chilli, slicing and serving.

Vegan?
Swap dairy yogurt for a dairy-free yogurt alternative.

Gluten free?
Use a gluten-free asafoetida or omit this ingredient.

Make it a feast!
Serve this with one or more of the Traffic Light Chutneys (see page 196) or – like most Desi households do – with tomato ketchup!

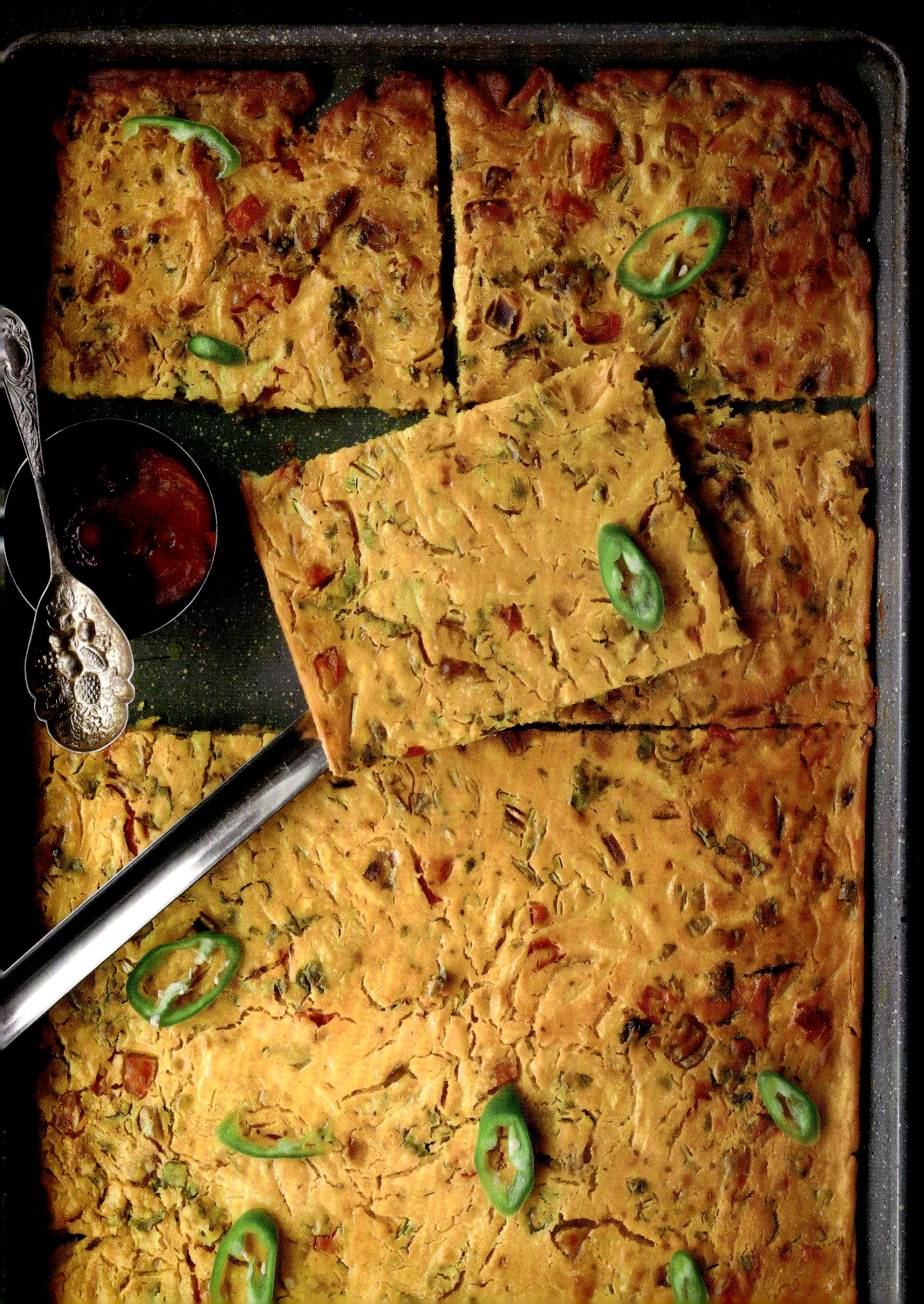

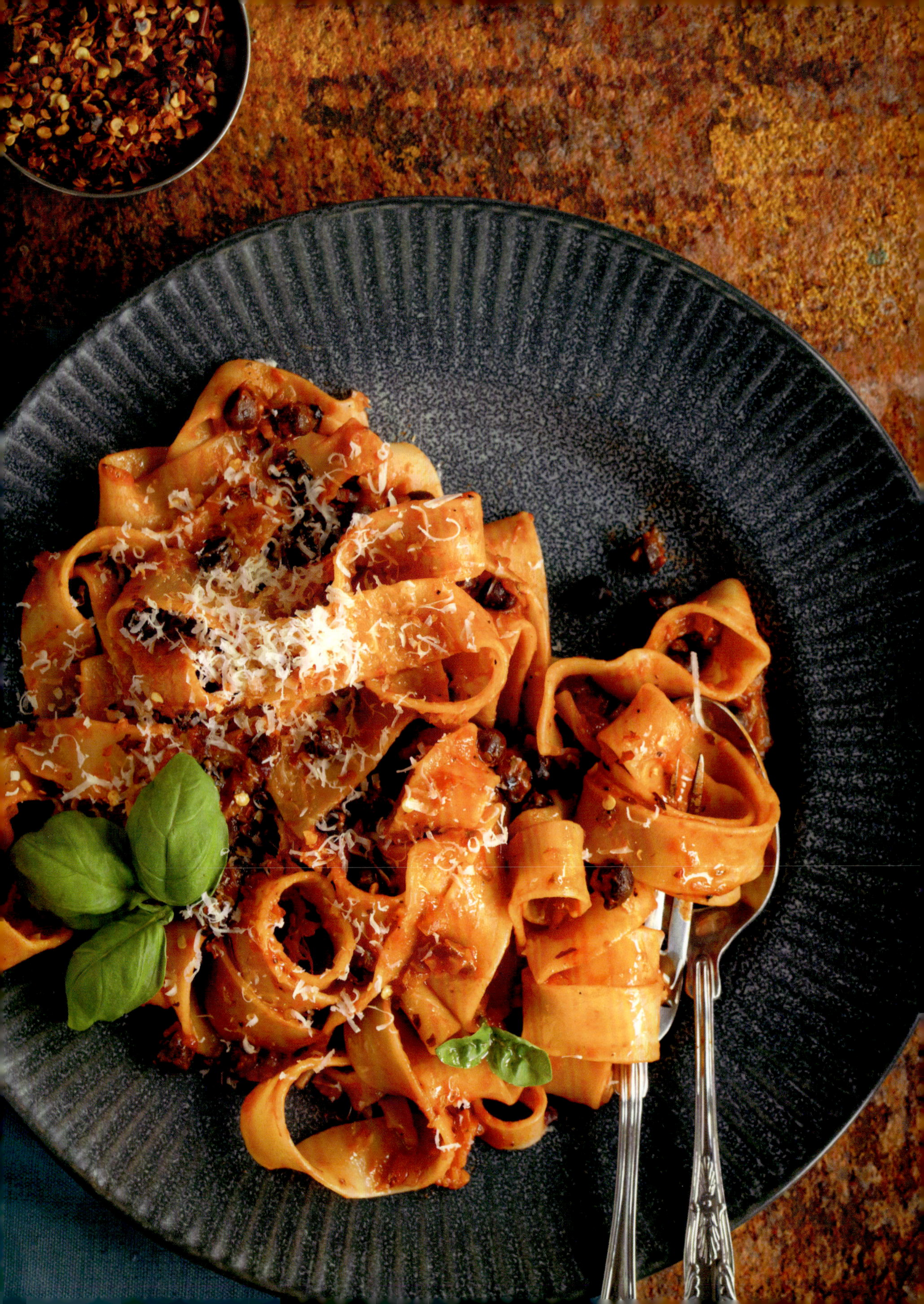

Black Chickpea 'Bolognese'

SERVES 4-6 • PREP: 20 MINS • COOK: 30 MINS

2 tbsp olive oil
1 onion, diced
1 carrot, finely diced
1 celery stalk, finely diced
1 dried Indian bay leaf
½ tsp fennel seeds
2 large garlic cloves, minced
1 hot red chilli, finely chopped
3-4 dried porcini mushrooms, soaked and finely minced
2 tbsp tomato purée (paste)
400 g (14 oz/1¾ cups) can tomato passata (strained tomatoes) or chopped tomatoes
6 sundried tomatoes, chopped
1 tsp concentrated tamarind paste or 1 tbsp balsamic vinegar
300 ml (10 fl oz/1¼ cups) vegetable stock
1 tsp dried oregano
¼ tsp salt
¾ tsp freshly ground black pepper
¼ tsp sweet smoked paprika
75 ml (2½ fl oz/generous ⅓ cup) single (light) cream
1 x 400-g (14-oz) can black chickpeas, drained
300 g (10½ oz) pappardelle, or your favourite pasta to pair with ragu-style sauces

To garnish
A few sprigs of fresh basil
Chilli flakes
As much grated (shredded) vegetarian hard cheese or other Parmesan alternative as you like

A warming, spiced take on bolognese, made with robust black chickpeas (kala channa). These are typically smaller than white chickpeas (garbanzo beans), with a nuttier flavour and more robust texture which is largely down to their thicker skins. Canned black chickpeas work well and save time, but feel free to soak and cook dried black chickpeas, if you wish.

1. Heat the oil in a large, heavy-based pan. Add the onion, carrot, celery, bay leaf and fennel seeds. Sauté for 5 minutes, or until softened. Next, add the garlic, chilli, mushrooms and tomato purée (paste). Cook for a further 3 minutes before tipping in the tomato passata (strained tomatoes), sundried tomatoes, tamarind paste or balsamic vinegar, vegetable stock, dried oregano, salt, pepper, smoked paprika, cream, black chickpeas and 350 ml (11¾ fl oz/scant 1½ cups) water. Mix well and bring to a simmer. Cover the pan with a tight-fitting lid and simmer over a low heat for 20 minutes.

2. Bring a pan of water to a boil and cook the pasta for 3 minutes less than the cooking time stated in the packet instructions. It should be quite al dente. Drain, reserving around 300 ml (10 fl oz/1¼ cups) of the pasta cooking water.

3. Add the pasta to the sauce, along with some of the pasta cooking water. The pasta will finish cooking in the sauce. If it feels too dry, add more of the pasta cooking water. Keep stirring until the sauce coats the pasta.

4. Serve immediately, finished with basil sprigs, chilli flakes and grated (shredded) cheese.

Vegan?
Swap the cream and cheese for dairy-free alternatives.

Gluten free?
Use your favourite gluten-free pasta.

(V) (GF) (VG)

Halloumi Fries Chaat

SERVES 2 • PREP: 20 MINS • COOK: 5 MINS

250 g (9 oz) halloumi,
   cut into thick fries
2 tbsp cornflour (cornstarch)
2 tbsp oil

For the masala yogurt
125 g (4½ oz/½ cup)
   full-fat Greek yogurt
¼ tsp cumin seeds, roasted
   and crushed
½ tsp dried mint
¼ tsp Chaat Masala
   (see page 263)
2 tsp sugar
2 tsp lemon juice

For the toppings
2 tbsp tamarind chutney
Green Coriander and Mint
   Chutney (see page 197)
2 tbsp chopped red onion
2 tbsp diced tomato
2 tbsp pomegranate seeds
2 tbsp sev (fried gram flour
   noodles)
A few sprigs of fresh mint

Vegan?

Try this with Fauxneer (my vegan paneer, see page 251) or substitute the halloumi for great big potato wedges. I've never met a potato I didn't like. Use any unsweetened vegan yogurt in place of Greek yogurt.

The squeakiest chaat there ever was. Pan-fried halloumi doused with masala yogurt, tamarind chutney, spicy coriander (cilantro) and mint chutney, onions, crunchy sev and juicy bursts of pomegranate makes this dish the definition of a party in your mouth.

1. In a bowl, whisk up all the ingredients for the masala yogurt. Cover and refrigerate until required. This can be done up to 24 hours in advance.

2. Toss the halloumi fries in the cornflour (cornstarch). Heat the oil in a non-stick frying pan (skillet) and fry the halloumi fries on all sides until golden.

3. Arrange the halloumi fries in a bowl or on a plate. Top with a drizzle of masala yogurt (you might want to save some to serve on the side) and both chutneys, the chopped onion, diced tomato, pomegranate seeds, sev and mint sprigs. Serve immediately.

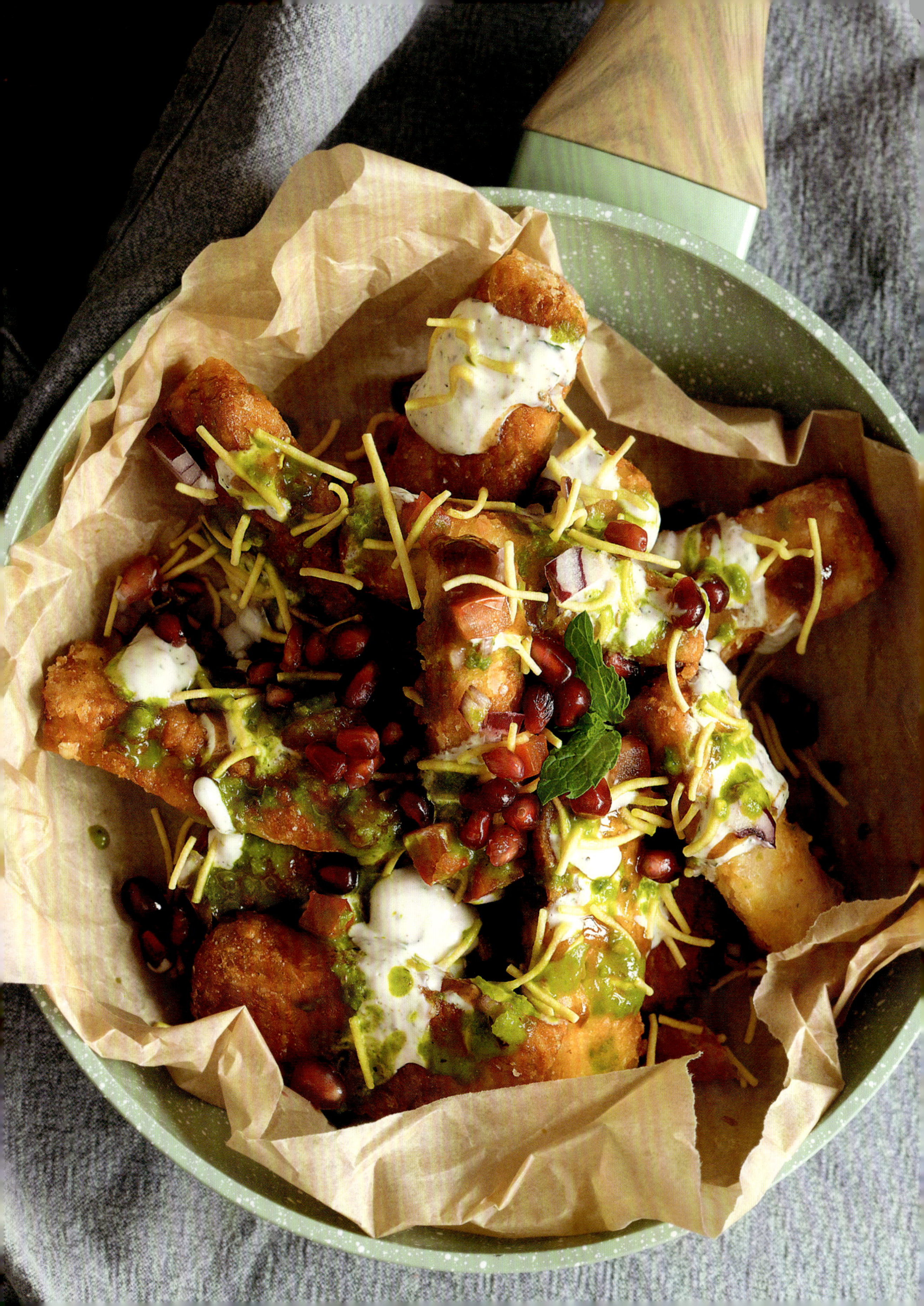

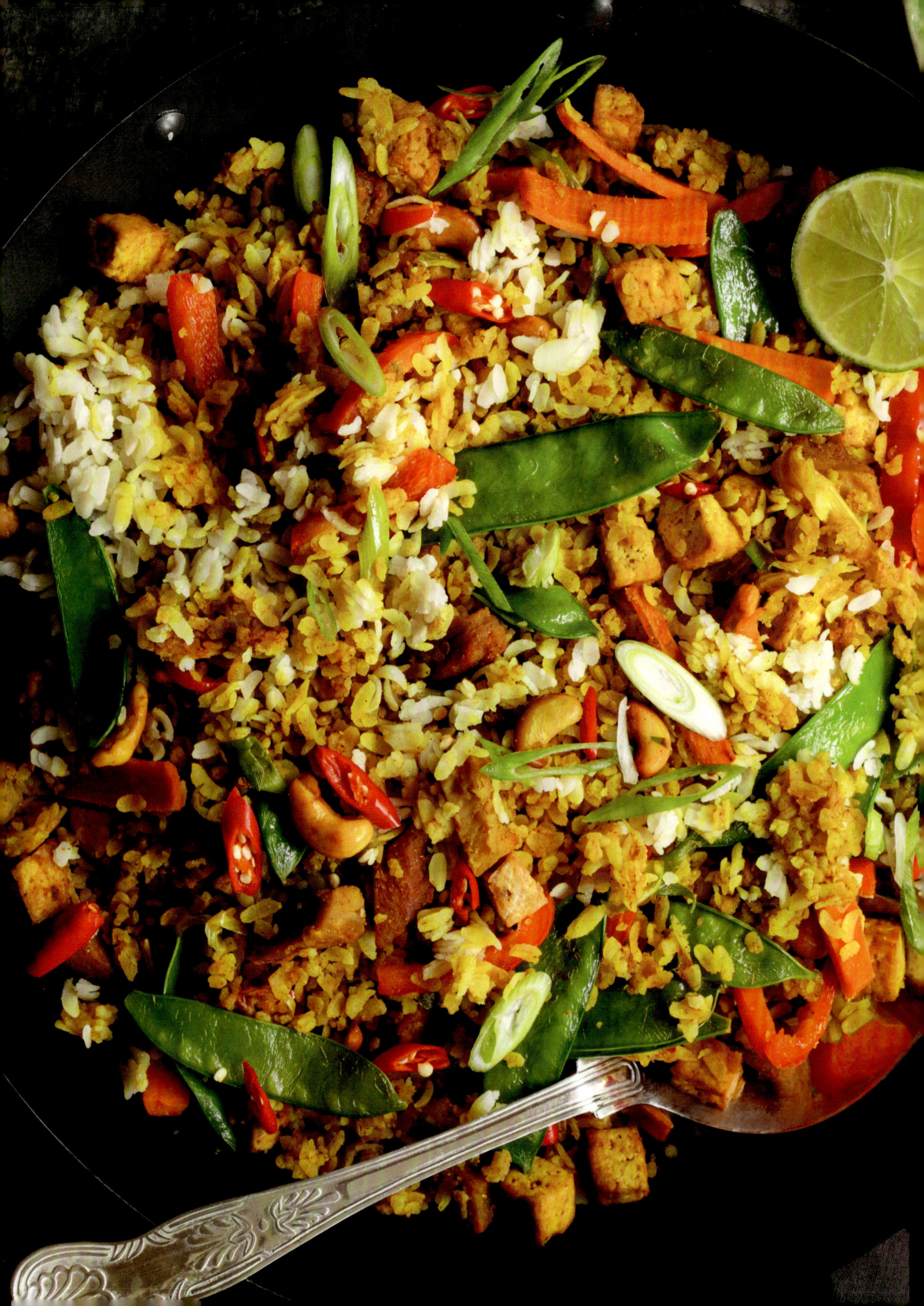

Singapore Poha

SERVES 4-6 • PREP: 20 MINS • COOK: 20 MINS

Poha is a variety of flattened rice treasured across India. Since the grains of rice are already pre-soaked, roasted and flattened during the manufacturing process, they take minutes to cook at home. You can spice poha up in many ways. The typical Gujarati way to do this is with loads of fried potatoes, onions, nuts, mustard seeds and curry leaves. In place of rice vermicelli, these separate, flaky grains of flattened rice satiate any cravings for Singapore noodles from my local Cantonese takeaway.

Ingredients

- 300 g (10½ oz) medium thick poha (see Note below)
- 3 tbsp oil
- 200 g (7 oz) firm tofu, pressed and cut into small cubes
- 150 g (5¼ oz) your favourite vegan chicken-style pieces
- 10 cashews
- 3 garlic cloves
- 3–4 bird's eye chillies, finely chopped
- 4 spring onions (scallions), finely sliced diagonally, some greens reserved to garnish
- 1 carrot, finely sliced diagonally
- 1 red bell pepper, finely sliced
- 100 g (3½ oz) mangetout (snow peas), halved diagonally
- 2½ tbsp Madras Curry Powder (see page 273)
- 1 tsp Chinese 5-spice
- ½ tsp ground white pepper
- 2 tsp sugar
- 1 tsp salt
- ½ tsp MSG
- 1 tbsp light soy sauce
- 1 tbsp toasted sesame oil
- Lime halves, to serve

Method

1. Place the poha in a colander. Pour 2 litres (70 fl oz/8½ cups) of hot but not boiling water over the poha until all the grains are soaked through. Allow to stand while you prepare the rest of the ingredients.

2. Heat the oil in a wok. Add the tofu cubes and fry on all sides until golden. Use a slotted spoon to transfer the tofu to a plate lined with kitchen paper. Repeat this for the vegan chicken-style pieces. Once crispy, transfer to the plate alongside the tofu.

3. In the remaining oil, add the cashews, garlic, chillies, spring onions (scallions), carrot, bell pepper and mangetout (snow peas). Stir-fry over a very high heat until slightly softened. Return the tofu and vegan chicken-style pieces to the wok along with the curry powder, Chinese 5-spice, white pepper, sugar, salt, MSG and soy sauce. Continue to cook for a minute before adding 250 ml (8½ fl oz/1 cup) water.

4. Fluff up the grains of poha with a fork to separate them. Immediately add the poha to the wok and toss to coat the grains in all the spices. Cook for 2–3 minutes until heated through. Once hot, drizzle with the sesame oil and scatter over the reserved spring onion greens. Serve with lime halves for squeezing over.

Note

Buy dried poha (sometimes called flattened rice or rice flakes) in bags at Indian grocery stores. There are different grades from thick to thin. I tend to stick to medium for most dishes.

Gluten free?

Use a gluten-free soy sauce or tamari. Ensure your vegan chicken-style pieces are free from gluten or substitute with a gluten-free tempeh, or more tofu.

Keema Jackets

SERVES 4 • PREP: 15 MINS • COOK: 45 MINS

Deeply spiced and smoky keema is the equivalent of a weighted blanket for baked potatoes. Soya mince is my go-to substitute for traditional minced (ground) meat, although a mashed-up block of firm tofu also works well. Give the spuds a head start prior to going into the oven by microwaving just until they begin to soften up.

1. Preheat the oven to 220°C/200°C fan/425 °F/Gas mark 7.

2. Wash the potatoes and leave them a little damp. Prick the skins all over with a fork and microwave on high power for 10–12 minutes, or until they've softened up a bit.

3. Arrange the potatoes in a roasting tray (sheet pan) and drizzle with 1 tablespoon of the oil and sprinkle with salt. Rub the oil and salt over the potatoes to coat. Bake in the preheated oven for 30 minutes, or until the skins are crispy, wrinkled and baked to perfection.

4. Meanwhile, make the keema. Heat the remaining 2 tablespoon of oil in a large, heavy-based pan (preferably one with a tight-fitting lid). Add the bay leaf, onion and carrot. Sauté for 10 minutes, or until the onion has softened and caramelised.

5. Next, add the soya mince and cook over a medium-high heat, stirring all the time until cooked through and lightly browned in places, about 4 minutes.

6. Add the chillies, garlic, ginger and tomato purée (paste). Sauté for a further minute before adding in half the garam masala (the rest is added at the end), ground coriander, ground cumin, ground turmeric, chilli powder, smoked paprika, salt, sugar and soy sauce. Stir well. Cook for a minute over a low heat before tipping in the tomato passata (strained tomatoes) and 250 ml (8½ fl oz/1 cup) water. Mix again and bring to a boil.

7. Once the keema in the pan is boiling, stir together the milk and cornflour (cornstarch) in a bowl. Immediately pour this into the keema and stir well until the sauce thickens very slightly and becomes a little glossy.

8. Place the lid on the pan and turn the heat down to low. Simmer the keema for 20 minutes. The longer you cook it, the more intense and wonderful the flavours will be. Add the peas during the final 5 minutes of cooking time to keep them bright green.

9. Finish the keema with the remaining garam masala, the dried fenugreek leaves, fresh mint and coriander (cilantro).

10. Split open the baked potatoes, add a knob of butter to each one and fluff up the insides with a fork. Spoon the keema over the top of the potatoes and sprinkle with as much, or as little grated (shredded) cheese as you like.

---

4 large baking potatoes
3 tbsp oil
¼ tsp salt
A few knobs of butter for inside the baked potatoes
80 g (2¾ oz/¾ cup) grated (shredded) Cheddar, or Gouda, to serve

For the keema
1 dried Indian bay leaf
1 large onion, finely diced
1 carrot, finely diced
500 g (1 lb 2 oz) soya mince (meatless grounds, see notes if you're using dried)
2 hot green chillies, finely minced
2 garlic cloves, minced
1 tsp minced root ginger
1 tbsp concentrated tomato purée (paste)
2 tsp Garam Masala (see page 259)
2 tsp ground coriander
1 tsp ground cumin
½ tsp ground turmeric
1 tsp Kashmiri chilli powder
½ tsp sweet smoked paprika
2 tsp salt
½ tsp sugar
1 tsp light soy sauce
600 g (1 lb 5 oz /2¾ cups) tomato passata (strained tomatoes)
175 ml (6fl oz/¾ cup) whole (full-fat) milk, cold
2 tsp cornflour (cornstarch)
100 g (3½ oz/½ cup) frozen peas, defrosted
½ tsp dried fenugreek leaves
1 tbsp chopped fresh mint leaves
1 tbsp chopped fresh coriander (cilantro) leaves and stems

Note

If you're using dried soya mince, you'll need to prepare around 175 g (6¼ oz) according to the packet instructions. Once soaked in hot water, I like to drain it through a sieve (strainer) and then rinse under warm water to remove the strong 'beany' smell. Squeeze out any excess water and weigh to ensure you have the 500 g (1 lb 2 oz) needed for this recipe.

Vegan?

Replace the Cheddar with your favourite dairy-free cheese alternative. Use vegan butter. Whole milk can be substituted with any plant-based milk.

Gluten free?

Swap the soy sauce for tamari or a gluten-free soy sauce.

Not Curry

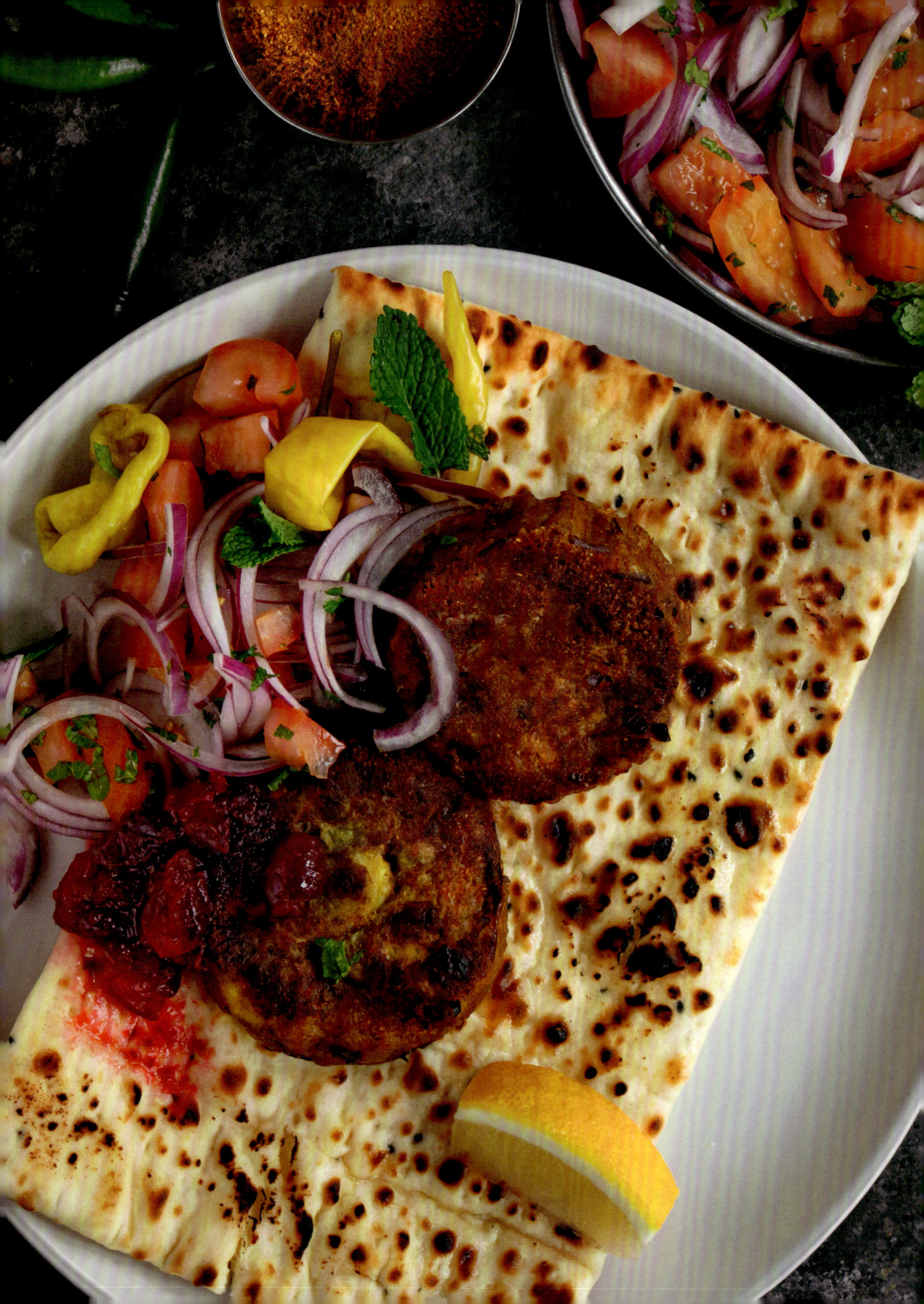

Bubble and Seekh Kebabs

SERVES 4 • PREP: 50 MINS, PLUS 30 MINS RESTING • COOK: 30 MINS

For the kebabs
2 tbsp oil, plus an extra 3–4 tbsp for shallow-frying the kebabs
1 large onion, finely chopped
3 tbsp gram flour
2 garlic cloves, minced
1 tsp minced root ginger
3 tbsp Seekh Kebab Masala (see page 271)
300 g (10½ oz) mashed potato, cold
100 g (3½ oz) Brussels sprouts, cooked and roughly mashed, cold
150 g (5¼ oz/1⅓ cup) grated (shredded) Cheddar
½ tsp salt

To smoke the kebabs
1 piece activated charcoal
2 cloves
1 tsp ghee

Vegan?
Use any plant-based cheese in place of Cheddar and use Vegan Ghee (page 244) or oil in place of ghee.

Make it a feast!
Serve these fabulous little bubble and seekh kebabs with cranberry sauce, naan or pitta, onion and tomato salad, lemon wedges, pickled chillies and fresh mint.

This is a wicked way to use up leftovers. This version of the British comfort classic bubble and squeak sees mashed potato and Brussels sprouts amped up with traditional seekh kebab masalas. An optional step includes charging the kebab mixture with the smoke of live charcoal and ghee. It's a technique seen mostly across the northern states of India and takes a just a few minutes. The barbecue flavour payoff is off the charts.

1. Heat the 2 tablespoons of oil in a pan (one that comes with a tight-fitting lid). Add the onion and fry over a low heat until caramelised, about 10 minutes. Add the gram flour and continue to cook for 2 minutes, or until golden. Add the garlic, ginger and seekh kebab masala. Stir well.

2. Tip in the mashed potato, sprouts, Cheddar and salt. Roughly mash everything together using a potato masher.

3. Using heatproof tongs, hold the charcoal over an open flame until it glows orange. Pop a small metal bowl inside the pan on top of the kebab mixture. Using the tongs, carefully place the hot charcoal into the bowl. Drop the two cloves on top of the charcoal and then very slowly spoon the ghee over the coal. It will immediately begin to smoke. Quickly cover the pan with a tight-fitting lid and allow to sit for 2–3 minutes.

4. Remove the lid and then use the tongs to carefully remove the metal bowl from the pan and set it down in the sink, on a heatproof mat if necessary. Extinguish the charcoal with cold water. The kebab mixture is now beautifully clove smoked.

5. Once cool, form the kebab mixture into 8 equal patties. Refrigerate for 30 minutes until firmed up.

6. Working in batches, pan-fry the kebabs a few at a time, depending on the size of your pan. Try not to move them too much during the first few minutes of cooking as the cheese can stick to the pan and break the kebabs. They will take around 3 minutes per side to turn golden brown.

Chestnut Manchurian

SERVES 4 • PREP: 25 MINS • COOK: 20 MINS

For the chestnuts
4 tbsp cornflour (cornstarch)
1½ tbsp self-raising flour
¼ tsp salt
1 tsp light soy sauce
2 tsp mirin (or any rice wine)
350 g (12⅓ oz) cooked and peeled chestnuts (I use the handy vacuum-packed kind)
Oil, for deep-frying

For the sauce
2 tbsp oil
6 garlic cloves, minced
2–3 green chillies, sliced diagonally
2 tbsp tomato purée (paste)
1 red onion, cut into wedges and separated into petals
1 green bell pepper, cut into strips
2 tbsp dark soy sauce
1 tsp distilled white vinegar
¼ tsp white pepper
½ tsp MSG
1 tsp sugar
½ tsp salt
1½ tbsp cornflour (cornstarch) mixed with 2 tbsp water

Gluten free?

Switch the flour for a gluten-free self-raising flour. Use tamari in place of soy sauce or try a gluten-free soy sauce.

Battered chestnuts in a hot and sour Indo-Chinese sauce. I love the sweetness and starchy texture of chestnuts alongside the sticky, fire-red Manchurian sauce. A simple cornflour (cornstarch) slurry creates a glossy, dynamite sauce that clings to each craggy chestnut. Use cooked, vacuum-packed chestnuts to save your fingers from the tedious job of peeling. And if chestnuts aren't your thing, make this with button mushrooms, cauliflower florets, new potatoes or, in fact, any protein of your choice. A mound of steamed jasmine rice or noodles to serve is essential.

1. To prepare the chestnuts, whisk together the cornflour (cornstarch), self-raising flour, salt, soy sauce and mirin with 50 ml (1¾ fl oz/scant ¼ cup) cold water until smooth.

2. Heat enough oil to deep-fry the chestnuts in a work or heavy-based pan with high sides. Once the oil temperature reaches 180°C (355°F), tip the chestnuts into the batter and coat each one well. One at a time, carefully lower each chestnut into the hot oil, taking care not to overcrowd the pan. Working in as many batches as necessary, deep-fry the chestnuts until they're crispy all over. Remove from the oil with a slotted spoon and allow to drain in a colander while you make the sauce.

3. To make the sauce, heat 2 tablespoons of oil in a wok until smoking hot. Add the garlic and chillies, sauté for a few seconds before adding in the tomato purée (paste). Cook for a further few seconds before adding the onion, bell pepper, soy sauce, vinegar, white pepper, MSG, sugar and salt. Stir-fry for 2 minutes, or until the vegetables have softened a little. Now add 300 ml (10 fl oz/1¼ cups) water (or more for a saucier Manchurian) and bring to a boil.

4. Give the cornflour and water slurry a quick mix before stirring this into the wok with the veggies. Continue to cook, stirring, over a high heat until the sauce thickens and turns glossy.

5. While the sauce is bubbling, fold in the battered chestnuts and serve immediately.

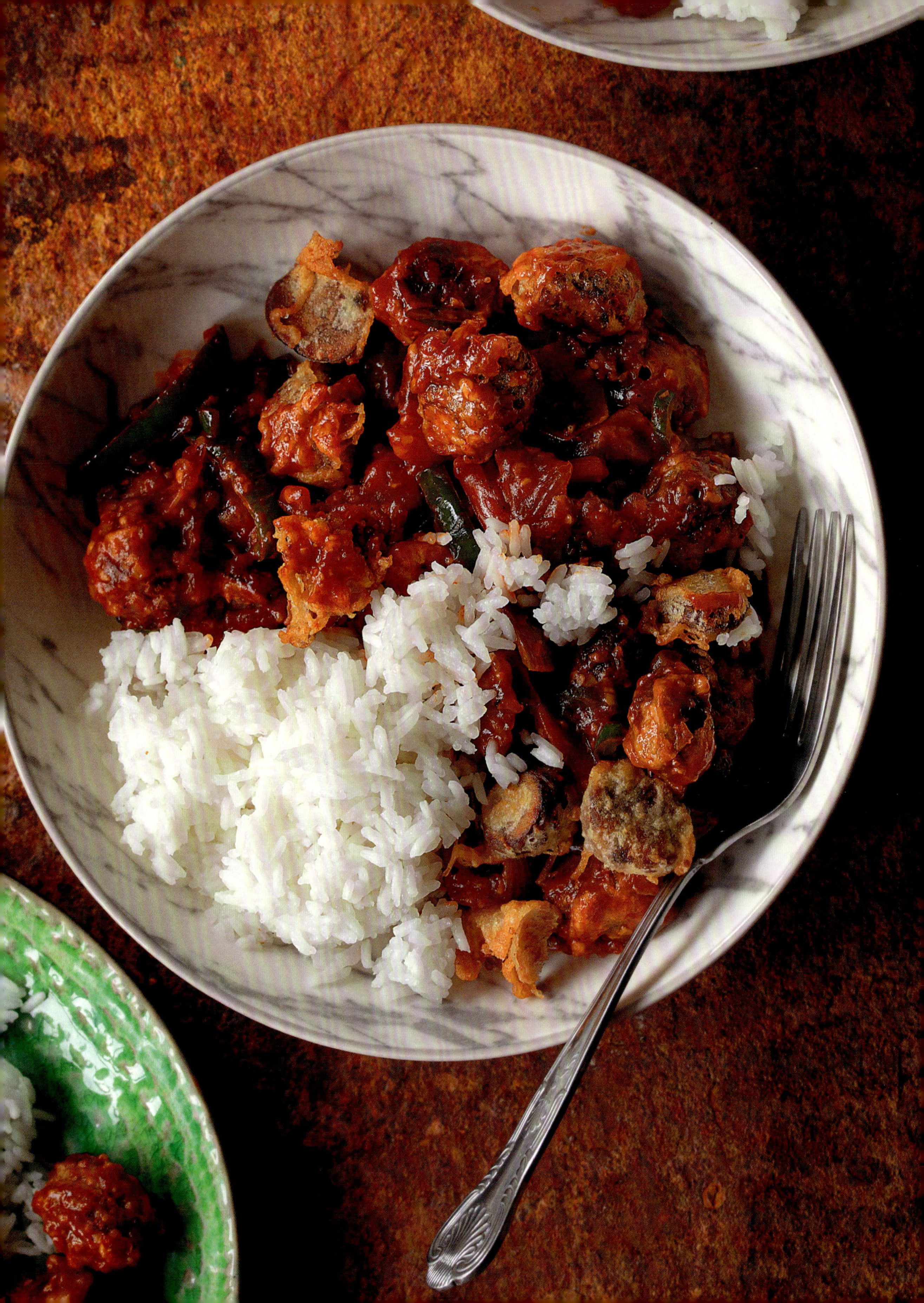

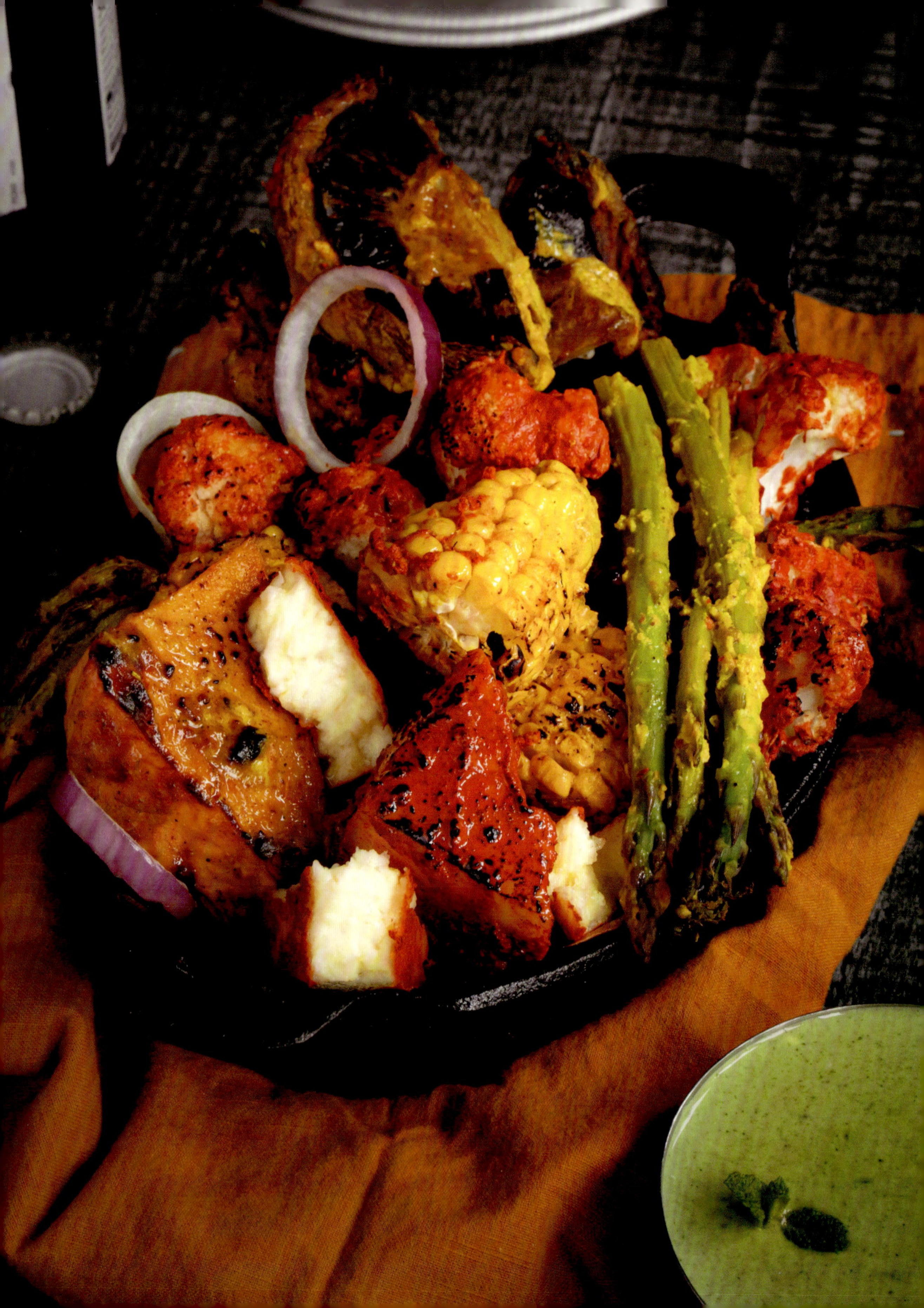

Meatless Mixed Grill

SERVES 4–6 • PREP: 30 MINS, PLUS 30 MINS MARINATING • COOK: 35 MINS

1 large corn-on-the-cob (ear of corn), husk removed and cob cut into 4–5 pieces
¼ cauliflower, broken into large florets
100 g (3½ oz) asparagus spears, woody part of stems snapped off
1 sweet potato, peeled and cut into large chunks
2 large Portobello mushrooms, thickly sliced
250 g (8¾ oz) paneer, halloumi or firm tofu, cut into large chunks
Sliced onion, to serve

For the red 'tandoori' marinade
2 tbsp gram flour
100 g (3½ oz/scant ½ cup) plain yogurt
2 tbsp Tandoori Masala (see page 269)
2 tsp lemon juice
2 garlic cloves, minced
2 tsp grated (shredded) root ginger
1 tsp salt
2 tbsp edible mustard oil

For the yellow 'achaari' marinade
100 g (3½ oz/scant ½ cup) plain yogurt
2 tbsp Achaar Masala (see page 264), or alternatively, use 3 tbsp Indian lime pickle
2 tbsp gram flour
2 garlic cloves, minced
½ tsp ground turmeric
½ tsp salt
2 tbsp edible mustard oil

The 'mixed grill' is a flagship meat-heavy offering at British curry houses. Here's a take on it, prepared entirely with vegetables and plant-based proteins. A duo of red and yellow marinades keeps the flavours fresh, and the dish colourful and exciting. Go all out and make both or, if you're in a hurry, double up on one marinade. Sizzler optional, although unquestionably exciting.

1. To make the red 'tandoori' marinade, first toast the gram flour in a small pan for a few minutes, stirring continuously until it's a nutty shade of pink. Whisk together all the ingredients for the marinade, except the mustard oil but including the toasted gram flour. Once smooth, heat the oil in the same pan used to toast the gram flour. Allow it to heat until smoking hot. Carefully pour the oil over the whisked marinade to temper the spices. It will sizzle and crackle (as well as smell incredible). Whisk once more until everything is well mixed.

2. To make the yellow 'achaari' marinade, toast the gram flour in a small pan for a few minutes, stirring continuously until it's a nutty shade of pink. Whisk together all the ingredients for the marinade, except the mustard oil but including the toasted gram flour. Once smooth, heat the oil in the same pan used to toast the gram flour. Allow it to heat until smoking hot. Carefully pour the oil over the whisked marinade to temper the spices. Whisk once more until everything is well mixed.

3. Marinate your chunks of veggies, mushrooms and paneer, halloumi or tofu in the red and yellow marinades. Feel free to mix and match the marinades and ingredients to your heart's content. Pop a combination of half the ingredients in the red and the same for the yellow marinade, if you're unsure of what you might like. That way you get a wide choice. Cover and allow to marinate for 30 minutes, or for up to 24 hours in the fridge.

4. Preheat the oven to 200°C/180°C fan/390°F/Gas mark 6.

5. Arrange the marinated veg, mushrooms and cheese or tofu in a large roasting tray (sheet pan). Roast in the preheated oven for 30 minutes, or until everything has cooked through and softened.

6. Pop the pan under the grill (broiler) for 5 minutes, turning the ingredients halfway through the cooking time to create a smoky, crusty char on the outside. Serve on a sizzler piled high with sliced onions if you're feeling fancy.

Note

Edible or food-grade mustard oil is usually made with a blend of mustard and vegetable oils. It's available in most South Asian stores, but if you can't get it or don't fancy buying a bottle, add 2 teaspoons of English mustard powder to the marinade and use your usual vegetable oil as directed in the recipe.

Vegan?

Replace the yogurt with any unsweetened plant-based yogurt.

Make it a feast!

Much like its meaty counterpart, this 'mixed grill' can be served as either a starter or main course. British curry house law states it must be served with a refreshing mint yogurt. To make mint yogurt, mix Green Coriander and Mint Chutney (see page 197) with an equal part of plain yogurt. A basket of pillowy naan (see page 164) will make it a complete meal.

Chilli Fauxneer: Vegan Chilli Paneer

SERVES 4 • PREP: 30 MINS • COOK: 15 MINS

3 tbsp oil

250 g (8¾ oz) Fauxneer (my vegan paneer, see page 251) or regular paneer, cut into 1-cm (½-inch) cubes

4 garlic cloves, minced

2 green chillies, sliced diagonally

2 green bell peppers, sliced into 3-cm (1-inch) strips

1 large red onion, cut into wedges and separated into petals

4 spring onions (scallions), sliced diagonally, some greens reserved to garnish

1 tbsp light soy sauce (if you want a darker colour, use dark soy sauce)

2 tsp dark soy sauce

1 tsp sugar

1 tsp distilled white vinegar

½ tsp ground white pepper

¼ tsp MSG

Gluten free?

Use gluten-free soy sauce or tamari in place of both light and dark soy sauce.

I was introduced to Indo-Chinese food in the late nineties, when 'fusion cooking' didn't carry with it an aroma of identity crisis. British curry houses were no longer the only Indian option when eating out in the UK. Korma? What was that? Balti, bhuna and phall? I'd never heard of them. Growing up in a Gujarati household meant that I was accustomed to oro (the Burnt Aubergine and Spinach Curry on page 110) and rotli. I'd nod and smile as my friends raved about the dishes they relished during their weekend visit to the local Indian restaurant. I had no idea what half of the dishes were. I felt like a fraud. Bombay potatoes? Were they like the bateta nu shaak my mum made at home? We rarely ate out at Indian restaurants in those days. Indeed, the vegetarian options were limited to random frozen mixed vegetables swimming in generic curry sauces. As the millennium approached, more and more options bubbled up, beginning with areas populated with a high density of Indian locals. Leicester, Wembley and Southall were all on the radar. We visited often. I was in Leicester when I first read the words 'Indo-Chinese fusion dishes' on a restaurant menu. I wanted to know more. I therefore made it my mission to try them all. Chilli paneer was the first dish I fell in love with. Here's a vegan take on it that uses my recipe for Fauxneer, a creamy, vegan paneer substitute you'll have to try to believe.

1. In a wok, warm the oil over a medium heat. Add the cubes of Fauxneer (they should sizzle a little) and stir-fry until golden all over. Transfer the fried Fauxneer to a colander or sieve (strainer) and set aside.

2. Turn the heat up under the wok and allow it to become smoking hot. Add the garlic and chillies. Stir-fry for a few moments, but do not let them brown. Tip in the peppers, onion, spring onions (scallions) – saving some greens, light and dark soy sauces, sugar, vinegar, white pepper and MSG. Stir-fry for 2 minutes over a very high heat.

3. Return the fried Fauxneer to the wok and toss well to combine. Heat through and serve immediately garnished with the remaining spring onion greens.

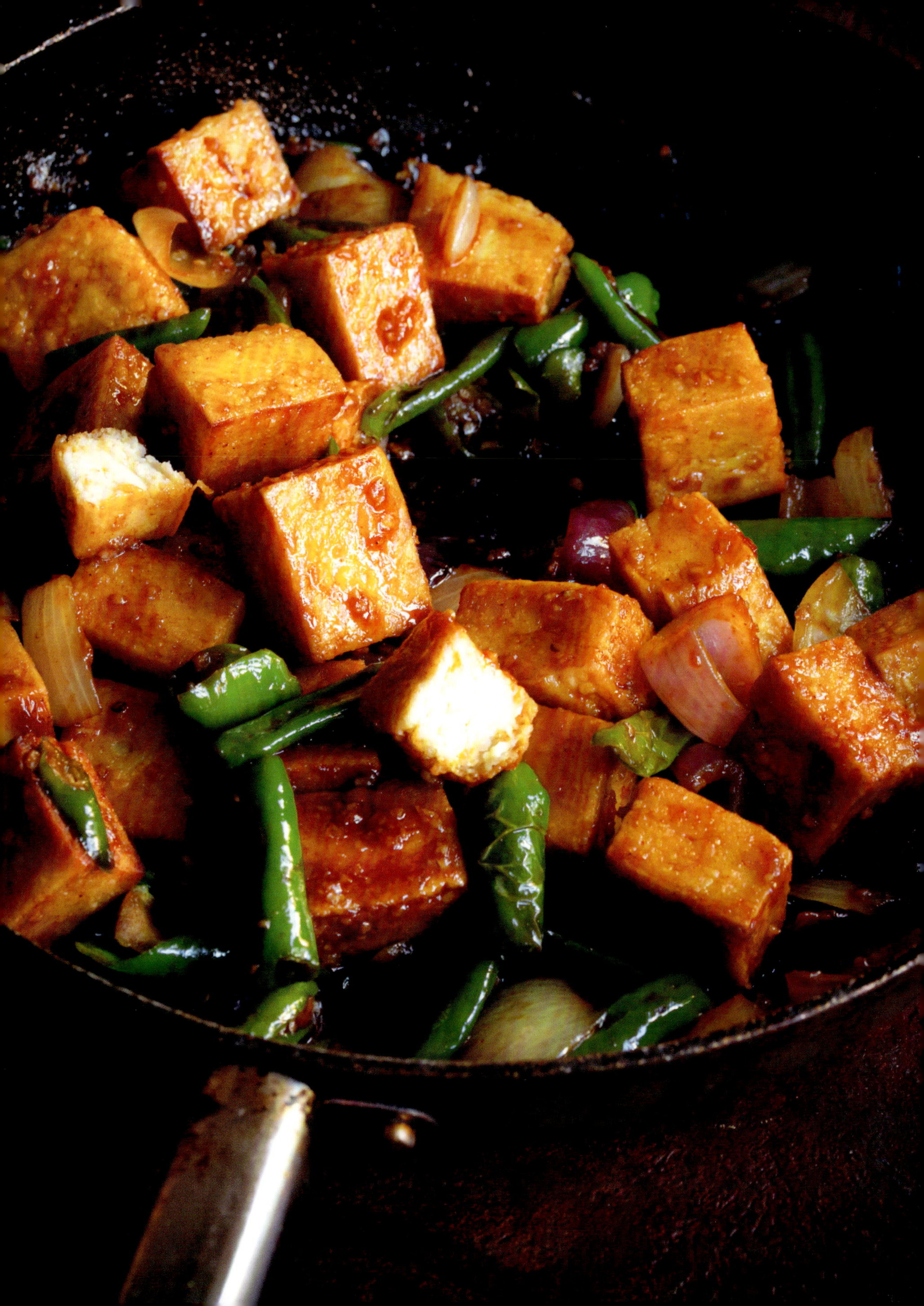

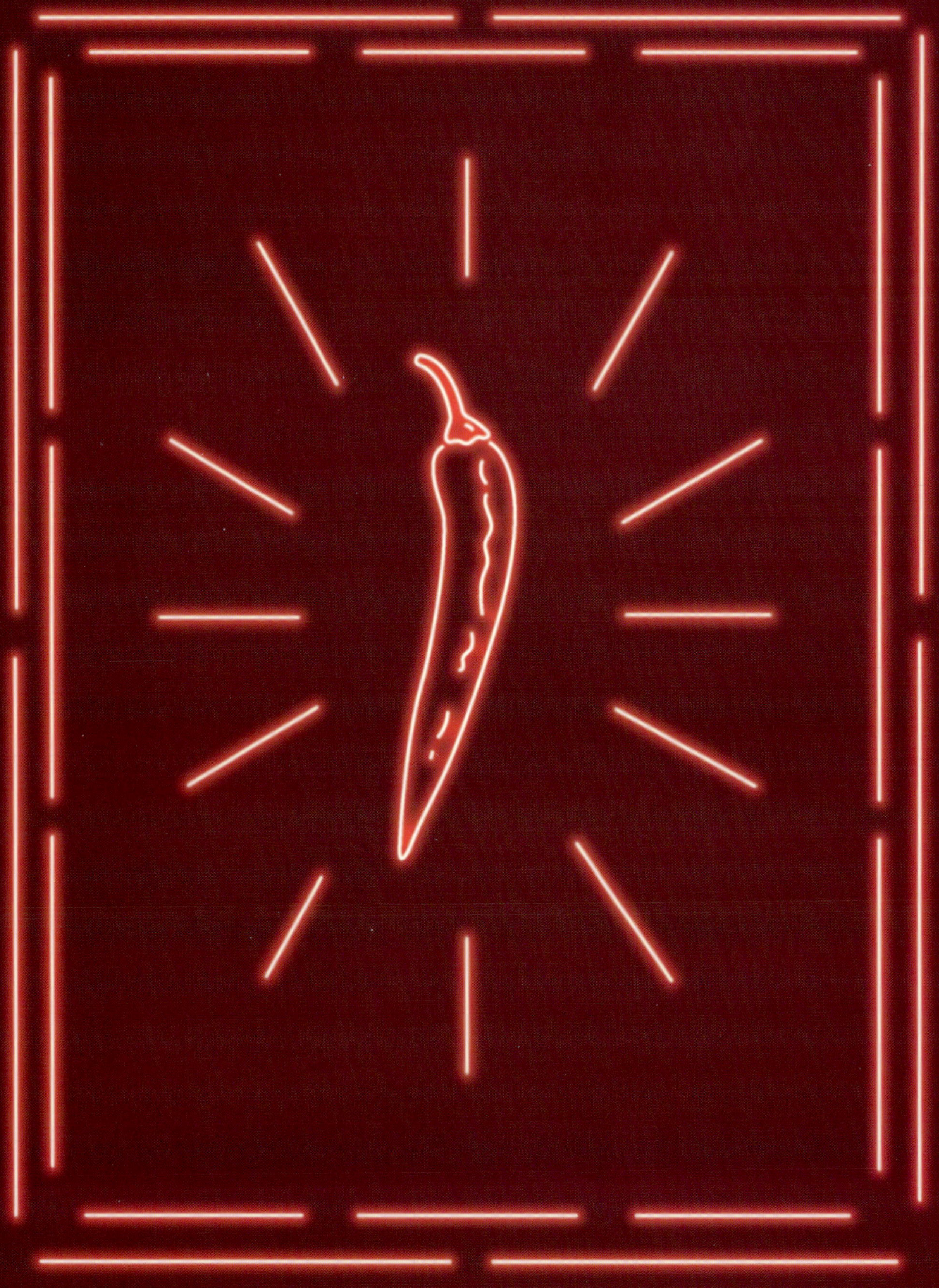

Curry

It tastes better when you eat it with your hands.

The world of curry is a vast galaxy of possibilities; some are bold and bright; others are the kind to make your belly glow with their mellow hum. Often, they are deeply rich in colour, with lustrous sauces and the ideal balance of sweetness and spice. Splashes of cream, coconut milk, yogurt, tomato purée (paste), blitzed boiled onions and even pastes made from nuts or seeds can form the perfect base for these velvety preparations. Texturally, dry curries are usually quite the opposite, often made with many of the ingredients I've mentioned, but not always. The spices are cooked and vegetables or proteins are added, while the liquid evaporates, leaving behind morsels of masala-cloaked goodness to scoop up with roti. These are the ideal starter curries for weaning children, for they lack the drippiness of their juicy counterparts. When my son was learning to eat Indian food with his hands, I taught him to tear off a piece of roti and 'pinch like a crab' - a technique he grasped quickly and easily, especially for his favourite Cauliflower and Pea Makani (see page 113), kidney beans and sweetcorn and classic Gujarati-style koru bateta nu shaak, which is more of a curried roughly mashed potato than any Bombay potato-style dish you'd find on a western Indian restaurant menu.

The tradition of eating with the right hand goes back to ancient Vedic teachings. It's a conscious step towards mindful eating, creating a connection with the food we eat by using all our fingers. Each finger is said to represent an element (space, air, fire, water and earth), and through the act of bringing the fingers together to eat, we unite energies to nourish the soul. There are various mudras (hand gestures) adopted specifically for eating, each one suited to consuming different dishes. Bread, rice, vegetables and fruits all have their unique mudras. The practice is an ancient art, evoking the senses through physical touch. India's first Prime Minister, Jawaharlal Nehru, once said, 'Eating biryani with fork and knife is like making love through an interpreter.' I remember this every time I pick up cutlery to eat biryani. I think the physical relationship we forge with our food can help us attune to the present moment - something we struggle with in today's bustling modern world. In this way, I see the motion of bringing the hand to the mouth as an act of self-love, in the physical and spiritual sense. Whilst it's common for cutlery to be set out at the modern Indian table, most of the people I know who grew up eating with their hands will leave those knives and forks untouched. It simply tastes better when you eat it with your hands. I vividly remember my first meal at a curry house with friends. I was in my mid-teens. Instinctively, I used the fingers of my right hand to tear the naan on my plate, using it as a medium to scoop up the channa masala beside it. I didn't even clock that my actions were being watched, the curious eyes of my companions studying this tear and scoop style of eating. We spent the rest of the meal practicing techniques for tearing bread, using just the first four fingers, then trying to envelope as much curry as possible inside without letting it drip down our spangly Y2K attire.

Some curries dance on the belt between what's traditionally deemed to be curry (depending on where you come from), achaar (pickle) and even daal. Achaari bhindi (okra stir-fried with pickling spices), sambharo (sautéed cabbage, carrots and chillies), channa daal and dudhi (daal stewed with bottlegourd) are all examples of classic dishes that blur lines, flitting between curry status and something else. Some might say that the word 'curry' is a meaningless, catch-all term, others that it is a term of convenience when describing a main dish commonly eaten with roti, rice or dosa. To me, the word doesn't feel lazy and can be conducive to conveying a particular style of dish. That said, it's important to acknowledge that behind the term is a wealth of regional nuances, which warrant their own recognition. There are so many types of curry, each with their own method of preparation and commonly used spices. Whilst it's true that many curries have unique names rooted in centuries of tradition and with ties to ancestral lands, there are also dishes that have journeyed with people, evolving as they go. Many of these are simply named after their core ingredients, followed by the word 'curry' or 'masala' - and that often feels appropriate. In our Gujarati home, we use the word 'shaak'. Shaak comes from the Sanskrit term shakahara, which refers to a vegetarian diet, although strictly speaking, not all shaaks are vegetarian. Going shaak shopping is the Sunday afternoon adventure to buy the vegetables to make shaak during the week.

Dry-style curries, or shaak, formed the backbone of what I ate growing up in a Gujarati home - my mum would curry everything from okra, aubergines (eggplants) and ivy gourds, to parsnips, Brussels sprouts and broad beans. All of them were my favourites, except for stuffed baby aubergines which looked unquestionably adorable in their raw state, but once cooked, resembled a line-up of musty old socks. Instead, I preferred the flame-cooked oro, the Gujarati equivalent of North India's famous Baingan ka bhartha. This is a dish of large aubergines fired over flames or coals, until they're completely blackened on the outside. It sounds intimidating at first, but it's almost impossible to overcook the aubergines due to their high water content, so you can't really go wrong. It's a case of the longer the better when it comes to building the foundations of flavour. After a good 15 minutes over a high, direct flame, the aubergine will have a charred, papery crust and the inside will be softened to a pulp. Peel off the skin and the flesh is infused with smoke, ready to be tossed with chopped tomatoes, spices and an almost illegal number of garlic cloves. A handful of leafy spinach brightens up the entire dish. At home, we enjoy this kind of curry with Everyday Roti (see page 157), and it transforms the humble aubergine and a sad bag of spinach into something quite stellar.

'I've brought yer some runner beans. I'll bring yer some broad beans next time. See what yer mek of 'em,' said Mr Sykes, a retired customer in my parent's West Yorkshire shop and a particularly well-seasoned allotment gardener. This would happen often, and with many of our kind friends in the village. Mum would see it as a challenge, à la Ready, Steady, Cook, and try to figure out what she could make with a kilo each of courgettes (zucchini), peas and summer squash. Often, they were fashioned into some sort of curry, which would then be packed into containers and distributed back to the very customers who provided the produce - a sort of currying of favours. Their wonderful friends, Eric and Andrea, would swing by to drop off bouquets of rhubarb destined for jars upon jars of Rhubarb Chhundo (see page 235), a type of sweet, sticky chilli chutney, quite like mango chutney. It was deep pink in colour, spreadable and delicious in cheese sandwiches, on buttered crumpets and, of course, with our beloved Gujarati thepla (spicy fenugreek chapatis).

Drawing inspiration from my mother's penchant to curry every seasonal vegetable, fridge scrap and allotment surplus, this collection of recipes will, I hope, help to invigorate your usual curry antics. It features an unctuous Brown Butter Cauliflower and Pea Makhani (see page 113), ideal for mopping up with naan or rice, a spicy Mangalore-style Savoy Cabbage Ghee Roast (see page 129), which puts a whole head of crinkly cabbage to work, and a Dumpling Handi (see page 122), which never fails to bring me home no matter where I am.

Finishing touches

Ten beautiful ways to garnish Indian curries

1. Tadka
Spices tempered in hot fat (find out more in the daal chapter).

2. Fresh or dried herbs
Coriander (cilantro), mint, dill, holy basil, dried fenugreek leaves, fried curry leaves.

3. Oils
Roghan, a chilli oil scooped from the oil that floats on top of a long-simmered curry. Collect and jar this liquid bronze (keep it in the fridge) and use as a drizzle for daal. It's especially tasty on White Daal (see page 140).

4. Toasted nuts and seeds
Coconut, sesame seeds, melon seeds, poppy seeds, lotus seeds, almonds, cashews, peanuts, pistachios.

5. Flowers
Edible rose petals, jasmine flowers, hibiscus, coriander flowers, mustard flowers.

6. Dairy, et al
Ghee, cream, coconut milk, butter, plain yogurt, buttermilk.

7. Fresh aromatics
Onions (pickled, fried, raw), root ginger matchsticks, pickled or fresh turmeric matchsticks, chillies (fresh, fried or flakes).

8. Fruit
Pomegranate, lemons, limes, tomatoes, sultanas.

9. Chutney
See options on page 196.

10. Namkeen
Sev, gathia, puffed rice, boondi, fried shoestring potatoes.

V VG GF

Burnt Aubergine and Spinach Curry

SERVES 4 • PREP: 20 MINS • COOK: 50 MINS

3 large aubergines (eggplants) (about 1 kg/2 lb 4 oz)
2 tbsp oil
1 tbsp cumin seeds
½ tsp asafoetida (optional)
1 large onion, finely chopped
1 whole head of garlic (about 8 large cloves), peeled and finely minced
3 hot green chillies, finely chopped
1 x 400-g (14-oz) can chopped tomatoes
1 tsp ground coriander
1 tsp ground cumin
¼ tsp ground cinnamon
½ tsp ground turmeric
1 tsp sugar
2 tsp salt
250 g (8¾ oz) baby leaf spinach, rinsed and squeezed of excess water

To serve

3–4 hot green chillies, sliced
½ small red onion, sliced
2 tbsp chopped fresh coriander (cilantro)
Lemon wedges

Sometimes you've just got to burn your food. I learnt to cook this dish when I was 12 years old and it blew my mind. After seeing my mother do it dozens of times before, I thought it was suitably daring to incinerate aubergines (eggplants) over an open flame. It went against everything I thought to be true about Indian vegetarian food. However, the very beauty of it is that whilst the outside of the aubergine burns to a crisp (think baba ghanoush), the inside is cooked until it's butter-soft and smoky. By the way, the whole head of garlic listed in the ingredients is not an error and makes this curry pop like no other.

1. Prick holes all over the aubergines (eggplants) and place one on each burner of a gas hob (stovetop). Turn on the flame to high and cook the aubergines for 8 minutes. Do not move them during this time. Once 8 minutes have passed, using heatproof tongs, carefully turn the aubergines over and cook the other sides for 8 minutes. Again, do not move them. Steam will escape from the holes you've made. It's important not to leave the kitchen during this time and to open a window. Once charred on the outside, transfer the aubergines to a plate and set aside to cool.

2. Heat the oil in a large pan. Once the oil is shimmering, add the cumin seeds and asafoetida (if using). Cook for 15 seconds and then add the onion. Allow the onion to cook over a medium heat until golden brown, about 10 minutes. Add the garlic and chillies and cook for a further 2–3 minutes to soften and mellow.

3. Tip in the canned tomatoes and add the rest of the ingredients, except the spinach. Simmer for about 15 minutes, stirring frequently until the sauce is thick and the oil begins to separate from the tomatoes, pooling at the sides of the pan.

4. While the sauce is cooking, check the aubergines have cooled enough to handle. Split each aubergine lengthways and scrape out the soft flesh onto the plate. It's okay if some burnt skin comes away with the flesh, but remove any large pieces. Roughly chop the aubergine flesh and add it to the tomato sauce along with the spinach. Discard the burnt aubergine skin but tip any juices from the plate into the curry too – it's loaded with flavour. Cook, stirring all the time, for a further 5 minutes or until the spinach has wilted and the excess water has evaporated.

5. Scatter over the sliced green chillies, red onion and fresh coriander (cilantro). Serve with the lemon wedges for squeezing over.

Notes

If fresh spinach is unavailable, a few blocks of frozen spinach will also work perfectly well.

If you do not have a hob or stovetop with a gas burner, blacken the aubergines under the grill (broiler), although the flavours may not be quite as intense.

Gluten free?

Use a gluten-free asafoetida or omit this ingredient.

Make it a feast!

Everyday Roti (see page 157) is the perfect scooping buddy for this intensely flavoured curry.

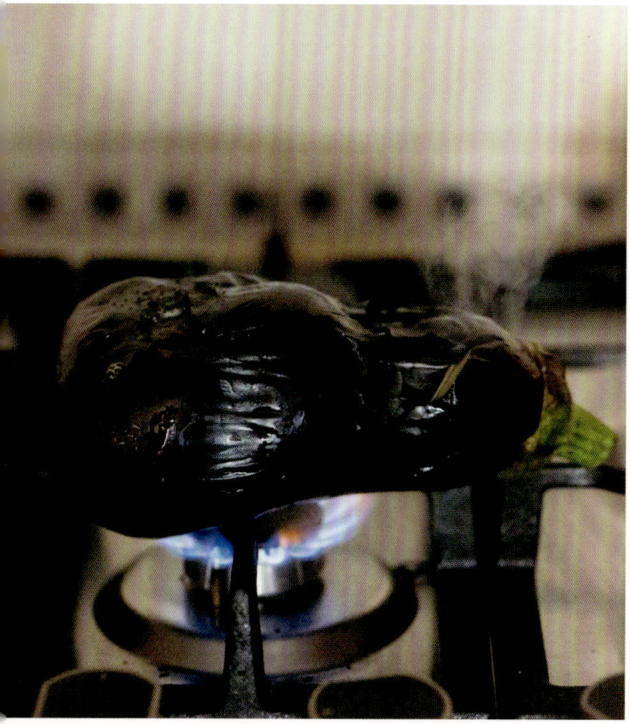
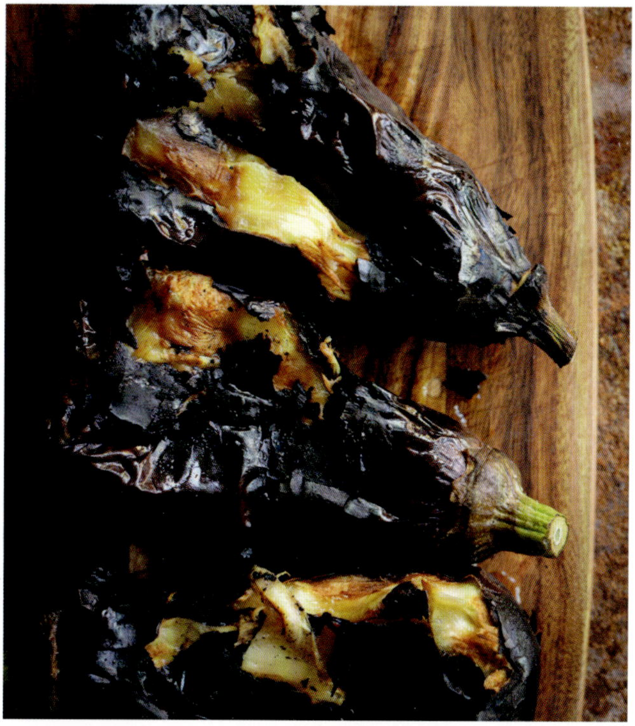
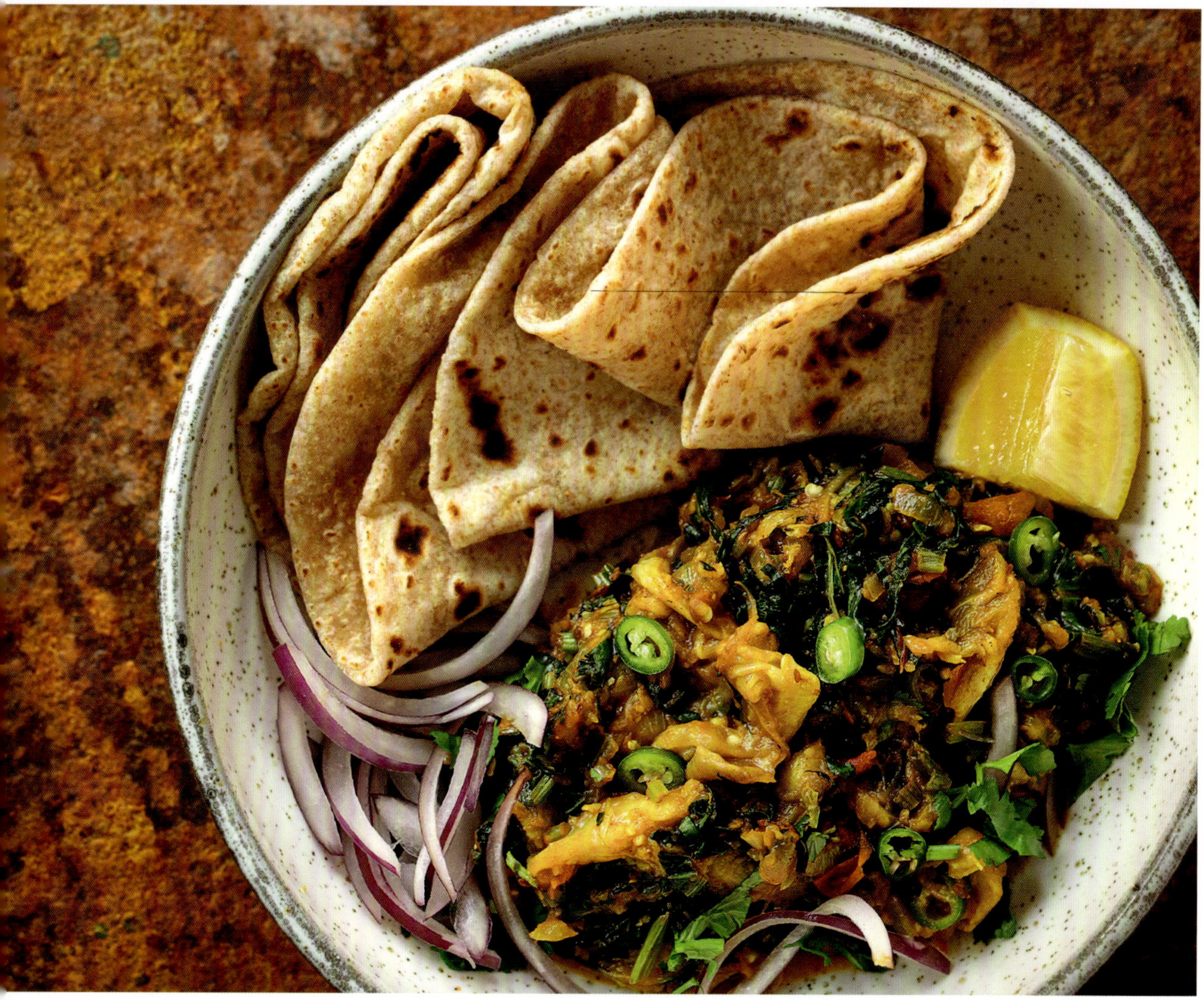

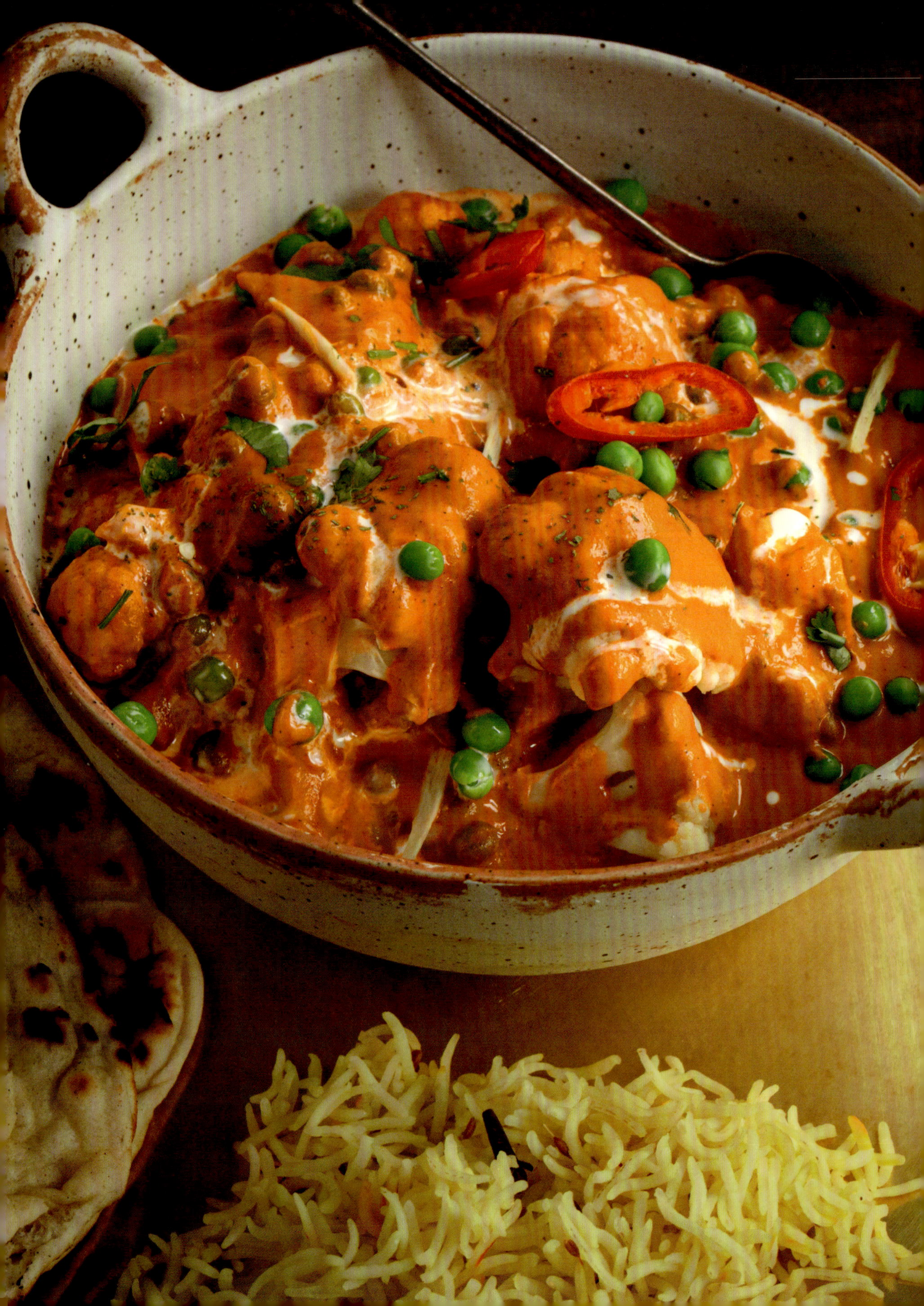

Brown Butter Cauliflower and Pea Makhani

SERVES 6 • PREP: 20 MINS • COOK: 40 MINS

600 g (1 lb 5 oz) cauliflower, broken into bite-sized florets

300 g (10½ oz/1½ cups) peas, fresh or frozen

1½ tsp salt

2 tbsp light brown sugar

1 tsp dried fenugreek leaves, plus extra to finish

2 green cardamom pods, seeds ground, to finish

100 ml (3½ fl oz/scant ½ cup) double (heavy) cream, plus extra to garnish

1 tbsp chopped fresh coriander (cilantro), to garnish

Sliced red chilli (optional), to garnish

For the sauce

15 unsalted, raw cashews

2–4 whole dried Kashmiri chillies

4 green cardamom pods, cracked

½ tbsp coriander seeds

½ tsp cumin seeds

1 onion, cut into rough chunks

500 g (1 lb 2 oz/scant 2¼ cups) tomato passata (strained tomatoes)

500 ml (17 fl oz/2 cups) hot water

150 g (5¼ oz/scant ¾ cup) unsalted butter

1 tbsp crushed garlic, about 3 cloves

½ tbsp grated (shredded) root ginger

1 tbsp concentrated tomato purée (paste)

¼ tsp ground turmeric

½ tsp Kashmiri chilli powder

1½ tbsp Garam Masala (see page 259)

Butter chicken who? Kundan Lal Gujral of Moti Mahal fame's signature creation of butter chicken is undisputedly one of India's most popular dishes. Here's my vegetarian take on the Delhi wonder-turned-global-icon, murgh makhani, using brown butter, cauliflower florets and peas. One sure-fire way to make butter taste more buttery is to brown it, initiating a Maillard reaction. Without getting too scientific, the process of cooking the butter to the point of golden toastiness causes a series of chemical reactions between amino acids and sugars from the lactose in butter. It's like regular butter, but with a golden glow-up.

1. Boil or steam the cauliflower until slightly softened, but not fully cooked. A fork should go through, but with some resistance at the centre. Drain and set aside.

2. To make the sauce, first dry fry the cashews, dried chillies, cardamom pods, coriander seeds, cumin seeds and onion in a non-stick saucepan for 5–6 minutes, or until fragrant and the whole spices and nuts have toasted. Pour in the tomato passata (strained tomatoes), and water. Cover with a tight-fitting lid and simmer over a medium heat for 15 minutes. Uncover and allow to cool slightly before transferring the mixture to a high-powered blender. Set aside, but do not blend yet.

3. Give the pan a rinse and wipe. Add the butter to the pan. Keep the heat low to ensure the butter browns slowly and evenly, without burning. Cook, stirring continuously. The butter will go from being yellow, to having large bubbles, then foamy, and, finally, a deep amber colour, rather like golden syrup. Some foam will subside and there will be toasted milk solids at the bottom of the pan. There's no need to skim off any foam or remove any sediment, this is brown butter, not ghee. The brown butter will smell incredibly buttery and nutty. This is a core building block of flavour in this curry. This process should take around 5 minutes from start to finish.

4. Add the garlic, ginger, tomato purée (paste), ground turmeric, Kashmiri chilli powder and garam masala to the brown butter. Cook for 1 minute and then switch off the heat.

5. Pour the brown butter mixture into the blender with the other ingredients and blend everything together until completely smooth and silky.

6. Return the sauce to the pan and add the cauliflower, peas, salt, sugar, dried fenugreek leaves (rubbed between your palms), ground cardamom seeds and double (heavy) cream. Once it comes to a simmer, cover the pan with the lid and cook for a final 5–10 minutes at a low simmer, until the cauliflower is tender and cooked to your liking. Finish with an extra swirl of cream, more dried fenugreek leaves, fresh coriander (cilantro) and rings of red chilli.

Notes

Infuse this curry with Indian dhaba-style flavour using the smoke of live charcoal and ghee. Follow the steps for the dhungar technique in my recipe for Bubble and Seekh Kebabs (see page 97). If you have guests, it's particularly fun to do this at the dinner table right before serving.

Make it a feast!

Serve with your favourite style of naan (see page 164) or basmati rice.

Tiger Pav Bhaji

SERVES 6 • PREP: 1¼ HOURS, PLUS 2¼ HOURS RESTING • COOK: 1½ HOURS

An ode to Mumbai's iconic street dish, my take on pav bhaji is served with the sesame-crackled tiger bread reminiscent of the tea-time chip butties of school days. It's a simple fact of life that tiger bread always tastes better with a thick smear of salted butter. Indian street-food law also dictates that when it comes to pav bhaji, butter is mandatory, use of cutlery is not. Roarsome.

For the pav bhaji masala
- 2 tbsp Garam Masala (see page 259)
- 2 tsp Kashmiri chilli powder
- 1¼ tsp ground cinnamon
- 1 tsp ground fennel
- 1 tsp ground coriander
- 1 tsp ground cumin
- 1 tsp ground turmeric
- 2 green cardamom pods, seeds crushed

For the pav bhaji
- 150 g (5¼ oz/scant ¾ cup) salted butter
- 2 dried Indian bay leaves
- 1 large onion, finely chopped
- 4 large garlic cloves, minced
- 2 tsp minced root ginger
- 690 g (1 lb 8 oz/3 cups) tomato passata (strained tomatoes) or canned tomatoes
- 250 g (9 oz) potatoes, peeled and roughly cubed
- 200 g (7 oz) cauliflower, broken into small florets
- 175 g (6¼ oz) red bell pepper, roughly chopped
- 150 g (5¼ oz) sweet potatoes, peeled and roughly cubed
- 100 g (3½ oz) carrots, roughly chopped
- 100 g (3½ oz/⅔ cup) frozen peas
- 2 tsp salt

For the pav bhaji garnishes
- 1 large red onion, finely chopped
- 2 large tomatoes, finely chopped
- 2–3 fresh chillies, chopped (optional)
- 50 g (1¾ oz/¼ cup) finely chopped fresh coriander (cilantro)
- 50 g (1¾ oz/scant ¼ cup) salted butter

Method for the bhaji

1. First, mix all the ingredients for the pav bhaji masala in a small bowl and set aside.

2. Next, make the pav bhaji mixture. Heat 100 g (3½ oz/scant ½ cup) of the butter in a large saucepan. Add the bay leaves and chopped onion and cook over a medium heat, until the onions are soft and golden brown, about 8 minutes. Add the garlic and ginger. Cook for a few minutes before tipping in the tomato passata (strained tomatoes). Bring to a boil.

3. Add all the pav bhaji masala to the pan and stir well. Simmer for 1–2 minutes before adding the vegetables, salt and 1 litre (34 fl oz/4¼ cups) water. Cover the pan with a tight-fitting lid and cook over a medium heat for 30 minutes, stirring often.

4. Remove the lid from the pan and switch off the heat. Use a potato masher to mash the pav bhaji mixture, or alternatively blend using a handheld stick (immersion) blender, to create a coarse-textured bhaji mixture, similar to bolognese.

5. Return the pan to the heat and continue to cook, covered, for 20–30 minutes. Stir often as the mixture can stick to the bottom of the pan and burn. Adjust the consistency with more water, if necessary. Stir in the remaining 50 g (1¾ oz/scant ¼ cup) butter and taste to check the seasoning. The texture of the bhaji mixture should be coarse and runny, like lava. The longer you let this simmer, the better it tastes – but do stir often. You can transfer the bhaji mixture to a slow cooker and keep it on low for up to 6 hours.

6. Garnish the bhaji mixture with onions, tomatoes, chillies, fresh coriander (cilantro) and yes, more butter.

Method for the tiger pav

1. In a large bowl, combine the flour, milk powder, yeast, sugar and salt. Add the warm water and mix to form a shaggy dough. Knead the dough for 7–8 minutes until smooth and elastic. Add the softened butter and continue to knead the dough for a further 5 minutes, until soft.

2. Place the dough in a large, greased bowl, cover with cling film (plastic wrap) and allow to rise in a warm place for 90 minutes, until doubled in volume.

3. Punch the dough back and knead briefly. Divide the dough into 12 equal portions and shape each piece into a smooth ball by folding it in on itself and pinching at the base.

4. Arrange on a large baking sheet dusted with a small amount of flour. Leave space between each pav to allow for rising. Cover the tiger pav loosely with cling film and allow to rise in a warm place for 45 minutes, until they're puffy and risen.

For the tiger pav

500 g (1 lb 2 oz/3¾ cups) strong white bread flour

30 g (1 oz/¼ cup) skimmed milk powder

14 g (4½ tsp) fast-action dried yeast

2 tbsp sugar

1 tsp salt

300 ml (10 fl oz/1¼ cups) warm water

60 g (2 oz/¼ cup) unsalted butter, soft

For the crackle topping

50 g (1¾ oz/⅓ cup) rice flour

3 g (1 tsp) fast-action dried yeast

2 tbsp toasted sesame oil

1 tsp soft dark brown sugar

¼ tsp salt

115 ml (3¾ fl oz/scant ½ cup) warm water

To serve

75 g (2⅔ oz/⅓ cup) extra butter, for toasting the buns

Lemon wedges

Vegan?

Swap the butter for a dairy-free butter alternative. Replace the milk powder in the tiger pav with an equal quantity of additional bread flour.

Make it a feast!

This is a complete meal, but you could add extra zing and vibrancy with one or more of my Traffic Light Chutneys (see page 196).

5. Meanwhile, preheat the oven to 210°C/190°C fan/410°F/Gas mark 6½.

6. To make the crackly tiger topping, combine all the ingredients in a bowl. Beat with a fork until it forms a smooth and glossy paste.

7. Once the tiger pav finish proving for the second time, gently spoon or brush over the tiger topping paste. Make sure each pav is evenly and generously coated.

8. Bake the tiger pav in the preheated oven until risen, golden and crackly all over, about 20 minutes. Rotate the baking sheet halfway through the cooking time to make sure the pav brown evenly. Remove from the oven and allow to cool.

9. Before serving, split each tiger pav in half and spread with softened butter. Toast in a hot pan and serve with the vegetable bhaji and lemon wedges for squeezing over.

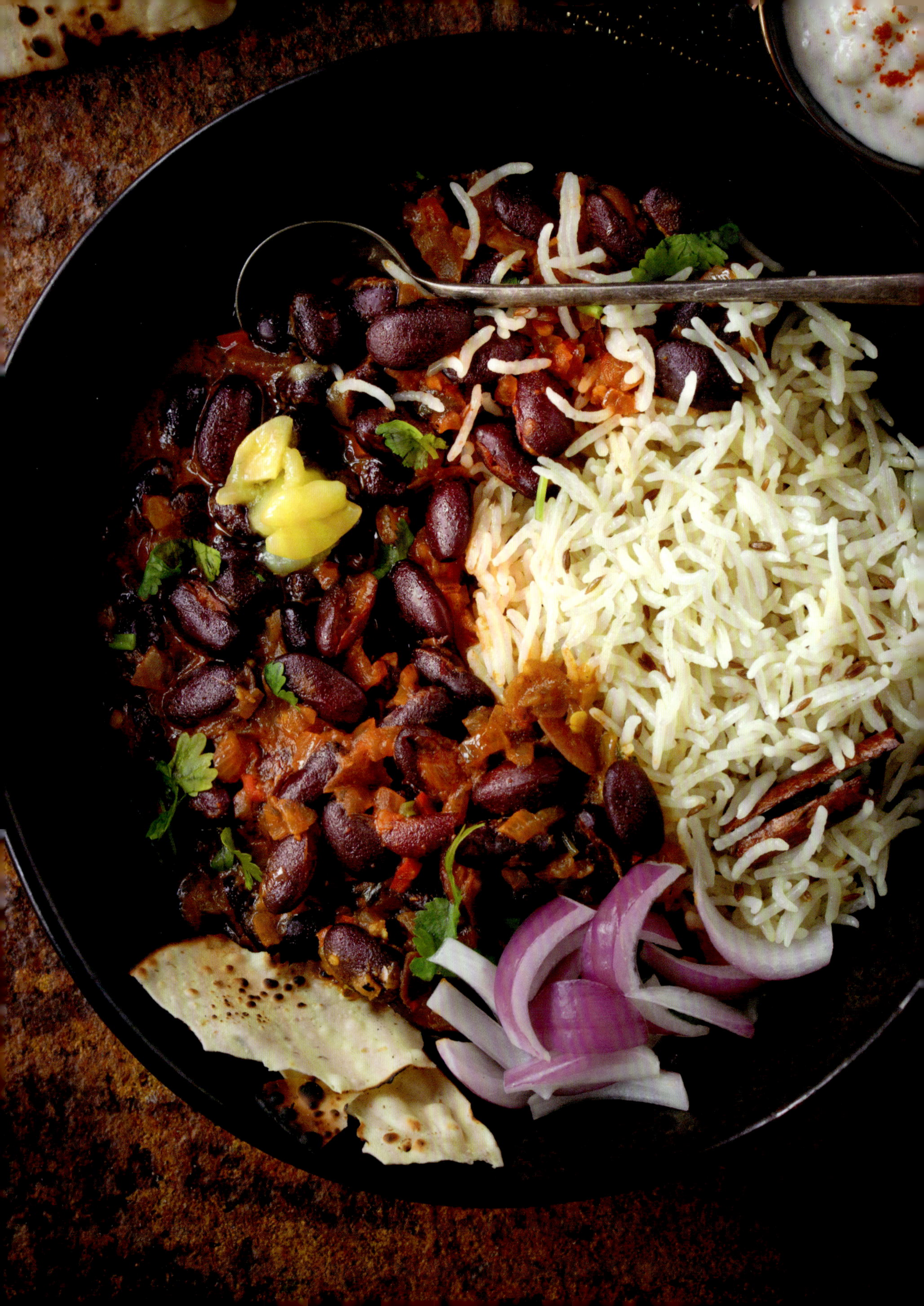

Coconut Rajma

SERVES 4-6 • PREP: 10 MINS • COOK: 30 MINS

There are few meals in life more comforting than beans and rice. Rajma (red kidney beans) and rice is a treasured North Indian combo. Here's my coastal version, influenced by the maharage ya nazi (coconut beans) of my East African family background.

3 tbsp ghee or oil
2 large onions, finely diced
1½ tsp salt
1 tsp sugar
2 garlic cloves, chopped
2 whole red chillies, finely chopped
¼ tsp asafoetida (optional)
1 large dried Indian bay leaf
1 black cardamom pod
2 cloves
½ tsp ground turmeric
½ tsp ground ginger
4 green cardamom pods, seeds ground
2 tbsp concentrated tomato purée (paste)
1 x 400-ml (14-fl oz) can full-fat coconut milk
2 x 400-g (14-oz) cans red kidney beans in water, drained and rinsed
1 tsp Garam Masala (see page 259)
½ tsp dried fenugreek leaves, rubbed between your palms
Cooked rice, to serve

1. In a large pot, heat the ghee or oil until shimmering. Add the onions, salt and sugar. Cook over a medium heat, stirring often, until they turn a deep golden brown. The salt will speed up the process, which will take around 12 minutes in total.

2. Add the garlic, chillies, asafoetida, bay leaf, black cardamom pod, cloves, ground turmeric, ground ginger, ground cardamom seeds and tomato purée (paste). Cook for 2 minutes and then add the coconut milk and 150 ml (5 fl oz/scant ⅔ cup) water. Stir well to combine.

3. Tip in the drained beans and bring to a boil. Cover and cook over a low heat for 15 minutes.

4. Finally, add the garam masala and dried fenugreek leaves,. Stir well and serve with rice.

Vegan?

Nothing brings out the butteriness of beans quite like ghee. However, if you would like to make a vegan version of this, try using my Vegan Ghee (see page 244) or oil.

Gluten free?

Use a gluten-free asafoetida or omit this ingredient.

Make it a feast!

Serve with rice, poppadoms and a salad of raw onions and chillies.

Broccoli Miloni

SERVES 4 • PREP: 35 MINS • COOK: 40 MINS

450 g (1 lb) broccoli
250 g (9 oz/1 cup) plain Greek yogurt
85 g (3 oz/⅓ cup) almond butter
2 tbsp gram flour
4 garlic cloves, minced
1 tbsp grated (shredded) root ginger
1 tsp white pepper
1 tsp ground turmeric
1 tsp nigella seeds
1 tsp salt
2 tbsp edible mustard oil

For the rest of the curry
2 tbsp oil
1 tsp cumin seeds
1 large onion, finely sliced
2-3 green chillies, chopped
2 garlic cloves, minced
2 tsp minced root ginger
100 g (3½ oz) leaf spinach
25 g (¾ oz) fresh fenugreek leaves
¼ tsp ground turmeric
1 tsp coriander seeds, ground
2 tsp Garam Masala (see page 259)
8 fresh, whole mint leaves
300 ml (10 fl oz/1¼ cups) double (heavy) cream
½ tsp salt
1 red chilli, finely sliced, to garnish
1-2 tbsp toasted, flaked (slivered) almonds, to garnish

Mustard-crusted, roasted broccoli florets in a silky spinach and fenugreek gravy – a fail-safe way to enjoy your greens. Use every part of the broccoli from leaf to stalk. The almond butter and mustard marinade is rocket fuel for veg.

1. Trim the very base of the broccoli but leave the stem intact. Break off the broccoli florets into bite-sized pieces. Chop the stem into small cubes and tear off the leaves. Set these aside. Blanch the broccoli florets in a large pan of boiling water for 3 minutes. Drain and refresh in ice-cold water. Once cold, drain well in a colander while you make the marinade.

2. In a large bowl, whisk together the Greek yogurt, almond butter, gram flour, garlic, ginger, white pepper, ground turmeric, nigella seeds and salt.

3. Heat the mustard oil in a small saucepan until smoking hot. Carefully pour the oil directly onto the marinade and allow to sizzle. Whisk well, then add the drained broccoli florets and toss to coat.

4. Preheat the oven to 220°C/200°C fan/425°F/Gas mark 7.

5. Arrange the broccoli florets in a roasting tray (sheet pan) and roast in the preheated oven for 15-20 minutes, or until slightly charred around the edges.

6. To make the sauce, heat the oil in a pan. Once the oil is shimmering, add the cumin seeds and chopped onion. Cook the onion for a couple of minutes until translucent but not browned.

7. Next, add the chillies, garlic, ginger, broccoli stems and leaves, spinach, fenugreek leaves, ground turmeric and ground coriander seeds. Continue to cook over a medium-low heat for 2 minutes. Pour in 200 ml (7 fl oz/generous ¾ cup) water, cover, and cook for a further 5-10 minutes, until everything has softened.

8. Remove the pan from the heat. Stir in the garam masala and mint leaves, then pour in the cream. Transfer the mixture to a blender and blitz until smooth and creamy.

9. Return the sauce to the pan and bring to a very gentle simmer. Season with the salt. Add the roasted broccoli, reserving some pieces to garnish (if you're feeling fancy). Heat through and serve sprinkled with sliced red chillies and toasted almonds.

Make it a feast!

This gorgeous green curry is delicious with Everyday Roti (see page 157) or Garlic and Coriander Naan (see page 164). I often enjoy it as it is, along-side a simple bowl of rice.

Vegan?

Replace the Greek yogurt with any dairy-free yogurt alternative and the cream with either oat cream or coconut milk.

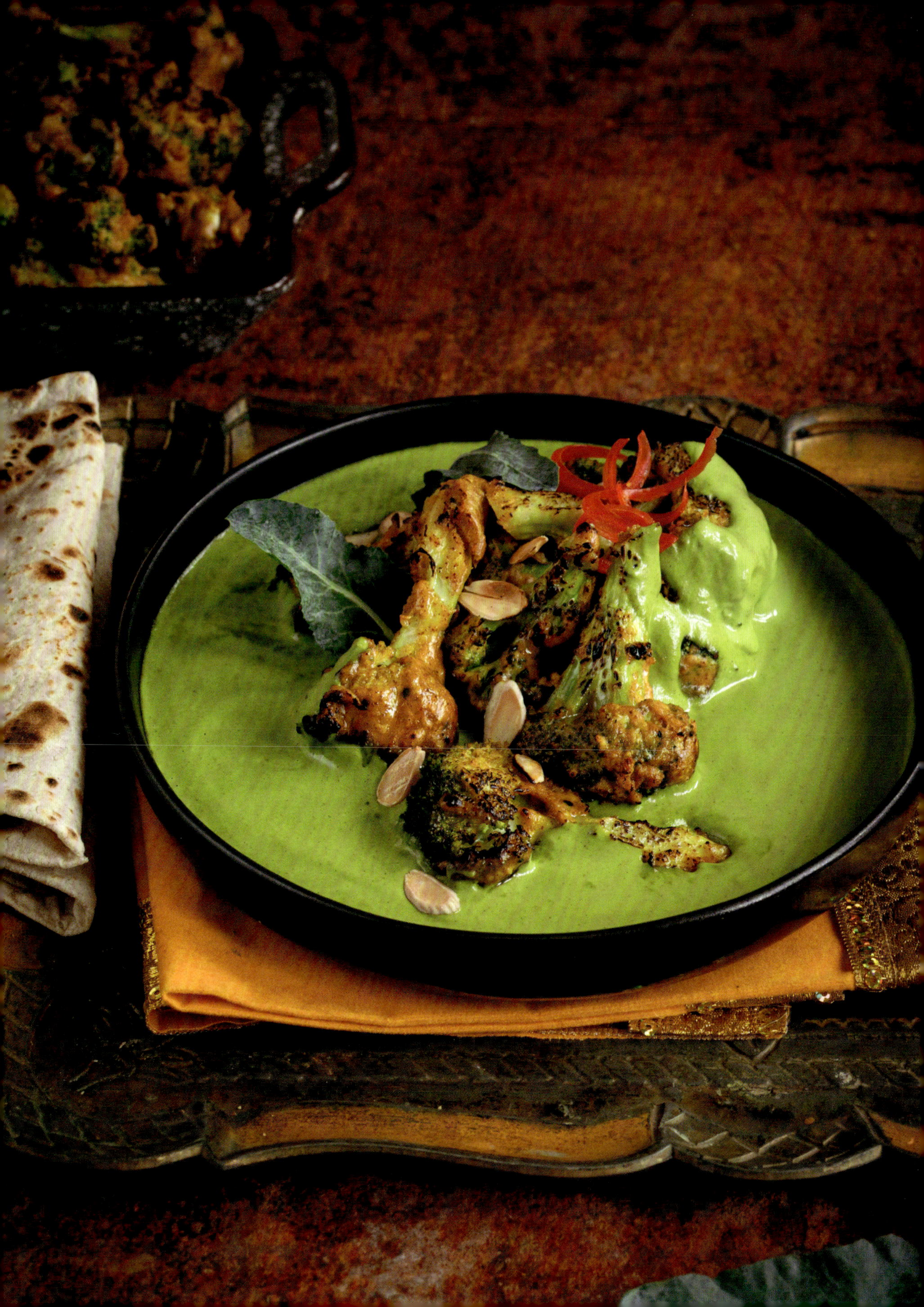

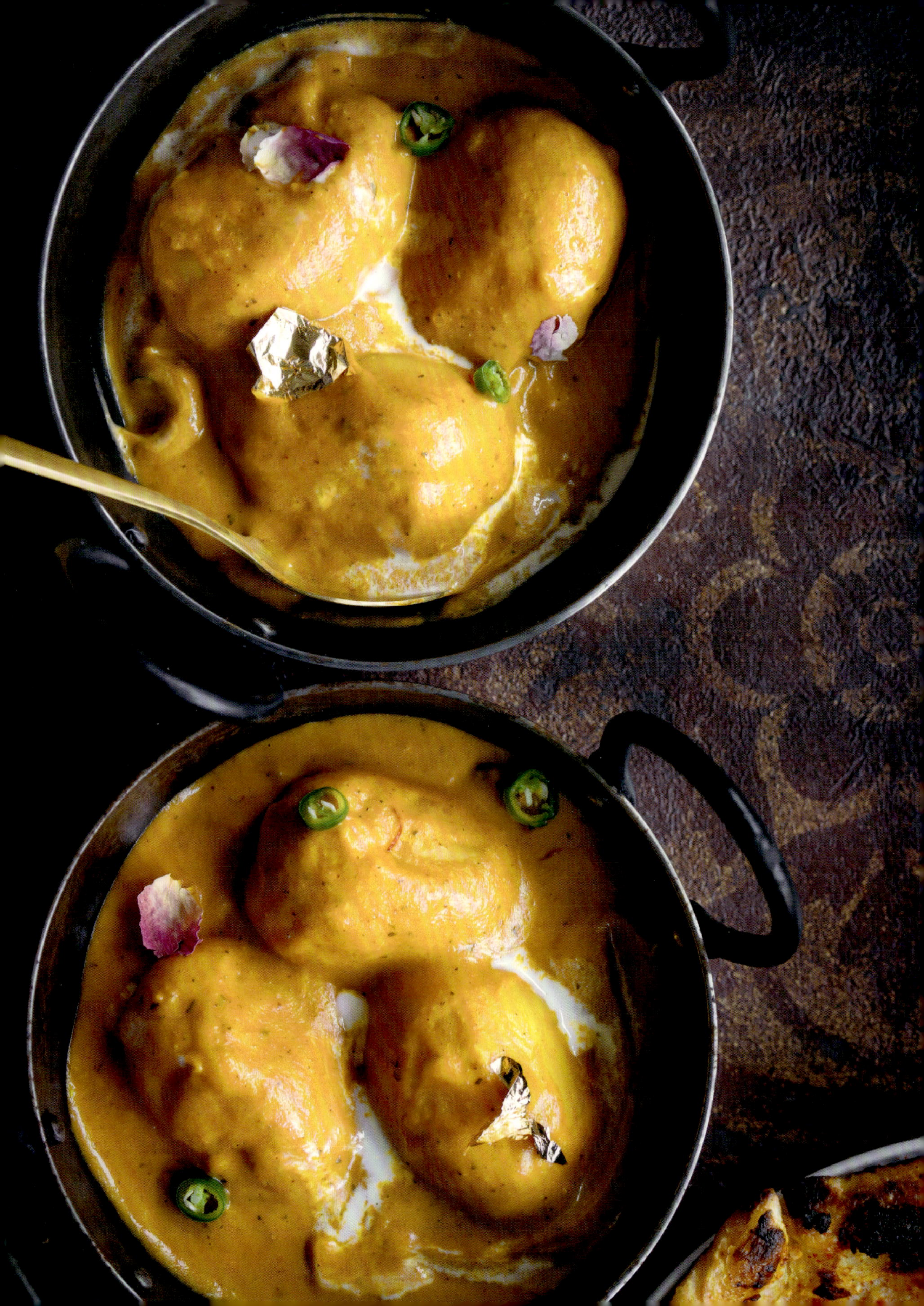

Shahi Potatoes

SERVES 4 • PREP: 20 MINS • COOK: 50 MINS

450 g (1 lb) new potatoes
1 tbsp ghee
1 tsp cumin seeds
1 tsp coriander seeds
½ tsp fennel seeds
2 cloves
2.5-cm (1-inch) cinnamon stick
3 green cardamom pods, cracked
1 black cardamom pod
1 dried Indian bay leaf
2 red chillies, roughly chopped
2 red onions, cut into wedges
2 garlic cloves, minced
2 tsp grated (shredded) root ginger
60 g (2 oz) blanched almonds
60 g (2 oz) dried unsweetened mango or apricot
4 large tomatoes, cut into wedges
8-10 saffron threads
1½ tsp salt

For the tempering
1 tbsp ghee
2.5-cm (1-inch) piece root ginger, cut into matchsticks
2 tsp Kashmiri chilli powder
¼ tsp ground turmeric
80 ml (2¾ fl oz/⅓ cup) double (heavy) cream, plus extra for swirling on top
1 tsp dried fenugreek leaves
2 green cardamom pods, seeds ground

For the optional garnishes
Green chilli rings
Edible dried rose petals
Edible gold leaf

A right royal affair. Expect nuts, fruitiness, saffron, cardamom and copious amounts of ghee in shahi dishes inspired by the food of the Mughal Empire (Persian influences aplenty). The Mughal dastarkhwān (tablecloth) was renowned for groaning with opulent feasts of biryanis, kebabs, koftas and naan. As a centre of fine arts, architecture and crafts, it comes as no surprise that Mughlai cuisine was rich in many ways, too. Today, a flourishing branch of the culture lives on through Indian cuisine, particularly across the Northern and Eastern states. Hero ingredients were historically meat heavy, but potatoes add filling warmth in its absence. Most Mughlai recipes include a sweetening element (often sugar) to balance the heat of the spices and compliment the richness of the dish. As dried fruits are such an integral part of the recipes from India's historical royal kitchens, it feels right to include dried mango or apricots in this mild and creamy potato curry. The blitzed tender mango also does wonders for the textures here.

1. Prick the potatoes all over with a fork. Place them in a saucepan of room temperature water and bring to a boil. Cover with a lid and simmer until the potatoes are fork tender. Drain in a colander and allow to cool. Once cool, peel off the skins with your fingers – they should come away easily. Set the potatoes aside.

2. Heat 1 tablespoon of ghee in a large saucepan. Add the whole spices and allow to sizzle for 20-30 seconds and then add the chillies, red onions, garlic, ginger, almonds, mango or apricot pieces, tomatoes, saffron, salt and 250 ml (8½ fl oz/1 cup) water. Stir well and cover with a lid. Simmer over a medium-low heat for 10-15 minutes, or until everything is soft. Allow to cool down. Remove and discard the bay leaf, black cardamom pod and cinnamon stick.

3. Transfer the mixture to a blender. Blend until completely smooth and creamy. Pass the mixture through a sieve (strainer) to remove any unwanted skins and seeds from the tomatoes and spices. Add 300 ml (10 fl oz/1¼ cups) water to the blender and swish around to catch the rest of the sauce. Pass this through the sieve and into the sauce too.

4. Prepare the tempering in the same pan. Heat the ghee until melted. Add the ginger matchsticks, Kashmiri chilli powder and ground turmeric. Return the strained sauce to the pan and stir well. Add the potatoes. Cover and simmer over a medium-low heat for 15-20 minutes, or until the sauce has thickened and the potatoes are meltingly soft but still holding their shape.

5. Switch off the heat and stir in the cream, dried fenugreek leaves (rubbed between your palms) and ground cardamom seeds.

6. Serve hot, garnished with an optional swirl of cream, chilli rings, rose petals and gold leaf.

Vegan?
Simply switch the ghee and cream for plant-based alternatives. A great deal of obligatory creaminess comes from the almonds anyway.

Make it a feast!
Serve with piles of naan (see page 164), steaming Zafrani Mushroom Pulao (see page 173) and live your best life.

(V) (VG)

Dumpling Handi

SERVES 4-6 • PREP: 20 MINS • COOK: 40 MINS

100 g (3½ oz) French beans, trimmed and halved
2 large carrots, cut into coins
165 g (5¾ oz/1 cup) sweetcorn kernels
60 ml (2 fl oz/4 tbsp) oil
½ tsp mustard seeds
½ tsp cumin seeds
¼ tsp asafoetida
1 tsp grated (shredded) root ginger
2 garlic cloves, minced
1 x 400-g (14-oz) can chopped tomatoes
2 tsp Kashmiri chilli powder
½ tsp ground turmeric
1 tsp sugar
½ tsp salt

For the dumplings

125 g (4½ oz/1 cup) chapati flour
2 tbsp gram flour
1 tbsp fine semolina
3 tbsp chopped fresh fenugreek leaves (or 1 tsp dried fenugreek leaves)
1 tsp Kashmiri chilli powder
1 tsp sugar
½ tsp salt
⅛ tsp baking powder
¼ tsp ground turmeric
1 garlic clove, minced
1 tsp lemon juice
¼ tsp asafoetida
1 tbsp oil
55 ml (1¾ fl oz/scant ¼ cup) hot water
Oil, for deep-frying

A word of advice: try not to eat all the fried dumplings before they hit the curry (and I'm talking from experience here). It's easily done, but friends and family may not forgive quite so easily. A handi is a round claypot that gives curries, daal and rice dishes a unique, earthy flavour. You could use an Indian or Chinese claypot (the kind used for making claypot rice). In the absence of these, a heavy-based casserole dish will do the job.

1. To make the dumplings, place all the ingredients except the hot water in a large bowl and stir well. Add the hot water and stir with a spoon until cool enough to handle. Knead to form a dough, about 5 minutes. Cover the dough with a damp dish towel and allow to rest for 15 minutes. Hot water hydrates the semolina effectively.

2. Boil the French beans, carrots and sweetcorn kernels until three-quarters cooked. They should be almost done and still retain their bite. If you're using canned sweetcorn, set it aside as there's no need to pre-cook it. Drain the vegetables and set aside.

3. Divide the dough into 15 g (½ oz) portions. Roll each portion of dough into a ball. Heat the oil for deep-frying in a deep, heavy-based pan. Once the temperature reaches 180°C (355°F), carefully lower the dumplings into the hot oil and deep-fry until slightly risen and golden, around 4-5 minutes. Do not overcrowd the pan with too many dumplings at once and so work in batches, if necessary. Use a slotted spoon to remove the dumplings from the oil and place in a colander or sieve (strainer) to allow any excess oil to drip away.

4. Meanwhile, heat the oil in a large claypot (handi) or use a casserole dish. Add the mustard seeds and wait for them to crackle before adding the cumin seeds, asafoetida, ginger, garlic, tomatoes, chilli powder, ground turmeric, sugar and salt. Pour in 200 ml (7 fl oz/generous ¾ cup) water, stir well and bring to a boil. Add all the vegetables to the pan and cover with a lid. Simmer over a medium-low heat for 10 minutes.

5. Add the deep-fried dumplings to the pan. Give the curry a very brief stir, place the lid back on the pan and simmer for a final 5 minutes.

Make it a feast!

This curry will never not give me Gujarati village vibes. It's a true taste of home. The fenugreek dumplings are hearty enough to not make you miss bread or rice, but if you eat this with roti or bhature, you'll be a very happy person. Bonus points are awarded for a side of plain yogurt.

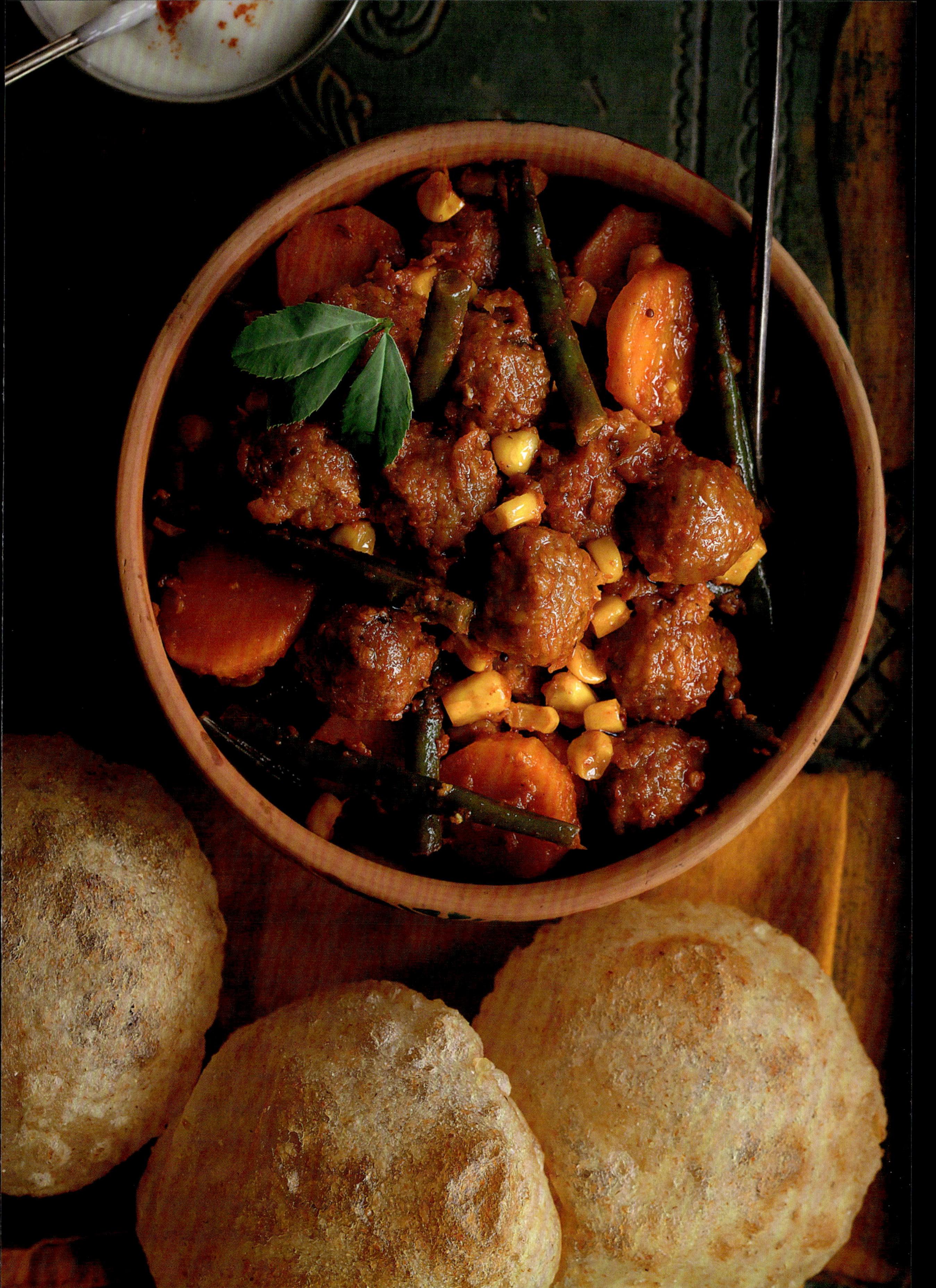

Scorpion Tikka Masala

SERVES 4 • PREP: 35 MINS, PLUS 1 HOUR SOAKING AND 30 MINS MARINATING • COOK: 40 MINS

250 g (8¾ oz) paneer, cut into 2-cm (¾-inch) cubes
100 g (3½ oz) okra, washed and thoroughly dried with a clean dish towel
1 large red bell pepper, cut into approximately 2-cm (¾-inch) pieces
1 large onion, cut into wedges and separated into petals

For the marinade
75 g (2⅔ oz/⅓ cup) thick plain yogurt
2½ tbsp Tandoori Masala (see page 269)
1 tbsp gram flour
1 tbsp lemon juice
1 tsp salt
3 tbsp edible mustard oil

For the scorpion sauce
2 tbsp oil
1 large onion, diced
4 garlic cloves, chopped
1 tbsp grated (shredded) root ginger
1 dried Scorpion chilli pepper, soaked in hot water for 15 minutes
10 cashews, soaked in hot water
2 tbsp concentrated tomato purée (paste)
150 ml (5 fl oz/scant ⅔ cup) pineapple juice
2 tsp ground coriander seeds
1 tsp ground cumin seeds
1 tbsp sweet smoked paprika
½ tsp ground turmeric
400 g (14 oz/1¾ cups) tomato passata (strained tomatoes)
2 tsp Garam Masala (see page 259)

This recipe gets its name from the supremely spicy Trinidad Scorpion chilli pepper that amps up the tikka masala sauce. It ranks among the hottest chillies in the world. But fear not, the base of this curry is fruity and creamy, providing the perfect balance of spice to blanket grilled tandoori okra, paneer, onions and bell peppers. If you can't find dried Scorpion chilli peppers, use fresh Scotch bonnet instead or, in a pinch, a dash of the hottest chilli sauce you can get your hands on. This recipe is a tribute to the many Indo-Trinidadian and Tobagonians who first arrived in Trinidad and Tobago from India as indentured labourers between 1845–1917.

1. Soak wooden bamboo skewers in cold water for an hour. Alternatively, you can use metal kebab skewers.

2. Start by making the marinade for the paneer and vegetables. In a large bowl, whisk together all the ingredients for the marinade except the mustard oil. Heat the mustard oil in a small saucepan until smoking hot. Carefully pour the hot oil into the whisked marinade and allow to sizzle for a few seconds before whisking in. This will temper the spices.

3. Add the paneer, whole okra, bell pepper and onion to the marinade and mix well to coat. Cover and allow to marinate at room temperature for 30 minutes (or as much time as you have).

4. In the meantime, make the scorpion sauce. Heat the oil in a medium saucepan. Add the onion and sauté until it's a rich golden brown. Next, add the garlic, ginger, Scorpion chilli pepper, cashews and tomato purée (paste). Cook, stirring continuously, for a further 30 seconds before adding the pineapple juice, ground coriander seeds, ground cumin seeds, sweet smoked paprika and ground turmeric. Stir well and cook for a further 30 seconds. Once the oil begins to separate from the sides of the pan, add the tomato passata (strained tomatoes). Cover the pan and simmer over a medium-low heat for 15 minutes.

5. Remove the lid from the pan and switch the heat off. Allow to cool for 15 minutes and then blend the sauce until smooth. Pass it through a sieve (strainer) and pour it back into the pan for a silky, restaurant-style finish.

6. Bring the sauce back to a gentle simmer. Once it begins to bubble, mix in the garam masala, ground cardamom seeds, dried fenugreek leaves, sugar, salt and cream. Keep the sauce simmering over a low heat for 10 minutes.

7. Preheat the oven to 240°C/220°C fan/465°F/Gas mark 9. Thread the marinated paneer, okra, bell pepper and onion onto the skewers, alternating the ingredients in a way that looks pretty to you. Leave a 2.5-cm (1-inch) space at the top and base of each skewer. Place the skewers on a baking tray, resting the free space at the tops and bottoms of the skewers on the edge of the tray, so the ingredients are suspended above the base of the tray and not resting directly on it. You can also place the skewers on a greased rack inside the tray. Pop the tray into the oven for 10–12 minutes.

4 green cardamom pods, seeds removed and ground
1 tsp dried fenugreek leaves, rubbed between your palms
2 tbsp light soft brown sugar
Salt, to taste
300 ml (10 fl oz/1¼ cups) double (heavy) cream, plus an extra 2 tbsp to garnish
Fried onions, to garnish
Chopped fresh coriander (cilantro), to garnish

8. To finish off the skewers, allow them to cool slightly, just enough so you can touch the handle. Hold each skewer directly over an open flame on your hob (stovetop) burner (don't put it down) and roll to char the outside. Be careful not to burn yourself and open a window before you start. This gives the tikka an amazing tandoori flavour. You could skip this part, but it makes a huge difference to the final flavour.

9. Using a fork, carefully remove the tikka pieces from the skewers and drop them into the hot scorpion sauce. Bring everything to a gentle simmer for a few minutes before serving. Finish the dish with a swirl of cream and scatter over the crispy fried onions and fresh coriander (cilantro).

Note

The paneer and vegetable tikka can also be cooked on a preheated griddle pan or on the barbecue. Turn and cook on all sides until grill marks appear, around 8–10 minutes.

Vegan?

Swap paneer for tofu, cooked potatoes or cauliflower. Use any plant-based yogurt in the marinade. Oat cream is the best replacement for dairy cream in this recipe, but you could also use coconut milk.

Make it a feast!

Serve alongside Butter Naan (see page 164), Achaari Matoke (see page 185) and Nectarine Kachumber (see page 193). Finish the meal with a cooling bowl of White Chocolate Rasmalai (see page 213) to smother the flames of the Scorpion chilli pepper!

Curry 125

Root Veg Jalfrezi

SERVES 4 • PREP: 20 MINS • COOK: 40 MINS

2 parsnips, peeled and cut into thick wedges
1 carrot, peeled and cut into thick wedges
1 large potato, peeled and cut into thick wedges
½ small swede, peeled and cut into thick wedges
3 tbsp ghee or oil
1 tsp cumin seeds
½ tsp nigella seeds
½ tsp fennel seeds
¼ tsp fenugreek seeds
4 large garlic cloves, crushed
2 tsp grated (shredded) root ginger
2 tbsp tomato purée (paste)
¾ tsp ground turmeric
2 tsp Kashmiri chilli powder
½ tsp freshly ground black pepper
1 large onion, cut into wedges and separated into petals
1 tsp Garam Masala (see page 259)
1 tsp dried fenugreek leaves
1 tsp salt

To garnish
1–2 red chillies, sliced
2 tbsp chopped fresh coriander (cilantro)
1-cm (½-inch) piece root ginger, cut into matchsticks

Mixed roots tossed in a heady concoction of spices. Whilst some of the techniques used to make jalfrezi have strong Asian influence, the original jalfrezi of Eastern India was very much created to cater to European tastes. Under colonial rule, Bengal, the home of jalfrezi was a major hub for the British East India Company. A medley of vegetables and protein were stir-fried to create 'a spicy dish designed for the British palate', or jhāl porhezī.

1. Preheat the oven to 220°C/200°C fan/425°F/Gas mark 7.

2. Place the root veg in a large roasting tray (sheet pan) and add 1 tablespoon of the melted ghee. Toss well. Roast in the preheated oven for 18–20 minutes, or until tender and lightly browned on the outside. Use a spatula to move them around in the tray halfway through the cooking time.

3. Heat the remaining ghee in a smoking hot wok. Add the cumin seeds, nigella seeds, fennel seeds and fenugreek seeds. Sauté for a few seconds before adding the garlic, ginger, and tomato purée (paste). Cook the tomato purée for 2 minutes and then add 240 ml (8 fl oz/scant 1 cup) water and the ground turmeric, chilli powder and black pepper. Stir well and simmer uncovered for 10 minutes, or until everything is reduced, thickened and the masalas begin to pull away from the ghee at the sides of the pan.

4. Once you notice it start to pool, add the onions, garam masala, dried fenugreek leaves (rubbed between your palms) and salt. Stir-fry for 2–3 minutes, or until the onions soften. Next, tip in the roasted root veg and toss everything well to coat.

5. Garnish with sliced red chillies, chopped coriander (cilantro) and root ginger matchsticks before serving.

Vegan?
Swap the butter-based ghee for Vegan Ghee (see page 244) or use oil.

Make it a feast!
Serve alongside Naan (see page 164) or Bhature (see page 162) and Pink Peppercorn Pickled Onions (see page 240). Finish with fridge-cold White Chocolate Rasmalai (see page 213).

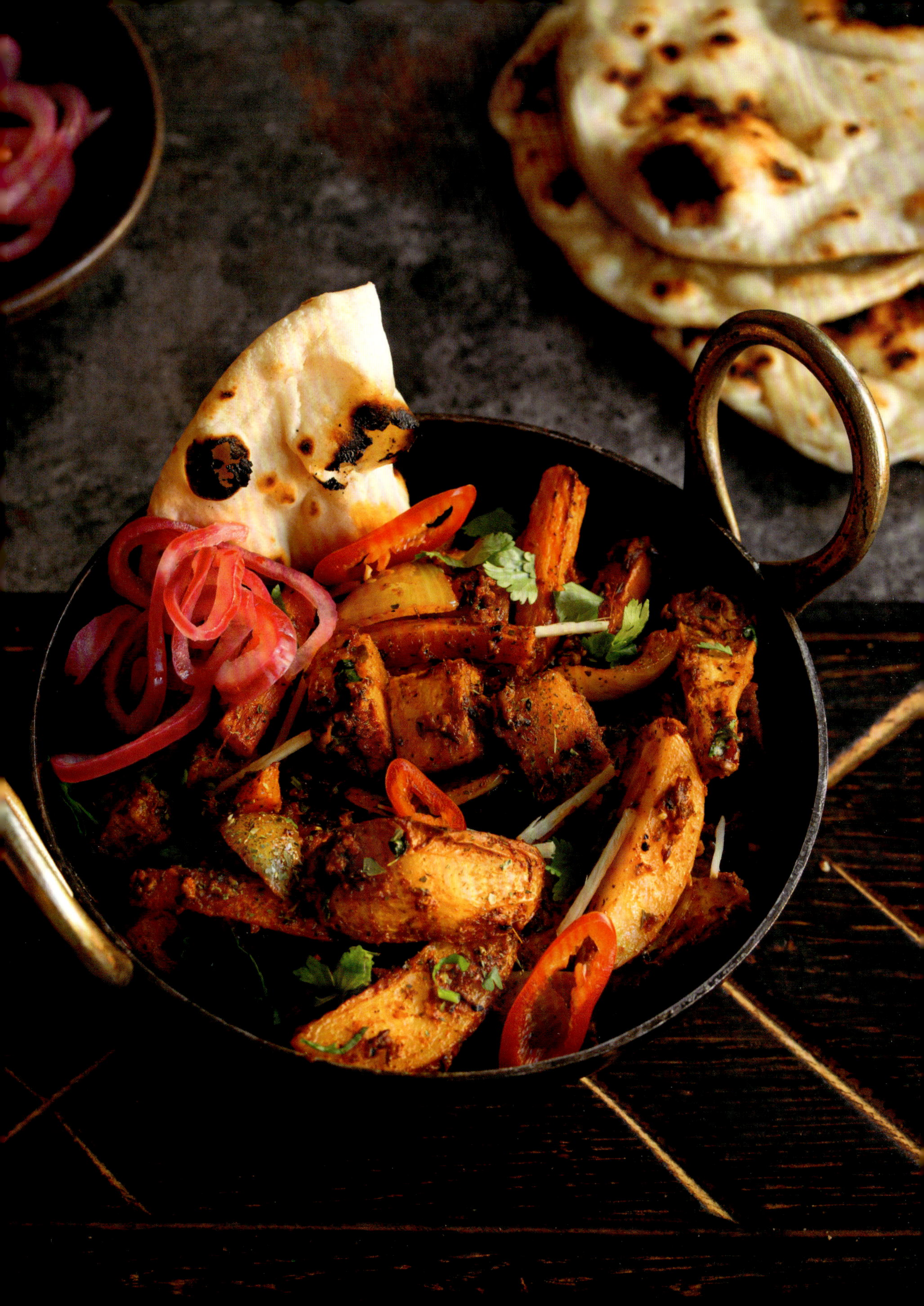

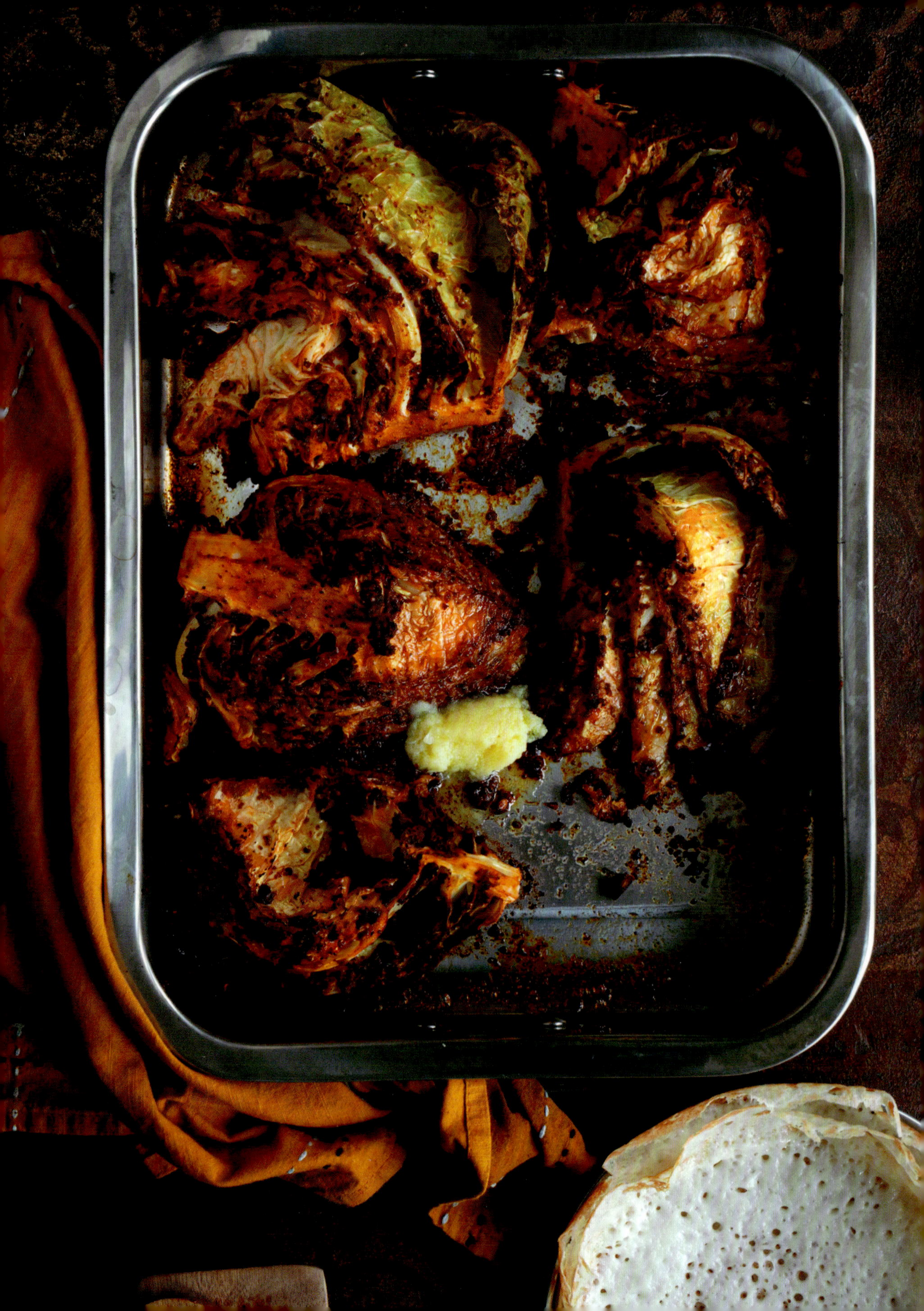

Savoy Cabbage Ghee Roast

SERVES 4 • PREP: 20 MINS, PLUS 20 MINS SOAKING • COOK: 70 MINS

V | GF | VG

8 unsalted raw cashews
1 tbsp coriander seeds
1 tsp cumin seeds
1 tsp fennel seeds
1 tsp black peppercorns
1 tsp mustard seeds
½ tsp fenugreek seeds
2 cloves
1 star anise
10–12 curry leaves
3 tbsp Kashmiri chilli powder
¾ tsp ground turmeric
10 garlic cloves
1 tsp concentrated tamarind paste
1 tsp salt
6 tbsp melted ghee
1 large head Savoy cabbage

Vegan?
Use Vegan Ghee (see page 244) in place of butter-based ghee.

Make it a feast!
Serve this South Indian-inspired roast with appam, dosa or rice.

Note
Some commercial tamarind pastes are far saltier than others. Be sure to taste yours before adding the salt. You can start by adding half the amount of salt and then, if necessary, increase the amount once the ghee-roast masala paste is ready.

I've never treated a head of cabbage with this much respect in my life. Give hardy Savoy cabbage a serious rani treatment with Mangalorean-style ghee-roast masalas. Massage the spices into the crevices of the cabbage and over every inch of its crinkly skin. Roast until the leaves wilt and become butter soft for a bountiful payoff.

1. Soak the cashews in hot water for 20 minutes. Drain and set aside.

2. In a dry frying pan (skillet), roast the coriander seeds, cumin seeds, fennel seeds, black peppercorns, mustard seeds, fenugreek seeds, cloves, star anise and curry leaves over a medium-low heat for 6–7 minutes until toasted and aromatic. The curry leaves should turn dry and brittle. Allow to cool and then grind to a fine powder.

3. Blend together the ground roasted spices, chilli powder, turmeric, soaked cashews, garlic, tamarind paste and salt, along with the melted ghee and 150 ml (5 fl oz/scant ⅔ cup) water. If it's too thick, add a touch more water until you have a very smooth, paste-like consistency.

4. Remove the outer leaves of the cabbage. Split the cabbage into six large wedges. Trim away enough of the tough stem to remove any pieces that would be unpleasant to eat, but not so much that the wedges fall apart.

5. Rub the cabbage wedges all over with the ghee-roast masala paste and arrange them in a large roasting tray (sheet pan).

6. Preheat the oven to 210°C/190°C fan/410°F/Gas mark 6½.

7. Cover the tray with kitchen foil and allow to sit on the side until the oven has preheated.

8. Roast the cabbage in the preheated oven for 50 minutes, or until soft and tender. Remove the foil and baste the cabbage wedges with any masalas and ghee in the base of the tray.

9. Return the tray to the oven and continue to roast the cabbage uncovered for a further 10–12 minutes, or until some of the cabbage leaves have browned and charred in places.

10. Baste with the remaining masalas from the tray once more before serving.

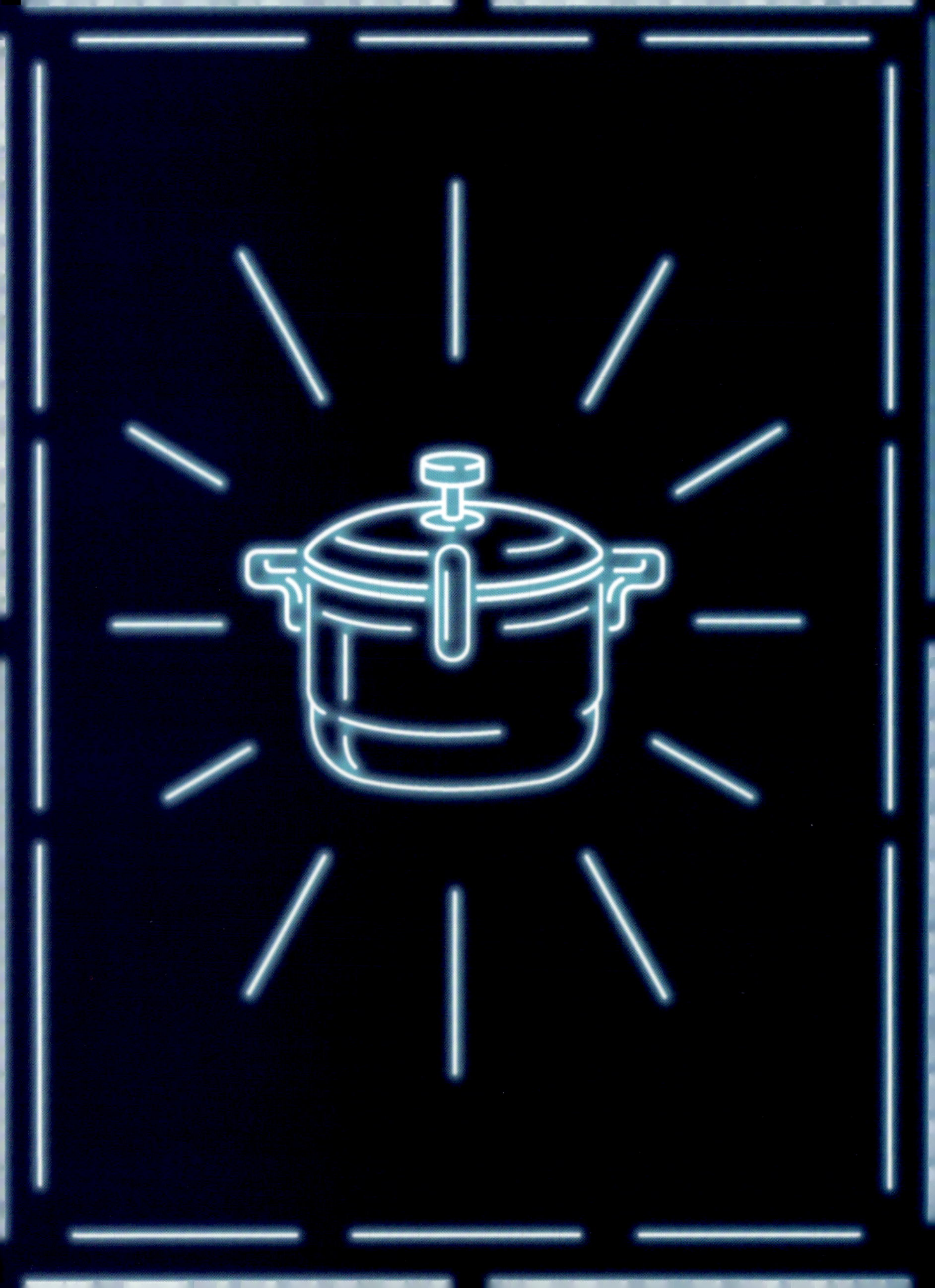

Daal

Don't forget the tadka!

Most kids fear creepy crawlies, the monster that lives under the bed or the villain from their favourite movie. Not me, though; I was afraid of the pressure cooker. 'HISSSSSSSSSSSS' is the venting sound my mum's battered old Prestige made, like a mongoose fighting a snake. Standing within a three-metre radius of the thing stirred up suspense, like the menacing Jaws theme tune. You knew the great white shark was circling, waiting to strike, but you just didn't know when. On Saturday mornings, the release of the furious pressure cooker served as my alarm clock, signalling that there was Teenage Mutant Ninja Turtles and Saved by the Bell to watch on telly, Coco Pops for breakfast and urad (Gujarati black daal) for lunch. Even now, when the pressure releases from a tightly sealed vat of bubbling daal, my heart thumps something rotten.

As ominous as they can be, my kitchen equipment hall of fame would be incomplete without one of these traditional pressure cookers. Their power to cook all manner of daals, as well as beans and veggies, such as chickpeas (garbanzo beans), potatoes and aubergines (eggplants), quickly is luring enough to forget the whistle drama. The rubber seal around the edge of a pressure cooker ensures every bit of steam stays trapped inside, building an intense heat that rapidly softens food. Once the pressure reaches a certain limit, the whistle hops up like a screaming Mandrake pulled from its terracotta pot in the Hogwart's Herbology class. The time that a classic stovetop pressure cooker takes to soften daal is usually measured in these 'whistles'. For example, a small split daal, like red masoor, may take only two whistles to cook, whereas robust black lentils only soften enough after eight whistles. I've included a handy guide overleaf to help you achieve perfect tenderness for the most popular types of daals in Indian cookery.

Washing and soaking

Prior to cooking any daal, I recommend giving the pulses a thorough wash in cold water, changing the water at least three times. Really rub the surface to remove any dirt. I will typically soak most varieties of daal in boiling hot kettle water for at least an hour, along with a small pinch of bicarbonate of soda (baking soda), which helps the pulses to soften quickly. Soaking makes daal easier to digest. For heartier types with their skins still on, like whole urad, I recommend soaking for 8 hours or overnight. Discard the soaking liquid and give everything a final rinse before draining and using.

The nitty gritty

In some cases, you may find it useful to sift through the pulses to reduce the likelihood of small stones making their way into your lovely pot of daal. As tedious as it sounds, in my youth, this is a job I'd sit at the table and do for mum. Some say stones were added to superficially increase the weight of the pulses, or it could simply have been down to poor processing. Whatever the reason, it's something to be mindful of as there's nothing worse than expecting a smooth bite of daal and then shocking your molars with a well-camouflaged nugget of grit. Your dentist will thank you. Since the quality of most commercially sold daals is much better than it used to be, nowadays I only really do this for whole black gram daal (urad), whole mung beans (moong) and split mung beans (moong) daal - stones are less conspicuous in a batch of dark-coloured daals.

How many whistles, mum?

When learning to make daal, my first task was to figure out how many whistles of a pressure cooker it takes to cook each variety. Split lentils typically take less time, whilst the chunkier kinds call for longer. Mum to the rescue. Here's Momma Feasts' guide to cooking different types of daals in a pressure cooker. The amounts below make enough for around 6 people (mum-sized portions), but reduce the quantity if necessary. Every style of daal is unique. The water measures given below are just enough to cook the daal, so you can freely adjust the thickness according to your preference. If you're following a specific recipe, stick to the quantities given in the list of ingredients. Always season your daal at the end of the cooking process as salt can prevent beans, pulses and lentils from softening. If a recipe requires you to drain your cooked daal, reserve some of the cooking liquid. Like pasta water is revered as the nectar of the gods for its magical thickening properties (i.e., starch), daal water can be used in very much the same way. Add some liquid back in if the daal is beginning to look a little too thick for your liking.

TYPE OF DAAL (325 g/11½ oz of beans, pulses or lentils)	MINIMUM SOAKING TIME (in hot water with ⅛ tsp bicarbonate of soda/baking soda)	COOKING WATER	NUMBER OF WHISTLES (from the pressure cooker)
Black chickpeas (garbanzos) *kala channa*	8 hours or overnight	1 litre (34 fl oz/4¼ cups)	9
White chickpeas (garbanzos) *kabuli channa*	8 hours or overnight	1 litre (34 fl oz/4¼ cups)	8
Red kidney beans *rajma*	8 hours or overnight	1 litre (34 fl oz/4¼ cups)	5
Whole black gram daal *urad*	8 hours or overnight	1 litre (34 fl oz/4¼ cups)	9
Black-eyed beans (peas) *chora*	8 hours or overnight	1 litre (34 fl oz/4¼ cups)	3
Whole mung beans *moong*	1 hour	1 litre (34 fl oz/4¼ cups)	3
Split yellow gram daal (chickpeas) *channa daal*	30 minutes	1 litre (34 fl oz/4¼ cups)	2
Whole green lentils *sabut masoor*	30 minutes	1 litre (34 fl oz/4¼ cups)	2
Split black gram daal with skin *urad daal chilka*	30 minutes	1 litre (34 fl oz/4¼ cups)	4
Split pigeon peas *toor daal*	30 minutes	1 litre (34 fl oz/4¼ cups)	5
Split mung beans (yellow) *moong daal*	30 minutes	1 litre (34 fl oz/4¼ cups)	2
Split black gram daal (white) *urad daal*	30 minutes	1 litre (34 fl oz/4¼ cups)	4
Split red lentils *masoor daal*	30 minutes	950 ml (32 fl oz/4 cups)	2

If you don't have a pressure cooker

It's entirely possible to cook daal without using a pressure cooker, however, in doing so, expect the cooking time to double. Some daal recipes require you to cook the lentils prior to adding other ingredients whilst others are one-pot affairs where the lentils are added to pre-tempered masalas. In either case, you will need to use a large, heavy-based pot with a tight-fitting lid and simmer until the beans, pulses or lentils are tender. Since more steam is likely to escape from a regular pot, you'll need to keep topping the pot up with hot water. The amount you'll need to add depends on the size and density of the lentils (split, skinless lentils need less, whereas robust lentils like whole urad require more). In any case, the lentils should be very soft and for some recipes, like Pasta Daal (see page 143) and White Daal (see page 140), they should be of a liquid or flowing consistency. Timings and the amount of water required may vary depending on the style of the dish you're cooking.

Tadka (a.k.a Vaghaar, Baghaar, Chhonk)

If we were talking about wrestling and not daal, tadka would be the ultimate finishing move. A tempering of hot ghee, mustard seeds, cumin, asafoetida, cinnamon and curry leaves go in to my most simple everyday daal. The reason why tadka is done in ghee or oil and not in other liquids is because many of the flavour compounds in the spices we use are fat soluble, so to make the most of each one, we tadka them. Only then are they able to show their true colours, like a peacock unfurling his feathers. When the dance of the mustard seeds ensues and that familiar crackle is followed with a waft of heady spices, you know the daal is almost done. Note that ghee and oil are used specifically for tadka because butter burns at high temperatures. However, the world of tadka is vast and diverse depending on the dish you are making. Like most Indian dishes, the masalas used are region specific, informed by centuries of age-old tradition. But that doesn't mean you can't experiment if you want to. Tadka can be as simple as a few spices and aromatics, or it can call for 15 different ingredients ranging from seeds and nuts to aromatics and fresh herbs.

Like most Gujaratis, I grew up preparing tadka at the beginning of the cooking process. It's considered to be the foundation of the meal, so most daal, curry and rice dishes start this way. The purpose of blooming whole spices at the beginning and then adding the daal is so that they simmer slowly, drawing out flavours as the dish cooks. However, many recipes call for the tadka to be prepared separately and then poured in at the end. Both styles have their merits; the former gives the daal the benefit of a deep infusion, whereas a tadka done at the end offers a welcome whoosh of flavour. For example, Karnataka's famous daal and rice pot, bisi bele bhath, typically calls for two elaborate tadkas to top and tail the dish. The choice is yours – but please, don't forget the tadka!

Every passionate Indian cook must have an arsenal of daal recipes, so a collection of recipes dedicated to the delights of lentils follows. The Pasta Daal (see page 143) my dad would make for my brother and I in mum's absence is a one-pot meal that bypasses the requirement to roll roti and cook rice; a winner for those who fancy a filling shortcut. Try White Daal (see page 140) for a delicious change of pace from restaurant favourite, Black Daal. Black Pepper Tadka Daal (see page 136) is basically central heating for the soul.

V **GF** **VG**

Black Pepper Tadka Daal

SERVES 4 • PREP: 15 MINS, PLUS 30 MINS SOAKING • COOK: 40 MINS

For the daal
100 g (3½ oz/½ cup) split red lentils
75 g (2⅔ oz/⅓ cup) split yellow gram daal
25 g (⅛ oz/⅛ cup) whole black gram daal
⅛ tsp bicarbonate of soda (baking soda)
2 tbsp ghee
1 onion, grated (shredded)
1 tbsp grated (shredded) root ginger
1 large tomato, finely chopped
½ tsp ground turmeric
½ tsp freshly ground black pepper
750 ml (25 fl oz/3 cups plus 2 tbsp) hot water
½ tsp Garam Masala (see page 259)
1½ tsp salt

For the tadka
2 tbsp ghee
1 tsp cumin seeds
1 tsp coarsely ground black pepper
2 spring onions (scallions), sliced diagonally
2 fresh green chillies, slit lengthways

A celebration of black pepper that was, at one time, more valuable than gold. Before chillies arrived in India with the Portuguese around 1500, black pepper was the most efficient way to infuse spicy heat into meals. Indian cooks were well accustomed to cooking with black pepper, and so they knew exactly what to do when chilli peppers arrived from the Americas and Caribbean islands. Today, both are mainstays of the modern kitchen. Most of the heat in this daal comes from the gentle warmth of good old black peppercorns. I add them at two separate stages during the cooking process to ensure the pepperiness kicks right the way through. Mixing three varieties of daal not only makes this nutritious, but it also gives the daal a uniquely creamy consistency you'll dream about for days.

1. Combine all three daals in a bowl. Rinse the daals in plenty of cold water, rubbing them between your palms to remove any surface dirt. Repeat this process, changing the water 3 or 4 times. Pour freshly boiled water over the daals, along with the bicarbonate of soda (baking soda) and allow to soak for 30 minutes. Drain well.

2. Heat the ghee in a pressure cooker or pressure pot (if you don't have one, see the notes below). Add the onion and cook over a medium-low heat, stirring all the time, for about 10 minutes or until well browned. Next, add the ginger, tomato, ground turmeric and black pepper. Mix well and cook for a further 2 minutes.

3. Tip the drained daals into the pot along with the hot water and bring to a boil. Place the lid securely on the pot.

4. Cook over a medium heat for about 20 minutes. For regular pressure cookers, this will be approximately 5 whistles. If using a pressure pot, select the stew/soup function for 20 minutes.

5. Once cooked, carefully release the steam from the pot and open the lid. You can also allow it to stand and cool by itself. There really is no way you can overcook this daal.

6. Add the garam masala and salt. Beat the daal with a balloon whisk for 90 seconds, until creamy. Beating the mixture with a whisk gives it a wonderful, creamy texture. I recommend it for any style of daal. Keep the daal over a low heat while you prepare the tadka.

7. In a separate small pan, heat the ghee for the tadka. Add the cumin seeds, black pepper, spring onions (scallions) - reserve some greens to garnish, and green chillies. Cook, stirring all the time, until the spring onions have browned very slightly and the chillies have blistered white on the outside. Since the ghee should be very hot, this process should take no longer than 20-30 seconds to prevent the spices from burning.

8. Immediately pour the hot tadka over the simmering daal and mix well. Garnish with spring onion greens for extra freshness if you like.

Notes
If you don't have a pressure cooker or pressure pot, you can simmer the daal in a pan with a tight-fitting lid until the lentils are tender. You'll need to keep topping the pan up with hot water (an additional 250 ml/8½ fl oz/1 cup of water).

Vegan?
Swap ghee for your favourite vegan spread or oil, or Vegan Ghee (see page 244).

Make it a feast!
Serve alongside plain rice, jeera rice or with garlic naan.

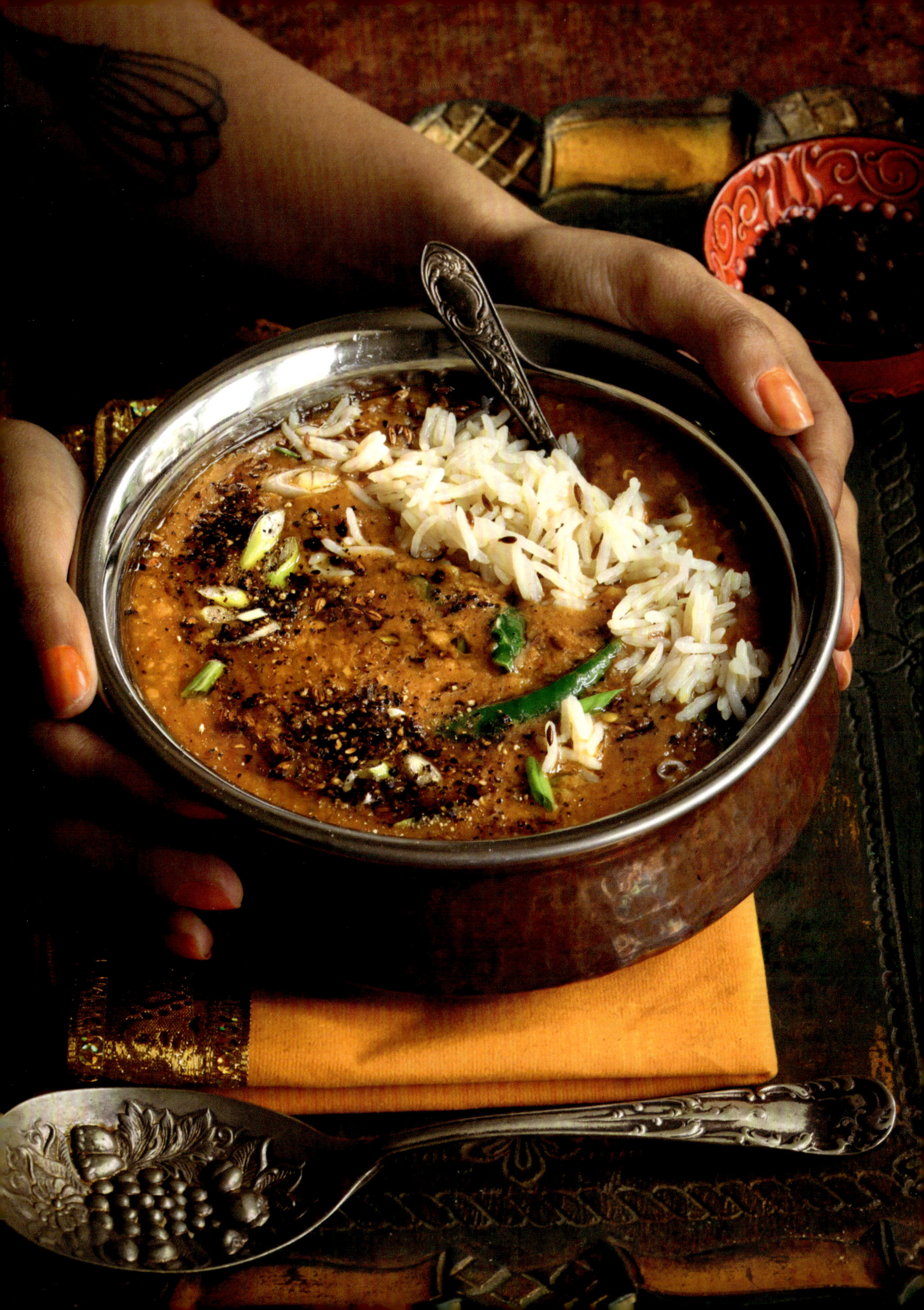

Black Daal

SERVES 4-6 • PREP: 20 MINS, PLUS 8 HOURS SOAKING • COOK: 1 HOUR

220 g (7¾ oz/1¼ cups) whole black gram daal
⅛ tsp bicarbonate of soda (baking soda)
1.2 litres (40 fl oz/5 cups) water, at room temperature
2 tbsp ghee
1 tsp cumin seeds
¼ tsp asafoetida
1 dried Indian bay leaf
2 large pieces black stone flower
2 black cardamom pods
5-cm (2-inch) cinnamon stick
3 large garlic cloves, crushed
2 tbsp minced root ginger
2 whole green chillies, slit lengthways
350 g (12⅓ oz) fresh or canned tomatoes blended
2 tsp Kashmiri chilli powder, or to taste
¼ tsp ground turmeric
2 green cardamom pods, seeds removed and ground
1 tsp ground coriander seeds
1 x 210-g (7½-oz) can kidney beans
50 g (1¾ oz/scant ¼ cup) butter or ghee
1 tbsp Garam Masala (see page 259)
1 tsp dried fenugreek leaves, rubbed between your palms
2 tsp salt, or to taste
100 ml (3½ fl oz/scant ½ cup) double (heavy) cream
2-cm (¾-inch) piece root ginger, cut into matchsticks

Black Daal or Daal Makhani isn't typical Indian home cooking. It's slow food that's unmistakably rich, in the unadulterated style we expect from restaurants, but that doesn't mean you can't make an excellent version at home. This recipe calls for whole black gram daal (urad) which has a robust, wholesome and creamy texture. Restaurant chefs simmer it for hours, often over coals, for a deep smokiness. I achieve this at home by finishing the daal with a lit stick of cinnamon soaked in ghee. This method is derived from dhungar, the Persian-inspired, coal-smoking method favoured by the Mughals and widely adopted in North Indian cookery.

1. Rinse the daal in plenty of cold water, rubbing it between your palms to remove any surface dirt. Repeat this process, changing the water 3 or 4 times. Pour freshly boiled water over the daal along with a pinch of bicarbonate of soda (baking soda) and allow to soak for 8 hours or overnight.

2. Drain the daal well through a colander, tipping away the soaking liquid. Give the daal a final rinse under running water. The water should run clear.

3. Next, add the daal to a pressure cooker or pressure pot, cover with the room temperature water and cook with the lid on until tender. For a regular pressure cooker, this will be approximately 9 whistles. For a pressure pot this will be 30 minutes (the stew/soup function does a good job of cooking the daal through.) If you don't have a pressure cooker or pressure pot, you can simmer the daal in a pot with a tight-fitting lid until tender. You'll need to keep topping the pot up with hot water (approximately an additional 500 ml (17 fl oz/2 cups). In any case, the daal should be very soft. It's better to overcook than to undercook here. Do not drain the daal.

4. Heat the ghee in a large pot. Earthenware imparts great flavour if you have one. Add the cumin seeds, asafoetida, bay leaf, black stone flower, black cardamom pods, cinnamon stick, garlic, ginger and green chillies. Allow to sizzle for 10–20 seconds before adding the tomatoes, chilli powder, ground turmeric, ground cardamom seeds and ground coriander seeds. Cook this out, stirring continuously for 10–15 minutes.

5. Tip in the cooked daal along with the cooking liquid and the kidney beans in their water. Mix well. Cover and simmer for 30 minutes, stirring often to ensure the daal doesn't stick to the base of the pan. Alternatively, transfer the daal to a slow cooker and cook on low for up to 8 hours.

6. Add the butter or ghee to the daal. Using a sturdy spoon or ladle, mash the daal against the base and sides of the pan to crush some of them, then whisk this for a minute or so. This is what thickens the daal for a luxuriously creamy, restaurant-style finish. Finally, add the garam masala, dried fenugreek leaves, salt, cream and ginger matchsticks. Mix well and simmer for 10 minutes, then switch off the heat.

To serve

5-cm (2-inch) cinnamon stick
1 tbsp ghee
1 tbsp double (heavy) cream
2 tbsp crispy fried onions
1 tbsp chopped fresh coriander (cilantro) leaves
¼ tsp dried fenugreek leaves (rubbed between your palms)
2-cm (¾-inch) root ginger, cut into matchsticks

Vegan?

Swap the butter or ghee for Vegan Ghee (see page 244) or use oil. Use any plant-based cream to finish the daal.

Gluten free?

Use a gluten-free asafoetida or omit this ingredient.

Make it a feast!

Serve alongside any, or all, of the options from my Naan Party (see page 164) and Tomato, Tulsi and Burrata Salad (see page 189) for a zip of freshness.

7. To serve, soak the cinnamon stick in melted ghee for at least 10 minutes.

8. To smoke the daal, hold the cinnamon stick with heatproof tongs. Light the cinnamon stick and lay it directly on the surface of the daal. Cover the pot with a lid and allow to smoke for 60–90 seconds. Stir the daal to put out the flame.

9. Garnish the daal with the cream, crispy fried onions, fresh coriander (cilantro), dried fenugreek leaves and ginger matchsticks.

White Daal

SERVES 4-6 • PREP: 10 MINS, PLUS 30 MINS SOAKING • COOK: 25 MINS

220 g (7¾ oz/1¼ cups) split black gram daal
⅛ tsp bicarbonate of soda (baking soda)
950 ml (32 fl oz/4 cups) water, at room temperature
1 tbsp finely chopped tomato
3 green chillies, minced
2 tsp minced root ginger
2 garlic cloves, minced
Juice of 1 large lemon
1 tbsp sugar
1¼ tsp salt, or to taste
1 tbsp chopped fresh coriander (cilantro), to serve
spicy chilli oil, to serve (optional)

For the tadka
3 tbsp ghee
1 star anise
3 whole cloves
2.5-cm (1-inch) cinnamon stick
1 tsp cumin seeds
½ tsp mustard seeds
2 dried red chillies, whole
¼ tsp asafoetida
4-5 curry leaves

Black Daal's laid-back cousin. This simple White Daal is a 30-ish minute affair. It calls for split black gram daal (urad daal), which is actually white in colour. Since it's split and skinless, it cooks in a fraction of the time that it takes to cook whole black gram. Don't let its plain appearance fool you; this daal sports big, zesty flavours and a rib-sticking creamy texture.

1. Rinse the daal in plenty of cold water, rubbing it between your palms to remove any surface dirt. Repeat this process, changing the water twice more. Soak in boiling hot water with the bicarbonate of soda (baking soda) for 30 minutes.

2. Drain the soaking water from the daal. (You can use this liquid to feed your houseplants – they will love it!) Give the daal a final rinse under running water. The water should run clear.

3. Next, add the daal to a pressure cooker or pressure pot, cover with the room temperature water and cook with the lid on until tender. For a regular pressure cooker, this will be approximately 4 whistles. For a pressure pot this will be 10 minutes (the stew/soup function does a good job of cooking the daal through). If you don't have either of these pots, simmer the daal in a pot with a tight-fitting lid until tender. You'll need to keep topping the pot up with hot water and keep an eye on it, since the urad tends to foam and overflow. In any case, the daal should be cooked enough so that you can mash them with the back of a spoon.

4. Carefully release the steam from the pressure cooker or pot and add the tomato, chillies, ginger, garlic, lemon juice, sugar and salt. Whisk the daal using a balloon whisk. Continue to boil for 10 minutes and top up with water depending on how thick you prefer it. If you like it on the thicker side, continue to boil the daal until the desired consistency is reached.

5. For the tadka, heat the ghee in a small pan. Add all the ingredients for the tadka. Allow the spices to crackle for a few seconds.

6. Immediately pour the hot tadka over the daal. Garnish with the chopped coriander (cilantro) and some spicy chilli oil, if preferred.

Vegan?
Swap the butter-based ghee for Vegan Ghee (see page 244) or use oil.

Gluten free?
Use a gluten-free asafoetida or omit this ingredient.

Make it a feast!
This daal is delicious alongside my Zafrani Mushroom Pulao (see page 173), or any kind of vegetable rice.

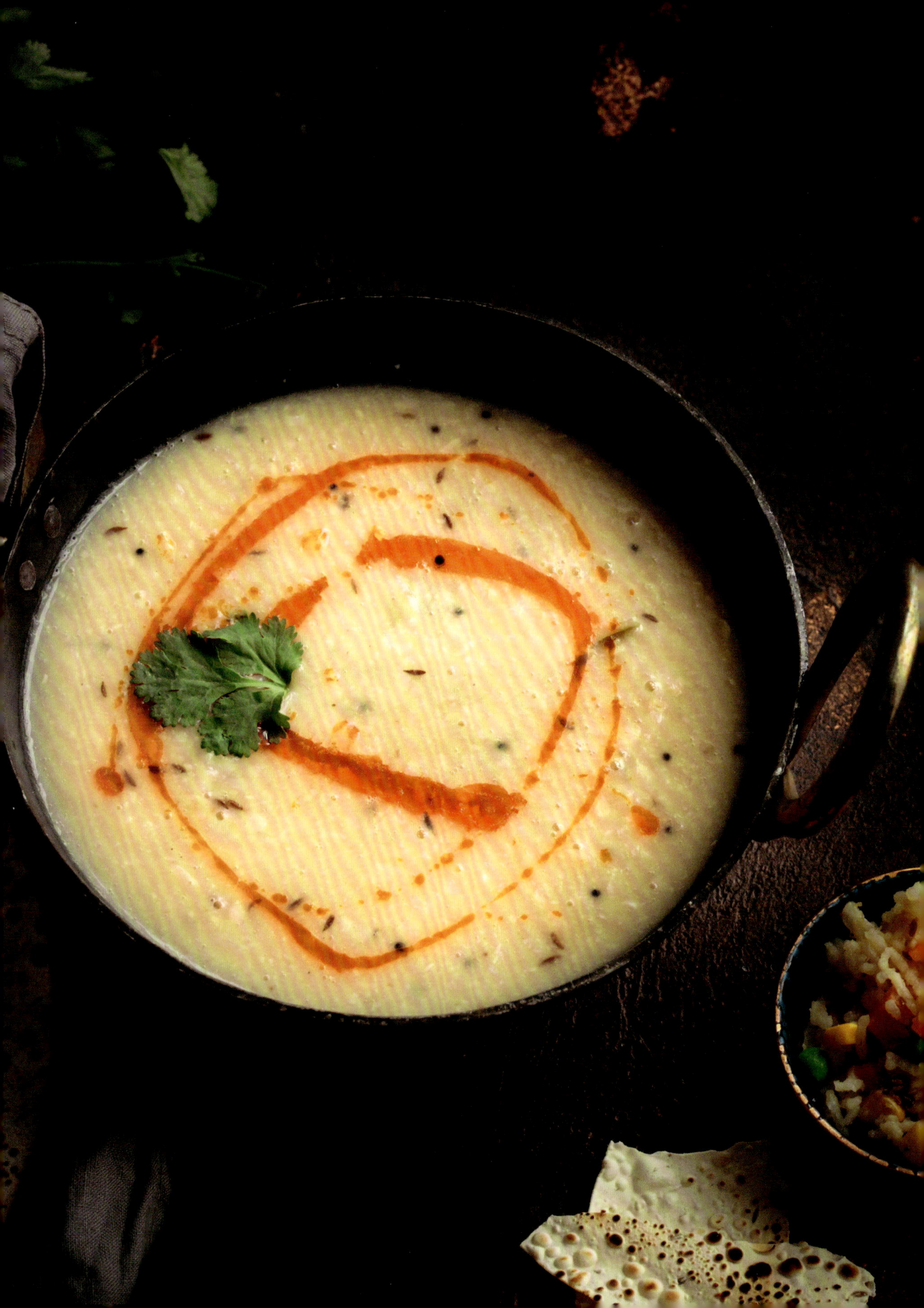

To Sanjana
with love from Dad xxx

Pasta Daal

200 gm toor dal
1.5 L hot water
1 tbsp grated
2-3 green ch
200 gm tinn
1 tsp gro
jui
1½
2

Temp
bsp ghee

stai
cloves
1 dried
½ tsp
1 tsp
10 pea

Pasta Daal

SERVES 4-6 • PREP: 15 MINS, PLUS 30 MINS SOAKING • COOK: 40 MINS

For the daal
- 200 g (7 oz/1 cup) split pigeon peas
- ⅛ tsp bicarbonate of soda (baking soda)
- 1.5 litres (50 fl oz/6⅓ cups) hot water
- 1 tbsp grated (shredded) root ginger
- 2-3 green chillies, finely chopped
- 200 g (7 oz) chopped tomatoes (canned or fresh)
- 1 tsp ground turmeric
- 1 tbsp jaggery or brown sugar
- Juice of 2 large lemons
- 1½ tsp salt

To temper the daal
- 1 tbsp ghee
- ½ tsp mustard seeds
- 1 tsp cumin seeds
- 5-cm (2-inch) cinnamon stick
- 1 star anise
- 1 dried red chilli
- 2 cloves
- 5-6 curry leaves
- ¼ tsp asafoetida
- 10 peanuts
- 10 cashews

To serve
- 150g (5 oz) spiral-shaped pasta of your choice
- 2 tbsp chopped fresh coriander (cilantro) (optional)

My dad's approach to cooking has always been sensible. Looking back, I notice that whenever it was his turn cook dinner, he would use up every scrap of food. His cooking style is a product of his early life in East Africa as one of 11 siblings. This recipe for Pasta Daal is a fine example of his frugality. A favourite of mine growing up, it's central heating for the soul and puts yesterday's daal to good use. This is a Gujarati-style daal we usually enjoy with rice, but the winding crevices of spiral pasta shapes quite flawlessly flood with daal. This is an Indo-Italian friendship that was meant to be. P.S. After a long simmer, the nuts turn so soft and creamy. People will fight over them.

1. Rinse the daal in plenty of cold water, rubbing it between your palms to remove any surface dirt. Repeat this process, changing the water twice more. Soak in boiling hot water with the bicarbonate of soda (baking soda) for 30 minutes.

2. Drain the daal and add to a pressure cooker. Cover with 1 litre (34 fl oz/4¼ cups) room temperature water and close the lid. Cook for 5 whistles. If you're using a pressure pot, cook on high pressure for 15 minutes. Carefully release the steam. The daal should be mushy, almost liquid. Strain the daal into a large bowl to ensure it's a smooth, flowing consistency or briefly whiz with a handheld stick (immersion) blender. Set aside.

3. To temper the daal, heat the ghee in a large, heavy-based pan. Add the mustard seeds and allow them to crackle. Next, add the cumin seeds, cinnamon stick, star anise, dried red chilli, cloves, curry leaves, asafoetida, peanuts, and cashews. Sauté over a low heat for 1-2 minutes, or just until the cashews begin to brown slightly.

4. Add the ginger and fresh chillies to the pan. Cook for 30 seconds and then tip in the tomatoes. Add the ground turmeric and jaggery, stir well and allow the masala to come to a gentle simmer. Stir continuously to encourage the jaggery to melt into the masala.

5. Carefully pour the daal mixture into the masala along with an additional 500 ml (17 fl oz/2 cups) hot water, lemon juice and the salt. Bring to a boil, stirring, then lower the heat and simmer gently for 20 minutes. Stir frequently to ensure the daal does not settle at the base of the pan. If you feel the daal is too thick, thin it out with more water. (Boiling the daal is imperative as this process extracts more flavour from the spices, resulting in a tastier daal.)

6. Cook the pasta according to the packet instructions. Drain well and stir into the hot daal.

7. Ladle into bowls and top with a dollop of ghee or butter to soothe your soul. Garnish with chopped coriander (cilantro) if you like.

Note
If you don't have a pressure cooker or pressure pot, you can simmer the daal in a pot with a tight-fitting lid until the lentils are tender. You'll need to keep topping the pot up with hot water (approximately 250 ml/8½ fl oz/1 cup water).

Vegan?
Swap the butter-based ghee for Vegan Ghee (see page 244) or use oil.

Gluten free?
Use your favourite brand of gluten-free pasta. Check the asafoetida is a gluten-free variety, since many brands blend it with wheat flour. If you can't find a gluten-free asafoetida, simply leave it out.

Make it a feast!
A spoonful of cold plain yogurt on the side is always a welcome addition.

Dry Daal

SERVES 4 • PREP: 15 MINS, PLUS 30 MINS SOAKING • COOK: 35 MINS

Not an oxymoron. It may or may not surprise you that daal is not always prepared in a stew-like or soupy fashion. Contrary to the texture daal is known for in the West, it's very common for Indian homes to make dry daal dishes, akin to curry. These dry-style lentils are usually paired with a runny dish like kadhi (tempered hot buttermilk), but they also make for filling meals all by themselves. Like most things worth scooping, I like to scoop up my dry daal with roti or paratha. The warm flavours of this ghee-drizzled dry daal bring instant gratification on cold winter evenings. This version is made with split mung beans (yellow moong daal), but it's just as delicious with whole green mung beans (moong).

For the daal
- 200 g (7 oz/1 cup) split mung beans
- ⅛ tsp bicarbonate of soda (baking soda)
- 2.5-cm (1-inch) cinnamon stick
- 4 cloves
- 1 black cardamom pod
- 1 dried Indian bay leaf
- 3 tbsp ghee
- 1 tsp cumin seeds
- 1 tbsp minced root ginger
- 1 tbsp minced garlic
- 4 green chillies, slit lengthways
- ¼ tsp asafoetida
- 2 tomatoes, finely chopped
- ¼ tsp ground turmeric
- ½ tsp chilli powder
- 1 tsp freshly ground black pepper
- 1 tsp salt

To garnish
- 2-cm (¾-inch) piece of root ginger, cut into matchsticks
- Crispy fried onions
- 1 tbsp melted ghee
- 2 tbsp chopped fresh coriander (cilantro)

1. Rinse the daal in plenty of cold water, rubbing it between your palms to remove any surface dirt. Repeat this process, changing the water twice more. Soak in boiling hot water with the bicarbonate of soda (baking soda) for 30 minutes.

2. Fill a large pan with water and add the daal, along with the cinnamon stick, cloves, black cardamom pod and bay leaf. Bring to a rolling boil and cover with a tight-fitting lid. Cook the daal for around 20 minutes, or until it's tender when pressed but holds its shape otherwise. (Think of it like cooking pasta to the al dente stage.) Drain the daal and whole spices in a sieve (strainer) or colander, reserving 100 ml (3½ fl oz/ scant ½ cup) of the cooking liquid.

3. Heat the ghee in the same pan. Add the cumin seeds, ginger, garlic, chillies and asafoetida. Allow to sizzle for 30 seconds before adding in the tomatoes, ground turmeric, chilli powder, black pepper and salt. Cook for 5 minutes, stirring continuously, until the ghee begins to separate from the tomatoes around the sides of the pan.

4. Tip the cooked daal into the pan, along with the whole spices and a couple of tablespoons of the reserved cooking liquid. Stir well. Cover and cook over a very low heat for 6–8 minutes. If it feels much too dry, or the daal is still a little too firm for you, add a touch more water and continue to cook gently with the lid on.

5. Remove the lid, turn up the heat to high and stir with a spatula for a few minutes to let any excess moisture escape – this is a dry daal after all. Each lentil should still be robust enough to hold its shape without turning to paste as you stir.

6. Garnish with the ginger matchsticks, crispy fried onions, a drizzle of ghee and chopped coriander (cilantro).

Note
For once, I don't recommend using a pressure cooker for this particular daal recipe (sorry ancestors). If you're planning to cook split mung beans in a soupy fashion, it's fine to use a pressure cooker, but for dry daal, it's best to follow the method in this recipe. The pressure cooker takes no prisoners when it comes to cooking daal to a pulp and, although desirable for many daal dishes, that is not required here. Each lentil should be cooked through, but not to the point of mashing under gentle pressure.

Vegan?
Swap the butter-based ghee for Vegan Ghee (see page 244) or use oil.

Gluten free?
Use a gluten-free asafoetida or omit this inredient.

Make it a feast!
Scoop up mounds of this Dry Daal with Everyday Roti (see page 157).

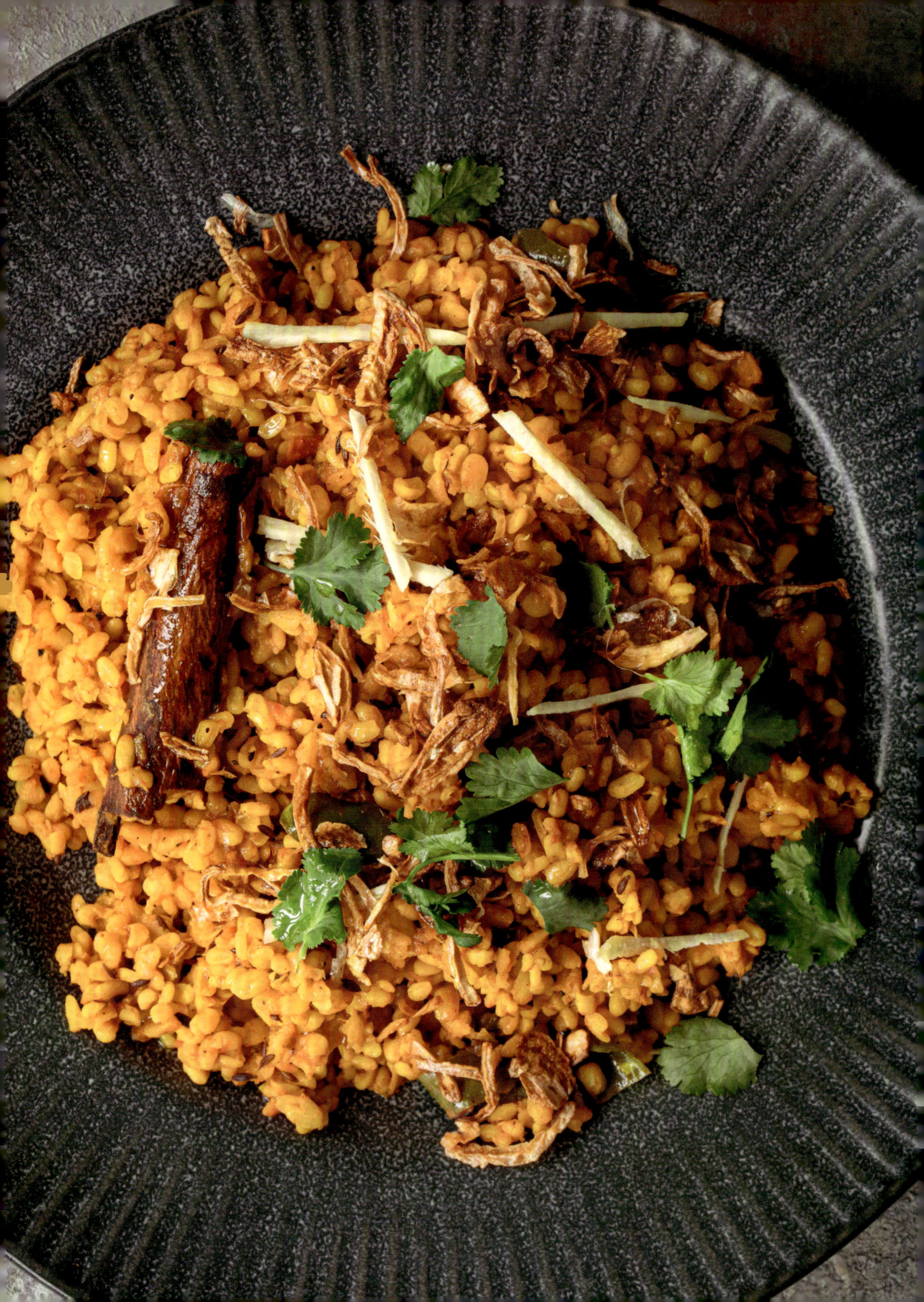

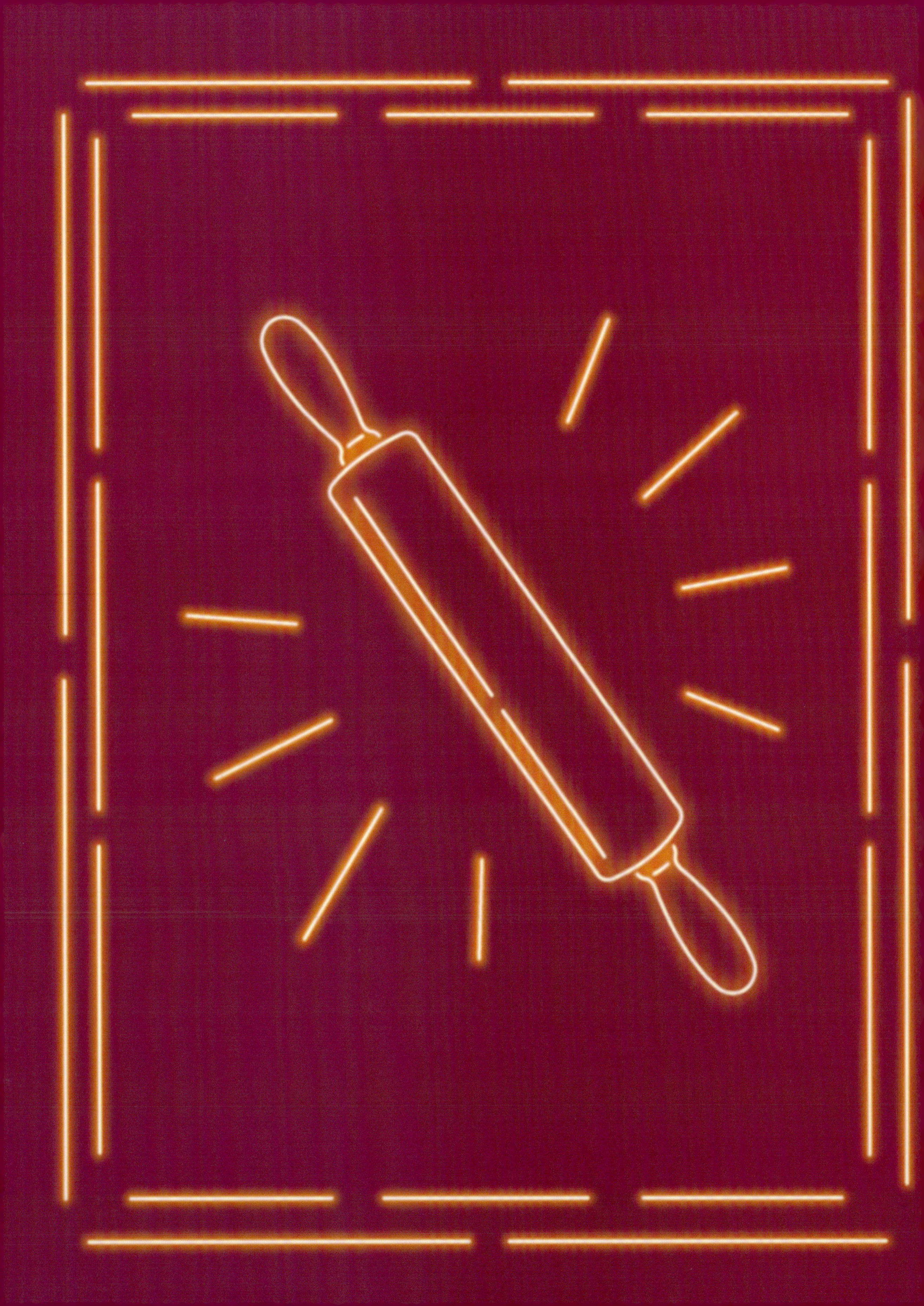

Roti AND Rice

The roti can feel your emotions.

The accessibility and versatility of roti and rice make them some of the biggest food heroes in an Indian cook's playbook. They're the basics, yet their simplicity can often make the techniques involved feel daunting. They need not be. Rice is thought to have been cultivated in the Indian subcontinent since as early as 5000 bc. Plain, boiled rice is a mainstay of the Indian kitchen since it goes with just about everything. Biryani and pulao are more likely to be reserved for special occasions, but these days, anything goes and shortcuts are forever welcome. A weekend biryani can be quite the treat, when time permits! In a similar way, chapati is seen to be the chief of everyday breads, whilst the more indulgent naans, parathas and fried breads are eaten less often. Dosa, pav, rice, roti and breads made from other grains, like millet, cornmeal and sorghum, are also treasured elements of everyday family meals, depending on their background. In the case of our Gujarati home, 80 per cent of the time, dinner was shaak and rotli (curry and chapati) or daal bhaat (daal and rice). On special occasions it was all four (daal, bhaat, shaak, rotli). It could be banquet-worthy or simplified for everyday eating. The point is that every dish has its place on the table. In the absence of cutlery, breads serve as effective utensils for scooping up curries, daals and pickles in the Indian home. For the more dextrous, compressing rice between the fingers to create a spoon-like indentation in the scoop is the greatest way to enjoy a meal.

Learning to make roti and rice are some of the most useful skills I've learnt in life. Not only because they're fuel for the day, but because for people of South Asian heritage, they're at the core of our culinary traditions and represent the notion of food itself. Roti and rice are the bread and butter of the home: simple, filling, inexpensive and readily made with few ingredients. Rotis don't have to be perfectly round to taste good, but they must be rolled flat and cooked through. As for rice, it can be prepared in several different ways, depending on the meal, from biryani and pulao to rice-based varieties of dosa, khichdi and plain boiled rice. These 'basics' are portrayed as uncomplicated but cooking them doesn't always feel simple. When there are very few ingredients at play, there's pressure to hone your techniques. There's not a lot to hide behind. I'd like to show you the steps I follow to ensure my roti and rice hit the spot.

The middle finger method

Yes, it's not a myth, it exists. I grew up trying to decipher the Asian method for cooking rice (a.k.a. the middle finger method or knuckle method). It calls for measuring the amount of water required by touching the surface of the rice with the middle finger, approximately 2.5 cm (1 inch). Almost every Asian will tell you it always works, while simultaneously applying their own rules. Coming from a family where an aversion to kitchen scales is enmeshed into our DNA, I was taught 'the middle finger method' for cooking rice. This is an age-old technique by which soaked rice is placed into a saucepan with enough water to reach the second line of the middle finger; that is, when the finger is placed touching the top of the rice.

Put into practice, the method is subject to discrepancy and depends on many factors, from the unique form of your hands, the width of the pan, the variety of rice and the intensity of the heat source. The ancestors might be shaking their heads at my doubt, but inconsistent results aren't my favourite. Teaching people to cook Indian food through various forms of media all these years has meant I've had to embrace the kitchen scales. In my home, measuring by eye (or by fingers, fists and Cornflakes bowls) is strictly reserved for cooking for pleasure, not functionality.

No, your roti doesn't need to be round

The wheaty smell that floods a home when the first leopard-spotted roti comes off a battered steel tawa surrounds me with a comfort that can only be compared to a warm hug from your favourite aunty wearing her fuzziest fleece. My love of roti is unwavering, innate, something infused into the very core of my being. It was love at first sniff. It's the sort of smell that makes your stomach gurgle and feel like an empty pit as soon as you detect a waft coming from the kitchen. Food smells are powerful, and often serve as passageways into the best and worst moments of our lives. I still delight in the smell memory (smemory, maybe?) of roti cooking on an old Primus stove at my grandparents' home in Kenya; a heady mix of toasted wheat, burning steel and kerosene.

As a child, I was utterly fascinated by the process of making roti at home. To think that you could produce a balloon of bread from just flour, water and oil was mind blowing. Aged four or five, I'd make raggedy, uneven flatbreads using a mini roti-making set my aunty bought me. It was from Popat Stores on Ealing Road in Wembley, a suburb of north-west London. It's an institution of an Indian cookware shop and a place we'd visit every summer holiday. My brother would browse comics featuring his favourite Hindu gods and demons, while I'd eyeball the old-school CorningWare dishes, catering-size pots so big I could neatly curl up inside one, and of course, the kids' cookware section. In this aisle was a pink and green-rimmed miniature wooden roti board and tiny rolling pin. Up until that moment, I'd never wanted anything more in my life (except for the Mr Frosty I never quite managed to convince my parents to buy). It had to be mine. Mum's sister, Nimu masi, saw the desperation in my eyes and very kindly bought it for me. To this day, it's one of the best gifts I've ever received.

Something I was taught at the very beginning of my Indian bread-making journey was that it's not only the rolling technique that makes for the perfect stack of roti – it's also the cook's mood! The roti can feel your emotions. Essentially, this refers to a few basic techniques. The first is to knead the dough less than you think you should.

Overdeveloping the gluten makes the roti chewy. Therefore, for a softer finish, knead the dough only for a couple of minutes. In addition to this, bind the dough with hot water, which inhibits gluten formation and produces a tender chapati. A touch of oil will also keep the cooked chapati pliable and primed for tearing and scooping.

The second piece of advice is to roll with gentle pressure. Up and down, with a light touch, almost hovering. Getting the roti to automatically turn as you roll is when you know you've mastered it. I'd know when my mum was having a bad day because on those days her rotis wouldn't balloon up as they usually did – her rolling in those moments was far too vigorous. Wide-eyed, I'd peer over our cooker, roti after roti, puffing up like giant hot-air balloons suspended over the Maasai Mara. I'd seen the colourful, lolly-striped balloons in the summer of '94 and they had immediately captivated my soul. The suspense that built up as they rose from flatbreads to footballs was one of the magical moments that led me to fall in love with cooking that little bit more. I was soon inspired to learn the craft of making roti, our daily bread. Every day, I would roll out the same piece of dough repeatedly, like it was Play-Doh and by the end of it, my poor dad would have to eat the splat-shaped biscuit. 'Map of Africa', we'd call it. I'd present my frisbee roti to him with such pride. Of course, he'd tell me it was delicious and that I was becoming a pro. Thanks, Dad. All that practice meant that I did, eventually, produce my very own hot-air balloon rotis.

Styles of bread vary across India, and they've travelled far and wide. Generally speaking, wheat and cornmeal are most commonly used in breads from the North, rice, lentils and millet in the South, multi-grain breads using millet and sorghum in the West, and a combination of rice, lentils and wheat in the East. Having said this, in these modern times, ingredients are widely available and, therefore, a variety can be enjoyed by all. Various iterations of roti, paratha and poori exist in every corner of the globe, from the Indian Ocean to Africa and the Caribbean, all the way to the South Pacific.

In this chapter, we'll explore a handful of Indian bread and rice recipes for everyday as well as some for special occasions. I hope these recipes and tips inspire you to create your own roti and rice magic at home.

Tawa or no tawa

A tawa is a flat or concave frying pan (skillet) used for preparing a variety of breads and curries. For roti, naan and paratha, I use either steel or anodised aluminium tawas, although clay is the most traditional option. I find they give the bread great browning and flavour. If you can't find any of these, a cast-iron frying pan works wonders. Non-stick frying pans will also do the job, but the browning and therefore the toasty flavour may not be quite so pronounced.

Roti and Rice **151**

Rice

There are many camps when it comes to cooking rice. There are those who swear by the middle finger method to cook rice by absorption, and those who prefer the pasta-style method. Some rice is best steamed (see Sticky Hakka Fried Rice on page 174). The point is, there are lots of different methods, each suited to the type of rice and the cooks' preference. I come from a family who adopt the pasta-style method and while it produces amazing results, I still went against the grain and began using the absorption method (sorry, mum). Rice rebel.

Choose the best quality rice insofar as your budget allows. Basmati is always a great choice and there are plenty of options for it in supermarkets. The word 'basmati' means aromatic, and it lives up to the name. For example, short-grain rice, like West Bengal's Gobindobhog, is a stellar option for khichdi, since this variety has so much aroma and creaminess. For khichdi, any short-grain or even broken rice can be used. Since we're striving for a creamy finish, using long-grain basmati would be counterintuitive. In the '70s, my mother's father would use pudding rice to make seriously creamy pressure-cooker khichdi.

How to cook rice (pasta-style method)

Ideal for cooking long-grain varieties of white rice but can also be used for short-grain varieties. The method calls for washed and soaked rice to be boiled in a large pot filled with plenty of water, the same as if you were cooking pasta. The water is later drained and the rice is allowed to stand until the steam dissipates. This is the way in which rice is parboiled for making biryani (before being layered with meats and/or vegetables).

Pros:	Cons:
• Every grain of rice will be long and separate. • Takes the guesswork or measuring out of cooking rice.	• You'll lose a bit of the natural rice aroma.

1. Place the rice in a sieve (strainer) and wash in plenty of cold running water, until the water begins to run mostly clear. This cleans the rice and removes excess starch from the surface to encourage separate grains.

2. Soak the rice in cold water for a minimum of 30 minutes to soften the grains. This might feel like an additional and unnecessary step, but it removes surplus starch from within the grains and promotes even cooking. The longer the rice soaks, the shorter the cooking time.

3. Fill a large, heavy-based pan with water and bring it to a boil. You can add whole spices like cinnamon sticks, cardamom pods and cloves, if you like a more aromatic rice, otherwise leave it plain. Add salt once the rice is almost at boiling point as the water will take longer to come to a boil if you salt it at the beginning. The amount of water you use is irrelevant since it just needs to be enough for the grains of rice to move around freely. Think of it as if you were cooking pasta. Foamy white starch from the rice will rise to the surface, so do watch the pot in case it overflows.

4. After around 7–8 minutes of continuous roll boiling over a high heat, the rice should be around 80 per cent cooked. The best way to test if the rice is done is quite simply to try a grain. It should be tender, with a very little bite. Think al dente, remember. The rice is going to continue to cook as it stands, so cooking to full doneness at this point will result in a batch of overcooked rice later.

5. Drain the rice though a colander or sieve (strainer), leaving it to stand, uncovered, for 20 minutes.

6. You can drizzle the rice with melted ghee or butter at this point. Allow the excess steam to do the work of an expensive scented candle and fill your kitchen with the fragrance of the cooked rice. The rice will continue to cook in the residual heat.

7. After the elapsed time, the rice grains should look like they're reaching for the sky (the top layer will 'stand to attention'). This is when you know the grains are cooked to perfection.

8. Gently fluff up the grains with a fork and serve.

How to cook rice (absorption method)

Ideal for cooking short-grain varieties of white rice, or if you don't want to lose too much of the natural aroma of the rice. The rice will need to be washed and soaked, then cooked with a measured amount of water. Using this method, the rice should be left to stand, covered, for 20 minutes after it's removed from the heat source.

Pros:	Cons:
• Preserves the natural aroma of the rice (particularly nice if you're cooking something fragrant like basmati). • Can produce lovely and long grains, but the rice will hold more starch. I prefer the texture of rice cooked this way as it's naturally a bit stickier.	• You'll have to measure the water to rice ratio (2:1).

1. Place the rice in a sieve (strainer) and wash in plenty of cold running water, until the water begins to run mostly clear. This cleans the rice and removes excess starch from the surface to encourage separate grains.

2. Soak the rice in cold water for a minimum of 30 minutes to soften the grains. This might feel like an additional and unnecessary step, but it removes surplus starch from within the grains and promotes even cooking. The longer the rice soaks, the shorter the cooking time.

3. Drain the soaked rice and place it in a heavy-based pot (one with a tight-fitting lid). To the pot, add 2x the volume of water to the amount of dried unsoaked rice you're cooking. Add a pinch of salt and any whole spices you wish to use. Bring the water to a rolling boil. Allow the rice to roll boil over a high heat for 5 minutes. Once almost all the water has evaporated and only a few bubbles are visible through the surface of the rice, switch off the heat and cover the pot with a tight-fitting lid.

4. Do not remove the lid for at least 20 minutes. Curiosity kills the rice. Make yourself a cup of tea instead.

5. After 20 minutes, remove the lid. The rice should be perfectly cooked as the excess water has been absorbed into the grains, finishing off the process in steam.

6. You can drizzle with melted ghee or butter at this point. As with the above method, the rice grains should look like they're reaching for the sky (the top layer will 'stand to attention'). This is when you know the grains are cooked to perfection.

7. Fluff up the grains with a fork and serve. This method will require a more vigorous fork through to fluff up the rice than the first technique.

A side-by-side comparison of the two rice cooking methods. The same variety of rice was used for both. Each batch was washed and soaked for 30 minutes prior to cooking.

There was no significant flavour difference between the two tests. The pasta-style method lacked a little aroma in comparison to the batch cooked using the absorption method. Having said this, the grains separated much more easily when forked through. The grains of the batch prepared using the absorption method were slightly plumper. Due to a higher level of starch remaining in the rice, the grains were not as separate after sitting a while. Both methods produce excellent results, however, so choose whichever one suits you best.

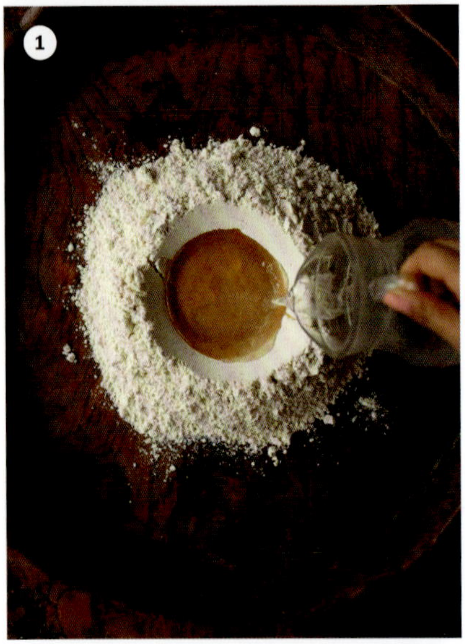
1

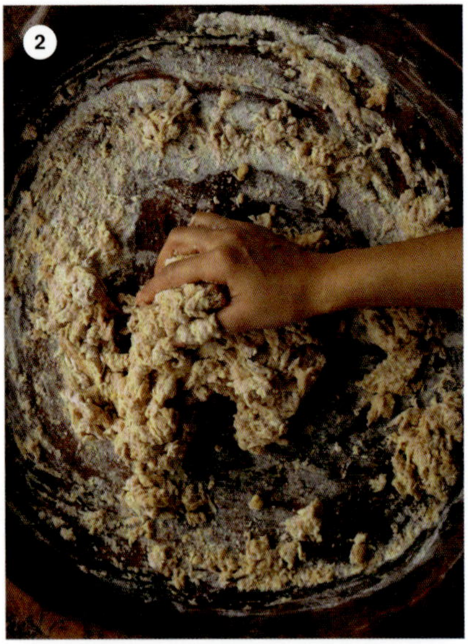
2

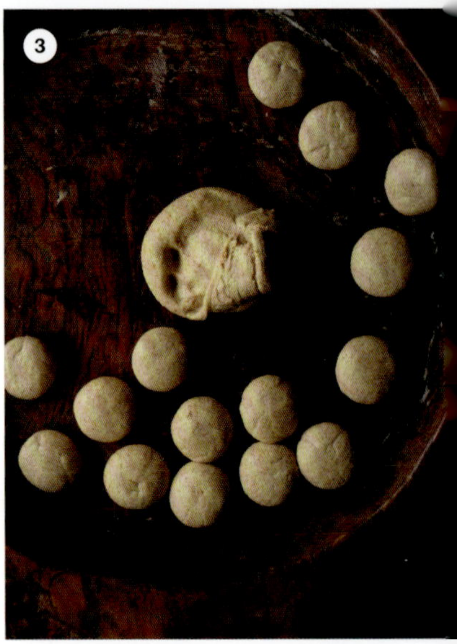
3

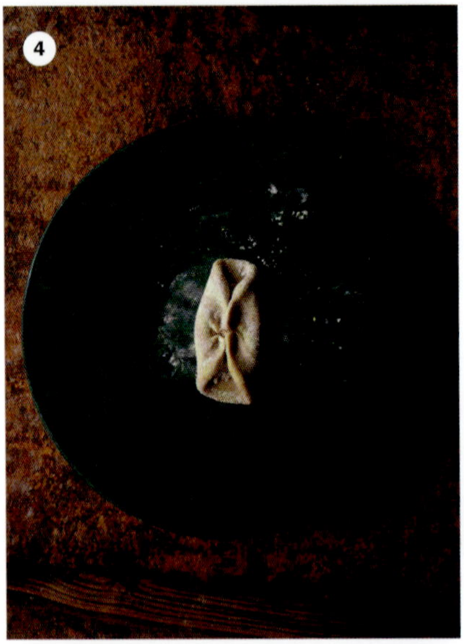
4

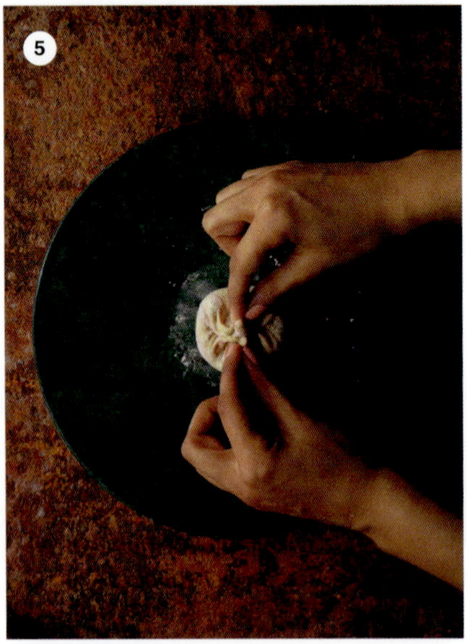
5

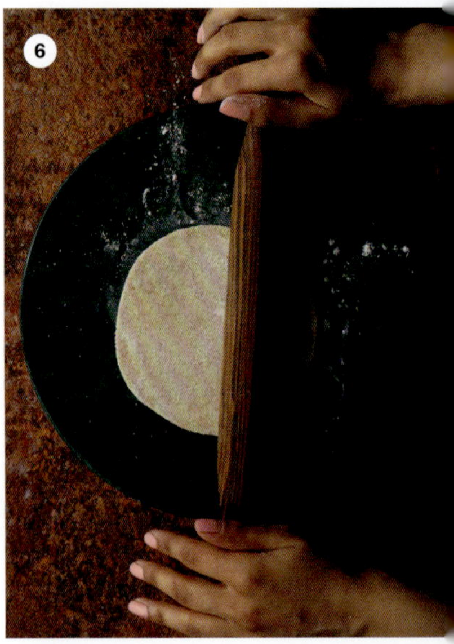
6

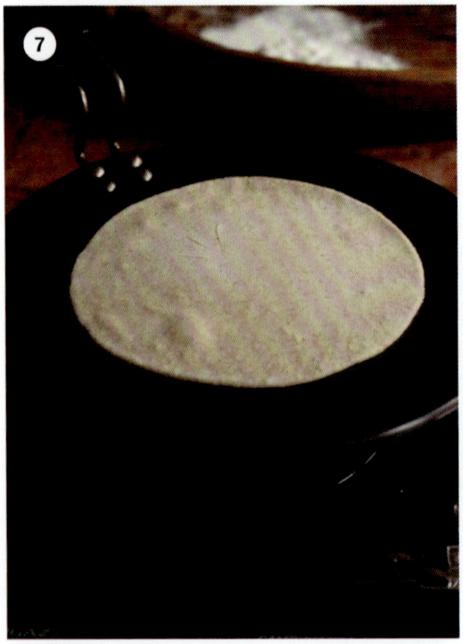
7

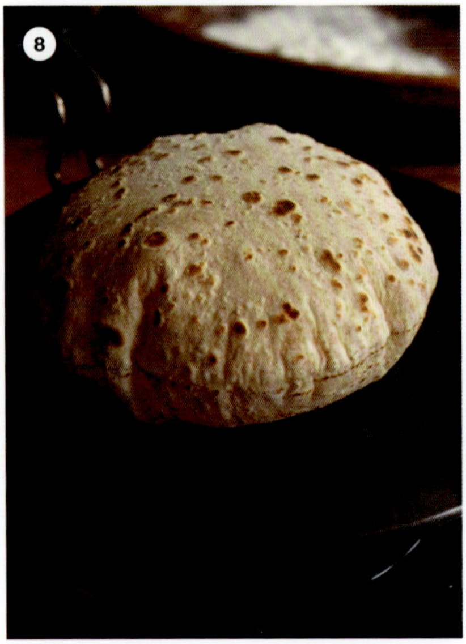
8

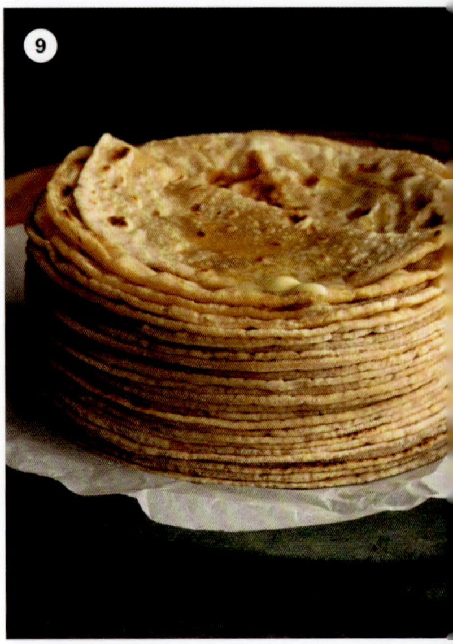
9

Everyday Roti

MAKES 8 ROTIS • PREP: 45 MINS, PLUS 15 MINS RESTING • COOK: 20 MINS

V VG

375 g (13¼ oz/3 cups) wholewheat chapati flour
50 ml (1¾ fl oz/scant ¼ cup) oil
175 ml (6 fl oz/¾ cup) freshly boiled water

Make it a feast!

Serve alongside any curry or use as wraps.

As far as day-to-day cooking goes, soft roti (also called phulka or rotli in my mother tongue of Gujarati) are the glue that sticks everything on the Indian dinner table together. They scoop up curry and daal, pickle, and everything in between. The smoky, wheaty smell that emanates from a roti tawa brings on an instant tummy rumble, no matter one's age. The best flour for making Indian roti is wholewheat flour, also called atta. This is a perfect balance of the right texture and flavour for soft roti. It's a misconception that rotis need to be round. They simply need to be evenly rolled in order that they are evenly cooked. Don't sweat the small stuff.

1. To make the dough, place the flour in a large bowl with deep sides. Make a well in the centre and add the oil and boiled water (1). Mix with a spoon to create a rough, shaggy dough and leave for 2 minutes. Then knead for 2–3 minutes, or until soft (2). Cover with a damp dish towel and allow to rest for 15 minutes.

2. To make the roti, roll the dough into small ping pong ball-sized pieces (3). Keep some flour on a plate for rolling out. Preheat a tawa over a medium heat. Allow it to heat up for 5 minutes. Get your rolling board and rolling pin ready or roll out directly on a clean surface. If you're using a rolling board, it's a good idea to keep a dish towel under the board so it doesn't move around while you roll.

3. Take a piece of dough and roll it between your palms, flattening it slightly. Dip each side in flour. Roll it once up and down with the rolling pin. Take a pinch of flour, place it in the middle of the dough and then, using your index finger and thumb and starting from the outer edges, pinch it closed (4, 5). This step isn't something everyone traditionally does, but it's what my mum taught me for soft roti that rise beautifully.

4. Flatten the dough using your palm and dip each side again in flour. Next, begin rolling the dough in a circular motion, teasing the dough to spin around with each rolling (6). If you can't do this, pick up the roti with one hand and move it a quarter of a turn. The aim is to create a round-ish roti with an even surface, that's around 2 mm (⅛ inch) in thickness and 15 cm (6 inches) in diameter. Remember, they don't have to be perfectly round.

5. To cook the roti, place the roti on the preheated tawa and cook on one side until little bubbles appear on the surface – around 10 seconds (7). Flip it using a metal turner or heatproof spatula. Do not be tempted to do this with your fingers – burns are no fun. Cook on the second side until small, even brown spots appear all over the bottom of the roti – around 30 seconds. Flip it again. Now, this is the rising side. Don't worry if your rotis don't rise the first few times you try it. It comes with practice. They'll still taste delicious. Cook until darker, less evenly spread patches appear on the bottom – around 15–20 seconds (8). Flip the roti again and place it this side up on a kitchen paper-lined plate. Spread with butter or ghee, if desired.

6. Repeat this process for all the dough, stacking the roti as you finish cooking each one (9). You can keep them warm in an insulated container or a lidded casserole dish (Dutch oven) lined with kitchen paper.

Laccha Paratha

MAKES 6 PARATHA • PREP: 45 MINS, PLUS 1½ HOURS RESTING • COOK: 15 MINS

400 g (14 oz/3¼ cups) plain (all-purpose) flour or wholewheat chapati flour
1 tsp salt
2 tsp sugar
225 ml (7⅔ fl oz/1 cup minus 1 tbsp) lukewarm water
2 tbsp ghee (or oil)
170 ml (5¾ fl oz/¾ cup) oil, plus extra for rolling

Notes

Use all plain (all-purpose) flour and warm milk or warm coconut milk to knead for Malabar Parotta. You can also add an extra teaspoon of sugar, since this variety is usually on the sweeter side. They're perfect with spicy dishes like my Savoy Cabbage Ghee Roast (see page 129).

Add a clove or two of minced garlic to the dough for gorgeous garlic bread flavours. Particularly good with Black Pepper Tadka Daal (see page 136).

Drop a large pinch of saffron into the full amount of boiling water and allow to infuse for 30 minutes. Once the water temperature has dropped to lukewarm, bind the dough with it to make daffodil-hued saffron parathas. These parathas are particularly evocative of Mughlai cuisine and pair wonderfully with a creamy North Indian-style curry, daal or grill.

Make it a feast!

Serve alongside any curry or as a wrap for Beetroot Paneer Tikka (see page 74) or Achaari Matoke (see page 185).

Vegan?

Swap ghee for oil, or Vegan Ghee (see page 244).

Roti's flakier cousin. The vortex of layers depends on the elasticity of the dough, so it's important to knead it long enough to develop the gluten. You should be able to stretch the dough so thin you could read a newspaper through it. For me, laccha paratha are at their happiest when served alongside daal.

1. Place the flour in a large mixing bowl with deep sides. Add the salt and sugar and stir to combine. Make a well in the centre and pour in the water. Mix to create a rough, shaggy dough.

2. Once the dough comes together, turn it out onto a large, clean work surface and knead for 5 minutes (1) until smooth and elastic. Add 2 tablespoons of ghee and continue to knead for a further 10 minutes until the dough is very smooth and stretchy. Return to the bowl, cover with cling film (plastic wrap) and allow to rest at room temperature for 1 hour. The longer you rest the dough, the flakier the paratha will be. You can also refrigerate the dough (tightly wrapped in cling film) for up to 24 hours. Allow the dough to come to room temperature before making the paratha.

3. Divide the rested dough into 6 equal portions and roughly roll into balls. Keep them covered in cling film when you are not working the dough.

4. Lightly oil the work surface. Take one piece of dough and press it out, either using your hands or a rolling pin until it's so thin you can see through it (2). Spread the entire surface with about 1 tablespoon of oil. It's fine if there are a few holes in the dough.

5. Working from the longest edge, roughly concertina the dough into a long snake (3). Coil the long piece of dough up into a spiral (4), tucking the loose end underneath.

6. Repeat for the remaining dough balls (5) and then cover once more with cling film. Allow the prepared dough spirals to rest for 30 minutes.

7. Pat or roll a rested spiral of dough into a rough circle, about 17 cm (6½ inches) in diameter using either your hands or a rolling pin (6,7). It doesn't need to be perfectly round.

8. Place a tawa or frying pan (skillet) over a medium heat. Allow to warm for a minute or two. Carefully place the rolled paratha on to the pan. It's okay if it pulls out of shape a little. Cook for 90 seconds on each side, or until golden all over (8).

9. Pop the cooked paratha on a clean dish towel, pick up the sides and clap it between your hands four or five times, rotating it between claps to reveal the flaky goodness (9).

10. Repeat this process for all the parathas.

11. Serve immediately or stack in an insulated container lined with a clean dish towel to keep warm.

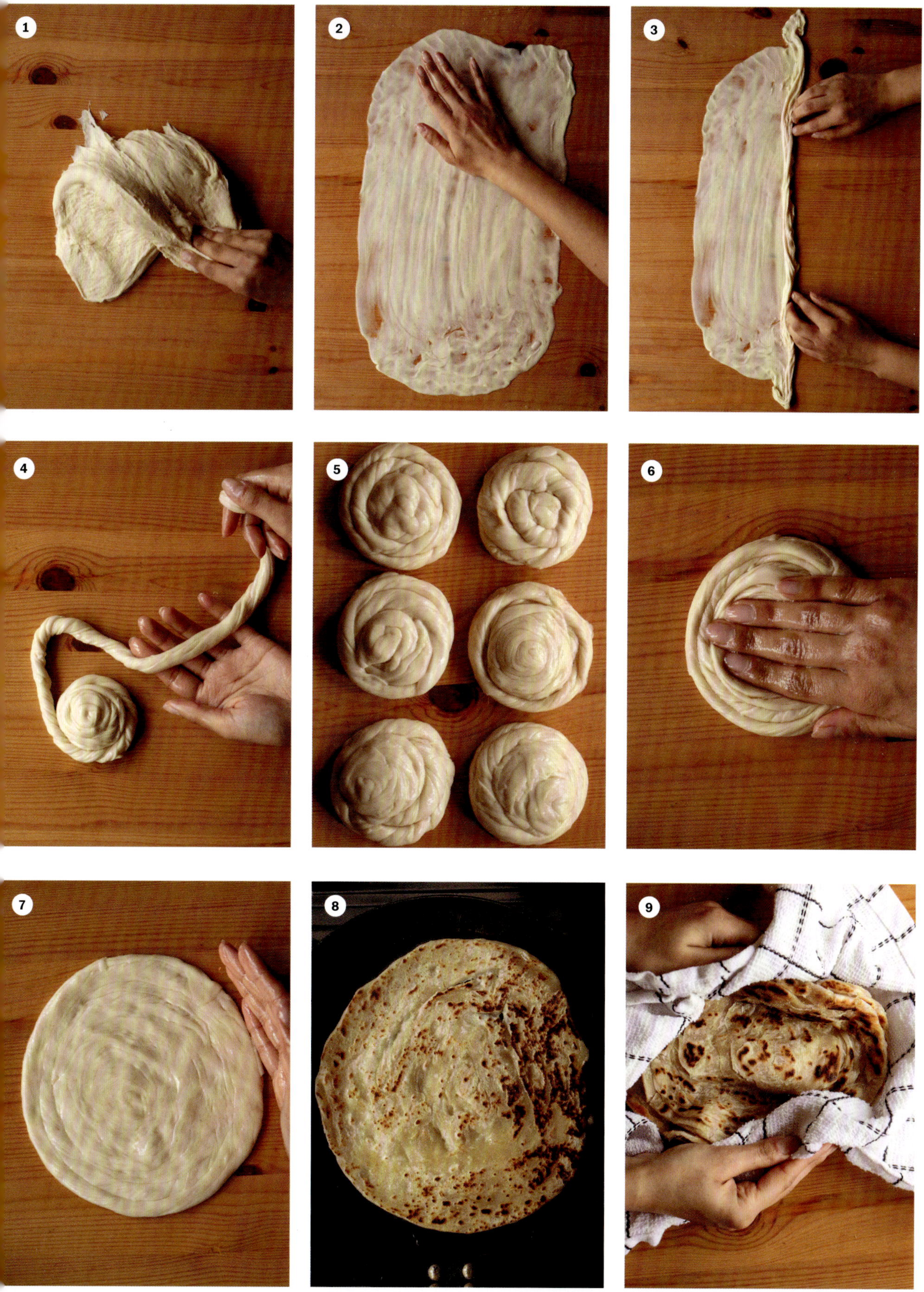
1
2
3
4
5
6
7
8
9

Halloumi and Mint Paratha

MAKES 6 PARATHA • PREP: 45 MINS, PLUS 20 MINS RESTING • COOK: 20 MINS

V

185 g (6½ oz/1½ cups) wholewheat chapati flour
1 tbsp gram flour
¼ tsp salt
130 ml (4⅓ fl oz/½ cup) warm water
½ tbsp oil
2 tbsp ghee or oil

For the halloumi and mint filling
225 g (8 oz) halloumi, soaked in hot water for 10 minutes
1–2 green chillies, finely chopped
¼ tsp ground cinnamon
¼ tsp nigella seeds
1 tbsp finely chopped fresh mint leaves

For the honey butter
60 g (2 oz/¼ cup) salted butter
2 tbsp honey

Make it a feast!
Try these for brunch, lunch or dinner with achaar and a cup of Masala Chai (see page 24).

Everyone's favourite squeaky cheese brings big flavours to flatbread with these Indo-Mediterranean stuffed paratha. Yeah, of course potatoes are the all-time classic filling, but bread stuffed with cheese and herbs will forever be the harbinger of comforting food contentment. Slather liberally with honey butter and serve with fridge-cold pickle for brunch, lunch or as a simple dinner.

1. To make the dough, mix the wholewheat chapati flour, gram flour and salt in a large bowl. Make a well in the centre and gradually add the warm water. Use your hands to bring the mixture together. Once it starts to look less like a shaggy mixture and more like a dough, knead for 2–3 minutes. Add the oil and continue to knead for a further 2 minutes until smooth and soft. Cover the dough with a damp dish towel and allow to rest for 15–20 minutes.

2. To make the filling, drain and gently squeeze the soaked halloumi between kitchen paper to remove any excess moisture. Grate (shred) the halloumi into a bowl and then add the rest of the ingredients for the filling. Use your hands to mix and gently knead the filling to create a soft and pliable stuffing. It should form a ball when squeezed together. Set aside.

3. Divide the rested dough into 6 portions and roll into balls. Divide the filling into 6 equal portions.

4. Roll or pat out the dough to about 6 cm (2½ inches) in diameter. Place a portion of the filling on top, bring the dough around the filling, slowly stretching the dough to encase. Pinch the dough together to fully enclose the filling inside. There should be no gaps or holes. Dust with additional flour.

5. Place the dough on a rolling board or clean work surface and gently use your middle three fingers (palm-side down) to pat the dough into a thick disc, starting from the centre and working your way outwards. This helps to distribute the filling evenly.

6. Use a rolling pin to gently roll the paratha in a circular motion, between the centre and edges, but not too much over them. You can use your hands to turn it as you roll. Once the paratha reaches the desired size (around 20–22 cm/8–8½ inches), carefully roll up and down a few times to even out the surface. The paratha is now ready to be cooked.

7. Slap the paratha down onto a preheated tawa or frying pan (skillet) and cook over a medium heat for 30–40 seconds. Flip the paratha over with a spatula and apply a very small amount of ghee or oil all over the surface. Allow this side to cook for a minute before flipping it over and applying ghee or oil on the second side. Once it's golden brown all over, remove from the pan. Keep warm on a plate lined with kitchen paper or in a clean dish towel while you cook the remaining paratha.

8. Blend together the butter and honey and brush the hot paratha with this honey butter before serving.

Other excellent paratha fillings

The world of stuffed paratha is vast and there are so many delicious options when it comes to filling ideas. In all of the options listed below, ensure the ingredients are very finely minced or grated (shredded), and are as dry as possible. This will prevent moisture from leeching into the dough and causing tears. Half-cook grated or minced veggies and squeeze them dry before adding garam masala and any aromatics. Vegetables like grated mooli (daikon), cauliflower, carrots and onions can be salted, rested and squeezed to remove any excess liquid. The vegetable juice can be used to bind the paratha dough. If you find your filling is still too wet, sprinkle instant mashed potato powder (potato flakes) into the mixture and stir well to absorb the unwanted excess liquid. Here are some of the most popular ones:

Aloo Paratha
(the famous of them all, made with spicy mashed potatoes. Try making them with my Samosa filling on page 46)

Mooli Paratha
(grated daikon or white radish)

Gobi Paratha
(scrambled cauliflower)

Daal Paratha
(spicy mashed lentils)

Paneer Paratha
(spiced Indian cottage cheese. Try making these with my Masala Paneer on page 248)

Matar Paratha
(mashed green peas)

Keema Paratha
(minced (ground) meat or soya)

Pyaz Paratha
(grated onions)

Bhature

MAKES 12 • PREP: 25 MINS, PLUS 8 HOURS STANDING AND 2 HOURS RESTING • COOK: 15 MINS

700 g (1 lb 8¾ oz/5½ cups) self-raising flour
2 tbsp semolina
1 tbsp sugar
1½ tsp salt
100 ml (3½ fl oz/scant ½ cup) oil, plus extra to rub over the dough
125 g (4½ oz/½ cup) plain yogurt
200 ml (7 fl oz/scant 1 cup) warm water

For the starter
¼ tsp fast-action dried yeast
1 tbsp sugar
100 ml (3½ fl oz/scant ½ cup) warm water
1 tbsp plain (all-purpose) flour

Note
I use a yeast-based starter for the dough, as well as self-raising flour for fabulous flavour and magnificent puffiness.

Vegan?
Use your favourite unsweetened, plant-based yogurt.

Make it a feast!
Pair with chole (try the recipe that goes with the samosas on page 46) and Fried Caper Raita (see page 194) for a satisfying meal.

I take comfort in the fact that almost every culture and cuisine has a style of deep-fried bread they hold dear. Like a warm pillow of cosiness. India has a handful, from poori and luchi to fulecha and bhature. These fluffy and crispy bhature from North India are one of these wondrous breads that rise magically in hot oil.

1. A day ahead, begin by stirring together the ingredients for the starter in a bowl. Cover with cling film (plastic wrap) and allow to stand in a warm place for a minimum of 8 hours.

2. In a large bowl with high sides, mix the self-raising flour, semolina, sugar, salt, oil, yogurt, warm water and rested starter. Combine to form a shaggy dough and then knead for 10 minutes until smooth, soft and elastic.

3. Rub a tablespoon of oil onto the surface of the dough and place it in a large bowl. Cover the bowl with cling film and allow the dough to prove in a warm place for 2 hours.

4. Knock any air out of the dough. It won't rise a great deal. Divide the dough into 12 equal portions and roll into balls. Cover with cling film.

5. Heat the oil to 200°C (390°F).

6. Take one ball of dough and lightly dab it in some cold oil. You don't want to dust the dough with flour for this as it will fall off in the oil and burn, causing the oil to blacken.

7. Roll out the dough to around 5 cm (2 inches) wide. Carefully place it directly in the hot oil, turning with a slotted spoon after a few seconds and gently pressing the surface to encourage it to rise. If the oil is not hot enough, the bhature won't rise. Each bhature will take around 1 minute to cook. Remove from the oil, allowing any excess oil to drip away, and place in a large colander. After a few minutes you can move the bhature to a tray lined with kitchen paper if your colander is small.

8. Repeat the rolling and frying process until you have a pile of warm bhature ready to be scooped up with your favourite curries or daal and raita.

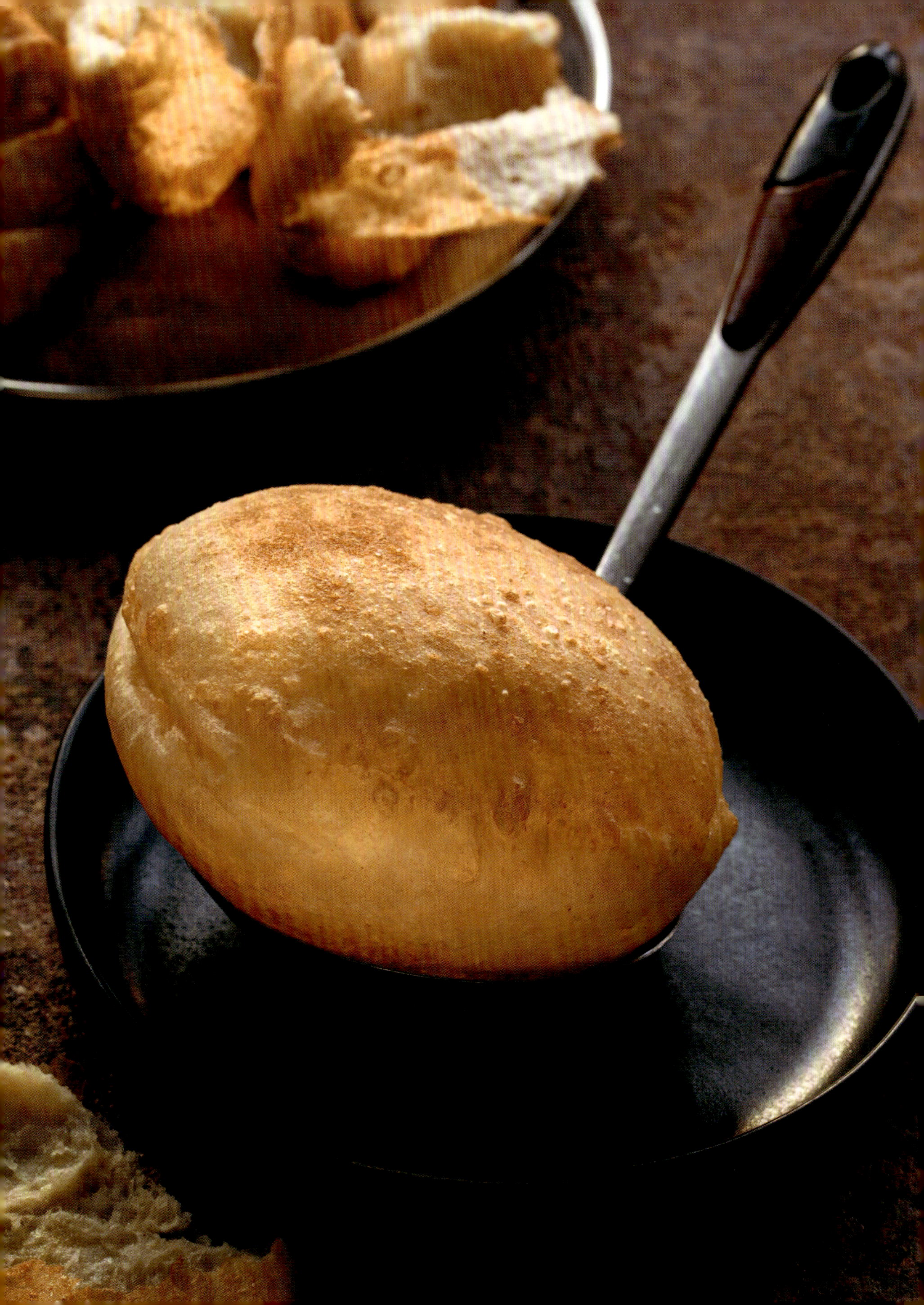

Naan Party

MAKES 6 NAANS OR 18 COIN NAANS • PREP: 10 MINS, PLUS 30 MINS RESTING • COOK: 20 MINS

For the base dough

- 325 g (11½ oz/2½ cups) self-raising flour
- 1 tbsp sugar
- ¾ tsp salt
- 1 tsp baking powder
- 1 tbsp oil plus extra to rub over the dough
- 2 tbsp full-fat plain yogurt
- 150 ml (5 fl oz/scant ⅔ cup) warm water
- 55 g (2 oz/scant ¼ cup) salted butter, melted

Note

If you prefer not to cook the naan over an open flame, it can be cooked on both sides in a very hot, dry frying pan (skillet) or under the grill (broiler).

One dough, six flavours. Which will you choose: Butter Naans; Garlic and Coriander Naans; Peshawari Naans; Marmite and Sesame Naans; Chilli-cheese Naans; Kalonji Coin Naans? This is my go-to recipe whenever I crave the tender chew of a puffy, blistered naan. The bread is made without yeast, which means it takes relatively little time to prepare, yet still produces naans that sport a coveted bubbly char. If you have a gas hob (stovetop), try the upside-down pan technique to cook the naan over an open flame – the naans will taste like they were made in a real tandoor. The word 'naan' is of Persian origin and is an umbrella term for bread in its many wonderful forms. Today, there are hundreds of styles of naan prepared across the Indian subcontinent. Some are enriched and/or yeasted, some are sweet, many are savoury or spicy. They can be stuffed, layered, infused or slathered. Naan can make for delicious sides to curries and daals, be served alongside tea, or stuffed with so much filling that they can be enjoyed as full meals in themselves.

For Butter Naans

1. To make a plain naan, mix together the flour, sugar, salt and baking powder in a large plate with high sides or bowl. Mix to combine.

2. Make a well in the centre and add the oil and yogurt. Add the warm water and use your fingers to begin mixing it with the yogurt and oil. Bring the flour to the centre a little at a time and mix to create a sticky dough. Knead for 8-10 minutes, or until smooth and soft. The mixture may feel a little sticky, but that's okay. Do not add any extra flour.

3. Cover the dough with a very thin film of oil, place it in a bowl and cover with a damp dish towel. Allow to rest for 30 minutes.

4. Divide the rested dough into 6 equal portions; each portion should weigh around 85g (3 oz). Keep the dough covered with a damp dish towel to prevent it from drying out.

5. Lightly flour a clean work surface. Take one portion of dough and use your middle three fingers (palm-side down) to gently pat it into a thick disc. Use a rolling pin to gently roll the dough in a circular motion, between the centre and edges. Do not apply too much pressure. You can use your hand to turn it as you roll. Once it reaches the desired size (15-18 cm/6-7 inches in diameter, depending on how thick or thin you like your naan), you can either keep the naan round or gently pull one end to create a teardrop shape.

6. Heat a tawa or large frying pan (skillet) over a medium-high heat (about 4-5 minutes). Do not use a non-stick pan for this cooking method. I use a steel or aluminium (aluminum) tawa.

7. Apply a thin layer of water to the back of the naan to moisten the surface. Very carefully place the naan on the preheated tawa, water-side down. Cook for 30-40 seconds, or until small bubbles appear on the surface of the naan. Pick up the pan by the handle (use an oven glove if it's very hot) and flip the pan upside down to cook the naan directly over the flame. The water will ensure the naan sticks to the pan. Cook until charred spots appear all over the surface of the naan. The naan will continue to cook from both sides. You'll be able to see when it's charred to your liking. Use a metal spatula or turner to gently release the naan from the tawa or pan.

164 Sanjana Feasts

Vegan?

Use unsweetened plant-based yogurt for the naan dough and brush with either shop-bought vegan butter or Vegan Ghee (see page 244).

8. Brush the spotty side of the naan with melted butter. Wrap in a clean, dry dish towel to keep warm while you roll and cook the remaining dough for the rest of the naans. After making the first naan, stack the second butter-side down to prevent the dish towel from getting greasy. Repeat this sandwiched stacking process for the remaining naans.

Roti and Rice 165

For Garlic and Coriander Naans

Make the naans as directed. Mix up a topping of garlic and coriander (cilantro) butter by melting 55 g (2 oz/scant ¼ cup) salted butter in a pan and adding 2 finely chopped garlic cloves. Allow the garlic to sizzle in the butter for 1 minute before adding 2 tablespoons of finely chopped fresh coriander leaves and stalks. Brush the cooked naans with the garlic and coriander butter before serving.

For Marmite and Sesame Naans

Make the naans as directed but add 1 teaspoon of freshly ground black pepper to the dough. Mix up a topping of Marmite butter by beating together 30 g (1 oz/⅛ cup) softened unsalted butter and 2 teaspoons of Marmite or other yeast extract with a fork. Toast 2 tablespoons of white sesame seeds in a dry frying pan (skillet) until lightly golden, about 2 minutes. Set aside. Brush the cooked naans with the Marmite butter and sprinkle with the toasted sesame seeds before serving.

For Chilli-cheese Naans

Make the dough for the naans as directed, but while the dough is resting, prepare a chilli-cheese stuffing and tandoori butter.

For the chilli-cheese stuffing: In a bowl, use the back of a spoon to squish together 200 g (7 oz/1¾ cups) grated (shredded) low-moisture mozzarella, 100 g (3½ oz/scant 1 cup) grated Cheddar, 1 tablespoon double (heavy) cream and 4 minced hot chillies. Set aside. For the tandoori butter: Take a separate bowl and mix 55 g (2 oz/¼ cup) softened salted butter and 1 teaspoon tandoori masala (either store-bought or homemade, see page 269).

To shape the naans, divide the rested dough into 6 equal portions and roll into balls. Divide the stuffing into 6 equal portions, each weighing about 50 g (1¾ oz). Lightly flour a rolling board or clean work surface. Roll or pat out a piece of dough into a disc around 4 cm (1½ inches) in diameter (1). Place a portion of the stuffing on top (2), bring the dough around the stuffing and pinch it together to fully enclose it inside (3, 4, 5). It should look like a dumpling. There should be no gaps or holes for the stuffing to escape from during rolling.

Continue rolling, shaping and cooking the naans from step 5 as directed above. Roll carefully to ensure the dough doesn't tear (6, 7, 8, 9). If it does, I recommend cooking the naans under the grill (broiler) otherwise you might be left with a cheesy mess all over your hob (stovetop). Brush the cooked, blistered naans with the tandoori butter before serving.

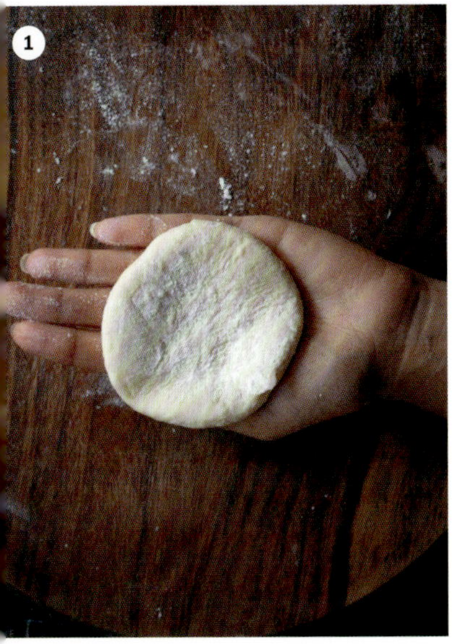
1

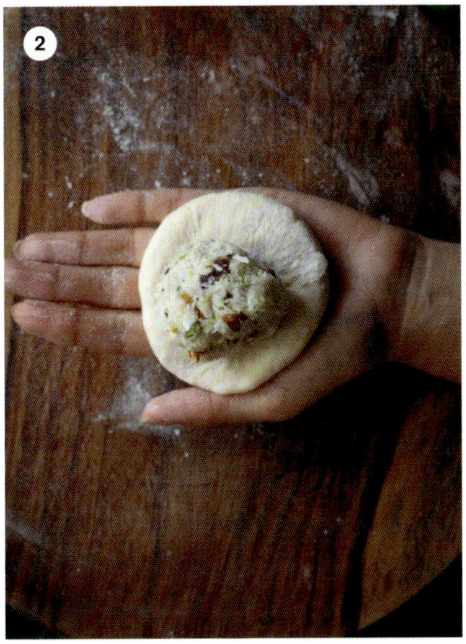
2

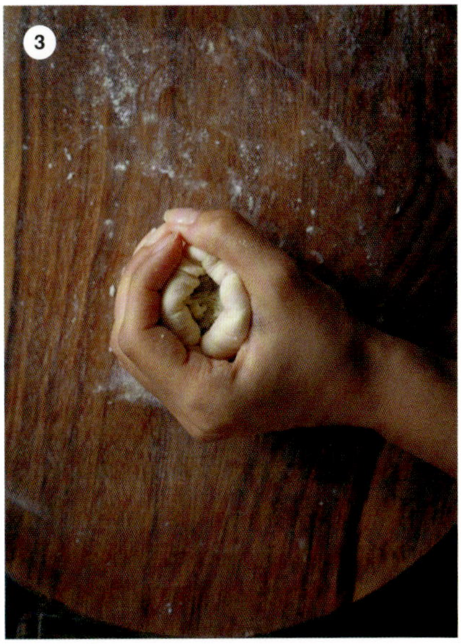
3

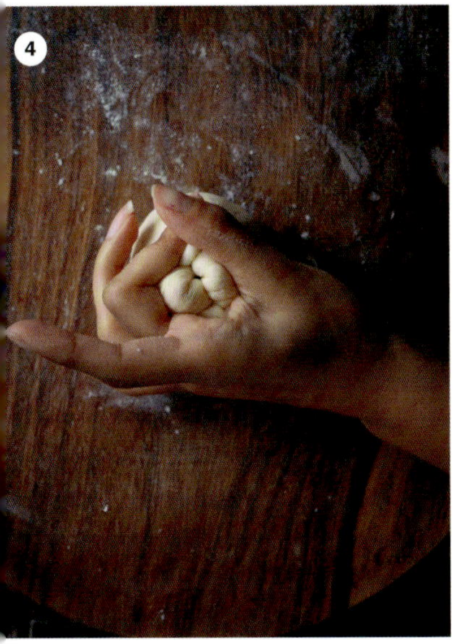
4

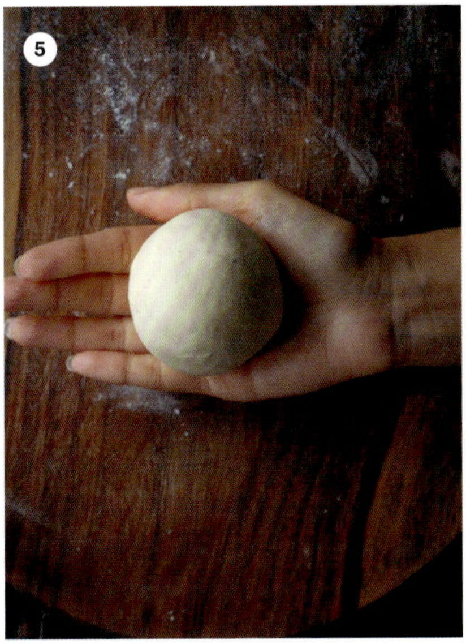
5

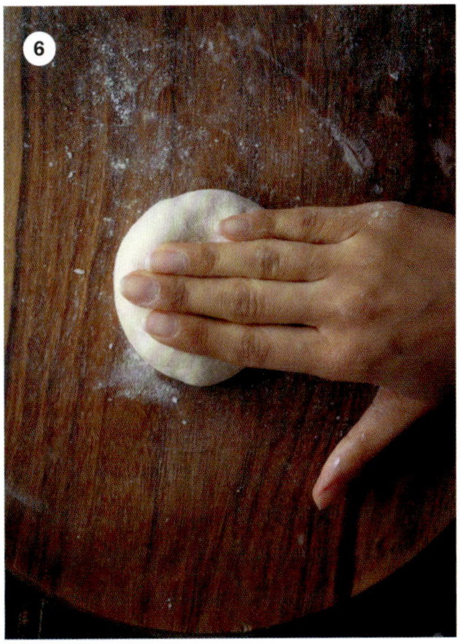
6

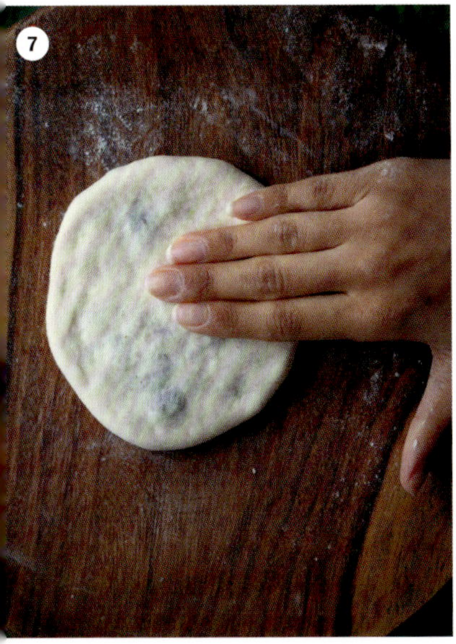
7

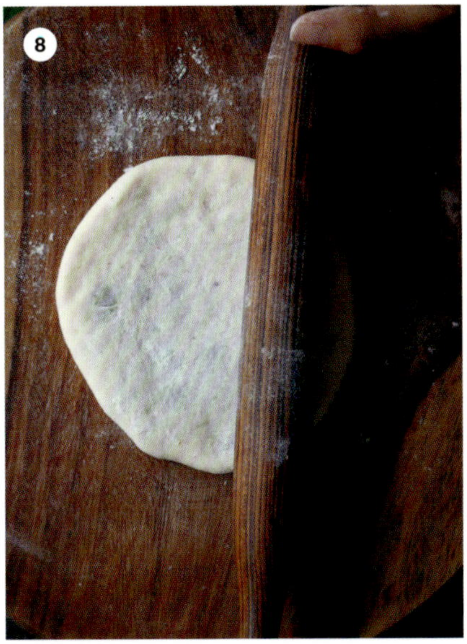
8

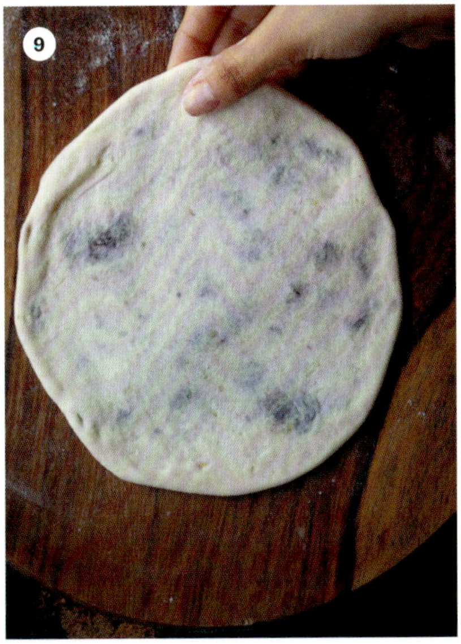
9

Pictured:

1. Butter Naans
2. Garlic and Coriander Naans
3. Marmite and Sesame Naans
4. Chilli-cheese Naans
5. Peshawari Naans
6. Kalonji Coin Naans

Notes

Desiccated coconut can be used in place of coconut milk powder. However, it must be blitzed prior to using and an additional 1 tablespoon of cream added to the stuffing to compensate for the richness of coconut milk powder.

For Peshawari Naans

Make the dough for the naans as directed, but while the dough is resting, prepare a sweet stuffing and saffron milk.

For the sweet stuffing: In a bowl, use the back of a spoon to squish together 2 tablespoons of chopped golden sultanas, 4 tablespoons of double (heavy) cream, 110 g (4 oz) coconut milk powder, 2 tablespoons of ground almonds (almond flour), 2 tablespoons of ground pistachios (pistachio flour), 2 tablespoons of golden syrup and the ground seeds of 4 green cardamom pods. Set aside.

For the saffron milk: Take a separate bowl and mix 2 tablespoons of warm milk with a pinch of saffron.

To shape the naans, divide the rested dough into 6 equal portions and roll into balls. Divide the stuffing into 6 equal portions, each weighing about 45 g (1½ oz). Lightly flour a rolling board or clean work surface. Roll or pat out a piece of dough into a disc around 4 cm (1½ inches) in diameter. Place a portion of stuffing on top, bring the dough around the stuffing and pinch it together to fully enclose it inside. It should look like a dumpling. There should be no gaps or holes for the stuffing to escape from during rolling.

Continue rolling, shaping and cooking the naans from step 5 as directed above. Roll carefully to ensure the dough doesn't tear. Brush the cooked, blistered naans with the saffron milk and melted ghee or butter before serving. (You'll need around 2 tablespoons of ghee or butter in total for all the naans.)

For Kalonji Coin Naans

Make the dough for the naans as directed. Divide the rested dough into 18 equal portions and keep covered. Pat out the naans with three fingers (palm side down) and press a pinch of nigella seeds (kalonji) into the top of each one. (You'll need around 2–3 tablespoons of nigella seeds in total for all the naans.) Moisten the undersides of all the coin naans and cook them a few at a time using the upside-down pan method on page 164. If you don't feel comfortable doing the upside-down method, the naans can be cooked in a very hot frying pan (skillet) or under the grill (broiler). They will take less than a few minutes to cook through. Brush the cooked coin naans with either plain butter or garlic and coriander (cilantro) butter.

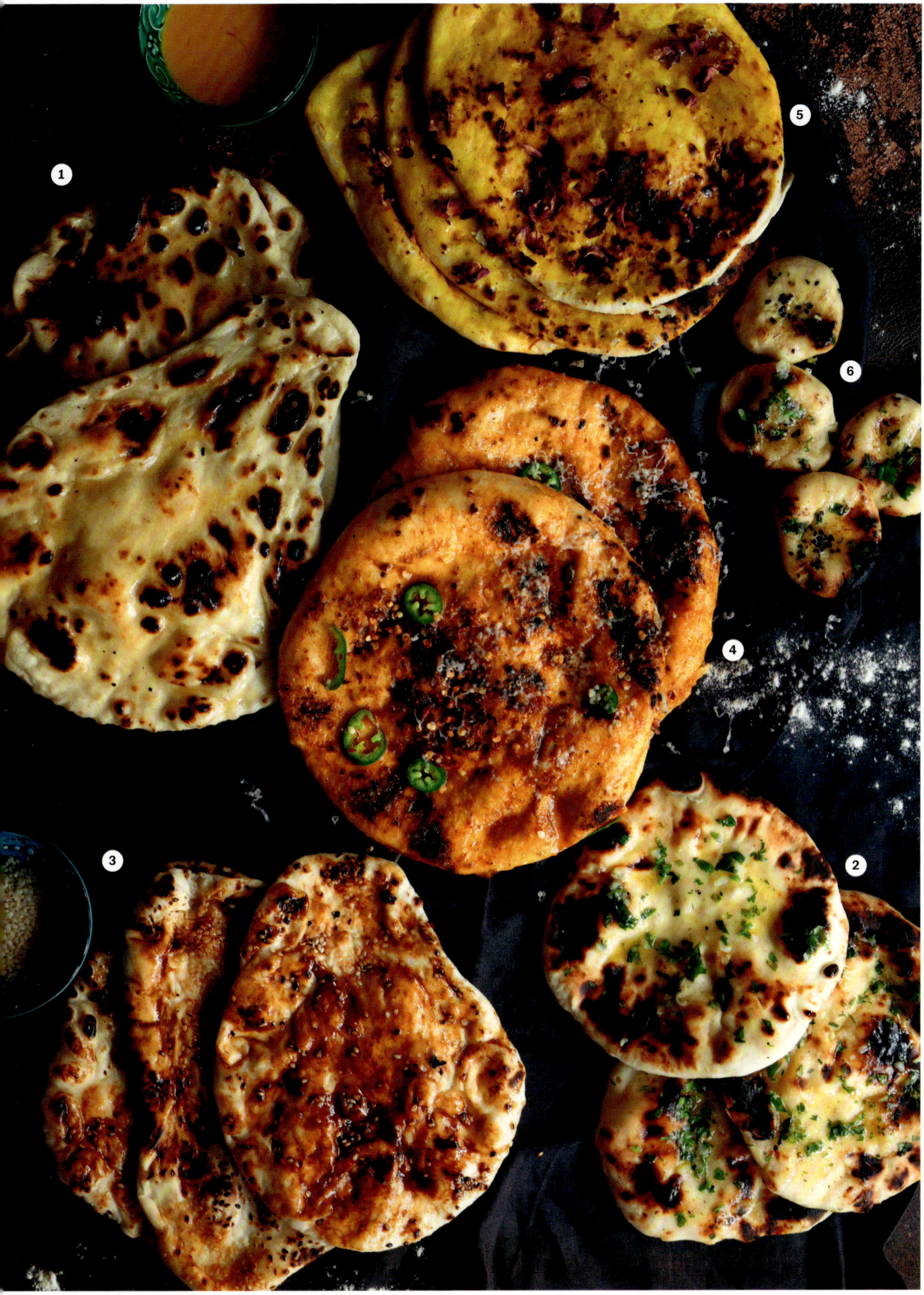
1
5
6
4
3
2

Scotch Khichdi with Ghee-roast Tomatoes

SERVES 4 • PREP: 10 MINS, PLUS 2 HOURS SOAKING • COOK: 20 MINS, PLUS 10 MINS STANDING

75 g (2⅔ oz/1 cup) Scotch broth mix
200 g (7 oz/1 cup) short-grain rice
50 g (1¾ oz/¼ cup) split mung beans with skin on
4 tbsp ghee
5-cm (2-inch) cinnamon stick
2 cloves
2 tsp cumin seeds
¼ tsp asafoetida
1 onion, finely chopped
2 tsp grated (shredded) root ginger
2 green chillies, minced
1¼ tsp salt
½ tsp ground turmeric
½ tsp freshly ground black pepper
1.3 litres (44 fl oz/5½ cups) hot water, plus extra for soaking the Scotch broth mix

For the ghee-roast tomatoes
300 g (10½ oz) cherry tomatoes on the vine
2 tbsp melted ghee
¼ tsp cumin seeds, coarsely cracked in a mortar with a pestle
⅛ tsp salt

Vegan?
Use Vegan Ghee (see page 244) in place of ghee.

Gluten-free?
Use gluten-free asafoetida or omit this ingredient.

This ghee-beaten rice and daal dish is the equivalent of chicken soup for the soul in Indian homes. According to 9 out of 10 Desi aunts and uncles, khichdi fixes everything from a dodgy tummy to your neighbour's best mate's cousin's leaky car radiator. Not really, but you know what I mean. Khichdi is the kind of dish that brings comfort to broken spirits or after a long holiday away. The worst kept secret in my family is that a packet of Scotch broth mix makes for an excellent addition to a humble bowl of khichdi. This twist is inspired by the adaptability of Indians who, back in the day, couldn't source all the ingredients for their beloved khichdi when they first arrived in the UK.

1. Wash well and drain the Scotch broth mix. Place the mix in a bowl and pour over enough hot water so the water level is 2 cm (¾ inch) above the surface of the mix. Leave to soak for 2 hours.

2. Combine the rice and mung beans in a sieve (strainer). Wash well under cold, running water and allow to drain.

3. Heat 2 tablespoons of the ghee in a pressure cooker. Add the cinnamon, cloves, cumin seeds and asafoetida. Allow to sizzle for a few seconds before adding the onion, ginger, chillies and salt. Sauté for 5–6 minutes until the onions have softened and started to brown. Stir in the ground turmeric and black pepper.

4. Drain the Scotch broth mix and add it to the pressure cooker with the drained rice and mung beans. Pour in the hot water. Bring to a boil.

5. Cover with the lid and cook over a medium heat for 4 whistles (about 18 minutes if you're using an electric pressure pot). If you're using a conventional gas or electric hob (stovetop), don't whack the heat up too high as the khichdi can burn on the base of the cooker.

6. Preheat the oven to 210°C/190°C fan/410°F/Gas mark 6½.

7. While the khichdi is cooking, place the cherry tomatoes in a roasting tray (sheet pan). Pour over the melted ghee and sprinkle with the cumin seeds and salt. Shake the pan to evenly coat the tomatoes. Roast in the preheated oven for 15 minutes, or until soft, blistered and slightly jammy inside.

8. Switch off the heat and allow the khichdi to stand for 10 minutes. Carefully release the steam from the pressure cooker and remove the lid. Add the remaining 2 tablespoons of ghee and beat it into the khichdi with a wooden spoon. If the rice and lentils have absorbed all the water and it feels too thick, loosen with a little extra hot water.

9. Pile the khichdi into bowls and top with the ghee-roast tomatoes, along with any tomato juices and ghee from the roasting pan.

Notes

You'll find Scotch broth mix in the dried lentil section of your local supermarket. It's sometimes called soup broth mix or simply broth mix. It must be soaked prior to using. I'm an advocate of the hot soak method as it cuts down the soaking time. You can also cold soak the broth mix overnight and drain before using.

If you are unable to source Scotch broth mix, you can mix your own batch. In a clean, dry jar, simply combine 100 g (3½ oz) of pearl barley with 20 g (¾ oz) of red lentils, 15 g (½ oz) each of yellow split peas and marrowfat peas.

Split mung beans are split, skinned whole mung beans. They're perfect for khichdi since they cook in about the same time as the rice. You'll find them in Indian supermarkets. If you can't find split mung beans, replace them with the same quantity of Scotch broth mix.

Short-grain rice or broken rice produce the creamiest results. You can use any variety. I keep inexpensive Patna rice or Sona Masoori handy for this. Gobindobhog is fragrant and wonderful, albeit more costly. Thai Jasmine rice or even short-grain pudding rice are also fine to use. If basmati is the only rice you have to hand, this may also be used, although the finished dish may not be quite as velvety. Khichdi is so forgiving.

Amp up the protein content by reducing the quantity of rice to 175 g (6¼ oz) and adding 25 g (¾ oz) quinoa.

Roti and Rice **171**

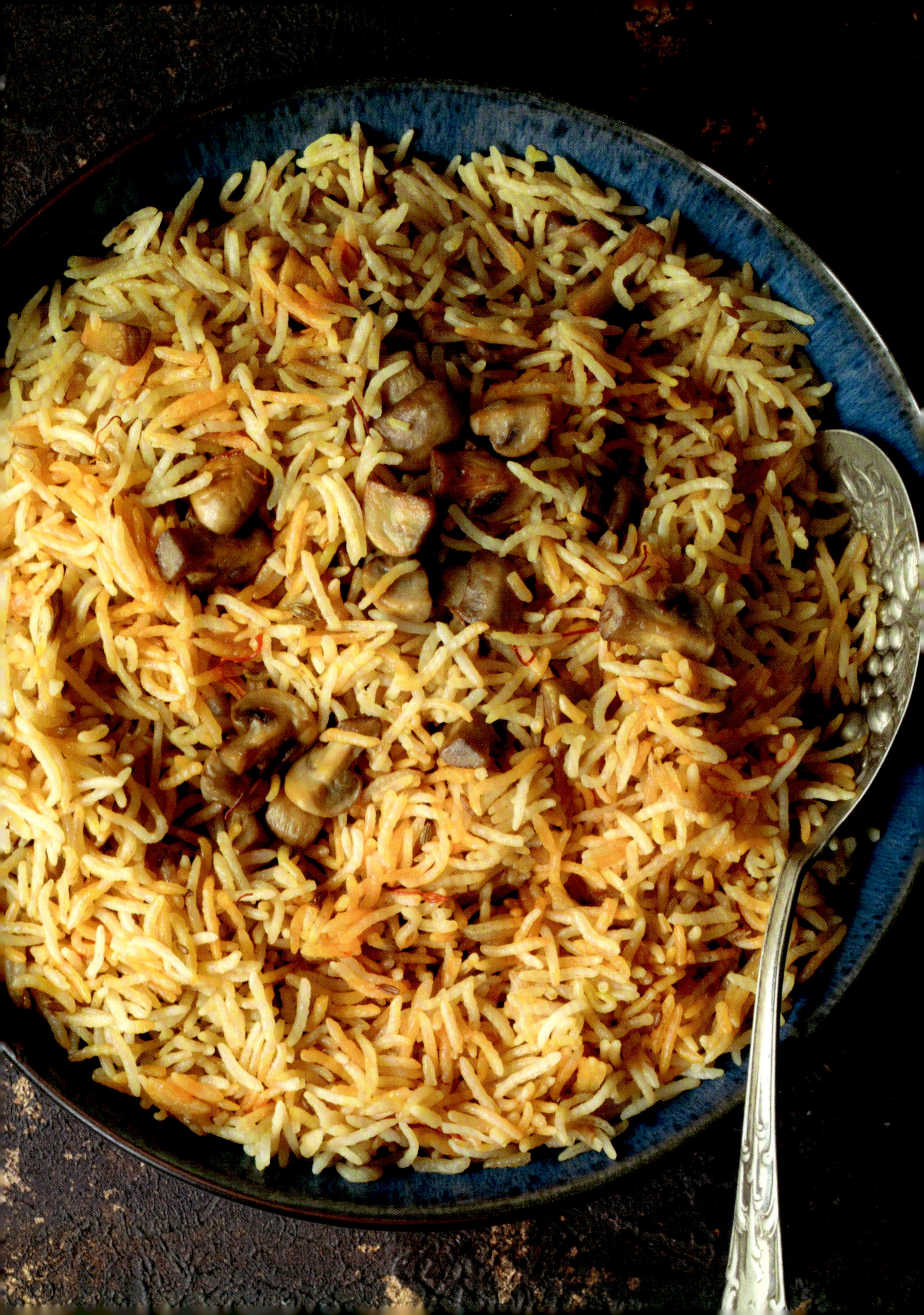

Zafrani Mushroom Pulao

SERVES 4 • PREP: 10 MINS, PLUS 30 MINS SOAKING • COOK: 25 MINS, PLUS 20 MINS STANDING

250 g (8¾ oz/scant 1½ cups) long-grain basmati rice
2 tbsp ghee or oil
1 large onion, finely and evenly sliced
1 tsp cumin seeds
½ tsp fennel seeds
2 cloves
1 green cardamom pod, cracked
¾ tsp salt
200 g (7 oz/2 cups) baby button mushrooms, quartered
A small pinch of saffron strands
500 ml (17 fl oz/2 cups) boiling water

Vegan?

Replace the butter-based ghee with Vegan Ghee (see page 244) or use oil.

Make it a feast!

This delicious restaurant-style pulao pairs well with just about any curry or daal. I love it with Brown Butter Cauliflower and Pea Makhani (see page 113), Black Pepper Tadka Daal (see page 136), Black Daal (see page 139) and Curry Leaf Tomato Soup (see page 81).

Just a bowl of fragrant saffron and mushroom rice. The trick to bags of flavour in any pulao is, first and foremost, to sauté soaked and drained rice in ghee. For grains so long they could moonlight as noodles, it's imperative you wash and soak the rice for anything up to 2 hours, but even 10 minutes will do if that's all the time you have. My favourite part of any pulao or biryani is the crispy rice skirt at the bottom of the pot. To achieve this, remove the lid after the 20-minute rest time and whack the heat up to high for 6-7 minutes. Allow the rice to sit for a further 5 minutes (uncovered) and flip from the base using a flat spatula to reveal the golden bottom.

1. Place the rice in a sieve (strainer) and wash in plenty of cold running water, until the water begins to run mostly clear. This cleans the rice and removes excess starch from the surface to encourage separate grains. Transfer to a bowl and add enough cold water so the water level is 5 cm (2 inches) above the surface of the rice. Allow to soak for 30 minutes.

2. Melt the ghee in a large non-stick saucepan (one that has a tight-fitting lid). Add the onion, cumin seeds, fennel seeds, cloves, cardamom pod and salt. Cook over a medium heat for 5 minutes, or just until the onion begins to brown at the edges.

3. After 30 minutes soaking time, drain the rice in a sieve or colander and allow all the water to drip away.

4. Add the mushrooms to the pan and cook, stirring often, until the mushrooms begin to turn lightly golden brown.

5. Tip the drained rice into the pan and use a spatula to turn the rice in the onion and mushrooms, taking care not to break the grains. Cook for a few minutes, or until all the grains are coated in ghee and begin to turn a shade darker. At this stage, add the saffron.

6. Pour in the boiling water and give the rice a brief stir. Allow to hard boil for 5 minutes, or until most of the water has evaporated. Once there is only a small amount of water bubbling at the surface of the rice, place the lid on the pan and turn down the heat to low. Simmer gently for a further 5 minutes and then switch off the heat. Do not lift the lid at any point. Allow the rice to stand with the lid on for 20 minutes. Remove the lid and fluff up the grains with a fork before serving.

Sticky Hakka Fried Rice

SERVES 4 • PREP: 30 MINS • COOK: 10 MINS

V VG GF

8 spring onions (scallions), white parts finely sliced diagonally, and green parts cut into long, thin strips
3 tbsp oil
2 large garlic cloves, crushed
6 dried Kashmiri chillies
1 carrot, cut into matchsticks
1 green bell pepper, cut into matchsticks
100 g (3½ oz) Chinese cabbage or white cabbage, shredded
60 g (2 oz) baby corn, sliced diagonally
60 g (2 oz) mangetout (snow peas), sliced diagonally
500 g (1 lb 2 oz/3¼ cups) cooked sticky rice, cold
1 tbsp dark soy sauce
2 tsp sugar
½ tsp ground white pepper
½ tsp salt
¼ tsp MSG
250 g (8¾ oz) fried tofu pieces, to serve

Notes

If you're cooking a large batch of sticky rice, consider using two tiers of the steamer so it cooks evenly. If you can't do this, you may need to give the rice a little shimmy halfway through the cooking process to ensure it cooks evenly. Make sure all your utensils and cookware are wet or the rice will stick to them!

You can use leftover home-cooked sticky rice for this recipe, or do as I often do, which is to cunningly buy a packet of microwave rice.

Gluten free?

Use gluten-free soy sauce or tamari in place of dark soy sauce.

A wholesome dish, and by that I mean pleasingly stodgy. This quick wok-fried rice pairs well with fried tofu. Any leftover, cold sticky rice is fine to use. If sticky rice isn't your thing, you can swap it for jasmine, basmati or even brown rice.

1. Place the spring onion (scallion) greens in a bowl of ice-cold water. Refrigerate until needed.

2. Heat the wok until smoking hot. Add the oil and garlic, dried chillies, spring onion whites, carrot, bell pepper, cabbage, baby corn and mangetout (snow peas). Stir-fry over a very high heat for a minute or two.

3. Add the cooked rice, soy sauce, sugar, white pepper, salt and MSG. Break up any clumps of rice with a spoon and toss everything together to combine. This might take a few moments as this variety of rice sticks together more than other types. Be patient and know that the rice at the bottom of the wok is crisping up for a gorgeous texture in the meantime.

4. Spoon the fried rice into bowls and top with hot fried tofu and the spring onion greens, which should have curled up like pretty ribbons on a Christmas present.

How to make your own sticky rice

1. First, some of the surface starch needs to be removed from the rice. Place the rice in a sieve (strainer) and wash in plenty of cold running water, until the water begins to run mostly clear. Drain the rice and then pour over enough boiling water so the water level is 3 cm (1 inch) above the surface of the rice. Allow to soak at room temperature for 30 minutes.

2. After 30 minutes soaking time, drain the rice in a sieve (strainer) and rinse under cold running water until the water runs mostly clear. Allow to drain for a few minutes.

3. Set up a steamer with enough water in the bottom to cook for 30-40 minutes without running dry. Don't worry too much if it does run dry, you can always top it up with more boiling water later.

4. Thoroughly dampen a double-layered, large sheet of parchment paper with water (the paper needs to be about 6 cm/2½ inches larger than the width of the steamer). Line the steamer with the paper and top with the soaked rice. Level the rice and bring the sides of the paper up around the rice. You can also use a very damp muslin for this, but the doubled-up parchment paper makes for an easier clean-up later.

5. Once the rice is neatly tucked inside the paper blanket, cover with a tight-fitting lid and steam over a medium-high heat for 30-35 minutes, or until cooked through. Like pasta, the best way to check the rice for doneness is to taste it. It should be soft, a little chewy (not crunchy) and, most importantly, sticky.

6. Remove the rice from the paper by turning it out onto a plate and peeling the paper away. Do this while the rice is still warm to reduce the number of grains that stick to the paper, although this is inevitable for some of them. Try to prise as many off as you can.

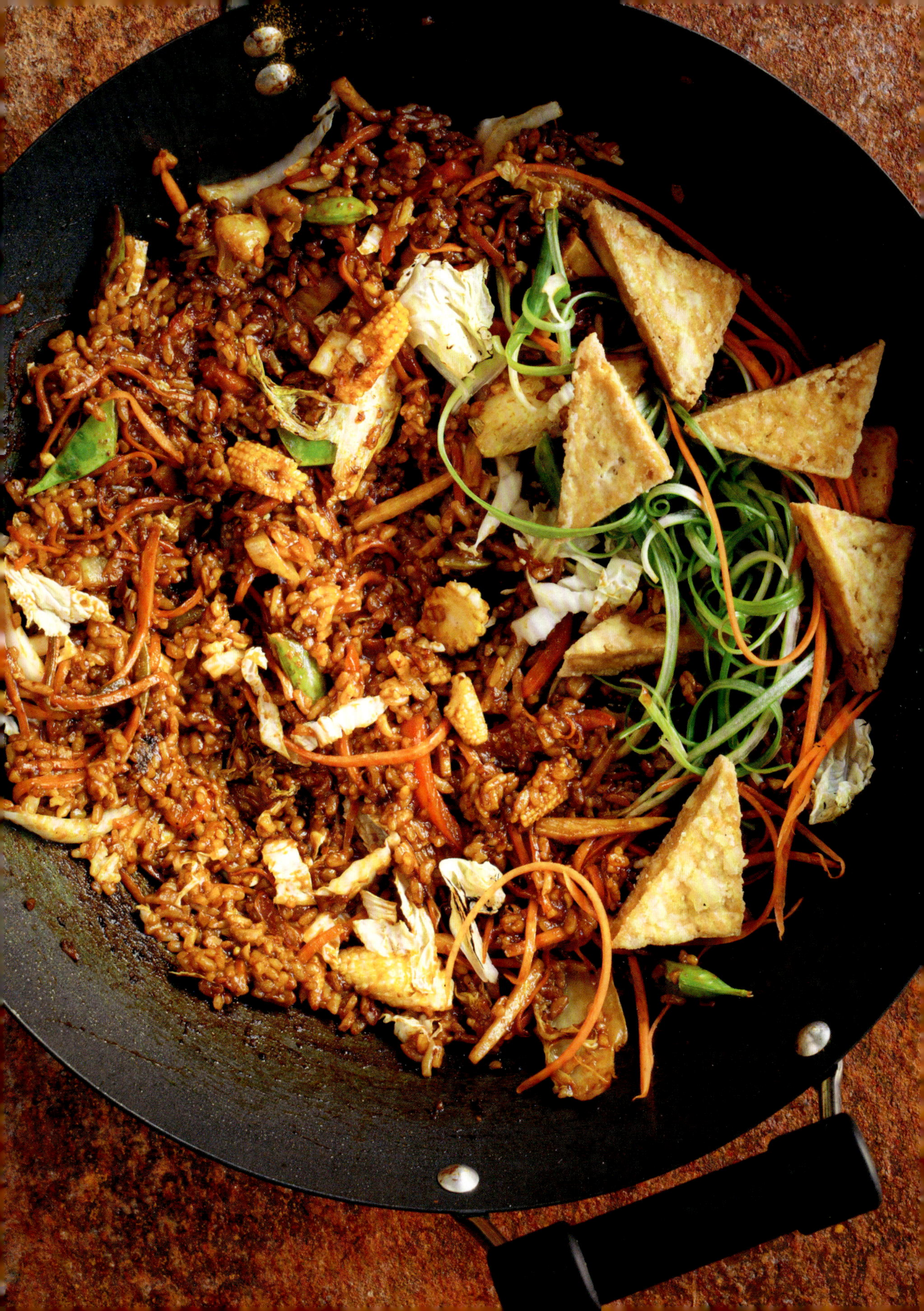

Ruffled Biryani

SERVES 6 • PREP: 40 MINS, PLUS 1 HOUR SOAKING • COOK: 80 MINS

For the rice
225 g (8 oz/1¼ cups) long-grain basmati rice
1 tsp salt
5-cm (2-inch) cassia bark or cinnamon stick
2 green cardamom pods, cracked
3 cloves
1 tbsp edible dried rose petals (optional)

For the vegetables
1 tbsp ghee or oil
½ tsp cumin seeds
80 g (2¾ oz/½ cups) cashews
1 tbsp tomato purée (paste)
2 tbsp All-in-One Biryani Masala (see page 260)
150 g (5¼ oz/⅔ cup) plain yogurt
350 g (12 oz) potatoes, cut into large chunks and fried until golden
200 g (7 oz) cauliflower florets, fried until lightly golden
150 g (5¼ oz) carrots, sliced into batons and steamed until 75 per cent cooked
100 g (3½ oz/⅔ cup) peas (I use frozen)
100 g (3½ oz) bell peppers (any colour), sliced into large pieces
1 large onion, sliced and fried until golden and crispy
200 g (7 oz) paneer, cubed and fried until golden

Purists will insist that there is no such thing as vegetarian biryani since it has almost always been prepared with meat. If you're one of these people, look away now. South Asia's most traditional biryanis are cooked in a Persian-inspired method called dum pukht. This refers to a seal of dough placed around the rim of the cooking pot so the food inside cooks in steam. The seal ensures that steam builds up inside the pot, plumps up the rice grains and infuses them with the flavours of spiced veg, crispy onions and saffron. Once you crack the seal open, the dum (which translates as 'warm breath') will escape and you'll be ready to pile mounds of biryani onto your plate. This Ruffled Biryani takes inspiration from the dum method, but it isn't traditional. My recipe dispenses with the traditional pastry seal and pot lid to make way for an arrangement of crisp filo (phyllo) pastry rosettes. They nestle on top of saffron milk-streaked rice and since the ruffles are brushed with butter, the entire biryani soaks up the golden drips from above. It really is the veggie biryani of dreams.

1. First, prepare the rice. Place the rice in a bowl. Gently wash it in plenty of cold water. Tip the water away and repeat with fresh water another 2–3 times. Drain the rice and then pour over enough cold water so the water level is 3 cm (1 inch) above the surface of the rice. Allow to soak at room temperature for 1 hour.

2. After 1 hour soaking time, drain the rice in a sieve (strainer) and rinse under cold running water until the water runs mostly clear. Allow to drain for a few minutes.

3. Fill a large pot with around 2 litres (70 fl oz/8½ cups) water. Add the salt, cassia bark or cinnamon, cardamom pods, cloves and edible rose petals, if using. Bring to a boil over a medium-high heat.

4. Add the soaked rice and bring to a boil again. Simmer over a medium heat until the rice is 80 per cent cooked. It should break when you press a grain between your fingers, but not smush. Drain in a colander and set aside.

5. Next, prepare the vegetable mixture. Heat the ghee or oil in a large frying pan (skillet) or saucepan. Once the ghee has melted, add the cumin seeds and allow to sizzle for 20 seconds. Add the cashews, tomato purée (paste) and biryani masala and cook for a further 30 seconds. Add the plain yogurt and cook, stirring continuously, for about 2 minutes until the paste cooks through. It's ready when the oil separates from the paste. Turn the heat down to low. Add the potatoes, cauliflower, carrots, peas, peppers, fried onions and paneer. Stir well. Pour in 150 ml (5 fl oz/scant ⅔ cup) water and bring to a boil. Cook for no longer than 2 minutes and then switch off the heat.

6. Preheat the oven to 200°C/180°C fan/390°F/Gas mark 6. Grease a 25-cm (10-inch) springform cake pan or pie dish with a small amount of oil.

7. To layer the biryani, spread one-third of the rice over the bottom of the pan. Top the rice with half of the vegetable mixture, some mint leaves, coriander (cilantro) leaves and fried onions. Add another layer of rice and the remaining half of the vegetable mixture. Gently flatten the layers – don't press down too hard. Top with some mint leaves, coriander leaves and more fried onions. Layer in the final one-third of the rice. Pour over the saffron milk and sprinkle some coriander leaves on top.

For the biryani

1 tbsp chopped fresh mint leaves

2 tbsp chopped fresh coriander (cilantro) leaves

1 large onion, sliced and fried until golden and crispy

150 ml (5 fl oz/scant ⅔ cup) hot milk, infused with a large pinch of saffron strands

For the filo pastry ruffles

500 g (1 lb 2 oz) filo (phyllo) pastry sheets

200 g (7 oz/scant 1 cup) butter, melted

Vegan?

Use Vegan Ghee (see page 244) or vegan butter and any unsweetened, plant-based yogurt of your choice. Tofu is a great substitute for paneer, but feel free to skip the paneer altogether and use only vegetables.

Make it a feast!

Serve with Fried Caper Raita (see page 194), or any other raita of your choice.

8. For the filo (phyllo) pastry ruffles, take the first sheet of filo pastry and generously brush it with the melted butter. Keep the rest of the pastry covered with a damp dish towel to prevent it from drying out. Scrunch the pastry up from one end to the other, like a rough concertina. Take one end and coil it into a spiral or rosette. You don't have to be neat — in fact, the more rustic, the better.

9. Place the scrunched, buttered filo pastry on top of the rice, starting from the outside edge and working in towards the centre. Repeat with the remaining filo pastry until all the rice is covered by ruffled pastry. This pastry top will help the rice and spices gently steam in the oven whilst the surface becomes golden and crispy.

10. Bake uncovered in the preheated oven for 45 minutes until the filo pastry top is golden and crispy.

Roti and Rice 177

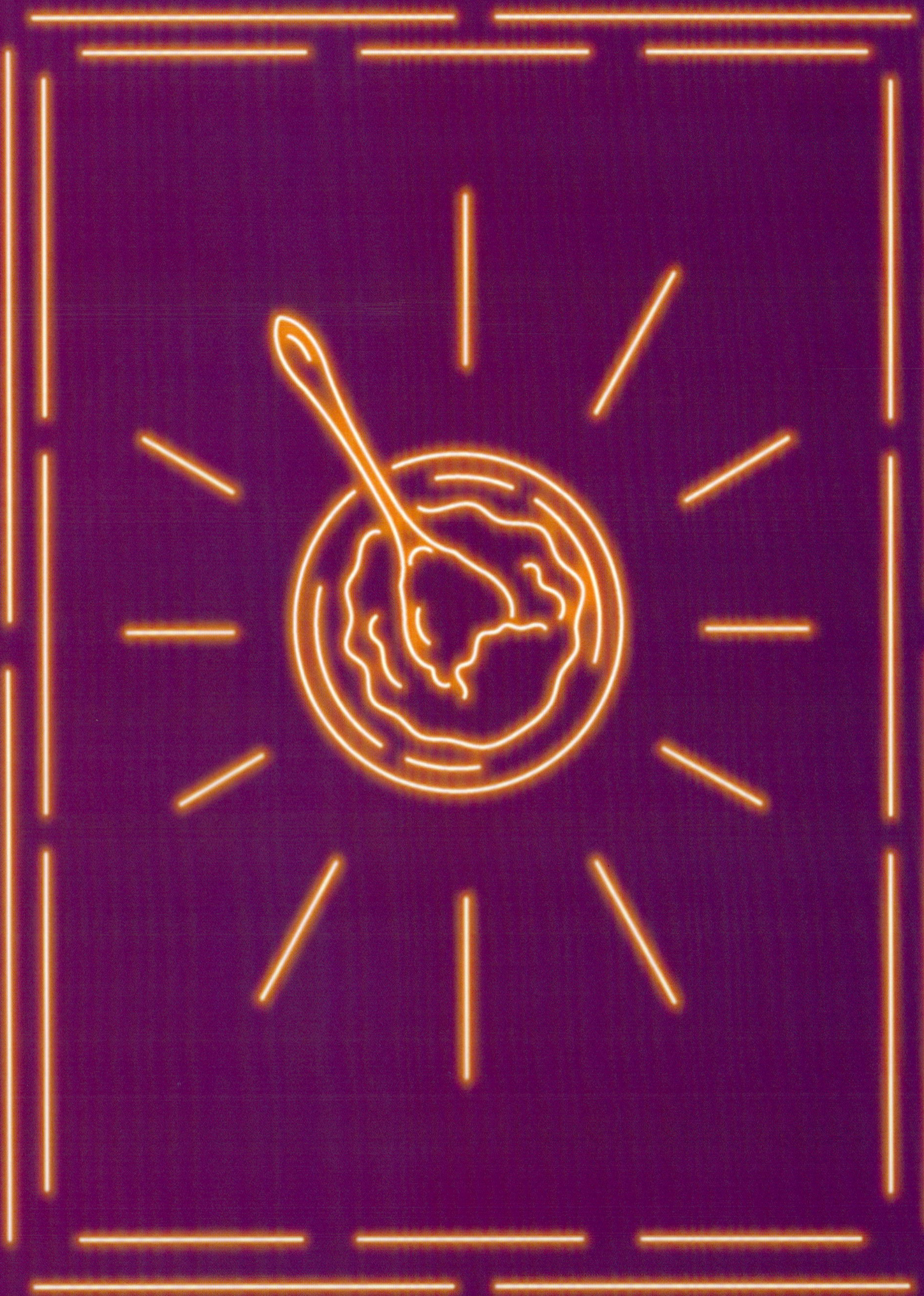

Sides

A final pop.

Indian meals often feel incomplete without a little something on the side: a mouth-puckering chutney, cooling raita or fresh salad, to name a few options. They round off a meal and temper the flavours of a main dish to offer balance and vibrancy. It's no wonder the concept of the thali is an indispensable element of Indian cuisine. Since we first eat with our eyes, these small add-ins, like embellishments on a sari, can elevate a meal. For example, biryani without raita on the side is great, but biryani with raita on the side is exquisite. Samosas are perfectly good by themselves, but samosas with a zingy chutney or two is a whole new level of delicious. Sides can make a meal pop, and I love a good pop with my food.

It was midnight. I woke from a dream (probably featuring Leo DiCaprio as my teenage beau) to the clang of a pot, followed by a slow glug coming from the kitchen. No, we weren't being robbed (and it certainly wasn't Leo coming to sweep me off my feet). It was my dad making chips (potato fries). You see, he would often crave chips as an almost midnight snack. It's a family quirk. All 11 of his siblings were known for it too. It's a quirk carried over from their childhood in East Africa, where masala chips bore a legacy for being cooked at all hours, usually on the agasi (rooftop), filling the entire street with the welcoming aromas of fried tubers and kerosene. A cheeky plate of home-cooked chips, sliced medium-thin from a potato and freshly fried, before the clock strikes twelve is hard to resist. He still does it, but he uses the air fryer now. Once lifted from the pool of bubbling oil, these golden chips would be doused with an array of sauces and spices. At first, the smell is that of pure spud, then later of chilli sauce, lemon juice, cumin, coriander seeds and black pepper. It's a heatwave of tang and it fills every corner of the house, much to the despair of the person who earlier cleaned the kitchen from top to bottom. My brother would join Dad in his feast of fries – an excuse to stay up late on a school night, no doubt. I'd sit alongside and listen to Dad tell stories of eating masala chips with his brothers and sisters, usually serving them with a glass bottle of cola and processed cheese from a can.

Whilst I may not be a fully fledged member of the Almost-midnight Masala Chips club, I have adopted Dad's recipe for Almost-midnight Masala Chips (see page 182) into my meal rotation. These fries pair well with almost anything, as well as being a spot-hitting snack all by themselves. Loosely based on a Kenyan recipe for Poussin Chips, which usually combine margarine, paprika, garlic, ginger, pepper and lemon or vinegar for an addictive, slick red coating, this style of marinade was traditionally used for chicken, hence the word 'poussin', which originates from French. The culinary landscape of East Africa is a melting pot of flavours and techniques, from South Asia and the Middle East to Europe and the Americas. To say that a simple bowl of chips embodies trade, migration and the culinary prowess of generations is no overstatement.

In this chapter, you'll find recipes for some of my most trusty sides dishes, each one bringing their own flavours to the table. They serve to brighten up more traditional Indian meals, as well as complete some of the non-curry dishes in this book, such as Gunpowder Tofu (see page 70), Spicy Bean Tawa Burgers (see page 77) and Singapore Poha (see page 93). My best advice is to follow the flavours and let your instincts help you mix and match.

Almost-midnight Masala Chips

SERVES 4 • PREP: 10 MINS • COOK: 20 MINS

500 g (1 lb 2 oz) frozen chips (potato fries)
1 tbsp Chips Masala (see page 272)
1 tbsp chopped fresh coriander (cilantro) leaves
Lime wedges, to serve

My dad's masala chips (potato fries) are the kind of thing I could eat with any meal, and at any time of the day. Lunch? Yes. Dinner? Why not. Midnight snack? Absolutely! With a hot and sour thump from the chilli and baobab fruit powder in the chips' masala, they're inspired by the fresh flavours of Mombasa, the coastal Kenyan city in which Dad spent much of his youth. I use frozen French fries for convenience, but if you have the time, you can make your own chips from fresh potatoes. I'll leave the choice of thin fries or chunky chips up to you.

1. Cook the chips (potato fries) according to the packet instructions.

2. While hot, toss the chips with the chips masala.

3. Pile the chips onto a large plate, scatter over the chopped coriander (cilantro) and serve with lime wedges for squeezing.

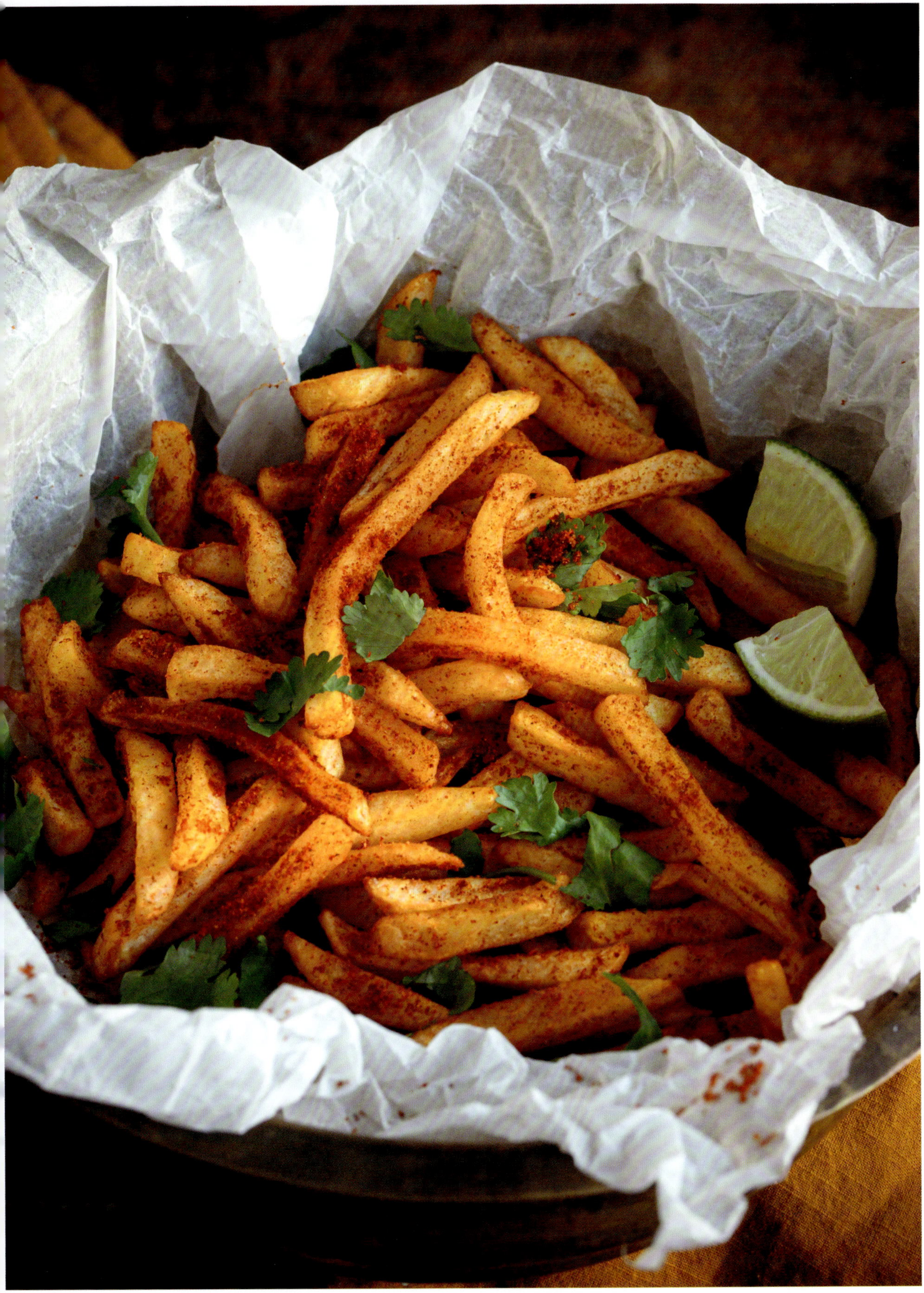

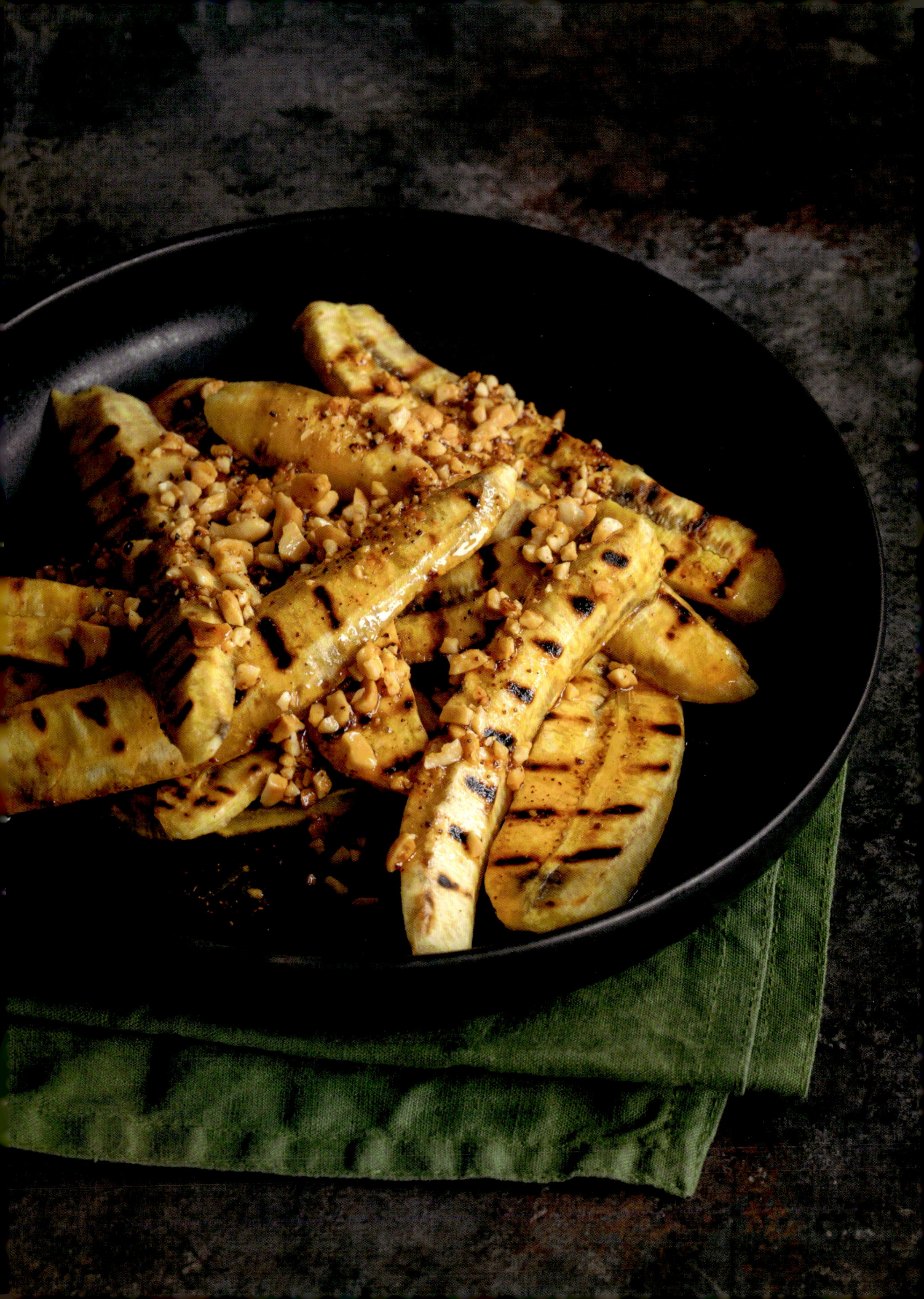

Sizzling Achaari Matoke

SERVES 4 • PREP: 10 MINS • COOK: 20 MINS

5 matoke, around 500 g (1 lb 2 oz)
4 tbsp oil
¼ tsp salt
2 tbsp unsalted roasted peanuts, coarsely ground
2 tsp Achaar Masala (see page 264)

Not an unripe banana, not an unripe plantain. Matoke are the small, green banana doppelgangers loved across East Africa. They're suitably starchy, versatile and, rather like potatoes, they're a blank canvas for any flavours you wish to throw at them. Here's a version with sizzling achaari oil (pickling spices) and peanuts. Buy matoke in chunky bunches from African and Asian greengrocers or from well-stocked markets.

1. Prick holes in the matoke skins and arrange them in a steamer. Make sure the water isn't touching them and place a tight-fitting lid on the pot. Steam for 10 minutes, or until slightly soft but not cooked all the way through. To test if they're done, poke a fork into the matoke – it should break through but be met with some resistance. Remove the matoke from the steamer and allow to cool for 5 minutes.

2. While they're still warm, peel the matoke. If you let them cool too much, it will be difficult to get the skins off. In any case, you can always use a knife to remove some of the skin if it proves difficult. Slice the peeled matoke into long pieces. Pour 1 tablespoon of the oil and a sprinkling of salt over the matoke and rub gently onto each piece, taking care not to break them.

3. Preheat a griddle pan until smoking hot. Lay the pieces of matoke onto the griddle and cook for 1–2 minutes per side, or until grill marks appear. Transfer to a serving plate.

4. Heat the remaining 3 tablespoons of oil in a pan until smoking hot. In a bowl, combine the peanuts and achaar masala. Carefully pour the hot oil directly on top of the peanuts and allow to sizzle for a moment before stirring.

5. Drizzle the achaari oil (including the peanuts) over the grilled matoke before serving.

Mogo Dirty Fries

SERVES 4 • PREP: 20 MINS • COOK: 40 MINS

500 g (1 lb 2 oz) fresh or frozen cassava
2 tbsp oil
1½ tsp Garam Masala (see page 259)
1 tsp black salt

For the cheese sauce
125 g (4½ oz/1 cup) grated (shredded) mature (sharp) Cheddar
100 g (3½ oz/scant 1 cup) grated (shredded) Red Leicester cheese
1½ tbsp cornflour (cornstarch)
½ tsp sweet smoked paprika
1 x 410-g (14½-oz) can evaporated milk
2 tbsp brine from a jar of pickled jalapeños

To serve
100 g (3½ oz) lettuce, shredded
1 small red onion, finely diced
1 large tomato, finely diced
½ green mango, peeled and diced (optional)
20 g (¾ oz) pickled jalapeños
20 g (¾ oz) sev (fried gram flour noodles)

Make it a feast!
Enjoy these fries as a snack with drinks.

Gluten free?
Check the ingredients label on any shop-bought sev to be sure it's gluten free.

Wedges of golden cassava, also known as mogo to East African Indians. Derived from the Swahili word 'muhogo', the misnomer refers to yucca roots, a tuber that grows underground. It is a staple carbohydrate in many parts of the world, from Africa and South America to China and beyond. Treat them very much like potatoes. In this recipe, the roasted root receives a smattering of nacho-inspired cheese sauce, jalapeños, lettuce, onions, tomatoes, raw green mango and sev.

1. If using fresh cassava, peel off the rough brown skin and chop it into thick fries. Steam or boil the cassava fries until tender but still holding their shape. If using frozen cassava, boil or steam it straight from frozen (this might take a little longer). Drain and allow to stand for 15 minutes. Peel off any tough, stringy fibres from the edges and core if there are any.

2. Preheat the oven to 220°C/200°C fan/425°F/Gas mark 7.

3. Toss the cassava fries in oil. Roast in the preheated oven for 20-25 minutes, or until golden brown, turning halfway through the cooking time. Take care not to break the fries.

4. While the cassava fries are cooking, make the cheese sauce. Mix the cheeses with the cornflour (cornstarch) and smoked paprika to coat. In a saucepan, bring the evaporated milk to a gentle simmer. Switch off the heat. Add the cheeses and beat well using a whisk. Add the jalapeño brine. Use a handheld stick (immersion) blender or conventional blender to blend the cheese sauce. It will transform into a thick, glossy sauce. Return to the pan and heat through.

5. Toss the roasted cassava fries in the garam masala and black salt. Pour a blanket of cheese sauce over the top and garnish with the shredded lettuce, diced onion, tomato and mango, pickled jalapeños and sev. Serve immediately with any remaining cheese sauce served in a bowl for dipping.

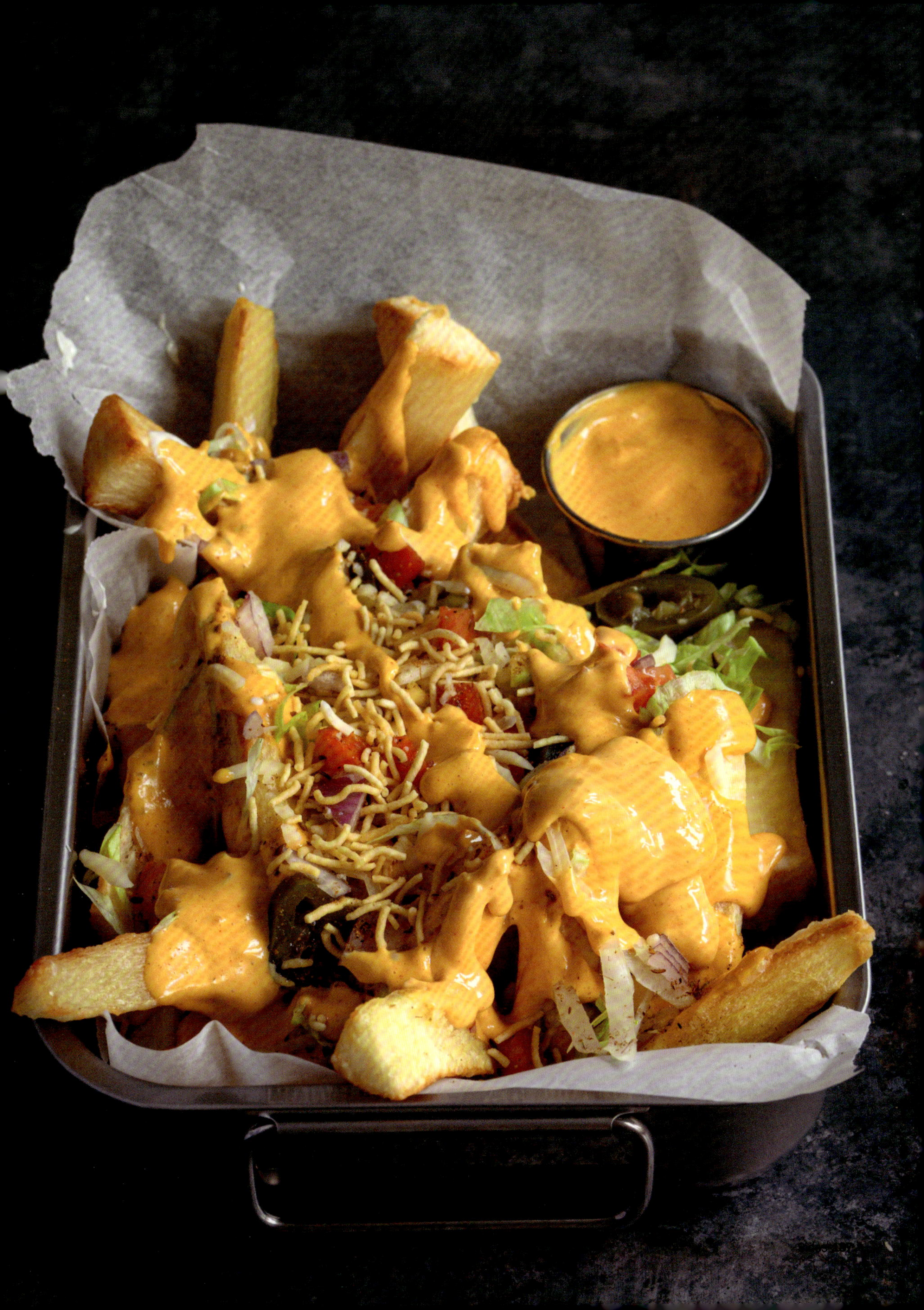

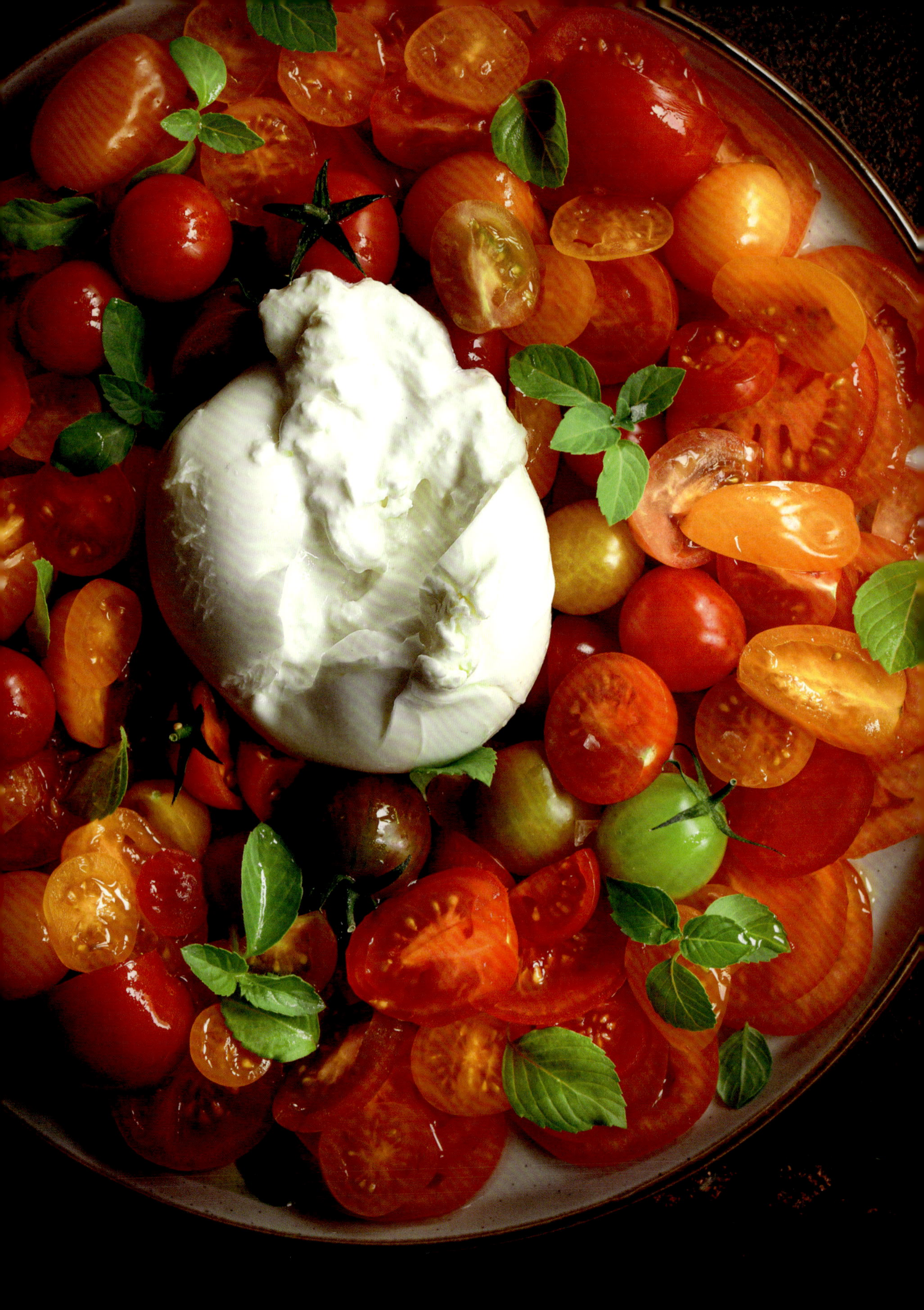

Tomato, Tulsi and Burrata Salad

SERVES 4 • PREP: 10 MINS, PLUS 10 MINS STANDING

V GF VG

750 g (1 lb 10 oz) mixed tomatoes of your choice
1 ball vegetarian burrata
20 g (¾ oz) fresh holy basil (tulsi) or Thai basil leaves
¼ tsp Chaat Masala (see page 263)
3 tbsp extra-virgin olive oil

Vegan?

Omit the burrata or replace it with a few handfuls of cashews boiled in hot water for 10 minutes and then drained.

Make it a feast!

Goes particularly well alongside Gunpowder Tofu (see page 70) or Pudla Traybake (see page 86).

The holy basil (tulsi) plant has a prominent place in Ayurveda, and it's an important symbol in Hindu religious traditions. I addressed the tulsi plant in our home as 'Tulsi-ji', a term of respect in our culture. It was notoriously peppery smelling; a waft that followed us down the stairs from the sunny windowsill where it thrived for many years. I remember drinking sweet milk steeped with tulsi leaves at the Hindu temple after it was offered to Lord Vishnu. Here's a play on those flavours featuring sweet tomatoes, creamy burrata and our beloved Tulsi-ji.

1. Slice the tomatoes into bite-sized pieces, as evenly or as unevenly as you like. I go for halves, wedges and quarters depending on the size of the tomato. Arrange them on a large serving platter.

2. Place the burrata in the centre of the platter and then scatter over the holy basil leaves. Sprinkle with the chaat masala and drizzle with the olive oil. Allow to stand for 10 minutes at room temperature before serving.

Sides

Wedge Salad Chaat

SERVES 4 • PREP: 20 MINS

1 large iceberg lettuce

For the blue cheese dressing
150 g (5¼ oz/⅔ cup) thick Greek yogurt
100 ml (3½ fl oz/scant ½ cup) buttermilk
50 g (1¾ oz/scant ¼ cup) mayonnaise
25 g (¾ oz) blue cheese, crumbled
2 tsp apple cider vinegar
½ tsp sugar
½ tsp freshly ground black pepper
½ tsp Chaat Masala (see page 263)
¼ tsp salt

For the other toppings
8 tbsp bottled tamarind chutney
8 tbsp Coriander and Mint Chutney (see page 197)
1 small red onion, finely chopped
1 tomato, finely diced
4 tbsp sev (fried noodles)
4 tbsp pomegranate seeds
16–18 whole cashew nuts
1 tbsp chopped fresh coriander (cilantro) leaves

Make it a feast!
Goes particularly well alongside Spicy Bean Tawa Burgers (see page 77).

Gluten free?
Check the ingredients label on any shop-bought sev to be sure it's gluten free.

I never thought I would take such pleasure in demolishing a wedge of lettuce; that is, until I ate this. A chunk of cold, crisp iceberg dressed in a blanket of blue cheese buttermilk dressing, with a pick 'n' mix of Indian chaat toppings. This is a refreshing side dish, and also makes for a great starter.

1. Quarter the lettuce, keeping the stem intact so the wedges hold together. Wash well in cold water and set aside in a colander to drain.

2. To make the dressing, whisk together the yogurt, buttermilk, mayonnaise, blue cheese crumbles, cider vinegar, sugar, black pepper, chaat masala and salt in a bowl.

3. Place the lettuce wedges onto individual serving plates or a large platter. Drench the wedges with the blue cheese dressing, chutneys, onion, tomato, sev, pomegranate seeds, cashew nuts and chopped coriander (cilantro).

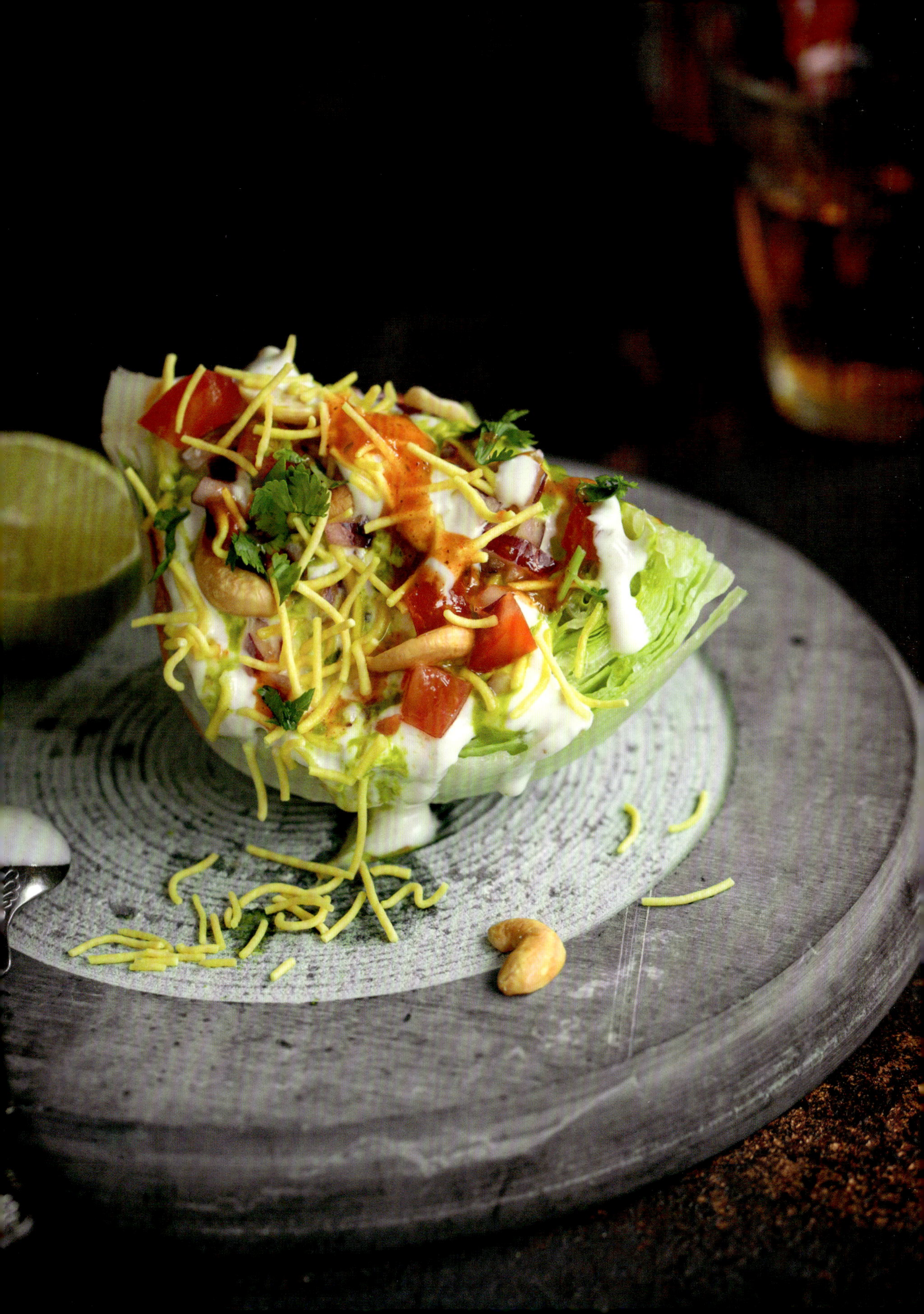

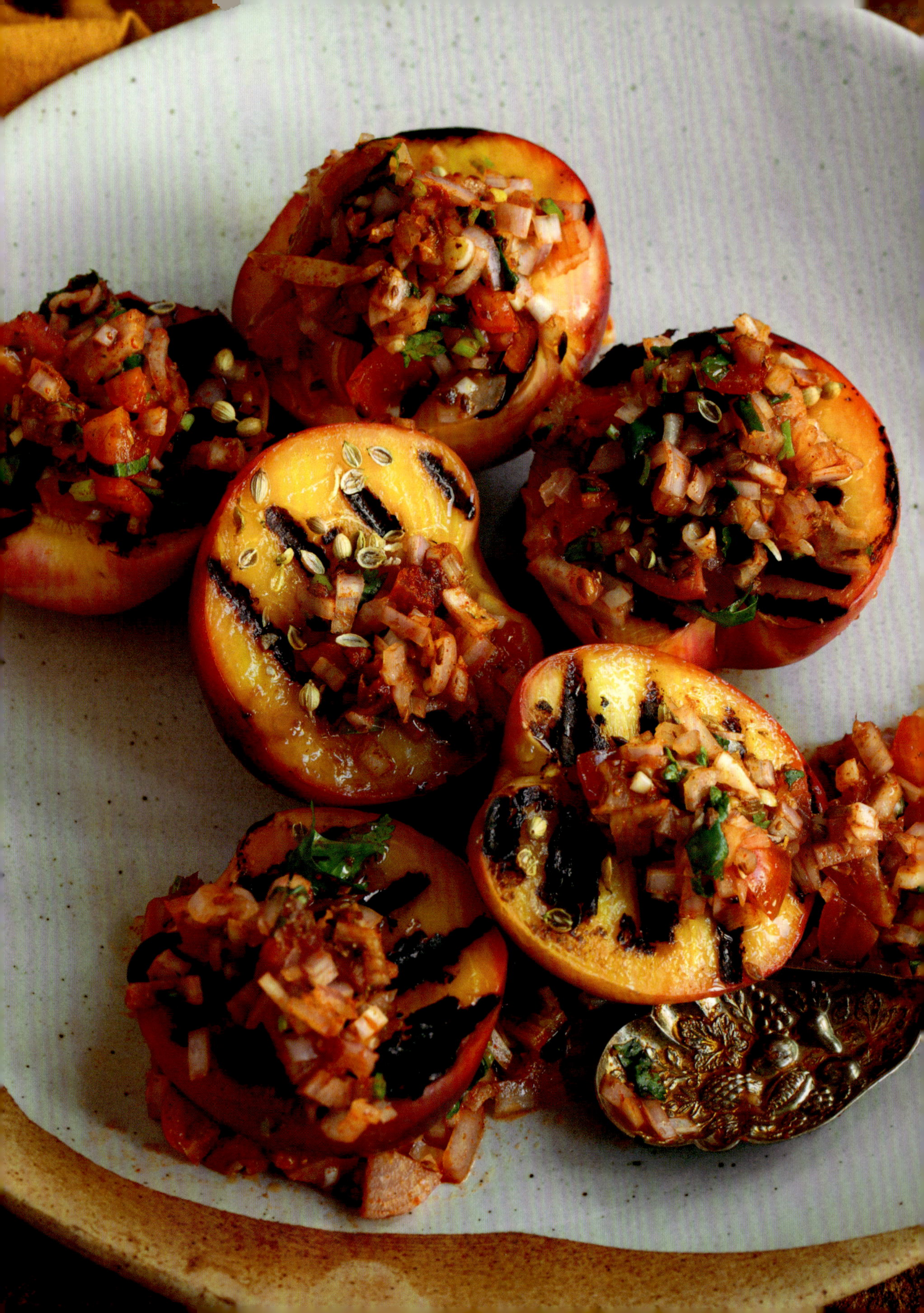

Grilled Nectarine Kachumber

SERVES 6 • PREP: 10 MINS • COOK: 5 MINS

3 ripe nectarines, halved and pitted (stoned)
1 tsp cumin seeds
1 tsp coriander seeds
1 red onion, finely diced
1 large tomato, seeds removed and finely diced
½ tsp Kashmiri chilli powder
2 tbsp chopped fresh coriander (cilantro)
1 tbsp oil
¼ tsp salt
1 tbsp lemon juice

Kachumber is a haphazardly chopped salad that goes with just about everything. I like to add a fruity element to the traditionally spicy salad in the form of grilled nectarines. Grilling the nectarines takes a mere few minutes and lends a fruity caramelisation to this hero of the Indian side world.

1. Preheat a griddle pan until smoking hot. Arrange the nectarine halves in the pan, cut-side down. Allow to cook until char marks appear. Remove from the pan and set aside to cool.

2. Toast the cumin and coriander seeds in a dry frying pan (skillet) until fragrant. Coarsely crush them in a mortar with a pestle.

3. In a bowl, combine the onion, tomato, toasted cumin and coriander seeds, chilli powder, chopped fresh coriander (cilantro), oil, salt and lemon juice. Cover and allow to macerate in the fridge for 30 minutes.

4. Assemble the dish just before serving by placing spoonfuls of the kachumber on top of the griddled nectarine halves.

Make it a feast!

You can very easily transform this into a starter or light main by serving the nectarine halves alongside pieces of toasted ciabatta and crumbled fresh paneer or feta.

Fried Caper Raita

SERVES 4 • PREP: 15 MINS, PLUS 30 MINS CHILLING • COOK: 5 MINS, PLUS 15 MINS COOLING

100 g (3½ oz) capers, drained
1 tsp cumin seeds
100 g (3½ oz) cucumber (no need to peel)
400 g (14 oz/1½ cups) full-fat Greek yogurt
1 small garlic clove, minced
1 tsp sugar
¼ tsp English mustard powder
½ tsp black salt
Oil, for frying
A pinch of Kashmiri chilli powder, to garnish

Vegan?

Use your favourite dairy-free yogurt in place of the Greek yogurt. Try to find something nice and thick if you can. If the yogurt is already sweetened, skip the sugar in the recipe.

Make it a feast!

A bowl of cool raita is especially joyful when it's sitting next to biryani. The refreshingly cold yogurt and spicy rice is a festivity of textures and flavours. Try it with Ruffled Biryani (see page 176) or your favourite Indian breads.

Some of us sneak globs of chocolate spread and peanut butter straight from the jar. I take my spoon to the fridge for quiet spoonfuls of raita. This recipe takes the famous Indian yogurt dip on a fleeting trip around the Med with pops of crispy, salty, fried capers. Scoop, drizzle or dunk – it's your choice.

1. Spread out the drained capers on top of a few sheets of doubled-up kitchen paper. Pat them dry to remove as much moisture as you can.

2. Toast the cumin seeds in a dry frying pan (skillet) for a few minutes until fragrant. Coarsely crush them in a mortar with a pestle or use a rolling pin.

3. Cut the cucumber in half lengthways and use a spoon to remove the seeds. Dice the cucumber flesh into very small pieces. Set aside about a tablespoon for garnishing later.

4. In a bowl, combine the yogurt, diced cucumber, toasted cumin, garlic, sugar, mustard powder and black salt. Cover and refrigerate for a minimum of 30 minutes, or until needed.

5. Heat around 1–2 cm (⅓–¾ inch) oil in a deep, heavy-based pan. Place all the capers onto a slotted spoon or spider suitable for frying. Once the oil has reached a moderately hot temperature, around 160°C (320°F), add the capers all at once. Fry the capers for 2–3 minutes, moving them continuously, until lightly browned and crispy. Switch off the heat. Remove the capers from the oil and drain on a plate lined with kitchen paper. Allow to cool for 15 minutes.

6. Stir one-third of the capers into the chilled raita and sprinkle the rest on top. Garnish with the reserved diced cucumber and a pinch of Kashmiri chilli powder. Serve cold.

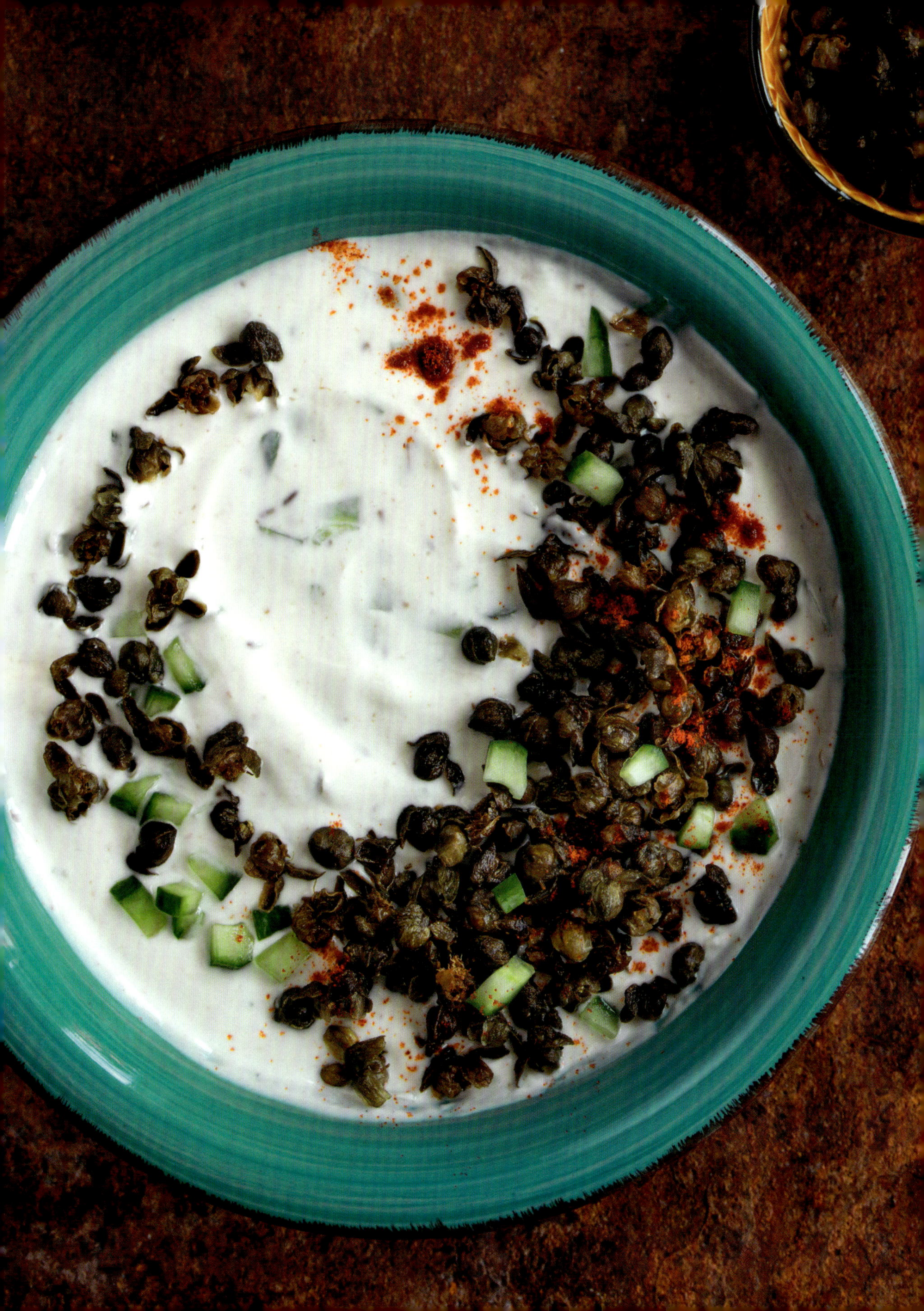

(V) (VG) (GF)

Traffic Light Chutneys

Stop. Wait. Go. These colourful Traffic Light Chutneys brighten up any dinner table and were made for spooning, dunking and drizzling. Serve them alongside all your favourite Indian dishes like samosas and bhajiya (pakora), as well as for chaats and smattered on hot chips (potato fries). There's a chutney to suit everybody in this selection. 'Red' is hot and spicy, 'Amber' is fruity and mild, and 'Green' is herby and aromatic. Try them all and pick your favourite.

Red Chilli Chutney
MAKES AROUND 125 ML (½ CUP)

1½ tsp cornflour (cornstarch)
1 tbsp Kashmiri chilli powder, plus 1 tsp
2 tbsp jaggery, grated (shredded)
2 tbsp lemon juice
1 tbsp ground fennel seeds
¾ tsp salt

Fiery flavours balanced with sweet jaggery and sharp lemon. This is a quick, no-blender chutney that you simply simmer, chill and serve. The thickening agent is cornflour (cornstarch), which gives the chutney a finish glossier than L'Oreal's hottest new lippy. If you don't have jaggery to hand, simply replace it with brown sugar.

1. In a small bowl, stir together the cornflour (cornstarch) and 60 ml (2 fl oz/4 tbsp) cold water.

2. Pour 175 ml (6 fl oz/¾ cup) water in a saucepan and bring to a boil. Add the Kashmiri chilli powder, jaggery, lemon juice, ground fennel seeds and salt. Whisk well. Once the mixture comes to a rolling boil, add the cornflour slurry. Continue to whisk until thickened and glossy, around 90 seconds.

3. Remove the pan from the heat and allow to cool to room temperature. Refrigerate for at least 30 minutes before serving.

Amber Mango and Coconut Chutney
MAKES AROUND 420 ML (1¾ CUPS)

200 ml (7 fl oz/generous ¾ cup) full-fat coconut milk
200 g (7 oz) peeled and chopped ripe mango (frozen works a treat)
50 g (1¾ oz) unsweetened dried mango pieces, roughly chopped
1 small garlic clove, roughly chopped
¼ tsp ground turmeric
¼ tsp freshly ground black pepper
Zest of 1 lime
½ tsp salt
2 tbsp finely diced red onion

A sweet and mild chutney packed with fruity flavours. This quick and easy mango-based chutney is made creamy with coconut milk and packs a zing with fresh lime zest. I use two types of mango (both dried and fresh) for intense flavour and a zippy tang.

1. To a small saucepan placed over a medium heat, add the coconut milk, fresh (or frozen) mango, dried mango, garlic, ground turmeric, black pepper, lime zest and salt. Bring to a boil and cover the pan with a lid. Simmer for around 10 minutes, or until the dried mango has softened. Allow to cool.

2. Place the mixture into a blender and blitz until smooth and creamy (or alternatively use a handheld stick (immersion) blender). You may need to add around 50 ml (1¾ fl oz/ scant ¼ cup) water to adjust the consistency. Stir in the diced onion.

3. Pour the chutney into a bowl and cover. Chill for a minimum of 1 hour before serving.

Green Coriander and Mint Chutney

MAKES AROUND 275 ML (1½ CUPS)

85 g (3 oz) fresh coriander (cilantro), including leaves and stalks
15 g (½ oz) fresh mint leaves
30 cashews, soaked in hot water for 30 minutes and then drained
3 thin green chillies (adjust according to your taste)
1 garlic clove
2 tbsp fresh lemon juice
½ tsp salt
1 tbsp sugar, plus 1 tsp
65 ml (2¼ fl oz/¼ cup) ice-cold water

My go-to smooth and creamy, street-style green chutney for drizzling over chaats, spreading in sandwiches and dipping bhajiya (pakora). This recipe is super aromatic and medium hot in flavour since you can add as few or as many chillies as you like. If you prefer a milder chutney, feel free to stir in some plain yogurt. Using ice-cold water will gift you the most vibrant green chutney.

1. Place all the ingredients in a blender. Blitz until everything is coarsely chopped.

2. Scrape down the sides of the blender jar to make sure everything blends evenly. Add a splash more water if you need to.

3. Blend again to achieve a smooth, creamy chutney.

4. Pour the chutney into a bowl and cover. Chill for a minimum of 1 hour before serving.

Note

It's an excellent, time-saving idea to freeze portions of chutney in ice-cube trays. They're ideal for serving alongside snacks when you have unexpected guests, or unexpected cravings of the solo kind. Simply pour into ice-cube trays, cover and freeze for up to 6 months. Pop the chutney cubes out of the tray, place into small bowls and defrost in the microwave. They are a great standby option and make preparing dishes that require a few different chutneys (such as chaats) a breeze.

Three great thickeners for chutneys

1. Nuts

Unroasted cashews, peanuts and almonds are all great options and impart very little additional flavour for a creamy but clean finish. I like to maximise their creaminess by soaking them in hot water for 30 minutes prior to blending. Think of them as doing the same job as pine nuts in pesto.

2. Cornflour

Cornflour (cornstarch) is a good option if you need a quick way to thicken without altering the core flavours of the chutney. It imparts no additional flavour and produces a shiny, pourable chutney.

3. Gathiya

This is an old Kenyan favourite. Made from fried gram flour noodles and effective at creating a thick paste when blitzed with herbs and aromatics. In fact, gathiya as the core ingredient of chutney is a very typical chutney to enjoy with daal kachori and daal bhajiya in Mombasa. Unlike the other two options, these have a deeply nutty flavour and often contain carom seeds, chilli powder and salt (which is why they make for excellent chutneys all on their own).

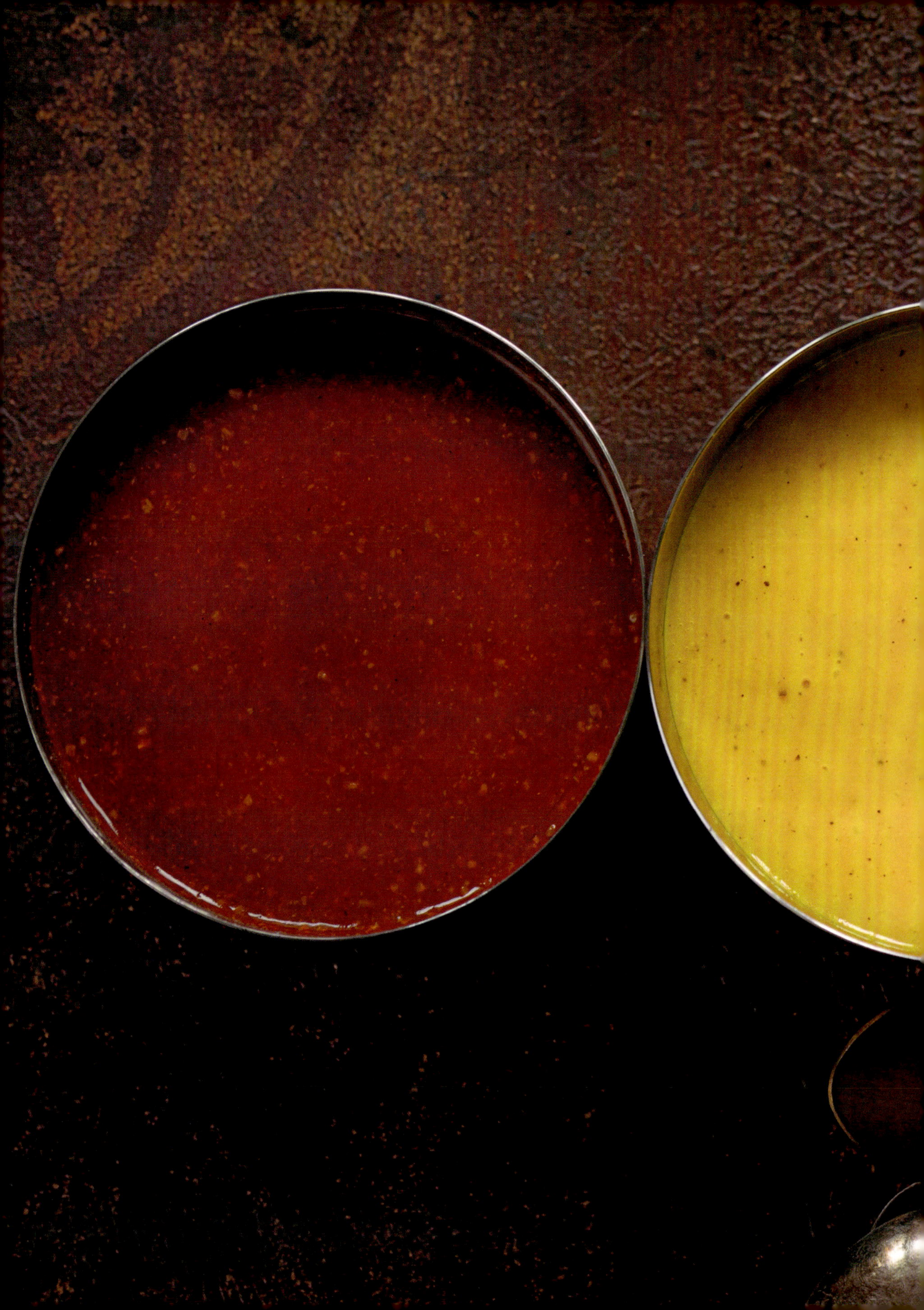

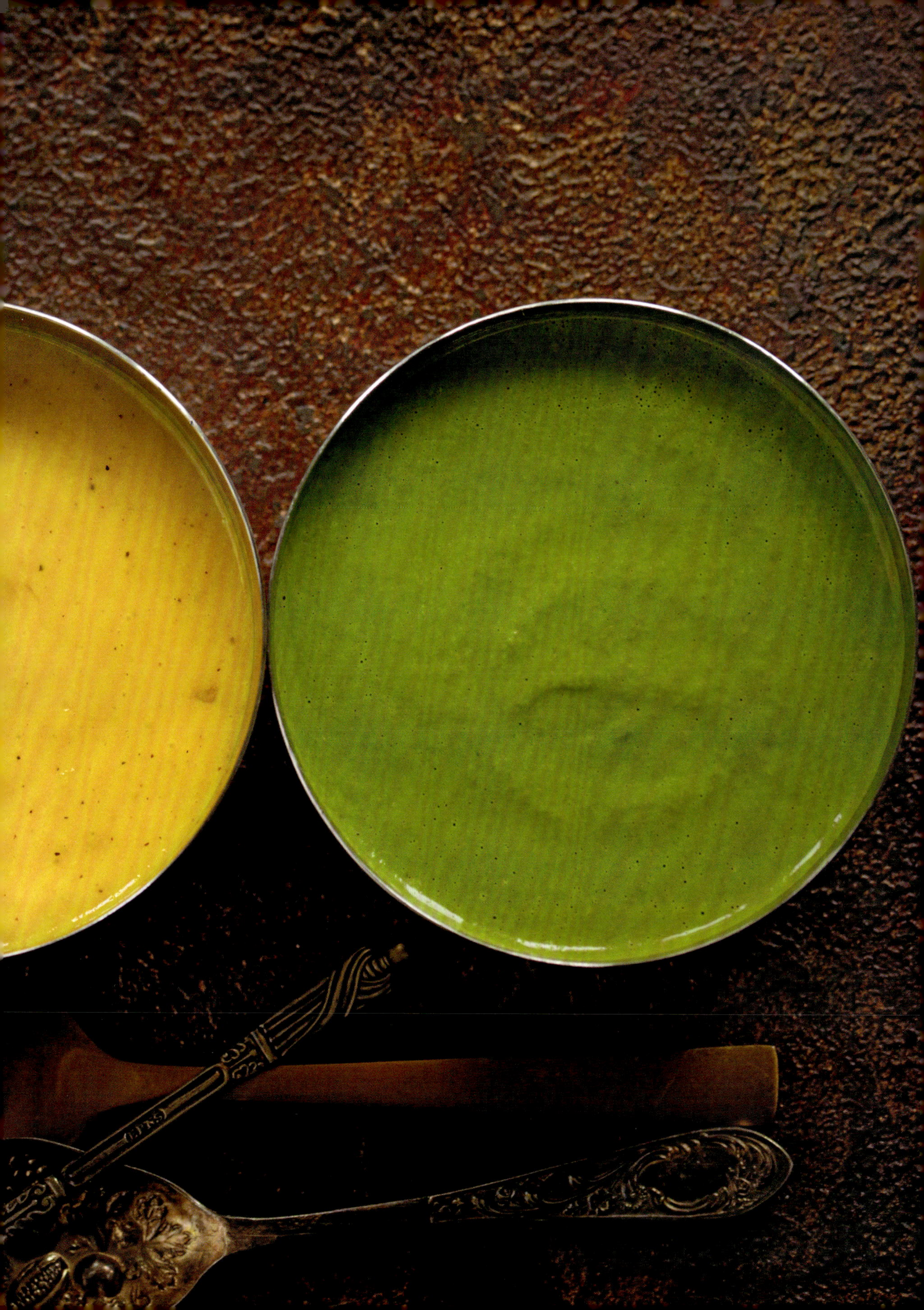

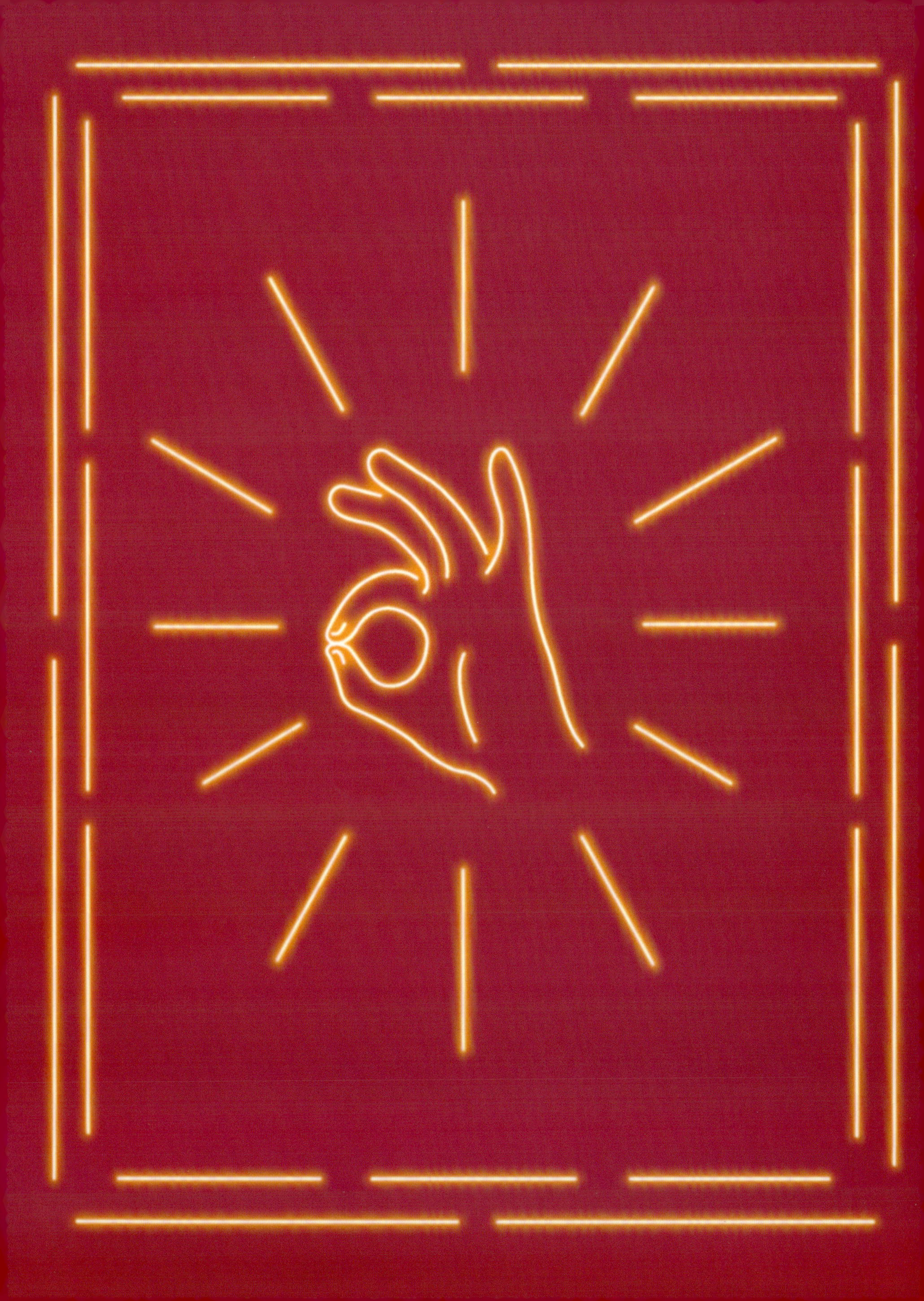

Sweets

Life is like a box of mithai.

My Nanabapu was a mithaiwala, a confectioner of Indian sweets (candies). He wore a flat cap and cooked with giant steel pots at Kakira sugar plantation on the shores of Lake Victoria, Uganda. Odhavji Haridas Thanky stirred vats of bubbling syrup and milk, with thoughts of perfecting his next great recipes for jalebi, mohanthal, boondi and halwa consuming his days with the same passion people would later devour his sweets. He was the eldest son of a large farming family in Gujarat. At the age of 14 he became an apprentice to his brother-in-law, a chef who worked for a wealthy family in Mumbai. During this time, drought and poor harvest badly affected the family farm and, as the eldest child, he took the decision to join a merchant by the name of Nanji Kalidas on a journey across the Indian Ocean to East Africa. It was the 1930s and with India and parts of Africa under the control of the British Empire, it was common for migrant Indian workers to cross borders in search of work, to support their families. It was there Nanabapu applied his cooking skills, aged just 16, preparing sattvic meals (plant-based whole foods aligned with the teachings of Ayurveda) for locals and other migrants. In the years to come, he flourished, travelling with associates across South Africa to Johannesburg and later to Mozambique. Nanabapu spoke in Gujarati, his mother tongue, peppered with Afrikaans, English and Portuguese. He collected words like recipes, each one reflective of the melting pot of people with whom he spent time cooking with and for. Food was their common language. After leaving Mozambique, he continued his travels across East Africa, meeting Mohanlal Modha, another chef and businessman who would later become my great, great uncle on my father's side. Armed with experience and a solid work ethic, he took a job as a personal chef to the Madhvani family, of the Madhvani Group in Uganda. It was here he was able to spend his days preparing feasts so plentiful they made tables groan. His final job before migrating to Britain was in Nairobi, Kenya, my mother's birthplace, as the head confectioner of the mithai shop, which he owned in partnership with his brothers. By the age of 18, Nanabapu married, fathered a child, and then tragically became a widower. He went on to remarry and had seven more children, of which six survived. The family moved around a lot, going wherever work was available. Britain was the next leg of the journey.

It was in the UK that Nanabapu lost his second wife (my Nanima). Their youngest child was just five. He became a single father of seven children, and a member of a marginalised community in Britain during the 1970s. On a modest salary, Nanabapu provided his children with a safe home in which to sleep, a loving parent they could talk to and, of course, perpetually full bellies. As a man whose love language was food, he grew his own fruits and vegetables and always kept a well-stocked pantry. My mother recalls his Chartreuse-coloured mango murabba freckled with whole cardamom seeds with a bittersweet nostalgia, much like murabba itself. She ate this fruity, spiced jam (preserves) with buttered rotli after school.

Much of Nanabapu's life was spent mastering his craft in other people's kitchens. Connecting with communities through the language of food was what truly cultivated joy in his heart. In his later years, he cooked for local Gurdwaras in Southampton, putting on giant spreads of Indian sweets, samosas and other savouries for the hundred people-strong congregations. He also worked in a factory to make ends meet. Like many parents, he strived to provide a bright future for his children.

Nanabapu passed his passion for cooking on to my mother. She is the guardian of his recipes and cooks Indian sweets like, well, the daughter of a mithaiwala. Growing up, I watched her create mountains of sweet thalis to take to the temple at festival time. She'd pour molten burfi (milk fudge) into steel plates, beat halwa shimmering and slick with ghee in pans the size of my torso. I'd soak up every moment like hot jalebi bathing in sugar syrup. I always knew what to expect, yet each year, her thalis managed to take my breath away.

With sugar syrup coursing through my veins, it later came as no surprise that I loved venturing into Indian sweetshops as a nipper, especially around Diwali. Wide-eyed and full of wonder, the shopkeepers would see me peering through their glass cases at the majestic displays of endless halwa, burfi, penda, jalebi, kaju katli, mohanthal gulab jamun, rasmalai and everything in between. I very quickly became an expert at getting free samples. My dad would always ask me what I'd like in my special box of sweets. I'd think long and hard about which ones would make the cut – it was a very important decision. To this day, he still buys me my own box of sweets and even if I'm not there to choose them, somehow he always picks my favourites. The sweets that always stood out were Bombay Halwa. They were bright and beautiful like the glittery jelly shoes I wore on summer days. Apart from burfi, they're one of the only sweets that come in a rainbow of colours: rows of translucent pink, yellow, green and orange jellies (jellos) studded with jewel-like pistachios and cashews. For me, it was always the pink ones. As an avid fan of C.S. Lewis's *The Lion, the Witch and the Wardrobe*, it reminded me of Jadis, the White Witch's wicked Turkish Delights that were conjured up to encourage Edmund's betrayal.

It was 1995 and I had begged my dad for a costume tiara from Bombay Stores in Bradford all summer. He finally caved in after some heavy persuasion and a nice little daal kachori pick-me-up from Kaushy Patel's Gujarati snack shop, Prashad. This was pre Gordon Ramsay declaring it his 'Best Restaurant' and long before it even became a dine-in establishment. In those days, we would be treated to some Indian snacks from Bradford's only vegetarian mithai shop one Sunday a month. Kaushy Aunty would always sneak me gulab jamun freebies as I peered through the glass counter of the chiller. She wore black kajal around her eyes and a huge smile on her face. I've always loved gulab jamun. I love their caramel brown colour and the way they glisten from almost every angle. I love their spongy texture and how they ooze cardamom syrup from the very first bite. I love them warm with vanilla ice cream. And sometimes with Devonshire custard. But what I love the most about gulab jamun is just how delicious they taste cold, straight from the fridge, when nobody is looking.

After loading up the boot of my dad's red VW Golf with savoury snacks, mithai and fruit and veg from the abundantly stocked Pakistani shop, Al-Halal, we'd head over to Bombay Stores; my happy place. Passing through the doors of Bombay Stores was like stepping onto the set of a Bollywood movie. A labyrinth of colourful saris and lenghas, glass counters filled with glimmering costume jewellery, incense and 'Aladdin' shoes with the curly toes as far as the eye could see. I'd have the 'Bombay Stoooooores' jingle from Zee TV adverts playing on loop in my head. The heavy scent of musty old Indian newspapers lingered in every corner. The smell of newspaper ink emanated from the saris – they were folded inside each sari to keep the fabric straight and the scent permeated every silky fibre. I took long, deep breaths and revelled in the anticipation of finally getting a tiara. Playing dress-up was always the same after that day. My go-to persona was a princess. Finally, I was no longer 'Little Diesel', a wresting protégé my brother had fashioned based on the infamous WWF (now WWE) character. Why? Because now I sported a tiara. I had arrived.

The first time I wore it outside the house was to the temple's Diwali fancy dress. I dressed up as the gopi, Radha. In Hinduism, she is a milkmaid and partner of Lord Krishna. Decked out in a shiny aubergine-coloured skirt and top (two sizes too big) and my mum's maroon lipstick, I felt like a million dollars. She gave me a faux beauty spot à la Cindy Crawford and painted my nails with her best bottle of fuchsia Revlon nail polish.

I lost the fancy dress competition to my brother. He was Shankar bhagwan (Mahadeva, an incarnation of Lord Shiva). He held a trident made of cardboard crisp boxes from our parent's corner shop, wrapped in foil, and a large rubber snake around his neck. Mum did a stellar job with his costume. I was happy with second prize, a box of Milk Tray, and my tiara still firmly on my head. Third prize went to my cousin, Vishal, who wore a long, grey school sock on his nose to resemble the trunk of the elephant god, Ganesha. It's a day I'll never forget, not only because of the glitz and glam, but because we all ate a lot of Indian sweets that day.

The sweet recipes in this chapter are based on my profound love of traditional Indian flavours; citrusy cardamom, warming cinnamon, the headiness of a few strands of saffron, the creamy realms of milk powder and condensed milk, a European introduction to the Subcontinent. However, many of my desserts take a gentle pivot into the world of treasured western dessert forms. Cakes, crumbles, buns and brownies are transformed by the addition of my favourite spices and more. Be ready to explore the foundations of Indian sweetmaking with my recipes for Sticky Toffee Gulab Jamun (see page 206) and White Chocolate Rasmalai (see page 213), whilst still enjoying well-known elements of the delicious sweets we all love. The Cardamom Jam Sponge (see page 219), Bourbon Biscuit Laddoos (see page 227) and Apple and Guava Crumble (see page 210) will, I hope, comfort your inner child with nostalgic flavours too.

Top: Nanabapu (Odhavji, my maternal grandfather) and my mum (Jyotsna)

Bottom left, clockwise from the top: Bindu, Nutan, Geeta, me, Vishal

Bottom right: Nanima (Jamna, my maternal grandmother)

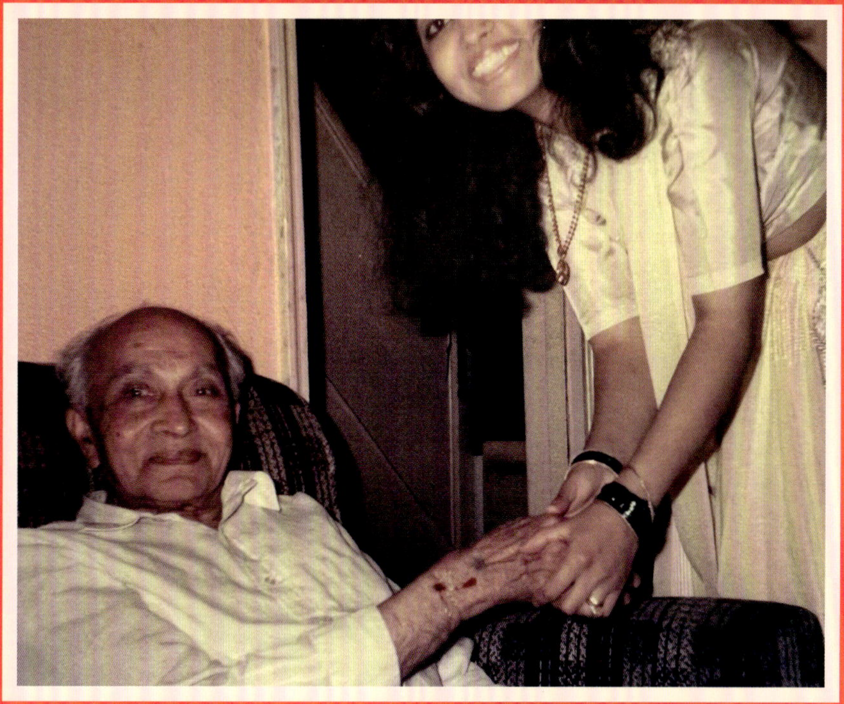

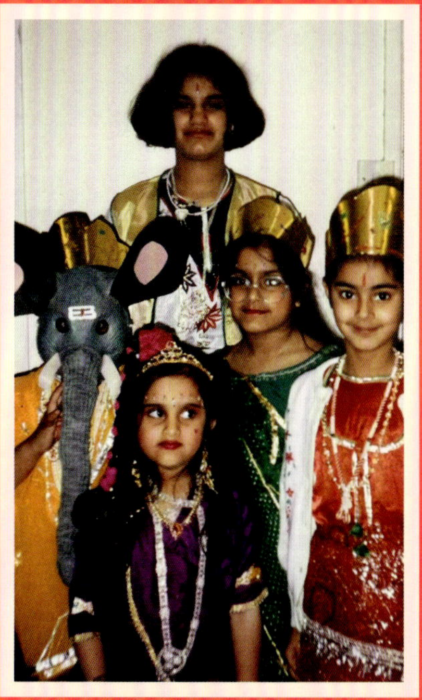

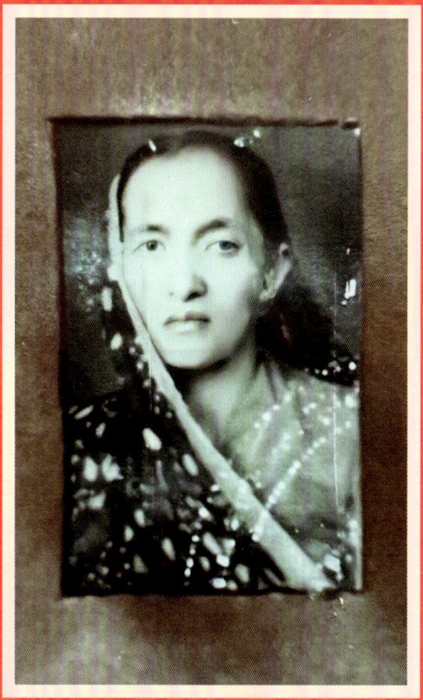

Sticky Toffee Gulab Jamun

MAKES 30 • PREP: 35 MINS, PLUS UP TO 48 HOURS RESTING • COOK: 45 MINS

For the jamun (fried milk balls)

60 g (2 oz) paneer
150 g (5¼ oz/scant 1¼ cups) full-fat milk powder
80 g (2¾ oz/⅔ cup) plain (all-purpose) flour
1 tbsp fine semolina
½ tsp bicarbonate of soda (baking soda)
2 tbsp melted salted butter
6 green cardamom pods, seeds ground
160 ml (5½ fl oz/⅔ cups) whole (full-fat) milk, at room temperature
1 litre (34 fl oz/4¼ cups) oil, for deep-frying
Edible dried rose petals, to decorate
Pistachio nibs, to decorate
Cream, crème fraîche or ice cream, to serve

For the sticky toffee sauce

300 g (10½ oz/generous 1¼ cups) unsalted butter
300 g (10½ oz/1½ cups) soft light brown sugar
600 ml (20 fl oz/scant 2½ cups) double (heavy) cream
A pinch of saffron (12-14 strands)
1 tbsp rose water
½ tsp flaky sea salt

Notes

The assembled, but unbaked toffee sauce-drenched gulab jamuns also freeze beautifully for up to 3 months.

This is a great dessert to make ahead of time. Everything can be prepared up to 48 hours in advance.

Gulab jamun, the most iconic of desserts, traditionally refers to spongy, caramelised milk balls bathed in a light sugar syrup. Swap the syrup dunk for a glossy sticky toffee sauce to pour over and you have a collision of heritage flavours from the Indian subcontinent and those reminiscent of a great British school dinner pudding.

1. On a clean work surface or platter suitable for kneading, grate (shred) the paneer. Using the heel of your palm, spread the paneer as thinly as possible across the work surface in a long, sliding motion. Apply enough pressure to press out any graininess and gather the mixture together again. Repeat this action 30-40 times until all traces of graininess have disappeared and the paneer is soft and smooth. This should take 5-6 minutes. Do not use a food processor.

2. To the paneer, add the milk powder, flour, semolina, bicarbonate of soda (baking soda), melted butter and ground cardamom. Use your fingers to crumble the mixture together. Add the milk and bring together to form a soft, sticky dough.

3. Knead the dough for 7-8 minutes until very smooth and soft. It might feel a bit sticky but do not add any more flour. The flour and semolina will hydrate and swell as the dough rests. Wrap the dough in cling film (plastic wrap) and allow to rest for 10 minutes.

4. Roll the dough into approximately 30-32 balls, each weighing 15 g (½ oz). Roll them between your palms using firm pressure to ensure the surface of each ball is smooth and free of any cracks. (If any of the milk balls are cracked, they will break in the oil, so it's important to ensure they're ultra-smooth.)

5. Heat the oil in a large pan, suitable for deep-frying. Once the temperature reaches 140°C (285°F), fry the milk balls in small batches of 4 or 5 at a time. Keep them moving all the time and do not overcrowd the oil as this will cause the temperature to drop. Don't let the oil go above 150°C (300°F) at any time. Continue frying until all the milk balls are evenly golden on the outside, about 5 minutes. Drain on absorbent kitchen paper and set aside.

6. To make the sauce, melt the butter in a pan and add the brown sugar. Stir to melt everything together. Once the sugar begins to bubble, carefully whisk in the cream and add the saffron. Continue to cook over a medium heat, whisking all the time, until the sauce thickens and turns a toffee colour, about 5-6 minutes. Be careful as it will bubble. Do not let it get too dark as the sauce will continue to cook in its residual heat as it cools. Once the desired toffee shade has been reached, switch the heat off and whisk in the rose water and sea salt.

7. Arrange the jamuns in a heatproof oven dish and pour the toffee sauce over the top. Cover the dish and refrigerate for up to 48 hours.

8. Just before serving, preheat the oven to 200°C/180°C fan/390°F/Gas mark 6. Uncover and bake in the oven for 8-10 minutes, until everything is just heated through and the toffee sauce is bubbling at the sides.

9. Decorate with edible dried rose petals and pistachio nibs. Serve hot with cold cream, crème fraîche or, dare I say it, ice cream.

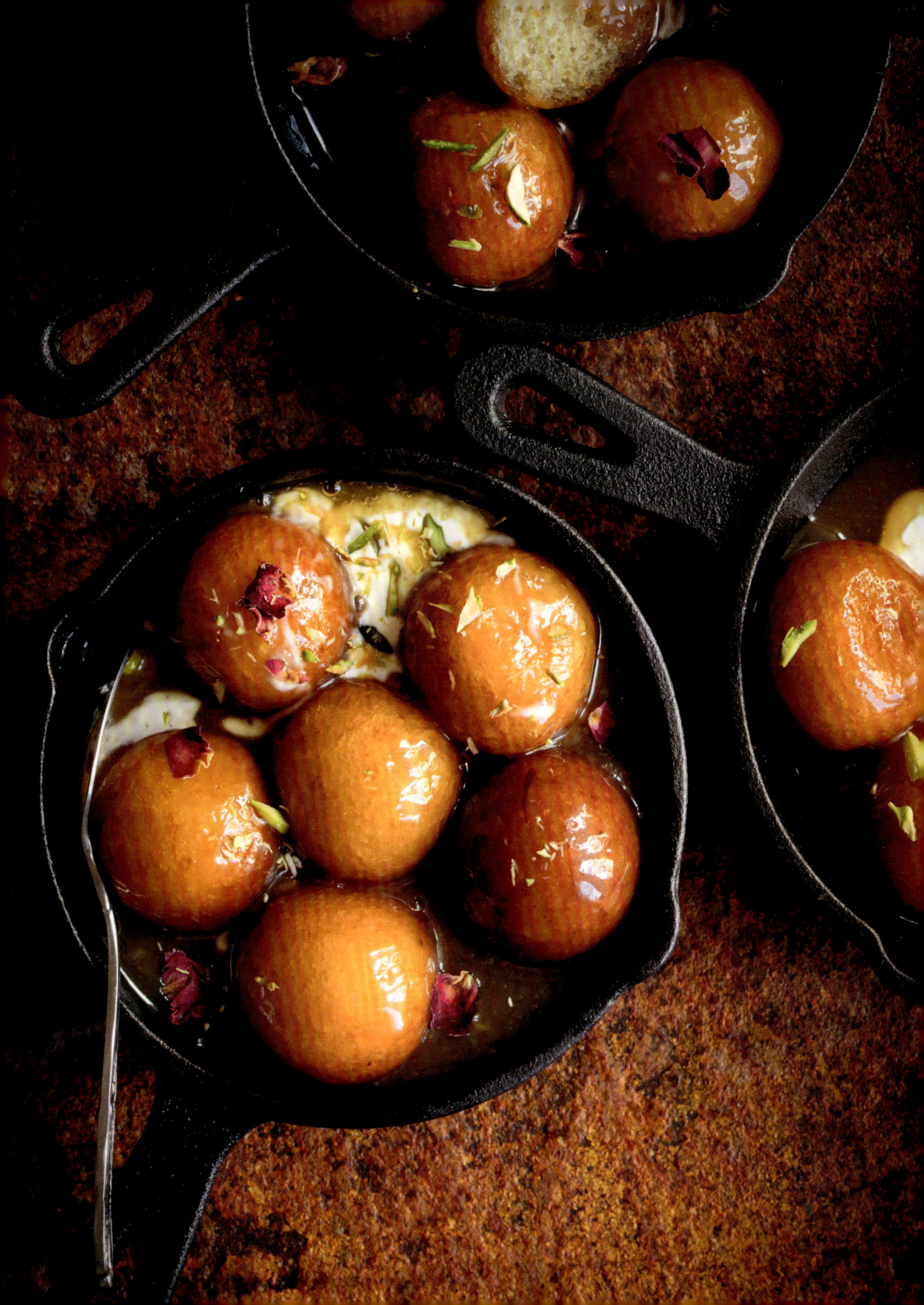

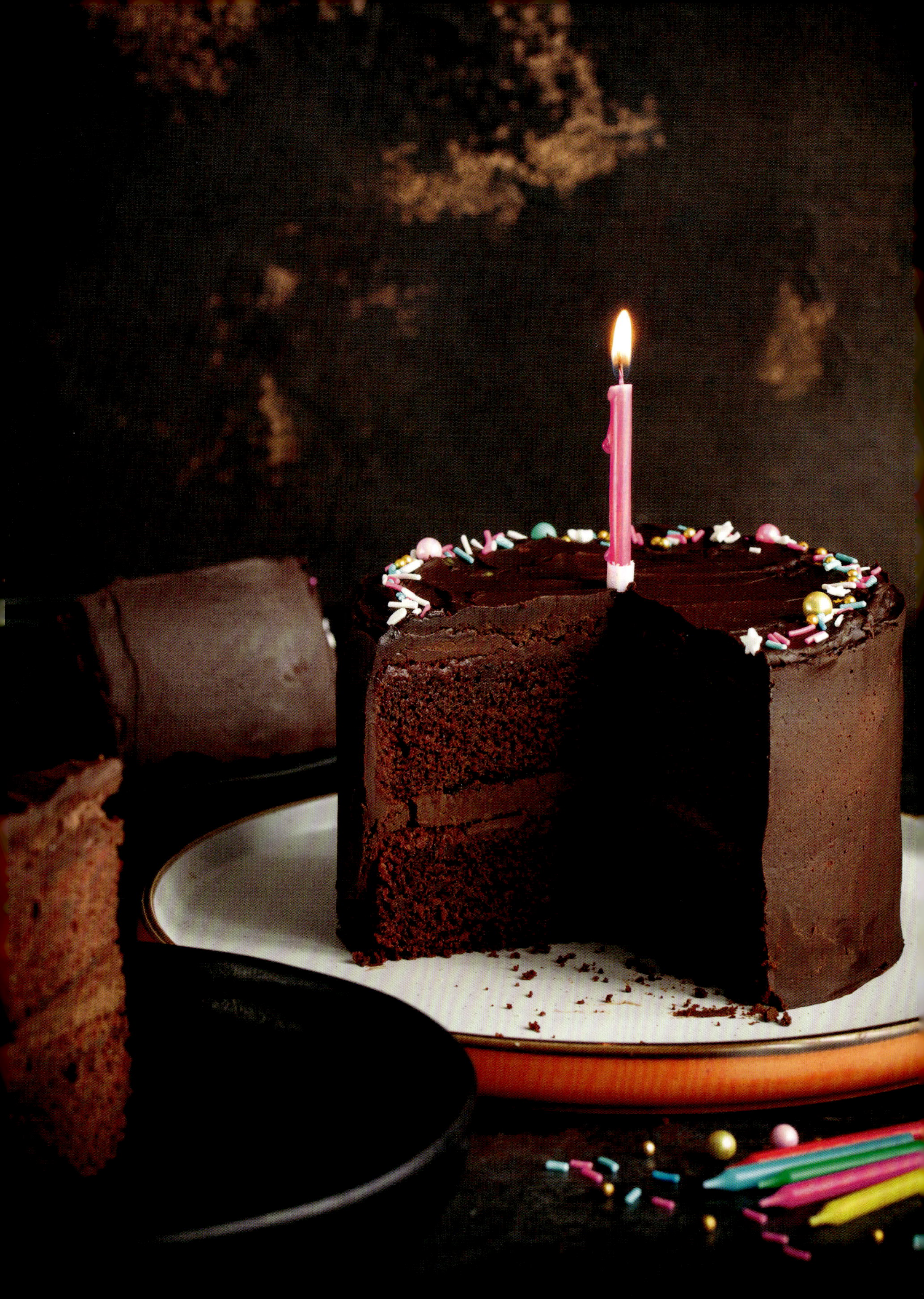

Cinnamon Chocolate Fudge Cake

SERVES 10 • PREP: 20 MINS, PLUS 1 HOUR CHILLING • COOK: 45 MINS

For the chocolate sponge
350 ml (11¾ fl oz/scant 1½ cups) whole (full-fat) milk
1 tbsp distilled white vinegar
1 tsp vanilla bean paste
1 tsp espresso powder dissolved in 2 tbsp hot water
175 ml (6 fl oz/¾ cup) vegetable oil
300 g (10½ oz/scant 2½ cups) plain (all-purpose) flour
65 g (2¼ oz/scant ⅔ cup) unsweetened cocoa powder
275 g (9¾ oz/1⅜ cups) soft light brown sugar
2 tsp ground cinnamon
1½ tsp bicarbonate of soda (baking soda)
⅛ tsp salt

For the whipped ganache
175 ml (6 fl oz/¾ cup) whipping cream
400 g (14 oz) dark (bittersweet) chocolate
175 g (6¼ oz/¾ cup) salted butter, softened
75 g (2⅔ oz/⅜ cup) soft light brown sugar

This decadent chocolate fudge cake is subtly spiced with a cinnamon cocoa sponge and whipped ganache. Light brown sugar gives the cake a rich caramel flavour and a shot of espresso intensifies the chocolatiness. Serve by the wedge.

1. Preheat the oven to 180°C/160°C fan/355°F/Gas mark 4. Grease and line two 15-cm (6-inch) baking pans.

2. To make the sponge, whisk together the milk and vinegar in a jug (pitcher). Allow to stand for 5 minutes before whisking in the vanilla, espresso and oil.

3. In a large mixing bowl, sift together the flour, cocoa powder, sugar, ground cinnamon, bicarbonate of soda (baking soda) and salt.

4. Pour the wet ingredients into the flour mixture and beat with a hand-held balloon whisk for 40–50 seconds, until smooth. Do not overmix the cake batter. If you're using a stand mixer or electric beaters, you will need to reduce the mixing time to no more than 30 seconds.

5. Divide the cake batter between the two prepared baking pans. Rap the pans on the countertop 5 or 6 times to encourage any air bubbles to come to the surface. Bake in the preheated oven for 45 minutes, or until a wooden toothpick inserted into the centre of the sponges comes out clean.

6. Once baked, remove from the oven and allow the sponges to cool in the pans for 10 minutes. Run a sharp knife around the edge of the sponges to release them from the pans and turn the cakes out on to a wire cooling rack. Allow to cool completely.

7. To make the ganache, heat the cream in a saucepan. Just as it begins to boil, switch the heat off and add in the chocolate, butter and sugar. Stir gently until everything has melted. Allow to cool to room temperature and then refrigerate for an hour, until thick and almost set. If it becomes too hard, leave it out at room temperature and allow to soften.

8. Using a stand mixer or electric beater, whip the ganache until it turns a shade paler and becomes light and fluffy.

9. If the sponges have domed a little, you can level the tops using a sharp, serrated knife, or leave them as they are for a more rustic look.

10. To assemble the cake, sandwich the sponges with some of the whipped ganache. Spread the rest of the ganache over the top and sides of the cake and smooth out using an offset spatula. Decorate as you prefer. I add a few sprinkles around the edge of the cake, but you can also pipe rosettes with the ganache if you like.

Vegan?
Swap the milk for any plant-based milk alternative. Dairy-free cream and butter can be used in the ganache. Be sure to check that your chocolate is free from dairy too!

Make it a hot chocolate cake like this...
Bake the cake batter in a greased 30-cm (12-inch) bundt or baking pan for 60–65 minutes, or until a wooden toothpick inserted into the centre of the sponge comes out clean. Allow to cool in the pan for 10 minutes and then turn the cake out onto a wire cooling rack for a further 10 minutes. Slice, plate up and pour the melted ganache over the top.

Apple and Guava Crumble

SERVES 6 • PREP: 20 MINS • COOK: 45 MINS

500 g (1 lb 2 oz) apples, such as Granny Smith or Bramley
500 g (1 lb 2 oz) ripe guavas
75 ml (2½ fl oz/⅓ cup) spiced dark rum
1 tbsp cornflour (cornstarch)
175 g (6¼ oz) guava jelly or guava jam (preserves)

For the crumble topping
100 g (3½ oz/scant 1 cup) self-raising flour
40 g (1½ oz/½ cup) rolled oats
½ tsp ground cinnamon
30 g (1 oz/¼ cup) Demerara sugar
80 g (2¾ oz/⅓ cup) salted butter, cold

Vegan?
Plant-based spread is fine to use in place of butter in this recipe.

Gluten free?
A gluten-free self-raising flour works perfectly well in place of regular self-raising flour in this crumble topping. If oats cannot be tolerated, use an equal measure of ground almonds (almond flour) in their place.

Tart apples, fragrant guava, spiced rum and a toasty, oaty topping come together in this warming crumble. If you can, go for Granny Smith or Bramley apples for a sharp contrast to the sweet guava jelly. If you don't have them, any eating apples lurking at the bottom of the fruit bowl will do. Serve with custard or ice cream for nostalgia, or do as I do and enjoy with a spoonful of cardamom mascarpone.

1. Preheat the oven to 180°C/160°C fan/355°F/Gas mark 4.

2. Peel and core the apples. Chop into large chunks, about 2 x 2 cm (¾ x ¾ inch).

3. Peel and core the guavas. Chop into large chunks and transfer to a plate. Using the back of a fork, mash them to a pulp (this is why it's important they're ripe).

4. Pass the mashed guava through a sieve (strainer), catching the pulp in a bowl. Press it with the back of a spoon to remove all the seeds (we don't want those in the crumble).

5. In a 20 x 24-cm (8 x 9½-inch) oven-safe baking dish or pie dish, combine the apples, guava pulp, rum and cornflour (cornstarch). Mix well to combine.

6. Chop the guava jelly into small cubes and scatter them over the fruit mixture. If you're using guava jam (preserves), dot blobs of the jam on top.

7. In a separate bowl, combine all the ingredients for the crumble topping except the butter. Grate (shred) the butter into the mixture using the coarse side of a cheese grater. Quickly rub everything together using your fingertips until the mixture resembles coarse breadcrumbs.

8. Scatter the crumble mixture over the macerated fruit and jelly.

9. Bake in the preheated oven for 40–45 minutes or until the crumble topping is crunchy and golden.

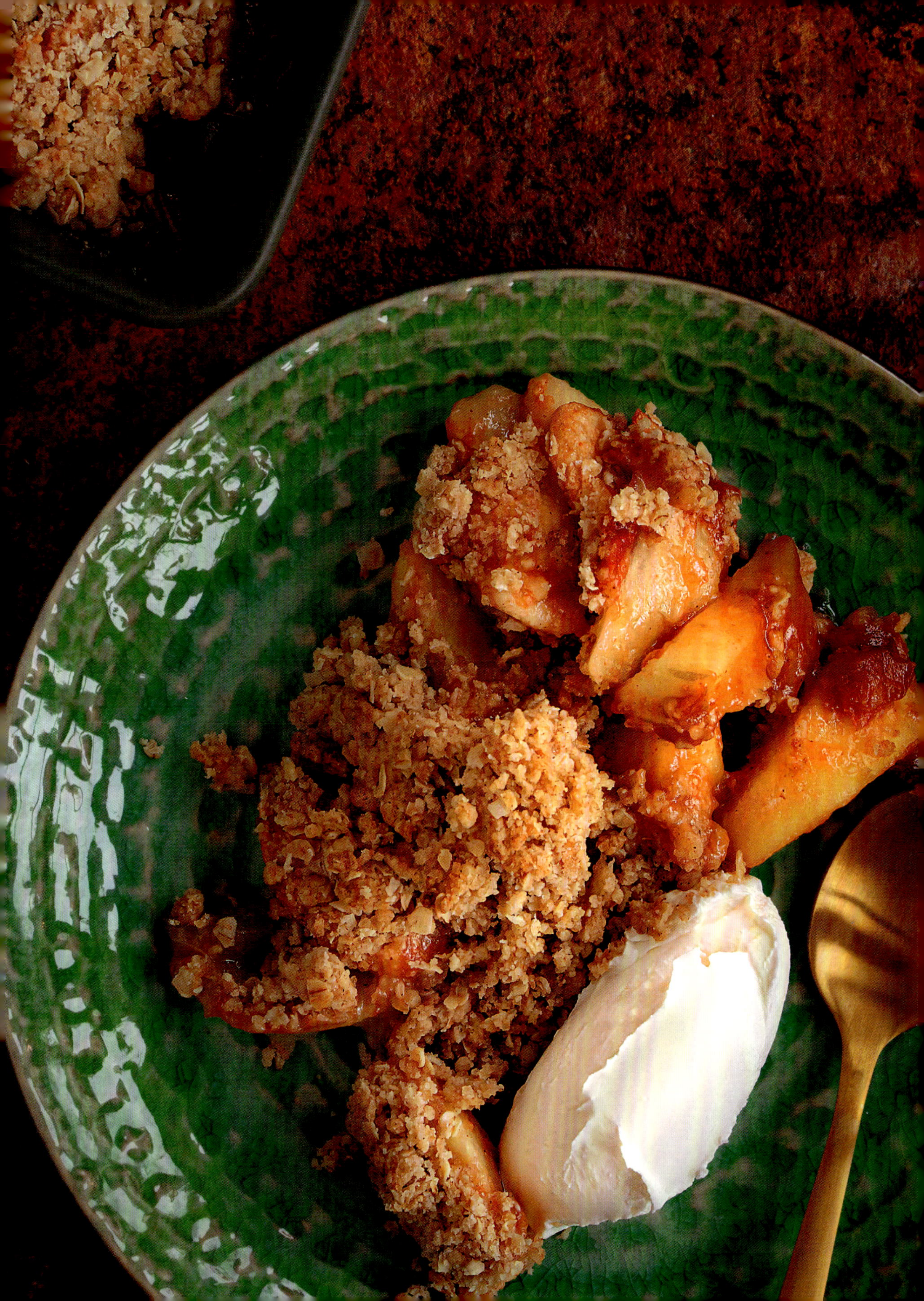

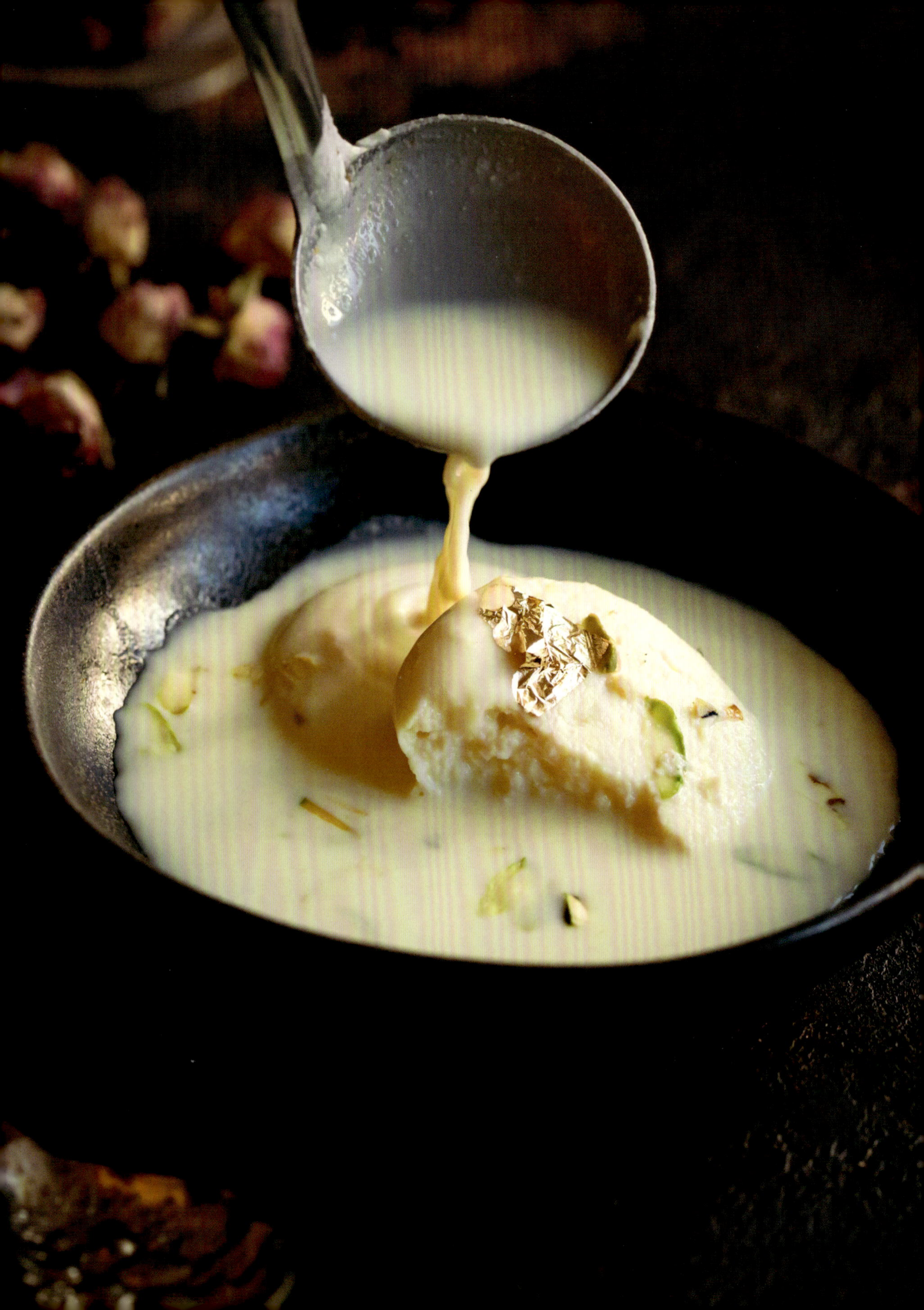

White Chocolate Rasmalai

SERVES 4 • PREP: 1 HOUR • COOK: 2 HOURS 50 MINS, PLUS 8-10 HOURS CHILLING

For the white chocolate milk
- 1 litre (34 fl oz/4¼ cups) whole (full-fat) milk
- 300 ml (10 fl oz/1¼ cups) double (heavy) cream
- 250 g (9 oz) white chocolate, chopped into small pieces
- 1 vanilla pod (bean), split lengthways and seeds scraped out
- 4 green cardamom pods, seeds ground
- A small pinch of saffron
- 1 tbsp flaked (slivered) almonds
- 1 tbsp flaked (slivered) pistachios

For the rasmalai
- ½ tsp oil, for greasing the base of the pan
- 2 litres (70 fl oz/8½ cups) whole (full-fat) milk
- 2 tbsp lemon juice, mixed with 1 tbsp cold water
- 1 litre (34 fl oz/4¼ cups) ice-cold water

For the sugar syrup
- 500 g (1 lb 2 oz/2½ cups) white granulated sugar
- 1 tsp lemon juice
- 2 tsp cornflour (cornstarch), mixed with 2 tbsp cold water
- 1 litre (34 fl oz/4¼ cups) ice-cold water

To decorate
- 8-10 edible dried rose petals (optional)
- Edible gold or silver leaf (optional)

Soft and spongy cheese dumplings soaked in sweet white chocolate, cardamom and saffron milk. Traditional Bengali rasmalai is served with a more classic style of spiced milk, however this version readily satisfies my inner eight-year-old's penchant for a Milkybar. Rasmalai is typically served chilled – just as chilled as you'll feel after you've eaten two or three.

1. For the white chocolate milk, pour the milk and cream into a large, heavy-based saucepan and bring to a gentle simmer. Add the white chocolate, vanilla seeds and split pod (bean), ground cardamom seeds and saffron strands. Bring to a boil and then turn the heat down to low. Allow to simmer, uncovered until reduced by half, about 40 minutes. Stir often to avoid the milk burning on the base of the pan. Once reduced, remove the pan from the heat, cover with a lid and set aside.

2. When cool, strain the white chocolate milk to remove any skin that may have formed during the boiling process. Pop any saffron strands back into the milk. Stir in the almonds and pistachios.

3. For the paneer, rub the base of a large, heavy-based saucepan with the ½ teaspoon of oil. (This makes cleaning up much easier.) Pour the milk into the oiled pan and bring to a rolling boil over a medium heat. Do not turn the heat up too high or the milk will burn. Turn off the heat and add the lemon and water mixture a tablespoon at a time, stirring briefly between each addition until the milk curdles. Once the curds have separated from the whey, add the ice water to stop the cooking process. Allow to stand for 5 minutes.

4. Line a colander with damp muslin or cheesecloth and place it in the sink. If you want to reserve the whey for another recipe, place the colander in a large bowl to catch the drained liquid. Carefully pour the mixture into the lined colander. Remove the bowl from under the colander (if using) or otherwise let the whey drain away. Rinse the curds under cold, running water to remove any sourness from the lemon juice.

5. Gather the corners of the cloth to enclose the curds. Gently twist the cloth to remove any excess moisture. Place the bundle back inside the colander resting on a plate or bowl. Apply approximately 1 kg (2 lb) of pressure on top of the bundle. You can use 3 or 4 cans of beans, a pan of water or anything stable that is heavy enough to press out the excess whey. Allow to press for 30 minutes.

6. For the sugar syrup, combine 2 litres (70 fl oz/8½ cups) of water with the sugar and lemon juice in a large, deep saucepan. Clip a sugar (candy) thermometer to the side to the pan. Bring to a boil and allow to boil until the syrup reaches 'thread' consistency (105°C/220°F). Turn the heat down to very low and cover the pan with a lid.

continued overleaf

Sweets 213

7. To make the rasmalai pieces, remove the weight from on top of the paneer bundle and unwrap. Place the paneer on a clean work surface and dab with kitchen paper to remove any excess moisture. Break the paneer into rough pieces and knead it with your hand. Using the heel of your palm, spread the paneer as thinly as possible across the work surface in a long, sliding motion. Apply enough pressure to press out any graininess and gather the mixture together again. Repeat this action 40-50 times until all traces of graininess have disappeared. This should take 10-12 minutes.
Do not use a food processor. The paneer should be soft and smooth, not grainy or greasy. If the dough feels oily, it has been overworked.

8. Divide the paneer into 24 equal pieces. Lightly oil your hands and roll each piece into a ball. Roll them between your palms using firm pressure to ensure the surface of each ball is smooth and free of any cracks. Lightly press to form a disc or patty, about 3 cm (1 inch) in diameter.

9. Bring the syrup back to a rolling boil (105°C/220°F). Add the cornflour (cornstarch) and water slurry and stir briefly. Next, carefully drop 6 of the rasmalai pieces into the hot syrup. Do not overcrowd the pan as the pieces will inflate to double or triple their size during cooking. Place the pan back on the heat and cover with the lid.

10. Boil hard for 15 minutes until the rasmalai pieces have at least doubled in size. Keep a kettle or separate pan of hot water near and quickly ladle hot water into the pan every 5 minutes during the cooking process. This will ensure the sugar syrup remains at the same consistency. If the rasmalai pieces are turning dark, the syrup is too concentrated. Add more hot water and bring it back to (105°C/220°F). Do not at any point add cold water.

11. Once the 15 minutes are up, turn the heat down and gently remove the cooked rasmalai pieces with a slotted spoon, draining the excess syrup. Place in a bowl of ice-cold water immediately to halt the cooking process. Allow to sit in the water for 3 minutes and then, very gently, press each piece between your palms to remove excess liquid and flatten slightly. Slide the rasmalai pieces into the white chocolate milk.

12. Repeat the process a further three times for the remaining batches of rasmalai pieces. Ensure the sugar syrup is the correct consistency throughout by adding more water at regular 5-minute intervals during the boiling process. Use a timer for best results.

13. Once all the rasmalai pieces have been added to the white chocolate milk, cover the pan and refrigerate for 8-10 hours for the rasmalai pieces to absorb the milk. Garnish with the optional edible dried rose petals and edible gold or silver leaf.

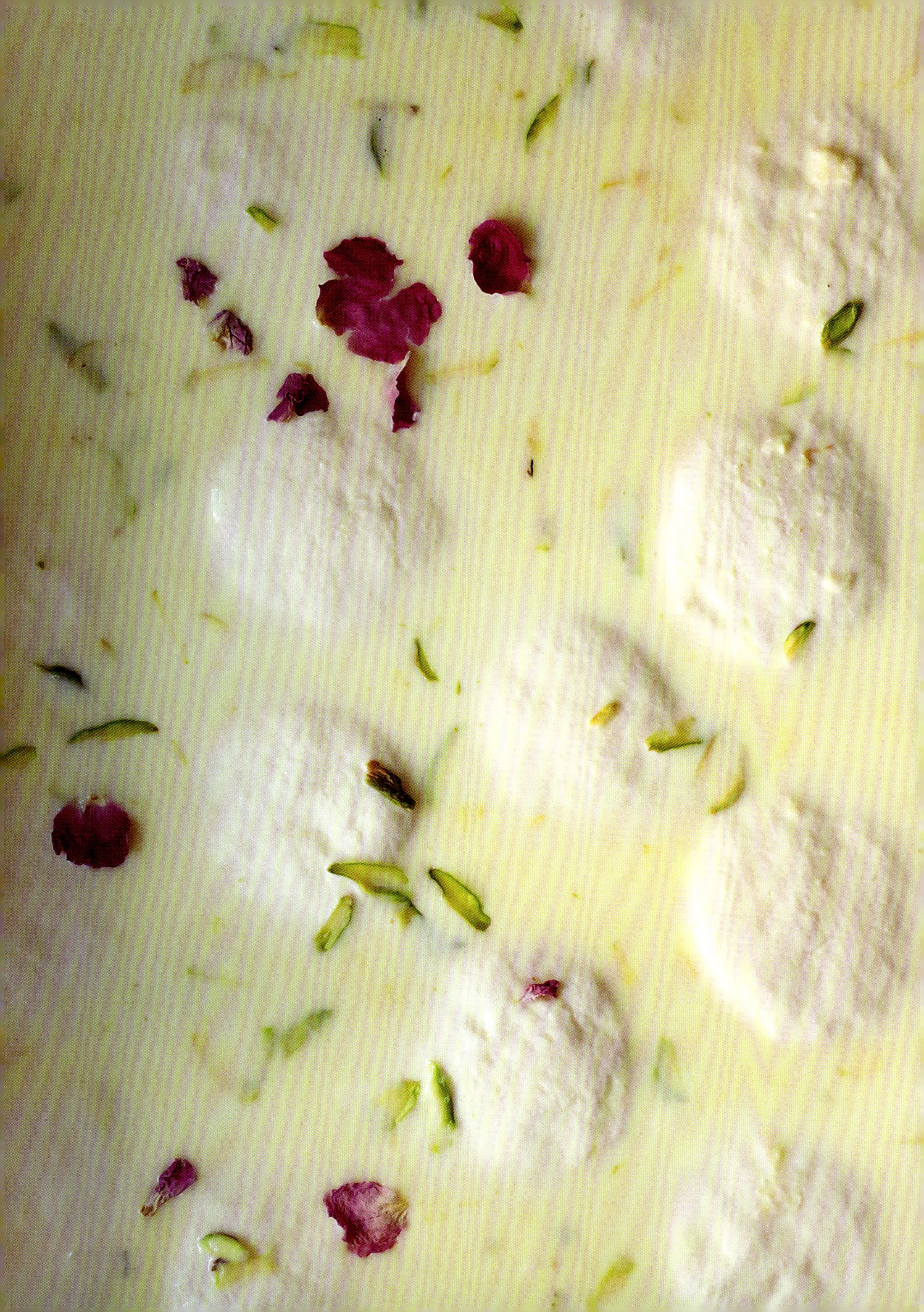

Badtameez Brownies

SERVES 12 • PREP: 25 MINS • COOK: 40 MINS

125 g (4½ oz/½ cup) unsalted butter

200 g (7 oz) dark (bittersweet) chocolate

220 g (7¾ oz/1¾ cups) plain (all-purpose) flour

40 g (1½ oz/⅜ cup) unsweetened cocoa powder

1 tsp ground cinnamon

2 tsp strong espresso grounds or powder

1 tsp baking powder

150 ml (5 fl oz/scant ⅔ cup) aquafaba (liquid from a can of unsalted chickpeas (garbanzo beans)

125 g (4½ oz/⅝ cup) soft light brown sugar

125 g (4½ oz/½ cup) granulated white sugar

75 g (2⅔ oz) milk chocolate, cut into hefty chunks

75 g (2⅔ oz) blonde chocolate, cut into hefty chunks

80 g (2¾ oz/¾ cup) salted roasted pecans

This recipe title is to be said in the most harrowing Bollywood villain voice possible... Presenting the biggest, baddest brownies you'll ever eat. 'Badtameez' is a Hindi word used to refer to someone who is utterly wicked. Think Amjad Khan's character, Gabbar (complete with his terrifying mafia moustache), from the 1975 movie, Sholay. Blonde chocolate, milk chocolate, coffee, cinnamon and salted pecans run through these dark, dense and chewy brownies.

1. Preheat the oven to 180°C/160°C fan/355°F/Gas mark 4. Grease and line a 20-cm (8-inch) square non-stick cake pan with parchment paper. Leave a 3-cm (1-inch) overhang at two sides of the pan that you can use to lift the brownies out.

2. Melt the butter in a heavy-based saucepan. Keep the heat low to ensure the butter browns slowly and evenly without burning. Cook, stirring continuously. The butter will go from being yellow to having large bubbles, then foamy, and finally turn a deep amber colour, rather like golden syrup. Some foam will subside and there will be toasted milk solids at the bottom of the pan. There is no need to skim off any foam or sediment as this is brown butter, not ghee. The brown butter will smell incredibly buttery and nutty. This process should take around 5 minutes from start to finish. Switch the heat off and add the chopped dark (bittersweet) chocolate. Whisk until the chocolate has melted and set aside to cool.

3. Sift together the flour, cocoa powder, ground cinnamon, espresso and baking powder in a mixing bowl.

4. In the bowl of a stand mixer fitted with the whisk attachment, whisk the aquafaba until frothy, about 3 minutes. Add a few tablespoons of each of the sugars and continue to whip until peaks form, about 3 minutes. Add the remaining sugars and whip for a further 4 minutes, until glossy peaks form.

5. With the mixer running at slow speed, drizzle the cooled chocolate butter mixture into the beaten aquafaba meringue. Once incorporated, switch off the mixer.

6. Add the sifted dry ingredients to the chocolate meringue mixture and mix on slow speed until thick and smooth. Do not overmix.

7. Fold the milk and blonde chocolate chunks and pecans into the meringue mixture.

8. Spoon the mixture evenly into the prepared brownie pan and level the surface using the back of a spoon or spatula.

9. Bake in the preheated oven for 35 minutes or until the top of the brownies is crackly. They will still have a little bit of a wobble until they cool. Allow to cool completely in the pan. Lift the brownies out of the pan and, using a sharp knife and wiping the blade between each cut, slice the brownies into squares.

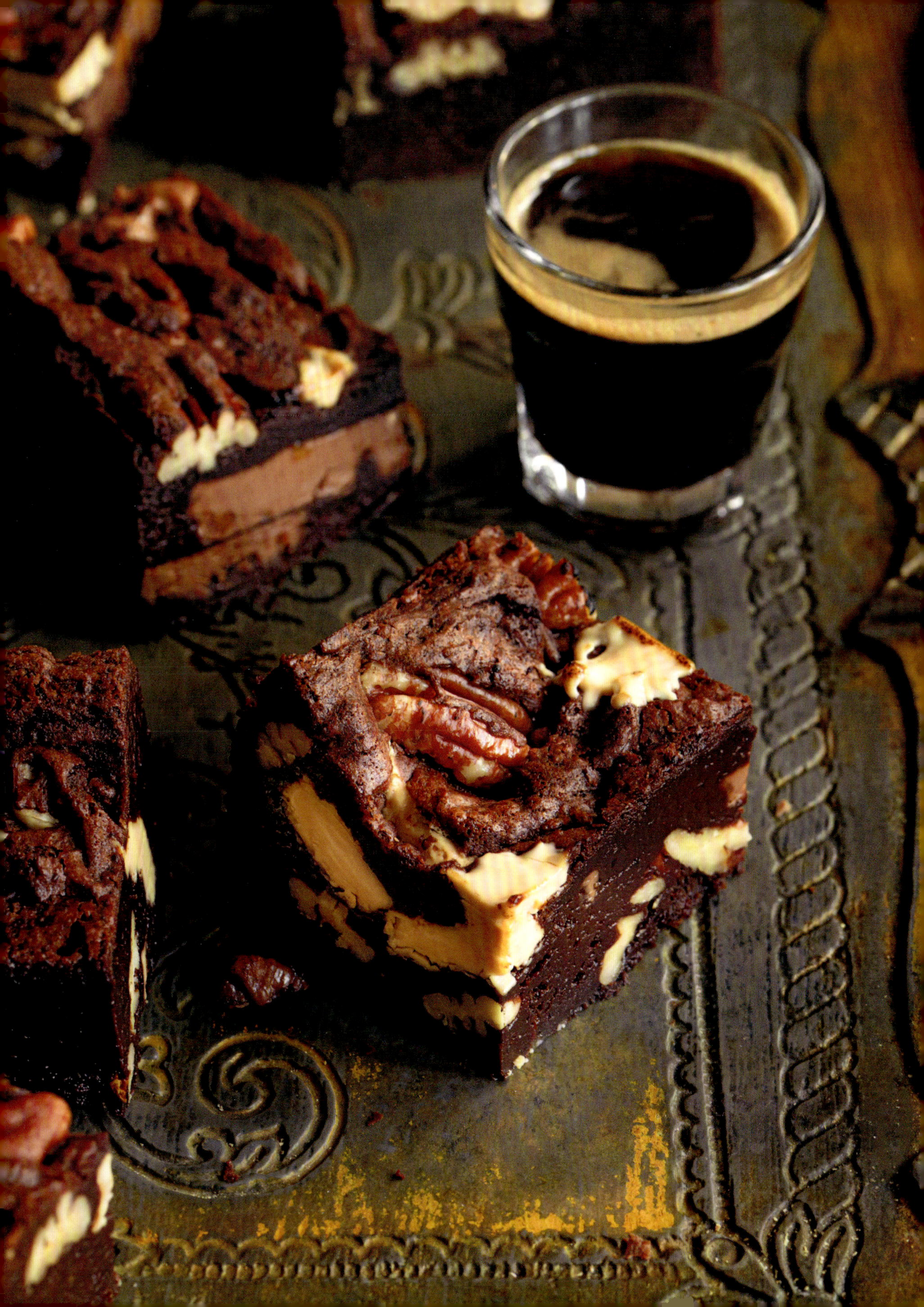

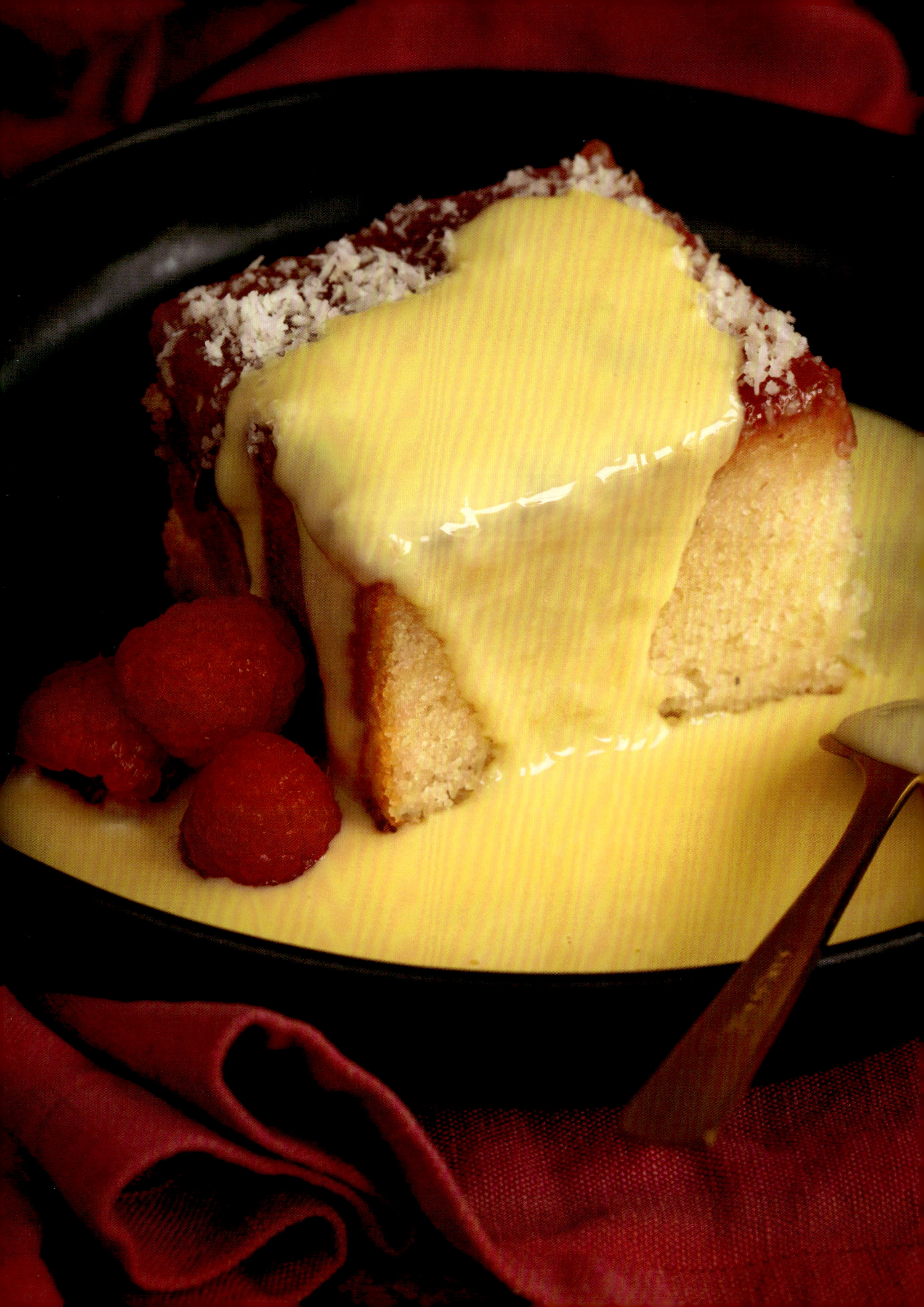

Cardamom Jam Sponge

SERVES 8-10 • PREP: 20 MINS • COOK: 45 MINS

480 ml (16¼ fl oz/scant 2 cups) whole (full-fat) milk, at room-temperature
2 tsp lemon juice
340 g (12 oz/2¾ cups) self-raising flour
300 g (10½ oz/1⅓ cups) caster (superfine) sugar
2 tbsp cornflour (cornstarch)
¾ tsp baking powder
25 g (¾ oz/scant ¼ cup) full-fat milk powder
6 green cardamom pods, seeds finely ground
¼ tsp fine salt
180 ml (6 fl oz/¾ cup) neutral oil (such as vegetable)
1 tbsp vanilla extract
200 g (7 oz/⅔ cup) seedless raspberry jam (preserves)
3 tbsp desiccated coconut
Vanilla custard, to serve
Fresh raspberries, to serve

This is reminiscent of the giant trays of steamed sponge pudding served up at school, albeit a slightly more grown-up version. A substantial pinch of cardamom in the sponge batter, as well as raspberry jam (preserves) and a flurry of coconut, gives this old favourite a simple but sensational revamp.

1. Preheat the oven to 180°C/160°C fan/355°F/Gas mark 4. Grease and line a 30 x 20 x 5-cm (12 x 8 x 2-inch) rectangular traybake pan with parchment paper.

2. In a jug (pitcher), stir together the milk and lemon juice. Allow to stand for 10 minutes.

3. Sift the flour, sugar, cornflour (cornstarch), baking powder, milk powder, ground cardamom and salt into a large bowl.

4. Whisk the oil and vanilla extract into the milk mixture which should have thickened slightly.

5. Pour the milk mixture into the dry ingredients and whisk until the batter is relatively smooth. Do not overmix the batter – no longer than a minute by hand or 30 seconds if using an electric beater.

6. Fill a roasting pan halfway with boiling water. Place this on the bottom rack of the oven to create some steam.

7. Pour the batter into the prepared traybake pan. Rap the pan on the countertop a few times to encourage any air bubbles to come to the surface. Bake on the centre rack of the preheated oven (with the tray of water positioned on the rack underneath) for 40–45 minutes, or until a wooden toothpick inserted into the centre of the sponge comes out clean. Do not open the oven door for at least the first 35 minutes of cooking.

8. Remove the sponge from the oven and allow to cool in the pan for 10 minutes before turning it out onto a wire cooling rack.

9. Spoon the jam (preserves) into a heatproof bowl and microwave for 20–30 seconds to loosen. Stir well.

10. Spread the jam over the still-warm sponge and sprinkle with desiccated coconut.

11. The only legal way to serve this is to cut the sponge into hefty squares, drench it in as much hot custard as your heart desires and add some fresh raspberries on the side (optional).

Pistachio Bread and Butter Pudding

SERVES 4 • PREP: 20 MINS • COOK: 1 HOUR

4 large slices of white bread
50 g (1¾ oz/scant ¼ cup) unsalted butter, softened
75 g (2⅔ oz) dark (bittersweet) chocolate chunks (optional – alternatively, use white or milk chocolate)
1½ tbsp cornflour (cornstarch)
250 ml (8½ fl oz/1 cup) whole (full-fat) milk, plus an extra 3 tbsp
125 ml (4¼ fl oz/½ cup) double (heavy) cream
150 g (5¼ oz) pistachio cream
30 g (1 oz/⅛ cup) caster (superfine) sugar
1 tsp almond extract

To sprinkle on top

2 tbsp roasted pistachios, crushed
A large pinch of edible dried rose petals (optional)
2 tsp icing (confectioners') sugar, to dust

The toasty top of a bread and butter pudding is the equivalent of a corner piece of brownie, or that craggy, cheese-crusted edge of lasagne. The crunchy corners of this one peek through a soft-baked pistachio custard like a shiver of sharks, fins exposed. Dust with icing (confectioners') sugar and finish with crushed roasted pistachios. Dark chocolate (bittersweet) is optional, but highly recommended.

1. Preheat the oven to 180°C/160°C fan/355°F/Gas mark 4.

2. Spread the slices of bread with a generous amount of butter. Stack the slices on top of each other and cut into triangles.

3. Arrange the bread triangles in a 23-cm (9-inch) buttered pie dish or baking dish. Scatter the chocolate chunks on top of the bread (if using).

4. In a small bowl, stir together the cornflour (cornstarch) and the 3 tablespoons of milk.

5. Heat the rest of the milk in a saucepan. Whisk in the double (heavy) cream, pistachio cream, caster (superfine) sugar, almond extract and cornflour slurry. Whisk continuously until the mixture thickens and just comes to a simmer, but do not allow it to boil.

6. Slowly pour the hot milk mixture over the bread in the dish.

7. Bake in the preheated oven for 40–45 minutes, or until the edges of the bread are toasty.

8. Just before serving, scatter over the roasted pistachios and edible dried rose petals and dust with icing (confectioners') sugar.

Note

Pistachio cream is available to buy online and from Italian grocers. Look for a jar labelled with 'pistachio cream', not pistachio paste or pistachio butter. Pistachio cream has added sugar and milk to create a creamy spread, rather like everyone's favourite chocolate and hazelnut spread. If you can't find it, try making your own or swap it for peanut butter. Top the pudding with crushed, roasted peanuts for a chocolate-peanut bread and butter pudding. If you do this, you can leave out the almond extract.

Make it a feast!

For a decadent dessert, serve this bread and butter pudding hot with frozen berries and pouring cream.

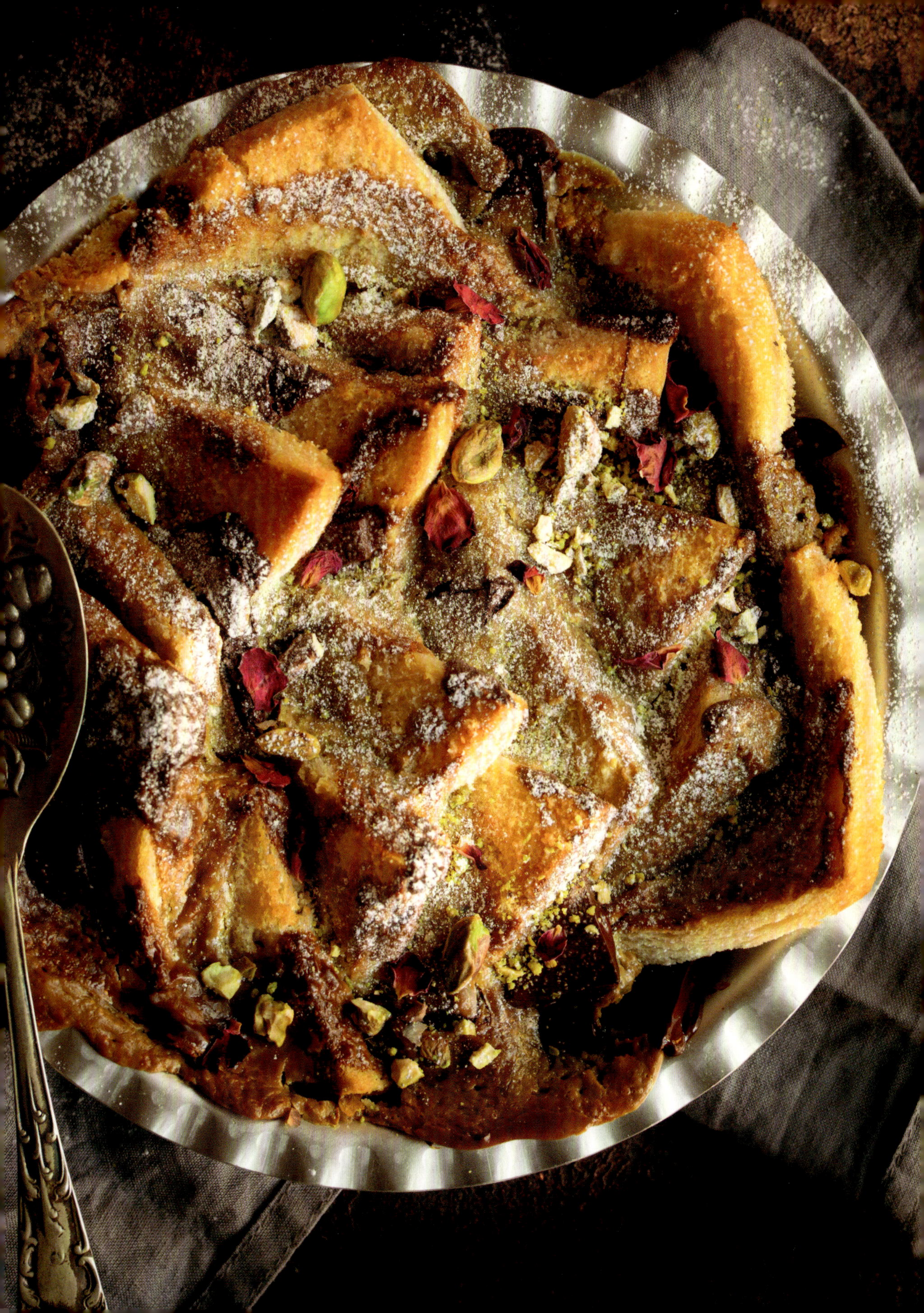

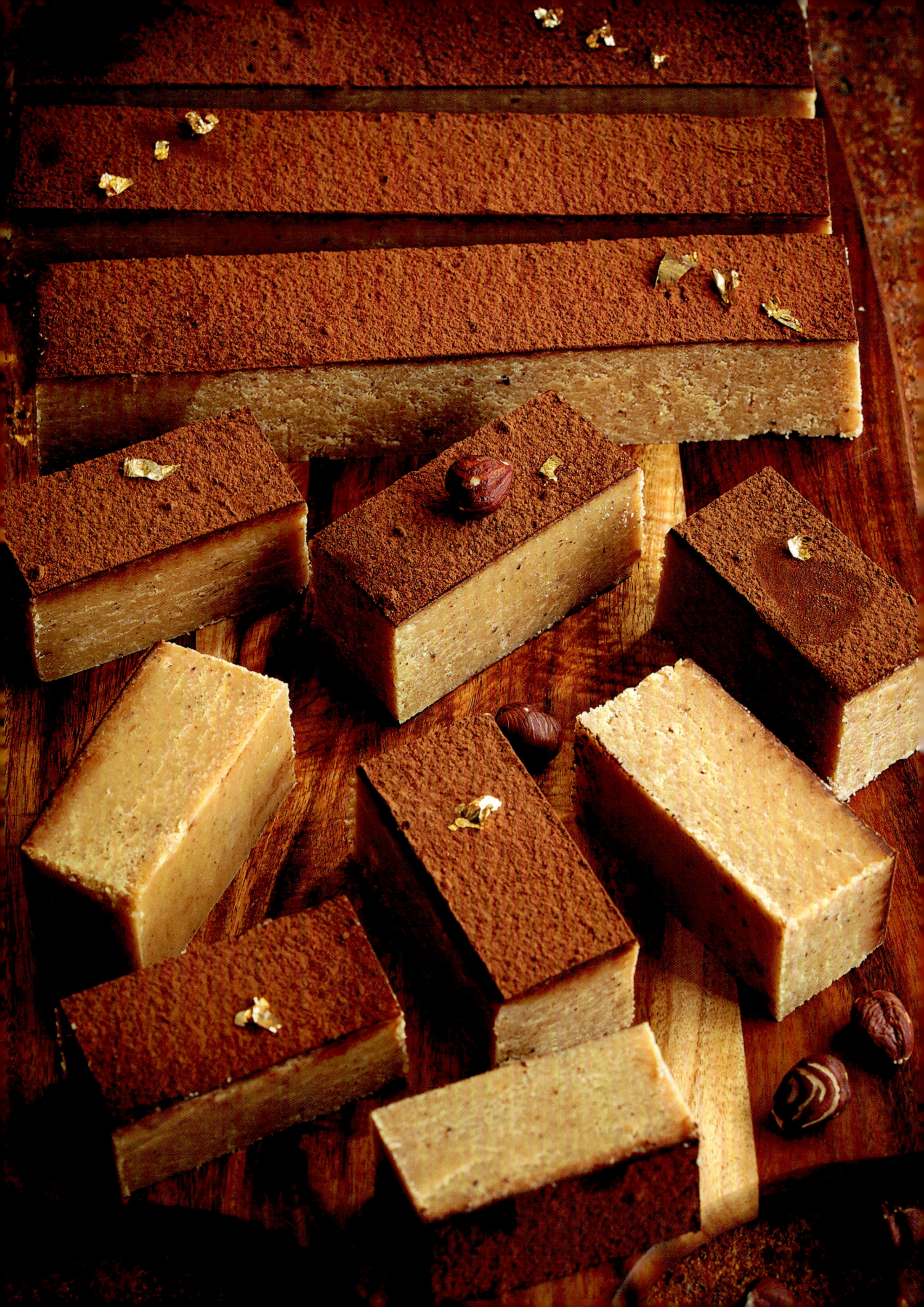

Hazelnut Cocoa Burfi

MAKES 18-20 PIECES • PREP: 30 MINS • COOK: 45 MINS, PLUS 2½ HOURS COOLING AND CHILLING

180 g (6¼ oz/1¼ cups) whole hazelnuts

130 g (4½ oz/½ cup) salted butter

300 ml (10 fl oz/1¼ cups) whole (full-fat) milk

415 g (14½ oz/3¼ cups) full-fat milk powder

250 g (8¾ oz/1¼ cups) soft light brown sugar

1 tsp vanilla extract

2 tbsp unsweetened cocoa powder

Edible gold leaf, to decorate (optional)

No festival or special occasion is complete without burfi. This fudgy-textured milk sweet is traditionally very sweet, with a melt-in-the-mouth texture. Here's a deeply nutty version made with roasted hazelnuts, salted brown butter and cocoa powder, all of which balance that obligatory sweetness. These flavours remind me of the creamy hazelnut filling of a very popular chocolate bar. This is especially good after a meal, alongside a shot of espresso.

1. Preheat the oven to 160°C/140°C fan/320°F/Gas mark 3. Line a 30 x 20 x 5-cm (12 x 8 x 2-inch) rectangular traybake pan with parchment paper, leaving an overhang of 3 cm (1 inch) at both of the widest sides.

2. Place the hazelnuts on a baking tray and roast in the preheated oven for 12-14 minutes. Remove from the oven and allow to cool completely. Once cool, place the hazelnuts on a clean dish towel and scrunch to close. Rub the hazelnuts in the towel to remove as many skins as possible. It's fine if some are left on. Place the hazelnuts in a food processor and pulse until they resemble ground almonds (almond flour).

3. Over a low heat, melt the butter in a large, non-stick saucepan. Cook, stirring continuously. The butter will go from being yellow in colour, to producing large bubbles, followed by foam, and then finally it will become a deeply golden colour, rather like golden syrup. Some foam will subside and there will be toasted milk solids at the bottom of the pan. There's no need to skim off any foam or sediment, this is brown butter, not ghee. This process should take around 7 minutes from start to finish.

4. To the brown butter, add the roasted and ground hazelnuts, milk, milk powder and sugar. Stir well and bring to a boil. It will thicken quite quickly. Cook this mixture over a low heat, stirring continuously for 20 minutes, or until thick and paste-like, rather like stiff mashed potato. Add the vanilla extract and continue to stir until incorporated.

5. Press the hot burfi mixture into the prepared pan. Use an offset spatula to flatten the surface. Allow the burfi to cool to room temperature. Cover and refrigerate for 30 minutes.

6. Carefully lift the burfi slab out of the pan. The parchment should come away easily. Using a sieve or fine-mesh strainer, dust the burfi with cocoa powder and decorate with the optional gold leaf. Use a sharp knife to cut the burfi into pieces. Serve at room temperature.

Scruffy Milo Rolls

MAKES 8 · PREP: 20 MINS, PLUS 1½ HOURS RESTING · COOK: 18-20 MINS

½ tsp fast-action dried yeast
150 ml (5 fl oz/scant ⅔ cup) warm milk
250 g (8¾ oz/2 cups) strong white bread flour
2 tbsp caster (superfine) sugar
¼ tsp salt
2 tbsp oil

For the filling
3 tbsp softened unsalted butter
2 tsp Milo, ground to a coarse powder (use crushed Malteasers if you can't find Milo)
1 tsp unsweetened cocoa powder
1 tsp ground cinnamon

For the frosting and topping
75 g (2⅔ oz/¾ cup) icing (confectioners') sugar
1 tbsp whole (full-fat) milk
2 tbsp Milo, ground to a coarse powder

When I was five, I told my grandad I loved the baby bananas I got to eat at his home in Kenya. The next day, he brought home an entire branch of baby bananas, hacked directly from the tree, just for me. From that moment on, I knew I was at home there. During the six weeks I spent visiting family in Mombasa we went on safari and saw the wildest animals. But for me, the best part was hanging out on the apartment roof drinking Milo with my brother and cousins. If you've never tried this malted chocolate wonder, think crushed Malteasers destined to be stirred into hot or cold milk. It was so good we'd sneak spoonfuls directly from the can. This recipe takes me back to Bapuji's house, complete with a Cheshire Cat chocolatey smile.

1. Sprinkle the yeast into the warm milk and give it a brief whisk. Allow to stand for 10 minutes until frothy.

2. Sift the flour, sugar and salt in a large bowl. Pour in the milk mixture and oil. Knead in the bowl (or on a clean work surface if you prefer) until soft and smooth, around 5 minutes.

3. Place the dough in a large, greased bowl and cover the bowl with cling film (plastic wrap). Keep in a warm place for an hour, until doubled in size. This might take longer if the room is cold.

4. Meanwhile, make the frosting. In a small bowl, mix the icing (confectioners') sugar and milk until smooth and a runny consistency is achieved.

5. In a separate bowl, combine the ingredients for the filling.

6. Knock back the dough and form it into a ball. Roll the dough out into a large, wide rectangle, about 30 x 15 cm (12 x 6 inches). Spread the soft filling over the dough and roll into a long, tight log. Using a sharp knife, cut the log into 8 equal pieces.

7. Place the rolls in a 25-cm (10-inch) greased cake pan, cut-side-up leaving some room around each one. Cover with cling film and allow to rise in a warm place for 30 minutes.

8. Preheat the oven to 190°C/170°C fan/375°F/Gas mark 5.

9. Bake in the preheated oven for 18–20 minutes, or until risen and golden on top. Remove from the oven and drizzle with the frosting while the rolls are still warm. Spoon or sprinkle generous amounts of crushed Milo over the top. Serve warm or at room temperature.

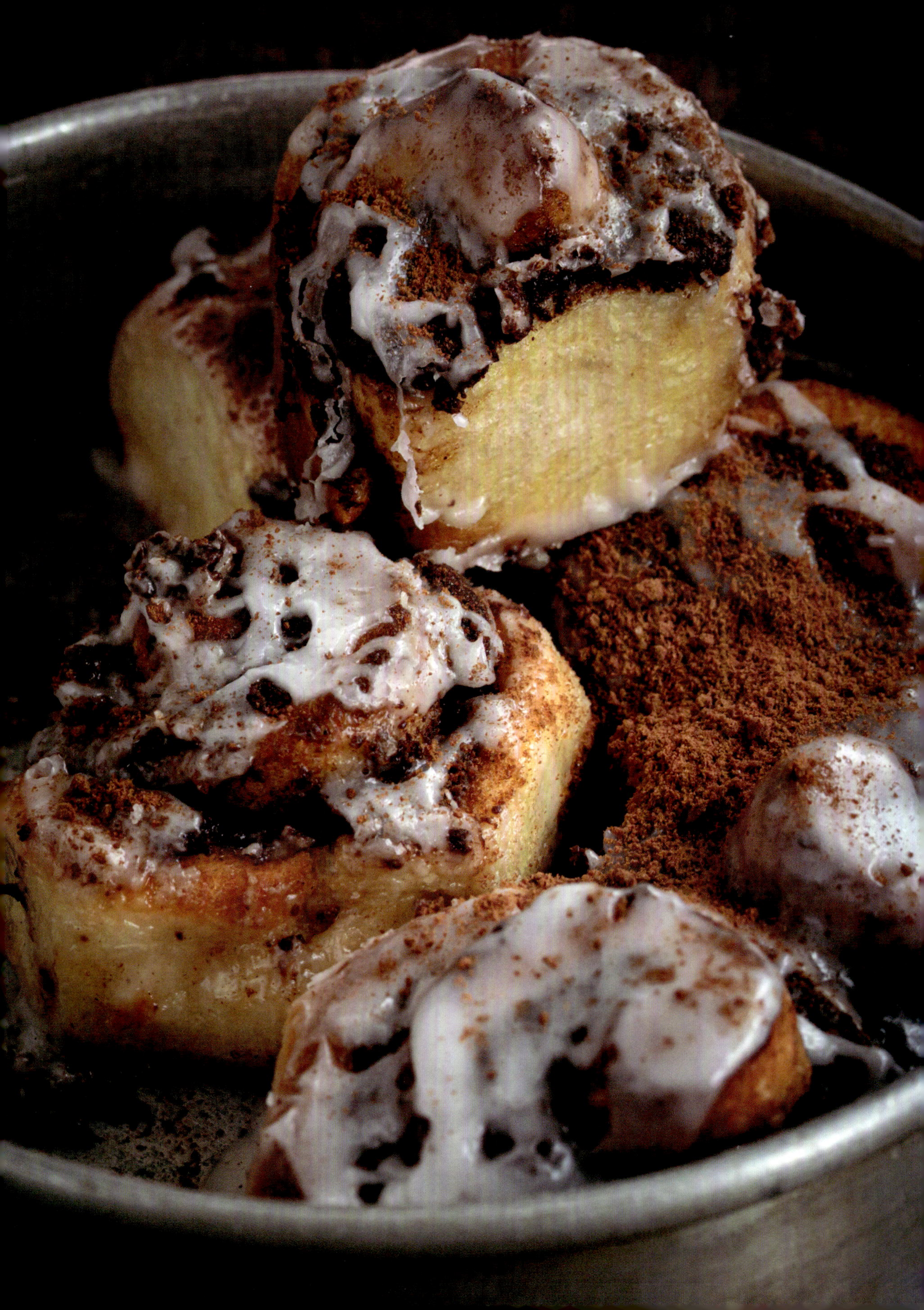

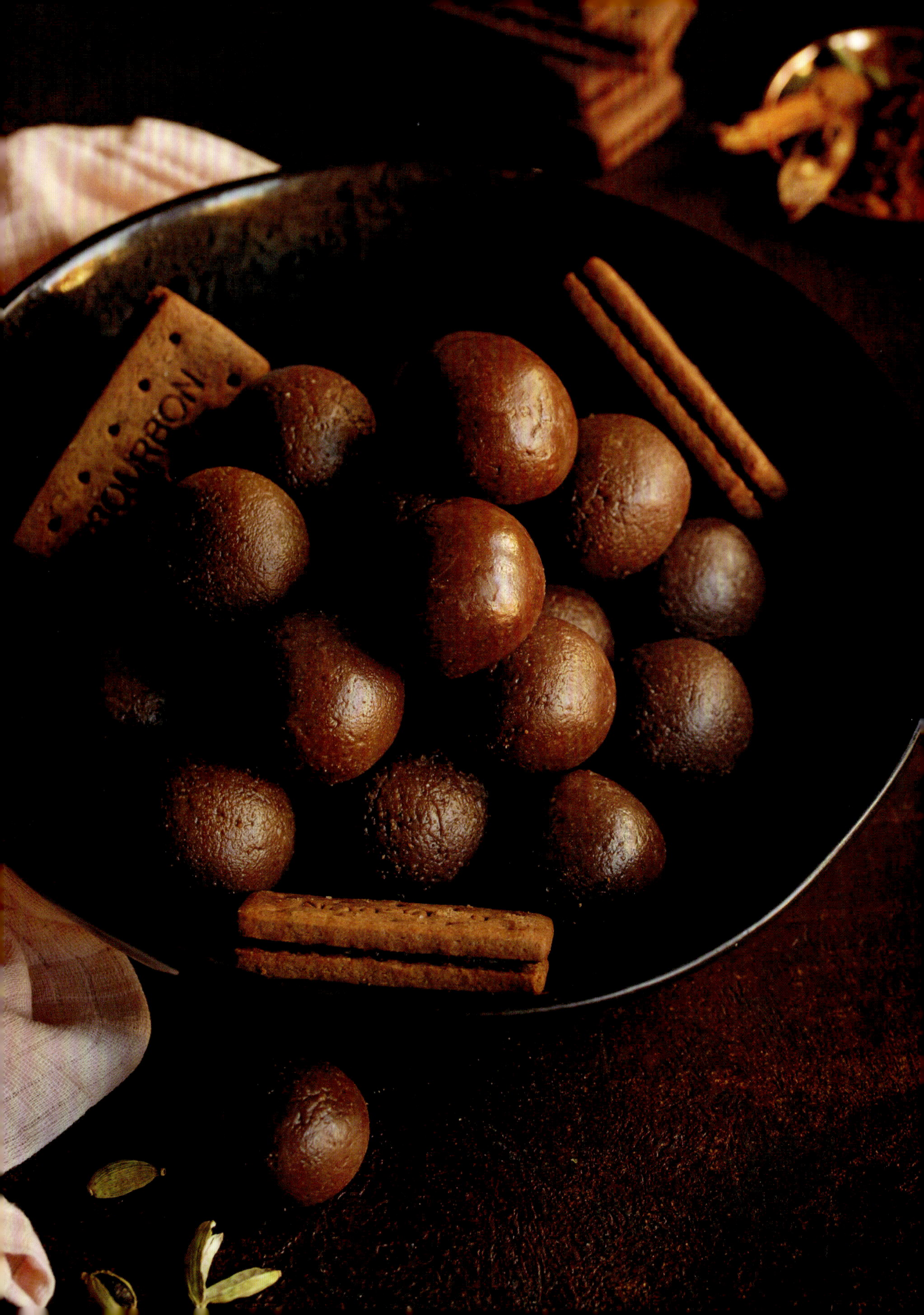
BOURBON

Bourbon Biscuit Laddoos

MAKES 20 LADDOOS • PREP: 30 MINS • COOK: 5 MINS, PLUS 2 HOURS RESTING

300 g (10½ oz) Bourbon biscuits (cookies), broken in half

100 g (3½ oz/¾ cup) full-fat milk powder

190 g (6¾ oz/⅔ cup) sweetened condensed milk

50 ml (1¾ fl oz/scant ¼ cup) warm water

6 green cardamom pods, seeds removed and finely ground

¼ tsp ground mace

Storage

Store in an airtight container in the fridge for up to a week. Allow the laddoos to come to room temperature before serving.

Notes

If Bourbons aren't your thing, this recipe works just as well with Custard Creams and Oreos.

Laddoos are a popular sweet to gift during religious and cultural festivals. Jazz these up for sharing with friends and family by decorating them with edible flowers, edible gold or silver leaf, nuts, melted chocolate, or a combination of them all.

Variations on the laddoo can be found across India, from coconut and puffed rice, to gram flour, nuts, sesame and even ground-up, leftover roti. My mother always told me that you can turn anything into a laddoo. Here's my joyful interpretation of her disclosure, featuring Bourbon biscuits (cookies) (a.k.a. the best biscuits in the world). These fudgy Bourbon biscuit balls come together in minutes. An (almost) no-cook recipe you can gift to your friends and family, or to yourself.

1. Pulse the biscuits (cookies) in a food processor until they resemble fine breadcrumbs. Alternatively, pop them into a clean plastic bag and bash with a rolling pin. The biscuit crumbs should be fine, as though you are preparing a cheesecake base. Pour the biscuit crumbs into a large bowl and stir in the milk powder.

2. In a small saucepan, combine the sweetened condensed milk, water, ground cardamom seeds and mace. Warm over a low heat until it just starts to bubble, but do not allow it to boil. Switch the heat off.

3. Pour the condensed milk mixture into the biscuit crumbs and stir with a spoon until cool enough to handle.

4. Bring the mixture together using your hands. Work it until you are able to form the mixture into a ball without it crumbling. If it feels too dry, add a teaspoon of warm water until you can form a ball.

5. Divide the mixture into 20 equal portions. Roll each piece into a ball between your palms under firm pressure until smooth on the surface. Allow to stand at room temperature for a couple of hours before eating.

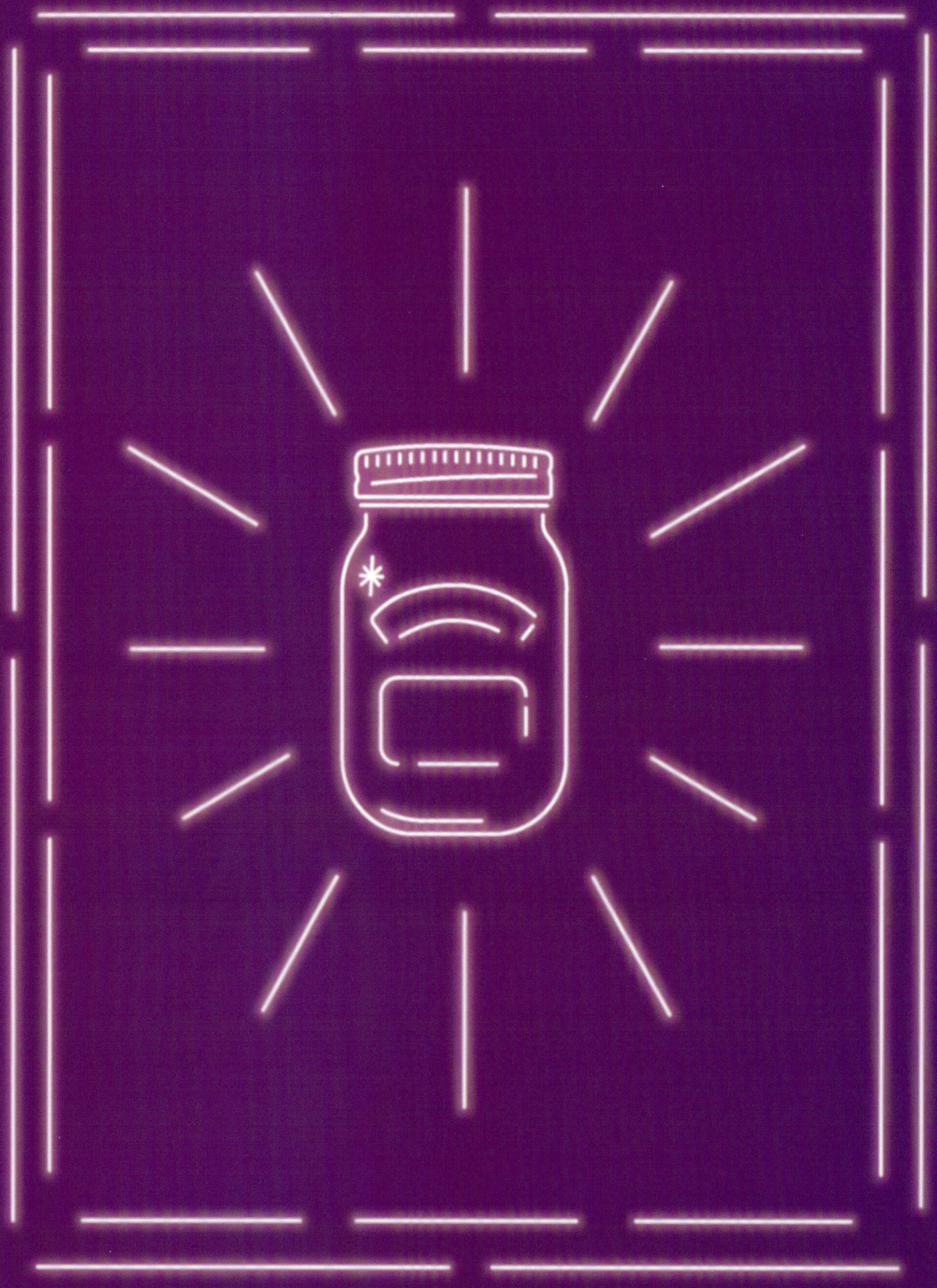

FRIDGE
Stash

Emergency condiments and more.

There is a hoard of jarred goodies in my fridge that often forms the basis for the meals I am yet to physically eat but have already mentally devoured. Condiments are often perceived to be either a dip or an afterthought – a sauce, pickle or chutney smudged onto the plate to 'round it off'. Whilst condiments can very much complete a meal, it is also true that they can step in as the initial inspiration for it. For example, I find myself first craving the mouth-puckering tang of homemade Cheat's Achaari Marmalade (see page 234) alongside aloo paratha fresh off the smoky tawa. I spiritually savour the sweetness of my Baa's katki keri (diced mango pickle) with thepla (fenugreek chapatis), the astringency of Mum's raw Garlic Chutney (see page 239) stirred into creamy sweet potato mash, or the herbal freshness of Dad's Green Coriander and Mint Chutney (see page 197) in a hefty Mumbai sandwich. Here, the frequent theme is that each dish is shaped through the nucleus of flavour that is the big, bad condiment at the back of the fridge. The meal is born in reverse.

My baa had a wicked sweet tooth; she was known for her mango chutneys, which would be left out on the rooftop under the beating Mombasa sun to macerate and cure in their own juices and added pickling ingredients. Katki keri was her speciality. She would use Kenyan green mangos, painstakingly cutting each one into tiny dice and mixing with sugar, salt, chilli and cumin. After a few days in the sunshine, the mango would transform into a syrupy concoction, ready to be jarred, distributed to family members and finally, scooped up with thepla for supper. My favourite part was being the first to break the crust of crystallised sugar at the side of the jar, scraping the grainy mass into my plate along with the translucent gems of sticky mango. Baa's dinner table was never complete without her stainless-steel pickle tray, suferia (cooking pot) of curry, kachumber (onion and tomato salad), chaas (chilled yogurt drink) and green chillies to accompany the meal.

I like to think of Indian condiments as a pick-and-mix that's ready to take your taste buds on the ride of their life. In lieu of sherbet lemons, there's lemon achaar which comes with bags of tang. For a whack of aniseed ball flavour, we opt for a chhundo. Amla ki murabba is the bonbon of the preserve world, made with sour Indian gooseberries. Since there's a signature sweet chutney in practically every region of India, the options for fruit lovers are endless. Chutney doesn't just refer to preserves, but also to fresh preparations (not unlike salsa), which last just a few days in the fridge. Chutneys can be wet or dry, cooked or raw, take five minutes to prepare or five days. Chutney, achaar, athanu, oorugaai, avakaya and loncha all allude to types of South Asian pickles. Some are deeply spicy and pungent, preserved with oil, others are fresh, brined or pickled, whilst many are sweet and sticky overlapping the border between jam (preserves) and candied fruit. The word 'achaar' is of Persian origin, introduced by the Mughals and adopted into Hindi, which is spoken throughout India, but predominantly in northern and central states. Although pickles are known by many different names throughout India's 22 official languages and various regional dialects. Many are available from stores ready to eat in all their spicy glory. They can be of excellent quality and are a great inroad into exploring the wealth and diversity of India's regional cuisines.

Whilst any raw mango can be used for pickling, cooks call upon several favourites depending on what's produced locally. Due to their firm flesh and sourness, raw mangos are perfect for preserving since their tartness can be balanced with the additions of salt and sugar. Many mango chutneys are made with sour raw mango varieties such as Rajapuri and Ramkela (although there are many more). These hard, green-skinned mangos provide a satisfying fruit pastille-like chew when cooked. Other fruits such as quince, dates and pineapples are also popular for making sweet achaars.

Spotting customers of my parents' newsagents hauling a glut of seasonal and locally grown fruits would warm my heart. It was their kindness that sparked curiosity into what we could preserve next. Buckets of Mrs Wood's crab apples, Mr Syke's cooking apples, the other Mr Sykes's garden plums and Eric's rhubarb would find their way into our stockroom, each one destined to go from lost to lovely with the addition of spices and a little imagination. In this chapter, I'm sharing a Rhubarb Chhundo (see page 235) and a Cheat's Achaari Marmalade (see page 234), both inspired by my favourite sweet Indian preserves, but rejigged using shortcuts to make life easier.

Cans of fruit, jams (preserves) and marmalades, packets of dehydrated and crystallised fruit, as well as pre-pickled vegetables, form the basis for some of my favourite recipes for making Indian condiments, quickly and effectively. For example, a jar of thinly shred orange marmalade is a flawless vehicle to carry spicy and salty achaar masala. Once you've heated everything through, it can all be piled back into its original jar, ready to be eaten in sandwiches, on crackers with cheese or with your favourite poppadoms and flatbreads.

Of course, many condiment options are salty, spicy and/or garlicky enough to floor a vampire. I've included my family recipe for Garlic Chutney (see page 239), complete with 40 cloves of raw garlic for anyone bold enough to dip into it alongside a meal. If raw garlic isn't for you, it's still worth making for the sheer fact that it can be spooned into any meal you're cooking, from curries and daals, to soups, pasta sauces and marinades. The flavour of the raw garlic chutney mellows once it's cooked, plus you won't have to peel garlic cloves and chop chillies every time a recipe calls for them.

Vegetables such as cauliflower, turnips, onions and carrots are also popular for pickling – these deeply savoury achaars are especially delicious with added chillies and small Indian limes. To add interest to a meal, eat them alongside parathas, rotis or thepla – an option which is particularly handy in empty-fridge emergencies. With each condiment, there's an opportunity to introduce elements such as sweetness, sourness, saltiness, chilli heat and aromatic heat to a meal. There's no need to cram your fridge with every variety, rather, it's a case of mixing and matching until you curate your personal collection of faithfuls. If you're making big batches, you can also gift a few jars to friends and family. Don't reserve them just for Indian meals either. In particular, they can introduce a great deal of interest and flavour to cheese boards, marinades and sauces.

Here, I include an assortment of pickles, chutneys and fridge staples that I like to eat as part of my meals and to incorporate into the recipes I cook. I generally keep these core fridge heroes on standby: gor keri; garlic chutney; mixed chilli pickle; Punjabi-style lime achaar; mango, papaya, or rhubarb chhundo; spicy pickled onions; gunpowder; achaari marmalade; amba haldi (brined white turmeric); and ker (a caper-like berry from Rajasthan, which is most often brined, pickled or curried). Go forth and create your own personal collection of fridge heroes.

The homemade Paneer (see page 247), Masala Paneer (see page 248) and Fauxneer (my vegan paneer, see page 251) are best eaten fresh within 24 hours but can last up to three days in the fridge when stored in an airtight container. Ghee can be kept inside or outside the fridge depending on how quickly you're likely to use up the batch. I tend to store my ghee in the fridge to prolong its shelf life.

Opposite:
1. Ghee (page 243)
2. Vegan Ghee (page 244)

Fridge Stash 233

Cheat's Achaari Marmalade

PREP: 5 MINS • COOK: 10 MINS

1 x 450-g (1-lb) jar of store-bought marmalade (I use fine-cut Seville orange)
2 tsp Kashmiri chilli powder
2 tsp Achaar Masala (see page 264)
1 tsp salt
2 tbsp oil
½ tsp whole coriander seeds
¼ tsp asafoetida

Note
This marmalade can be stored for up to a month.

Gluten free?
Use a gluten-free asafoetida or omit this ingredient.

Try this!
Pop a slab of feta into an oven-safe dish. Drizzle with olive oil and top with sprigs of fresh thyme. Bake in a preheated oven at 220°C/200°C fan/430°F/Gas mark 7 for 10–12 minutes. Top the feta with a dollop of Achaari Marmalade and serve with crackers.

A dressed-up jar of marmalade, jam (preserves) or compote is my secret weapon when it comes to making achaars, pickles and chutneys. It's a fantastic way to save time and energy while also stocking up the fridge with special condiments. This cheat's marmalade-based achaar calls for a jar of store-bought marmalade and a handful of spices. Enjoy it alongside Indian meals or relish it in toasted sandwiches, alongside baked cheeses or as part of cheese boards. P.S. This works just as well with orange, lime and lemon marmalade too!

1. Gently warm the marmalade in a saucepan. Mix in the chilli powder, achaar masala and salt. Set aside.

2. Heat the oil in a separate pan until smoking hot. Add the whole coriander seeds and asafoetida. Immediately pour this hot oil over the marmalade. Cover and allow to stand for 10 minutes before mixing well.

3. Meanwhile, sterilise the jar the marmalade came in and then pour the warm marmalade back in. Secure the lid and allow to cool completely.

4. Refrigerate for 24 hours before eating.

Rhubarb Chhundo

PREP: 5 MINS • COOK: 20 MINS, PLUS 10 MINS STANDING AND 24 HOURS CHILLING

1 x 540-g (1 lb 3-oz) can rhubarb in light syrup
½ tsp cornflour (cornstarch) mixed with 1 tbsp water
65 g (2¼ oz/⅓ cup) white granulated sugar
½ tsp salt
1½ tsp fennel seeds, ground
1 tsp Achaar Masala (see page 264)
1 tsp Kashmiri chilli powder
1 tsp oil
1 star anise
2–3 dried Kashmiri red chillies
¼ tsp asafoetida

Note
This chhundo can be stored in the fridge for up to a month.

Gluten free?
Use a gluten-free asafoetida or omit this ingredient.

Try this!
Stir a blob of this Rhubarb Chhundo into plain yogurt and serve with any type of poppadom, paratha or roti.

Transform a can of rhubarb (or any canned fruit for that matter) into a sweet and spicy chhundo. Rather endearingly, the word 'chhundo' means mush in Gujarati and is typically used to refer to sticky chutneys made with fruit. Canned fruits like rhubarb, peaches, plums, mango, apples, cherries, pears and pineapple all have stellar chhundo potential.

1. Simmer the rhubarb and syrup from the can until reduced by half. Do this in a saucepan over a medium-low heat and try not to stir it too much to preserve some of the chunky rhubarb texture.

2. Mix the cornflour (cornstarch) slurry into the rhubarb, along with the sugar and salt. Cook for a further 2–3 minutes, then remove the pan from the heat.

3. Add the ground fennel seeds, Achaar Masala and chilli powder, but do not stir. Let these spices sit on top of the fruit.

4. In a separate pan, heat the oil until smoking hot. Add the star anise, dried chillies and asafoetida. Pour this over the rhubarb and spices. Cover and allow to stand for 10 minutes before mixing well.

5. Meanwhile, sterilise a jar and then pour the warm chhundo into the jar. Secure the lid and allow to cool completely.

6. Refrigerate for 24 hours before eating.

Overleaf:
1. Cheat's Achaari Marmalade
2. Rhubarb Chhundo

Fridge Stash

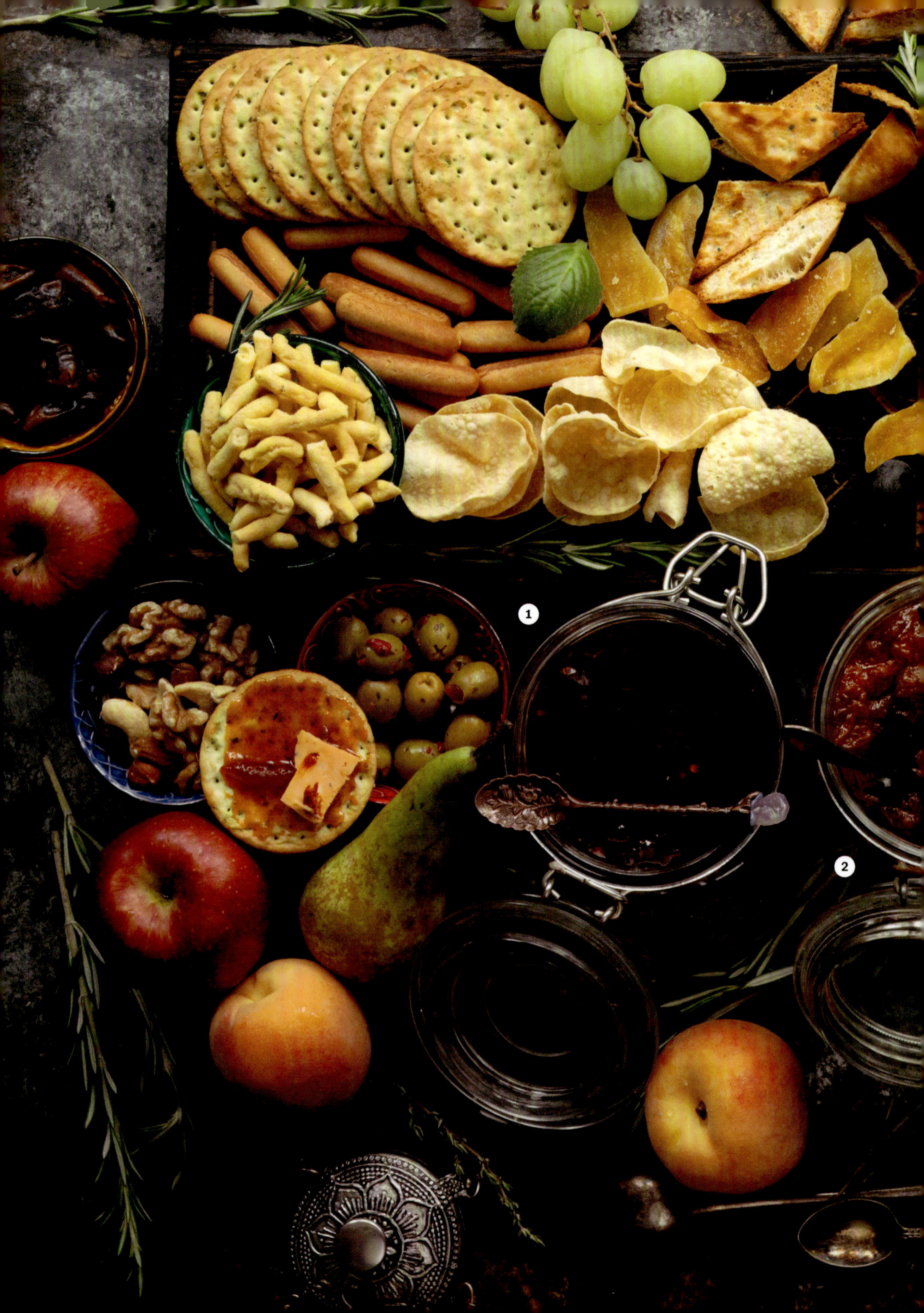
1
2

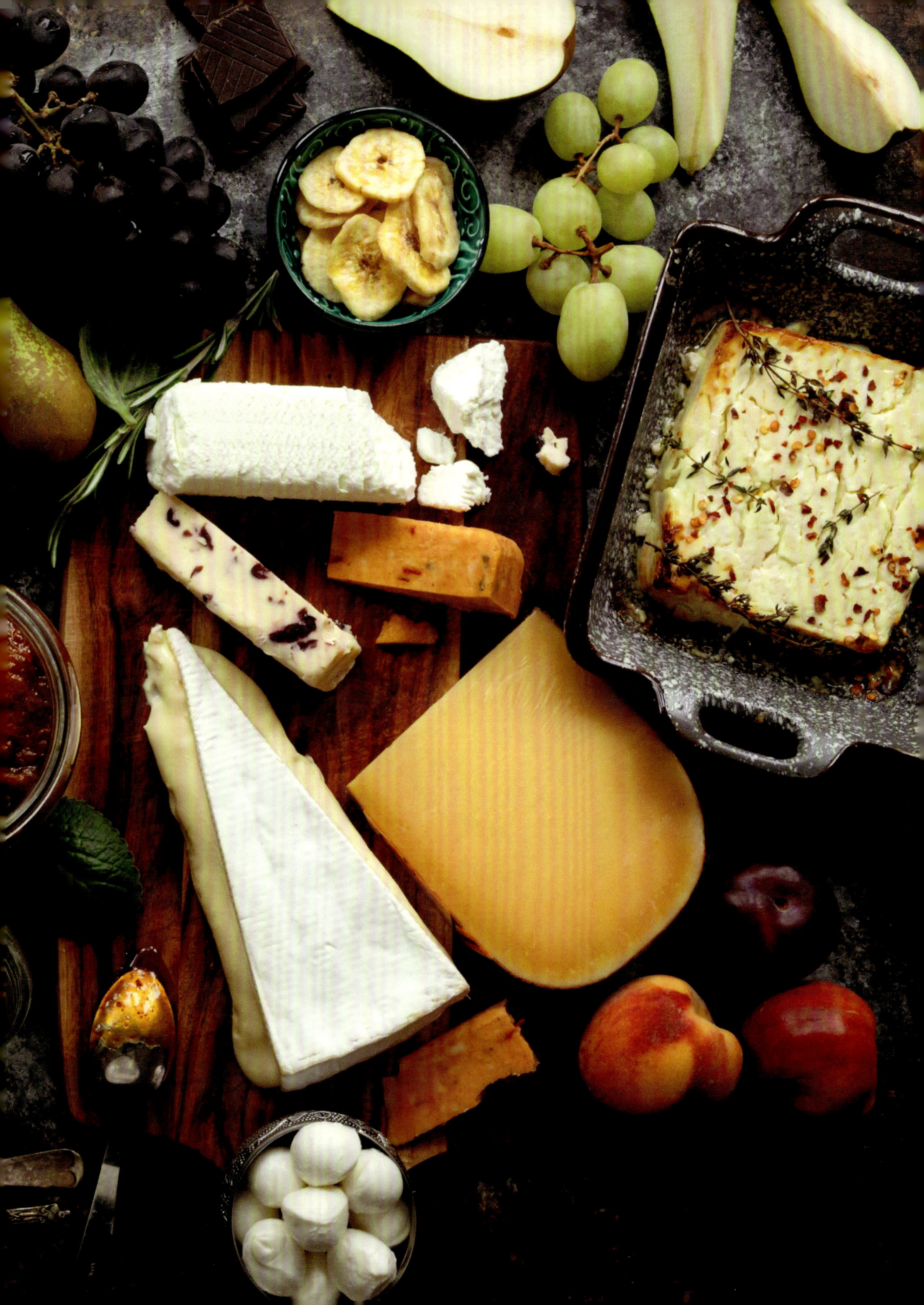

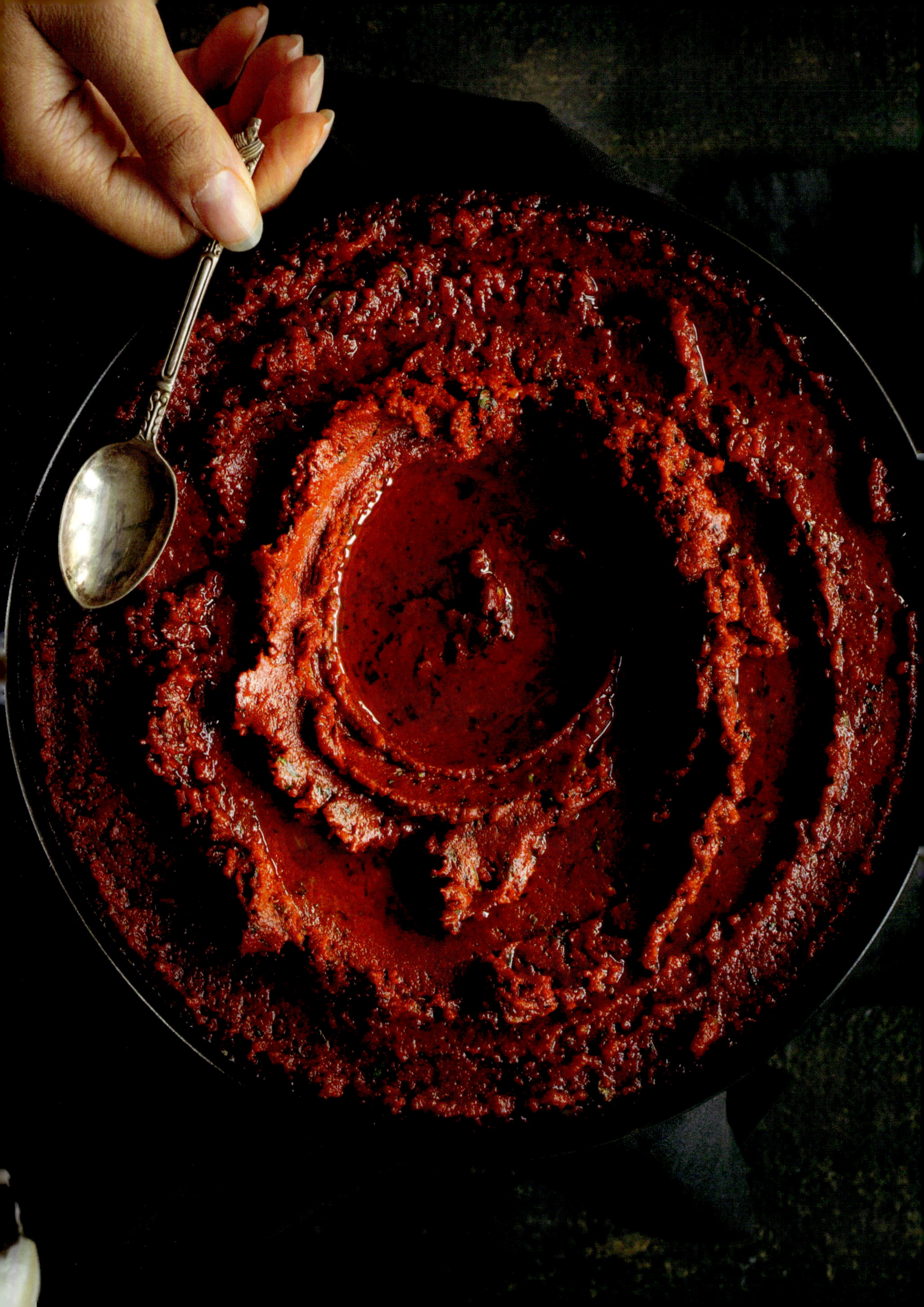

Chutney with 40 Cloves of Garlic

PREP: 25 MINS

V VG GF

- 3–4 large bulbs of garlic (about 40 cloves)
- 1 tbsp salt
- 400 g (14 oz) Kashmiri chilli powder
- 120 g (4¼ oz) fresh coriander (cilantro), very finely chopped
- 290 ml (9¾ fl oz/1¼ cups) oil (any flavourless oil or olive oil, if you like the taste)

A no-cook affair. This is the chutney to rule all chutneys; it is always in my fridge. All you need is garlic, chilli powder, coriander (cilantro), salt and oil. This is simple Kathiyawadi village fare from the heart of Gujarat. Kathiyawad is a peninsula off the western coast of India, in the region of Saurashtra and it's where my family come from. As this is good old-fashioned farmer food, leave the blender in the cupboard and make it by hand.

1. Using a pestle and mortar, pound the garlic cloves and salt together to make a coarse paste. Do not use a blender as this will dramatically change the texture. If you don't have a pestle and mortar, crush the garlic using a garlic press.

2. Use a wooden spoon or spatula to mix the crushed garlic, chilli powder, chopped coriander (cilantro) and oil together in a large bowl. Keep mixing until the chutney resembles a very thick paste. If it feels dry, keep mixing, pressing at the sides of the bowl with the spoon or spatula to encourage the garlic and coriander to release more liquid. If the paste still feels too dry after 3–4 minutes of pressing and mixing, gradually add some additional oil, 1 teaspoon at a time, until everything comes together and forms a very thick paste. A coarse finish is traditional and is perfect.

3. Pile the mixture into a large, sterilised jar, packing it down as tightly as you can. Top with a layer of oil to preserve the chutney.

Note

This chutney can be stored in the fridge for up to 2 weeks. Remember to top up the jar with oil after every use.

I recommend seeking out Kashmiri chilli powder for this recipe. It has a mild heat and therefore can be used in large quantities without singeing your nose hairs clean off. Kashmiri chilli powder also has a vivid colour, which makes this chutney so beautifully red.

Three ways to use your garlic chutney

1. For a quick dip, stir ½ teaspoon of chutney through 250 g (9 oz/ 1 cup) thick Greek yogurt. For raita vibes, you can also add a few tablespoons of finely diced cucumber.

2. Breathe life into cheese on toast by spreading a thin layer of garlic chutney onto the toast before topping with cheese and grilling to melt.

3. Swirl into mashed potato. This garlic-fuelled mash is particularly delicious on top of pies, but there's also no shame in eating it by the spoonful, straight from the bowl.

Pink Peppercorn Pickled Onions

PREP: 10 MINS • COOK: 5 MINS, PLUS 2 HOURS CHILLING

V VG GF

2 red onions
160 ml (5½ fl oz/⅔ cup) distilled white vinegar
2 tsp pink peppercorns, cracked
2 tbsp sugar
3 tsp sea salt

Note
These pickled onions can be stored in the fridge for up to 2 weeks.

After 10 minutes of prep and very little effort on your part, these Pink Peppercorn Pickled Onions are the gift that keep on giving. Serve them in and alongside anything and everything.

1. Finely slice the onions into rings. The thinner you slice the onions, the quicker they 'pickle'. Pop these into a sterilised jar.

2. Mix the remaining ingredients together a saucepan with 200 ml (7 fl oz/scant 1 cup) water. Bring to a boil and stir to dissolve the sugar and salt.

3. Pour the hot pickling liquid over the onions in the jar and close the lid. Give the jar a gentle shake to ensure everything is submerged. Allow to cool completely and then store in the fridge. You can enjoy them after they've chilled in the fridge for 2–3 hours.

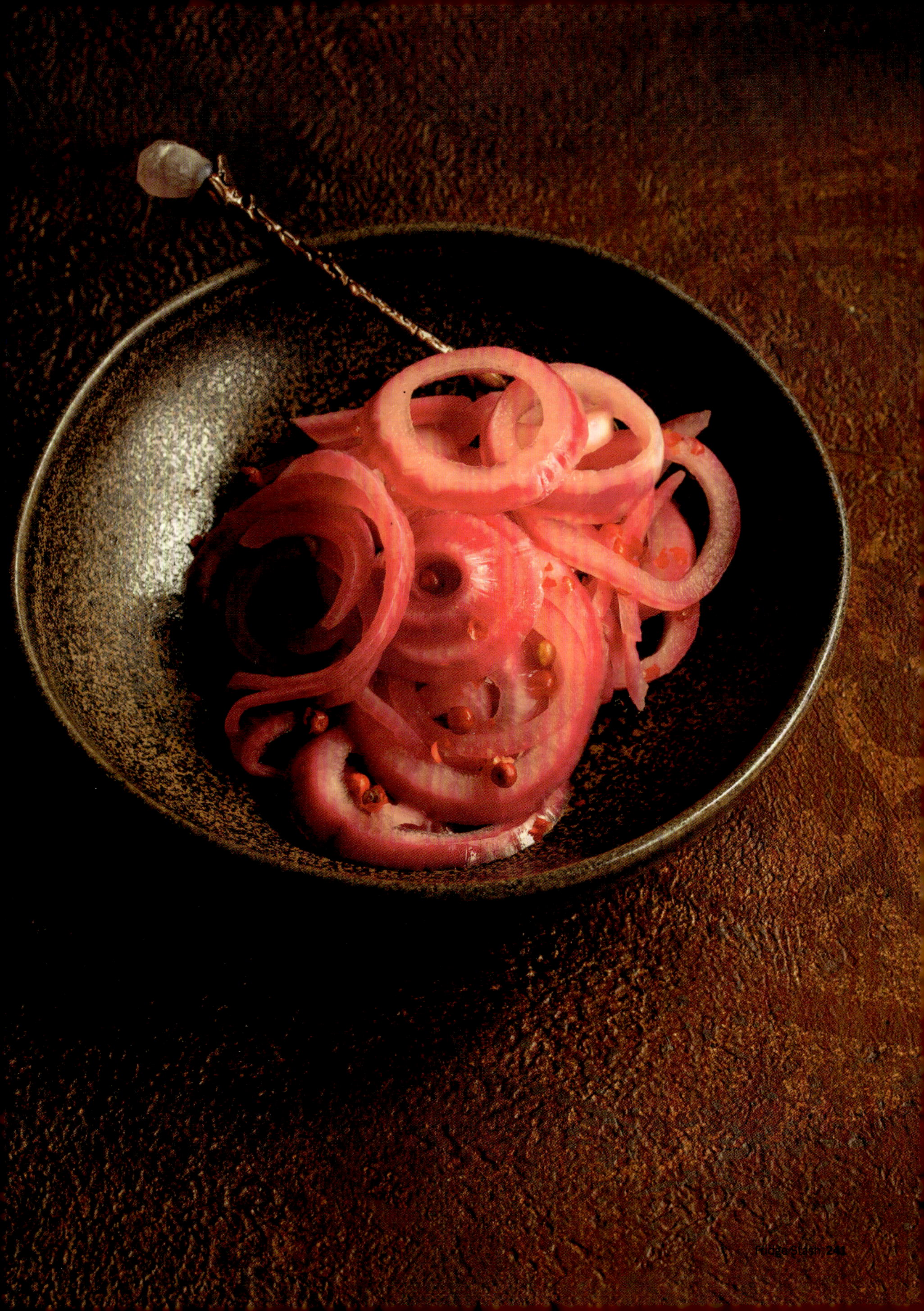

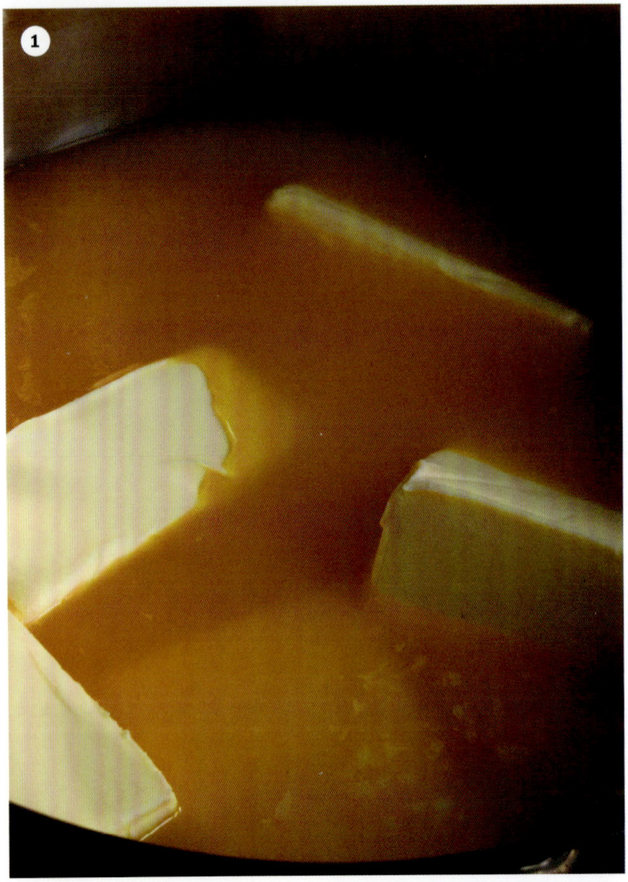
1

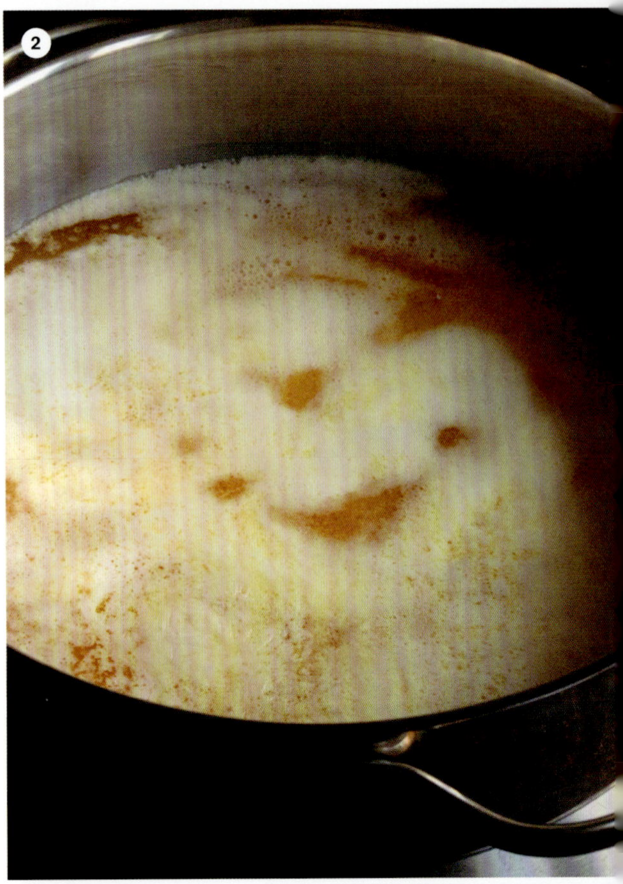
2

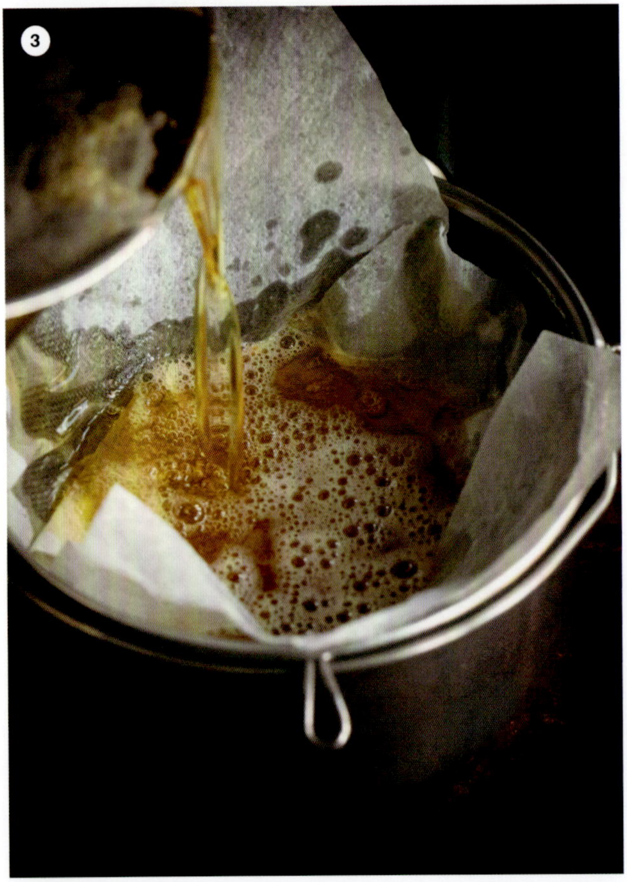
3

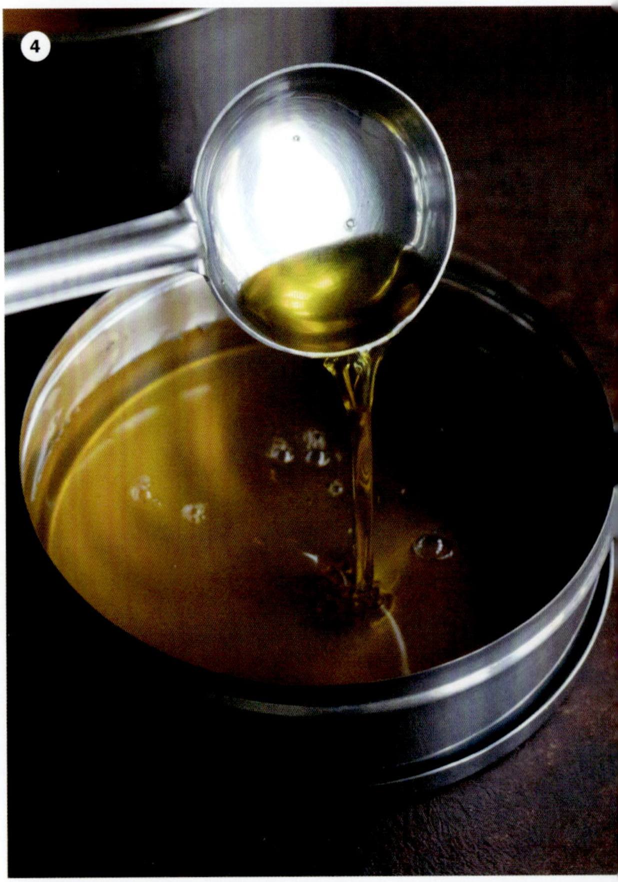
4

Ghee

MAKES AROUND 425 G (15 OZ) • PREP: 5 MINS, PLUS 25 MINS STANDING • COOK: 25 MINS

500 g (1 lb 2 oz/2¼ cups) unsalted butter

Storage

Ghee is fine to store in a cool, dry and dark place for a good 3 months, but you can extend the life of your batch by keeping it in the fridge. How you choose to store it depends on how quickly you think you'll get through the batch.

Note

Leftover milk solids from the ghee-making process can be used to add richness to roti, paratha or naan dough. In the Gujarati community, we use them to make a thick, unleavened biscuit bread called bhakri.

Unsalted or salted butter?

Unsalted butter results in a smaller deposit of milk solid sediments at the base of the pan. Be mindful that salts will clump together with the sediment, so if you're using salted butter, there will be double the scraps. Using unsalted butter gives you a little more ghee for your rupee.

Clarified butter, or ghee, is a bedrock of Indian cooking. It doesn't burn like butter does and can therefore be used for cooking at very high temperatures. It also has a unique flavour of its own that's not quite butter or brown butter. Since ghee is often called for in recipes like daal and curry, as well as on bread and in sweets, I always keep it handy. The process of making ghee is a one-ingredient job, and it can be made in larger quantities if you don't want to commit time to preparing ghee often. I prefer making ghee at home over buying a can from the store (which often has a lingering smell that I can't quite get on board with). The clarifying process is a piece of cake, and the flavour payoff is grand. FYI, this will fill your entire house with the smell of buttery cinema popcorn.

1. Begin by melting the butter in a heavy-based pan (1). Try to use a pan that's light in colour as it can be difficult to see the colour of the butter when the pan is black or dark grey. Keep it over a moderately low heat. It's important the butter doesn't start to brown.

2. Once melted, continue to cook the butter. It will turn from cloudy to foamy (2). Do not stir the butter since the milk solids need to settle at the bottom of the pan. Always keep an eye on the pan. The buttery foam tends to billow up and can overflow if you're not paying attention. I usually make ghee while I'm making roti or something that requires me to stand next to the hob (stovetop).

3. After around 15 minutes of gentle melting and bubbling, the ghee will turn a few shades darker – a light buttercup (not amber, and certainly not brown). At this point, immediately remove the pan from the heat as it will retain heat and continue to cook the ghee. Allow the ghee to stand for 20–25 minutes at room temperature to cool slightly.

4. While the ghee cools, place a sieve (strainer) over a large jug (pitcher) or lipped pan. Line the inside of the sieve with 1-ply of kitchen paper. You can use muslin too, but I find that separating the layers of 2-ply kitchen paper produces a crystal-clear result.

5. Very carefully pour the warm ghee into the lined sieve (3). The kitchen paper will filter the ghee, catching the burnished milk solids. Pour slowly and allow the ghee to drip through into the vessel underneath. When you get to the end, the majority of the milk solids from the butter will be lurking at the base of the pan. Go ahead and filter as much as you can through the kitchen paper. Do not throw the milk solids away, they can be put to good use (see Note).

6. Once the ghee has been filtered, you can pour it into a sterilised jar or clean can, ready for use in all your recipes (4). Allow to set at room temperature. The gorgeousness of ghee is often measured by how clear it is in its melted state, as well as how grainy it is once solid.

[V] [VG] [GF]

Vegan Ghee

MAKES 500 G (1 LB 2 OZ) • PREP: 5 MINS • COOK: 25 MINS

500 g (1 lb 2 oz) refined coconut oil
2 carrots, grated (shredded)
4 tbsp sweetcorn kernels

Storage

This vegan ghee can be stored in a well-sealed jar inside the fridge for up to 6 months.

Notes

Be sure to use refined coconut oil in this recipe, and not unrefined. The key difference between the two varieties is that unrefined coconut oil has a very prominent coconut flavour, whilst refined is totally odourless.

Like real ghee, this vegan ghee has a very high smoke point thanks to the coconut oil. This means it's suitable for high-heat cooking such as preparing tadka for daal.

You don't have to throw the strained veggies away; you can use them in all kinds of recipes from fritters to samosas.

Just three ingredients and 30 minutes is all you need to produce a plant-based ghee alternative that has a remarkably buttery flavour. When I dab this liquid amber vegan ghee on roti and naan, my friends and family can't tell that it's not the real deal. You won't believe how I make it...

1. Melt the coconut oil in a large, deep saucepan over a low heat.

2. Add the carrots and sweetcorn kernels and allow to cook over a very low heat for 20 minutes. The carrots and corn should always be just very slowly bubbling around the edges. Do not turn the heat up too high or they will fry. You're looking to extract all the colours and flavours from the veggies very slowly, rather than cooking them. The oil will slowly transform from clear white to liquid amber. The colour of the carrots and buttery aroma of the corn magically create something very ghee-like in appearance and flavour.

3. Place a small sieve (strainer) over a sterilised jar or clean can. Strain the ghee into the jar, allowing any pieces of carrot and sweetcorn to be caught in the sieve. Do not throw the veggies away, they can be put to good use (see Note below).

4. Allow to set at room temperature. Since coconut oil sets at room temperature, this vegan ghee sets and takes on a beautiful graininess, just like butter-based ghee.

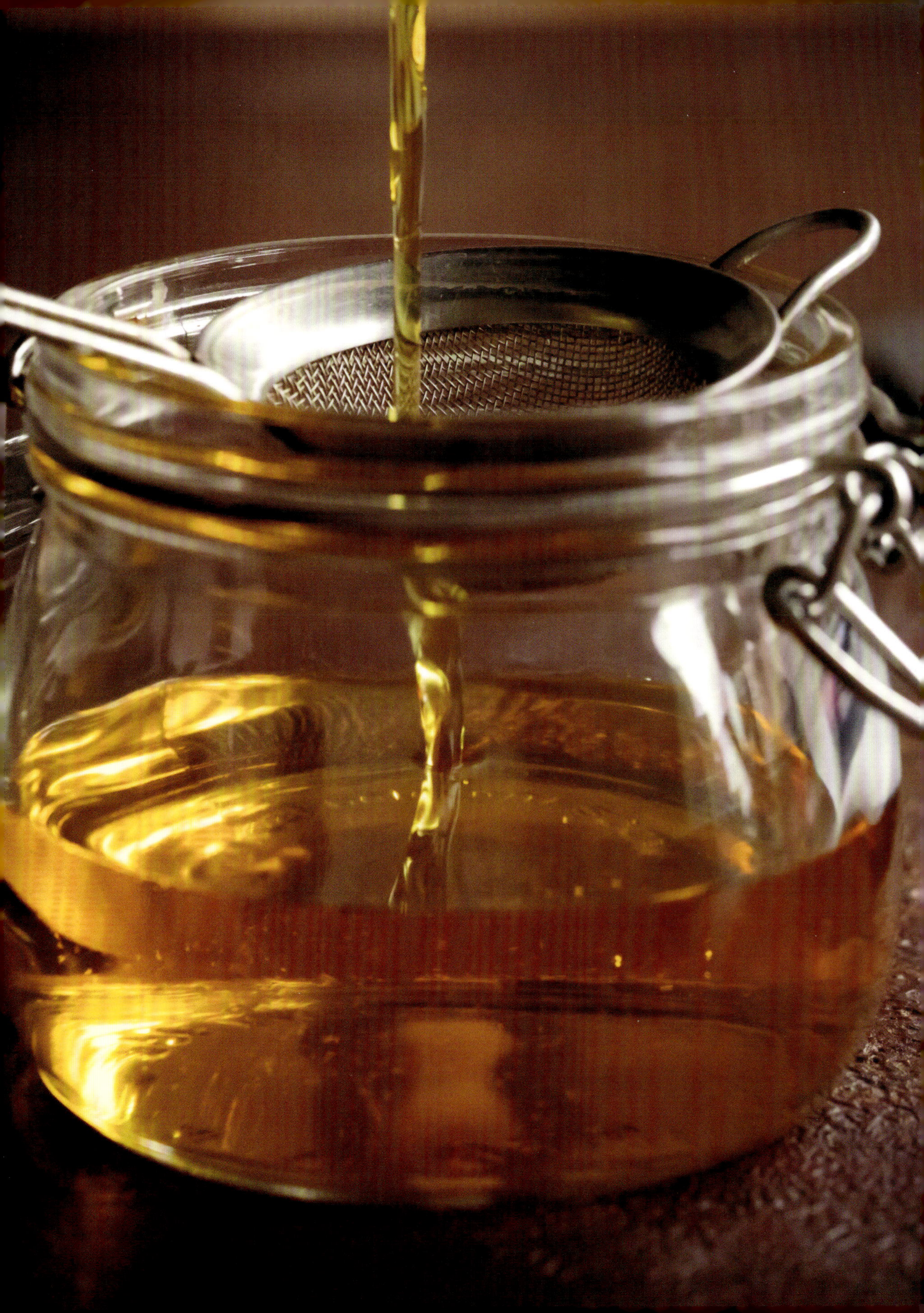

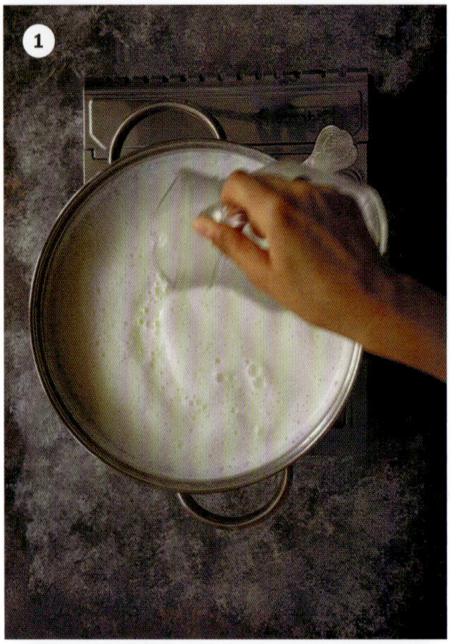
1
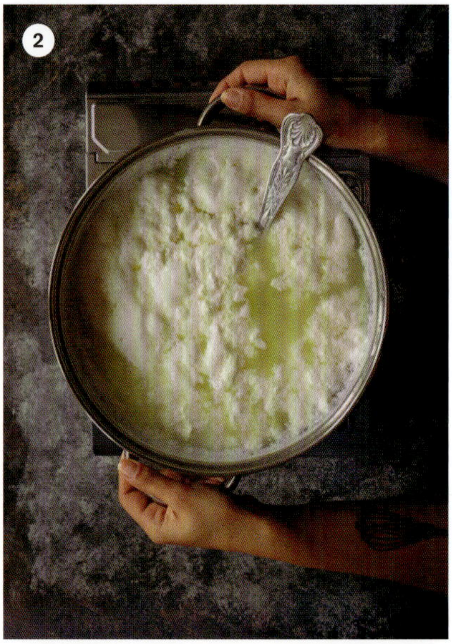
2
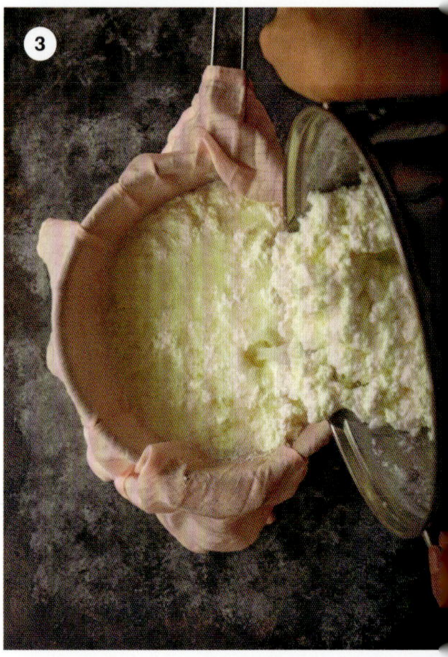
3
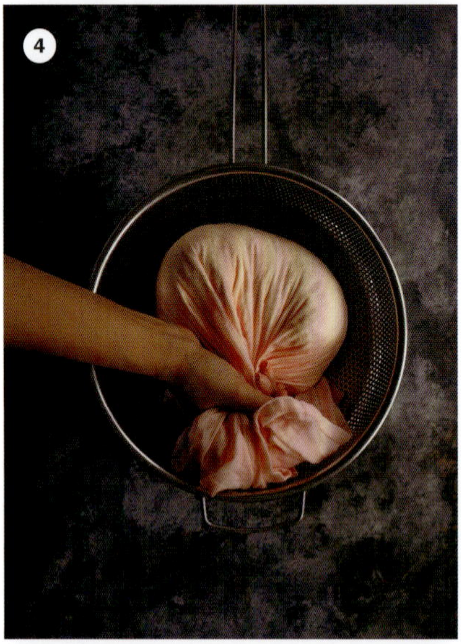
4
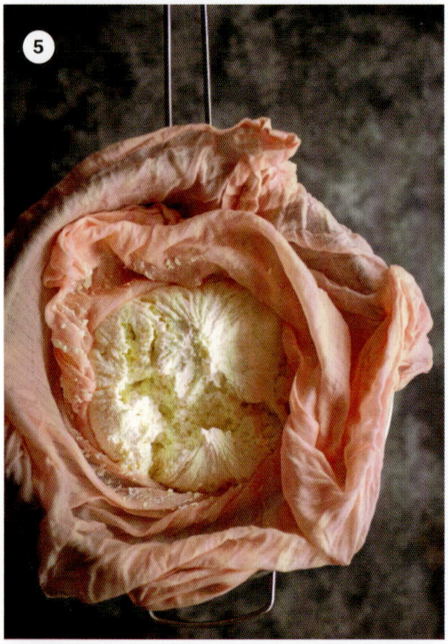
5
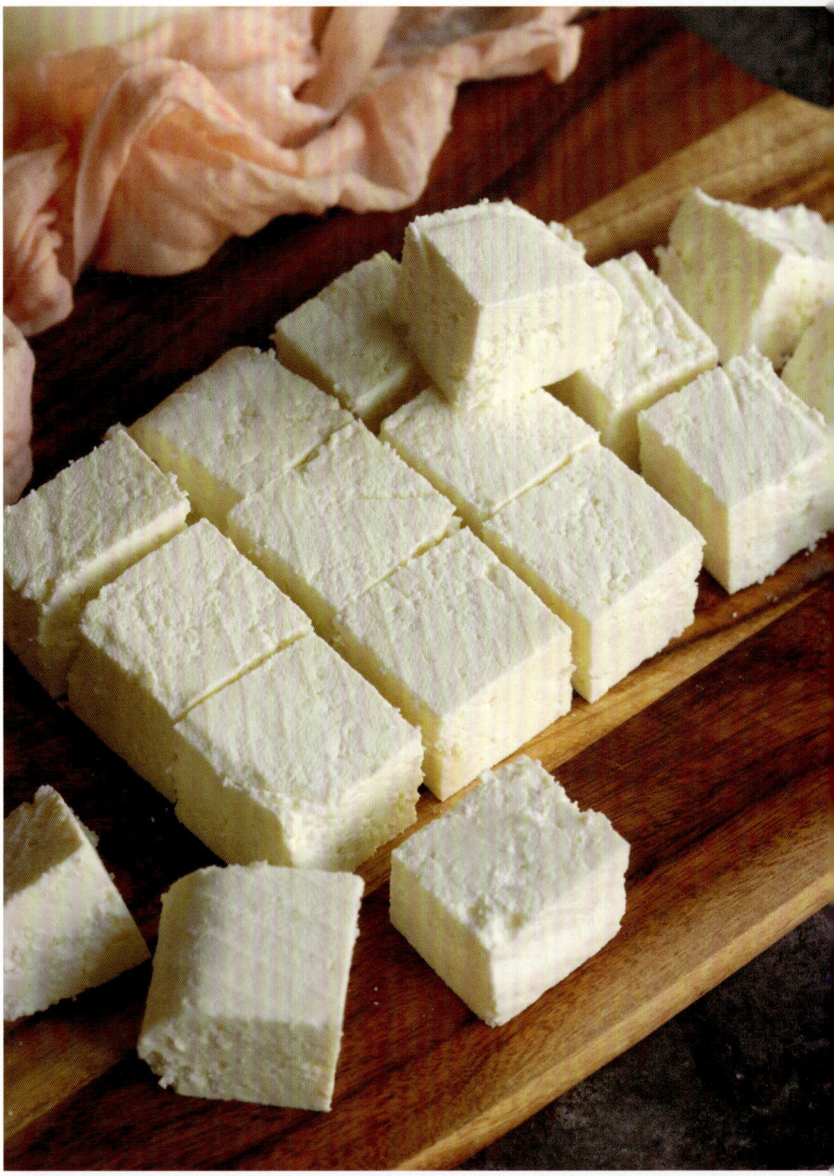

Paneer

MAKES APPROX. 500 G (1 LB 2 OZ) • PREP: 10 MINS • COOK: 25 MINS

65 ml (2¼ fl oz/¼ cup) distilled white vinegar
¼ tsp oil, to grease the base of the pan
1.5 litres (5 pints/10½ cups) whole (full-fat) milk (at least 3% fat)

Storage

Homemade paneer will keep well in the fridge for up to 3 days. Wrap it well to ensure it doesn't dry out.

Notes

Try to find the least homogenised, least processed milk possible for better yield. If the milk is overly processed, it will not curdle or may produce only a small amount of curds. This is because the heating process integral to lasting shelf life damages the proteins in the milk. Whole (full-fat) milk with at least 3% fat produces good-quality paneer. For very soft and creamy malai paneer, use fresh gold top milk.

Instead of vinegar, you can also use lemon juice, citric acid, yogurt or even leftover whey from a previous batch of paneer to curdle the milk.

For 2.5 litres (4½ pints/10½ cups) milk, you'll need the following quantities of either:

100 ml (3½ fl oz/scant ½ cup) lemon juice mixed with 250 ml (8½ fl oz/1 cup) water

or 1 tsp citric acid mixed with 250 ml (8½ fl oz/1 cup) water

or 100 g (3½ oz/scant ½ cup) sour plain yogurt whisked with 2 tbsp water

or 250 ml (8½ fl oz/1 cup) sour whey

Soft and squidgy homemade paneer for curries, paratha fillings, chilli paneer, samosas and more. This simple recipe includes tips for making fresh paneer that tastes like it just came from the dairywala.

1. In a bowl or jug (pitcher), stir the vinegar into 200 ml (7 fl oz/scant 1 cup) water.

2. Use kitchen paper dipped in the oil to grease the base of a saucepan. This stops the milk from burning on the bottom. Pour the milk into the pan and warm over a medium heat. Do not stir the milk too much as you don't want to create too much froth. Do not leave the milk unattended; it can boil over quite quickly. Once the milk comes to a boil, switch off the heat.

3. Slowly add the vinegar mixture to the pan (1) and stir the milk very gently to disperse. Imagine slowly drawing a figure of eight in the pan. If the milk isn't curdling, add more of the vinegar mixture until it does.

4. You will know the paneer is ready when the curds look like little white clouds floating in a greenish-yellow coloured liquid (2). (This is the whey, which you can save for baking.)

5. Line a colander or sieve (strainer) with a clean, damp muslin or cheesecloth. Place the lined colander over a large bowl to catch the drained whey. Pour the mixture into the lined colander and allow the whey to drain out (3).

6. Next, transfer the bundle of drained curds (along with the muslin) to a bowl while you pour the whey into another bowl or simply swap it with another bowl.

7. The curds now need to be washed to remove any excess acidic flavour. Pour plenty of warm water over the cheese and agitate with a spoon to wash away the sourness. I use around 1 litre (34 fl oz/4¼ cups) water for this process. Try not to rinse the curds too much.

8. Wrap the muslin over the top of the curds, as flat as you can get it. Press gently with your hands to drain off any excess water (4). Place a flat plate over the top of the muslin and weigh the curds down with something heavy (like a few cans of beans, a mortar or a few heavy books) to drain off any remaining water and lightly set the paneer. The heavier the weight you apply, the firmer set and more compact the paneer will be. You can use the paneer after around an hour of draining and pressing, but it may not be as sturdy as the kind you get from food stores (5). This is fine if you plan to crumble the paneer. For curries, skewers and stir-fries, you may want to leave the paneer pressed for longer. For a very cube-able paneer, you might choose to leave it pressed in the fridge overnight.

Masala Paneer

What can I do with leftover whey?

The possibilities are endless! Use it in sweet and savoury baking and, in particular, cake and bread baking. You can also use leftover whey for making Indian bread like roti, thepla, naan, paratha and bhatura. Or add it to your morning smoothie for a low-fat protein boost. Kadhi made with leftover whey is deliciously sour. It's super nutritious and versatile. Keep it bottled in a clean container for up to 2 weeks.

Note

I particularly love this paneer stuffed inside bread, or grilled and served as an accompaniment to salad.

Infuse the cheese with a handful of herbs and spices to give it a beautiful flavour and colour from within. My recipe uses ground black pepper, root ginger, chilli flakes and fresh coriander (cilantro) leaves. However, you can customise your block of masala paneer to your taste by using your favourite herbs and spices. Use exactly the method outlined on the previous page to make homemade paneer. After washing and squeezing the curds dry, mix in the following:

½ tsp salt
¼ tsp freshly ground black pepper
½ tsp chilli flakes
½ tsp grated (shredded) root ginger or ginger paste
1 tbsp chopped fresh coriander (cilantro) leaves

Press the paneer as usual. It's ready for using in all your favourite paneer recipes after about an hour.

What other herbs and spices can I add to masala paneer?

This recipe is highly customisable and can be transformed with just a few changes to the herbs and spices used. Here are some of my favourite paneer flavour infusions:

Indo-Chinese
Chinese 5-spice, ginger paste, green chillies, chopped spring onions (scallions).

Mediterranean-ish
Sliced olives, chopped sundried tomatoes, garlic paste, fresh basil.

Jamaican Jerk-inspired
Ground allspice, dried thyme, dried garlic powder, chopped Scotch bonnet chilli.

Tex-Mex style
Smoked paprika, ground cumin, dried onion powder, chopped coriander (cilantro).

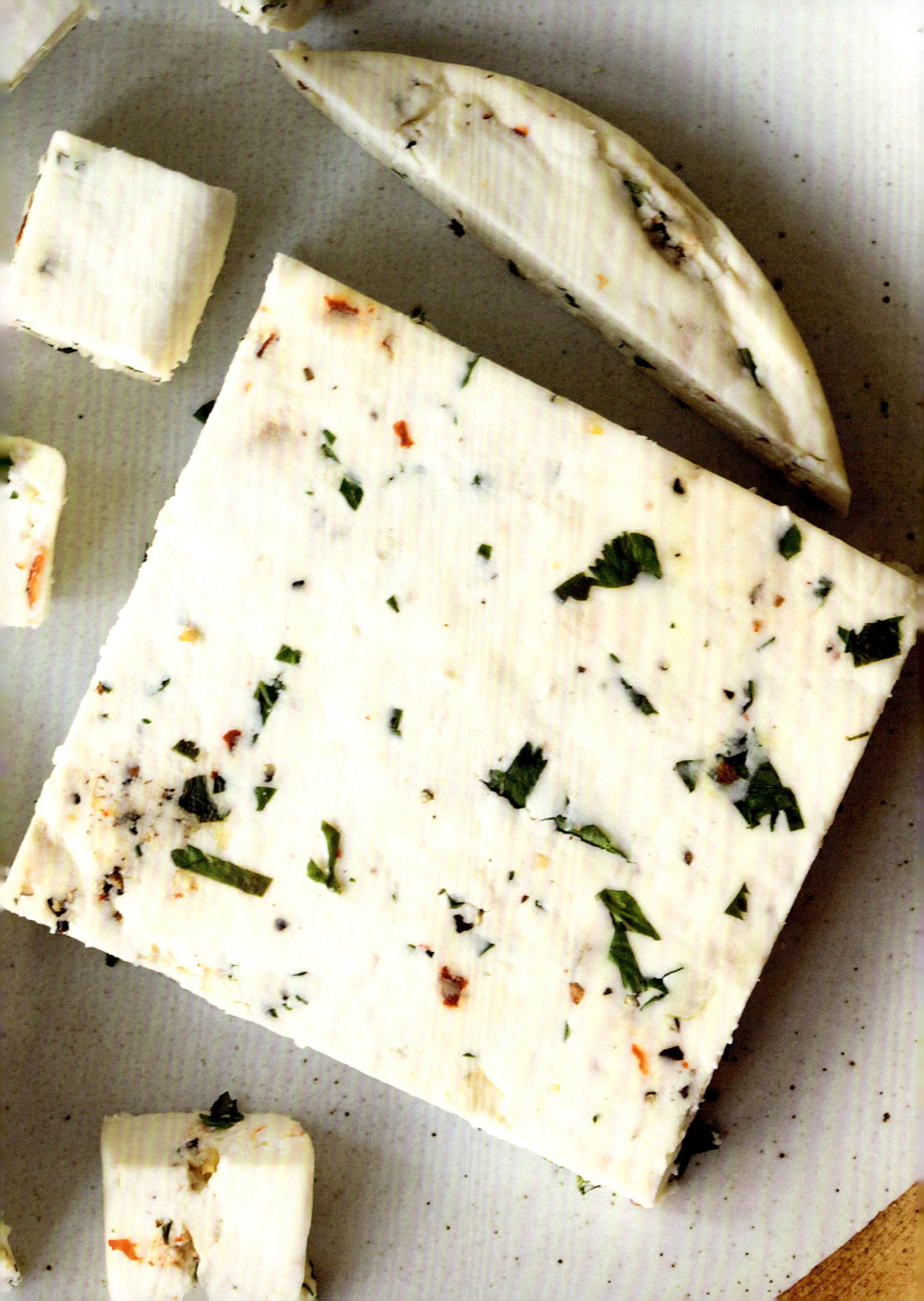

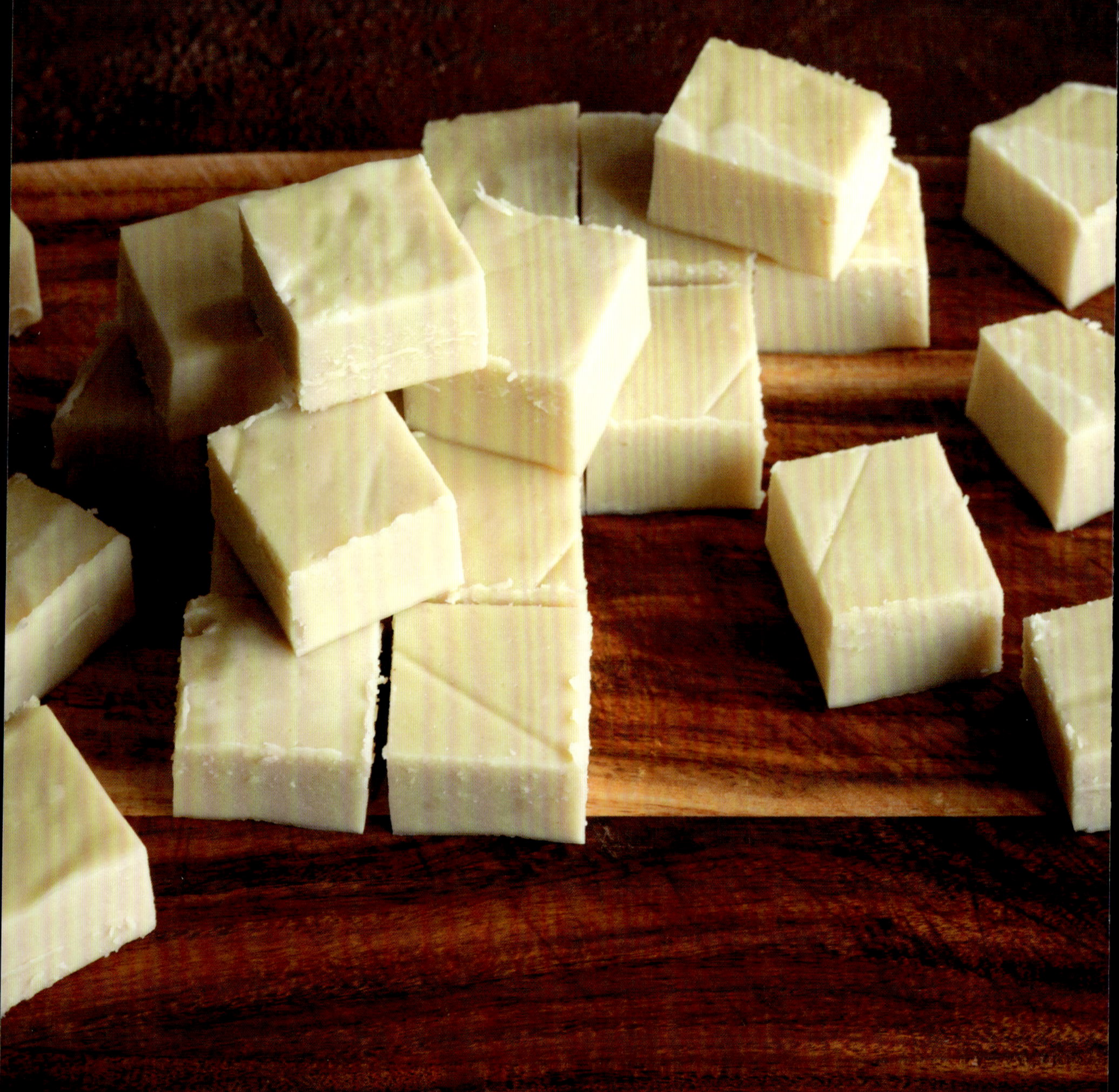

Fauxneer: My Vegan Paneer

MAKES APPROX. 600 G (1 LB 5 OZ) • PREP: 20 MINS • COOK: 1 HOUR

100 g (3½ oz) unsalted cashews
300 g (10½ oz) silken tofu, drained
140 g (5 oz/1 cup) rice flour
1 tbsp cornflour (cornstarch)
2 tbsp nutritional yeast flakes
¼ tsp lemon juice
3 tbsp oil
½ tsp salt
60 ml (2 fl oz/4 tbsp) water

Notes

A high-powered blender is essential for this recipe. It will ensure the cashew and tofu mixture is well emulsified for the creamiest, dreamiest paneer substitute.

Be sure to steam the Fauxneer over a gentle heat to prevent it from bubbling up or doming too much. You might notice a slight dome after steaming but this should sink back down flat within a few minutes.

If you're not using the Fauxneer straight away, keep it wrapped in the fridge for up to 48 hours. You can freeze Fauxneer, but it may lose some of its creamy texture.

To say that this recipe is anything less than mind-bending to perfect would be an epic understatement. After dozens upon dozens of tests, I have finally produced a plant-based paneer that I'd say is on a par with real-deal dairy paneer. My vegan paneer, or Fauxneer, is pleasingly creamy yet firm enough to use in curries and stir-fries, as well as to scramble for samosa and paratha fillings. It fries and grills, but it never melts, so it's suitable for skewering to make vegan tandoori paneer. Try the Chilli Fauxneer or Vegan Chilli Paneer (see page 102) to witness it in action.

1. Place the cashews in a pan of boiling water. Simmer for 15 minutes until the cashews have completely softened. Drain well.

2. Place all the ingredients in a high-powered blender and blitz until completely smooth. You may need to pause to scrape down the sides. It should be totally smooth, like lotion, and with no gritty cashew pieces.

3. Set up a steamer with a flat base and cover with a tight-fitting lid. Allow it to preheat for 5 minutes.

4. Grease an 18-cm (7-inch) round pan with oil and line the base with parchment paper. Check the pan fits inside the steamer first.

5. Pour the thick cashew and tofu mixture into the pan and smooth out the surface. Give it a few raps on the countertop to encourage any large air pockets to come to the surface and pop.

6. Carefully place the pan in the steamer and cover. Simmer over a low heat for 40 minutes or until the Fauxneer is firm and bouncy. Keep it covered the whole time and do not be tempted to peek.

7. Remove the pan from the steamer and allow to cool completely at room temperature.

8. Run a sharp knife around the sides of the pan to loosen the Fauxneer and turn the slab out onto a cutting board. Slice into cubes, strips, grate (shred) or crumble depending on your paneer recipe.

Fridge Stash

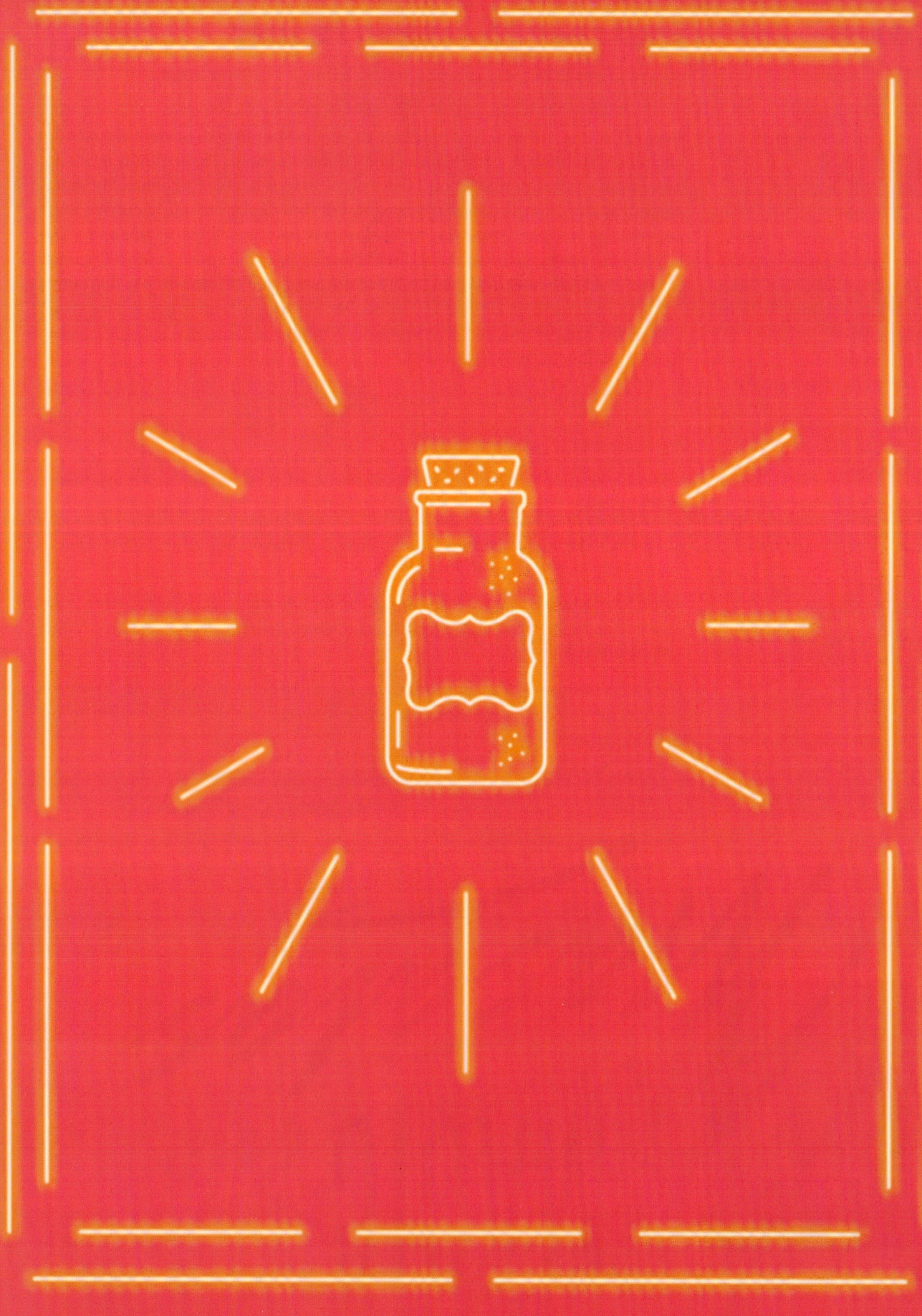

MAGIC
Masalas

A kiss of life for everyday meals and more.

Composing pre-mixed masala blends needn't feel overwhelming. It requires thought and an understanding of the spices, but it's very much like learning to drive. Once you've got it, you've got it for life. Crafted well, masala blends can showcase a cook's experience when it comes to the merits of leveraging the power of various spices. To understand what every spice brings to the party, how it interacts with others in the mix, as well as how they will collectively flavour a meal, calls for foresight. The orchestration of spice blends is a strategy. Nail your formula, nail the dish. Hot, pungent and bitter spices can be offset by sweeter ones. Herbal, citrusy and menthol-forward spices introduce a freshness that stands up to warmer ones. Woody spices enjoy the company of floral flavours. Banded together, they can create magic in our meals. Coming from a Gujarati home, the cuisine of my heritage isn't laden with masalas. We use them sparingly, in a way that complements the flavours of an overall dish. For example, the Gujarati samosa carries a trifecta of flavours: hot, sour, sweet. The filling is a hodgepodge of chilli and lemon-laced potatoes, peas and carrots, as well as a truckload of onions. Cinnamon and cloves support the onions by imparting sweetness, whilst harmonising the zesty lemon and hot chilli. Balance.

Collecting whole spices to grind and sprinkle into food was never common practice for me. Neither were extra masalas kept on hand in neatly labelled containers, as they are now. Small batches might have been made on demand whenever something called for a medley of ground masalas. The strongest spices were within daal masala, samosa masala, kachori masala and chai masala – sometimes these were made at home, store-bought or gifted by friends or family (who had made it at home, in bulk). These are the masalas that were traded and treasured. It wasn't unusual to receive a 2 kg (4½ lb) bag of chai masala from an auntie in Kenya. My dad and his many siblings would shuffle Santa-like sacks of masalas and snacks between cars at family weddings, since these were the rare occasions during which the clan were reunited.

Most Gujarati dishes are based around spicy, sour, sweet and salty foods. A balance of each element is carefully curated in dishes like puran puri (sweet daal-stuffed bread) and kadhi (a hot, sweet, sour and spicy tempered buttermilk), daal-bhaat, dhokra, khandvi and chutneys. To achieve this, jaggery, salt, lemon and chilli are all staple ingredients in the Gujarati kitchen. Our meals relied on a slow release of aromatic flavours using whole spices, which is why many Gujarati recipes require a tadka to be carried out at the beginning, rather than at the end. Ground, whole masalas rarely make an appearance, but when they do, they are typically limited to snacks. The ground masalas we rely upon in everyday cooking are based around spices that have a cooling effect on the body (according to Ayurveda), such as coriander seeds, cumin seeds and fennel seeds. Warming spices like cinnamon, cloves and star anise are typically used in their whole form. To do so effectively, the flavours are released slowly in hot fat through the tadka process. This creates a mellow flavour throughout the dish, rather than a whack at the end, which is what roasted ground masalas offer. For example, garam masala – a warming ground spice mix from the North – finishes a dish with a kick of spice.

For me, cooking and eating a lot of Gujarati food has rendered other styles of regional Indian dishes a treat, for they require additional thought, time and preparation. Exploring other regional dishes of India is as demanding as exploring the cuisines of unfamiliar countries. The ingredients may overlap, but the nuances are vast. Fermenting batter for Mysore dosa, mastering Punjabi saag, balancing masalas for pav bhaji and kneading and poaching chhena (paneer) for Bengal's melt-in-the-mouth dessert, rasmalai, have been major projects. I have invested a lot of time and effort into studying the dishes I never learned from my family and cooked them repeatedly until they were right. Likewise, blending spices is crafty. It requires research, thoughtfulness and understanding how each spice interacts with the others in the mix. Saffron and cardamom are great friends in sweet and savoury dishes. Fennel seeds balance the bitterness of fenugreek seeds. Together, dried mango powder and black salt make a sherbet you'll want to sprinkle on everything. Black cardamom and rose create a mesmerising floral smokiness in rice dishes and kebabs. Cloves can explode …

All spices have different roasting times and so, if you do have time, dry roast each one individually in a small frying pan (skillet) to ensure every player brings its A-game. If you don't have time to roast them separately, I recommend that you at least take the process of roasting everything together as slowly as time permits, and over a low heat. This will ensure the oils are released gently and you can keep an eye on the spices so that nothing burns. I usually dry roast all my spices together, very slowly until aromatic. I don't recommend roasting spices in the oven unless you're particularly eagle eyed. If you do try to oven roast spices, do it one ingredient at a time and take care not to burn them. Lightly bash cloves and cardamom pods in a mortar with a pestle prior to roasting – they can pop and project themselves out of the pan.

Not all pre-mixed masalas require you to roast the whole spices prior to grinding. You can simply pre-roast the ones you intend to stir into the finished dish as a final flourish or eat as they are alongside a meal. Garam masala, chaat masala, achaar masala and gunpowder are all used in this way, and therefore elements of the masala creation involve some cooking.

I recommend making masalas in relatively small batches to ensure they remain as fresh as possible. You can extend the shelf life of masalas with cooked elements, added oils or daals by storing them in the fridge, or even in the freezer. I've found that these freshly ground masalas can be used sparingly in comparison to store-bought packets. Since the spices haven't been laying around in box for a while, they pack a Muhammad Ali-esque uppercut.

My expertise in blending mixed masalas comes from a lot of eating, a lot of trials and many errors. It really is the best way to learn. I have faith that this collection will breathe life into all your old favourites, as well as fuel new discoveries.

Magic Masalas 257

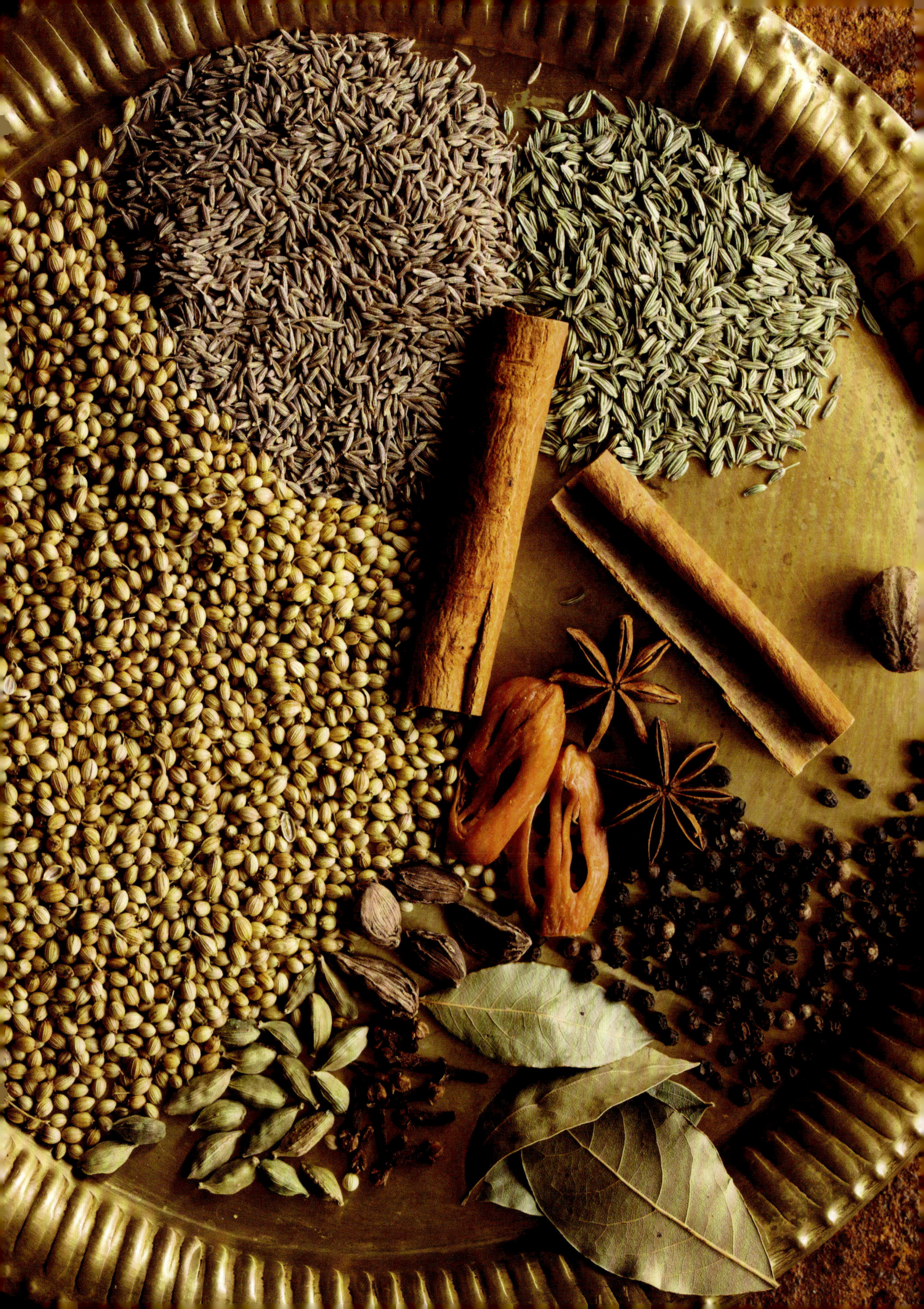

Garam Masala (the warming one)

40 g (1½ oz) coriander seeds
30 g (1 oz) cumin seeds
20 green cardamom pods
4 dried Indian bay leaves
5 black cardamom pods
12 cloves
2 blades mace
12-cm (5-inch) cinnamon stick or cassia bark, bashed into small pieces (15 g/½ oz)
2 star anise, bashed into small pieces
10 g (⅓ oz) fennel seeds
5 g (⅙ oz) black peppercorns
1 small nutmeg, bashed to pieces in a pestle and mortar

Storage

Store this garam masala in a clean, dry airtight container, preferably somewhere cool and dark. It will keep for up to 6 months, but it's best used within 3 months.

A cracker of a blend using whole roasted spices. Use this versatile and warming combination of mixed whole spices to jazz up any North Indian dish, from curry and pulao to samosas, snacks and parathas. The cooler climate calls and rich Mughlai and Central Asian influences on North Indian cuisine are very well suited to the 'garam' (warm) spices in garam masala. It is a flavour protagonist in many North Indian sub-cuisines, including (but not limited) to Awadhi, Rajasthani, Bihari, Punjabi and Himachali. Every region, and indeed, every home will have their favourite blend of spices.

The use of garam masala extends far beyond the borders of India. Indeed, garam masala is popular in Pakistani, Sri Lankan, Nepalese, Bangladeshi, African, Caribbean and Afghan cuisines. Garam masala is a blend that also features heavily in British Indian restaurant cookery.

1. Heat a dry frying pan (skillet) or saucepan over a low heat. Add all the spices and stir to combine. Cook over a very low heat for 10 minutes, stirring continuously to ensure the spices don't burn. If you have time, roast all the spices one by one, giving each spice a good 3–4 minutes (depending on size) to toast up. Allow to cool.

2. Pile the spices into a spice grinder. Blend until the mixture becomes a fine powder. You might need to stop and stir everything once or twice to ensure all the spices are getting some blade time.

3. Sift the masala to ensure no large pieces or whole spices remain. If they do, just blend them again and sift into the rest of the mixture.

All-in-One Biryani Masala (the fragrant one)

20 cloves
20 black peppercorns
15 green cardamom pods
4 black cardamom pods
20-cm (8-inch) cinnamon stick or cassia bark
3 dried Indian bay leaves
2 blades mace
5 dried red chillies
4 large pieces black stone flower (about enough to cover your palm)
2 tbsp edible dried rose petals
2 tbsp coriander seeds
2 tsp cumin seeds
2 tsp carom seeds
1 tbsp dried garlic
2 tsp ground ginger
2 tsp ground turmeric
1 tbsp salt
2 tsp sugar

Storage

Store this biryani masala in a clean, dry airtight container, preferably somewhere cool and dark. It will keep for up to 6 months, but it's best used within 3 months.

As a dish, biryani is very much a labour of love. If someone takes time out of their day to layer up this multi-stage wonder, you know you hold a special place in their heart. Making biryani requires thought, impeccable timing and soul. I like to begin by making my own masala.

I roast whole spices until the oils are released and become fragrant. It's as satisfying to make as it is to eat. Plus, everything is fresh and you get to see exactly what goes into the blend. My biryani masala is an all-in-one recipe. I include dried chilli, garlic and ginger in the masala, so you don't need to add their fresh counterparts when you cook your biryani.

1. Heat a dry frying pan (skillet) or saucepan over a low heat.

2. Add all the whole spices and toss to combine. Cook over a low heat for about 2 minutes, stirring continuously.

3. Add the powdered spices, salt and sugar. Toss again and cook, mixing continuously to ensure the masala doesn't burn. This shouldn't take longer than 2 minutes. Allow to cool.

4. Pile the spices into a spice grinder. Grind until the mixture becomes a fine powder. You might need to stop and stir everything once or twice to ensure all the spices are getting some blade time.

5. Sift the masala to ensure no large pieces or whole spices remain. If they do, just blend them again and sift into the rest of the mixture.

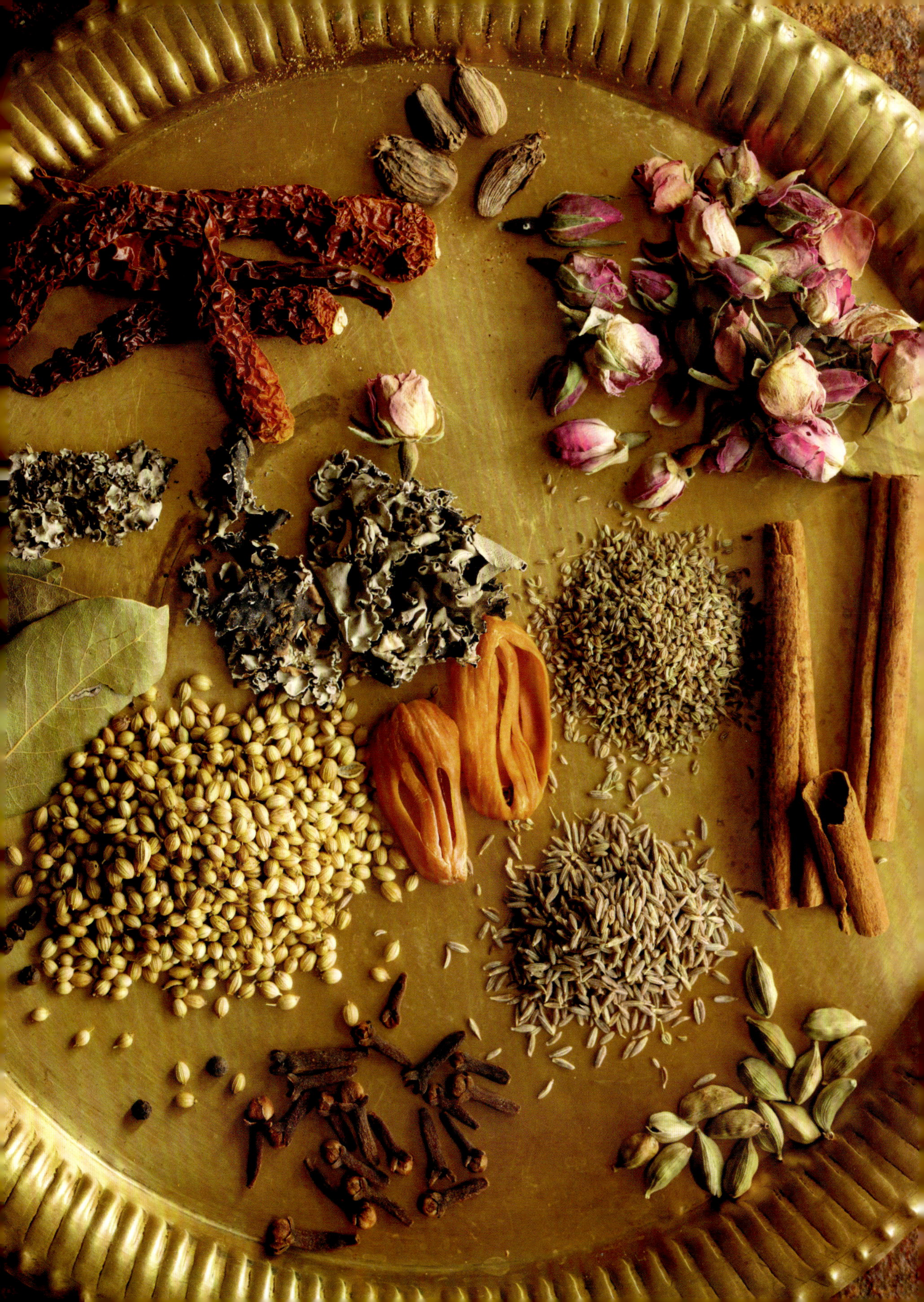

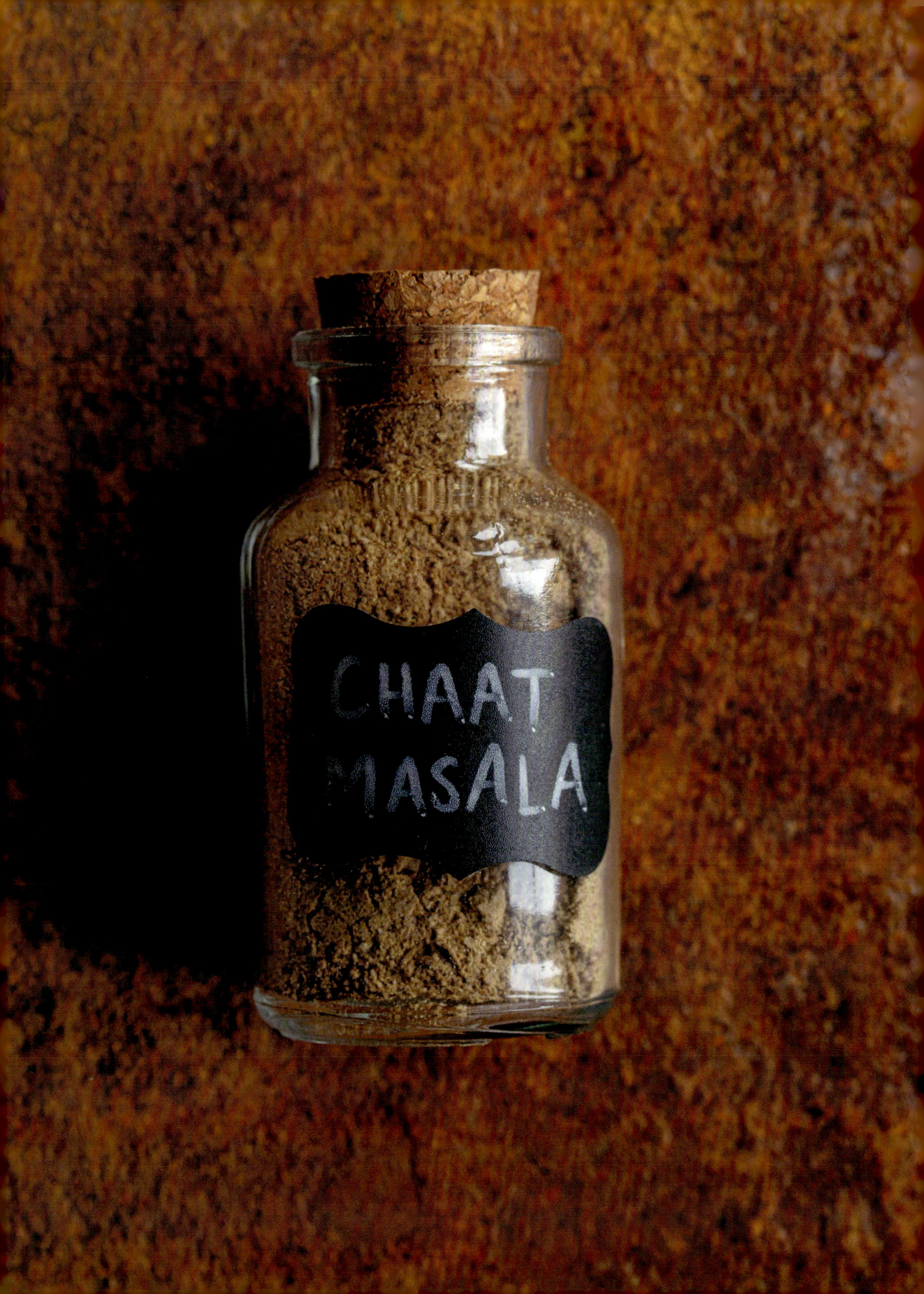
CHAAT
MASALA

Chaat Masala (the funky one)

40 g (1½ oz) cumin seeds
60 g (2 oz) dried mango powder
15 g (½ oz) black salt
5 g (⅙ oz) freshly ground black pepper
5 g (⅙ oz) sugar

Storage

Store this chaat masala in a clean, dry airtight container, preferably somewhere cool and dark. It will keep for up to 6 months but is best used within 3 months.

An essential addition to any chaat. This supremely sour combination of dried mango, toasted cumin seeds and funky black salt can raise anything from the dead. Don't let the short list of ingredients fool you, this masala packs a punch. Use sparingly until you acquire a taste for it. Once you start, you'll be sprinkling it on everything from chaats and salads, to roast potatoes and fruit! If you can handle heat, try piercing a few holes in whole, thin, green chillies (the long jwala variety, also called Indian finger chillies). Deep-fry the chillies in hot oil until blistered white on the outside. Remove from the oil with a perforated spoon and sprinkle with chaat masala. These are sublime eaten alongside snacks, with street foods like pav bhaji, and they can be used as a wicked garnish.

1. Heat a dry frying pan (skillet) or saucepan over a low heat.

2. Add the cumin seeds and dry roast for 4–5 minutes until toasted and aromatic. Allow to cool.

3. Add the cumin, along with the other ingredients, to a spice grinder or pestle and mortar. Grind until the mixture becomes a fine powder.

Achaar Masala (the pickling one)

1 tsp oil
10 g (⅓ oz) fenugreek seeds
5 g (⅙ oz) asafoetida
60 g (2 oz) Kashmiri chilli powder
25 g (¾ oz) dried mango powder
20 g (⅔ oz) split yellow mustard seeds
5 g (⅙ oz) salt

Storage

Store this achaar masala in a clean, dry airtight container, preferably somewhere cool and dark. It will keep for up to 4 months but is best used within 2 months. After this, it will begin to lose its flavour and aroma. If kept too long, the masala may turn rancid due to the oils in the spices. Prolong the life of your achaar masala by storing it in the fridge.

Spoiler: It's not just used for pickling. Achaar masala is so fiery and flavoursome that it can add oomph to just about any marinade, dry rub or curry. It's common to see achaari dishes on restaurant menus, usually in the selection of curries. Achaari potatoes, okra and protein-based dishes are ones I see most often. They can be saucy or dry, although the latter is more common. The achaari element refers to spices such as mustard seeds, chilli powder, fenugreek seeds and asafoetida, which are typically included in Indian achaars (pickles) and preserves. The flavours are astringent and potent, so a little achaar masala goes a long way. Mix with plain yogurt and roasted gram flour (besan) to make an excellent marinade for your barbecue favourites.

I like to mix achaar masala with hot oil and then pour this over roasted vegetables, noodles or dumplings for something uniquely delicious.

Rai kuria (split yellow mustard seeds) are the little yellow guys that live inside yellow mustard seeds. They're hot and spicy in flavour and traditionally used for pickles and preserves in Indian cookery. My family make a mean green chilli chutney with them. If you can't find split mustard seeds at your local South Asian store or online, swap them for an equal measure of English mustard powder.

1. Heat a dry frying pan (skillet) or saucepan over a low heat.

2. Add the oil and fenugreek seeds. Allow to sizzle gently for a minute before adding the asafoetida. Remove from the heat and allow to cool.

3. Add the roasted fenugreek seeds and asafoetida, along with all the other ingredients to a spice grinder. Grind until you obtain a slightly coarse but uniform powder.

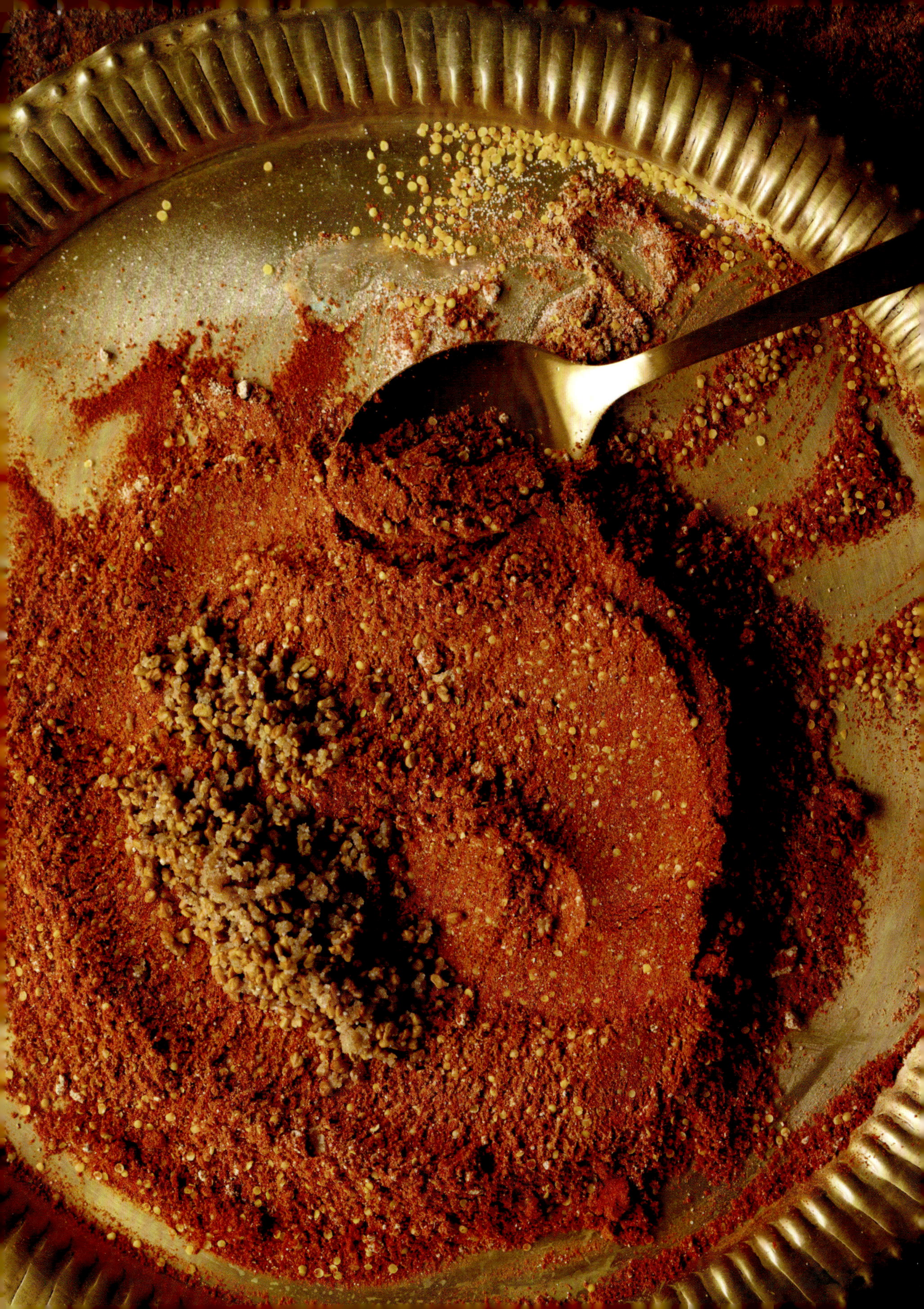

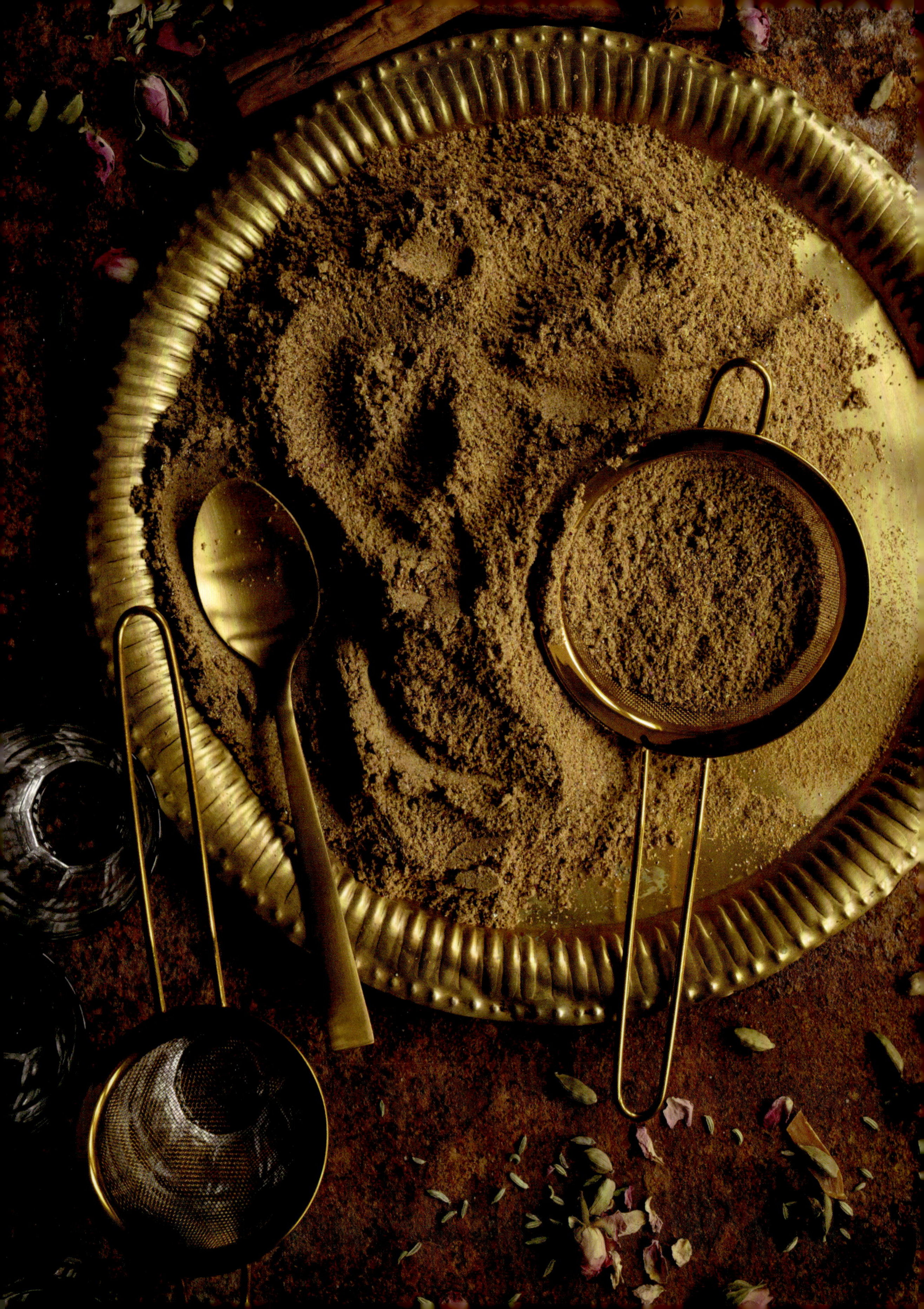

Chai Masala (the tea one)

100 g (3½ oz) ground ginger
80 g (2¾ oz) green cardamom pods
60 g (2 oz) black peppercorns
30 g (1 oz) cinnamon sticks
20 g (⅔ oz) edible dried rose petals
15 g (½ oz) cloves
10 g (⅓ oz) fennel seeds
3 blades mace
1 vanilla pod (bean)

Storage

Store this chai masala in a clean, dry airtight container. It will keep for up to 3 months. After this, it will begin to lose its flavour and aroma.

This chai masala recipe delivers aromatic flavours as well as a whack of dried ginger and peppercorns. I firmly believe that when cool, aromatic spices and warming spices work in tandem, beautiful things happen. For me, it's the spiciness of the ginger and peppercorns, offset by cooling cardamom, that takes a standard cuppa chai to the next level. Recipes vary from place to place and seasonally, too. During winter, warming spices are added with a heavy hand, whereas cooling spices are the workhorses in summer months.

There's no need to toast the spices prior to grinding when making chai masala. The heat of the blade while grinding will do the hard work. The spices are boiled with the tea, so that takes care of the rest of the infusion.

Bonus: You can also use this chai masala to make masala coffee, masala hot chocolate and in cakes, pastries and other baking recipes too. Whilst chai masala is readily available in stores, I think this homemade version is very good and I hope you will enjoy it too.

1. Add all the spices, including the ones that are already ground to the jar of a spice grinder or coffee grinder. Grind to a fine powder. Stop halfway to stir the spices and make sure everything is properly ground.

2. Sift the chai masala into a bowl to ensure there are no longer any large spice fragments left in. Grind again until fine.

Gunpowder (the explosive one)

50 g (1¾ oz) split yellow gram daal
25 g (¾ oz) split black gram daal
2 tbsp basmati rice
2 tbsp sesame seeds
15 large dried mild red chillies
4–5 fenugreek seeds
15 curry leaves
½ tsp asafoetida
1 tsp salt

Storage

Store this gunpowder in a clean, dry, airtight container in the fridge for up to a month.

Gunpowder, or podi, is a chief masala in South Indian cookery. It varies in hundreds of ways, calling upon various daals, aromatics and vegetables. Much like other masalas, there is no single definitive recipe. Each blend of gunpowder differs regionally, and from home to home. It can be used for cooking and as a condiment.

Three ways to enjoy gunpowder:

- Serve gunpowder as an accompaniment to any South Indian meal. Place a small mound of gunpowder on the side of a plate of dosa, appam or rice. Make a well in the centre of the mound and add a few teaspoons of smoking hot ghee. Mix as you eat, varying the amount you take according to your spice tolerance – it's quite fun!

- Mix gunpowder with yogurt and add to stir-fried dishes like Gunpowder Tofu (see page 70). The daal, rice and yogurt blend to create a crust that clings to veggies and proteins, taking them from bland to blast-off in moments.

- Gunpowder Nuts to go with drinks. Toss assorted nuts in a drizzle of oil and then sprinkle with gunpowder. Roast in the oven until toasty and fiery.

1. Roast both types of daal and the rice together in a dry frying pan (skillet) set over a medium-low heat, stirring continuously until they're a nutty brown colour, about 15 minutes.

2. Add the rest of the ingredients and continue to dry roast for 5 minutes, stirring all the time. Remove from the heat and allow to cool completely.

3. Transfer to a spice grinder or coffee grinder, then grind to a fine powder.

Tandoori Masala (the smoky one)

2 tbsp coriander seeds

2 tbsp cumin seeds

4 tsp black peppercorns

4 tsp dried fenugreek leaves

½ tsp citric acid

4 green cardamom pods

1 black cardamom pod

70 g (2½ oz) Kashmiri chilli powder

2 tbsp smoked paprika

2 tsp ground turmeric

4 tsp Garam Masala (see page 259)

Storage

Store this tandoori masala in a clean, dry, airtight container, preferably somewhere cool and dark. It will keep for up to 6 months but is best used within 3 months.

When it's time to grill Indian style, there is no party without tandoori masala. The iconic red marinade that clings to charred skewers and kebabs. The name refers to the clay oven in which the masala-marinated ingredients are cooked in. Burning hot, the tandoor reaches temperatures in excess of 450°C (850°F). The bright red masala is the one that makes for the most magical grills, kebabs and breads. I always have a batch of in my store cupboard ready to be mixed into yogurt for barbecues and indoor grill nights. It works with practically everything. If you can't find citric acid, substitute a teaspoon of dried mango powder, or simply omit and remember to add a generous squeeze of lemon to your yogurt marinade. This is my go-to recipe for making any kind of tikka dish. Tikka simply refers to bite-sized 'pieces' of any ingredient(s).

Since much of my grilling is done indoors, I like to add smoked paprika to the masala to achieve that familiar smoky depth, since it's almost always too cold outside to fire up the barbecue.

You can also smear your naans, rotis and parathas with tandoori butter for deeply delicious and spicy flatbreads to accompany any Indian meal.

1. Add the coriander seeds, cumin seeds, peppercorns, dried fenugreek leaves, citric acid and green and black cardamom to a pestle and mortar. Bash until you obtain a very fine powder.

2. Mix the powder with the remaining ground ingredients.

SEEKH KEBAB MASALA

Seekh Kebab Masala (the 'meaty' one)

1 tbsp gram flour (besan)
2 tsp coriander seeds
2 tsp cumin seeds
1 tsp carom seeds
2 dried Indian bay leaves
6 dried red chillies
1 star anise
8 cloves
10 black peppercorns
3 tsp ground ginger
1 tsp dried mango powder
2 tsp dried garlic powder
1½ tsp dried mint

Storage

Store this seekh kebab masala in a clean, dry airtight container, preferably somewhere cool and dark. It will keep for up to 6 months but is best used within 3 months.

A deeply savoury blend of mostly warming spices. Seekh kebab masala is usually used for kebabs, koftas and other meat preparations. With the Mughal Empire, the ingredients and cooking techniques of Central Asia came to India. A wealth of dishes from shammi kebabs, galouti kebabs, chapli kebabs, and of course seekh kebabs (named after the skewer they're cooked on). These Nawabi dishes infused the food culture of many parts of Northern India and modern-day Pakistan.

I use this spice mix in many vegetarian dishes for its ability to add bold, nutty and herbal flavours to just about any ingredient, especially those with meaty textures. Try using it for plant-based kebabs, koftas, grills, burgers and mince dishes. Jackfruit, tofu, root vegetables, paneer, halloumi, tempeh, soya chunks, soya mince and seitan all love it.

1. Heat a dry pan over a medium-low heat. First dry roast the gram flour for 2–3 minutes until golden and nutty. Remove from the pan and set aside.

2. Next, add the whole spices: the coriander seeds, cumin seeds, carom seeds, bay leaves, red chillies, star anise, cloves and black peppercorns. Sauté for 30 seconds. Next, add the dry spices: the ground ginger, dried mango powder (amchur), garlic powder and dried mint. Sauté for 10–15 seconds and then remove from the heat. Add everything to the gram flour and allow everything to cool completely.

3. Grind the masala in a high-powered blender or coffee grinder until fine.

Chips Masala
(the Indo-East African one)

2 tbsp chilli powder
2 tsp baobab powder
1 tsp sweet smoked paprika
1 tsp garlic powder
1½ tsp salt
2 tsp sugar

Storage
Store this chips masala in a clean, dry airtight container, preferably somewhere cool and dark. It will keep for up to 6 months but is best used within 3 months.

Note
You'll find baobab powder in health food stores or online.

A hot and sour masala for sprinkling on chips (potato fries). This simple mix-and-sprinkle masala requires no blender. A zap of sherbet freshness comes courtesy of baobab powder, a seed from the fruit of East Africa's indigenous baobab tree. The fruit is a hard shell covered in velvety green fuzz. Crack it open to reveal hundreds of creamy white powdery seeds caught in a web of wispy, orange fibres. The seeds are duck face-inducingly sour. The powder is either harvested from the seeds or the seeds are candied to make a local sweet called mabuyu in Swahili. Inspired by the sour, hot and sweet flavours of mabuyu, this chips masala is a blend you'll want to sprinkle onto any kind of root vegetable or crispy snack. It's also excellent on popcorn.

1. Add all the ingredients to a clean, dry jar. Tightly screw the lid onto the jar and shake to combine the powders together.

2. Sprinkle this masala over chips (potato fries) or use as a seasoning for grilled corn, roasted cassava (mogo) or slices of raw green mango.

Madras Curry Powder (the all-purpose one)

4 tbsp coriander seeds
2 tbsp cumin seeds
2 tsp mustard seeds
1 tsp fenugreek seeds
½ tsp black peppercorns
1 star anise
3 cloves
3 green cardamom pods
10 curry leaves
½ tsp chilli powder
1 tbsp ground turmeric
2 tsp onion powder
1 tsp garlic powder
1 tsp ground ginger
1 tsp ground cinnamon

Storage

Store this Madras curry powder in a clean, dry airtight container, preferably somewhere cool and dark. It will keep for up to 6 months but is best used within 3 months.

A good-quality, all-purpose curry powder is great for adding spice to rice, noodles, sauces and soups. I find I get the most use out of Madras curry powder when I'm making Indo-Chinese dishes and fusion recipes. A handful of recipes in this book, such as my Madras Mac and Cheese (see page 62), Singapore Poha (see page 93) and Paneer Katsu Curry (see page 84), call for it.

Curry powder is an all-in-one affair used for adding a generic Indian curry flavour to all sorts of dishes, much like the many types of masala powders there are. The concept of curry powder was entirely a British construct, created to mimic the Indian flavours enjoyed in the Subcontinent while under British rule (1858-1974). It was later introduced to other countries occupied by Britain. Before long, curry powder reached almost every part of the world, from Eastern and Southern Africa to the Pacific and Indian Ocean, the Caribbean, China, Malaysia and Japan. Today it has a place in my kitchen cupboard beside other masala mixes I use often, such as Garam Masala (see page 259), Biryani Masala (see page 260) and Achaar Masala (see page 264).

1. Heat a dry frying pan (skillet) over a medium-low heat. Roast the coriander seeds, cumin seeds, mustard seeds, fenugreek seeds, black peppercorns, star anise, cloves, cardamom, and curry leaves over a low heat. Stir continuously to ensure none of the spices burn. The process will take around 8–10 minutes. Remove the pan from the heat and transfer these spices to a plate to cool completely.

2. Grind the roasted spices in a high-powered blender or coffee grinder to a very fine powder. Add the ground spices and blitz once more to incorporate.

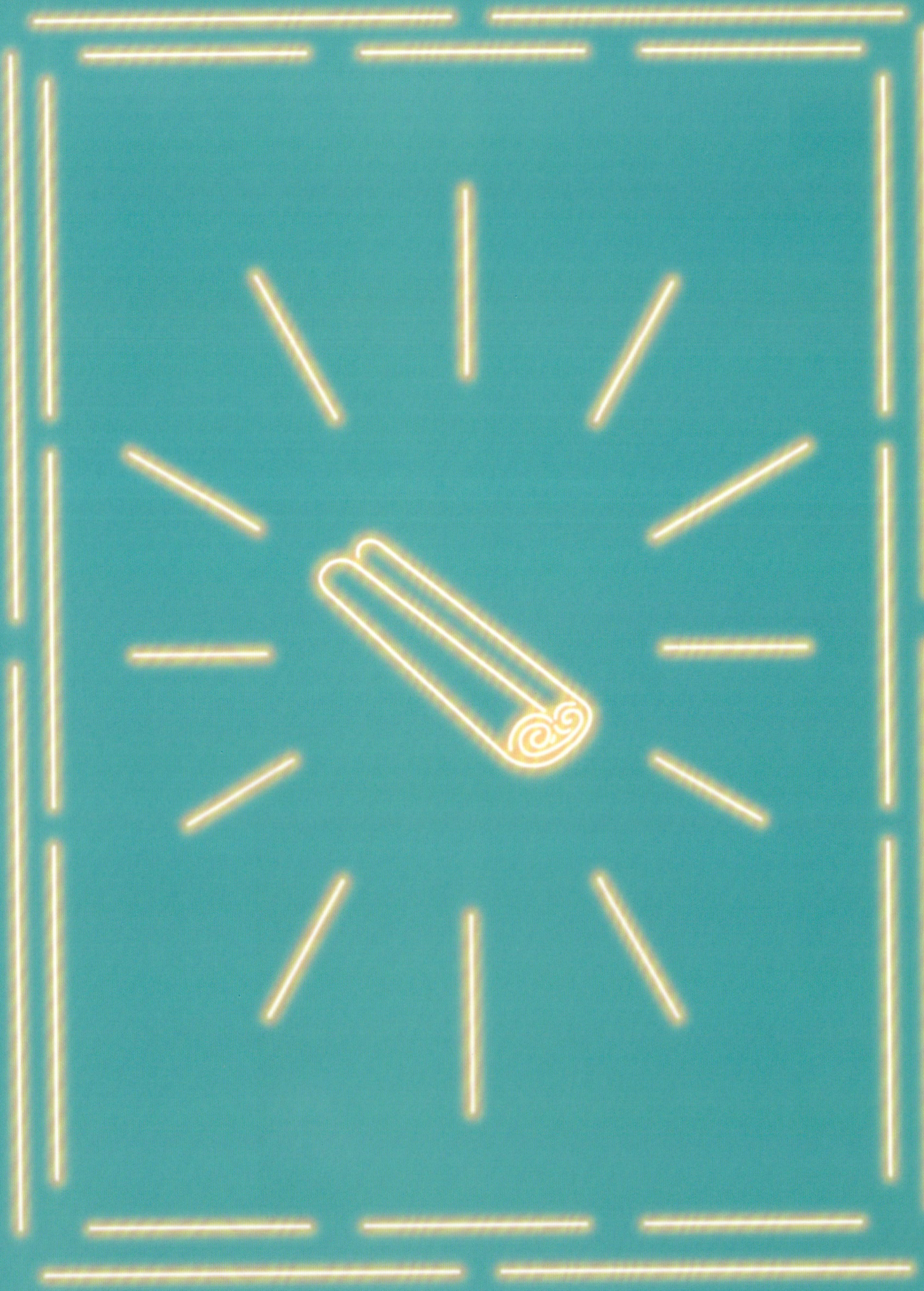

MY Indian-ish Pantry

Where all meals begin.

Every Indian pantry or store cupboard I've experienced has always smelled the same. First comes the rush of spice. Go closer and the starchy aroma of rice and earthy grains begin to plant the seeds of potential meals. A lingering scent of buttery ghee, the sack of onions still in their skins and a feint waft of 'cellar'. Ours was a Victorian-era hole-in-the wall we'd have to crawl into and use a torch to locate ingredients. My Nanabapu's pantry was a walk-in through the living room with rows of spices stored in recycled bottles of his favourite grapefruit juice. Bapuji's came with the addition of stainless-steel catering pots and flour bins so huge I could fit inside. Of the dozens of steel dabbas and ceramic pots on the shelf, my Baa had memorised exactly what was stashed inside each one, no labels required. Everything had a place. My Masi's had potatoes in wicker baskets and garlic hanging on hooks on the inside door. My Kaka's is through the home office, with purpose-built shelves and tremendous lighting. No torch required. Mine is a set of kitchen cupboards: one for flours, one for spices, one for cans and another for beans and lentils. Each set-up may look different, but Indian pantries contain almost identical ingredients and always smell like you just walked in on a masala party.

In our family home, we stored our supplies in empty sweet jars. My mother would wash and dry the surplus jars from the store, using them to hold rice, khichdi mix, gram flour, lentils, beans and pulses. Since chapati flour was required every day, it would be bought 10 kg (22 lb) at a time and stored in its own flour bin. Large stocks of spices would be kept in airtight containers, with a selection of them destined to be decanted into the spice tin that lived in the kitchen cupboard. Mum's storecupboard was modelled on her father's. She recalls childhood trips to Harnam Singh's Punjabi grocers on Derby Road in Southampton. It was the only Indian store around for miles. In those days, the choice was limited to ground spices and pre-packaged masala mixes. Once Ugandan Asians arrived in the UK during the 1970s, the range of ingredients available grew. Shopkeepers would wait by the airport or travel to the docks to receive stock. Fresh Asian vegetables were still limited, so daal became an even bigger staple than it already was. Local vegetables formed the basis for curries, as well as a reliable stock of canned vegetables. They bought frozen peas every Saturday and, since there was no freezer in the house, the bag would be kept in a bowl of cold water in the back garden, ready to be used the next morning. If there was nothing in the house, curry and sliced white bread or Ritz crackers and achaar would be on standby.

A functional, but not necessarily overstocked pantry is the basis for many great Indian meals. They do not have to be extensive, nor intimidating. There really is no need to go out and buy everything on this list. Instead, I suggest selecting a few recipes you like and keeping the ingredients you need to make them to hand. The range of standby ingredients you choose can expand organically, alongside your cooking repertoire. Indeed, if you only want to stick to a handful of Indian recipes, keep your collection small, and replenish as you need. That way you know that your ingredients are fresh and bright for the recipes you do like to include in your regular meal rotation. If you're concerned about not using up ground spices before they dull, buy whole spices and grind them yourself. A coffee grinder is a great way to whip up small batches of fresh masala when you have the time.

I cook Indian food almost every day, yet in my solo parent home, I keep a smaller selection of ingredients, since I usually cook for two. It's a world apart from the flour bins and oil drums of my parents' and grandparents' eras. Keeping my storecupboard lean, yet diverse allows me to save space and money, but doesn't limit the food I'm able to cook. Small packets of spices, lentils and flours are available to buy everywhere. I buy small cans of beans to keep handy for post-school cooking and if I know I'm not going to use the whole thing, I'll rinse the beans, use what I need and then freeze the rest for another meal, another day. Frozen vegetables are a mainstay and can help to bulk out everything from curries and paratha fillings, as well as for samosa stuffing and simple vegetable pulao.

How to make curry out of anything

The secret behind my mother's superpower is about to be revealed. If you have any vegetables or lentils you want to make a basic, everyday curry out of, this is the formula for how to do it. It's a very unspecific guide, but it generally works for the simplest vegetarian curries and daals.

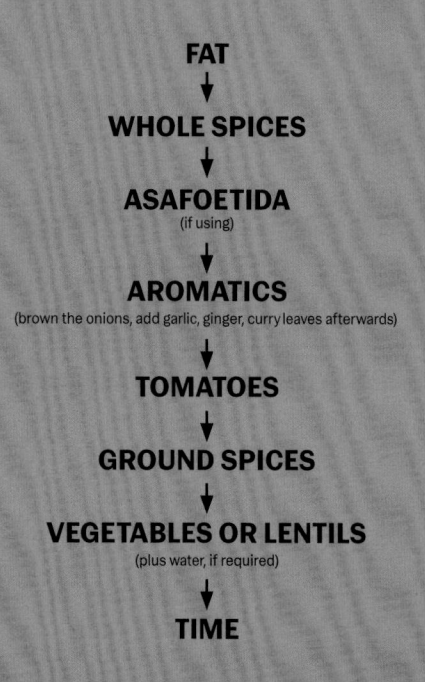

FAT
↓
WHOLE SPICES
↓
ASAFOETIDA
(if using)
↓
AROMATICS
(brown the onions, add garlic, ginger, curry leaves afterwards)
↓
TOMATOES
↓
GROUND SPICES
↓
VEGETABLES OR LENTILS
(plus water, if required)
↓
TIME

After slow or quick cooking, the dish can be garnished with fresh coriander (cilantro) before serving.

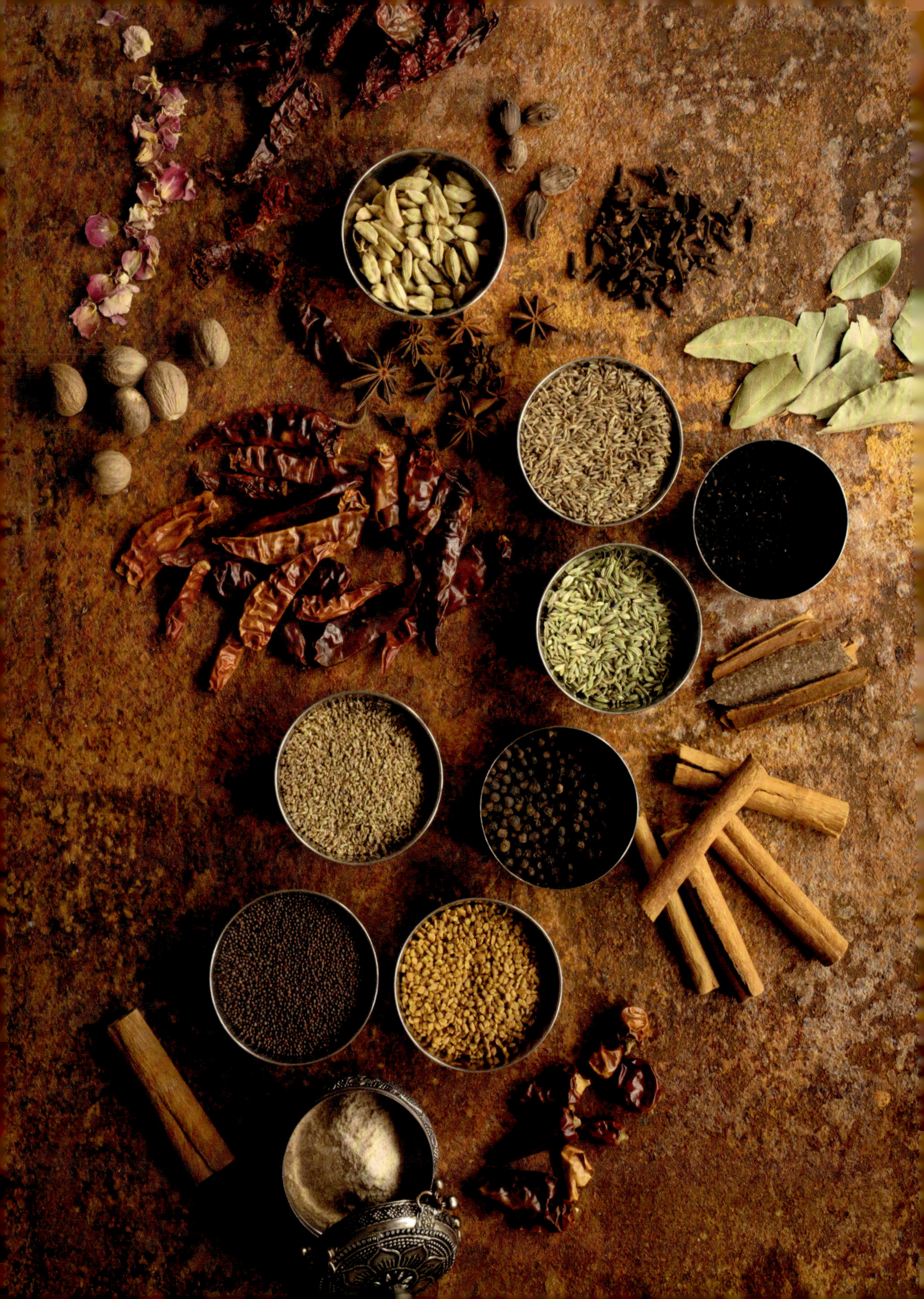

SPICES

WHOLE

In my kitchen, whole spices are used both in their whole form and ground for masala mixes that sing with flavour. Rice and daal dishes usually call for whole spices to be tempered in hot fat (tadka), since they impart a gentle infusion of flavour in comparison to a punchy powder. The downside to this is that you'll need to remember to remove large whole spices from the dish prior to serving. I usually just leave them in and tell diners to set them aside when they come across spices like whole cloves, cardamom pods, bay leaves and pieces of cassia bark or cinnamon stick in their dish. There really is nothing worse than biting down on a rogue clove mid-biryani. Small or seed-like whole spices are fine.

Black cardamom (moti elaichi)
A larger variety of cardamom, which is typically dried over an open flame prior to packaging. It imparts very much of the same eucalyptus-like flavour as its green cousin, but with a smokier side. Ideal for savoury dishes, varieties of black cardamom are also used in Nepalese, Bhutanese and Chinese cuisines respectively. Crush the pod lightly before adding to a dish. For me, black cardamom is a must in Black Daal (see page 139), rice dishes and other warmly spiced comfort meals. It's not interchangeable with green cardamom.
  Pairs well with: asafoetida, bay leaves, black peppercorns, black stone flower, chilli, coriander seeds, ginger, star anise, turmeric.

Black peppercorns (kali mirch)
Peppercorns are second in command to chillies when it comes to adding deep heat to dishes. Keep whole peppercorns handy and bash in a pestle and mortar as needed for the biggest flavours.
  Pairs well with: bay leaves, cumin seeds, curry leaves, ginger, mace, turmeric.

Black stone flower (dagad phool)
Whilst it's called 'flower', dagad phool (Hindi) is in fact, a type of fungus/dried lichen. The black petal-like shape of the fungi grows on stones. Another name for it is pathar ke phool, which means 'stone flower'. It has an unmistakable, characteristic musky aroma. Think mellow woody perfume, but not at all like Grandad's Old Spice. It adds background fragrance and umami notes to masalas and is a must in biryani. I find that once I start eating a dish with dagad phool in it, I can't stop.
  Pairs well with: black and green cardamom, cloves, edible dried rose petals, fennel seeds, fenugreek, mace, nutmeg, star anise.

Carom seeds (ajwain)
Tiny speckles of carom seeds often appear in batters for fried foods, and in gram-flour based dishes, for it's considered to be an excellent digestive aid. The flavour is not a far cry from thyme, but with herbal celery undertones. The fleshy, peach fuzz-covered leaves of the ajwain plant can be battered and fried to make bhajiya (pakora).
  Pairs well with: bay leaves, chilli, cumin seeds, curry leaves, ginger, turmeric.

Cinnamon or cassia bark (dalchini)
Buy either true cinnamon or cassia bark (also known as Chinese cinnamon or wild cinnamon). Both are widely used in the Indian kitchen across savoury and sweet dishes. Add whole cinnamon sticks to tadka. I often soak a stick of cinnamon in melted ghee, set it alight and pop it into a pot of daal to give the dish a smoky cinnamon warmth. Try my Black Daal recipe (see page 139) to have a go at this yourself.
  Pairs well with: asafoetida, bay leaves, chilli, cloves, coriander seeds, cumin seeds, curry leaves, nutmeg, star anise, turmeric.

Cloves (laung)
Not just for toothaches and mulled wine. Shaped like a tiny mace (the weapon, not the spice), cloves have a deep medicinal flavour. Use them sparingly in tadka (be careful because they can explode). Cloves are a warming spice used in an abundance of Indian dishes from daal and rice to garam masala and chai masala. Pick them out of biryani prior to serving unless you're feeding it to your enemies.
  Pairs well with: asafoetida, black peppercorns, chilli, cinnamon, green cardamom, nutmeg, star anise, turmeric.

Coriander seeds (dhania)
With sprightly citrus undertones, there's very little coriander seeds don't pair well with. Coarsely crush them and add to samosa and paratha fillings, curries, snack dishes, pickles and chutneys.

Pairs well with: asafoetida, carom seeds, chilli, cumin seeds, dried mango powder, fennel seeds, ginger, turmeric.

Cumin seeds (jeera)
Another all-rounder spice integral to the flavour foundations of many dishes cooked in the Indian kitchen. It has a deeply savoury flavour and is often added to tadka when making savoury dishes. Dry roast your cumin until golden. You'll experience one of the best food smells in the world through the plume of smoke that comes from bashing the roasted cumin. Be sure to sprinkle this onto yogurt-based dishes like raita, chaat and lassi.

Pairs well with: asafoetida, black salt, carom seeds, chilli, cinnamon, coriander seeds, dried mango powder, fennel seeds, ginger, mint, turmeric.

Dried Indian bay leaves (tej patta)
Meaning 'pungent leaf', dried Indian bay leaves have a uniquely aromatic and woody flavour. This type of bay leaf has a different flavour to European laurel bay leaves. They're used in savoury dishes as well as sweets. Add them sparingly to tadkas and remove once the dish is cooked.

Pairs well with: black cardamom, black peppercorns, chilli, cinnamon, cloves, coriander seeds, cumin seeds, green cardamom, mace, star anise, turmeric.

Dried Kashmiri chillies (Kashmiri lal mirch)
These deep red and wrinkly chillies are prized for their colour and mild level of heat. Use whole in tadka for a gentle warmth. Dried Kashmiri chillies can also be rehydrated in hot water and blended to make chutneys and marinades. Try my recipe for Savoy Cabbage Ghee Roast (see page 129) to witness this in action.

Pairs well with: everything. Add whole dried Kashmiri chillies to tadka, along with other whole spices, asafoetida and aromatics.

Edible dried rose petals (gulab ki pankhudiyaan)
The petals of edible varieties of rose can be dried and used as garnishes for both sweet and savoury dishes, as well as ground into masalas for a delicate floral undertone.

Pairs well with: black cardamom, black peppercorns, black stone flower, cinnamon, cloves, cumin seeds, fennel seeds, green cardamom, mace, nutmeg, saffron, screwpine water, vanilla.

Fennel seeds (saunf)
These little green seeds have a liquorice or aniseed-like taste with a sweetness. They're used across almost all regional Indian cuisines in both savoury and sweet dishes, as well as in drinks. Use them in their whole form or grind into a powder. Fennel seeds are often candied in a sprinkle-like fashion to make a post-meal mouth freshener and digestive aid. It's also an ingredient in paan (various nuts, seeds, syrups and oftentimes tobacco wrapped in betel leaves).

Pairs well with: black peppercorns, chilli, cinnamon, cloves, cumin seeds, fenugreek seeds, ginger, mustard seeds, nutmeg, turmeric.

Fenugreek seeds (methi)
These little brown seeds carry a caramelised bitterness that adds depth to mostly savoury dishes, pickles and ground masala blends. Use the whole seeds sparingly in tadka for daal and curry. When preparing tadka, add them at the very end as they brown quickly and can make the dish taste acrid.

Pairs well with: asafoetida, black peppercorns, chilli, coriander seeds, cumin seeds, fennel seeds, mustard seeds, nigella seeds, turmeric.

Green cardamom (elaichi)
The strong menthol flavour of green cardamom is used across both savoury and sweet dishes. Since the flavours do well to cut richness, it makes chai masala sing, shahi qormas and makhanis dance, and breathes life into milk-based desserts. Green cardamom can be bought either in pods or as seeds. It's not interchangeable with black cardamom.

Pairs well with: cinnamon, cloves, edible rose petals, nutmeg, saffron, star anise.

Mustard seeds (sarson)
This usually refers to small black mustard seeds. They have a pungent flavour and add warmth to a dish. When frying mustard seeds in oil for tadka, wait for them to finish popping before adding the next ingredient. Yellow mustard seeds (rai kuria) are often reserved for pickling, but they can be used in lieu of black mustard seeds if they're all that's available. The leaves of the mustard plant produce sarson ka saag, the peppery greens used to make one of Punjab's most cherished dishes.

Pairs well with: bay leaves, cinnamon, cloves, cumin seeds, curry leaves, fennel seeds, fenugreek seeds, nigella seeds.

Nigella seeds (kalonji)
You'll recognise these little black seeds from naan. A common addition to breads, pastries, rice dishes, chutneys and curries. The flavour is like that of dried oregano and toasty onions. Try using them as a topping for savoury cheese scones.

Pairs well with: asafoetida, bay leaves, chilli, cumin seeds, fennel seeds, fenugreek seeds, mustard seeds, turmeric.

Star anise (badian or chakri phool)
Undoubtedly one of the most visually stunning spices in the storecupboard. The warm sweetness of star anise adds depth to daal, rice dishes, masala blends and when it's infused into sticky, fruity preserves and chutneys.

Pairs well with: asafoetida, black peppercorns, chilli, cinnamon, cloves, curry leaves, ginger, white pepper.

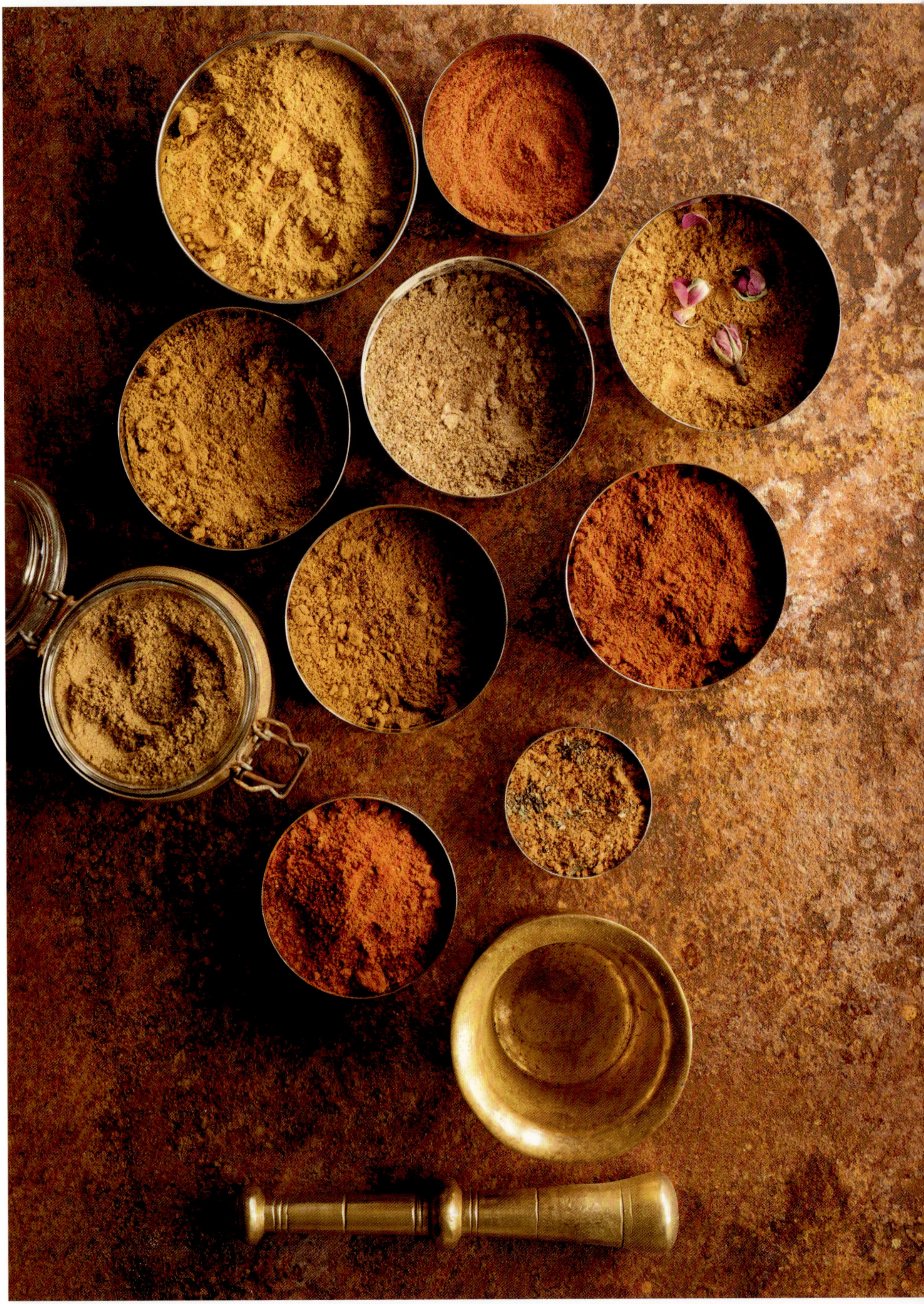

GROUND

Many of these pre-ground spices are a quick way of incorporating big flavour into a meal. They do not need to be tempered – in fact, putting them in hot oil will burn them in the blink of an eye. When cooking with ground spices (store-bought or ground at home), try to reduce the time they're in contact with a dry mixture over high heat. Add the ground spices once a high moisture or liquid element of the recipe has been added, such as tomatoes or water. For dry-style curries, you can mix the ground spices with a few tablespoons of water prior to adding it to the mixture. This will prevent the masalas burning so you're not frantically trying to toss them into the pan to evenly coat the ingredients.

Asafoetida (hing)
Asafoetida is technically a gum derived from tree resin. Buy tubs of pre-ground asafoetida in Indian supermarkets. Once opened, keep it well sealed and away from other masalas – it can overwhelm your spice cupboard. Asafoetida is typically pounded into a powder and is often mixed with wheat or rice flour to prevent caking and clumping. To use, first sizzle a small pinch in warm fat to release the natural aromas. The flavours are pungent, so very little is needed. According to Ayurveda, it is said to be an excellent digestive aid, so you'll often find it is used alongside beans and lentils. It is widely used as a substitute for onions and garlic in Jain cuisine and during periods of religious fasting, due to its potent allium-like flavour.
Pairs well with: bay leaves, cinnamon, cloves, cumin seeds, curry leaves, mustard seeds.

Baobab powder
The sour powder derived from the fruit of the baobab tree, native to East Africa. It's a powerhouse of vitamin C and tastes a lot like sherbet. I use it as a souring agent. Sprinkle onto grilled vegetables, fruits, breakfast dishes and use in dressings and marinades.
Pairs well with: asafoetida, chilli powder, coriander seeds.

Black salt (kala namak)
You'll find that commercially sold ground black salt is often pink in colour. It's used primarily to give dishes like chaats, chutneys and other street foods a uniquely explosive slap of sulphur-like saltiness. The smell is as potent as can be and a little goes a long way. It's a flavour that grows on you the more you become accustomed to it. Use it in vegan scrambled tofu or other bhurji (scrambled) dishes to add a pronounced 'eggy' flavour.
Pairs well with: cumin, dried mango powder, turmeric.

Chilli powder
A storecupboard essential. Some chilli powders are hotter than others. You'll find various types in Indian supermarkets, from mild Kashmiri chilli powder and deggi mirch (made from a blend of red peppers and Kashmiri chillies, much like a mild paprika), to extra hot chilli powder. Mild chilli powders can be used in larger quantities and impart a wonderful colour, especially when combined with turmeric. Hot chilli powders are bolshy and bring pure heat.
Pairs well with: everything.

Dried fenugreek leaves (kasoori methi)
The grand finale for any curry or daal that's a little sweet, starchy or rich. It's also excellent on grills and tandoori dishes, adding an herbal element to smoky kebabs and kofta. Many breads like thepla, paratha and naan also call for the magic of kasoori methi. Finish off a dish with a flurry of kasoori methi rubbed between the palms. This action releases its flavours and imparts a gentle bitterness. Store-bought kasoori methi is quite potent so add it in small quantities. It's a star ingredient in my Root Vegetable Jalfrezi (see page 126).
Pairs well with: black cardamom, black peppercorns, chilli, cinnamon, cloves, coriander seeds, cumin seeds, fennel seeds, ginger, green cardamom, turmeric.

Dried mango powder (amchur)
A powder made from dehydrated raw (green) mango. Adds a tart edge to chaat masala, samosa fillings, chutneys, curries and snacks. Add a pinch to drinks, like cocktails and sodas, for happy fruitiness.
Pairs well with: asafoetida, black salt, carom seeds, coriander seeds, cumin seeds, fennel seeds.

Ginger

The fresh, warm flavour of dried, ground ginger is the backbone of many styles of chai masala. Ground ginger is commonly added to curries in the colder northern regions of India. In parts of South India, ground ginger is added to masala blends. Ground ginger can bring more intense heat than fresh root ginger, so shouldn't be used as a direct substitute – if ground is all that's available, use half the quantity compared to fresh root ginger.

Pairs well with: black peppercorns, carom seeds, chilli, coriander seeds, cumin seeds, fennel seeds, mint, nutmeg, star anise, turmeric.

Mace (javitri)

The red web-like coating that hugs the nutmeg kernel. This heady spice turns bright orange once dried and, like nutmeg, should be used sparingly. The flavours are in a league of their own. Grind to a powder and add to masala blends and rich Indian sweets.

Pairs well with: cinnamon, cloves, cumin seeds, edible dried rose petals, fennel seeds, ginger, saffron, vanilla.

Nutmeg (jaiphal)

Buy whole nutmeg kernels and grate them at home for the freshest flavour. If you're adding it to a mixed masala blend, be sure to give it a few solid whacks in a pestle and mortar to crack it into pieces first. Your blender will thank you for it. It's important to always use nutmeg sparingly.

Pairs well with: bay leaves, black and green cardamom, black peppercorns, cinnamon, cloves, coriander, ginger.

Saffron (kesar)

Saffron is a spice collected from the saffron crocus. It imparts a heady, earthy fragrance to dishes as well as a deep yellow hue. It's said the name saffron comes from the Arabic word 'asfar' meaning yellow. By weight, saffron is the most expensive spice in the world and nobody can argue over prices when each crocus contains just three single strands of pure saffron, handpicked by light-fingered saffron collectors. Iranian, Greek and Spanish saffron are all widely available and are of excellent quality. A little goes a long way. Saffron is not fat soluble, so dissolve it in water or milk prior to using.

Pairs well with: black peppercorns, black stone flower, edible dried rose petals, green cardamom, mace, nutmeg, fennel seeds, vanilla.

MIXED MASALAS

Some favourite masala blends from my kitchen. These are the mixes I use most often and commit to making at home on a regular basis. Having said this, store-bought varieties are widely available and can be of good quality.

Achaar Masala
The pickling one. Recipe on page 264.
Try these recipes with Achaar Masala: Meatless Mixed Grill (see page 101), Achaari Matoke (see page 185)

Biryani Masala
The fragrant one. Used specifically for cooking the legendary rice dish, biryani. Aromatic spices loved for their heady warmth and floral quality. Recipe on page 260.
Try this recipe with All-in-One Biryani Masala: Ruffled Biryani (see page 176).

Chaat Masala
The funky one. If you're a fan of all things sour, you'll love this street-style masala mix. It contains black salt, which has a distinctive sulphur flavour – it's a love/hate situation so try a small batch to begin with. Sprinkle on chaats, raita and other yogurt-based dishes, and if you dare, in sandwiches. Recipe on page 263.
Try these recipes with Chaat Masala: Halloumi Fries Chaat (see page 90), Wedge Salad Chaat (see page 190).

Chai Masala
The tea one. Recipe on page 267.
Try this recipe with Chai Masala: Masala Chai (see page 24)

Chips Masala
The Indian-East African one. Hot and sour masala for sprinkling on chips (potato fries). This simple mix and sprinkle masala requires no blender. A zap of sherbet freshness comes from baobab powder, a seed from the fruit of East Africa's baobab tree. Recipe on page 272.
Try this recipe with Chips Masala: Almost-midnight Masala Chips (see page 182)

Garam masala
The warming one. A warming blend of pre-roasted and ground spices. When a recipe calls for garam masala, it most commonly refers to a northern Indian-style of garam masala. Recipes can vary greatly, with each state, manufacturer and home having their own preferences. Note that there are also regional blends of garam masala, which celebrate the spices most popular in each cuisine. Recipe on page 259.
Try these recipes with Garam Masala: Chole Samosa (see page 46), Tiger Pav Bhaji (see page 114), Brown Butter Cauliflower and Pea Makhani (see page 113), Black Daal (see page 139).

Gunpowder
The explosive one. A hot and fiery concoction of roasted daal and whole spices. Gunpowder is a South-Indian treasure and can be served with dosa, idli, rice and more. Recipe on page 268.
Try this recipe with Gunpowder: Gunpowder Tofu (see page 70).

Madras Curry Powder
The all-purpose one. Recipe on page 273.
Try these recipes with Madras Curry Powder: Madras Mac and Cheese (see page 62), Singapore Poha (see page 93), Paneer Katsu Curry (see page 84).

Seekh Kebab Masala
The 'meaty' one. Cool, smoky, herbal and savoury. The combination of spices in this blend is ideal for adding depth and dimension to proteins and robust root vegetables. Recipe on page 271.
Try this recipe with Seekh Kebab Masala: Bubble and Seekh Kebabs (see page 97).

Tandoori Masala
The smoky one. Recipe on page 269.
Try these recipes with Tandoori Masala: Scorpion Tikka Masala (see page 124), Meatless Mixed Grill (see page 101), Desi-inspired French Bread Pizza (see page 65).

WHAT'S IN YOUR MASALA TIN?

This is one of the most deeply personal questions you can ask any Indian cook. Don't ask it on a first date. Here's the lowdown on mine, based on the spices I use most often in my own cooking (and what's the most conducive setup for following the recipes in this book). If you're new to Indian cookery, consider it a starting point for building your masala tin, adapting as you go.

Cinnamon sticks or cassia bark
(broken otherwise they won't fit in the tin and rarely do I use a giant whole one in any dish)

Cloves

Coriander seeds

Cumin seeds

Garam masala

Green cardamom pods

Kashmiri chilli powder

Mustard seeds

Turmeric

Asafoetida is kept in a separate tub but always in close vicinity to the masala tin, so it doesn't overpower everything else

Ultimately, the purpose of the masala tin is to make your life easier. Nobody wants to be rifling through the cupboard looking for various packets while cooking a mighty daal. Think of the spices in your masala tin as your trusty sidekicks.

Rations

'Rations' is a loanword from British English. It's the term used to refer to long-life ingredients such as flour, rice and daal. Here, it doesn't have the wartime connotations of rationing, but rather alludes to the things you would buy in bulk or keep a surplus of at home. Flour or rice, lentils and spices mean you can always put a meal on the table regardless of whether fresh ingredients are available.

In Kenya, my father's family of 13 and their many guests would get through a lot more than modern-day families, which is why big quantities were the norm back then (this also explains why I come from such a long line of lentil enthusiasts). My Baa would shop once a month and in the absence of refrigeration (and certainly no freezers), fresh food was consumed quickly and frugally. The rest of the time, pantry ingredients were sufficient, wholesome even. Now, we buy our ingredients in much smaller quantities for our much smaller families while still creating the same warming comfort food. Here are some I like to keep handy.

My Indian-ish Pantry **287**

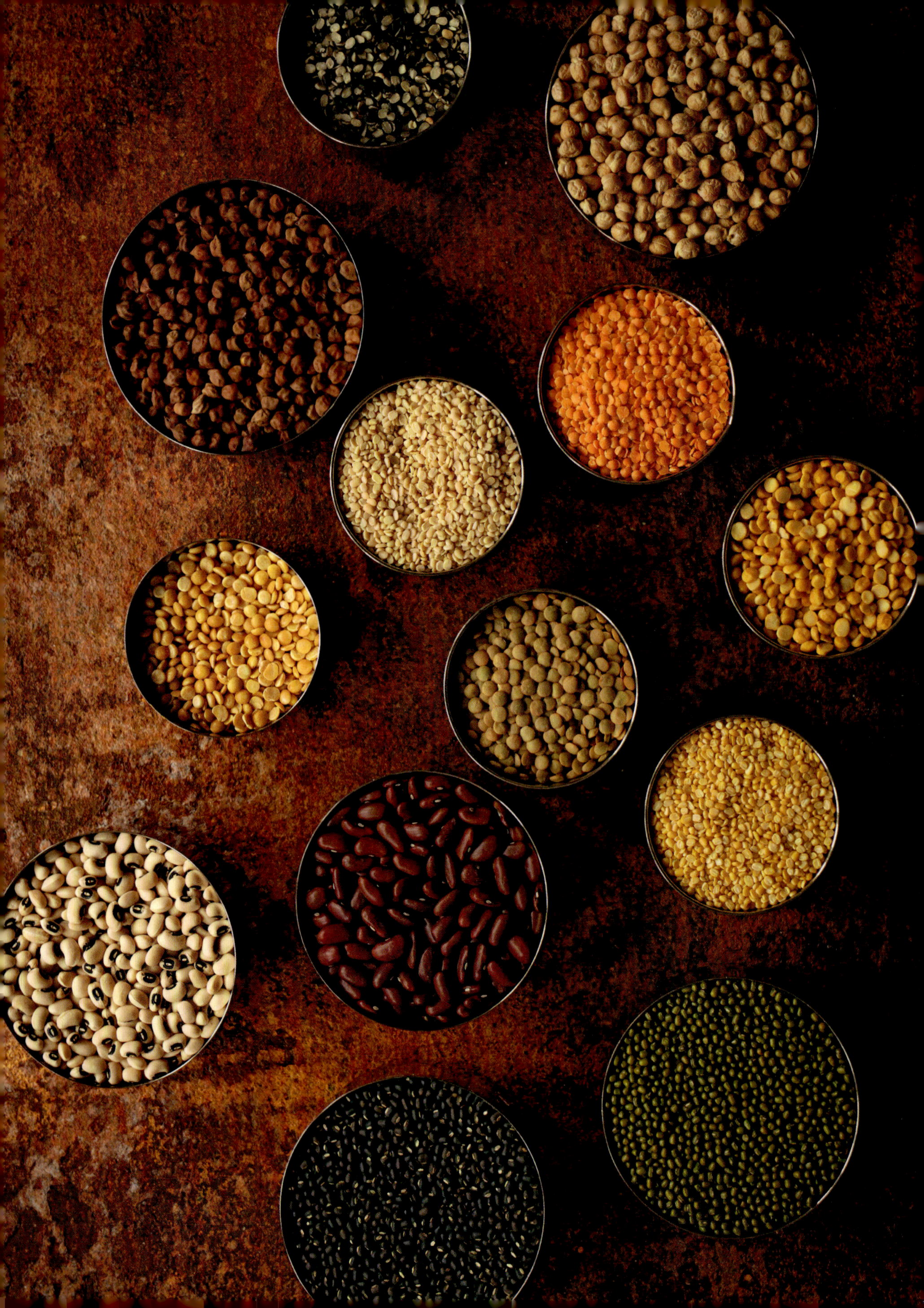

DAAL (LENTILS)

Split black gram daal (urad daal)
Split urad is made from black daal (of daal makhani fame, see page 139). Without their tough skins, these small white lentils cook in a fraction of the time. Protein-rich urad daal has a unique ability to add structure to dishes. Once cooked, it becomes remarkably viscous. It has the power to impart creaminess into daals, give bounce to idli and vada and create the crispiest dosa.

Split mung beans with skin (moong daal chilka)
Split moong with the skin on. Use it for everyday daal and in khichdi. If you can't find moong daal chilka, you can use this skinless moong daal in its place.

Split mung beans without skin (moong daal)
An everyday favourite made from split, skinless moong beans. Use these small yellow lentils for making dry curries and tadka daal, as well as steamed and fried snacks such as dhokla, bhajiya (pakora) and dosa.

Split pigeon peas (toor daal)
Yellow split pigeon peas cook down to a smooth and flowy consistency, making them an excellent all-rounder for everyday tadka daal. Toor is often found in two forms: one oily and one dry. A slick of oil is said to prevent pests and preserve the daal for a longer shelf life. In any case, the daal should be washed well and soaked prior to cooking so any variety will do.

Split red lentils (masoor daal)
One of the most accessible lentils. Masoor daal, also known simply as split red lentils, are usually found in their split form. Whole is fine to use too, but might take a little longer to cook. Moon-shaped red masoor are particularly handy to stow away as they're quick to cook and make a mean tadka daal.

Split yellow gram daal (channa daal)
Yellow gram, or channa daal is made with split black chickpeas. They're used for preparing all manner of daals, vegetable-laced curries, or they're soaked and ground into pastes, batters and doughs for snack making. Gram flour is simply channa daal, milled into flour.

Whole green lentils (sabut masoor)
Versatile whole green masoor, are perfect round buttons used for making dry curry, stew-like daal and fragrant pulao. This is one to always keep in your daal arsenal. Since green masoor takes no time at all to cook, if making pulao, you can simply add pre-soaked masoor to the ghee and spices along with soaked and drained rice. These lentils are ideal for pulao as they hold their shape beautifully alongside grains of fluffy basmati. Once cooked, they can turn a khaki or brown colour.

PULSES AND BEANS

Cooking pulses and beans from a dried state requires very little effort on your part, just a little foresight. If the process doesn't suit, there are cost-effective time savers to hand. For example, a can or jar of cooked chickpeas (garbanzo beans) or kidney beans can be saviours when time is scarce. Pressure cookers and electric pressure pots make light work of cooking dried pulses and beans.

Like daal, lentils need to be washed well to remove any surface dirt, changing the water 3-4 times, or until it runs clear. They will also require a soak. Soaking times will vary depending on the pulse or bean you're cooking, but I find a hot soak (in boiling water), with a small pinch of bicarbonate of soda (baking soda) added will soften them up swiftly.

Black chickpeas (kala channa)
Black chickpeas, otherwise known as horse gram, are robust and filling. In India, they're commonly used in horse fodder, hence the name.

Dried kidney beans (rajma)
Kidney beans are perfect in dishes like rajma (see page 117) and Black Daal (see page 139). Growing up, a simple preparation of Gujarati-style kidney beans and sweetcorn nu shaak would be the perfect belly filler after a long day at school. Shaak is the Gujarati word for a sauté, stew or curry.

Dried white chickpeas (Kabuli channa)
Kabuli channa, or white chickpeas (garbanzo beans), are a staple in any Indian pantry and a home cooking hero. Whilst chickpeas are now thought to have originated in Turkey, they're known as Kabuli channa in India since they were once believed to have come from Afghanistan. It's possible India's first encounter with them was via Afghan traders. You don't need to keep both dried and canned chickpeas to hand, just one or the other will do.

Mung beans (moong)
Whole green mung beans are relatively quick cooking, unlike black gram daal (urad). They have a sage green skin and earthy flavour. Use them to make daals and dry curries. Sprout mung beans over a couple of days to make your own beansprouts or semi-sprouted mung beans, which are typically used for salads and curries. Maharashtra's famous street dish, misal pav is a spicy, stew-like preparation of sprouted lentils served with soft bread buns.

Soya
Soya granules and chunks are sources of protein and used in vegetarian keema dishes, curries and stir-fries. Rehydrate them in boiling water, drain, rinse well and squeeze the soya dry to remove the lingering smell of dog biscuits (it goes away, I promise). For soya mince, a speedy 10-minute soak will do. For larger soya chunks, 30 minutes is the minimum soak time.

Whole black gram daal (urad)
Black daal in its whole form, with the skin on. This is a starchy, creamy daal that requires a long soak and cooks up to be so silky and luxurious in texture. It is most known for being the star of the show in Black Daal (see page 139).

RICE

Poha
Flattened or beaten rice. Rice is pre-soaked, roasted and flattened during the manufacturing process and sold dry, in packets much like regular rice. It takes minutes to cook at home, calling for a brief soak and drain prior to cooking. Poha can also be fried in very hot oil to make what's basically crispy rice cereal except we season with salt and chilli to make Indian snack mixes. There are different grades of poha from thick to thin and the most common varieties are made from white rice. Corn poha, red rice poha and sago poha are also available. I tend to stick to standard white rice 'medium' thick poha for most dishes. At home, store poha exactly as you would store rice. A renowned take on the ingredient is a street-style preparation called Indori Poha, hailing from the central region of Madhya Pradesh.

Rice
I generally keep no more than two varieties of rice for Indian cooking in the house at any one time. The first is a long-grain basmati, like Golden Sella, for biryani, pulao and plain boiled rice. The second is a short-grain variety, such as Sona Masoori, for khichdi, kheer, idli and dosa. If I'm out of Indian short-grain rice, fragrant Thai jasmine rice, such as Hom Mali, is a wonderful substitute in all these dishes and is widely available in supermarkets.

My Indian-ish Pantry

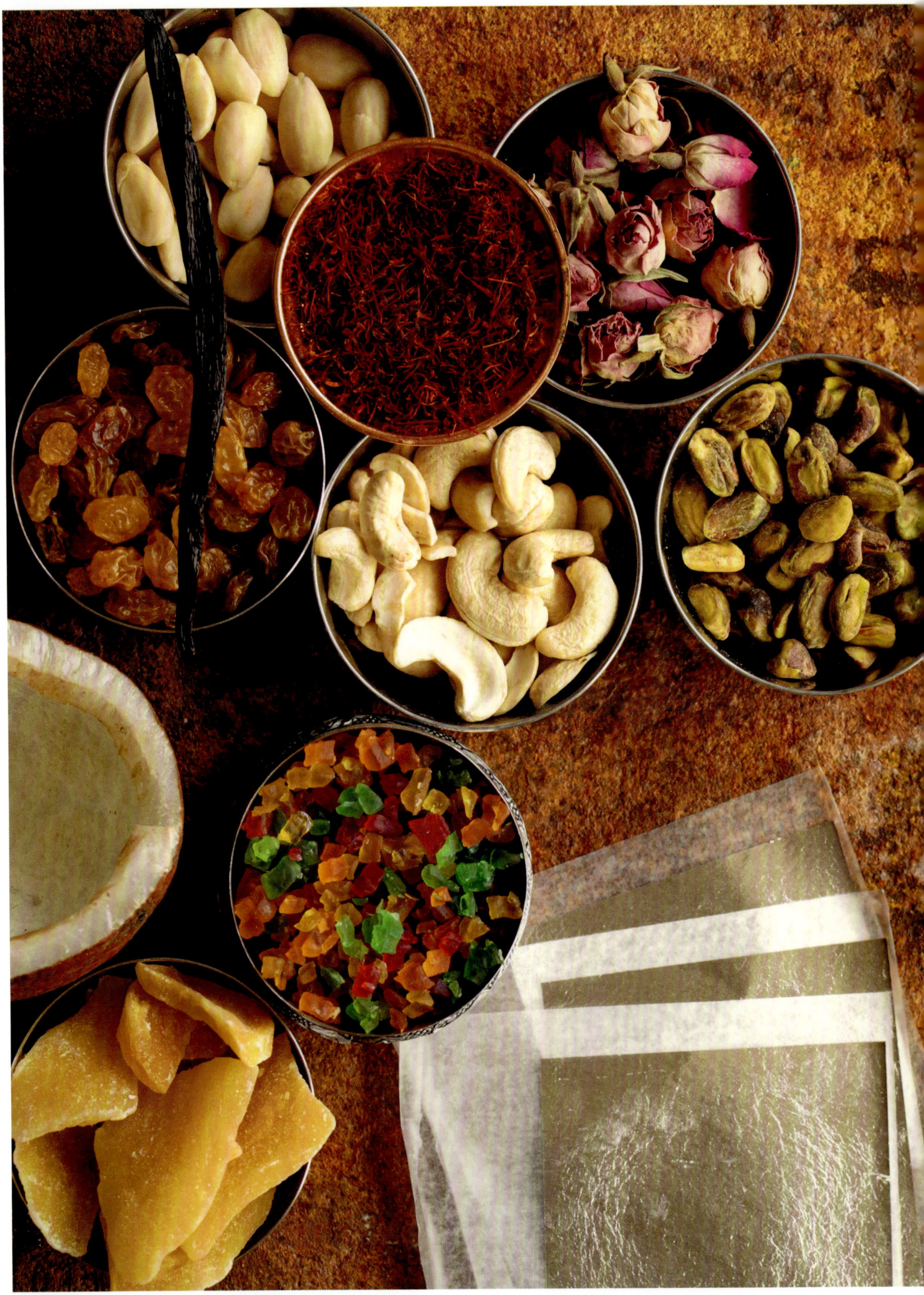

NUTS, SEEDS, DRIED FRUITS, ETC

Dehydrated onions for frying or pre-made fried onions
Crispy and wispy golden fried onions (birista) are an excellent addition to just about any rice dish, and delicious when used as a garnish for daal and curry. The pre-fried versions you can buy in stores tend to have a staleness about them, so go for dehydrated onions and fry them yourself at home. They need just a couple of seconds in hot oil. The onion flavoured oil can then be used for tadka or added to marinades.

Dried coconut
There are plenty of options, so choose what suits your cooking style best. I make the most use of unsweetened desiccated coconut in my kitchen, but whole dried coconuts, ready for grating, blending or shaving are also available if you want to keep your options open. I keep a stash of coconut milk powder or blocks of creamed coconut handy for the days I don't have a fresh coconut or can of coconut milk.

Flower waters
Rosewater and screwpine water (kewda) are both typically found in the Indian storecupboard. Their prevalence is telling of North India's historical Persian connection via the Mughal Empire. Use sparingly in rice dishes like biryani, as well as in desserts and drinks.

Full-fat milk powder
Used for making a plethora of Indian sweets from gulab jamun to burfi. Milk powder tends to absorb smells, so store it in a well-sealed airtight container in a cool, dark place. Full-fat milk powder and skimmed milk powder are not interchangeable ingredients.

Peanuts, cashews, pistachios, almonds
Soak nuts in hot water or boil until soft prior to blending. This creates smooth, creamy pastes used for giving curries a rich and creamy foundation. In Mughlai cookery, a combination of nut or seed pastes (primarily almonds, cashews, pistachios and white poppy seeds) would be used in addition to yogurt, ghee and cream to create some of the most luxurious dishes to come from royal kitchens. Think qorma, pasanda and rezala.

If you need nut paste for a recipe but don't have any nuts in the pantry, or if you're short of time, a form of pure nut butter such as almond butter or cashew butter may be substituted in a pinch. This is a handy option for curries and marinades.

One of my favourite parts of making Gujarati daal is adding whole raw peanuts and cashews and simmering until they turn soft and creamy. Cooking them like this gives the dish a beautifully unique dimension. Similarly, simmering pistachios in kheer (rice pudding) produces a glorious texture.

Unless you use nuts in large quantities, buy in small batches to prevent them from turning rancid. The cupboard is an obvious place to keep them, but you can extend the shelf life of nuts by storing them in the freezer.

Sesame seeds, white poppy seeds
Seeds are useful for many dishes, for snack mixes, for topping savoury nibbles and sweet treats. Like nuts, many recipes call for them to be soaked in hot water and ground into pastes to add richness to sauces. Since nuts are a common allergen (and not to mention, expensive), white poppy seeds are a less costly substitute for almond or cashew paste in many rich curries, chutneys, marinades and masala pastes.

Tamarind
Buy it in paste form or as a block, which you'll need to soak and strain. This is integral to South Indian cookery but less commonly used in North Indian cuisine. If you don't use tamarind often and so feel it's not worth buying, replace it with a mixture of lemon or lime juice and sugar. Before using, taste the product. Many brands contain a lot of added salt and so you may need to adjust the seasoning in your dish accordingly.

Tutti frutti, glacé cherries, golden sultanas
Non-essential nice-to-haves, like the baking sprinkles in the back of the cupboard. Tutti frutti is candied papaya or watermelon rind tinted with various artificial colourings to produce a confetti-style assortment for cookies, buns, cakes and rusks. Glacé or candied cherries are used in very much the same fashion, and often alongside tutti frutti. Supremely sweet, retro and nostalgic. Sultanas are dried green grapes used for baking, rice dishes, puddings, snack mixes and breads.

Jaggery
Unrefined cane sugar. Think of it as turbo-charged brown sugar. Jaggery is to Indian cooking, what palm sugar is to South-East Asian cooking. Very sweet, bags of flavour and surprisingly rich in iron. Usually used in small amounts for savoury cooking (namely in daal or sambar, and in stuffings for bread) and more generously for sweets (candies) like laddoos and burfis. Available in many varieties. Light and dark. Blocks, pastes and powders. They sometimes come in blocks that look like the ghosts in Pac-Man. Blocks can be grated (shredded) at home or nuggets can be chiselled off and dropped directly into the dish, depending on what you're cooking. Particularly solid chunks can be microwaved for 30–40 seconds to soften. It will save you from doing a mid-recipe bicep workout. If you don't have it, use brown sugar instead.

CANS, BOTTLES AND JARS

Baked beans
How else will you make Masala Baked Beans? (See page 73.)

Chopped tomatoes
Forms the basis of many curries, daals, soups, stews and chutneys. Tomato passata (strained tomatoes) is great for sauces destined to be smooth and creamy (without skins and seeds).

Chutneys, pickles and achaars
Whilst I much prefer a frozen chutney, bottled tamarind chutney and chilli sauces tend to be quite fit for chaats and impromptu dipping. Various fresh and herby chutneys, as well as sticky fruit-based chutneys, chilli pickles, achaars and pickled turmeric, all have a special place in my fridge. Enjoy alongside an Indian meal, as they are with a simple flatbread, or stir through dishes to add reams of flavour. A word of warning: if you eat at a South Indian restaurant, the chutneys are so good you may be inclined to order a large selection, with just a side of idli, dosa, vada or uttapam.

Coconut milk
Adds creaminess to curries, daals, chutneys, sweets and puddings. A great way of incorporating flavour into breads and dosa.

Concentrated tomato purée (paste)
Use alone if you don't have fresh or canned tomatoes to hand. Give curries an intense tomato kick with both concentrated tomato purée and canned or fresh tomatoes.

Fruits and vegetables
Sweetcorn, green beans, peas, artichokes, jarred bell peppers and green jackfruit are all great options to keep on standby.

Lemon juice
A bottle of lemon juice is a handy souring agent to use when fresh isn't available. It can also be diluted with water and used to separate milk when making paneer.

Pulses and beans
No need for soaking and pressure cooking. Canned chickpeas (garbanzo beans), kidney beans, butter beans, etc.

Tomato soup
Temper with curry leaves, ghee, cumin and cinnamon for a delicious Indian-style tomato soup (see page 81). Also great for tadka and in the absence of fresh or canned tomatoes, works for making makhani-style sauces. An old trick of the British Indian restaurant business.

FLOURS

Chapati flour (atta)

Wholewheat flour milled specifically for making roti, paratha and poori. Each brand varies and can produce different results even when following the exact same recipe. Until you find a brand you like, I recommend buying it in small bags. Seasoned cooks will know the pain of sliding a heaving great 10-kg (22-lb) bag of chapati flour off a supermarket shelf and carrying it over the shoulder to the checkout. It's the Desi cook's fireman's lift. We do it with sacks of rice and onions too. If you can't find chapati flour, try mixing equal parts plain (all-purpose) white flour and wholemeal flour and pulsing in a food processor until the bran is less coarse. This isn't the ideal solution since the bran can cause tears if it hasn't broken down enough, but it works fine in a pinch.

Chakki gold is a variety of chapati flour that incorporates wholewheat but is finely milled for fewer rough bits of bran. Due to the powdered bran, it has a 'golden' colour, hence the name. You can even hear the husks of wheat crackle as the roti bakes on the tawa. Multigrain and gluten-free chapati flours are now readily available in stores and may involve slightly different methods of preparation to the roti recipe in this book.

Chapati flour can also be used for making various dumplings, pastries, cookies, confectionery and noodle-based dishes.

Cornmeal, millet flour and sorghum flour

These flours are used primarily for making various types of roti. These tend to be thick and/or biscuity and form part of larger region-specific meals. For example, cornmeal roti (makki ki roti) spread with white butter and a bowl of steaming saag is one of the great wonders of Punjabi cuisine. Millet roti (bajra na rotla) with burnt aubergine (eggplant) curry (oro), melted ghee and a chunk of jaggery is quintessential Gujarati village fare. In Maharashtra, sorghum flour rotis are typically served with green garlic and chilli chutney (thetcha) and gram flour curry (zunka).

Gram flour (besan)

Also known as chickpea flour or besan. This type of flour is made from milled skinless black chickpeas (Bengal gram). It's found at the heart of many recipes from bhajiya (pakora) and dhokla, to pithla to pudla as well as other styles of dumpling. In curries and marinades, gram flour can be mixed with yogurt and used as a thickener. Toasted gram flour acts as a binder in kebabs. Sev and gathiya are both fried snacks that call for a spiced gram flour dough to be extruded or rolled and slid into hot oil. In desserts, gram flour is often roasted in ghee to make sweets like besan laddoo, boondi, mohanthal and besan burfi. Since gram flour is free from gluten, it isn't ideal for creating stretchiness in bread dough, although it can be mixed with other flours to provide flavour and structure to doughs in tandem. I like to add a small amount of gram flour to paratha dough for lovely nutty aromas.

Rice flour

A multi-purpose flour made from pure rice that's been ground to a fine powder. Dosa, breads, dumplings, snacks and sweets can all call for rice flour so it's worth keeping some. Adding rice flour to batters can do wonders for the crispiness of your final fritters. Dusting your work surface with rice flour instead of wheat flour when making roti will create far less mess.

Semolina

Not just for pudding. Whilst semolina makes for fantastic halwa, it can offer crispiness to pastries and snacks, provide structure in bread recipes like poori and Bhature (see page 162), be cooked into a spicy South Indian breakfast porridge called sooji upma and form the basis of lacy rava dosa.

My Indian-ish Pantry **297**

FATS AND OILS

Coconut oil
Like ghee, coconut oil has a high smoke point and is used interchangeably with ghee throughout regions, predominantly in Southern parts of India. Note that coconut oil comes in two varieties (refined and unrefined). Refined is flavourless and odourless whilst unrefined has a distinct coconut aroma.

Ghee
The clarified butter at the heart of Indian cookery, and across multiple regions. Ghee has a high smoke point and, therefore, is ideal for frying and tempering spices and vegetables. It's also used in rice, breads, sweets (candies) and as a condiment.

Mustard oil
Coveted in marinades for its fiery depth and astringency. Make sure it's smoking hot before carefully pouring over ground spices and yogurt or use in pickles and tadka. Take a deep breath because the crackly sounds and heady aroma is a next level ASMR experience. In Europe, edible or food-grade mustard oil is usually made with a blend of mustard and vegetable oil. Most pure mustard oils are labelled for external use only due to food laws. Edible or blended mustard oil is available in most South Asian stores, but if you can't get it or don't fancy buying a bottle, try blending a ratio of three parts any vegetable-based oil to one part English mustard powder.

Olive oil
I use olive oil and extra virgin olive oils sparingly. They have lots of flavour and so don't always pair well with Indian dishes. Indeed, their low smoke point also means olive oils are not ideal for things like tadka. However, I do prepare some salads and Indian fusion dishes with olive oil. For example my Black Chickpea Bolognese (see page 89) and my Tomato, Tulsi and Burrata Salad (see page 189).

My Indian-ish Pantry **299**

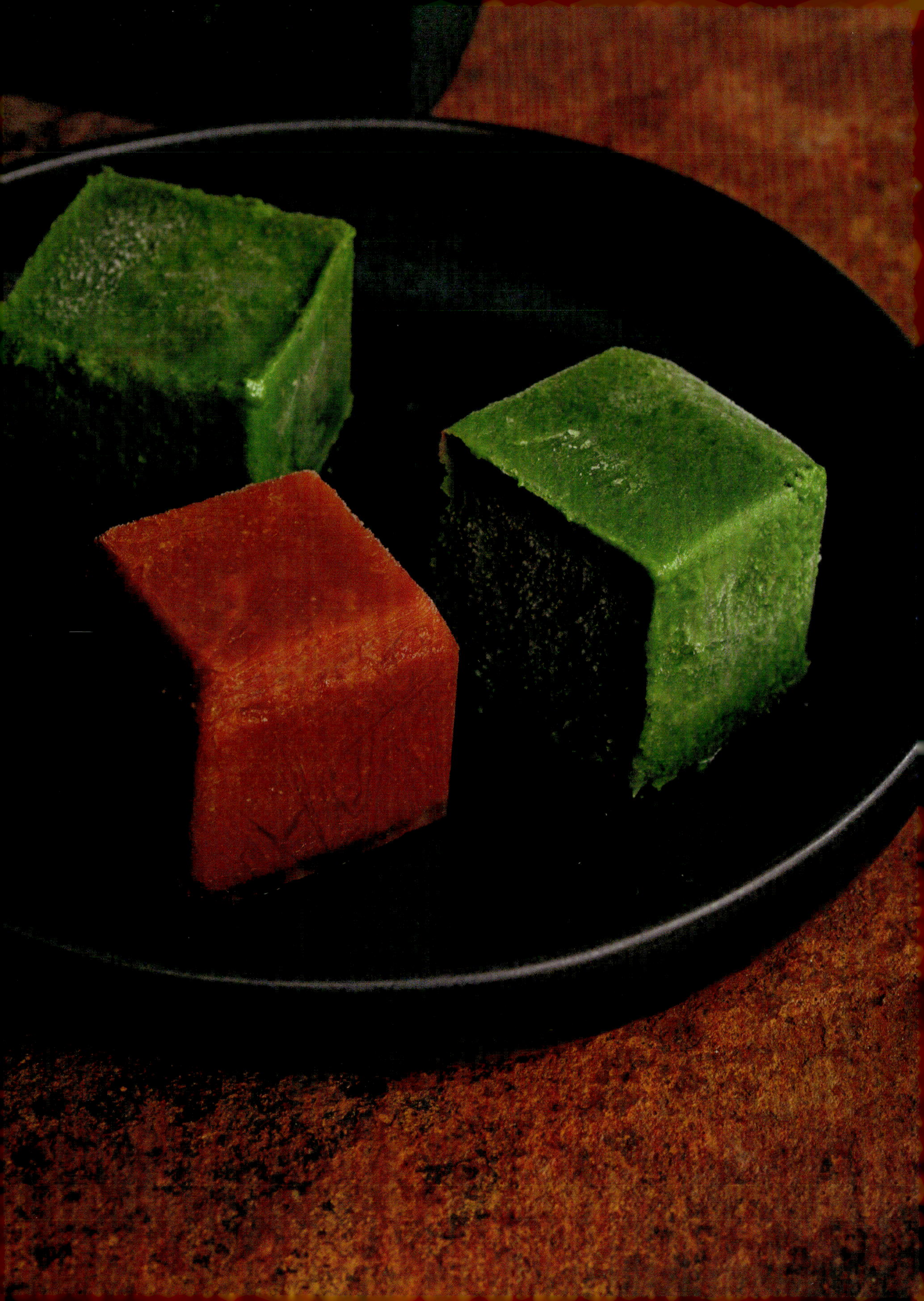

FREEZER

Chilli
Green chilli is frequently called upon. Cubes of frozen green chilli can be bought or prepared from a paste of fresh chillies. Extend the life of fresh chillies by washing, drying and snapping off the stems at the base of the chilli (do not snap the actual chilli flesh). Store in a piece of kitchen foil lined with kitchen paper.

Chutneys (opposite)
Having a stash of chutneys in the freezer is a sure-fire way to know you're winning at life. Last-minute guests won't know what hit them when you dish up a chutney or two alongside snacks. Make fresh chutneys (like the ones on page 198) in batches and freeze them in small portions (freezer-safe containers, freezer bags, or in covered ice-cube trays). Pop them out as required and defrost in the microwave. These are also ideal if you fancy a midweek chaat but don't have the time to make a couple of different chutneys.

Curry leaves
Depending on your location, curry leaves can be tricky to find. If you can, buy a few bags at a time as they freeze particularly well. Strip the curry leaves from the stems (reserve the stems and woody stalks), wash the leaves very well and thoroughly dry. Pack both the leaves and stems into freezer bags and freeze for up to 6 months. The stems are chock-full of magic and can be added to a pot of simmering daal for massive flavour.

Garlic and root ginger
Garlic-ginger paste is a common ingredient in Indian recipes. Frozen cubes are much more pleasant than jars since they don't contain added vinegar. Generally, if a recipe calls for garlic-ginger paste it will be a ratio of 3:1 garlic to ginger. In this book, I have detailed recipes with the exact amounts of fresh garlic and root ginger as I like to be able to control the intensity of both ingredients. You'll notice from the recipes in this book that a recipe might only call for one or the other – I don't think both garlic and ginger are always necessary. However, if you would prefer to save time, frozen cubes of mixed garlic-ginger paste can be useful to keep in the freezer. They are available to buy mixed and separate. If preparing batches from fresh, freeze portions in ice-cube trays and pop them out when required.

Grated coconut
Frozen grated (shredded) coconut is excellent for making chutneys. Defrost it a little and then add straight to a blender along with fresh coriander (cilantro), mint, garlic, lemon juice, salt and sugar. The chill from the iced coconut keeps everything vibrant. Use defrosted frozen coconut as a garnish, in breads, in burfi and other sweets (candies). Blend with water and squeeze through a muslin or cheesecloth for homemade coconut milk.

Roti, paratha, etc
Packs of frozen roti, paratha, naan, thepla, idli, puttu and idiyappam are perfect for the days you need some quick complementary carbs to go with your main meal.

Snacks
Whilst you can't beat freshly made, frozen snacks can still satisfy a craving when time is in short supply. Some of my favourite pre-made frozen Indian snacks are samosas, spring rolls, kachori, aloo tikki, medu vada and idli sambhar.

Vegetables
Frozen veggies are often an excellent time saver. Usually frozen very soon after picking, frozen vegetables are a lot fresher than you might think. Bags of frozen mixed veg, as well as peas, French beans, cubes of spinach, cassava and Indian greens are all excellent to have on standby. Some of my favourite greens for Indian meals are okra (bhindi), cluster beans (guvar), hyacinth beans (valor), fenugreek leaves (methi) and drumsticks (saragwo). I like to keep these in the freezer in case I can't get to the Indian supermarket.

INDO-CHINESE AND FUSION

Curry powder
Shock, horror. I believe that, in many recipes, there is a time and a place for curry powder. Indeed, a good-quality curry powder is key to many of my Indo-Chinese and fusion recipes from Singapore Poha (see page 93) to Paneer Katsu Curry (see page 84). Whilst I generally don't add curry powder to Indian dishes, I find it an excellent all-rounder to incorporate into fusion recipes that call for mild spice. Sometimes a coriander, fennel, cumin and fenugreek seed-heavy flavour and turmeric colour are all that's required to add the layer of spice necessary. This is when a jar of curry powder shines. Since it imparts a generic curry flavour into many dishes, a Madras-style curry powder is perfect for fried rice, noodles, spring rolls and sauces. I often make a batch with little to no chilli in for acclimatising my son's taste buds to Indian flavours in a gentle way.

MSG
Monosodium glutamate (MSG) is a flavour enhancer, also known as ajinomoto. It's a crystallised product that resembles grains of salt and a source of glutamates (the stuff that gives savoury food a unique umami richness). MSG can be produced via natural or synthetic processes. Mushrooms, tomatoes, onions, cheese, milk, soy sauce, miso, broccoli, peas and yeast extract are just a handful of vegetarian sources of glutamic acid, from which the product is made. Fermented beetroot (beets) or corn starch, as well as sugar cane, are all used to commercially produce MSG in most cases. I add a small amount of MSG to most of my Indo-Chinese dishes and love the savoury dimension it offers. If you choose not to cook with it, simply omit it from the recipe.

Sesame oil
A drizzle of sesame oil added at the end of the cooking process is the way to finish off a batch of fried rice and noodles. Sesame oil is also widely used in the regional cuisines of South India, where it is known as gingelly oil.

Soy sauce
Light soy sauce for potent saltiness, dark soy sauce for a beautiful, rich colour. I keep both handy. Tamari is a good substitute for those with a gluten intolerance, however it's always best to check the label to be sure it's suitable for your needs.

White pepper
Black pepper can also be used, but the deep heat of white pepper gives Indo-Chinese dishes a special edge.

EQUIPMENT

From the kadai that's said to have inspired the word 'curry', to masala tins for storing spices, tawas for making roti, rice and other flat-top delicacies, there are a few cooking vessels and utensils I use often in my kitchen. If you don't have them, alternatives are suggested below (where possible).

Handi
A pot-bellied cooking basin, often made from clay or copper. Find them in South Asian cookware shops. A clay handi used for cooking pulao, biryani, daals and curries will impart the most wonderful earthy flavour into the meal. It should be soaked in water for 30 minutes prior to cooking (this will prevent shattering) and allowed to air-dry thoroughly after each use. Over time, the handi will develop a non-stick patina on the inside, rather like a carbon steel wok.

A good alternative: heavy-based casserole dish (Dutch oven).

High-powered blender, spice grinder or coffee grinder
If you find yourself keen on making batches of homemade masalas, a coffee grinder is a handy piece of equipment to stow away in the cupboard. For wet mixes like chutneys, sauces and lentil or rice-based dosa batters, a high-powered blender will make blitzing a breeze.

A good alternative: if you fancy a workout, you can also pound masalas in a pestle and mortar. This is best done when making masalas in very small batches.

Kadai
A kadai, or karahi, is a multipurpose cooking bowl used for making all manner of Indian dishes like curries, stir-fries and for tempering daals. Like some woks, the kadai is characterised by its loop-shaped handles. These heavy-based pots are used across the Indian subcontinent, as well as in the cuisines of the Indian Ocean and the Caribbean. Paper-thin handkerchief rotis called roomali roti are typically cooked on top of an inverted kadai. Some say it's the kadai after which the curry was named. The name can also refer to a specific style of curry cooked in the vessel, although in truth, anything can be cooked in a kadai.

A good alternative: well-seasoned carbon steel wok.

Pestle and mortar
A centuries-old kitchen essential. Crush or pound spices, herbs and aromatics in any kind of mortar with a pestle. Great for releasing stress, plus you get a nice meal at the end. I believe my Baa's serene disposition was a result of her relieving tension by squatting on the floor, bashing spices in her giant pestle and mortar. The heavy ones are the most effective. Rough granite would be my first choice. A brass pestle and mortar are often used for tea spices and Indian sweet making.

A good alternative: end of a rolling pin and a shatterproof bowl (plus some elbow grease).

Pressure cooker
The golden child of the Indian equipment cupboard. Pressure cookers are handy for cooking all manner of lentils, vegetables and khichdis quickly. Use them to make curries and daals in as little as 10 minutes. Traditional Indian pressure cookers come with a whistle on top that shrieks as soon as the built-up pressure inside is ready to vent. The cooking process is measured by the number of whistles sounded by the pot. They're noisy and nostalgic.

A good alternative: electric pressure pot.

Tavitho (stainless steel turner)
Used for turning rotis as they cook on a tawa. Those who have been cooking roti for years have developed the superpower of turning roti with their bare fingertips. It's done swiftly and effortlessly, like people who walk over hot coals. For those of us without asbestos fingers, we flip with a trusty tavitho. Our tavitho is a family heirloom, engraved with my paternal grandfather's name. It's the same one from his kitchen in Kenya. Some people like to gift engraved jewellery, Indians prefer to gift engraved cookware!

A good alternative: any metal turner or spatula.

Tawa
An Indian tawa is, for want of a better description, a flat-top griddle. It can be made from iron, steel or aluminium (aluminum). This style of cookware has multiple uses in Indian cookery, from cooking flatbreads and dosa, to street-style specialities like pav bhaji, tawa pulao (rice), noodles, curries, buns and burgers. If you don't have a tawa, you can use a non-stick frying pan (skillet) instead. The goal is to create a golden, crispy exterior and a frying pan will do a similar job.
  A good alternative: non-stick frying pan or flat-top griddle.

Velan/Belan (rolling pin)
An Indian rolling pin isn't essential since any rolling pin can be used for making roti and other Indian breads. Having said this, the tapered ends of thin Indian rolling pins can be conducive to getting the roti to spin by itself as you roll – a skill most coveted. Chunky western-style rolling pins can be more difficult to manoeuvre. The thinnest rolling pins in an Indian cook's kitchen are used for making puri, which are usually smaller and thinner than roti, naan, paratha and bhature. If you'll be making more of the latter, choose a mid-size rolling pin with tapered ends, like the one pictured.
  A good alternative: any kind of lightweight rolling pin.

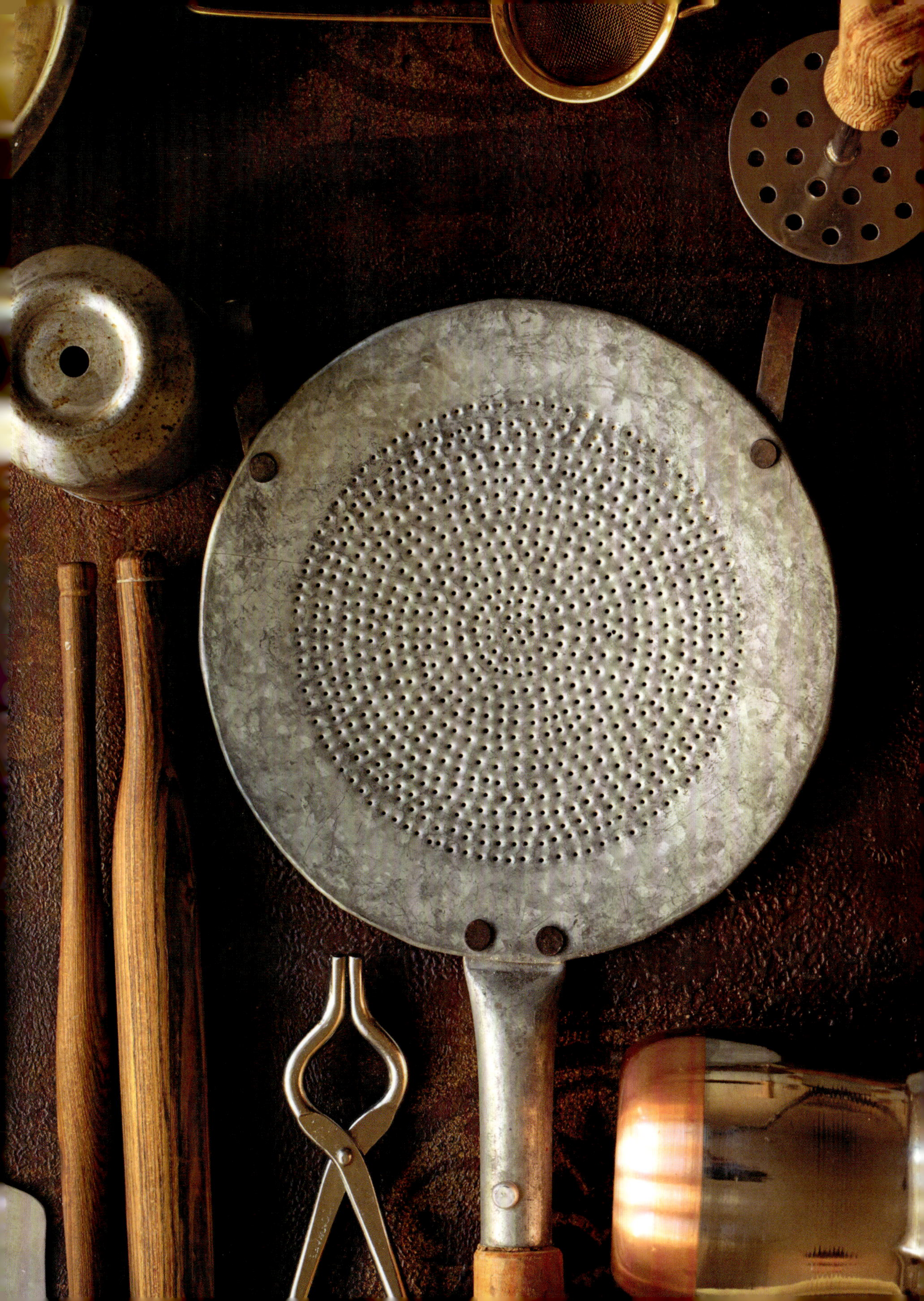

OVEN TEMPERATURE GUIDE

ELECTRIC °C	ELECTRIC (FAN ASSISTED) °C	ELECTRIC °F	GAS MARK
140°C	120°C	285°F	1
150°C	130°C	300°F	2
160°C	140°C	320°F	3
180°C	160°C	355°F	4
190°C	170°C	375°F	5
200°C	180°C	390°F	6
210°C	190°C	410°F	6½
220°C	200°C	425°F	7
230°C	210°C	445°F	8
240°C	220°C	465°F	9

Build-a-thali: menu ideas

Inspired by the North

Artichoke Pakora (see page 55),
Brown Butter Cauliflower and Pea Makhani (see page 113),
Black Daal (see page 139),
Butter Naan (see page 164),
Zafrani Mushroom Pulao (see page 173),
Pink Peppercorn Pickled Onions (see page 240),
Sticky Toffee Gulab Jamun (see page 206)

Inspired by the East

Root Vegetable Jalfrezi (see page 126),
Garlic and Coriander Naan (see page 166),
White Chocolate Rasmalai (see page 213)

Inspired by the South

Vermicelli Upma 'Summer Rolls' (see page 66),
Savoy Cabbage Ghee Roast (see page 129),
Gunpowder Tofu (see page 70),
Rice,
Amber Mango and Coconut Chutney (see page 196),
Cardamom Jam Sponge (see page 219)

Inspired by the West

Scotch Khichdi with Ghee-roasted Tomatoes (see page 170),
Rhubarb Chhundo (see page 235),
Apple and Guava Crumble (see page 210)

Indo-Chinese

Indo-Chinese Bhajiya (see page 51),
Chestnut Manchurian (see page 98),
Sticky Hakka Fried Rice (see page 174),
Red Chilli Chutney (see page 196)

Easy

Meatless Mixed Grill (see page 101),
Almost-midnight Masala Chips (see page 182),
Traffic Light Chutneys (see page 196),
Bourbon Biscuit Laddoos (see page 227)

Vegan

Vegan Chilli Paneer (see page 102),
Coconut Rajma (see page 117),
Everyday Roti (see page 157),
Achaari Matoke (see page 185),
Cinnamon Chocolate Fudge Cake
(vegan option, see page 209)

Gluten free

Shahi Potatoes (see page 121),
Zafrani Mushroom Pulao (see page 173),
Black Daal (see page 139),
Tomato, Tulsi and Burrata Salad (see page 189),
Hazelnut Cocoa Burfi (see page 223)

GLOSSARY

A mixture of Hindi, Gujarati and Swahili, with some words interchangeable across other Indian languages. I speak none of these languages very well, but like others of a third-culture generation, I have successfully enmeshed the mother tongues into my everyday English well enough that I can communicate with my family as well as read recipes, enjoy movies and music. Mingling words from the various languages of our backgrounds is just another kind of mash up central to diasporic culture. You'll find many of my recipes combine languages, which is reflective of the way we speak in our British Indian home.

Food

Bhajiya – Another word for pakora (crispy gram flour fritter)

Bun maska – bread and butter. A favourite in Irani cafes and a treasure of Parsi cuisine (Parsis are Indians who are descended from Persian Zoroastrians).

Chaat – a refreshing dish whereby the main component is adorned with yogurt, one or more chutneys, fried gram flour noodles and more. Often sprinkled with tangy chaat masala.

Chai nashta – tea and snacks

DBSR – daal, bhaat, shaak, rotli (lentils, rice, curry, roti), a complete Gujarati meal

Dhokla/dhokra – steamed savoury cakes. Can be made from soaked and ground lentils (fermented), gram flour, rice flour, or other types of grain.

Ghee – clarified butter

Karak chai – strong masala tea

Katki keri – Gujarati mango chutney with pieces of diced mango

Khichdi – a comforting dish of rice and lentils cooked together

Masala – blend of spices, or used to describe a dish cooked with spices

Masala chai – tea with spices

Murabba – spiced fruit jam (preserves), similar to chutney

Nankhatai – sweet semolina biscuits (cookies)

Paneer – mild and creamy cheese made from whole (full-fat) milk

Poori – deep-fried wholewheat bread

Sattvic – plant-based whole foods aligned with the teachings of Ayurveda

Tadka – spices and aromatics tempered in hot oil

Thali – a food adventure on a plate! Think of a thali as a personalised buffet, where you get to mix and match dishes at will. We're talking spicy curry, daal, pickles, breads, rice, sweets and more. This is traditionally a meal presented and eaten from a banana leaf, but thali plates can come in all sorts of materials. Every thali is typically a curation of dishes from a specific region of India, or tailored for special occasions. Truth be told, I see them as an opportunity to put together eclectic and exciting meals I'd like to eat and share with friends.

Thepla – Gujarati masala chapati

Tikki – morsel, or pieces

People

Baa – paternal grandmother

Bapu – paternal uncle (male sibling older than your father)

Bapuji – paternal grandfather

Fai – paternal aunt

Kaka – paternal uncle (male sibling younger than your father), or mother or father's sister's spouse

Mama – maternal uncle

Masi – maternal aunt

Nanabapu (or *Nana*) – maternal grandfather

Nanima (or *Nani*) – maternal grandmother

Objects

Belan/velan – rolling pin

Handi – cooking pot made from brass or clay

Khandni ne dusto – pestle and mortar

Sansi – potholder

Suferia – cooking pot (Swahili)

Tavitho – metal turner for flipping roti

Tawa – flat or concave griddle pan made from aluminium, clay, steel or cast iron. Usually used for making bread but can be useful for fried rice and dishes like pav bhaji.

Miscellaneous

Chutki – a pinch (i.e., ek chutki – one pinch)

Mudra – hand gesture

Mutthi – a fistful (i.e., ek mutthi – one fistful)

TIPS AND TRICKS

Balance: Made a dish too spicy? Add a squeeze of lemon juice and a pinch of sugar to mellow the heat.

Beans: Alkaline water can help in softening the skins of pulses and encourage lentils to cook faster. Adding a tiny pinch of bicarbonate of soda (baking soda) to the water does the trick. If your dried beans are particularly old and won't soften, this can help resurrect them.

Beat: Right before deep-frying bhajiya (pakora), beat the batter with your hands for a minute. The heat from your hands will begin to activate the raising agents (if you're using any) and the beating motion will trap in air bubbles for a light and crispy finish.

Boondi (1): Pearls of fried gram flour. They're made by pouring a flowy gram flour batter through a perforated spoon, perched directly above a pan of hot oil. The droplets form crispy balls not unlike 'scraps' from the chippy. Boondi are ready to use straight from the packet. Soak in hot water, drain and squeeze dry before adding to raita, or substitute the crispy (unsoaked) boondi for croutons in salads and soups.

Coconut (2): Give desiccated coconut the fresh treatment by soaking it in warm milk (either dairy or plant-based). This simply rehydrates the coconut, making it ideal to use in lieu of fresh coconut in recipes. It's great for chutneys, snacks, upma and sweet recipes. In the absence of a can of coconut milk, blitz milk or water-soaked desiccated coconut in a blender and squeeze through a clean muslin or nut milk bag.

Curry leaves: Where I live, fresh curry leaves aren't always available in stores, or they can be expensive. When I stumble upon them, I buy a couple of bags to stash in the freezer, which proves to be quite handy when making daals, curries, upmas and snacks. Freshly frozen curry leaves hold much more aroma and flavour than their dried counterparts. To freeze, thoroughly wash and dry the curry leaves before freezing in an airtight container. They tend to splutter when adding them to tadka and so pat them dry once more prior to using, ensuring no water lingers on the leaves. Don't throw away the stems of the curry leaves – they contain heaps of flavour and are great for throwing into a pot of daal. Trim and freeze the clean, dry stems along with the leaves.

Daal water: If a recipe requires you to drain cooked daal, reserve some of the cooking liquid. Like pasta water, it's revered for being the nectar of the gods for its magical thickening properties (i.e., starch). Daal water can be used in the same way. Add some liquid back in if your batch of daal is beginning to thicken too much.

Dried fenugreek leaves (3): Dry fresh methi in the microwave to make your own kasoori methi. It tastes a million times better than store-bought and retains its vibrant green colour. Simply wash and dry a bunch of fresh fenugreek. Pick the leaves off the stems, retaining the stems for later (nothing will go to waste). Arrange the fenugreek leaves in a single layer on a microwave-safe plate. Microwave on high power for 3 minutes. Allow the leaves to cool completely. They should be a deep green colour and brittle to the touch. Pop the kasoori methi into an airtight container. It should always be rubbed between the palms and added to the dish at the end of the cooking process. Do not rub it to a powder prior to storing as it will quickly lose its flavour. Stir it in and/or use as a garnish. Finely chop the fenugreek stems, pop them into a freezer bag and stow in the deep freeze. Add a tablespoonful of fenugreek stems to the tadka whenever you're making daal or a curry. Their potency adds reams of flavour.

Khichiya baskets (4): Turn poppadoms or rice khichiya into baskets to hold salads and chaats. Fry them in a high-sided pan that's around twice the width of the cracker. The edges will lift and mould to the shape of the pan, creating a fillable bowl. Fill with chaat ingredients like boiled potatoes, black chickpeas, onions, tomatoes, masala yogurt and chutneys.

Nuts: Historically, nuts have been used throughout Indian cuisine as a means of adding richness to food. The chefs of Mughal emperors typically laced gravies with expensive nuts like almonds, pistachios and cashews. Food was one medium for demonstrating wealth. The

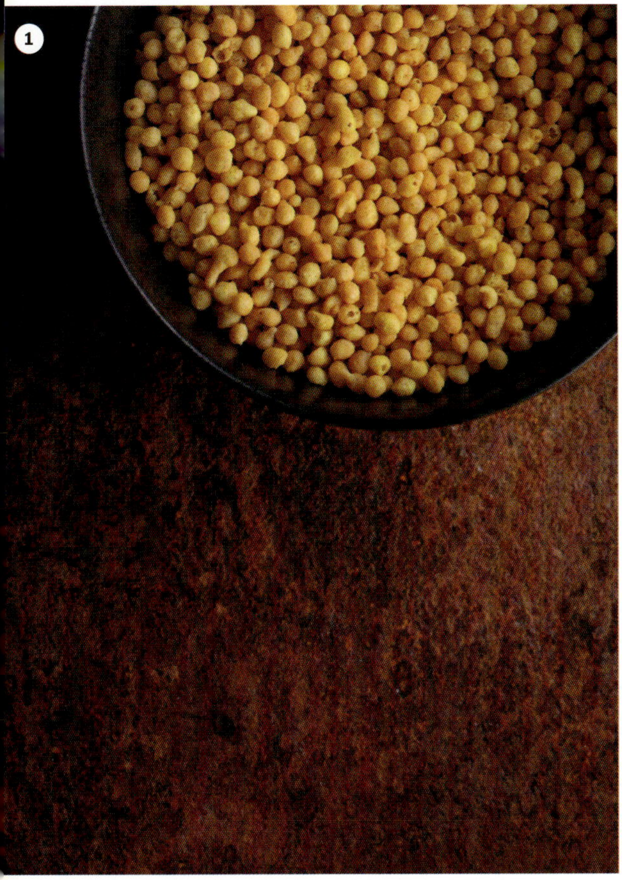
1

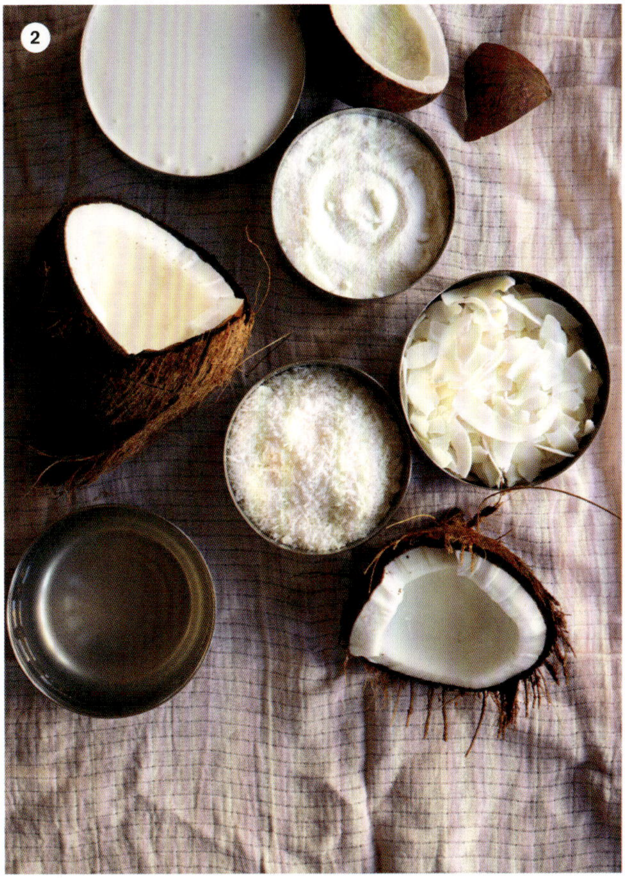
2

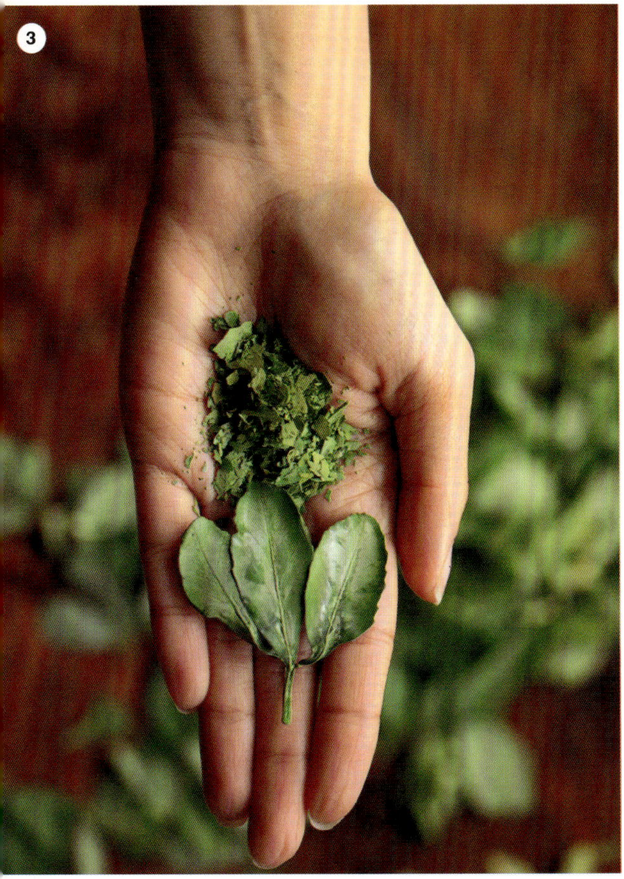
3

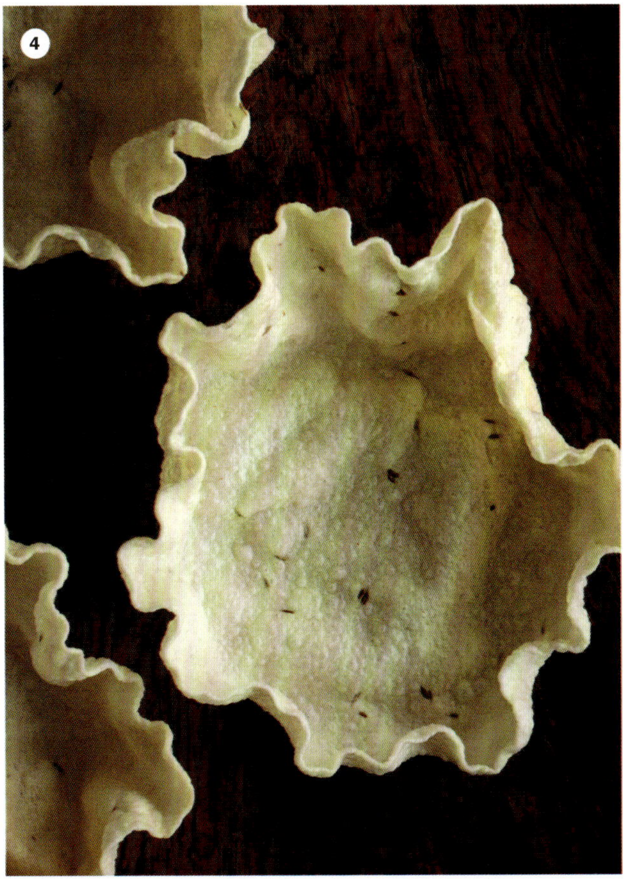
4

nuts would be boiled and blended to create very creamy pastes. These could be used as base gravies for qorma, bound into bread doughs to enrich, or to make koftas, kebabs and trays of glimmering sweets (candies). Today this practice is a handy way to impart creaminess into vegan dishes.

Roast: Dry-roast whole spices for the masala blends you are most likely to use at the end of a cooking process, such as garam masala or chaat masala. Spices you are more likely to spend time cooking out first can be ground without roasting. Roasted spices will lose their sparkle much faster than unroasted. Remember that the heat from your spice grinder will also cause flavour compounds of spices to release.

Saffron: Always dissolve saffron strands in hot water or milk. Saffron is not fat soluble so do not sprinkle this expensive ingredient directly into oil, ghee or butter.

Sour: Sour flavours are prized in most of India's regional cuisines. It's a balance of flavours that gives dishes a distinct level of sophistication. Here are some souring agents you can try, some more potent than others. Whilst all are widely available, each region has its favourites.

Buttermilk

Citric acid

Dried mango powder (amchur)

Dried mangosteen (kokum)

Dried pomegranate powder (anardana)

Lemon

Plain yogurt

Raw mango

Tamarind

Tomatoes

Spices: If you're concerned about not using up ground spices before they dull, buy whole spices and grind them yourself. Spice grinders or coffee grinders are great tools for whipping up small batches of fresh masala when you have the time. Alternatively, grind whole spices to fine powders using a pestle and mortar.

Sweeten: Jaggery is a type of unrefined cane sugar. It comes in light and dark colours, the latter carrying an intense caramel flavour. Grate (shred) or chisel off nuggets, depending on what you're cooking. If you don't have jaggery, use brown sugar as a substitute.

Temper: Also known as tadka, vaghaar, baghaar and chhonk. Begin or end a recipe by sizzling whole spices in hot fat. The flavour compounds in most spices are fat soluble so ensure every bit of aroma is released by beginning or ending a dish with this process. It usually applies to curries and daals but is also used for making snacks.

Unlikely hero: A spoonful of instant mashed potato powder (potato flakes) added to dry-style potato curries, aloo tikkis, paratha and samosa fillings can offer bonus fluffiness and bring potatoes together into joyful clouds that form fillings and patties. This is especially handy if your potatoes are a little on the watery side.

Yogurt: Plain yogurt is a fridge staple. Unless the recipe specifies another style, buy set yogurt from the Asian section at the supermarket as it tends to be on the sour side. Sour yogurt is suited to most types of Indian cookery since it introduces tanginess to balance heat. Beat it with a whisk prior to using.

Acknowledgements

With gratitude to my son and most honest taste tester, Bodhi; my parents, Harish and Jyotsna, for supporting me in everything I do. To Ravi, Surina, Cubir, Saiyuri and Arti. To our legend in the sky, Neel; the last thing you said to me was that I could write this book. For Krishna fai and Hiren bhai, for your encouragement. We love and miss you all deeply. To my family, the Natalyas. To Velji bapu for your eternal blessings. To Aliya and the entire team at Unbound, for putting your trust in me. To you, reader: Thank you for picking up my book. With love and laddoos.

Index

A
achaar masala 264, 285, 295
    cheat's achaari marmalade 234
    sizzling achaari matoke 185
all-in-one biryani masala 260
almonds 293
    shahi potatoes 121
almost-midnight masala chips 182
aloo croissants 41
amber mango and coconut chutney 196
apples: apple and guava crumble 210
    paneer katsu curry 84–5
aquafaba (chickpea liquid): badtameez brownies 216
aromatic garnishes for curry 109
artichoke pakora 55
asafoetida 283
asparagus: meatless mixed grill 101
aubergines (eggplants): burnt aubergine and spinach curry 110

B
baby corn: sticky hakka fried rice 174
    see also corn-on-the-cob; sweetcorn
badtameez brownies 216
baked beans 295
    masala baked bean toasties 73
balance 310
bananas: paneer katsu curry 84–5
Bangladesh 10
baobab powder 283
    chips masala 272
barley: Scotch broth mix 171
bay leaves 280
beans 134, 290, 295, 310
    baked beans 295
    black daal 138–9
    coconut rajma 117
    dry daal 144
    kidney beans 290
    masala baked bean toasties 73
    mung beans 290
    Scotch khichdi with ghee-roast tomatoes 170–1
    spicy bean tawa burgers 77
    split mung beans 289
beansprouts: Kolkata chow mein 78
    upma 'summer rolls' 66
beating 310
beetroot paneer tikka 74
belan (rolling pin) 304
bell peppers see peppers
bhaji, tiger pav 114–15
bhajiya, Indo-Chinese 51
bhature 162
biryani, ruffled 176–7
biryani masala 260, 285
biscuits (cookies): Bourbon biscuit laddoos 227
    Indian-inspired rocky road 45
    rusk 36
black beans: spicy bean tawa burgers 77

black cardamom 279
    all-in-one biryani masala 260
    garam masala 259
    tandoori masala 269
black chickpeas 134, 290
    black chickpea 'bolognese' 89
black-eyed beans (peas) 134
black gram daal 134, 289, 290
    black daal 138–9
    black pepper tadka daal 136
    gunpowder 268
    white daal 140
black peppercorns 279
    black pepper tadka daal 136
black salt 283
black stone flower 279
blenders 303
blue cheese dressing 190
'bolognese', black chickpea 89
boondi 310
bottled food 295
Bourbon biscuit laddoos 227
bread 147–50, 301
    bhature 162
    butter naans 164–5
    Cheddar and mango chutney loaf 38
    chilli-cheese naans 166
    Desi-inspired French bread pizza 65
    everyday roti 156–7
    garlic and coriander naans 166
    halloumi and mint paratha 160
    kalonji coin naans 168
    laccha paratha 158–9
    Marmite and sesame naans 166
    masala baked bean toasties 73
    Peshawari naans 168
bread and butter pudding, pistachio 220
British Raj 10
broccoli miloni 118
brown butter cauliflower and pea makhani 113
brownies, badtameez 216
Brussels sprouts: bubble and seekh kebabs 97
bubble and seekh kebabs 97
buns, raspberry and rosewater iced 52
burfi, hazelnut cocoa 223
burgers, spicy bean tawa 77
burnt aubergine and spinach curry 110
butter: butter naans 164–5
    garlic and coriander butter 166
    honey butter 160
    Marmite butter 166
    tandoori butter 65, 166
    see also ghee
buttermilk: blue cheese dressing 190

C
cabbage: Indo-Chinese bhajiya 51
    Kolkata chow mein 78
    sambharo spiral 82
    Savoy cabbage ghee roast 129
    sticky hakka fried rice 174
    see also red cabbage

cakes: badtameez brownies 216
    cinnamon chocolate fudge cake 209
canned food 295
capers: fried caper raita 194
caramel: sticky toffee gulab jamun 206
cardamom pods see black cardamom; green cardamom
carom seeds 279
carrots: carrot cake scones 56
    dumpling handi 122
    Indo-Chinese bhajiya 51
    Kolkata chow mein 78
    paneer katsu curry 84–5
    root veg jalfrezi 126
    ruffled biryani 176–7
    sambharo spiral 82
    Singapore poha 93
    spicy bean tawa burgers 77
    sticky hakka fried rice 174
    tiger pav bhaji 114–15
    upma 'summer rolls' 66
    vegan ghee 244
cashews 293
    brown butter cauliflower and pea makhani 113
    fauxneer 251
    green coriander and mint chutney 197
    Singapore poha 93
    upma 'summer rolls' 66
cassava: mogo dirty fries 186
cassia bark 279
    all-in-one biryani masala 260
    garam masala 259
    ruffled biryani 176–7
cauliflower: brown butter cauliflower and pea makhani 113
    meatless mixed grill 101
    ruffled biryani 176–7
    tandoori cauliflower cheese 69
    tiger pav bhaji 114–15
chaat, halloumi fries 90
chaat masala 263, 285
chai masala 20–3, 24, 267, 285
chakri 35
chapati flour 296
cheat's achaari marmalade 234
Cheddar and mango chutney loaf 38
cheese: blue cheese dressing 190
    bubble and seekh kebabs 97
    Cheddar and mango chutney loaf 38
    cheese sauce 69, 186
    chilli-cheese naans 166
    Desi-inspired French bread pizza 65
    halloumi and mint paratha 160
    halloumi fries chaat 90
    keema jackets 94–5
    Madras mac and cheese 62
    masala baked bean toasties 73
    spicy bean tawa burgers 77
    tandoori cauliflower cheese 69
    tomato, tulsi and burrata salad 189
    see also paneer

cherries, glacé 293
chestnut Manchurian 98
chevdo 35
chicken-style pieces (vegan): Singapore poha 93
chickpeas (garbanzo beans) 134, 290
    black chickpea 'bolognese' 89
    chole samosa 46–8
chilli powder 283
    achaar masala 264
    artichoke pakora 55
    chips masala 272
    chole samosa 46–8
    chutney with 40 cloves of garlic 239
    dumpling handi 122
    red chilli chutney 196
    Savoy cabbage ghee roast 129
    tandoori masala 269
    tiger pav bhaji 114–15
chillies 301
    aloo croissants 41
    beetroot paneer tikka 74
    black chickpea 'bolognese' 89
    broccoli miloni 118
    brown butter cauliflower and pea makhani 113
    burnt aubergine and spinach curry 110
    chestnut Manchurian 98
    chilli-cheese naans 166
    chilli fauxneer 102
    chole samosa 46–8
    coconut rajma 117
    Desi-inspired French bread pizza 65
    dried Kashmiri chillies 280
    dry daal 144
    green coriander and mint chutney 197
    gunpowder 268
    halloumi and mint paratha 160
    hara bhara rolls 42
    Indo-Chinese bhajiya 51
    keema jackets 94–5
    Kolkata chow mein 78
    Madras mac and cheese 62
    paneer katsu curry 84–5
    pudla traybake 86
    rhubarb chhundo 235
    sambharo spiral 82
    Scotch khichdi with ghee-roast tomatoes 170–1
    seekh kebab masala 271
    Singapore poha 93
    sticky hakka fried rice 174
    white daal 140
Chinese cabbage: Kolkata chow mein 78
    sticky hakka fried rice 174
chips (potato fries): almost-midnight masala chips 182
chips masala 272, 285
chocolate: badtameez brownies 216
    Bourbon biscuit laddoos 227
    cinnamon chocolate fudge cake 209
    hazelnut cocoa burfi 223

314 Sanjana Feasts

Indian-inspired rocky road 45
narangi hot chocolate 27
pistachio bread and butter pudding 220
scruffy Milo rolls 224
whipped ganache 209
white chocolate rasmalai 213–14
chole samosa 46–8
chow mein, Kolkata 78
chutneys 295, 301
  amber mango and coconut chutney 196
  Cheddar and mango chutney loaf 38
  chutney with 40 cloves of garlic 239
  garnishes for curry 109
  green coriander and mint chutney 197
  red chilli chutney 196
  thickeners 197
cilantro see coriander
cinnamon 279
  cinnamon chocolate fudge cake 209
cloves 279
  all-in-one biryani masala 260
coconut 293, 301, 310
  cardamom jam sponge 219
coconut milk 295
  amber mango and coconut chutney 196
  coconut rajma 117
  paneer katsu curry 84–5
  quick peanut-tamarind dip 66
coconut oil 298
  vegan ghee 244
coffee: badtameez brownies 216
  maple-cardamom masala coffee 28
coffee grinders 303
condensed milk: Bourbon biscuit laddoos 227
condiments 230–51
  cheat's achaari marmalade 234
  chutney with 40 cloves of garlic 239
  fauxneer 251
  ghee 242–3
  paneer 246–7
  pink peppercorn pickled onions 240
  rhubarb chhundo 235
  vegan ghee 244
cookies see biscuits
coriander (cilantro): almost-midnight masala chips 182
  chutney with 40 cloves of garlic 239
  garlic and coriander naans 166
  green coriander and mint chutney 197
coriander seeds 280
  garam masala 259
  Madras curry powder 273
  seekh kebab masala 271
  tandoori masala 269
corn-on-the-cob (ear of corn):
  meatless mixed grill 101

see also baby corn; sweetcorn
cornflour, thickening chutney 197
cornmeal 296
crackers: far far 36
  khichiya 36
cream: broccoli miloni 118
  cardamom cream 56
  pistachio bread and butter pudding 220
  scorpion sauce 124–5
  whipped ganache 209
  white chocolate rasmalai 213–14
cream cheese: Cheddar and mango chutney loaf 38
  Madras mac and cheese 62
croissants, aloo 41
crumble, apple and guava 210
cucumber: fried caper raita 194
  quick pickles 85
  upma 'summer rolls' 66
cumin seeds 280
  chaat masala 263
  garam masala 259
  Madras curry powder 273
  seekh kebab masala 271
  tandoori masala 269
curry 105–29, 277
  broccoli miloni 118
  brown butter cauliflower and pea makhani 113
  burnt aubergine and spinach curry 110
  coconut rajma 117
  curry leaf cream of tomato soup 81
  curry leaves 301, 310
  curry powder 302
  finishing touches 109
  gunpowder 268
  Madras curry powder 273, 285
  Madras mac and cheese 62
  paneer katsu curry 84–5
  root veg jalfrezi 126
  Savoy cabbage ghee roast 129
  scorpion tikka masala 124–5
  shahi potatoes 121
  Singapore poha 93
  tiger pav bhaji 114–15

D
daal 131–45, 289
  black daal 138–9
  black pepper tadka daal 136
  dry daal 144
  pasta daal 143
  white daal 140
daal water 310
dairy garnishes for curry 109
Desi-inspired French bread pizza 65
dips: quick peanut-tamarind dip 66
see also sauces
dressing, blue cheese 190
dried fruit 293
drinks: chai masala 20–3, 24
  maple-cardamom masala coffee 28
  narangi hot chocolate 27

dry daal 144
dumplings: dumpling handi 122
  white chocolate rasmalai 213–14

E
East Pakistan 10
eggplants see aubergines
equipment 303–4
evaporated milk: cheese sauce 186
everyday roti 156–7

F
far far 36
fats 298
fauxneer 251
fennel seeds 280
fenugreek leaves 283, 310
  tandoori masala 269
fenugreek seeds 280
  achaar masala 264
filo (phyllo) pastry: ruffled biryani 176–7
  sambharo spiral 82
finishing touches, curry 109
flours 296
flower waters 293
flowers, garnishes for curry 109
freezer ingredients 301
French beans: dumpling handi 122
fries: almost-midnight masala chips 182
  mogo dirty fries 186
fritters: artichoke pakora 55
  Indo-Chinese bhajiya 51
  sticky toffee gulab jamun 206
frosting (icing) 52, 224
fruit 295
  garnishes for curry 109
fusion ingredients 302

G
ganache, whipped 209
garam masala 259, 285
  broccoli miloni 118
  coconut rajma 117
  keema jackets 94–5
  root veg jalfrezi 126
  scorpion sauce 124–5
  tiger pav bhaji 114–15
garbanzo beans see chickpeas
garlic 301
  burnt aubergine and spinach curry 110
  chilli fauxneer 102
  chutney with 40 cloves of garlic 239
  garlic and coriander naans 166
  gunpowder tofu 70
  Kolkata chow mein 78
  tandoori butter 65
  tiger pav bhaji 114–15
garnishes, curry 109
gathiya 35
  thickening chutney 197
ghee 242–3, 298
  ghee-roast tomatoes 170–1
  Savoy cabbage ghee roast 129
  vegan ghee 244

ginger 284, 301
  chai masala 267
ginger biscuits (ginger cookies): Indian-inspired rocky road 45
gluten-free recipes 15
golden sultanas 293
  Peshawari naans 168
gram daal 134, 289, 290
  black daal 138–9
  black pepper tadka daal 136
  gunpowder 268
  white daal 140
gram flour 296
  pudla traybake 86
green cardamom 280
  all-in-one biryani masala 260
  Bourbon biscuit laddoos 227
  brown butter cauliflower and pea makhani 113
  cardamom cream 56
  cardamom jam sponge 219
  chai masala 267
  chole samosa 46–8
  garam masala 259
  maple-cardamom masala coffee 28
  raspberry and rosewater iced buns 52
  sticky toffee gulab jamun 206
  white chocolate rasmalai 213–14
green coriander and mint chutney 197
green lentils 134, 289
grinding spices 312
guava: apple and guava crumble 210
gulab jamun, sticky toffee 206
gunpowder 268, 285
gunpowder tofu 70

H
halloumi and mint paratha 160
halloumi fries chaat 90
handi (cooking pot) 303
hangover cure 73
hara bhara rolls 42
hazelnut cocoa burfi 223
herbs: garnishes for curry 109
  in paneer 248
Hindustan 10
holy basil (tulsi): tomato, tulsi and burrata salad 189
honey butter 160
hospitality 20

I
iced buns, raspberry and rosewater 52
icing (frosting) 52, 224
India 10
Indian hangover cure 73
Indian-inspired rocky road 45
Indo-Chinese bhajiya 51
Indo-Chinese ingredients 302
Indo-Chinese paneer 248
ingredients 275–302

Index 315

J

jaggery 294, 312
jalfrezi, root veg 126
jam sponge, cardamom 219
Jamaican jerk-inspired paneer 248

K

kachumber, grilled nectarine 193
kadai (cooking bowls) 303
kalonji coin naans 168
kebabs: beetroot paneer tikka 74
    bubble and seekh kebabs 97
keema jackets 94-5
khichdi, Scotch 170-1
khichiya 36
khichiya baskets 310
kidney beans 134, 290
    black daal 138-9
    coconut rajma 117
Kolkata chow mein 78

L

laccha paratha 158-9
laddoos, Bourbon biscuit 227
leeks: hara bhara rolls 42
lemon juice 295
lentils 134, 289
    black pepper tadka daal 136
    Scotch broth mix 171
lettuce: upma 'summer rolls' 66
    wedge salad chaat 190
lotus seeds: makhana 36

M

macaroni: Madras mac and cheese 62
mace 284
Madras curry powder 273, 285
Madras mac and cheese 62
makhana 36
Manchurian, chestnut 98
mangetout (snow peas): Singapore poha 93
mango chutney: Cheddar and mango chutney loaf 38
mango powder 283
    achaar masala 264
    chaat masala 263
mangoes: amber mango and coconut chutney 196
    shahi potatoes 121
maple-cardamom masala coffee 28
marinades: red 'tandoori' marinade 101
    tandoori marinade 69
    yellow 'achaari' marinade 101
marmalade: carrot cake scones with marmalade 56
    cheat's achaari marmalade 234
Marmite and sesame naans 166
marrowfat peas: Scotch broth mix 171
marshmallows: Indian-inspired rocky road 45
masala baked bean toasties 73
masala chai 24
masala paneer 248
masala yogurt 90
masalas 253-73, 285-6

achaar masala 264, 285
all-in-one biryani masala 260
biryani masala 285
chaat masala 263, 285
chai masala 267, 285
chips masala 272, 285
garam masala 259, 285
gunpowder 268, 285
Madras curry powder 273, 285
seekh kebab masala 271, 285
tandoori masala 269, 285
matoke, sizzling achaari 185
mayonnaise: blue cheese dressing 190
measurements 16
meatless mixed grill 101
Mediterranean-ish paneer 248
menu ideas 307
milk: cardamom jam sponge 219
    chai masala 20-3
    full-fat milk powder 293
    hazelnut cocoa burfi 223
    maple-cardamom masala coffee 28
    masala chai 24
    narangi hot chocolate 27
    paneer 246-7
    pistachio bread and butter pudding 220
    sticky toffee gulab jamun 206
    white chocolate rasmalai 213-14
millet flour 296
Milo: scruffy Milo rolls 224
mint: green coriander and mint chutney 197
    halloumi and mint paratha 160
mixed grill, meatless 101
mogo dirty fries 186
MSG (monosodium glutamate) 302
Mughal Empire 10
mung beans 134, 290
    dry daal 144
    Scotch khichdi with ghee-roast tomatoes 170-1
    split mung beans 134, 289
mushrooms: black chickpea 'bolognese' 89
    meatless mixed grill 101
    zafrani mushroom pulao 173
mustard oil 298
mustard seeds 281
    Madras curry powder 273

N

naan 164-9
    butter naans 164-5
    chilli-cheese naans 166
    garlic and coriander naans 166
    kalonji coin naans 168
    Madras mac and cheese with naan crumbs 62
    Marmite and sesame naans 166
    Peshawari naans 168
namkeen, garnishes for curry 109
narangi hot chocolate 27
nectarines: grilled nectarine kachumber 193
Nehru, Jawarhalal 107

nigella seeds 281
    kalonji coin naans 168
noodles: gathiya 35
    Kolkata chow mein 78
    sev 35
    upma 'summer rolls' 66
nutmeg 284
nuts 293, 310-12
    garnishes for curry 109
    thickening chutney 197
    see also cashews, peanuts etc

O

oats: apple and guava crumble 210
oils 298
    garnishes for curry 109
okra: scorpion tikka masala 124-5
olive oil 298
onions: beetroot paneer tikka 74
    bubble and seekh kebabs 97
    chilli fauxneer 102
    coconut rajma 117
    dehydrated onions 293
    gunpowder tofu 70
    pink peppercorn pickled onions 240
    see also spring onions
oranges: narangi hot chocolate 27
oven temperatures 306

P

Pakistan 10
pakoras, artichoke 55
paneer 246-7
    beetroot paneer tikka 74
    chilli fauxneer 102
    fauxneer 251
    hara bhara rolls 42
    masala paneer 248
    meatless mixed grill 101
    paneer katsu curry 84-5
    ruffled biryani 176-7
    scorpion tikka masala 124-5
    sticky toffee gulab jamun 206
    white chocolate rasmalai 213-14
pani puri 35
parathas 301
    halloumi and mint paratha 160
    laccha paratha 158-9
parsnips: root veg jalfrezi 126
pasta: black chickpea 'bolognese' 89
    Madras mac and cheese 62
    pasta daal 143
pastry: hara bhara rolls 42
    ruffled biryani 176-7
    sambharo spiral 82
    samosa pastry 46-8
peanut butter: quick peanut-tamarind dip 66
peanuts 293
    sizzling achaari matoke 185
pearl barley: Scotch broth mix 171
peas: brown butter cauliflower and pea makhani 113
    chole samosa 46-8
    hara bhara rolls 42
    keema jackets 94-5
    ruffled biryani 176-7

tiger pav bhaji 114-15
pecans: badtameez brownies 216
peppercorns: all-in-one biryani masala 260
    black peppercorns 279
    chai masala 267
    pink peppercorn pickled onions 240
    tandoori masala 269
peppers (bell): beetroot paneer tikka 74
    chestnut Manchurian 98
    chilli fauxneer 102
    gunpowder tofu 70
    Indo-Chinese bhajiya 51
    ruffled biryani 176-7
    scorpion tikka masala 124-5
    Singapore poha 93
    spicy bean tawa burgers 77
    sticky hakka fried rice 174
    tiger pav bhaji 114-15
Peshawari naans 168
pestle and mortar 303
phyllo pastry see filo pastry
pickles 295
    pink peppercorn pickled onions 240
    quick pickles 85
pigeon peas 134, 289
    pasta daal 143
pineapple juice: scorpion sauce 124-5
pink peppercorn pickled onions 240
pinto beans: spicy bean tawa burgers 77
pistachio cream: pistachio bread and butter pudding 220
pistachios 293
    Indian-inspired rocky road 45
pizza, Desi-inspired French bread 65
pizza sauce 65
poha 291
    Singapore poha 93
poppy seeds 293
porcini mushrooms: black chickpea 'bolognese' 89
potato fries see chips
potato powder, instant mashed 312
potatoes: aloo croissants 41
    bubble and seekh kebabs 97
    chole samosa 46-8
    keema jackets 94-5
    root veg jalfrezi 126
    ruffled biryani 176-7
    shahi potatoes 121
    tiger pav bhaji 114-15
pressure cookers 132-5, 303
pudla traybake 86
puff pastry: hara bhara rolls 42
pulao, zafrani mushroom 173
pulses 290, 295

Q

quick pickles 85

316 Sanjana Feasts

R

radishes: quick pickles 85
raisins: carrot cake scones 56
raita, fried caper 194
raspberry and rosewater iced buns 52
raspberry jam: cardamom jam sponge 219
rations 286
red cabbage: upma 'summer rolls' 66
red chilli chutney 196
red kidney beans 134, 290
    black daal 138–9
    coconut rajma 117
red lentils 134, 289
    black pepper tadka daal 136
    Scotch broth mix 171
red 'tandoori' marinade 101
rhubarb chhundo 235
rice 147–8, 152–77, 291
    coconut rajma 117
    cooking techniques 149, 152–5
    gunpowder 268
    ruffled biryani 176–7
    Scotch khichdi with ghee-roast tomatoes 170–1
    Singapore poha 93
    sticky hakka fried rice 174
    zafrani mushroom pulao 173
rice flour 296
    fauxneer 251
rice paper wrappers: upma 'summer rolls' 66
roasting spices 312
rocky road, Indian-inspired 45
rolls: hara bhara rolls 42
    scruffy Milo rolls 224
root veg jalfrezi 126
rose petals, dried 280
rosewater: raspberry and rosewater iced buns 52
roti 147–50, 301
    everyday roti 156–7
ruffled biryani 176–7
rum: apple and guava crumble 210
rusk 36

S

saffron 284, 312
    Peshawari naans 168
    shahi potatoes 121
    sticky toffee sauce 206
    white chocolate rasmalai 213–14
    zafrani mushroom pulao 173
salads: grilled nectarine kachumber 193
    tomato, tulsi and burrata salad 189
    wedge salad chaat 190
salt 283
sambharo spiral 82
samosa, chole 46–8
sauces: cheese sauce 69, 186
    curry sauce 84–5
    pizza sauce 65
    scorpion sauce 124–5
    sticky toffee sauce 206
    see also dips
Savoy cabbage ghee roast 129
scallions see spring onions
scones, carrot cake 56
scorpion tikka masala 124–5
Scotch broth mix 171
Scotch khichdi with ghee-roast tomatoes 170–1
scruffy Milo rolls 224
seeds 293
    garnishes for curry 109
    see also nigella seeds, sesame seeds etc
seekh kebab masala 271, 285
semolina 296
serving sizes 16
sesame oil 302
sesame seeds 293
    gunpowder 268
    Marmite and sesame naans 166
sev 35
    aloo croissants 41
shahi potatoes 121
Silk Route 10
Singapore poha 93
sizzling achaari matoke 185
snacks 23, 32–7, 301
snow peas see mangetout
sorghum flour 296
soup, curry leaf cream of tomato 81
sour flavours 312
soy sauce 302
soya 290
soya mince: keema jackets 94–5
spice grinders 303
spices: chai masala 23
    grinding 312
    ground spices 283–4
    in paneer 248
    roasting 312
    whole spices 279–81
    see also masalas and individual spices
spinach: broccoli miloni 118
    burnt aubergine and spinach curry 110
    hara bhara rolls 42
split mung beans 134, 289
sponge, cardamom jam 219
spring onions (scallions): chilli fauxneer 102
    Indo-Chinese bhajiya 51
    Singapore poha 93
    sticky hakka fried rice 174
star anise 281
sticky hakka fried rice 174
sticky toffee gulab jamun 206
sugar: jaggery 294, 312
    sugar syrup 213–14
sultanas (golden) 293
    Peshawari naans 168
'summer rolls', upma 66
swede: root veg jalfrezi 126
sweet potatoes: meatless mixed grill 101
    paneer katsu curry 84–5
    tiger pav bhaji 114–15
sweetcorn: dumpling handi 122
    spicy bean tawa burgers 77
    sticky hakka fried rice 174
vegan ghee 244
    see also corn-on-the-cob
sweetening 312
sweets 201–27
    apple and guava crumble 210
    badtameez brownies 216
    Bourbon biscuit laddoos 227
    cardamom jam sponge 219
    cinnamon chocolate fudge cake 209
    hazelnut cocoa burfi 223
    pistachio bread and butter pudding 220
    sticky toffee gulab jamun 206
    white chocolate rasmalai 213–14
syrup, sugar 213–14

T

tadka 135
    black pepper tadka daal 136
    garnish for curry 109
    white daal 140
tamarind paste 293
    quick peanut-tamarind dip 66
tandoori butter 65, 166
tandoori cauliflower cheese 69
tandoori masala 269, 285
tavitho (stainless steel turner) 303
tawa (griddle) 150, 304
tea: masala chai 20–3, 24
temperatures, oven 306
tempering 312
Tex-Mex style paneer 248
thickeners for chutney 197
tiger pav bhaji 114–15
tikka, beetroot paneer 74
toasties, masala baked bean 73
toffee: sticky toffee gulab jamun 206
tofu: fauxneer 251
    gunpowder 70
    Kolkata chow mein 78
    Singapore poha 93
tomatoes 295
    black chickpea 'bolognese' 89
    black daal 138–9
    brown butter cauliflower and pea makhini 113
    burnt aubergine and spinach curry 110
    chole samosa 46–8
    concentrated tomato purée 295
    curry leaf cream of tomato soup 81
    dumpling handi 122
    ghee-roast tomatoes 170–1
    grilled nectarine kachumber 193
    keema jackets 94–5
    pasta daal 143
    pizza sauce 65
    scorpion sauce 124–5
    tiger pav bhaji 114–15
    tomato, tulsi and burrata salad 189
    tomato soup 295
traffic light chutneys 196–7
tulsi (holy basil): tomato, tulsi and burrata salad 189
Turkish delight: Indian-inspired rocky road 45
tutti frutti 293

U

upma 'summer rolls' 66

V

vanilla: white chocolate rasmalai 213–14
vegan ghee 244
vegan paneer 251
vegan recipes 15
vegetables 295, 301
    pudla traybake 86
    see also peppers, tomatoes etc
vegetarian recipes 13
velan (rolling pin) 304
vermicelli: upma 'summer rolls' 66

W

wedge salad chaat 190
weights and measures 16
white chickpeas 134, 290
white chocolate rasmalai 213–14
white daal 140
white pepper 302

Y

yellow 'achaari' marinade 101
yellow gram daal 134, 289
    black pepper tadka daal 136
    gunpowder 268
yellow split peas: Scotch broth mix 171
yogurt 312
    beetroot paneer tikka 74
    bhature 162
    blue cheese dressing 190
    broccoli miloni 118
    fried caper raita 194
    masala yogurt 90
    red 'tandoori' marinade 101
    ruffled biryani 176–7
    tandoori marinade 69
    yellow 'achaari' marinade 101

Z

zafrani mushroom pulao 173

Unbound is the world's first crowdfunding publisher, established in 2011.

We believe that wonderful things can happen when you clear a path for people who share a passion. That's why we've built a platform that brings together readers and authors to crowdfund books they believe in – and give fresh ideas that don't fit the traditional mould the chance they deserve.

This book is in your hands because readers made it possible. Everyone who pledged their support is listed below. Join them by visiting unbound.com and supporting a book today.

Shanara Abdin, Khairoun Abji, Shailen Achar, Nikita Acharya, Bhvita Jani, John Adams, Bex Addis, Anjana Agarwal, Ramya Aggarwal, Sejal Aggarwal, Jo Aghera, Priyanka Desai Agrawal, Anisha Ahmed, AJ, Akhila, Bilqees Akhtar, Anisa Akinlami, Rebecca Aksamit, Ghaida Al Mutairi, Nosheen Ali, Sharon Ali, Syeda Ali, Zed Ali, Zarrin Ali, Claire Hawkins, Nileema Zodgekar Allerston, Heena Alli, Judith Allwang, Bella Amin, Divya Amin, Kirna Amin, Miral Amin, Neal Amin, Priti Amin, Sejal Amin, Trushar Amin, Akhil Amlani, Hasmita Amtha, Shivani Anand, Tina Anand, Janaki Anderson, Anju Andrews, Marie Antons, Susan Antony, Taruna Bolding, Anushruti, Mina Anwar, Sara Armstrong, Amanprit Arnold, Aakanksha Arora, Nital Patel Arora, Rohini Arter, Vaishnavi Arvind, Ash & Sid, Abigail Ashton, Dr Rajveer Athwal, Atika, Natalie Atkins-Sloan, Modupe Ayinde, Lina B, Sumaya Babamia, Komal Badiani, Bagdai, Renu Bagga, Parampreet Bahia, Vanisha Bahra, Priya Bahri, Amreet Bains, Anjna Bains, Suki Bains, Sharon Bakar, Emma Bal, Komal Balakrishnan, Jason Ballinger, Ramesh Bance, Salima Bandali, Ilona Bansal, Chandni Baptiste, Aahuti Barai, Isabella Barbato, Dominique Barcz, Bianka Esha Bargmann, Andy Barnes, Jo Barnes, Dan Barnett, Mansi Barot, Bini Barr, Kathryn Barraclough, Sara Barratt, Michael Barrett, Hazel Bartels, Swati H Barve, Ian Barwell, Archana Basnet, Steve Bass, Ashee Bathia, Chintal, Sam, Kush & Yash Bathia, Nita Bathia, Richard Bauld, Krupa Bava, Emma Bayliss, Colette Beaupre, Suzanna Beaupre, Marcus Beaver, Sally Bedford, Laura Bedi, Indie Beedie, Sundeep Bhogal, Hassan Beg, Sharifa Begum, Baba Belletti, Chitralekha Beniwal, Phillip Bennett-Richards, Sheetal Bentley, BG, Mandy Bhachu, Ciona Bhachu-Nankervis, Saarika Bhagat, Raj Jigna Bhagwati, Archana Bhakta, Mayuri Ishvar Bhakta, Punam Bhakta, Sonal Bhakta, Sonali Bhalsod-Patel, Baljit Bhamra, Dilber Bhamra, Bhavisha Bhandari, B Bharania, Maya Bhardwa, Jaina Patel, Mira Bhardwaj, Karishma Bharti, Nisha Bhat, Preeya Bhatia, Palak Bhatt, Priya Bhatt, Sneha Bhatt, Sharni Bhatti, Shetal Bhayani, Manisha Bhikha, Heenal Bhogaita, Rimmi Bhogal, Satnam Bhogal, Trisha Bhogayata, Freya Bhoja, Amisha Bhudia, Daxa Bhudia, Gayatri Bhudia, Shital Bhudia, Sonal Bhudia, Bina Bilimoria, Pritie Billimoria, Chris Bird, Rachel Bishop-Firth, David Blue, Bobworth, Julie Boora, Nitya Boora, Alexander Borg, Rumi Bose, Sumita Bose, Kate Boulton, Hattie Bowden-Howl, Andrew Boyce, Chris Boyce, Roma Bracey, Nicky Bramley, Jasdeep Brar, Sukhpal K Brar, Andy Brereton, Amanda Bressette, Eleanor Bridgman, Bina Briggs, Simon Briton, Alice Broadribb, Aditi Broomfield, Alexandra Brown, Duncan Bruce, Sam Brundish, Andrew Bryan, Jess Buck, Nicola Buckland, James Bucknall, Tania Buckthorp, Jita Buddhdev, Neeta Budhdeo, Mira Buhecha, Hina Buhecha, Little Bun, Archana Burlow, Shelly Butcher, Zohra Butt, Priya Buxton, Versha C, Nimisha Cacciatore, Anjali Caddies, Neelam Patel Caires, Jay Calderisi, Lindsey Callaghan, Claire Callow, Elaine Campbell, Victoria Cargill-James, Brian Carli, Sean Carroll, Michael Casner, Jovita Castelino, Sheena Castelino, Naveen Cavale, Faith Shakti Heyliger Cedarholm, Sonia Chadda, Pratap Chahal, Leon Chakrabarti, Sarah Chalmers Page, Guillaume Chambon, Kiran Chana, Rita Chana, Saranjit Chandan, Harshni Chandaria, Bharti Chandegra, Maya Chandegra, Tohral Chandegra, Simrun Chandhok, Merran Charles, Gurpreet Chatha, Rehana Chaudary, Yasmin Chaudhry, Irfan Chaudry, Sabiha Chaudry, Maleeha Mirza, Jaina Chauhan, Monica Chauhan, Nita Chauhan, Shivani Chauhan, Shruti Chauhan, Vishal Chauhan, Vishnu and Gauri Chauhan, Shwetha Cherukuri, Chhaya @ The Cardamom Pods, Varsha @ The Cardamom Pods, Jaimini Chohan, Kamaljit Chohan, Dimpy Chotai, Reena Chotai, Bhavna Chotalia, Dinita Chouhan, Juan Christian, Balkishan Chudasama, Devyani Chudasama, Jagruti Chudasama, Vik Chudasama, Dilip Chudgar, Shailly Chudhari, Sheila Chumber, Fazila Chunara, Chris Clark, Kalpa Clarke, Darya Classen, Felicity Cloake, Freyalyn Close-Hainsworth, Jo Coates, Tom Cockerill (Woodrow Studios), Teri Cole, Simon Colson, Sam Cook, Louise Cooke, Cookwitch, Faye Coopey, Jo Cosgriff, Charan Coulby, Andrea Courtois, Matthew Cowell, Joe Cox, Susheila Cox, Lucy Crawford, Michael Croke, Michael Cumming, Paul Cumming, Shilpa Cunniffe, The Cursons Family from Cape Town, H D, Anisha D'Cruz, Fatima Dadabhai, Radha Dainton, Naazneen Dalvi, Tasha Daly & Stefan Birkett, Priti Damle, Ashish Dasani, Ishita DasGupta, Hetal Dassani, Parina Dattani, Sruti Dattani-Patel, Maya Datwani, Nidhish Davda, Bijal Dave, Daksha Dave, Jayshree Dave, Kiran Dave, Krupa Dave, Rhea Dave, Varsha Dave, Kalpini Davé, Jiten Dave, Bina Dave, Sweetie Davé, Rohan Dave, Julie Davies, Anjali Daya, Jyoti Dayah, Urvi Dayal, Nilesh & Beena Dayalji, Farida Dedat, Zunaira Deen, Rapinder Deol, Trusha Depala, Anuja Desai, Binita Desai, Harshali Desai, Isha Desai, Jigsha Desai, Maitri Desai, Neha Desai, Nikita Desai, Priya Deshingkar, Samara & Aeshan Devani, Devika and Jonathan, Patric ffrench Devitt, Hema Dewal, Mandy Dhaliwal, Rieethaa Dhamne, Manisha Dhanak, Anisha Dhanani, Dipen Dhanani, Poojitha Dharmavaram, Sharon Dhesi-Cowper, Jesvir Dhillon, Pardeep Dhinsa, Bhanu Dhir, Kapil Dhir, Pragna Dhokia, Sangeeta Dhrona, Dhruv, Akshee, Ahren, Raj Dhugga, Dan Dhunna, Shefali Dhutia, Mira Dodhia, Priya Dodhia, Anita Dodia, Dolly, Anne Doran, Manjula Doshi, Rupal Doshi, Parisha Doughty, Paul Driver, Kate Dyer, John Edwards, Rachel Edwards, Jaime Elder, Bethan Ellis, John & Geri Ellis, Diana Emus, Reinhard Eschbach, Jacky Evans, Matthew Evans, Brett Eveleigh, Adam & Rachel Fairbank, Tennant Family, Dean Fearing, Meryl Feinstein, Deanna Fellows, Ben Finley, Lisa Finnimore, Reva Flay, Chris Fosten, Aaron T J Foulds, Thomas Fox, Gert Frahm-Jensen, Fran and Bro, Penelope Fried, Mani G, Neepa Gadhia, Indira Gadhvi, Avni Gairola, Reena Gajjar, Jay Gala, Ashish Galani, NRA Gall, Punita Gandecha, Pardeep Gandham, Reshma Gandhi, Sanjay Gandhi, Sheetal Gandhi, Sonal Gandhi, Arti Ganeshie, Sonia Ganeshwaran, Johan Gant, Shikha Gapsch, Russell Garlick, @garlicrosemaryandsalt, Krupa Germin, Felicity Ghani, Anjani Ghedia, Priya Ghelani, Samit Ghosh, Jasmin Ghuznavi, Ryan Gibberd, Ruth Gibbsmith, Alec Gibson, Manpreet Gill, Rina Gill, Roopal Gill, Satti Gill, Javeria Gilmore-Khan, GK, Emma Godden, Sarah Godwin, Bharti Gohel, Bhoomi Gohil, Leena Gohil, Meera Gohil, Pinki Gohil, Sanjay Gohil, Seema Gohil, Shilpa Gohil, Tiara Gohil, Khushil Gokani, Rina Gokani Thomas, Rebecca Good, Katie Goodall, Paul J Goodison, Scott Goodwin, Ami Gorasia, Chandan Gorasia, Harsha Gorasia, Vijyanti Gorasia, Darren Gordon, Madhu Prakash Gorecha, Harsha Gorsia, Dhareshni Gounden, Pravina Govind, Prerna Goyal, David Goyette, Maxine Grant, Ruchita Green, Mary Gregory, Charlotte Griffiths, Graham Griffiths, Noel Griffiths, Julie Griggs, Dimple Patel Ash Grove, Ushma Gudka-Chik, Ben "Curry Off" Guest, Katy Guest, Jo Guilor, Champa Gujjanudu, Rakshit Gulab, Aliya Gulamani, Ridhika Thakrar Gunawardene, Kamini Gupta, Seema Gupta, Shilpa Gupta, Sunitha Gupta, Phil H, Dan Hagedorn, Kajal Halai, Kala Halai, Tejal Halai, Debika Hall, Peter Hallsworth, Sarah Hamilton, Raj Hanspal, Alistair Hargreaves, Janvi Haria, Shashikant Haria, Andrea Harman, Becca Harper-Day, Ben Harris, Michael Harris, Fiona Harrison, Phil Harrison, Toni Harrison, Harsha, Victoria Hart, Ursula Hartley, Angelika Haselbacher, Sabera Hashim-Versi, Barry Hasler, Lauren Haslett, Andy and Emma Haynes, Rob Haynes, Namrata Hazariwala, Andrew Hearse, Stuart Hedges, Minal Hemraj, Jude Henderson, Harvinder Higgens, Philippa Higginson, Peter Hilty, Sonia Hindocha, Sumeet Hindocha, Jalpa Hingu, Maya Hira, Hiral, Chan Hirani, Dipti Hirani, Jayna Hirani, Joyti Hirani, Vanita Hirani, Vanisha Hirji, Tony Histed, Max Hoberman, Karen Holford, Cat Hollow, Kerenza Hood, Tom Hook, Francesca Hopkins, Amie Horgan, Sandra Horn, Izy Hossack, Ema Hossain, Shailee Howard, Helen Hubert, Monica Hucks, Claire Hugman, Larissa Hulme, Steve Hurley, Reshma Hussain, Tasneem Hussain, Mary Hyland, R I, Mitsu Ikeda, Shabana Islam, Farah Ismail, Ashia Ismail-Singer, Ivaan & Kush, Arthi Iyer, Anil J, William Jack, Shayan & Veer Jackman, Judith Jackson, Jasel Jadeja, Pratham Jadeja, Muntazir Jaffer, Divya Jagasia, Heenal Jagatia, Hemali Jagjivan, Mayoor Jagjiwan, Rajani Jain, Jaina, Sadiyah Jamal, Mike James, Hirsh Jamie, Shweta Jani, Nuha Jannat, Emma Jarvis, Samira Jasat, Anil Jassi, Habibah Javid, Jhalini Jawaheer, Monisha Jayakumar, Vee Jayaprakash, Christian Jeffery, Gopika Jem, Hithik Jemini, Simon Jerrome, Mark Jessett and Milly Brown, Hema Jetha, Neesha Jetha, Rina Jethwa, Heena Jhala, Alisha C. Jinabhai, Carmalita Jitendran, Moheni Jivan-Natha, Sharmila Jivan, Kejal Mistry, Harry Jobanputra, Paresh Jobanputra, Sarita Jogia, Bhavini Jogie, Deepti Jones, Mary Jordan-Smith, A. Joshi, Bhavna Joshi, Bina & Ketan Joshi, Chandani Joshi, Chandni Joshi, Jasmine Joshi, Jay Joshi, Nutan Joshi, Parul Joshi, Pratiksha H Joshi, Priya Joshi, Raveena and Naresh Joshi, Shinal Joshi, Shital Joshi, Shivani Joshi, Vaishaalee Joshi, Dhara Joshi, Surbhi Joshi, Hemini Jotangia, Joy of Cooking, Caroline Joyce, Judith & Kerry, Nushma Juwaheer, Rozina Kabani, Lara & Mikhil Kachalia, Hema Kachela, Kajal, Chand Kaka & Nimu Masi, Eish, Nu, Sienna & Ava, Asha Kalyan, Hema Kalyanji, Farzanah Kamal, Kimi Kamdar, Miten Kana, Hema Kanani, Mala Kanbi, Mahilini Kandasamy, Deeksha Kansagra, Kripa Kapadia, Rita Kapadia, Nikitasha Kapoor, Asha Kara, Pareesa Kara-Patel, Soniya Kara-Patel, Bhumika Karamshi, Neeta Karelia, Nira Karia, Shilpa Karia, Hemal Karsan, Dina Kashap London Ltd, Suraj Kataria, Katie, Sunny Katigbak, Gurleen Kaur, Harpreet Kaur, Harps Kaur, Harvi Kaur, Isha Kaur, Jagmeet Kaur, Manjeet Kaur, Navrup Kaur, Pardeep Kaur, Rajvinder Kaur, Rupinder Kaur, Mandeep Kaur-Bains, Kav Kaushik, Usha Kavasseri, Shital Kavia, Jill Kaye, Becky Kearns, Jane Kenneway, Tony Kennick, Nicky Kenning, Hershika Kerai, Chaya Keshwala, Hina Sofia Keval, Maymunah Khalifa, Humera Khalifa, Naila Khan, Shazia Khan, Fozia Khanam, Jag Khangura, Seema Khatani, Purnima Khatri, Sajida Khatri, Sapna Khimani, Charlotte Khunpha-Ridley, Khushbu, Deepali Kidambi, Preeti Kika, Kim, Janneke Kimstra, Shreenu King, Amie Knighy, Anjanee Kohli, Sabina Kola, Anuradha Kolhatkar, Komal & Nikhil, Kontikitoo, Roopa Kotak, Maya Kotecha, Neesha Kotecha, Raksha Kotecha, Rekha Kotecha, Yookti NomNomnivore Kotecha-Davda, Shetal Kotedia-Gadhia, Anisha Kothari, Shreena Kothari, Anjli Kothary, Joanne Koukis, Hanna Kozak-King, Krina, Karunya Krishnan, Christine Kubjacek, Kanaka Kulkarni, Supriya Kulkarni, Camini Kumar, Radhika Patole Kumar, Harish Kunverji, Oli Kyle, Jill Kyne, Emily Kyne, Lina Lad, Naina Lad, Nita Lad, Sweta Lad, Krupa Ladva, Ansuya Ladwa, Hitesh Ladwa, Mit Lahiri, Arti A Lakhani, Meena Lakhani, Neel Lakhani, Renuka Lakhani, Harkirat Kaur Lall, Jeanette Lamb, Sanjana Landry, Sally Langley, Nick Lansbury, Laughton Family (Jaya-Poornima-Jim), Robert Lax, Elizabeth Eva Leach, Ryan Leach, Tierney Leighton, Jamie Lemming, Victoria Lennon, Runesha Leo, Claire Lewis, Rick Lewis, Dimple Limani, Ekta Limbani, Josna Limbani, Victoria Lishman-Peat, Geoff Lloyd, Tessa Longbottom, Ashleigh Lowther, Ishmeet Rajbans Lydder, Heather Lyons, Mani M, Sejal M, Tara M, Sheetal Magdani, Palvi Mahajan, Vaishali Mahajan, Kapish Maharaj, Sunita Maharaj-Vidal, Sophie Mahbub, Faisal Shaan Mahmud, Churnjeet Mahn, Geeta Maini, Tara Maini, Bijal Majithia, Deesha Majithia, Trusha Majithia, Chaitra Makam, Anita Makwana, Janki Makwana, Madhvi Makwana, Marion Makwana, Trina Makwana, Veena Makwana, Priti Malde, Shenal Malde, Gita Malhotra, Devi Maliha, Pyaar & Angela, Serena Malik, Jyoti Malkan, Meena Manchoo-Bhana, Nikita Mandavia, Chandni Manek, Munira Mangalji, Manisha Mistry's Kitchen, Joti Manji, Kiran Manji, Megan Marie, Megha Maripuri, Bodhi Marullo, Kiran Marwaha, Sagar Masani, Steve Mash, Sonal Mashari, Neelam Mashru, Catherine Mason, Deepa Master, Jaspreet Matharu, Pavan Matharu, Neesha Mathur, Bhavisha Mawji, Kyle Maxwell, Dawood Mayet, Suzanna McAninley, David McBride, Bridget Rose McCall, Sam McCarthy, Peter McCowie, Lawrence McCrossan, Mim McDonald, Julian McEvoy, Marie McGinley, Carole McIntosh, Sierra McLeod, Darren McManus, Bhavna Mehta, Minal Mehta, Parikha Mehta, Priya Mehta, Rutesh Mehta, Suneeta Mehta, Tulsi Mehta, Nicolas Melicosta, Charnyla Mepani, Uroosa Mianoor, G Minhas, Madhu Mirpuri, Mahayno Mirza, Runjhun Misra, Aarti Mistry, Ashme Mistry, Bhavi Mistry, Bina Mistry,

318 Sanjana Feasts

Chaaya Mistry, Dina Mistry, Gemini Mistry, Jem Mistry, Jenna Mistry, Kapisha Mistry, Kate Mistry, Krina Mistry, Krishan Mistry, Minal Mistry, Neeta Mistry, Nikita Mistry, Nina Mistry, Nishma Mistry, Pooja Mistry, Preena Sandip Mistry, Priynka Mistry, Reena Mistry, Sandeep Mistry, Sapna Mistry, Sayjal Mistry, Seema Mistry, Tina Mistry, Vanita Mistry, Vickesh + Leena Mistry, Anita Mistry JAKYD, Beena Mistry-Kanani, Deepa Mistry-Patel, Shilpa Mistry-Patel, John Mitchinson, Roopal Modasia, Anand Modha, Chandni Modha, Dhruti Modha, Hina Modha, Hitesh Modha, Kartik Modha, Keren and Jitin Modha, Kishor Modha, Leena Modha, Minal Modha, Mr Modha, Niralee Modha, Pragna N Modha, Premkunj Modha, Ravi Modha, Shailesh Mohanlal Modha, Vish Modha, Suresh Modha, Ashmita Modha, Bansi Modha, Avni S. Gudka, Hiren N Modha, Maya Josephine Jacobs, Shyaama - Jyoti Modha, Archana Modha, Manju Modhwadia, Dhara Modi, Hema Modi, Jessie Modi, Tina Modi, Kavita Modi, Meena Modi, Lena Mohamed, Sarah Mohammad-Qureshi, Parminder Mohan, Rashmi Mohan, Nisha Mokashi, Christian Möllerström, Michelle Moltz, Rita Momin, Ken Monaghan, David Monteith, Kribarani Moodley, Peter Moore, Rita Morar, Vanisha Morar, Jeni Morgan, Reema Morjaria, Sonali Morjaria, Ed Morland, Janet Morson, Iain Morton, Indrajit Motala, Homayra Motara, Kiran Moyo, Mrs N, Karanjit Mudhar, Hummera Mughal, Priya Mulji, Shohrin Mulla, Jasmeen Munif-Field, Aishwarya Murali, Darren Murphy, Ami Murthy, Nadia Nadarajah, Sonal Nadiadhara, Jainita Nagar, Ravi & Jenna Nagar, Darshita Naik, Pooja Nainani, Prameela Nair, Payal Nakum, Rishi Nanavati, Neha Nandha, Sophie Nandha, Reshma Nangpal, Dina Sonpal, Hena Naranbhai, Priya Narayanan, Reshma Narsi, Prabhaben Nathu Vaghela, Deepa Nathvani, Dillon Nathwani, Panna Nathwani, Carlo Navato, Niti Nayee, Prakash D Nayee, Usha Nayee, Osmond, Christine and John Naylor, Aashni Nayyer, Rumeena Nazarali, Ned, Tania Nehme, Martin Nehmiz, Kay Nettle, Huong Nguyen, Candace Nicolls, Nichole Nigam, Luna Nightingale, Paul Nightingale, Nikita & Shivani, Nikki, Kaushik Nimisha Dhruv Bella, ù§Ô∏è, Heena Nirmal, Anita Nirmalsingh, Nisha, Nirupama Nishtala, Bala Noone, Brian Nordmann, Lesley Northfield, Douriya Nurbhai, Beth Nuyens, Sachin and Ravi O'Brien, Keavy O'Shea, Amy O'Sullivan, Jonathan O‚ÄôCarroll, Kajal Odedra, Seema Odedra, Bijal Odedra-Pinder, Maria Ogrady, Cynthia Okerfelt, Sheetal Olivier, Riya P, Kavita Pachchigar, Sashi Padarthy, Depa Padhiar, Rups&Raj Padhiar, Devhuti Padhra, Paula Page, Sarah Page-Alder, Neha Painaik, Poonam Palan, Nerali Panchal, Shweta Panchal, Sanjiv Panchani, Meera Panchasara, Namrata Panchmatia, Tina, Esmé & Damini Pancholi, Nuleen Panday, Bhavin Pandit, Jayshree Pandit, Poonam Pandit, Pragna Pandit, Vimal Pandit, Saajan Pandit, Avani Pandya, Darshna Pandya, Hema Pandya, Meghna Pandya, Rani Pandya, Chuch Panesar, Anjali Rupesh Pankhania, Chhaya Pankhania, Miran & Alexandra Pankhania, Tulsi Pankhania, Gwen Papp, Milan Parbhoo, Neelam Parbhoo, Kaajal Parekh, Prachi Parekh, Preeti Parekh, Neema Parikh, Rizwana Parkar, Sonal Parmanand, Velji Parmanand, Taramati Parmanand Bhadreshwara, Ami Parmar, Bansri Parmar, Bhavna Parmar, Jai Parmar, Kiran Parmar, Nisha Parmar, Shilpa Parmar, Shruti Parmar, Sonia Parmar, Sukhraj Parmar, Vaishali Parmar, Ramya Parthasarathi, Shilpa Parthasarathi, Deborah Partington, Madhukar Patani, Aayushi Patel, Alpa Patel, Amar Patel, Amita Patel, Amrit Patel, Aneeta Patel, Anita Patel, Ankita Patel, Any K Patel, Archanna Patel, Arti Patel, Arushi Patel, Beejal Patel, Bharat Patel, Bharti Patel, Bharvi Patel, Bhavesh Patel, Bhavika B Patel, Bhavini Patel, Bhavna Patel, Bhranti Patel, Bijal Patel, Bina Patel, Binal Patel, Binita Patel, Chandni Jadav Patel, Charuti Patel, Daksha Patel, Dakshaben Patel, Darsh Patel, Davina Patel, Dhara Patel, Dharam Patel, Dhruti Patel, Dhupal Patel, Dimple Patel, Dina Patel, Dipa Patel, Dipal Patel, Dylan Patel, Ekta Patel, Geeta Vadher Patel, Gopi Patel, Harish Patel, Harry Patel, Hasi Patel, Hasruty Patel, Heeral Patel, Hema Patel, Hemantkumar Patel, Hemma Patel, Heral Patel, Hinal Patel, Ila Patel, J Patel, Jag Patel, Jagdish R Patel, Janaki Patel, Janki Patel, Jaymala Patel, Jaymica Patel, Jayna Patel, Jinal Patel, Jyorti Patel, Kajal Patel, Kalpana Patel, Kalpita Sharma Patel, Kamila Patel, Kamini Patel, Karishma Patel, Keshvi Patel, Khyati Patel, Kiran Patel, Kirti Patel, Krishna Patel, Krupa Patel, Krupal Patel, Laxmi Patel, Leena Patel, Manisha Dhanak Patel, Meena Patel, Meera Patel, Meeta Patel, Meghna Patel, Menesha Patel, Milauni Patel, Mira Patel, Mitul Patel, Mukta Patel, Namisha Patel, Natasha Patel, Neha Patel, Nikki Patel, Nila Patel, Nilam Patel, Nimet Patel, Nipa Patel, Nipa Kanjiya Patel, Nirali Patel, Nirmala Patel, Nisa Patel, Nisha Patel, Nishma Patel, Paresh Patel, Parisha Patel, Parita J. Patel, Pasmina Patel, Pavuluri, Divya Patel, Payal Patel, Pooja Patel, Pragnya Patel, Prashant Patel, Priya Patel, Raksha Patel, Reema Patel, Reena Patel, Rekha Patel, Rina Patel, Roopal Patel, Roshni Patel, Ruchi Patel, Rupal Patel, Sachin Patel, Saloni Patel, Sam Patel, Sangeeta Patel, Sapna Patel, Sarina Patel, Seema Patel, Sefali Patel, Sheena Patel, Shinal Patel, Shraddha Patel, Shreelekha Patel, Shriya Patel, Sima Jitesh Patel, Snehal Patel, Sonal Patel, Sriya Patel, Stephanie Patel, Swaroop Patel, Tejal Patel, Tejal, Äúur_tejasty, Patel, Tina Patel, Trisha Patel, Trishna Patel, Trupti Patel, Tulsi Umesh Patel, Unnatie Patel, Urvashi Patel, Vaishali Patel, Vanisha Ricky Patel, Vijeta Patel, Viragni Patel, Zakeeya Tilly, Sonal Patel, Zinal Patel, Mitesh Patel - Drake & Case, Aarti Patel-Manoj, Shinal Patel-Thakkar, Jagruti Patel, Devya Patel, Kirpa Patel, Jaishri Nakum, Arti Patel, Krupa Patel, Chintal Patel, Kush & Yash Bathia, Priya Patel, Mruna & Dilesh Patel, Sejal Patel, Rasmeet Neote, Panna Pattani, Rupal Pattani, Meera Pattani-Shah, Sonal Gadhia Pattany, Kiki Pattni, Mamta Pattni, Meghna Pattni, Priya Pattni, Rajee Pattni, Shini Pattni, T Pattni, Ella Barnbrook, Raji Pau, Sejal Pau, Anju Pawar, Manisha Peck, Frankie Pellatt, Emily Peopall, Hugo Perks, Luke Perrett, laura Perry, Kalawatee Persad, Mandeep K Phull, Tajinder Phull, Prenisha Pillay, Dipti Pindoria, Hashmita Pindoria, Mina Pindoria, Tia Pindoria, Danielle Pines, Chris Plumley, Katherine Pole, Pooja & Rukey, Anokhi Popat, Sheena Popat, Rakhee Porter, Chloe Portman, Neha Powell, Purvi Prajapati, Pree, Preeyah, Harshan Premanand, Cornelia Prendiville, Preya Preya, Laura Price, Rab Prinjha, Prital, Beth Procter, Bhakti Purohit, Sumayyah Qureshi, Ashka Radadia, Bindi Radia, Jaymini Radia, Sonal Radia, Rads, Daniel Rafferty, Anita Raghvani, Nilupa Rahim, Tina Raichura, Sandeep Raithatha, Sheetal Raithatha, Akta Raja, Pratibha Raja, Sarb Raja, Shivani Raja, Kavya Rajagopala, Jannat Shah Rajan, Jaimini Rajanathan, Dharmesh Rajput, Jyoti Rajyagor, Meera and Mike, Bhavika Rakholia, Bharti Ram, Alpana Rama, Mika Ramachandran, Maitri Ramadhin, Suji Ramakrishnan, Reetesh Rambhai, Rishi Ramchandani, Sheetal Ramesh, Kavita Ramjee, Keshar Ramji Bhadreshwara, Ruth Ramsden-Karelse, Ramya & Satish, Arrti Ramyead, Sukhy Rana, Bharti Raniga, Sairoz Rashid, Annada D Rathi, Hina Rathod, Louise Rathod, Rakhee Rathod, Dharshi Ratnabalan, Shifally Rattan, Balbinder Rattu, M Rattu, Megha Rattu, Shreya Rawal, Jayshri Rayani, Reshma Raycoba, RB, Jessica Rees, Vicky Rehal, Cital Reil, Remy Marianne Rhodes, Steve Richards, Rishi & Tasvee, Sonal Ritin, Mary J Robb, Deb Roberts, Wyn Roberts, Bosco Rodrigues, Sujata Rodriguez, Debora Roncon, Roshni, Aarti Rostron, Karen Rowland, Priya Ruda, Sofia Rüdiger, Elizabeth Ruffell, Joe Osmond, S.Girach, Hennah Sacoor, The Sadarangani Family, Saffronly Saffron, Priya Saggar, Ravinder Sagoo, Jaina Saha, Sahar & Hafsa, Priya & Arun Sahni, Rav Sahota, Maleeha Saiyed, Saima Saleh, Khalima Salvador, Rekha Samani, Rithee Samani, Meena Samani, Ravi Benitez, Sushma Samonini, Manpreet Sandhu, Sandy Sandhu, Sanpreet Kaur Sandhu, Sandip & Vimee, Min Sangha, Sharan Sanghera, Meera Shah Sanghrajka, Congratulations Sanjana!, Meera Sankaran, Devina Sankhla, Ruchita Sarawgi, Katherine Sargent, Rebecca Sarjeant, Nandini Sarma, Morten Sau, Sonia Savla, Neil Scarlett, Eric Schnaubelt, Zalyn Schwartz, Sreelakshmi SD, Ayushi Sehmbi, Anita Sembi, Linda Sendowski, Sita Sethi, Visal Sethi, Daniel Sewell, Freda Shafi, Aarti Shah, Amit Shah, Anjali Shah, Avani A Shah, Beejal Shah, Beena Shah, Bijal Shah, Bina Shah, Binita Shah, C Shah, Chandni Shah, Chitra Shah, Darshna Shah, Davina Shah, Dipika Shah, Divyesh Shah, Harshi Shah, Harshni Shah, Heena Shah, Hema Shah, Hemali Shah, Ishita Shah, Jeena Shah, Jigna Shah, K and V Shah, Kapila Shah, Kavita Shah, Kaye Shah, Komal Shah, Krishna Shah, Kunal Shah, Kushal Shah, Lexy Shah, M Shah, Mauli Shah, Minoo Shah, Mittal Shah, Naina Vipul Shah, Neha Shah, Nesha Shah, Nilma Shah, Nirali Shah, Nita Shah, Nixha Shah, Parita Shah, Parul Shah, Prina Shah, Puja Shah, Rajul Shah, Reina Shah, Reshma Shah, Roshni Shah, Ruchi Shah, Runish Shah, Rupal Shah, Sajan Shah, Salma Shah, Saloni Shah, Sheetle Shah, Shilpa Shah, Shilpi Shah, Shirin Shah, Shital Shah, Shruti Shah, Sneh Shah, Sonali Shah, Sonia Shah, Suri and Dillon Shah, Teena Shah, Tejal Shah, Tejni Shah, Trishna Shah, Vijal Shah, Vihaan Shah & Diyan Shah, Kian and Sami Shah-Ackroyd, Shilpa Shah-Hertzberg, Krina Shah-Hirani, Roshni Shah-Oftadeh, Aarti Shah, Chirag Shah, Bansri Shah, Uma Shah, Niraj Shah, Bella Shah, Pranay Shah, Nikki Shah, Raksha Barai, Seema Patel, Preena Shah, Vik Rayit, Menaka Shah, Vishal Laladia, Alom Shaha, Deepa Anand Shahani, Hetal Shaikh, Nayna Shamji, Reshma Shamnarine, Nadia Shanaz, Shivani Shankar, Bhavesh Sharma, Mina Sharma, Teena Sharma, Vandna Sharma, Vishal Sharma, Heather Sharp, Andrew Shaw, Aims Shearing, Lydia Shears, Sheena, Sofia & Selena, Liz Sheppard, Chaitalee Sheth, Shivani Sheth, Shruti Sheth, Harjeet Shingadia, Nilisha Shivji, Sandie Shokar, Satya Shree, Rani Shrestha, Dhruma Shukla, Ritika Shukla, Amee Shukla-Kotecha, Muniza Siddiqui, Rukzana Sikkandar, Grace Simms, Meera Singadia, Dipika Singh, Gurpal Singh, Heena Singh, Namrata Singh, Rachel Singh, Roshika Singh, Nikita Sinha, Shilpa Siyani, Siyavam, Tony Slater, Purvi Smart, AJ Smith, Anika Smith, Billie Smith, Duncan Smith, Gareth Smith, Jo Smith, Sneha, Sheena Sodha, Sheena Solankey, Aarti Solanki, Deviyani Solanki, Disha Solanki, Heena Solanki, Ranjit Solanki, Solvester, Veena Soma-Barron, Sonal & Raj, Nisha Sondhe, Priya Soneji, Bhavna Soni, E Soni, Rachna Soni, Soni Soni, Vaishali Soni, Manisha Sonigra, Upasana Sonigra, Fellow Yorkie - Bhavesh Sonigra :), Heena Sood, Balwinder K Soor, Fawni Spottswood, Sri SRao, Shobana Sridharan, Priya Srinivasan, Uma Sriram, Wendy Staden, Charlotte Stark, Jamie Steel, Rory Steele, David Stevens, Sejal Sthankiya, Stinsons, Mishel Straminsky, Big Stu, Chris Styles, Louise Su, Akhil Suchak, Neha Sudame, Sanjeev Sudera, Neeta Sujeevan, Surya Sukumar, Jackie Sullivan, Nishi Sumaria, Safiya Sumra, Kiran Suri, Bhavisha Surti, Hema Suthar, Anne-Marie Svensson, Zeena Swier, Punam T, S T, Bansri Tailor, Krishma Tailor, Roshni Tailor, Bindya Tak, Shakunt Tambe, Pankhuri Garg Tamotia, Tani, Priti Tank, Roshni Tank, Sheetal Tank, Komal Tanna, Nimisha Tanna, Poonam Tanna, Tony Tassell, Tejal & Jamie, Tom Thackeray, Reshmi Thakerani-Chung, Ursula Mirani Thakker, Nandita Thakrar, Pooja Thakrar, Vaishali Thakrar, Sital Thankey-Lindemann, Daksha Narendra Thanki, Disha Thanki, Mital Thanki, Rakhee Thanki, Sanj Thanki, Prakash Thanky, Gina Thiara, Kam Thiara, Anna Thomas, Barbara Thomas, Kirsty Thomas, Carl Thompson, Sophie Thomsett, Alexander Thomson, Risha Thomson, Susan Thomson, John Thorpe, Jaz Tiara, Laxmi Tierney, Veeral Tolia, Will Tomlinson, Komal Toor, Amit Toprani, Sabine Tötemeyer, David Toyne, Lucy Traves, Aesha Tripathi, Shivangi Tripathi, Trishika, Abha Trivedi, Avni Trivedi, Parita Trivedi, Rakhee Trivedi, Andrew Truelove, Carney Turner, Rajan Tutt, Annelise Tyler, Radhika Unjiya, Urshula, Aarti Vadera, Aneesha Vadgama, Rekha Vadgama, Anjli Vadher, Mona Vadher, Sapna Chudasama Vadher, Hetal Vagadia, Priti Vagadia, Tulsi Vagjiani, Sita Vaja, Mona Vakil, Dipa Valambhia, Nina Valanju, Meera Valla, Flora van der Doelen, Shreya Vanmari, Minal Vara, Priya Vara, Suman Varadaraj, Sinu Varghese, Mala Varma, Anjna Varsani, Bindu Varsani, Diviya Varsani, Hinal Varsani, Nandhini Vasan, Janaki Vashee, Susan Vedhera, Bodhi Veer, Dintha Vekaria, Jyoti Vekaria, Mardula Vekaria, Neeta Vekaria, Tine Vekemans, Velisha, Sue Vickers-Thompson, Bharvi Vilkhu, Lucy Vince, Shahin Virani, Jasvir Virdi, Riya Visavadia, Vishma Vissandjee, Ameesha Vora, Arti Vora, Saz Vora, Apu Vyas, Ushma Vyas, Kosha Vyas-Patel, Jo W, Mukta Wad, Sachin Wadher, Nikita Wadher-Basra, Kim Wadhwa, Darshna Waghela, Mike Wallis, Walls of Bhangra, Mike Walsh, Laura Watson, Kim Watt, Colline Watts, Rhitika Webb, Richard Webb-Stevens Q.A.M., Richard Webber, Dimple Wedgewood, Alexandra Welsby, Durgā Welsh, Margaret White, Charlotte Whyte, Dharshini Wijayakumar, David Wilkinson, Shan Wilkinson, James Willard, Ross Williams, Phil Williamson, Chan Wilson, Nikita Wiseman, Oliver Wiseman, Nimish Shah, Peter Wood, Judith Wood-Archer, Babita Woodgate, Steve Woolley, Suki Wright, Sean Wyer, Tom Wyman, Stephen Xavier-Roberts, Shivani Yagnik, Anila Yarnal, Kaila Yates, Sravanthi Yellapragada, Farrah Yusuf, Zalak-Arya, Zenab Zavery,

Supporters 319

First published in 2024

Unbound

c/o TC Group,
6th Floor Kings House,
9-10 Haymarket, London,
United Kingdom, SW1Y 4BP

www.unbound.com

All rights reserved

© Sanjana Modha, 2024

All photographs taken by the author

The right of Sanjana Modha to be identified as the author of this work has been asserted in accordance with Section 77 of the Copyright, Designs and Patents Act, 1988. No part of this publication may be copied, reproduced, stored in a retrieval system, or transmitted, in any form or by any means without the prior permission of the publisher, nor be otherwise circulated in any form of binding or cover other than that in which it is published and without a similar condition being imposed on the subsequent purchaser.

Text design by Nathan Burton

A CIP record for this book is available from the British Library

ISBN 978-1-80018-296-7 (hardback)
ISBN 978-1-80018-297-4 (ebook)

Printed in China by C&C Offset Printing Co., Ltd.